Rochester Symposium on Developmental Psychopathology

Volume 5

DISORDERS AND DYSFUNCTIONS OF THE SELF

DEDICATION

We dedicate this volume to Robert N. Emde, Susan Harter, and Michael Lewis in recognition of their contributions to theory and research on the self in normal and atypical populations.

Rochester Symposium on Developmental Psychopathology

Volume 5

DISORDERS AND DYSFUNCTIONS OF THE SELF

EDITED BY

DANTE CICCHETTI & SHEREE L. TOTH

Mt. Hope Family Center
University of Rochester

UNIVERSITY OF ROCHESTER PRESS

First published 1994
Transferred to digital printing 2009

University of Rochester Press
668 Mt. Hope Avenue, Rochester, NY 14620, USA
www.urpress.com
and Boydell & Brewer Limited
PO Box 9, Woodbridge, Suffolk IP12 3DF, UK
www.boydellandbrewer.com

ISSN: 1056-6511
ISBN-13: 978-1-87882-231-4
ISBN-10: 1-878822-31-4

Library of Congress Cataloging-in-Publication Data
Rochester Symposium on Developmental Psychopathology (5th : 1991 : University of Rochester)
Disorders and dysfunctions of the self / edited by Dante Cicchetti & Sheree L. Toth
p. cm.—(Rochester Symposium on Developmental Psychopathology, ISSN 1056-6511 ; v. 5)
Based on the papers presented at the fifth Rochester Symposium on Developmental Psychopathology, held at Mt. Hope Family Center, University of Rochester, in Oct. 1991.
Includes bibliographical references and index.
ISBN 1-878822-31-49 (alk. paper)
1. Self—Congresses. 2. Mental illness—Etiology—Congresses. 3. Self in children—Congresses. 4. Self psychology—Congresses. 5. Developmenal psychology—Congresses. 6. Self-perception in teenagers—Congresses I. Cicchetti, Dante. II. Toth, Sheree L. III. Title. IV. Series: Rochester Symposium on Developmental Psychopathology. Rochester Symposium on Developmental Psychopathology ; v. 5.
RC455.4.S42R63 1991
616.89—dc20 93-24573

A catalogue record for this title is available from the British Library.

This publication is printed on acid-free paper.
Printed in the United States of America

Table of Contents

List of Contributors

CATHERINE AYOUB, PH.D.
Departments of Human Development and Psychology, Graduate School of Education, Harvard University, Cambridge, MA 02138
SIMON BARON-COHEN, PH.D.
Departments of Psychology and Child Psychiatry, Institute of Psychiatry, University of London, London SE5 8AF
MICHAEL CHANDLER, PH.D.
Department of Psychology, The University of British Columbia, Vancouver, BC V6T 1Y7
DANTE CICCHETTI, PH.D.
Mt. Hope Family Center, University of Rochester, Rochester, NY 14608
PATRICIA M. CRITTENDEN, PH.D.
Family Research Laboratory, University of New Hampshire
HOLLAND COLE, PH.D.
Department of Psychology, University of Delaware, Newark, DE 19716
KURT W. FISCHER, PH.D.
Departments of Human Development and Psychology, Graduate School of Education, Harvard University, Cambridge, MA 02138
SUSAN HARTER, PH.D.
University of Denver, Department of Psychology, Denver, CO 80208
ANNE HOGAN, PH.D.
Department of Psychology, University of Miami, Coral Gables, FL 33124
ROGER KOBAK, PH.D.
Department of Psychology, University of Delaware, Newark, DE 19716
CLAIRE B. KOPP, PH.D.
Department of Psychology, University of California at Los Angeles, Los Angeles, CA 90024-1563
DONNA B. MAROLD, PH.D.
Department of Psychology, University of Denver, Denver, CO 80208
JOHN MORIARTY, M.D.
Department of Neuropsychiatry, Institute of Neurology, University of London, London WC1N 3BG
PETER MUNDY, PH.D.
Department of Psychology, University of Miami, Coral Gables, FL 33124
GIL G. NOAM, ED.D., DIPL.PSYCH.
Laboratory of Developmental Psychology and Developmental Psychopathology, Harvard Medical School, Belmont, MA 02178

Frank W. Putnam, M.D.
National Institute of Mental Health, Bethesda, MD 20892
Mary M. Robertson, M.D.
Department of Neuropsychiatry, Institute of Neurology, University of London, London WC1N 3BG
Sheree L. Toth, Ph.D.
Mt. Hope Family Center, University of Rochester, Rochester, NY 14608
Gayle Valiant, Ph.D.
Laboratory of Developmental Psychology and Developmental Psychopathology, Harvard Medical School, Belmont, MA 02178
Drew Westen, Ph.D.
Department of Psychiatry, The Cambridge Hospital at Harvard Medical School, Cambridge, MA 02139
Natalie Wyer, Ph.D.
Department of Psychology, University of California at Los Angeles, Los Angeles, CA 90024-1563

Preface

This volume contains chapters that are the outgrowth of papers presented during, and the thought-provoking discussions generated at, the Fifth Annual Rochester Symposium on Developmental Psychopathology, held at Mt. Hope Family Center, University of Rochester, in October of 1991. The current volume, *Disorders and Dysfunctions of the Self,* reflects the importance of this construct, both historically and contemporaneously, for normal development as well as for psychopathology.

The study of self is an area of inquiry with a long and illustrious history. In many ways the extensive work that has been directed toward defining the self and articulating its role in human existence emphasizes its illusory nature. We can date a concern about the origins and functions of self to Aristotelian thought, with a continued presence in much of Western philosophy (Aristotle, 1965; Cicchetti & Beeghly, 1990a). More recent philosophers such as Daniel Dennett (1969, 1978), Robert Nozick (1981), and Derek Parfit (1975) have continued to focus on the self. In addition to philosophers, the exploration of the self has captured the attention of theoreticians in a range of disciplines, including anthropology, sociology, biology, clinical, developmental, personality, and social psychology, and psychiatry.

Throughout history, efforts to elucidate the self were largely non-empirical. While rich depictions of the self were offered by philosophers and psychoanalysts, these early theoretical formulations were based predominantly on thought experiments, observation, and clinical case description. Additionally, much work on the etiological role that assaults on the self exerted on the emergence of various forms of psychopathology relied on the retrospective recall of patients presenting with various disorders. Empirically based prospective examinations of the self have a much more recent history.

Due to their centrality in conceptualizations of development and in the emergence of psychopathology, theories of the self based in psychoanalysis and object relations theory deserve special mention. In this regard, the writings of Harry Stack Sullivan, D. W. Winnicott, and Heinz Kohut are among those that are particularly important, especially because their influences on current empirical approaches to the study of self and psychopathology are readily apparent in the current volume, as well as among the writings of scholars more broadly (Bretherton, 1987, 1991; Noam, Kohlberg, & Snarey, 1983; Sroufe, 1990; Stern, 1985; Westen, 1992).

According to Sullivan (1953), individual differences in the development of the self can be traced to tender versus anxious caregiving experiences during infancy. Although initially the infant is thought to organize good and bad caregiving experiences separately, gradually these separate personifications are viewed as being differentiated and integrated into representations of specific caregivers who are good and bad. It is out of these personifications that the infant also is viewed as creating conceptions of self, with "good me" emerging out of experiences with satisfying caregiving and with "bad me" stemming from caregiving experiences that were associated with anxiety. A third personification, "not me", is seen by Sullivan as resulting from experiences that are so anxiety-laden that they became inaccessible to awareness. The patterns acquired in early interactions are seen by Sullivan as forming the base for a dysfunctional self that will be carried into later relationships.

Consistent with Sullivan, Winnicott, a member of the British object relations school of psychoanalysis, views caregiving history as central in the development of self (Winnicott, 1965). According to Winnicott, the "good enough" mother provides an environment within which the infant can become an organized person. This requires that the caregiver be both responsive to the infant's needs and nondemanding when the infant does not need the caregiver. Unlike Sullivan's focus on the role of anxiety in future dysfunction, Winnicott stresses the role of both maternal under- and over-involvement in endangering the infant's self. While under-involvement is viewed as resulting in the lack of a stable self, over-involvement can lead to a "false self."

One of the most influential theoreticians to explore self in recent writings is Kohut (1971, 1977), whose view of human experience is very similar to that of both Winnicott and Sullivan with respect to the focus on the role of interpersonal relationships. For Kohut, the infant is viewed as being born into an empathic milieu of "selfobjects." It is through the responsivity of the "selfobjects" that the infant is provided with the experiences required for the development of the self. In order for this process to be successful, Kohut believes that the infant needs to be admired for displaying evolving capacities and, later, to form an idealized image of at least one parent that results in merger with the idealized selfobject. Over time, the gradual failure of the parent to "mirror" the child or to allow the idealization of the caregiver is thought to give rise to a healthy, cohesive self. However, empathic failure on the part of the caregiver is considered to inhibit the development of the intrapsychic structures required to regulate self-esteem effectively and to provide self-soothing functions, thereby contributing to the emergence of self pathology.

Stemming from the object relations tradition, the work of John Bowlby (1969, 1980) also is of considerable importance for current approaches to self, as his attachment theory has contributed to the operationalization of the quality of the parent-child relationship. Like prior theorists, Bowlby stresses the role of caregiving history in the development of working models of attachment figures, the self, and the self in relation to others and views these early mental representations as influencing future relationships. Unlike many self theorists, however, Bowlby places a greater emphasis on healthy development than on pathological development. In addition, Bowlby's incorporation of theories and research from beyond the parameters of psychoanalysis and object relations theory (e.g., ethology; developmental psychology) has resulted in a greater receptivity to the utilization of an attachment theory perspective in basic research endeavors. Researchers working within this theoretical framework are increasingly beginning to examine the role of maladaptive caregiving relationships in contributing to the emergence of inadequate internal working models of the self, and of the self in relation to others (Cicchetti, Cummings, Greenberg, & Marvin, 1990; Crittenden, 1990, this volume; Sroufe, 1990; Toth, Manly, & Cicchetti, 1992).

In view of its extensive theoretical history, one cannot help wonder why research on self has been relatively slow to emerge. Even more startling in relation to the role of self processes in the etiology of psychopathology, the dearth of prospective empirical work examining the links between the self and psychopathology is notable. To begin to address the reasons underlying this perplexing state of affairs, issues related to the operationalization of self surface as obstacles to conducting empirical work (Kagan, 1990, 1991). Unless agreement can be reached on what one is evaluating when assessing self, little consensus can emerge among investigators. Somewhat in reaction to the subjective approaches adhered to by psychoanalysts, investigators reaching prominence within the behavioral tradition advocated for a focus on observable behavior and a minimization of intrapsychic phenomena (e.g., Skinner, 1953). As a largely theoretical, non-observable entity, the study of self became less of a priority. This trend was bolstered by investigators operating within a Piagetian framework, who emphasized cognition over emotional experience (Cicchetti & Hesse, 1983). While psychotherapists, especially those of psychodynamic or psychoanalytic persuasions, continued to delve into the self, empirical work directed at self processes was minimized.

It has been only since investigators have sought to better define the construct of self and, concomitantly, to devise more valid measures of self that work on this entity has seen a renascence (Lewis & Brooks-Gunn, 1979). Despite the increase in research on self, as recently as 1983 Susan Harter concluded that there was a paucity of empirical work available on how the self develops and changes over the life course.

Not surprisingly, advances in our understanding of the development of self in normal populations were a pre-requisite for increasing our knowledge regarding the role of self processes in the etiology of psychopathology. In this regard, major contributions to normal development have been made by a number of researchers and theoreticians, including work on self-awareness (Kagan, 1981; Lewis & Brooks-Gunn, 1979), self-understanding (Damon & Hart, 1988), and self conscious emotions (Buss, 1980; H. Lewis, 1971; M. Lewis, 1963; Tomkins, 1963). Similar advances have been made with respect to the development of self- and emotion language (Bretherton & Beeghly, 1982; Bretherton, Fritz, Zahn-Waxler, & Ridgeway, 1986; Lutz, 1988), self-regulation (Kopp, 1981; Karoly, 1993), self-schemata (Markus, 1977), self-perception/evaluation (Harter, 1982, 1983; Stipek, Recchia, & McClintic, 1992), and self-concept (Epstein, 1973; Markus & Wurf, 1987; Wylie, 1979).

As the aforementioned approaches to the study of the self connote, multiple domains of development have been invoked in these investigations of the ontogenesis of self (see Cicchetti, 1991; Cicchetti & Beeghly, 1990a, b). Specifically, emotion (Emde, 1983; Sroufe, 1990), cognition (Kagan, 1981; Wellman, 1990), biology (Jaynes, 1976; Kagan, 1981), language (Bates, 1990; Snow, 1990), perception (Butterworth, 1990; Neisser, 1988), autobiographical memory (Main, 1991; McAdams, 1990), morality (Emde, Biringen, Clyman, & Oppenheim, 1991; Kagan, 1981), and motivational (Deci & Ryan, 1991; Ryan, 1991) approaches have all contributed to a more in-depth understanding of the self.

Interestingly, the advances within the arena of normal development begin to illustrate a trend within the study of self, namely, self is not viewed as a unitary construct, but as an aggregation of various components. Thus, rather than addressing "the self", researchers are articulating the aspects of self that they are focussing on (cf. Kagan, 1989, 1991). In this regard, the current volume can more accurately be viewed as an exploration of different aspects of the self as they relate to various dysfunctions and disorders of development. It must be stressed that it was only after the development of increasingly sound operationalizations of the self and an elaborated body of research on normal development of the self system that empirical work on perturbations of the self has been able to emerge.

In the past several decades, investigators have begun to utilize normal developmental theory and research to guide their quest to understand self disturbances in a variety of "high-risk" and psychopathological populations. Within a relatively short period of time, important insights have been made about the development of self pathology in autistic (Baron-Cohen, Tager-Flusberg, & Cohen, 1993; Hobson, 1990), handicapped (Kopp & Recchia, 1990), Down syndrome (Cicchetti, 1991), blind (Bigelow, 1991; Fraiberg, 1980), and maltreated (Cicchetti, 1991; Toth et al, 1992) children. Moreover, developmental approaches have elucidated our knowledge of self disturbances in a number of clinical conditions and in association with experienced trauma. Depression (Cummings & Cicchetti, 1990; Kegan, 1982; Radke-Yarrow, Belmont, Nottelman, & Bottomly, 1990; Zahn-Waxler & Kochanska, 1990), schizophrenia (Frith, 1992), sexual abuse (Cole & Putnam, 1992; Putnam & Trickett, 1993), and borderline personality disorder (Adler & Buie, 1979; Westen, 1990, 1991) all have been analyzed with respect to dysfunctions of self.

The influence of developmental theory derived from normal populations can be seen clearly throughout the current volume. Conversely, a number of authors have begun to discuss the influence of knowledge derived from work with atypical populations on theories of normal self development. It is this dynamic interplay between normal and abnormal that is the cornerstone of developmental psychopathology (Cicchetti, in press a, b), and that is elucidated throughout this volume. In fact, it is the very relevance of the self to both normal development and psychopathology that has contributed to its ascendance as a construct of major importance to the field of developmental psychopathology.

The contributors to *Disorders and Dysfunctions of the Self* reflect a group of premier developmentalists who are committed to elucidating the role of various aspects of the self for normal and atypical functioning. In fact, many of these individuals have made significant contributions to the realm of normal developmental theory before extending their expertise into the exploration of psychopathology. This capacity to integrate the fields of normal and atypical development as they relate to mental health and psychiatric dysfunction is noteworthy and, unfortunately, an all too rare endeavor (Cicchetti, in press b). It is our hope that the writings that continue to emanate from the yearly symposium on developmental psychopathology will provide a forum in which work that examines the interface between normal and abnormal processes can be recognized and highlighted. We believe that if we study a given behavioral or biological process in the light of an entire array of dysfunctional and disordered modifications, then we may be able to attain significant insight into the mechanisms of development not generally achieved through the study of non-disordered populations.

The volume begins with a chapter by Claire Kopp and Natalie Wyer on self-regulation in normal and atypical development. By examining self-regulation in normal and developmentally delayed youngsters, these authors provide a conceptual framework for better understanding the causes of noncompliance. Kopp and Wyer clearly demonstrate the importance of building on normal developmental theory in order to better understand self development in an atypical population.

Continuing with the prior authors' examination of self-regulation, the area of self development captured by self-control is examined through an analysis of children with Gilles de la Tourette Syndrome (GTS). Simon Baron-Cohen, Mary Robertson, and John Moriarty propose that a dysfunction in the development of the Intention Editor contributes significantly to the problems suffered by children with GTS. These authors also maintain that neuropsychological research in this area will be helpful not only in enhancing our knowledge of GTS, but also in elucidating the development of the self-control aspect of the self.

Peter Mundy and Anne Hogan again draw from a base of normal development in their approach to autism. Because social impairments are a hallmark of autism, investigators often have sought to understand this disorder in terms of a dysfunction of self development. In their chapter, Mundy and Hogan discuss how research based on a model of infant preverbal communication has illuminated the nature of the social deficits exhibited by young autistic children. The role that findings of work with autism have contributed to normal developmental theory also is described.

Drawing from a theoretical base of attachment theory, Patricia Crittenden provides an outstanding analysis of the role of internal representational models in the development of the self. This author's discussion of self development in infancy, preschool, and school-age children, as well as her examination of the links between self development and psychopathology, can serve as a powerful stimulus to facilitating research in this area.

In a further exploration of the role of early experience in the emergence of self development, Kurt Fischer and Catherine Ayoub provide a comprehensive and stimulating description of affective splitting and dissociation in normal and maltreated children. These authors build upon dynamic skills theory in their developmental analysis of splitting and, in the process, make significant contributions to both our understanding of normal development and the emergence of psychopathology.

Drew Westen utilizes clinical observation and extant research to examine the effects of a specific form of maltreatment, sexual abuse, on the structure of self development. In the course of his discussion, Westen articulates the criticality of delimiting various dimensions of the self and emphasizes the role of individual differences in the overall manifestation of the effects of sexual abuse. Despite the methodological challenges associated with disentangling the effects of sexual abuse on self development from issues such as insecure attachment relationships and multiple co-occurring forms of abuse, Westen views sexual abuse as potentially disruptive with respect to all aspects of the self.

In a fascinating chapter on dissociation, Frank Putnam focuses on dissociative disruptions in four components of self; self-agency, self-coherence, self-affectivity, and self-continuity. Putnam discusses dissociation as existing on a continuum and cautions against diagnosing dysfunction in children when a normal process may be operative. Again, the necessity of bringing an understanding of normal development to bear on issues of psychopathology emerges.

Roger Kobak and Holland Cole begin their chapter on adolescent autonomy and psychopathology by examining ways in which cognitive growth creates new opportunities for adolescents to meta-monitor, update, and revise working models of self and parents. The Adult Attachment Interview (George, Kaplan, & Main, 1985) is used as a window into the coordination of emotional, cognitive, and attentional capacities, processes considered to be necessary if representational models are to be updated. These authors suggest that insecure attachment strategies and reduced capacities for meta-monitoring may, under stressful conditions, increase an adolescent's risk for the emergence of psychopathological conditions such as depression and eating disorders. Implications for intervention as well as for a developmental pathways model of continuity and change in adolescent personality and adaptation are discussed.

Adolescent functioning, specifically as it relates to ego development and suicidal ideation and behavior, is the focus of the research described by Gil Noam and Gayle Valiant. These authors bring a clinical-developmental approach to bear on their examination of the effect that mental representations of self and relationships exert on the occurrence of psychopathology. In accord with the goals of developmental psychopathology, the role of this perspective in reformulating theories of normal development is presented.

Susan Harter and Donna Marold highlight their program of research on the evolution of a normative developmental model of self-esteem among adolescents. The link between self-esteem and depression is eloquently presented and efforts to examine the directionality between self-esteem and affect are reported. The implications of directionality for issues such as suicide and effective approaches to treatment are examined.

The volume concludes with a chapter by Michael Chandler, who reports on an ongoing program of research directed at delimiting a developmental explanation for the increase in suicidal behaviors during the adolescent years. Chandler's belief that suicidal adolescents have lost a sense of personal continuity during the stressful transitions of adolescence is extremely thought-provoking, especially so when viewed in the context of the conceptualizations of adolescent development and suicidality provided by Kobak and Cole, Noam and Valiant, and Harter and Marold.

Chandler's position that some forms of psychopathology are best understood not as developmental delay or arrest, but as the manifestation of a form of structural collapse brought about by the dangers associated with normal transitions from one stage of development to the next also is noteworthy and consistent with that of other contributors to this volume (cf. Noam & Valiant). For example, Fischer and Ayoub's analysis of maltreated populations admonishes us to consider the development of these individuals not as reflective of failed development, but as "sophisticated skills that generally parallel the skills of normal development, but that are built on the devastating dissociations that arise from their unfortunate lives."

We have been stimulated by the integration of theory and research with principles of normal development and atypical functioning that the authors of *Disorders and Dysfunctions of the Self* have brought to their work. While much research remains to be conducted that articulates the role of the self in the development of psychopathology, the current volume represents a compilation of the work being carried out by some of the leading thinkers in this area. The consistent incorporation of theory derived from normal development into the consideration of self dysfunction, the recognition that research on development in pathological populations can enhance our knowledge of typical ontogenesis, and the willingness to question theories based solely on findings obtained with either normal or atypical populations, reflect the realization of a central tenet of developmental psychopathology - the need to span the dualisms that exist between the clinical study of and research into psychopathological disorders and between basic and applied research (Cicchetti & Toth, 1991).

The unusual level of interest that recent advances in knowledge of normal self development have engendered on research activity on abnormal self processes has ushered in a great deal of energy, creativity, and productivity. We believe that success in realizing the potential for significant progress in our knowledge will depend in large measure on the ability to engage the inherently complex issues surrounding the study of the self in multi-disciplinary ways within a developmental psychopathology framework. If this approach is fostered, an exciting new era of theoretical and empirical advances on self-system processes is on the horizon.

Dante Cicchetti
Sheree L. Toth

REFERENCES

Adler, G. & Buie, D. (1979). Aloneness and borderline psychopathology: The possible relevance of child development issues. *International Journal of Psychoanalysis, 60,* 83–96.

Aristotle (1965). *de Anima.* New Haven, CT: Yale University Press.

Baron-Cohen, S., Tager-Flusberg, H., & Cohen, D. J. (1993). *Understanding Other Minds.* New York: Oxford University Press.

Bates, E. (1990). Language about me and you: Pronominal reference and the emerging concept of self. In D. Cicchetti & M. Beeghly (Eds.) *The Self in Transition: Infancy to Childhood,* (pp.165–182). Chicago: University of Chicago Press.

Bigelow, A. E. (1991). Hiding in blind and sighted children. *Development and Psychopathology, 3,* 301–310.
Bowlby, J. (1969). *Attachment and loss (Vol. I).* New York: Basic Books.
Bowlby, J. (1980). *Attachment and loss (Vol. III): Loss, sadness, and depression.* New York: Basic Books.
Bretherton, I. (1987). New perspectives on attachment relations: Security, communication, and internal working models. In J. Osofsky (Ed.), *Handbook of Infant Development* (Second Edition) (pp. 1061–1100). New York: John Wiley and Sons.
Bretherton, I. (1991). Pouring new wine into old bottles: The social self as internal working model. In M. Gunnar & L. A. Sroufe (Eds) *Minnesota Symposia on Child Psychology, Vol. 23: Self processes and development* (pp. 1–41). Hillsdale, NJ: Erlbaum Associates.
Bretherton, I. & Beeghly, M. (1982). Talking about internal states: The acquisition of an explicit theory of mind. *Developmental Psychology, 18,* 906–921.
Bretherton, I., Fritz, J., Zahn-Waxler, C. & Ridgeway, D. (1986). Learning to talk about emotion: A functionalist perspective. *Child Development, 57,* 530–548.
Butterworth, G. (1990). Self Perception in infancy. In D. Cicchetti & M. Beeghly (Eds.) *The Self in Transition: Infancy to Childhood,* (pp. 119–137). Chicago: University of Chicago Press.
Buss, A. (1980). *Self-consciousness and social anxiety.* San Francisco: W. H. Freeman.
Cicchetti, D. (1991). Fractures in the crystal: Developmental Psychopathology and the emergence of self. *Developmental Review, 11,* 271–287.
Cicchetti, D. (in press a). Developmental Psychopathology: Reactions, Reflections, Projections. *Developmental Review.*
Cicchetti, D. (in press b). Developmental Theory: Lessons from the study of risk and psychopathology. In S. Matthysse, D. Levy, J. Kagan, and F. Benes (Eds.), *Psychopathology: The Evolving Science of Mental Disorder.* New York: Cambridge University Press.
Cicchetti, D. & Beeghly, M. (1990a). Developmental perspectives on the self: A historical Review. In D. Cicchetti & M. Beeghly (Eds.) *The Self in Transition: Infancy to Childhood,* (pp. 1–15). Chicago: University of Chicago Press.
Cicchetti, D. & Beeghly, M. (1990b). *The Self in Transition: Infancy to Childhood.* Chicago: University of Chicago Press.
Cicchetti, D., Cummings, E. M., Greenberg, M. & Marvin, R. (1990). An organizational perspective on attachment beyond infancy: Implications for theory, measurement, and research. In M. Greenberg, D. Cicchetti and M. Cummings (Eds.), *Attachment in the preschool years* (pp. 3–49). Chicago: University of Chicago Press.
Cicchetti, D. & Hesse, P. (1983). Affect and Intellect: Piaget's Contributions to the Study of Infant Emotional Development. In R. Plutchik and H. Kellerman (Eds.), *Emotion: Theory, Research and Experience,* Vol. II, (pp. 115–169). New York: Academic.
Cicchetti, D. & Toth, S. L. (1991). The Making of a Developmental Psychopathologist. In J. Cantor, C. Spiker, and L. Lipsitt (Eds.), *Child Behavior and Development: Training for Diversity,* (pp 34–72). Norwood, NJ: Ablex.
Cohen, D. (1980). The pathology of the self in primary childhood autism and Gilles de la Tourette syndrome. *Pediatric Clinics of North America, 3,* 383–402.
Cole, P. & Putnam, F. (1992). Effect of incest on self and social functioning: A developmental psychopathology perspective. *Journal of Consulting and Clinical Psychology,* 60, 174–184.
Crittenden, P. (1990). Internal representational models of attachment relationships. *Infant Mental Health Journal, 11,* 259–277.

Cummings, E. M., & Cicchetti, D. (1990). Attachment, Depression, and the Transmission of Depression. In M. T. Greenberg, D. Cicchetti, and E. M. Cummings (Eds.), *Attachment during the preschool years,* (pp. 339–372). Chicago: University of Chicago Press.
Damon, W. & Hart, D. (1988). *Self-understanding in childhood and adolescence.* New York: Cambridge University Press.
Deci, E. & Ryan, R. (1991). A motivational approach to self: Integration and personality. *Nebraska Symposium on Motivation,* Vol. 38 (pp. 237–288). Lincoln, NE: University of Nebraska Press.
Dennett, D. (1969). *Content and consciousness.* London: Routledge and Kegan Paul.
Dennett, D. (1978). *Brainstorms: Philosophical essays on mind and psychology.* Cambridge, MA: MIT Press.
Emde, R. (1983). The prerepresentational self and its affective core. *The Psychoanalytic Study of the Child, 38,* 165–192.
Emde, R. N, Biringen, Z., Clyman, R., & Oppenheim, D. (1991). The moral self of infancy: Affective core and procedural knowledge. *Developmental Review, 11,* 251–270.
Epstein, S. (1973). The self-concept revisited or a theory of a theory. *American Psychologist, 28,* 405–416.
Fraiberg, S. (1980). *Insights from the blind.* New York: International Universities Press.
Frith, C. (1992). *The cognitive neuropsychology of schizophrenia.* Hillsdale, NJ: Lawrence Erlbaum.
George, C., Kaplan, N., & Main, M. (1985). *The Berkeley Adult Attachment Interview.* Unpublished protocol, Department of Psychology, University of California, Berkeley.
Harter, S. (1982). The perceived competence scale for children. *Child Development, 53,* 87–97.
Harter, S. (1983). Developmental perspectives on the self-system. In P. Mussen (Ed.) *Handbook of child psychology* (pp. 275–385). New York: Wiley.
Hobson, R. P. (1990). On the origins of self and the case of autism. *Development and Psychopathology, 2,* 163–181.
Jaynes, J. (1976). *The origins of consciousness in the breakdown of the bicameral mind.* Boston: Houghton Mifflin.
Kagan, J. (1981). *The second year: The emergence of self-awareness.* Cambridge, MA: Harvard University Press.
Kagan, J. (1989). *Unstable ideas: Temperament, cognition, and self.* Cambridge, MA: Harvard University Press.
Kagan, J. (1990). The concepts of self: A dialogue of questions without answers. In D. Cicchetti & M. Beeghly (Eds.) *The Self in Transition: Infancy to Childhood.* (pp. 363–383). Chicago: University of Chicago Press.
Kagan, J. (1991). The theoretical utility of constructs for self. *Developmental Review, 11,* 144–150.
Karoly, P. (1993). Mechanisms of self-regulation: A systems view. *Annual Review of Psychology, 44,* 23–52.
Kegan, R. (1982). *The evolving self.* Cambridge, MA: Harvard University Press.
Kohut, H. (1971). *The analysis of the self.* New York: International Universities Press.
Kohut, H. (1977). *The restoration of the self.* New York: International Universities Press.
Kopp, C. B. (1982). Antecedents of self-regulation: A developmental perspective. *Developmental Psychology, 18,* 199–214.
Kopp, C. B. & Recchia, S. (1990). The issues of multiple pathways in the development of handicapped children. In R. Hodapp, J. Burack, & E. Zigler (Eds.) *Issues in the developmental approach to mental retardation* (pp. 272–293). New York: Cambridge University Press.

Lewis, H. (1971). *Shame and guilt in neurosis.* New York: International Universities Press.

Lewis, M. (1992). *Shame: The exposed self.* New York: The Free Press.

Lewis, M. & Brooks-Gunn, J. (1979). *Social cognition and the acquisition of self.* New York: Plenum.

Lutz, C. (1988). *Unnatural Emotions: Everyday Sentiments on a Micronesian Atoll and Their Challenge to Western Theory.* Chicago: University of Chicago Press.

Main, M. (1991). Metacognitive knowledge, metacognitive monitoring, and singular (coherent) vs. multiple (incoherent) model of attachment: Findings and directions for future research. In C. M. Parker, J. Stevenson-Hinde, & P. Marris (Eds.) *Attachment across the life cycle* (pp. 127–159). London: Routledge.

Markus, H. (1977). Self-schemas and processing information about the self. *Journal of Personality and Social Psychology, 35,* 63–78.

Markus, H. & Wurf, E. (1987). The dynamic self-concept: A social psychological perspective. *Annual Review of Psychology, 38,* 299–337.

McAdam, D. (1990). *The person: An introduction to personality psychology.* New York: Harcourt Brace Jovanovitch.

Neisser, U. (1988). Five kinds of self-knowledge. *Philosophical Psychology, 1,* 35–59.

Noam, G., Kohlberg, L. & Snarey, J. (1983). Steps toward a model of the self. In B. Lee & G. Noam (Eds.) *Developmental Approaches to the Self* (pp. 59–141). New York: Plenum Press.

Nozick, R. (1981). *Philosophical explanations.* Cambridge, MA: Harvard University Press.

Parfit, D. (1975). Personal identity. In J. Perry (Ed.) *Personal Identity* (pp. 199–223). Berkeley: University of California Press.

Putnam, F. & Trickett, P. (1993). Child sexual abuse: A model of chronic trauma. *Psychiatry, 56,* 82–95.

Radke-Yarrow, M., Belmont, B., Nottelmann, E., & Bottomly, L. (1990). Young children's self-conceptions: Origins in the natural discourse of depressed and normal mothers and their children. In D. Cicchetti and M. Beeghly (Eds.), *The self in transition* (pp. 345–361). Chicago: University of Chicago Press.

Ryan, R. (1991). The nature of the self in autonomy and relatedness. In J. Strauss & G. R. Goethals (Eds.) *The Self: Interdisciplinary approaches.* (pp.208–238). New York: Springer-Verlag.

Skinner, B. F. (1953) *Science and Human Behavior.* New York: MacMillan.

Snow, C. (1990). Building memories: The ontogeny of autobiography. In D. Cicchetti & M. Beeghly (Eds.) *The Self in Transition: Infancy to Childhood,* (pp. 213–242). Chicago: University of Chicago Press.

Sroufe, L. A. (1990). An organizational perspective on the self. In D. Cicchetti & M. Beeghly (Eds.) *The Self in Transition: Infancy to Childhood,* (pp. 281–307). Chicago: University of Chicago Press.

Stern, D. (1985). *The interpersonal world of the infant: A view from psychoanalysis and developmental psychology.* New York: Basic Books.

Stipek, D., Recchia, S. & McClinic, S. (1992). Self-evaluation in young children. *Monographs of the Society for Research in Child Development,* (Serial No. 226, Vol. 57(1)), (pp. 1–83).

Sullivan, H. (1953). *Interpersonal theory of psychiatry.* New York: Norton.

Toth, S. L., Manly, J. T., & Cicchetti, D. (1992). Child maltreatment and vulnerability to depression. *Development and Psychopathology, 4,* 97–112.

Tomkins, S. (1963). *Affect, imagery, and consciousness, Vol. 2: The negative affects.* New York: Springer.

Wellman, H. (1990). *The child's theory of mind.* Cambridge, MA: MIT Press.

Westen, D. (1990). Toward a revised theory of borderline object relations: Implications of empirical research. *International Review of Psycho-Analysis, 17,* 661–694.

Westen, D. (1991). Social cognition and object relations. *Psychological Bulletin, 109,* 429–455.

Westen, D. (1992). The cognitive self and the psychoanalytic self: Can we put our selves together? *Psychological Inquiry, 3,* 1–13.

Winnicott, D. W. (1965). *The maturational processes and the facilitating environment.* New York: International Universities Press.

Wylie, R. C. (1979). *The self-concept, Vol. 2: Theory and research on selected topics.* Lincoln: University of Nebraska Press.

Zahn-Waxler, C. & Kochanska, G. (1990). The origins of guilt. In R. Thompson (Ed.), *Nebraska Symposium on Motivation, Vol. 36: Socioemotional Development.* (pp. 183–258). Lincoln, NE: University of Nebraska Press.

I Intersubjectivity, Joint Attention, and Autistic Developmental Pathology

PETER MUNDY & ANNE HOGAN

I. Introduction

Autism is a pernicious developmental disorder that handicaps approximately five to ten in every ten thousand individuals (Gillberg, 1988). Descriptions of this form of pathology have a considerable history (Frith, 1989). The modern description and nomenclature associated with autism, however, may be attributed to the coincidental but independent work of Kanner (1943) and Asperger (1944). Central to the work of both these clinicians was the observation that a serious disturbance in social development is fundamental to the nature of autism. Kanner (1944), for example, characterized the core disturbance of autistic children as "an inability to relate themselves in the ordinary way to people and situations from the beginning of life" (p. 31). This initial clinical hypothesis concerning the central nature of social dysfunction to autistic psychopathology has been verified empirically in numerous studies (Fein, Pennington, Markowitz, Braverman & Waterhouse, 1986; Howlin 1986; Mundy & Sigman, 1989) and codified in currently used diagnostic systems (Volkmar & Cohen, 1988).

Given the cardinal nature of social dysfunction in autism it may not be surprising that there have been numerous efforts to understand the nature of autism in terms of a disorder of self development. One of the first of these involved the attempt to describe self disorder in autism as an outcome of aberrations in psychodynamic process (e.g., Goldfarb, 1963). Indeed, this early psychoanalytic approach suggested that a gross deficiency in self identity and self/other differentiation was *the* pervasive and fundamental disturbance that gave rise to this disorder. However, studies of self recognition, using the mirror response paradigm, eventually indicated that young autistic children do display awareness of

Preparation of this manuscript was supported by a James W. McLamore award through the University of Miami. The first author would also like to express special thanks to Marian Sigman who, as both an enlivening mentor and an esteemed colleague, has been pivotal to much of the thought and data discussed in this chapter. Appreciation is also extended to Stephen Sheinkopf for his helpful comments on this chapter.

self and differentiate self from others (e.g., Dawson & McKissik, 1984; Ferrari & Matthews, 1983; Spiker & Ricks, 1984; See Rogers & Pennington, 1991 for a review). Thus, the early psychoanalytic notion of a pervasive deficit in all aspects of self development in autism was not supported by empirical inquiry. Nevertheless, the question of whether autism involves a disorder of self development remains a topic of contemporary interest.

Current research and theory explicitly approach this question from varied perspectives including the study of sensory and psychophysiological process (Ornitz & Ritvo, 1968), a model of inherent affectively mediated process (Hobson, 1990), and a model of representational cognitive processes (Rogers and Pennington, 1991). These contemporary approaches to the study of self pathology in autism are more circumscribed than the initial psychoanalytic view of a pervasive disturbance of self development. Indeed, new perspectives on the developmental nature of psychopathology and the multifaceted nature of self development conspire to suggest that the question, "Is impaired self development fundamental to autism ?", may be too broad and perhaps too simple.

Viewing autism from the perspective of developmental psychopathology, while also taking into account recent research on self-development, provides us with assistance in refining this question. First, in accord with a basic tenet of developmental psychopathology (Cicchetti, 1984), the characteristic deficits of autism appear to change with age and developmental level (Mundy & Sigman, 1989a; Rutter, 1984; Volkmar, Cohen, Bregman, Hooks, & Stevenson, 1989). Therefore, it is likely that the precision of attempts to understand the core phenomenon associated with this syndrome may depend on research and theory that focus on describing the nature of autism as it is manifest in specific developmental periods. Second, current theory and data also posit that self development may not refer to a single unitary construct, *the self*, but rather to a variety of constructs, *the selves*, that arise in response to different sources of information that impinge on the child (e.g., Neisser, 1991). Taken together, these two points suggest a more specific, two-part question regarding self development in autistic children. This question may be best framed as: "What aspects of self development are impaired in autism and how are these impairments manifest at different ages ?"

With this formulation as a guide, in the present chapter we strive to describe the psychopathology of a specific age range of autistic children in terms of a particular aspect of disordered self development. This chapter, in part, constitutes an elaboration of an earlier contribution to this Symposium that described how research on social and cognitive development in autism exemplifies a developmental approach to psychopathology (Sigman, 1989). Moreover, the content of this chapter owes much to data derived from collaborative studies conducted at UCLA (e.g., Kasari, Sigman, Mundy, & Yirimya, 1990; Mundy, Sigman, Ungerer and Sherman, 1986; Sigman, Mundy, Ungerer, and Sherman, 1986).

These studies have attempted to examine the social and cognitive characteristics of three to seven-year-old autistic children using various measures of nonverbal communication skills as a lens through which to view their developmental pathology. The gist of this research indicates that, early in development, an important aspect of the social disturbance of autism is characterized by a deficit in joint attention, a specific type of nonverbal communication skill. One interpretation of this finding is that this deficit, at least in part, reflects a disturbance in the autistic child's development of the capacity for intersubjectivity. In other words, according to Trevarthen and Hubley's (1978) definition of intersubjectivity, a joint attention disturbance may reflect an aspect of the developing interpersonal sense of self of autistic children that is manifest as an attenuated tendency to intentionally share the experience of objects or events with others.

This interpretation of the data on early nonverbal communication deficits holds much in common with at least two models of autism, one proposed by Hobson (1989, 1990) and one proposed by Dawson and Lewy (1989). This interpretation also appears to be relevant to models proposed by Baron-Cohen (1988) and Rogers and Pennington (1991). In this chapter we examine data on joint attention deficits as it relates to the possible nature of self disorder in autism and as it relates to these alternative psychological models of autistic pathology. We begin with an overview of the features of developmental theory that provide a link between research on nonverbal communication and research on early aspects of self development.

II. Nonverbal Communication

The typical development of nonverbal communication skills in the first two years of life may be conceptualized in terms of three phases (Bakeman & Adamson, 1984). In the 0- to 5-month-phase communication often involves face-to-face exchanges of affective signals between the infant and caregiver (Trevarthen, 1979; Tronick, 1989). In contrast to the dyadic phase, interactions in the second 6- to 18-month-phase increasingly are characterized by triadic exchanges (Bakeman & Adamson, 1984). These involve the child's use and response to eye contact and conventional gestures to coordinate the attention of self and another person vis-a-vis some third object or event that is external to the dyad (e.g., Bates, Benigni, Bretherton, Camaioni, & Volterra, 1979; Bruner & Sherwood, 1983; Leung & Rheingold, 1981; Sugarman, 1984). An example here might be an infant pointing to a toy while making eye contact with a caregiver. The third, or locutionary phase, overlaps with the second phase (12 to 24 months) and involves the child's increasing utilization of verbal communication. Herein the term nonverbal communication skills will be used primarily to refer to those behaviors that emerge in the second, triadic phase of early communication development.

At least three categories or functions of nonverbal communication behaviors have been described (Bates et al., 1979; Brunner & Sherwood, 1983; Seibert, Hogan & Mundy, 1982; 1984). Affiliative or social interaction behaviors involve the use of gestures and eye contact to elicit or maintain physical or face to face interaction between the infant and caregiver. Examples here include reaching to the caregiver with eye contact to elicit or maintain physical contact or taking turns rolling a ball back and forth with a caregiver to maintain face to face interaction. This type of nonverbal skill involves conventional gestures and may involve objects in the service of maintaining social interaction. However, it may be a transitional class of nonverbal behaviors because they do not appear to be as clearly triadic as the following categories of behavior.

Requesting skills involve the use of gestures and eye contact to elicit another person's aid in obtaining objects and events. Here the referent is clearly on an object or event that is external to the dyad, and the function of the communicative bid can be classified as instrumental or imperative. Examples include a child eliciting aid in reactivating a wind-up toy by giving it to a caregiver, or a child eliciting aid in obtaining an out of reach toy by combining eye contact and pointing to the object.

Joint attention behaviors comprise the third class of nonverbal communication skills. The infant uses these behaviors simply to coordinate or share attention with a social partner vis a vis-an-object or event. Here again the focus of the communicative bid is an object or event. Hence, joint attention exchanges are characteristically triadic. However, there is little instrumental signal value associated with the behaviors. Examples include the child making eye contact and pointing to a wind up toy that is active *but within reach* or holding and showing a ceased wind up toy to a caregiver. Thus, while joint attention and requesting are similar with regard to the type and form of the gestures used (e.g. pointing may be used for requesting or for joint attention), they may be discriminated based on the degree to which they serve declarative or imperative communicative functions (Bates, et al. 1979; Mundy, Sigman, Kasari & Yirmiya, 1988; Seibert, et al. 1982).

III. Nonverbal Communication as Indices of Self Development

In this section we present a sequence of theoretical assumptions that link measures of nonverbal communication skills to the study of self development in young children.

An important assumption concerning the second or triadic phase of infant communication development is that the intentionality of communicative bids becomes more apparent during this period of development (Bates, et al. 1979; Bretherton, 1991; Golinkoff, 1983). There are at least three characteristics of triadic nonverbal communication bids that demarcate the intentional nature of these behaviors (Bates, 1979; Bretherton, 1991). First, the systematic use of eye contact in conjunction with gestures suggests that infants in this phase are monitoring the potential reception of the signal value of their gestures. Second, the increasing use of socialized gestures in this phase, such as pointing or a palm-up arm extension for requests, suggests that the infant may have learned the signal value of specific types of hand, arm, and eye movements.

Perhaps the most impressive evidence for the intentional nature of communication comes from the observation that infants increasingly display the capacity to repair failed communicative bids in this phase (Golinkoff, 1983). An infant may initially point to a toy that is out of reach while using eye contact to monitor the reception of the signal. However, if a caregiver response is not forthcoming the infant may change or repair the signal through a variety of means, such as the addition of vocalizations or by changing the point to a reaching gesture. The use of repair in these bids is indicative of the intentional nature of triadic nonverbal communication.

With the assumption that triadic nonverbal communication is intentional has come the corollary assumption that nonverbal communication skills reflect aspects of infants' rudimentary awareness of self and other (Bretherton, 1991; Bretherton, McNew, & Beegly-Smith, 1981). The intentional use of a request bid, for example, may be dependent upon some understanding that others have an awareness and agency relative to a desired object, and that the awareness and agency of others may be effected by the systematic behaviors of the child. Furthermore, it may well be that different types of nonverbal communication reflect different dimensions of the infant's dawning awareness of self and other. This last assumption is consistent with models of infant development that have recently been espoused from divergent theoretical backgrounds.

Models of interpersonal development (Stern, 1985) and cognitive development (Wellman, 1992) are in surprising agreement on the basic elements of shared understanding of self and other that may be indicated by triadic nonverbal communication skills development. Stern (1985) has suggested that the social and communicative behavior of infants in this period (7- to 12-months) suggests that they have developed the capacity to share three aspects of mental states with others. Accordingly, infants in this period can understand that the self and others can: share *intentions* or a common goal orientation with regard to objects or events; engage in *joint attention* or a common visual perspective on objects or events; and share *affective states* or a common emotional response to objects or events. Similarly, Wellman (1992) has proposed that in this period of development infants understand people (self and other) in terms of three aspects of behavior: *desire*, or that people can seek to attain the same things or experiences; *perception*, or that people can see, hear feel the same object or event; and *emotion*, or that people may have the same affective reactions to objects or events.

At least two of the aspects of self awareness described by Stern and Wellman, intentions/desire and joint attention/perception, may be related to categories of nonverbal communication. With regard to the former, the understanding that self and other can share a common goal orientation may be involved in the capacity of the child to generate nonverbal request bids. The capacity to understand that both self and other can share a common visual perspective may be involved in both joint attention and request skills as these both involve reference (coordinating attention) to objects and events. Alternatively, the awareness of shared affect/emotion does not have a clear correlate in terms of the descriptions so far presented of the three nonverbal communication skills. However, as we will see later in this chapter, joint attention skills may involve this aspect of self awareness to a greater degree than do requesting skills. Thus, it may be that joint attention and requesting communication skills reflect both similar and different aspects of the development of self/other awareness in infants.

This hypothesis would suggest that developmental profiles, particularly uneven profiles, generated on measures of nonverbal communication development may be informative with regard to aspects of pathology of self development in young children. Therefore, data that pertain to the profile of nonverbal communication skills displayed by young autistic children are presented in the next section.

IV. Nonverbal Communication and Autism

In 1978 Frank Curcio published an observational study indicating that autistic individuals may suffer from a specific deficit in joint attention as opposed to requesting skills. Although this study was not well controlled, the basic finding of a specific deficit in the development of joint attention skills as opposed to requesting skills has subsequently been substantiated by numerous controlled studies (Baron-Cohen, 1989a; Loveland & Landry, 1986; Mundy, Sigman, & Kasari, 1990; Mundy et al. 1986; McEvoy, Rogers & Pennington, 1993; Wetherby & Prutting, 1984). Data from the UCLA studies may be used to illustrate the breadth of the relevant findings with regard to this phenomenon.

Several of our studies at UCLA used the Early Social-Communication Scales (ESCS; Seibert et al. 1982, 1984) to examine the facility of young autistic children with nonverbal social interaction, requesting, and joint attention behaviors while in interaction with a stranger. Observations with these scales have indicated that young autistic children tend to show a pattern of strengths and weakness on the behaviors comprising the social interaction and requesting scales. However, autistic children only displayed deficits on the joint attention behaviors as compared to MA, IQ, and language age matched children with mental retardation (Mundy et al. 1986; Mundy et al, 1990). The display of poorly developed joint attention skills is not only apparent in a tester structured interaction such as the Early Social-Communication Scales, but also may be observed in interactions with caregivers (Sigman et al. 1986). With regard to developmental level, these deficits in joint attention skills have been apparent in comparisons of children with verbal age estimates below 18 months and chronological ages below 48 months (Mundy et al. 1990; Mundy, Sigman, & Kasari, in press). Moreover, recent data suggest that joint attention deficits may be observed in autistic children before other types of deficits, such as those involving pretense play, may be observed (Mundy, Sigman & Kasari, 1993). Thus, a specific deficit in the emergence of joint attention skills appears to be an important characteristic of the early development of autistic children.

An examination of one type of behavior that occurs in all three categories of nonverbal communication skills may illustrate something of the specificity of autistic joint attention deficits. Eye contact may be used in social interaction, joint attention and requesting behaviors. Moreover, eye contact has long been regarded as an arena of general deficiency among autistic children (Mirenda, Donnellan & Yoder, 1983). However, on the Early Social Communication Scales autistic children made eye contact with the experimenter after the cessation of being tickled (social interaction eye contact) and made eye contact after removal of a toy or cessation of a mechanical toy (requesting eye contact) as frequently as did controls (Mundy et al. 1986). In contrast, compared to controls, this sample of autistic children displayed much less eye contact in joint attention contexts, such as eye contact while holding a toy or alternating eye contact between a tester and an active toy (Mundy et al. 1986). These findings were quite consistent with Rutter's (1978) hypothesis that autistic children do not display a pervasive deficit of eye contact, but rather one that is specific to certain social functions. In this case the functional deficit in eye contact appeared to involve joint attention rather than requesting or social interaction functions.

This is not the only type of specific behavior comparison that is possible. Pointing for joint attention as opposed to pointing for requesting is clearly deficient among autistic children (Baron-Cohen, 1989a; Mundy et al. 1986). Autistic children also display deficits in the joint attention behavior of showing as opposed to the similar requesting behavior of giving (Mundy et al. 1986). Indeed, the specificity of autistic joint attention deficits relative to matched controls with mental retardation has ranged from 80% to 94% in discriminant analyses (Lewy & Dawson, 1992; Mundy et al. 1986, 1990).

It is important to note, however, that autistic joint attention deficiencies are not absolute. Rather, young autistic children manifest an attenuated but observable tendency to display and respond to joint attention bids. Thus, overall deficits notwithstanding, individual differences in joint attention skills are also characteristic of autistic children and these individual differences turn out to be important.

Joint attention skills appear to be both concurrent and predictive correlates of individual differences in language acquisition (Loveland & Landry, 1986; Mundy et al. 1990; Mundy, Sigman, Ungerer, & Sherman, 1987). Moreover, individual differences in joint attention skills are associated with parental reports of the frequency and type of symptoms displayed by autistic children (Mundy, et al. in press). Finally, an individual child's joint attention skills may be sensitive to social context and stimulation (Lewy & Dawson, 1990), suggesting that joint attention skills may be a viable target for early intervention efforts.

Thus, research focussed on group or individual differences suggests that joint attention skill deficits are an important marker of the developmental disturbance that characterizes the early presentation of the syndrome of autism. However, joint attention skill deficits are not manifest in the nonverbal behavior of only developmentally immature children. Related skill deficits continue to be apparent in the nonverbal communicative behavior of older autistic children (Baron-Cohen, 1989a; Loveland & Landry, 1986) and in the verbal skills of higher functioning autistic children (Tager-Flusberg, 1992). Therefore, understanding the nature of this early emerging disturbance in social development is an issue of some consequence in the contemporary study of autism. One approach to this issue has been the comparative task analysis of nonverbal requesting and joint attention skills (Baron-Cohen, 1989a; Gomez, Sarria, & Tamarit, 1993; Mundy et al. 1986; 1993). That is, research and theory have been directed toward understanding why autistic children do relatively well with the development of requesting skills but relatively poorly with the development of joint attention skills.

V. The Comparison of Joint Attention and Requesting Skill

The validity of any comparison of joint attention and requesting skills rests on the assumption that measures of joint attention and requesting skills assess at least partially independent domains of development. Although independence is assumed on the basis of a functional analysis of these types of behaviors (e.g., Bates et al. 1979), little empirical data exists with regard to this issue. Extant data suggest that, within handicapped samples, requesting and joint attention skill development *are* significantly but only moderately correlated (Mundy, Seibert & Hogan, 1984; Mundy, Sigman, Kasari, & Yirmiya, 1988). Thus, these skill sets may be related, perhaps because they both may depend on understanding that self and other can share a common visual perspective. However, they are not so strongly related to suggest that thay are necessarily isomorphic in development.

It is also noteworthy that profiles of development across these two types of nonverbal skills appear to segregate with different organic syndromes of developmental disturbance. As noted above, deficits in joint attention skill but not requesting skill characterize the early development of children with autism. However, a different pattern appears to characterize another organic syndrome of developmental disorder. Young children with Down syndrome display more pronounced deficits in nonverbal requesting skills than joint attention skills (Mundy et al. 1988; Mundy, Kasari, Sigman & Ruskin, submitted). This segregation of specific types of nonverbal communication deficits with specific syndromes of developmental disorder suggests that nonverbal joint attention and requesting skills constitute at least partially independent behavior domains in early development. Moreover, it has been hypothesized that, in addition to cognitive and attention processes, these two types of nonverbal communication skills may differ with respect to the involvement of affective processes (Mundy et al. 1986).

The Affective Hypothesis

The term joint attention may suggest that behaviors in this domain serve only to coordinate or direct attention to objects or events. However, it is important to consider why young children engage in these types of attention directing acts. Let us briefly adopt a phenomenological approach to this issue. Imagine for a moment a situation when you have used pointing simply to direct the attention of another person to some object or event. Perhaps you have been for a walk with a friend in a park and noticed an unusual animal. You may have pointed to the animal to direct the attention of your friend without speaking so as to not disturb the object of your reference. In this imaginary scenario, do you think pointing was used to indicate something of interest? Do you think you would have expressed that interest through facial affect (e.g., eye brows up, eyes opened wide, mouth open) while pointing, or do you think your point would have been accompanied with neutral affect. Finally, why in the world did you not simply experience the event in solitude? Did you use pointing in an attempt to share or communicate the experience (e.g., your interest or surprise) with your friend?

It may be that you were using a joint attention gesture in an attempt to share an experience with your friend. Indeed, joint attention behaviors may be viewed as a mechanism through which the young (and old) may share their interest in, or experience of, objects and events with another person (Bruner, 1983; Mundy, Sigman, & Kasari, 1992; Rheingold, Hay & West, 1976). This assumption is not based solely on the type of phenomenological analysis outlined above, but also on extant theory and research in the developmental literature.

Werner and Kaplan (1963), among others, suggested that a fundamental aspect of social behavior involves the capacity to share experiences with others. Indeed, Werner and Kaplan hypothesized that prior to the development of intentional communication skills infant-caregiver interaction revolves around the capacity of both social partners to share experience. They state that early development (approximately 0- to 5-months) is characterized by the "primordial sharing situation" wherein interactions have the characteristic of "sharing experiences with others rather than communicating messages to others" (p.42). Presumably the medium for sharing experience in this early stage of development is the conveyance of, and response to facial and vocal indices of affect (e.g., Bakeman & Adamson, 1982; Klinnert, Campos, Sorce, Emde, & Svedja, 1983; Trevarthen, 1979; Werner & Kaplan, 1963).

Recent work suggests that the capacity to share affective experience becomes elaborated in the infant so that by the latter part of the first year affect is a social signal that may be used in reference to some object or event. In a very informative study Jones, Collins, and Hong (1991) examined the effect of an attentive or inattentive caregiver on the tendency of ten-month-olds to smile to the caregiver while engaged in toy play. Jones et al. reported that in the attentive caregiver condition the infants tended to more frequently smile at the toy, *and then* display the smile to the caregiver. Thus, in this study it appeared that caregivers were not eliciting the smiling behavior. Rather, the infants initiated the sharing of affective experience with regard to toy play in the attentive condition.

If the assumption that joint attention behaviors provide a mechanism for sharing experience in young children is valid then it follows that joint attention behavior may involve the conveyance of affect (Mundy & Sigman, 1989a,c). Moreover, if joint attention behaviors may be distinguished from requesting behaviors on the basis of the function of sharing experience, then, operationally these behavior domains may be distinguished by the degree to which they involve the conveyance of affect (Bruner, 1981). This hypothesis has been examined directly in two recent studies.

Kasari, Sigman, Mundy, and Yirmiya (1990) examined the nonverbal communication behaviors of autistic children and control samples of children with mental retardation or normal development. In this study Kasari et al. merged the ESCS paradigm (Seibert et al, 1982; Mundy et al, 1988) with the Maximally Discriminant Movement Coding System (MAX) developed by Izard (1979) to rate facial affect. This enabled observers to precisely rate facial affect in conjunction with the different types of nonverbal communication bids.

The results of this study indicated that autistic children typically displayed neutral affect when engaged in either joint attention or requesting behaviors. Alternatively, the majority of joint attention bids displayed by the normal and mental retardation control samples involved displays of positive affect. Moreover, in the normal sample joint attention behaviors were associated with the display of positive affect significantly more often than were request behaviors.

Using the merged ESCS/MAX paradigm developed by Kasari and her collegues, another study has examined the co-occurrence of affect and communicative behaviors for four types of joint attention and four types of requesting bids in a sample of 32 normal infants (Mundy, Kasari & Sigman, 1992). The results in this study indicated that more positive affect was displayed in conjunction with each of the four types of joint attention behavior relative to the set of requesting behaviors. On average, positive affect was displayed for over 50% of the duration of the display of all types of joint attention behaviors (range = 56% to 70%). Alternatively, the mean duration of positive affect displayed during requests did not exceed 36% for any type of these behaviors (range = 18% to 36%).

Thus, joint attention bids not only involve the coordination of attention vis-a-vis some object or event, but they also often involve the conveyance of affect. The latter characteristic distinguishes joint attention from requesting behaviors and presumably reflects some aspect of the child's response to, or experience of, the referent object or event. In terms of these, data joint attention deficits suggest that one part of the early developmental disturbance of autistic children is manifest as a deficit in the capacity to share affective states with others (Kasari et al, 1990; Mundy et al. 1993). This interpretation has implications for the description of the nature of self pathology presented by young autistic children.

VI. Joint Attention, Intersubjectivity and Self Development

In the introduction to this chapter it was noted that current theory suggests that self development does not follow a single course in development. Rather it may follow any of one of a variety of trajectories that arise in response to different sources of information that impinge on the child (e.g., Neisser, 1991). Neisser suggests that there are two early aspects of the self that develop in infancy: the ecological and interpersonal. These emerge prior to the conceptual aspects of the self that require sophisticated representational cognition. The ecological self involves the infants understanding[1] or sense of self awareness in reference to visual-spatial, tactile, auditory and other perceptual information concerning the child's nonsocial environmental surroundings. The interpersonal self is generated via the co-perception of actions of the self and related

[1] Understanding may be too cognitive a label for the process involved here since Neisser (1991) suggested that both types of selves derive directly from perception.

contingent actions of others. Thus, the interpersonal self appears to be generated from the perception of action states simulaneously shared by the child and other. Neisser's hypothetical construct of the interpersonal self is not necessarily dissimilar from Trevarthen and Hubley's construct of intersubjectivity, nor is it unrelated to the interpersonal and social cognitive models of Stern (1986) and Wellman (1992). Viewed from the perspective of the latter two models, the interpersonal self of Neisser could be further articulated to involve three arenas in which infants may experience co-perception of actions or experience between self or other. Infants may perceive self and other as sharing: 1) instrumental action states (e.g., "I" and "you" obtain the toy); 2) sensory action states (e.g., "I" and "you" see the toy); and 3) affective action states (e.g., "I" and "you" smile in regard to the toy).

The relation between Trevarthen and Hubley's (1978) construct of intersubjectivity and Neisser's (1991) interpersonal self is apparent in that both hypothetical constructs involve the capacity to engage in the co-perception and/or shared experience of objects and events. Moreover, to the degree that Stern's and Wellman's analyses of early aspects of self-other awareness serves to define three aspects of the interpersonal self, their analyses would also serve to point to three potential arenas of the development of intersubjectivity: instrumental intersubjectivity, sensory/perceptual intersubjectivity, and affective intersubjectivity.

Given this integration of models and constructs, how may the data on the nonverbal communication skills of autistic children be interpreted? First of all, the data seem to suggest that autistic children do not exhibit deficiencies on all aspects of the interpersonal self or the development of intersubjectivity. They do relatively well with the capacity to share instrumental intentions with others as is indicated by their relatively well developed object requesting behavior (Baron-Cohen, 1989a; Curcio, 1978; Mundy et al; 1986, 1990). This intact aspect of intersubjectivity in autism appears to go beyond object requests to include requests for social contact, as when young autistic children use gestures to request repetition of being tickled or touched (Mundy et al. 1986). Hypothetically, both requesting and joint attention may involve the capacity to share peception of objects with others. Thus, this arena of intersubjectivity may not be grossly disturbed among autistic children. This conclusion is consistent with the interpretation of data on understanding visual line of regard trials in older autistic children (Baron-Cohen, 1989a). Alternatively, joint attention, as opposed to requesting, may involve affective intersubjectivity and autistic deficits in the former may reflect a disturbance in the development of this facet of intersubjectivity.

We next consider the degree to which this conjecture fits with current psychological theories on the nature of autism.

VII. Affect and Pathological Process in Autism

The claim that young autistic children exhibit a disturbance in affective intersubjectivity predates research on joint attention development.

Kanner (1943) first suggested that a disturbance of the capacity for affective contact between the child and others was fundamental to the disorder. Hobson (1989) has most recently championed this position. His seminal work has suggested that the core disturbance of autism is the early onset of an affective disturbance that is ultimately manifest as an attenuated capacity to process and understand affective information. Hobson has also discussed the development of the self system and this aspect of autistic pathology (Hobson, 1990b; 1992). There is mixed evidence for a disturbance in the capacity to perceive and process affective information later in the development of autistic children (Hobson, 1986; McDonald et al., 1989; Ozonoff, Pennington & Rogers, 1990; Prior, Dahlstrom, & Squires, 1990; Tager-Flusberg, 1992; Yirmiya, Sigman, Kasari & Mundy, 1992). However, research on affect expression has provided empirical support for the early presentation of an affective related disturbance in autistic children.

Several studies have described disturbances in the capacity of young autistic children to convey affect to others (e.g. Dawson & McKissik, 1984; Ricks, 1979; Snow, Hertzig & Shapiro, 1986; Yirmiya, Kasari, Sigman & Mundy, 1989). These deficits do not appear to reflect a general disturbance in the display of affect (Yirmiya et al. 1989). Rather, the affective disturbance appears to reflect specific deficits in the social display of affect. Similar to the affective disturbance associated with joint attention behaviors, research has indicated that young autistic children display comparable levels of positive affect but less *socially directed* smiling than do controls (Dawson, Hill, Spencer, Galpert and Watson 1990). Moreover, young autistic children display fewer pride related responses to others, such as positive affect and an arms open posture, after achieving task mastery than do controls children (Kasari, Sigman, Baumgartner & Stipek, In press).

In conjunction with research on joint attention deficits, these studies strongly suggest that early in development young autistic children may have difficulty sharing affect with others or using affect in the context of social communication. This may be a fundamental aspect of the early manifestation of this disorder (e.g., Dawson & Lewy, 1989; Kanner, 1943; Hobson, 1986, 1989; Kasari et al. 1990; Mundy & Sigman, 1989). Moreover, as we have tried to argue in this chapter, this arena of disturbance may be associated with a specific anomaly in the autistic individual's developing sense of self and other. Hypothetically, several processes and mechanisms may be involved in this disturbance.

Attempts to understand the nature and repercussions of affective disturbance in young autistic children may vary according to the level of analysis chosen. A bottom-up perspective would attempt to identify the neurophysiological substrates of the apparent autistic disturbance in the capacity to share affective experience. Current research suggests that subcortical and brain stem structures may exert a critical influence (Courchesne, 1989; Dawson & Lewy, 1989b), or that an atypical functional balance between the cerebral hemispheres may contribute to early affective disturbance in autistic children (Fein et al. 1986). Two major neurochemical models also have been suggested. A general model of autistic dysfunction suggests that hyperserotonemia may be an important aspect in

TABLE 1 **Models of Autism and the Construct of Affective Intersubjectivity**

Model	Core Pathological Process	Relation to Affective Intersubjectivity
Theory of Mind (Baron-Cohen, 1988)	Cognitive impairment. Deficit in secondary representation leads to difficulty in understanding beliefs, feelings, and thoughts of others.	No clear relation to disturbed affective intersubjectivity, affective disturbance is an epiphenomenon of cognitive impairment.
Representational Mapping (Rogers & Pennington, 1991)	Neurocognitive. Frontal dysfunction leads to impaired capacity to coordinate representations of self and other.	Deficit in affective intersubjectivity flows directly from representational mapping deficit.
Arousal Model (Dawson & Lewy, 1989)	Cognitive & Affective. Impaired capacity to process & predict social events leads to over arousal and impaired social functioning.	Cognitive disturbance leads to arousal. This, in turn, leads to impaired affective intersubjectivity and this is a primary factor in the early development of autistic children.
Affect Model (Hobson, 1989)	Affective. An impaired capacity to process or express affect appropriately creates and impoverishment of information that is important to normal social cognitive development.	The disturbance in affective intersubjectivity arises directly from impairment in systems mediating early emotional development. A recent version of this model incorporates aspects of the representational mapping and arousal models (Mundy et al. 1993)

the etiology of behavior disturbance exhibited by at least a subset of autistic individuals (Ritvo, et al. 1970). In a model specific to social behavior, Panksepp and others have suggested that an early imbalance in systemic endorphins may have a critical effect on behavior development in young autistic children (Panksepp, 1979; Panksepp, Siving, & Normansell, 1985).

Alternatively, a top-down perspective leads to attempts to describe the psychological processes that may be involved in a developmental disturbance of affective intersubjectivity in young autistic children. Here several models may be considered. How these models may attempt to explain autistic joint attention deficits and related anomalies of affective intersubjectivity is outlined in Table 1 and discussed in some detail in the following sections.

The Theory of Mind Model

The proponents of the theory of mind model of autism have attempted to explain joint attention deficits in terms of representational cognitive processes (Baron-Cohen, 1988; Leslie and Happe, 1989). They have not directly addressed themselves to explanations of the affective component of joint attention that is manifest at least among young children. However, some theory of mind supporters may not agree that there is compelling evidence for early affective deficits in autism (Leslie & Happe, 1989), or if these deficits exist, that they are important to the nature of autism. Thus, the theory of mind proponents have not yet attempted to extend their model to the explication of early arising affective components of social communication deficits in autistic children (For a more complete discussion of the theory of mind model and joint attention, see Mundy, Sigman, & Kasari, 1993). Nevertheless, the theory of mind model does make a compelling attempt to explain joint attention deficits in young autistic children (Baron-Cohen, 1989b; Leslie & Happe, 1989).

To understand the Theory of Mind model recall the assumption that nonverbal communication skills reflect developments in the young child's understanding of self and other (Bretherton, 1991; Bretherton et al, 1981; Stern, 1985; Wellman, 1992). This model suggests that autistic children display deficiencies on joint attention, but not requesting skills, because the former involves cognitive processes attendant to understanding self and other that the latter does not involve (Baron-Cohen, 1989b; Mundy et al. 1986).

What type of cognitive processes may differentiate joint attention and requesting skills? As noted earlier, requesting may involve an understanding that self and other may share a common instrumental goal. However, as the work of Werner and Kaplan (1963) suggests, while requesting skills may involve understanding self and others as agents of action, joint attention skills may involve understanding self and other as agents of contemplation (Mundy et al. 1986). We have previously noted that both joint attention and requesting skills may involve understanding that self and other can share a common perception of objects and events. However, the theory of mind model suggests that understanding self and others as agents of contemplation may go beyond this understanding of common perceptual experience.

To understand other as an agent of action and to understand that self and other can share common percepts may require only that the child access representations of previously processed and stored action sequences, such as "other retrieves object" or "other turns eyes toward object". This may demand the representation of *overt* aspects of behavior and, thereby, the understanding of potential causal relations between self, other, and object. However, the cognitive processes involved in this may be of a relatively low order, involving what Mandler (1988) has described as sensorimotor or procedural representation of motor and perceptual acts.

Alternatively, if joint attention involves understanding other as an agent of contemplation, this may involve the capacity to represent more *covert* aspects of behavior such as the internal experience of seeing an object or event or thinking about an object and event (Baron-Cohen, 1988, 1989b). Theoretically, such a representational process would be of a higher order than that involved in requesting or sensorimotor representations. Such higher order representations might involve a conscious self awareness of perceiving and a representational scheme of other as capable of perceiving. This may, in turn, entail symbolic process (Baron-Cohen, 1989a; Mandler, 1988).

This cognitive/symbolic process hypothesis may be open to empirical inquiry. Measures of pretense play with objects constitutes an early measure of symbolic development in young children (Leslie, 1987). Moreover, young autistic children display marked difficulty on measures of pretense play (Baron-Cohen, 1987; Leslie 1988; Riquet, Taylor, Benaroya, & Klein, 1981; Sigman & Ungerer, 1984; Wing, Gould, Yeates & Brierly, 1977). Hence, examining the relations among the development of pretense play, joint attention, and requesting skills in autistic children provides one approach to the cognitive hypothesis under discussion.

This approach has guided a preliminary longitudinal study of 15 young autistic children and a language matched control sample of 15 children with mental retardation (Mundy, Sigman, & Kasari, 1993). The data from this study indicated that joint attention deficits were manifest by autistic children relative to controls during the initial assessment session. However, differences in symbolic play were not apparent at that time because neither the autistic nor control sample displayed sufficient amounts of symbolic play behaviors. Follow-up testing thirteen months later indicated that the autistic joint attention deficits were still displayed. In addition, sufficient development in play behavior had occurred to allow autistic play deficits to begin to emerge. Thus, these data were consistent with the hypothesis that the emergence of joint attention deficits may initially reflect a presymbolic arena of developmental disturbance in autistic children (Mundy & Sigman, 1989a,b; Sugarman, 1984; Wellman, 1992). If joint attention deficits arise before the types of representational skills involved in theory of mind are operative, then this model may need to be modified to be applicable to the early manifestations of joint attention deficits in autistic children. However, currently there is insufficient data to provide a definitive resolution to this important issue.

Representational Mapping and Affect

Rogers and Pennington (1991) have also recently presented a cognitive model of autism. Unlike the theory of mind model, this representational mapping model explicitly addresses both joint attention deficits and the possible early affective disturbance associated with this disorder. Indeed, this is a neurocognitive model that explicitly addresses the developing understanding of self and other in autistic children.

According to Rogers and Pennington, a disturbance of the prefrontal neocortex of autistic children may lead to a deficit in the capacity to form and coordinate cognitive representations of self and other. The process of coordinating representations of self and other is referred to as representational mapping. The central hypothesis of this model is that a disturbance of this capacity attenuates the development of all aspects of intersubjectivity in autistic children, including the capacity to share affective states, to share common motor action states (i.e., imitation of motor actions), and to share higher order aspects of cognition such as thoughts, beliefs, etc.

At first glance, the representational mapping process of Rogers and Pennington appears similar to the meta-representational process described by theory of mind researchers (e.g., Baron-Cohen, this volume; Leslie, 1987). However, Rogers and Pennington argue that the representational mapping process described in their model is operative in the course of development before the meta-representational process of the theory of mind model. Indeed, Rogers and Pennington appear to be describing a process analogous to the early developing co-perception of self and other that Neisser (1988) suggests is fundamental to the development of an infant's interpersonal self.

Rogers and Pennington argue that representational mapping is first manifest in normal development in the neonatal (0 to 3 months) capacity to imitate motor states. Borrowing from Malatesta and Izard (1984), they suggest that early imitation skills allow the infant to match their own affective display to the perceived adult affective displays. This provides a context for early shared affect that enables the child to learn about affect of self and others. Children with autism, however, do not engage in shared affective states because a representational mapping deficit inhibits the capacity for early motor imitation that, in turn, disrupts the ability of these children to enter into shared affective states.

This is a plausible and well articulated model. It incorporates accumulating evidence that a disturbance of a complex system involving the brain stem (e.g., Courchesne, 1991) and prefrontal cortex may give rise to difficulty with flexible and strategic attention regulation among autistic children. In this model the affective sharing deficit of autistic individuals is considered to be secondary to a basic cognitive or neurocognitive deficit. Moreover, this model leads to testable hypotheses.

According to this model, one might expect joint attention performance among autistic children to be associated with measures sensitive to frontal lobe functioning. This hypothesis has been explored in a recent study (McEvoy, Rogers, & Pennington, 1993). Data from this study indicated that autistic children exhibited significantly more perseverative responses on a spatial reversal task. According to McEvoy et al., this task is a measure of frontally mediated behavior. Moreover, in an analysis of data combined across autistic and control samples performance on the spatial reversal task was significantly correlated with joint attention behavior, as measured on the Early Social-Communication Scales, even after controlling for variance associated with diagnostic groups.

Serendipitously, relevant data have also been provided in a study of nonverbal communication in 13 children with intractable seizures (Caplan, Chugani, Messa, Guthrie, Sigman, Traversay, Mundy, & Phelps; in press). In this study positron emission tomography patterns of cerebral glucose metabolism were observed in the children prior to surgical intervention for their seizure disorder. The results indicated that preoperative glucose metabolism in the prefrontal region was significantly correlated with postoperative change measures of joint attention skills, again using the ESCS. Glucose uptake in other regions of the cerebrum (e.g. orbital, parietal, temporal) was not related to nonverbal development, and other types of nonverbal skills such as requesting were not associated with preoperative frontal metabolic rate.

At a minimum these data are consistent with the basic tenet of the representational mapping model that frontal functions, and deficits therein, may be associated with the disturbance of joint attention development among autistic children. However, these data do not speak directly to the construct of representational mapping. The construct of representational mapping is a broad one and a pervasive deficit in this mechanism would seem to lead to a complete loss of the capacity for intersubjectivity. Alternatively, we have proposed that autism is characterized by a specific disturbance intersubjectivity rather than a general deficit. If this is true then the representational mapping hypothesis may need to be honed to apply to specific arenas of coordinating representations of self and other. Indeed, it may be that early in development autism is characterized by a disturbance in the control of affect and representational thinking that combine to yield an especially pronounced deisturbance in the capacity to coordinate or simultaneously process the affect of self with information on the emotions of others (Mundy et al. 1993).

In addition, when considering representational mapping it is noteworthy that much of this model is based on two assumptions: a) the existence of neonatal imitation in normal development and b) evidence of a disturbance in imitation skills in autistic children. The first assumption is controversial. Considerable data has been presented in support of presence of imitation skills early in infancy (e.g., Meltzoff & Moore, 1989). However, a recent review of the literature (Anisfeld, 1991) suggests that there is too little information on this phenomenon to draw strong conclusions. Anisfeld notes that consistent evidence of neonatal imitation exists for only one type of behavior, tongue protrusion. Moreover, he maintains that the contiguity of adult and neonatal tongue protrusion found in several studies may be due to an orienting response rather than imitation. Thus, there are differences of opinion within the literature regarding whether motor imitation warrants the developmental primacy extended to it by the Rogers and Pennington model.

The second assumption of this model is less controversial. For the most part research has been consistent in suggesting that autistic children imitate the acts of others less frequently than do comparison children (e.g., Jones and Prior, 1985; Sigman & Ungerer, 1984). However, there are exceptions to these findings (Morgan, Cutrer, Coplin & Rodrigue, 1989). Moreover, even young autistic children seem to be quite responsive to being imitated by others (Dawson & Lewy, 1989). These data may suggest that the capacity of the autistic child to recognize coordination of acts of other with acts of self may not be pervasively impaired. The examination and resolution of this possibility may be of importance to the representational mapping model.

The Arousal Model

Another model that speaks directly to the affective sharing deficits of autistic children has been proposed by Dawson and Lewy (1989). This model is based on the long standing hypothesis that autistic children may have deficient arousal modulating systems (Hutt, Hutt, Lee & Ounsted, 1964; Ornitz & Ritvo, 1968). After acknowledging the methodological limits of the extant literature, these authors note that electrophysiological research suggests that autistic individuals display abnormally high values on measures of arousal and appear to respond to unpredictable and novel objects or events with indices of increased arousal and reduced information processing capacity. Dawson and Lewy extrapolate from this research that autistic children may have a restricted range of optimal stimulation and suggest that social stimulation, because of its relatively unpredictable nature, may frequently exceed these optimal stimulation limits. Thus, in social situations young autistic children may be handicapped by the frequent experience of overarousal.

Dawson and Lewy explicitly predict that this difficulty in arousal modulation could be expected to negatively affect the early formation of attachment relationships, the expression of emotions, and what they refer to as the interpersonal coordination of affect in autistic children. In regard to the latter, these authors suggest that very early on in development the autistic child's atypical arousal response to the unpredictable nature of social stimuli would decrease the likelihood that caregiver and child would experience shared affective states. For example, a smiling caregiver may be too arousing for the autistic child, eliciting a negative affective state rather than a shared positive experience. Moreover, in the context of overarousal, information processing would be reduced. Therefore, even if the affect of the child and caregiver matched, the child's processing of the match and opportunity to develop an intersubjective aspect of self would be impaired.

The importance of this model lies in its well reasoned discussions of the possible processes that may link basic neurophysiological disturbance with social deficits in autism. Moreover, this model also leads to explicit hypotheses that may be empirically examined. For example, this model may be construed to suggest that there should be some evidence of a disturbance in arousal modulation among autistic children during tasks that typically elicit joint attention bids in children.

Despite its strengths, this model would well be served by the clarification of several issues. First, it is not clear in the Dawson and Lewy model why autistic children should display uneven development across social skill development. How, for example, would this model explain data indicating that, during assessment with the Early-Social Communication Scales, young autistic children display relative proficiency at requesting objects or tickle interactions, but less facility with joint attention bids (Mundy et al. 1986)? Would the model need to suggest that joint attention situations presented in the Early Social-Communication Scales were less predictable and, therefore, more arousing than opportunities to request? This seems unlikely. The behavior and proximity of the experimenter to the child does not vary greatly in the Early Social-Communication Scales across joint attention, social interaction or requesting opportunities. Indeed, perhaps one of the least predictable and most arousing social episodes in this assessment occurs when the tester sings a song and tickles the child. However, autistic children respond with as much eye contact and gestural requests for repetition of the tickle as do children with mental retardation or typical development (Mundy et al. 1986).

A second, but related issue is that the arousal model does not present sufficient detail regarding the nature of the process that results in difficulty for autistic children in predicting social stimuli. This difficulty presumably reflects cognitive functions and these appear to be at the core of the causal pathway described by this model. That is, the model suggests that difficulty in predicting social events leads to overarousal which, in turn, leads to negative effects on the development of affective sharing.

Given the importance of the cognitive construct in this model, the arousal model would be enhanced by explication of the nature of this hypothetical cognitive process. One important question concerns when in development the difficulty with stimulus predictability begins. Does this disturbance disrupt the very beginnings of affective sharing in autistic children? If so, this would necessarily be a very early developing cognitive process since Dawson and Lewy (1989) note that affective sharing processes may typically have their onset in the second or third month of life.

The Affect Model

The models of Dawson and Lewy (1989) and Rogers and Pennington (1990) both suggest that a cognitive process deficit may undermine the development of affective sharing, the related aspects of intersubjectivity, and self-other awareness in autistic children. Alternatively, Hobson (1989, 1990) has cogently argued that there is a biologically based capacity for nonverbal interaction, and specifically shared affective experience, that is manifest in infancy. This hypothesis is based on theory espoused by Baldwin (1902), Stern (1985), Neisser (1988) and others. It also harkens back to Kanner's (1943) original position that autism reflects a deficiency in the biological systems that regulate the ability of children to develop affective contact with others.

The affect model suggests that early social behavior and the developing capacity for early affective sharing may not necessarily be regulated by cognition. It has been a seminal influence in the field as it has reminded us not to ignore the possibility that an early affective deficit, independent of cognitive disturbance, may play a role in autism. However, the model is not sufficiently explicit with regard to the process involved in the early affective deficit of autistic children. For example, is the affective disturbance manifest as a general deficit in the experience and display of emotions by young autistic children? Probably not, because autistic children appear to display a normal range of facial affect (Yirmiya, et al. 1989).

In considering the Kanner-Hobson suggestion of the possible primacy of an affective disturbance in autism, it may be useful to view early normal affective development from a framework similar to that of discrete emotions theory (e.g. Izard, 1977). With regard to the early development of affect this theory suggests that emotions may best be conceived as instinct-like behaviors with a range of elicitors that can provoke a particular response (Izard and Malatesta, 1987). In autism a biologically based disturbance may lead directly to an imbalance in the range of elicitors that provoke a particular affective response in autistic children. Panksepp's model of a neonatal imbalance in endogenous opiates among autistic children articulates one possible mechanism of this biological disturbance (Panksepp, 1979; Panksepp, et al. 1985; Sahley & Panksepp, 1987).

Panksepp suggests that social behavior is linked to the release and uptake of endorphins at prescribed central nervous system receptor cites. This uptake of endorphins or endogenous opiates serves to reward and potentiate social behavior. In autism, however, an elevation of central nervous system endorphin levels is thought to disrupt this inherent reward system for social behavior because endorphin receptors cites are chronically filled. Therefore, the biological feedback system that normally serves to make social behavior a prepotent stimulus for children early in development is attenuated. An extension of this model suggests that one specific effect may be a reduction of affective sharing among autistic children. Such an effect could be explained if we assume that affective sharing is one external marker of the degree to which very young children find social behavior to be intrinsically rewarding. Thus, linking the affect model with the Panksepp's neurochemical model of social behavior suggests that much of the social disturbance evinced by autistic children, including joint attention deficits, is due to a faulty biological positive feedback system that normally potentiates social behavior.

VIII. An Integration Across Models

The models described above provide the framework for current attempts to understand the nature of early disturbance of affective sharing in autistic children. Each of these models has much to offer, but none is definitive. Current problems associated with each model do not reflect inadequacies on the part of the model developers so much as they reflect inadequacies and limits of current knowledge with regard to the mechanisms of early normal social and emotional development (or perhaps limits in the present authors understanding of these models). Nevertheless, each model is heuristic and encourages the consideration of a diverse array of mechanisms in attempts to understand the nature of joint attention deficits in autistic children.

While these models differ in the psychological and neurological processes described, there is some consistency in the notion that a disturbance in the capacity to engage in shared affective states may be fundamental to the nature of autism. Regardless of the causal mechanisms, such an early arising disturbance may have important implications for the subsequent development of autistic children (Dawson & Lewy, 1989; Hobson, 1989; Rogers & Pennington, 1991).

We have previously attempted to describe the possible sequelae of early affective sharing deficits among young autistic children (Mundy et al. 1993). In brief, the description of this hypothetical process draws upon two threads of developmental theory. One of these is the assumption that the development of specific social and cognitive skills are tied to the provision of specific experiences or information to the cognitive system of the child (Fischer & Pipp, 1984). The other notion is that the process involved in the exchange of affect between the young child and others itself provides a unique source of information that plays a role in fostering the development of specific aspects of social cognition (Malatesta & Izard, 1984).

In the case of autism, regardless of the mechanism, the attenuation of early opportunities to engage in shared affect *vis-a-vis* objects is hypothesized to present a critical impoverishment of the information available to the developing autistic child (cf., Dawson and Lewy, 1989; Hobson, 1989). Accordingly, the autistic child would have fewer opportunities to compare their own affective experience of an object or event (proprioceptive or self affect) with the perceived emotion displayed by another person that corresponds to that external object or event (exteroceptive or other affect). This may be viewed as a disturbance in the co-perception of affect (Neisser, 1988) or the representational mapping between affect of the self and emotions of others (Roger's and Pennington, 1991). Regardless of terminology, the attenuation of opportunities to engage in shared affect may be one critical component of early autistic pathology.

These opportunities to compare self and other affect *vis-a-vis* a third reference may be necessary for children to develop a sense of the commonality between self affect and other affect. Hypothetically, this "sense" is embodied in the development of integrated cognitive representations of the affect of self and other. This type of integrated representation may ultimately enable children to interpret the affective displays of others via reference to detailed information on affect of self. That is, the child's cognitive analysis and integration of shared affective states may lead to a specific symbolic representational system that enables the child to interpret the affect of others "as if it were my own" (see Mundy et al. 1993).

In the autistic child a disturbance in this process of integrating representations may contribute to subsequent deficits in the social cognitive development among autistic children (Mundy et al. 1993). The processes described in this model are analogous, if not identical, to processes described in other models of autism (Dawson & Lewy, 1989; Hobson, 1989; Rogers and Pennington, 1991). Redundancy notwithstanding, this model has been presented to emphasize two points. First, an early affective disturbance may feedback on the child, diminishing the availability of important social information for autistic children. Second, since cognitive development is at least partially dependent on the information available to the child, such an early impoverishment may deflect the path of cognitive development in these children and contribute to the subsequent anomalies in social cognition that are characteristic of autistic children (Mundy et al. 1993). Thus, the early putative difficulty in engaging shared affect between self and other need not be regarded as a core deficit (Ungerer, 1989), but rather simply one of a variety of important developmental missteps that ultimately lead autistic children down an atypical and distressing developmental path.

IX. Atypical Nonverbal Communication and Developmental Psychopathology

The study of the early emergence of the self and related aspects of social cognition constitute a complex, but potentially valuable arena of inquiry with respect to psychopathology (Cicchetti, 1991). Moreover, as readers familiar with the basic tenets of Developmental Psychopathology are aware, there is (or at least should be) a well traveled two way street between research on normal and atypical paths of self development (Cicchetti, 1991; Hobson, 1990). That is, just as information on normal development should stimulate inquiry and knowledge relevant to psychopathology, research on abnormal development should stimulate research on normal aspects of ontology (Cicchetti, 1984; Sroufe & Rutter, 1984). Although it hopefully has been inferred throughout this chapter, let us now explicitly articulate how the research and theory that we have presented illustrates this tenet of Developmental Psychopathology.

Models of normal infant development and theory on the importance of nonverbal communication as a marker of early social and cognitive development (Bates et al. 1979; Bruner & Sherwood; 1983) give rise to much of the research that has been reviewed in this chapter. Moreover, recent developments in theory on early normal interpersonal and social-cognitive development (Neisser, 1991; Stern, 1985; Wellman, 1993) have provided a foundation for the new interpretation of autistic deficiencies in nonverbal communication that we have attempted to describe in this chapter. However, it is also clearly the case that research on nonverbal communication in atypical samples may inform and stimulate research among those interested in normal development.

Prior to the application of theory on nonverbal communication skills to atypical populations it was hypothesized that this skill domain constituted an important arena of social cognitive development that may be related to subsequent cognitive and linguistic skill acquisition (Bates et al. 1979; Bretherton, 1991; Bruner & Sherwood, 1983; Golinkoff, 1983; Sugarman, 1984). To date, it has been research on atypical populations that may have provided the most cogent support for this hypothesis. For example, two longitudinal studies have indicated that nonverbal communications skills predict language acquisition in children with autism (Mundy et al. 1990) and children with Down Syndrome (Mundy et al. submitted).

These data support extant models of the place and importance of nonverbal communication skills in early development. However, with the exception of earlier work (Bates et al. 1979; Bruner, 1981) the nature of nonverbal communication skills remains largely unexplored. In this regard, research on nonverbal communication in atypical children raises at least three issues for further study.

Young autistic children characteristically exhibit specific social deficits on early measures of joint attention skills. Older autistic children characteristically display specific social-cognitive deficits on theory of mind paradigms such as false belief tasks (Baron-Cohen, 1988; Perner & Wimmer, 1985). This confluence of deficits within one syndrome has suggested that there may be a link between the early social cognitive processes inherent to joint attention skill development and the types of social cognitive processes measured at age three and four in theory of mind paradigms (Baron-Cohen, 1989b; Mundy & Sigman, 1989b). Understanding the parameters of this hypothetical link may be an important issue for the study of normal development. Future studies may profitably address this issue through longitudinal research on individual differences in nonverbal communication and subsequent social cognition in both normal and atypically developing children.

Second, studies of atypical nonverbal communication development raise the issue of whether nonverbal communication skills reflect a monolithic domain or whether important differences exist between the development of different types of skills. As noted earlier, specific deficits in nonverbal requesting skills are more apparent in Down Syndrome while deficits in joint attention skills are more apparant in children with autism (Mundy et al. 1986; 1988). While the distinction between these two classes of skills has long been recognized (Bates et al. 1979), these findings suggests that they may differ in fundamental ways. As this chapter hopefully has already illustrated, exploring how these two skills may be different is important to understanding the nature of autism. In addition, attempts to understand the differences in these skills may be revealing with regard to normal development. For example, the hypothesis that nonverbal communication skills are related to later developing language skills (Bates et al. 1979) may be too broad. We may need to examine specific types of nonverbal communication skills to evelaute this hypothesized association. Thus, future research may explore the relative predict validity of measures of nonverbal requesting and joint attention skills for language development in normal toddlers.

Attempts to understand differences in atypical children's development of nonverbal communication also begun to push our understanding of the associated neurological mechanisms. In this chapter we described the convergence of studies by McEvoy et al (1993) and Caplan et al. (In press) which suggest that joint attention skills development may be closely tied to frontal cortical functions. This opens up an exciting arena of inquiry. For example, it may be possible to use existing methods for electroencephalogram (EEG) recording with infants and toddlers (Fox and Bell, 1990) to begin to explore the cortical activation correlates of nonverbal communication development in normal infants. This type of research could provide important information on early normal social-communication development as well as information pertinent to understanding the anomalies in nonverbal communication development that have been observed in children with autism and Down syndrome.

Finally, and perhaps most pertinent to the content of this chapter, attempts to understand differences in types of nonverbal communication skills have lead us to conclude that measures of joint attention skills reflect the capacity of the child to share affective components of subjective experience *vis-a-vie* an object or event. Thus, measures of joint attention skills provide an operationalization of one aspect of intersubjectivity and, as such, provide a tool with potential for basic and clinical research on the integration of affect and cognition in the developing interpersonal world of the young child (Mundy et al. 1992).

The research implications of this conjecture are considerable. For example, research and theory have long maintained that nonverbal communication development is related to the development of the attachment system in young children (Bretherton, Bates, Benigni, Camaioni, & Volterra, 1979). However, the details of this relation have not been clearly defined. The foregoing hypotheses, however, would suggest that the attachment system may be most directly related to the development of joint attention skills in children as both may be mediated by the child's tendency to share affective states with others. Moreover, if this hypothesis is valid then one might expect nonverbal communication measures, especially joint attention measures, to be sensitive to early perturbations in interpersonal development that are common to children who experience abusive life histories (see Cicchetti & Carlson, 1989, for review). While this hypothesis has received some recent attention (Coster, Gersten, Beeghly, & Cicchetti, 1989) a detailed analysis of the nonverbal communication skills of maltreated toddlers remains an important arena for future inquiry. Moreover, if the foregoing interpretation of the nature of nonverbal communication skills is valid, then the combination of research on the relation of nonverbal communication development to cortical functions, attachment, and the effects of maltreatment may provide unique information on important cognitive and affective processes that occur in the first years of life.

X. Conclusions

In concluding this chapter we would like to point out that autism is a disorder that, by definition, is first manifest early in development (American Psychiatric Association, 1986). Increasingly, knowledge garnered in studies of normal development are being brought to bear on the nature of autism with beneficial results. In this chapter we have discussed how research based on a model of infant preverbal communication has illuminated the nature of the social deficits that are manifest by young autistic children. Specifically, the research we described indicates that young autistic children present with a disturbance in a domain of preverbal communication development called joint attention skills. In keeping with one characteristic of developmental psychopathology (Cicchetti, 1984), this provides an example of how basic research on normal development may inform research in psychopathology.

In order to understand the nature of the deficit reflected in this disturbance we typically return to the developmental literature for advice. However, the normal developmental literature is not always prepared to answer the questions that arise in developmental research on psychopathology. For example, there was not a well articulated body of knowledge that would lend itself to understanding why autistic children may do well on nonverbal requesting skills, but poorly on nonverbal joint attention skills. Indeed it has been research on autism and Down syndrome that has alerted us to the possibility that these two dimensions of preverbal communication development may reflect at least partially independent domains (Mundy et al. 1992). It is often the case, then, that the explication of the results of applied developmental research in psychopathology is dependent upon going beyond the extant developmental literature to attempt to synthesize new and, hopefully, explanatory models.

We have attempted to do this by examining the affective components of different types of nonverbal communication behaviors. Moreover, in this chapter, we sought to extend this work by integrating extant theory on nonverbal communication, early interpersonal development, and social cognition in order to interpret joint attention development and its disruption in terms of disturbance in the early development of intersubjectivity and the self system of autistic children. In so doing we have described some of the common elements in proposals made by Niesser (1988), Stern (1986), Trevarthen and Hubley (1979) and Wellman (1992) and suggested that self development and the allied development of intersubjectivity proceed along varied paths. In turn, it was argued that the data on nonverbal communication development in young autistic children may indicate that early development in autistic children is not characterized by a pervasive disturbance of the capacity for intersubjectivity. Rather, early development in autism may be characterized by a specific type of disturbance within the general capacity for intersubjectivity. In young autistic children those aspects of intersubjectivity and self development that are associated with the capacity to experience or share common affective states with others appear to significantly disturbed.

Other examples of this type of synthesis abound in the current literature on nature of autistic developmental psychopathology (e.g., Baron-Cohen, 1988; Dawson & Lewy, 1989; Hobson, 1989; Rogers & Pennington, 1991). For example, attempts to understand the possible connections between early occurring deficits in autistic children such as joint attention skills and latter occurring deficits on social cognitive measures such as false belief tasks may contribute to new models of social cognitive development and the relations between affect and cognition in development (Mundy & Sigman, 1989; Mundy et al, 1992; Rogers & Pennington, 1991; Wellman, 1992). Thus, much of the research in autism, having originally been guided by the extant developmental literature, is now beginning to broach questions and issues that may inform and facilitate research on normal development. This type of feedback from the literature on the atypical, to the literature on the typical, is an ideal of developmental psychopathology.

REFERENCES

American Psychiatric Association (1987). *Diagnostic and statistical manual of mental disorders (Third Edition-Revised)*. Washington, D.C.: American Psychiatric Association.

Anisfeld, M. (1991). Neonatal imitation. *Developmental Review, 11*, 60–97.

Asperger, H. (1944). Die 'autistischen psychopathen 'im kindesalter. *Archiv fur Psychiatrie und Nervenkrankheiten, 117*, 76–136.

Baldwin, J. (1902). *Social and ethical interpretations in mental development.* New York: Macmillan.

Bakeman, R. & Adamson, L. (1984). Coordinating attention to people and objects in mother infant and peer-infant interaction. *Child Development, 55*, 1278–12.

Baron-Cohen, S. (1987). Autism and symbolic play. *British Journal of Developmental Psychology, 5*, 379–402.

Baron-Cohen, S. (1988). Social and pragmatic deficits in autism: Cognitive or affective? *Journal of Autism and Developmental Disorders, 21*, 37–46.

Baron-Cohen, S. (1989a). The autistic child's theory of mind: A case of specific developmental delay. *Journal of Child Psychology and Psychiatry, 30*, 285–297.

Baron-Cohen, S. (1989b). Joint-attention deficits in autism: Towards a cognitive analysis. *Development and Psychopathology, 3*, 185–190.

Bates, E., Benigni, L., Bretherton, I., Camaioni, L. & Volterra, V. (1979). *The emergence of symbols: Cognition and communication in infancy.* New York: Academic Press.

Bretherton, I. (1991). Intentional communication and the development of an understanding of mind. In D. Frye and C. Moore (Eds.), *Children's Theories of Mind: Mental States and Social Understanding,* (pp. 271–289). Hillsdale, NJ: Lawrence Erlbaum Associates.

Bretherton, I., Bates, E., Benigni, L., Camaioni, L. & Volterra, V. (1979). Relationships between cognition, communication, and quality of attachment. In Bates, E. et al. *The emergence of symbols: Cognition and communication in infancy,* (pp. 223–269). New York: Academic Press.

Bruner, J. (1981). Learning how to do things with words. In J. Bruner & A. Garton (Eds.) *Human grown and development,* (pp. 62–84). London, England: Oxford University Press.

Bruner, J. & Sherwood, V. (1983). Thought, language and interaction in infancy. In J. Call, E. Galenson, & R. Tyson (Eds.) *Frontiers of infant psychiatry,* (pp. 38–55). New York: Basic Books.

Caplan, R., Chugani, H., Messa, C., Guthrie, D., Sigman, M., Traversay, J., Mundy, P., & Phelps, M. (In press). Hemispherectomy for early onset intractable seizures: Presurgical cerebral glucose metabolism and postsurgical nonverbal communication patterns. *Developmental Medicine and Child Neurology.*

Cicchetti, D. (1984). The emergence of developmental psychopathology. *Child Development, 55,* 1–7.

Cicchetti, D. (1991). Fractures in the crystal ball: Developmental psychopathology and the emergence of self. *Developmental Review, 11,* 271–287.

Cicchetti, D. & Carlson, V. (1989). *Child maltreatment: Theory and research on the causes and consequence of child abuse.* New York: Cambridge University Press.

Courchesne, E. (April, 1991). *The theory of mind deficit in autism: Possible biological bases.* Paper presented at the Workshop on Theory of Mind in Research on Autism, Seattle, Washington.

Coster, W., Gersten, M., Beeghly, M. & Cicchetti, D. (1989). Communicative functioning in maltreated toddlers. *Developmental Psychology, 25,* 1020–1029.

Curcio, F. (1978). Sensorimotor functioning and communication in mute autistic children. *Journal of Autism and Childhood Schizophrenia,* 8, 282–292.

Dawson, G. & Lewy, A. (1989). Arousal, attention, and the socioemotional impairments of individuals with autism. In G. Dawson (Ed.), *Autism, nature, diagnosis, and treatment* (pp. 49–74) New York: Guilford

Dawson, G. & Lewy, A. (1989b). Reciprocal subcortical-cortical influences in autism: The role of attentional mechanisms. In E. Dawson (Ed.), *Autism, nature, diagnosis, and treatment* (pp. 144–173). New York: Guilford

Dawson, G. & McKissick, F. (1984). Self recognition in autistic children. *Journal of Autism and Developmental Disorders, 14,* 383–394.

Dawson, G., Hill, D., Spencer, A., Galpert, L. & Watson, L. (1990). Affective exchanges between young autistic children and their mothers. *Journal of Abnormal Child Psychology, 18,* 335–345.

Fein, D., Pennington, B., Markowitz, P., Braverman, M., & Waterhouse, L. (1986). Toward a neuropsychological model of infantile autism: Are the social deficits primary? *Journal of the Academy of Child & Adolescent Psychiatry, 25,* 198–212.

Fischer, K., & Pipp, S. (1984). Process in cognitive development: Optimal level and skill acquisition. In R. Sternberg (Ed.), *Mechanisms of cognitive development,* (pp.45–80). New York: W. H. Freeman.

Frith, U. (1989). A new look at language and communication in autism. *British Journal of Disorders of Communication, 24,* 123–150.

Fox, N. & Bell, M. (1990). Electrophysiological indices of frontal lobe development: Relations to cognition and affective behavior in human infants over the first year of life. In A. Diamond (Ed.), *The development and neural bases of higher cognitive functions* (pp. 677–698). New York: New York Academy of Sciences Press.

Gillberg, C. (1988). The neurobiology of autism. *Journal of Child Psychology and Psychiatry, 29*, 257–266.

Goldfarb, W. (1963). Self awareness in schizophrenic children. *Archives of General Psychiatry, 8*, 63–77.

Golinkoff, R. (1983). The preverbal negotiation of failed messages: Insights into the transition period. In R. Golinkoff (Ed.), *The transition from prelinquistic to linguistic communication*, (p. 57–78). Hillsdale, NJ: Lawrence Erlbaum Associates.

Gomez, C. & Tamarit, J. (1993). The comparative study of early communication and theories of mind: Ontology, phylogeny, and pathology. In S. Baron-Cohen, H. Tager-Flusberg & D. Cohen (Eds.), *Understanding other minds:Perspective from Autism*, (pp. 397–426). Oxford, UK: Oxford University Press.

Hobson, P. (1986). The autistic child's appraisal of expressions of emotion. *Journal of Child Psychology and Psychiatry, 27*, 321–342.

Hobson, P. (1989). Beyond cognition: A theory of autism. In G. Dawson (Ed.), *Autism: Nature, Diagnosis and Treatment*, (pp. 22–48). New York: Guilford Press.

Hobson, P. (1990a). On the origins of self and the case of autism. *Development & Psychopathology, 2*, 163–181.

Hobson, P. (1990b). On acquiring knowledge about people and the capacity to pretend. Response to Leslie (1987). *Psychological Review, 97*, 114–121.

Howlin, P. (1986). An overview of social behavior in autism. In E. Schopler and G. Mesibov (Eds.), *Social behavior in autism*, (pp. 103–131). New York: Plenum.

Hutt, S., Hutt, C., Lee, D. & Ounsted, C. (1965). A behavioral and electroencephalographic study of autistic children. *Journal of Psychiatric Research, 3*, 181–197.

Izard, C. (1979). *The maximally discriminant facial movement coding system*. Newark: Instructional Resources Center, University of Delaware.

Izard, C. (1977). *Human emotions*. New York: Plenum.

Izard, C. and Maltesta, C. (1987). Perspectives on emotional development: I. Differential emotions theory of early emotional development. In J. Osofsky (Ed.), *Handbook of infant development*, (2nd ed.) (pp. 494–554). New York: John Wiley.

Jones, V. & Prior, M. (1985). Motor imitation abilities and neurological signs in autistic children. *Journal of Autism and Developmental Disabilities, 15*, 37–46.

Jones, S., Collins, K. & Hong, H. (1991). An audience effect on smile production in 10-month-old infants. *Psychological Science, 2*, 45–49.

Kanner, L. (1943). Autistic disturbances of affective contact. *Nervous Child, 2*, 217–250.

Kasari, C., Sigman, M., Mundy, P. & Yirmiya, N. (1990). Affective sharing in the context of joint attention interactions of normal, autistic and mentally retarded children. *Journal of Autism and Developmental Disorders, 20*, 87–100.

Kasari, C., Sigman, M., Baumgartner, P., & Stipek, D. (In Press). Pride and mastery in children with autism. *Journal of Child Psychology and Psychiatry.*

Klinnert, M., Campos, J., Sorce, J., Emde, R. & Svejda, M. (1983). Emotions as behavior regulators: Social referencing in infancy. In R. Plutchnik & H. Kellerman, (Eds.), *Emotion: Theory, research and experience*, (Vol 2, pp. 57–86). New York: Academic Press.

Leslie, A. (1987). Pretense and representation: The origins of "theory of mind". *Psychological Review, 94* 412–426.

Leslie, A. (1988). Some implications of pretense for mechanisms underlying the child's theory of mind. In J. Astington, P. Harris, and D. Olson (Eds.), *Developing theories of mind*, (pp. 19–46). Cambridge: Cambridge University Press.

Leslie, A. & Happe, E. F. (1989). Autism and ostensive communication: The relevance of metarepresentation. *Development and Psychopathology, 1*, 205–212.

Leung, H. & Rheingold, J. (1981). Development of pointing as a social gesture. *Developmental Psychology, 17*, 215–220.

Lewy, A. & Dawson, G. (1992). Social stimulation and joint attention deficits of young autistic children. *Journal of Abnormal Child Psychology, 20*, 555–566.

Loveland, K. & Landry, S. (1986). Joint attention and language in autism and developmental language delay. *Journal of Autism and Developmental Disorders, 16*, 335–349.

Mandler, J. (1988). How to build a better baby: On the development of an accessible representational system. *Cognitive Development, 3*, 113–136.

Malatesta, C. & Izard, C. (1984). The ontogenesis of human social signals: From biological imperative to symbolic utilization. In N. Fox & R. Davidson (Eds.), *The psychology of affective development*, (pp. 161–206). Hillsdale, NJ:Erlbaum.

Mandler, J. (1988). How to build a better baby: On the development of an accessible representational system. *Cognitive Development, 3*, 113–136.

McDonald, M. A., Mundy, P., Kasari, C. & Sigman, M. (1989). Psychometric scatter in retarded, autistic preschoolers as measured by the Cattell. *Journal of Child Psychology and Psychiatry, 30*, 599–604.

McEvoy, R., Rogers, S. & Pennington, R. (1993). Executive function and social communication deficits in young, autistic children. *Journal of Child Psychology and Psychiatry, 34*, 563–578.

Meltzoff, A. & Moore, M. (1989). Imitation in newborn infants: Exploring the range of gestures imitated and the underlying mechanisms. *Developmental Psychology, 25*, 954–962.

Mirenda, P., Donnellan, A. & Yoder, D. (1983). Gaze behavior: A new look at an old problem. *Journal of Autism and Developmental Disorders, 13*, 397–409.

Morgan, S., Cutrer, P., Coplin, J., & Rodrique, J. (1989). Do autistic children differ from retarded and normal children in Piagetian sensorimotor functioning? *Journal of Child Psychology and Psychiatry, 30*, 857–864.

Mundy, P., Seibert, J. & Hogan, A. (1984). Relationships between sensorimotor and early communication abilities in developmentally delayed children. *Merrill-Palmer Quarterly, 30*, 33–48.

Mundy, P., Sigman, M., Ungerer J. A. & Sherman, T. (1986). Defining the social deficits in autism: The contribution of non-verbal communication measures. *Journal of Child Psychology and Psychiatry, 27*, 657–669.

Mundy, P., Sigman, M., Ungerer, J. A. & Sherman, T. (1987). Nonverbal communication and play correlates of language development in autistic children. *Journal of Autism and Developmental Disorders, 17*, 349–364.

Mundy, P. & Sigman, M. (1989a). The theoretical implications of joint attention deficits in autism. *Development and Psychopathology, 1*, 173–183.

Mundy, P. & Sigman, M. (1989b). Second thoughts on the nature of autism. *Development and Psychopathology, 1*, 213–217.

Mundy, P. & Sigman, M. (1989c). Specifying the nature of social impairment in autism. In G. Dawson (Ed.) *Autism: New perspectives on diagnosis, natures, and treatment*, (pp. 3–21). New York: Guilford Press.

Mundy, P., Sigman, M. & Kasari, C. (1990a). A longitudinal study of joint attention and language development in autistic children. *Journal of Autism and Developmental Disorders, 20*, 115–123.

Mundy, P., Kasari, C. & Sigman, M. (1992). Nonverbal communication, affective sharing, and intersubjectivity. *Infant Behavior and Development, 15*, 377–381.

Mundy, P., Sigman, M., & Kasari, C. (1993). The theory of mind and joint attention deficits in autism. In S. Baron-Cohen, H. Tager-Flusberg & D. Cohen (Eds.), *Un-*

derstanding other minds: Perspective from Autism, (p. 181–203). Oxford, UK: Oxford University Press.

Mundy, P., Kasari, C., Sigman, M., & Ruskin, E. (Submitted). Nonverbal communication and language development in children with Down syndrome.

Mundy, P., Sigman, M., & Kasari, C. (In press). Joint attention, developmental level, and symptom presentation in young children with autism. *Development and Psychopathology.*

Neisser, U. (1988). Five kinds of self knowledge. *Philosophical Psychology, 1,* 35–59.

Neisser, U. (1991). Two perceptually given aspects of the self and their development. *Developmental Review, 11,* 197–209.

Ornitz, E. & Ritvo E. (1968). Perceptual inconstancy in early infantile autism. *Archives of General Psychiatry, 18,* 76–98.

Ozonoff, S., Pennington, B., & Rogers, S. (1990). Are there specific emotion perception deficits in young autistic children. *Journal of Child Psychology and Psychiatry, 30,* 343–361.

Ozonoff, S., Pennington, B., & Rogers, S. (1991). Executive function deficits in high-functioning autistic children: Relationship to theory of mind. *Journal of Child Psychology and Psychiatry, 31,* 1081–1105.

Panksepp, J. (1979). A neurochemical theory of autism. *Trends in Neurosciences, 2,* 174–177.

Panksepp, J., Siving, S., & Normansell, L. (1985). Brain opiods and social emotions. In M. Reite & T. Fields (Eds.), *The psychobiology of attachment and separation* (pp. 3–49). New York: Aacdemic Press.

Prior, M., Dahlstrom, B. & Squires, T. (1990). Autistic children's social knowledge of thinking and feeling states in other people. *Journal of Child Psychology and Psychiatry, 31,* 587–601.

Rheingold, H., Hay, D. & West, M. (1976). Sharing in the second year of life. *Child Development, 83,* 898–913.

Ricks, D. (1979). Making sense of experience to make sensible sounds. In M. Bullowa (Eds.), *Before speech: The beginning of interpersonal communication* (pp. 245–268). New York: Cambridge University Press.

Riquet, C., Taylor, L., Benaroya, S., & Klein, L. (1981). Symbolic play in autistic, Down's and normal children of equivalent mental age. *Journal of Autism and Developmental Disorders, 11,* 439–448.

Ritvo, E., Yuwiler, A., Geller, E., Ornitz, E., Saeger, K., & Plotkin, S. (1970). Increased blood serotonin and platelets in early infantile autism. *Archives of General Psychiatry, 23,* 566–572.

Rogers, S. & Pennington, B. (1991). A theoretical approach to the deficits in infantile autism. *Development and Psychopathology, 3,* 137–162.

Rutter, M. (1978). Diagnosis and definition. In M. Rutter & E. Schopler (Eds.), *Autism: A reappraisal of concepts and treatment,* (pp. 1–25). New York:Plenum.

Sahley, T. & Panksepp, J. (1987). Brain opiods and autism: An updated analysis of possible linkages. *Journal of Autism and Developmental Disorders, 17,* 201–216.

Seibert, J. M., Hogan, A. E., & Mundy, P. C. (1982). Assessing interactional competencies: The Early Social-Communication Scales. *Infant Mental Health Journal, 3,* 244–245.

Seibert, J. M., Hogan, A. E., & Mundy, P. C. (1984). Developmental assessment of social-communication skills for early intervention: Testing a cognitive stage model. In Roslyn A Glow's (Ed.) *Advances in the Behavioral Measurement of Children, 1* Greenwich Connecticut: JAI Press, Inc.

Sigman, M. & Ungerer, J. A. (1984). Cognitive and language skills in autistic, mentally retarded, and normal children. *Developmental Psychology, 20,* 293–302.

Sigman, M., Mundy, P., Sherman, T. & Ungerer, J. A. (1986). Social interactions of autistic, mentally retarded and normal children with their caregivers. *Journal of Child Psychology and psychiatry, 27*, 647–656.

Sigman, M. (1989). The application of developmental knowledge to a clinical problem: The study of childhood autism. In D. Cicchetti (Ed.), *The emergence of a discipline: Rochester symposium on developmental psychopathology* (Vol 1, pp.165–189). Hillsdale, New Jersey: Lawrence Erlbaum Associates.

Snow, M., Hertzig, M. & Shapiro, T. (1987). Expressions of emotion in young autistic children. *Journal of the American Academy of Child and Adolescent Psychiatry, 26*, 836–838.

Spiker, D. & Ricks, M. (1984). Visual self recognition in autistic children: Developmental relationships. *Child Development, 55*, 214–225.

Sroufe, L. A., & Rutter, M. (1984). The domain of developmental psychopathology. *Child Development, 55*, 17–29.

Stern, D. (1985). *The Interpersonal World of the Infant.* New York: Basic Books.

Sugarman, S. (1984). The development of preverbal communication. In R. L. Schiefelbusch & J. Pickar (Eds.), *The acquisition of communicative competence* (pp. 23–67). Baltimore: University Park Press.

Tager-Flusberg, H. (1992). Autistic children's talk about psychological states: Deficits in the early acquisition of theory of mind. *Child Development, 63*, 161–172.

Trevarthen, C. (1979). Communication and cooperation in early infancy: A description of primary intersubjectivity. In M. Bullowa (Eds.), *Before speech: The beginning of interpersonal communication* (pp. 321–347). New York: Cambridge University Press.

Trevarthen, C. & Hubley, P. (1978). Secondary intersubjectivity: Confidence, confiders and acts of meaning in the first year. In A. Lock (Ed.), *Action gesture and symbol*, (pp. 217–243). New York: Academic Press.

Tronick, E. (1989). Emotions and emotional communication in infants. *American Psychologist, 44*, 112–119.

Ungerer, J. (1989). The early development of autistic children: Implications for defining primary deficits. In G. Dawson (Ed.), *Autism: Nature, diagnosis, and treatment* (pp. 75–91). New York: Guilford Press.

Volkmar, F. & Cohen, D. (1988). Issues in the diagnosis and classification of infantile autism. In B. Lahey & A. Kazdin (Eds.), *Advances in clinical child psychology* (pp. 1–35). New York:Plenum.

Volkmar, F., Cohen, D., Bregman, J., Hooks, M. & Stevenson, J. (1989). An examination of social typologies in autism. *Journal of the American Academy of Child and Adolescent Psychiatry, 28*, 82–86.

Wellman, H. (1993). Early understanding of mind: The normal case. In S. Baron-Cohen, H. Tager-Flusberg & D. Cohen (Eds.), *Understanding other minds:Perspective from Autism* (pp. 40–58). Oxford, UK: Oxford University Press.

Werner, H. & Kaplan, S. (1963). *Symbol formation.* New York: Wiley & Sons.

Wetherby, A. M. & Prutting, C. A. (1984). Profiles of communicative and cognitive-social abilities in autistic children. *Journal of Speech and Hearing Research, 27*, 367–377.

Wing, L., Gould, J., Yeates, S. R. & Brierly, L. M. (1977). Symbolic play in severely mentally retarded and autistic children. *Journal of Child Psychology and Psychiatry, 18*, 167–178.

Yirmiya, N., Kasari, C., Sigman, M. & Mundy, P. (1989). Facial expressions of affect in autistic, mentally retarded and normal children. *Journal of Child Psychology and Psychiatry, 30*, 725–735.

Yirmiya, N., Sigman, M., Kasari, C., & Mundy, P. (1992). Empathy and cognition in high functioning children with autism. *Child Development, 63*, 150–160.

II Self-Regulation in Normal and Atypical Development

Claire B. Kopp and Natalie Wyer

The Task: Mother has asked Willi to put his toys away.

Willi's verbal responses during the first minute or so:

at 30 months— Okay, You help me . . . . I don't want to . . .
at 36 months— Why? I never play with that . . . . . What?
at 42 months— Then we'll play with that? Put this away cause it's gonna break . . .
at 48 months— Okay, but first I'm gonna need the machine. Oh, I have to go to school . . . . All the toys are together

Willi is a child in one of our studies; his toy clean-up behaviors are representative of most normally developing young children we have observed. At 2 to 3 years, many children argue and often resist parent requests but by 4 years they know what is expected of them. Toy play, for example, is invariably followed by clean-up and there's not much point in arguing.

This chapter is about young children who begin to comply with the *rules of everyday life*, and those young children who find this challenge very difficult. Children who habitually noncomply to everyday rules present problems to themselves, their caregivers, teachers, and peers. The goal of this chapter is to offer ideas about the specific causes of noncompliance. Ideally, these ideas will promote new strategies for research and for long term remediative interventions. The chapter begins with a brief discussion of terminology. After establishing this frame of reference, it then describes self-regulation from a developmental perspective, highlighting what is required from parents and children to make self-regulation happen. The following section turns to individual differences in self-regulation. Here the primary goal is to understand why self-regulation (and compliance) is often problematic among young children who are developmentally delayed. The theme of cognition, along with its role in self-regulation, is repeatedly emphasized.

The final part of the chapter focuses on the self system where the underlying motivation is to address this thesis: the self system has cognitive elements, developmentally delayed children have cognitive difficulties, the self is important in self-regulation, ergo the self system of developmentally delayed young children may result in problematic self-regulation. We use the self literature with particular reference to early self development to examine what we know about self development among normal young children and those whose development is precarious. As will be seen, there is a marked void in the state of our knowledge of self development for developmentally delayed young children.

Terminology

Self-regulation is a construct that in general refers to young children's ability to be responsive to family and social demands and to gradually assume responsibility for their own behaviors with respect to these demands (Kopp, 1982). *Self-regulation* reflects a more advanced form of *self-control* in that the former is invoked more adaptively and thoughtfully than the latter (Kopp, 1982). Both kinds of monitoring rely on a self system in which young children understand that *their own actions and behaviors* will be judged by others with respect to appropriateness. In general, self-regulation and self-control refer to the broader aspect of children moving toward family and social norms. These two constructs encompass the term *compliance* which designates the child's ability to go along with very specific requests and rules. Developmentally, some forms of compliance precede the emergence of self-control and self-regulation.

Recently, we have adopted the term *standards for everyday behaviors* to refer specifically to the particular everyday rules parents establish for their young children (Gralinski & Kopp, 1993). These standards are further subdivided into categories that refer to the various kinds of rule requests parents ask of young children. These include rules around safety issues, respecting other family members' possessions, being polite (not kicking, biting, hitting), following family hygiene practices, helping in everyday family routines, and so forth. The use of categories has been invaluable because it has allowed us to examine the implicit developmental agenda that parents generate for everyday rule systems.

We also now use a more specific coding system for compliance (Gralinski & Kopp, 1993) than we did in the past (e.g., Vaughn, Kopp, & Krakow, 1984). Four compliance codes capture the complexity of young children's behaviors; the code also lends itself to analyses of the relative developmental maturity of compliance acts. The code is applied to parent reports of compliance as well as to observations made in the laboratory and in the child's home by the research team. *Compliance* signifies the child's ability to usually go along with a specific everyday request and to act accordingly. If dad says, "no running in the house" and most of the time Betts does not run in the house, her behavior would be coded as compliant. *Complies, sometimes on his (her) own* covers the instances when a child responds appropriately to an everyday rule sometimes by himself and sometimes with help from a caregiver (e.g., some mornings Jack folds his pajamas and puts them away, other mornings they lay scattered on the floor). *Compliance with assistance* refers to situations in which the child complies solely because someone is monitoring and helping almost every step of the way. Lastly, *noncompliance* concerns those caregiver requests that the child can not or will not go along with (e.g., no matter how often his mother reminds him, Robbie invariably interrupts her while she is on the telephone).

In this chapter, we use the construct of self-regulation to refer to the big picture of children moving to assume relative responsibility for many aspects of their social behavior. Compliance is used to talk about children becoming responsive to specific everyday rules. We will argue that the growth of compliance and self-regulation is predicated on a core set of processes. Some of these processes are themselves strongly linked to developmental phenomena (e.g., cognition, self, language skills) and some are less so (e.g., recurrent social interactions). However, self-regulation is as bound to cognitive development as it is to the infant and young child's willingness and ability to be part of ongoing affectional, emotional, and caring relationships.

The Self-Regulation Parent and Child Team

Parents

One of the *givens* of parenting is that young children need to be socialized to family and cultural conventions. Parents seem to intuitively sense what researchers have documented: children's self-regulatory activities have implications for contemporaneous family relationships and other social interactions, as well as for long-term social abilities, emotional well-being, and educational attainments (Harter, 1983; Kendall & Braswell, 1984; Masten, Best, & Garmezy, 1990). Although the content of socialization lessons and the techniques used to convey them to children may differ from one social group to another (e.g., Campos, Kermoian, & Zumbahlen, in press; Gralinski & Kopp, 1993; Rogoff, Sellers, Pirrotta, Fox, & White, 1975), there is consensus that the toddler and early preschool years are the time for lessons to begin.

The socialization challenge is not trivial. Initially parents must assume all responsibility for moving the child to respond to 'do's and 'don'ts for everyday standards (e.g., Gralinski & Kopp, 1993; Maccoby & Martin, 1983). To do this requires warmth and caring, an understanding of children's capabilities, and an intuitive sense of when to be firm in demands and when to be flexible (Gralinski & Kopp, 1993; Kopp, 1987).

Gradually as children become more competent, parents need to adopt a less directive stance and provide room for the child's attempts to master psychological independence (e.g., Crockenberg & Litman, 1990; Kuczynski, Kochanska, Radke-Yarrow, Girnius-Brown, 1987). Still later, parents must recognize when children are willing and able to monitor much of their own behavior. Overall, effective parenting for achieving child compliance involves being sensitive to the child, providing organization and routines in the child's life, and offering specific control strategies required in particular situations (see Kopp, 1987 for a summary of this parenting research literature). Connell (1990) states these kinds of parenting skills basically include: provision of structure, autonomy support for the child, and involvement.

The Child's Contribution

Early Developmental Trends

Short of physical coercion, parents can not bring about child compliance on their own. Children begin to comply when they begin to recognize they are members of a family (however defined) (Maccoby & Martin, 1983). This understanding, according to Kopp (1982, 1987, 1991), is based on fundamental developmental changes that occur in the child's cognition, her understanding of herself in relation to others, and her desire to be approved of by meaningful others. Thus in supportive rearing environments most young children are responsive to requests and assume some responsibility for their own behavior: they comply, modulate verbal and motor actions, control affect to some degree, and generally act in accordance with behavior standards in the absence of external monitors (e.g., Gralinski & Kopp, 1993; Kuczynski, 1984; Schneider-Rosen & Wenz-Gross, 1990; Vaughn, Kopp, & Krakow, 1984). There are upheavals: children resist—they cry, argue, assert their feelings of autonomy, and attempt to negotiate *better terms* from their parents (e.g., Klimes-Dougan & Kopp, 1991; Kopp, 1992; Kuczynski et al, 1987). However, the amount of resistance diminishes over time (Klimes-Dougan, 1992).

Precursor and Contributing Processes/Behaviors

Although Kopp's interest has focused on cognitive processes that underlie the child's path to compliance and self-regulation, there are other important processes (See Figure 1). Kochanska (1993) also notes that "multiple process may be activated in the phenomenon of behavioral control" (p 335). From a developmental perspective, the processes listed in Figure 1 do seem to be essential for self-regulation. They are themselves inter-related, albeit the how of the inter-relationships have yet to be empirically determined. Each process is discussed briefly; because cognition is a key theme of this chapter, cognitive processes receive additional emphasis.

Cognition. Elsewhere Kopp suggested that the ontogeny of child cognitive skills and the growth of a self system provide critical substrates for the evolution of compliance, and ultimately, for self-regulation (Kopp, 1982, 1987, 1992). In the 1982 article, Kopp emphasized processes of representation, recognition and recall memory. The point was made that very young children must be able to grasp some idea of what is expected of them. Representation and recall together allow the child to keep rules in mind and to retrieve appropriate information as required.

Kopp (1987) later added *attention deployment* as another key cognitive variable. She noted that on the one hand children must pay attention to others in order to learn the specifics of expectations (e.g., not touching hot objects), and that attention might be particularly important as very young children first become aware of these demands. Empirical support for this perspective is found in Schaffer and Crook's (1979, 1980) studies which indicated that attention to mother was tied to young toddlers' compliance to simple play requests. Alter-

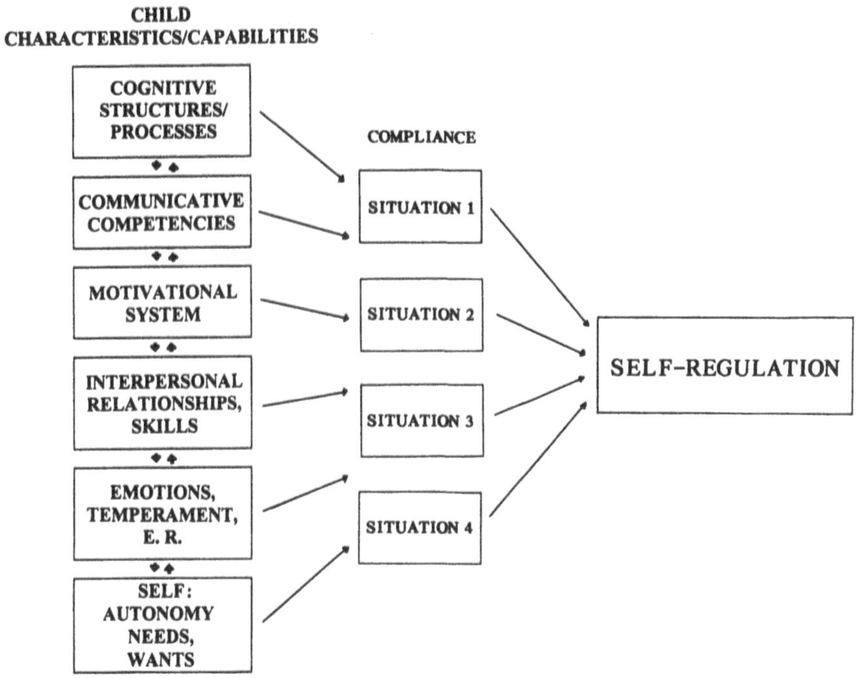

FIGURE 1 The processes involved in self-regulation.

natively, attention deployment is invaluable when used as strategic form of self-distraction for waiting tasks. The seminal research on this topic was done by Mischel and colleagues (see summary 1983) who demonstrated that preschoolers' (and school aged children) ability to delay gratification was related to their skill in turning attention away from desired objects. Subsequently, Kopp and colleagues extended the work to toddlers and young preschoolers and documented strategic-like behavior among normally developing two and three year olds in the service of waiting tasks (Vaughn, Kopp, Krakow, Johnson, & Schwartz, 1986).

Kopp (1987, 1992) also specifically discussed the issue of *comprehension of caregiver requests* which of course has ties to representational thinking. Although the mere comprehension of words and phrases is related to compliance in toddlers (Kaler and Kopp, 1990), Kopp (unpublished) has also proposed that: a) the acquisition of a knowledge base about everyday rules, and b) how this knowledge base is used across similar kinds of rule contexts will have a bearing on the child's ability to show consistency in compliance responses across time and across settings.

She further suggests that there may be several steps in the acquisition of knowledge regarding compliance to standards for behavior (see Table 1). In one of the first steps, the child acquires very particular information about an everyday rule—"you are not to touch your brother's toys". Learning about a specific

TABLE 1 Different levels of child understanding/responses with respect to rules for everyday standards for behavior

1. Associative reactions (e.g. behavioral inhibition) that are tied to caregiver directives.

   However, the child seems to have little or no comprehension of the communication. The child's reaction is probably a function of reading caregiver's intonation and affect.
2. Responses that are indicative of a primitive comprehension of rules. The child
   a) may understand single words (e.g., come, go) or simple phrases such as "don't touch the TV",
   b) may process a word or two and then guess the meaning of the entire phrase or sentence,
   c) point to a photograph/drawing of rule violation or rule compliance
   d) affirms rule by nodding yes
   e) shows evidence of familiar routine (e.g., child gets toothbrush when told it is time to brush teeth).
3. Shows procedural knowledge of rules, but cannot explain actions or reasons for same.
   a) follows a *script* for a familiar family routine (e.g., in the AM, gets out of bed, and stands in front of the toilet),
   b) walks to prohibited object (TV), looks at object, and does not touch it.
4. Can talk about everyday rules; verbalizations indicate an organization of rule ideas, rule themes, and principles.
   a) describes rules in terms of cause and effect relationships (e.g., knives are sharp and I could get hurt)
   b) generalizes information from one setting to another (e.g., if I'm not supposed to run in the street outside my house, I shouldn't run in the street when I visit my friend).
   c) generalizes from familiar setting to unfamiliar situation (e.g., I'm not supposed to yell indoors, when I go to a new store I'm not supposed to yell)
   d) deals with multiple representations (e.g., my toys go in the basket, my clothes go in the closet)
5. Verbal responses that indicate knowledge of how I should behave; assumes a self-evaluative component.
   a) goes up to another child as if to hit her, and then says, "I'm not supposed to hit; I will get in trouble".
   b) recognizes school rule, for example, and says, "I'm not supposed to bring my dolls to school; I will leave her at home".
6. Understands that rules that apply to self probably apply to others as well. Is exemplified by telling another that behavior is right/wrong or correct/incorrect for a particular situation, and, also understands why the behavior is appropriate or inappropriate.

rule may not entail major cognitive effort on the part of the child. Associative learning, imitative learning, or simple conditioned responses may be implicated. Thus when repeatedly admonished about his brother's toys, our little learner comes to realize that it is in his own best interests to avoid violating the brother toy rule. He may even go one step beyond and recognize that the rule about his brother's toys applies to his cousin's toys as well.

Another level of learning, one that demands considerably more cognitive effort, is involved when the child has to take the lesson learned in one or two very specific contexts and apply that lesson to other situations where possession rules apply (e.g., before you can call an object a possession, you must pay for it; other people's possessions include a variety of things ranging from homes to a kitchen utensil). In other words, effective compliance requires that the child learn an extension of a specific rule to more general instances. This is where the child has to reorganize or reclassify his knowledge—"I must not take or otherwise harm things that do not belong to me". In effect, the child has decontextualized the rule from its tie to the original rule scenario. Decontextualization allows adaptive rule compliance.

Self. The self serves to define an individual and to organize and integrate experiences in his or her world. It enables one to existentially go beyond one's ecological boundaries and to evaluate one's self in relation to others (Emde, Biringen, Clyman, & Oppenheim, 1991; Lewis, 1991). Stated another way, one of the self's functions is the "imposition of order in the world from a single, consistent vantage point, and the definition of the world from that vantage point" (Brownell & Kopp, 1991).

Brownell and Kopp describe a quasi developmental model for the self's functions. For immature infants, the self helps to integrate body-related experiences defining the physical boundaries of self and world. Once the physical self is relatively well established, the self functions to define social boundaries including the loci of social interactions. Next the self functions to outline the social and causal self in a social and causal world. Still later, as representation skills get better, the self functions to integrate knowledge of one's physical and social feelings, possessions, abilities, and future. In effect, the self is establishing personal boundaries.

By definition then, self-regulation imposes an active recognition—on the part of the child—that one's own personhood is involved with others' likes and dislikes of certain behaviors. The self in self-regulation includes the child's sense of "being", but a being that relates to other people, and to situations that have do's and don'ts associated with them. From one standpoint, we can talk about child compliance as a child doing his parents' bidding because his parents assist him. In contrast, self-regulation requires that the child recognize and understand his own responsibility for his behaviors within a rule system that others have established. Self-regulation does not mean blind obedience, the child can negotiate terms, but it does mean that after terms are negotiated the child more or less goes along with requests.

Self-regulation evolves slowly; however, there are early signs. To quote Kopp (1982), ". . . the self as an independent controller appears . . . in family routines where a young child proudly announces a self-initiated toy cleanup. An alternative form is observed in compliance situations where a child uses his or her body to erect an invisible barrier again the person issuing the command. . . . .Similarly, the self emerges when children transgress and reflect their awareness of their transgression with facial expressions, tears, and denial." (p 209).

Language. Spoken language provides children with the opportunity to work out their own feelings, to negotiate in situations they are unhappy about, and to handle conflicts (Bretherton, 1990; Dunn, Bretherton, & Munn, 1987; Klimes-Dougan, 1992). In our toy clean-up sessions language has been used in a variety of ways: to provide excuses for not cleaning up, "I'm too little", for gaining more play time, "let me play a little longer", and to plan a future action, "maybe we can take this thing (truck) up then we're gonna leave". Note these examples of language highlight its instrumental role in helping children maintain a sense of their own self integrity as caregivers urge them toward norms.

This perspective of language's part in self-regulation gives speech a more adaptive role in helping children monitor their own behaviors than was originally envisioned by Luria (1961). He contended that speech was used primarily as a regulatory tool to give one's self directions.

Motivational, Temperament, and Emotion Processes. The way these processes are implicated in compliance and conscience development has recently been summarized by Kochanska (1991, 1993) and need not be repeated here. Overall, Kochanska cogently argues that a moral self emerges from repeated interactions with others who are consistently emotionally available. This holds true for compliance, and indeed Stayton, Hogan, & Ainsworth (1971) were among the first to demonstrate the link between attachment relationships and early child compliance. Taking the interpersonal side one step further, Kochanska (1993) draws upon Emde and colleagues' writings. To wit, when young children establish a bond with parents through *affective attunement,* ". . . emotional signals function as inhibitors of forbidden acts. . ." (p 326). Kochanska (1991, 1993) also suggests that certain patterns of temperament influence the growth of conscience. Her line of reasoning is provocative and compelling, although the data she presents only partially support her perspectives, i.e., a measure combining impulsive behaviors along with temper tantrums was negatively correlated with later conscience development. But impulsivity, as Kochanska (1993) suggests, is a complex behavioral characteristic; it may interfere with compliance to prohibitions yet have no detrimental effects on the growth of morality.

From Kopp's perspective, it seems that young children are not inherently motivated to develop a conscience or to comply with everyday rules. They do, however, have incentives for compliance that come from their relationships with parents and others. When these relationships meet their emotional and self needs, then compliance and conscience development will follow in time.

Variability in the Parent and Child Team: A Shorthand Notation

Much of the preceding discussion has had a developmental essence; however, we now turn to an emphasis on individual differences in parents and children as these differences relate to facilitating or inhibiting self-regulation. We use a matrix to emphasize the role of variability in parenting skills and in child abilities.

The upper left quadrant of Figure 2 is a shorthand notation indicating that parent and children's behaviors critical for effective self-regulation are integrated, that is, parent and child are working as a team. The + within the parent cells is an abbreviated notation that signifies parents effectively provide the multidimensional competencies mentioned above. The + within the child cells

Child \ Parents	+	–
+	+ SR	? SR
–	? SR	– SR

SR = Self Regulation

FIGURE 2. The parent and child team for self-regulation.

signifies that a child has sufficient developmental maturity to understand the words and phrases embedded in parents' requests, some notion of the importance of everyday rules' (e.g., not hurting one's self or others), motivation to generally go along with parent requests, and a sense of belonging in a family system.

The three other cells indicate circumstances that arise in which parents and/or children contribute to a dysfunctional growth of child self-regulation. Specifically, the - in the parent cells signifies that one or more key dimensions of parenting vis a vis child self-regulation is dysfunctional or absent. For example, parents may be unable or unwilling to provide the socialization input that children require. Consequently, the child does not have the opportunity to learn rules for everyday behavior. The - in the child cells indicates dysfunction in cognitive skills, motivation, or some other aspect of child functioning that is intrinsic to the development of self-regulation. The - in both cells predicts the worst case scenario (lower right quadrant).

In this chapter, the focus is on situations in which parents provide appropriate input and structure to the child, but the child is unable or unwilling to receive and to acknowledge these guidelines. This is the situation depicted in the lower left quadrant of the matrix. The child limitation theme is the focus of the remainder of the chapter.

Problematic Non Compliance in the Early Years

Background

In general, research and clinical data indicate the path toward self-regulation is often undermined when young children are developmentally delayed, mentally retarded, have emotional disturbances, educational difficulties despite normal intelligence, or sensory disorders (e.g., deafness)(Camp, 1980; Douglas, 1979; Harris, 1978; Kopp, Krakow, & Vaughn, 1983). In particular, these children have been described as having difficulty complying with simple requests, controlling their actions, waiting, or modulating play interactions with their peers. Also, they may be unduly aggressive, show little regard for others' possessions, and be inattentive to their own and others' safety. Problems arise as early as the second and third years of life (Campbell, Szumowski, Ewing, Gluck, & Breaux, 1982).

Kopp and colleagues periodically focus on issues of compliance with developmentally delayed toddlers and preschoolers with the goals of documenting the nature of compliance difficulties and sorting out the reasons for same (Kopp, Klimes-Dougan, & Matheson, in preparation; Kopp, Krakow, & Vaughn, 1983; Kopp; Krakow, Johnson, & Kopp, 1983). The children in our studies are usually developmentally delayed with DQ or IQ scores falling between 60 and 80. The children's diagnoses include Down syndrome, developmental delay of unknown etiology, or delay as a consequence of preterm birth.

In subsequent paragraphs we will refer to a group of developmentally delayed children enrolled in our ongoing research project. These children are developmentally delayed preschoolers who are generally functioning with IQs between 60 and 80 (tested with the WPPSI). Their developmental age ranges from three and a half years to five years or so. These children are matched on developmental age to a group of normally developing children. Most of the children come from middle-class homes although education and income may be somewhat higher for the normally developing sample. In an initial examination of mothers' reports of family rule requests, we found no significant differences between mothers of delayed and normally developing children in the kinds of everyday rules they requested of their children (Kopp, Klimes-Dougan, & Matheson, in preparation).

Whereas normally developing young children periodically resist some everyday rules, many children with developmental disorders tend to be more resistant, more noncompliant with a problematic course of overall self-regulation. The children in our current study are no exception. As a group they have more difficulty complying with *everyday preschool rules* related to structured activities (e.g., staying in line, reading time); however, the children do relatively well at snack times and during unstructured play (Kopp, Klimes-Dougan, & Matheson, in preparation).

Overall then the data suggest that some difficulties for developmentally delayed children arise in structured situations that involve a group of children who are supposed to follow set routines. It is not difficult to imagine the behavioral implications for these children when they move to the more formal and structured learning environment of the elementary school where they will be expected to monitor their own behaviors without reminders. If they fail to do so, repeated teacher reprimands and possibly ostracism from other children will likely follow.

Reasons for Difficulties with Compliance: The Case of Developmentally Delayed Young Children

Is the Problem Due to Faulty Perceptions by Others?

Some have argued that the problems with compliance manifested by developmentally delayed young children are primarily due to the fact that many of these children are placed in situations (e.g., classrooms, playground) with chronologically aged-matched peers. Thus the children are judged by teachers, peers, and others as if they were on a par with their chronological age peers when in reality they are developmentally younger. They are, in other words, less behaviorally mature. According to this conceptualization, if then placed with younger aged children there would be no problems with compliance.

Is there evidence to support this thesis? In effect, this is the thrust of Zigler's (1968) developmental hypothesis[1] in which he argued that if one matches children on developmental age (or mental age), delayed and normal peers would show few or no behavioral differences because they are at the same level of development within an overall developmental sequence.

Data supporting Zigler's ideas have been reported; Weisz and Zigler (1979) and Cicchetti and Sroufe (1976) have documented similar sequential paths of development among groups of developmentally delayed infants and children and overall structural similarities in the behavioral repertoire.

Kopp has long contended that behavioral repertoires may differ in subtle but important ways even when developmentally delayed children are at the same general developmental level with their nondelayed peers (Kopp & Parmelee, 1979). A probable difference pertains to children's relative resources in their own behavioral repertoires. The richer the repertoire, the more likely a child can find adaptive solutions to challenging situations. Clinical impressions suggest that children with developmental delays have repertoires that are less rich than their agemates. Thus for example, the noncompliance often characteristic of delayed children may be a function of a constrained repertoire of strategies that could be adapted to meet caregiver demands.

Some empirical support has been garnered for the idea that there are variations in repertoires despite similarities in developmental age. For example, play behaviors of developmentally delayed toddlers were less rich, less mature, and less functional than the behaviors of their developmentally aged matched peers (Krakow & Kopp, 1983). In another study Rumsfeld (1989), working with Kopp, observed a small number of developmentally delayed preschoolers and found they had knowledge of some everyday routines (e.g., bedtime) but knew fewer routines than age-matched peers, offered limited elaboration about routines, and rarely made comments about 'do's' and 'don'ts.

Overall then, some differences in behavioral repertoires emerge even when children are matched on developmental age. The differences tend to surface in specific contexts. Thus it may be that certain situations make a greater claim on the delayed child's repertoire than do other situations, and he or she can not effectively respond. In an earlier part of this chapter, we enumerated some major components of cognitive functioning that were likely to be involved in self-regulation. The question that arises then is whether the problem is due to specific kinds of limitations in the child's repertoire of cognitive processing skills.

---

[1] Zigler's thesis was proposed in reference to children who were mentally retarded due to familial factors in contrast to children who are mentally retarded due to biological risk factors.

Cognitive Skills Limitations

Here, we describe a data set taken from our current study that elucidates some of the cognitive problems encountered by developmentally delayed children. Recall that earlier we mentioned that at least two kinds of knowledge are implicated in compliance. The first is factual knowledge—*stoves are hot, I can get burned.* The second kind of knowledge involves decontextualizing information learned in very specific situations such that the information can be applied across settings. In this study we examine children's knowledge of everyday rules and the reasons for these rules; the two kinds of knowledge were used as a basis for the tasks we designed.

The children were presented with three tasks (Kopp, Klimes-Dougan, & Matheson, in preparation). The first pertains to rule recognition. The task involves several pairs of line drawings in which one drawing depicts a child following a rule—not touching a vase that contains flowers—and the other drawing depicts a child not following the rule. Children are given each pair of drawings and informed, for example,: "This little girl's mother told her not to touch the flowers. Which little girl is touching the flowers?" The child's response can be given verbally or with gestures. Contrast analyses revealed no group differences between the delayed and normally developing children on this task—which involves very basic information about rules.

A second task asks children to generate rules for particular everyday situations. The task consists of four miniature *stage sets,* each approximately 12" long and 10" deep. Each set has both two and three dimensional representations of an everyday situation: kitchen and mini bathroom, playground, grocery store, and preschool play room. The child is asked to generate rules for each of these situations, and also to provide reasons for each rule. If answers are not forthcoming, the experimenter utilizes a series of graded prompts in an attempt to elicit rules. Overall, the delayed children had greater difficulty generating rules on their own, and when they generated rules they tended to make more mistakes about reasons for the rules. There were no group differences when children were provided with prompts for rules. Thus this task which provides visual representations (and memory cues) makes more cognitive demands on the child's information repertoire. With assistance, the delayed children can perform relatively similarly to their normally developing peers, without assistance they reveal some difficulty in generating rules and reasons for rules.

Whereas the first two tasks provide visual clues for the children, the third task relies on processing oral information. Our analyses to date indicate this task is the most difficult one for the developmentally delayed sample. Their error rate is high. Specifically, this is the task. The children are given a rule for a particular situation: "Jimmy's mommy has told him he can not run in the house". Then the child is asked if the rule applies to other situations: "Jimmy goes to his grandma's house, can he run in her house? Jimmy goes to the store with his mommy, can he run in the store? Jimmy goes to the playground, can he run there?" This challenging task requires the child to keep a rule in mind, and, generalize the rule from one context to another.

In sum, preliminary findings indicate that the repertoire of information about everyday rules is partially limited among developmentally delayed children. We are inclined to think that these limitations rather than negativism or willfulness contribute to noncompliance among delayed children. Parenthetically, it would seem essential for teachers and intervention specialists to systematically determine which rules developmentally delayed children actually understand and those that elude them. Specific interventions could be geared toward helping the children fill in gaps in their rule knowledge.

Is the Problem Partly a Function of Cognitive Constraints Within the Self System?

In recent years, cognitive components of the self system have received an extensive amount of attention (Case, 1991; Harter, 1986; Kilstrom, Cantor, Albright, Chew, Klein, Niedenthal, 1988; Markus, 1980; Rogers, 1981); there is little disagreement that the self system has cognitive underpinnings. Neisser (1988), for example, views the self system as encompassing personal memories (extended self), knowledge of one's own unique experiences (private self), and the network of theories and assumptions about social roles and conventions (conceptual self). He demarcates the developmental progression of these aspects of the self system from those that occur earlier (i.e., ecological and interpersonal selves).

Given that the self system is partly cognitive, that developmentally delayed children have cognitive difficulties, that the self is a critical component of self-regulation—then, the self-system among developmentally delayed young children may have problematic features. It may be that children who have cognitive limitations also have distortions in self-hood such that they do not perceive their own role within a rule system, do not evaluate their own skills in terms of what they can do and where they need help, or do not understand the intersection of their own desires and the needs/desires of meaningful others.

We have made some preliminary analyses of self in our ongoing study of developmentally delayed preschoolers and their age matched peers. Using the Instrumental Competence Scale (a teacher report measure developed by Lange, MacKinnon, & Nida, 1989), we arbitrarily selected self-related items some of which have cognitive elements (e.g., sets goals that expand abilities, finds novel ways to interest self, likes to engage in challenging activities, actively uses resources for help and information, takes pride in accomplishments) and compared responses for the delayed and normal children. Differences between the groups were significant.[2] At this point, we can infer that something is faulty in the developmentally delayed child's self system.

In the next section we explicitly focus on the self system. The section opens with a summary of ideas about the characteristics of early selfhood among

---

[2] We have wondered about the possible role of teacher bias in the measures they have filled out. Although we cannot directly assess bias, we do know that teacher observations about higher rates of noncompliance in the developmentally delayed sample are congruent with observations made by Es in our research group. Our observers do not know the developmental status of the children they observe.

normally developing infants and young children. We then use this information as a springboard to examine the knowledge base obtained with developmentally delayed children (from various diagnostic groups). The short-term goal is to identify what we know and what we need to know vis a vis the self. The long term goal is to understand the self system of developmentally delayed young children with respect to compliance and self-regulation.

The Self System

> To set the stage here, we again state the thesis that underlies our thinking: the self system has cognitive elements, developmentally delayed children have cognitive difficulties, the self is important in self-regulation, ergo the self system of developmentally delayed young children may result in problematic self-regulation.

The topic of early selfhood was not neglected in past years (e.g., Erikson, 1950; Escalona, 1963; Freud, 1966; Spitz, 1959); however, the last two decades have been witness to unprecedented attempts to understand the origins and maturation of self (e.g., Bretherton, 1985; Brownell & Kopp, 1991; Case, 1991; Cicchetti & Beeghly, 1990; Damon & Hart, 1982; Emde, Biringen, Clyman, & Oppenheim, 1991; Kagan, 1981; Harter, 1983; Lewis, 1991; Lewis & Brooks-Gunn, 1979; Mahler, Pine, & Bergman, 1975; Neisser, 1988, 1991; Sroufe, 1979; Stipek, Gralinski, & Kopp, 1990; Stern, 1985). A multitude of domains have been addressed in conceptualizations and in research. These include processes involved in self-development (e.g., precursors represented in parent-child relationships), the interpersonal context of self, the content of self, representations of selfhood, needs of self, agentic roles, working models, language and self, and the self system going awry.

Many of these topics are represented in Table 2 along with developmental trends that have been the subject of theoretical papers and empirical research. As can be seen in Table 2, shifts in emphasis occur as a function of age. During the earliest months of life, a preself is emerging with respect to recognition of separateness from another and establishishing interpersonal modes of communication. Somewhat later, there is additional growth and emphasis on locating the body in space and discovering the permanence and physical boundaries of the body. The second, third, and fourth years are marked by a burgeoning self system that depends on a growing cognition: consolidation of basic self categories, autonomy, self-evaluation, memories, and so forth.

In dealing with this rich and diverse developmentally oriented literature, Kopp (unpublished) has found it useful to impose an additional organizational structure on the themes embedded in Table 2. This strategy makes it easier to make comparisons between self development among normally developing young children and those that have developmental disorders. The structure contains the following categories: social interaction precursors and maintainers, physical elements, cognitive aspects, motivational aspects, and feeling/evaluative

TABLE 2 The Ontogeny of the Self System: The Early Years Theoretical Perspectives and Empirical Research

Birth to Three Months	
Birth to Two months	*Emergent self* (Stern, 1985) - organization of systems - physiological regulation
Two to Three months	*Core Self* - integration of behaviors - sense of distinct and separate self
Birth to Three months	*Existential self* (Lewis & Brooks-Gunn, 1979) - interest in social objects - self and other distinction
Early Infancy	*Ecological self* (Neisser, 1988; 1991) - self perceived in relation to physical environment - use of kinetic information *Interpersonal self* - emotional rapport and communication
First Three Months	*Sensory Orienting Stage* (Case, 1991) - orienting to others - model of "maternal landscape" - glimmering sense of agency
Three to Twelve Months	
Three to Eight Months	*Consolidation of Self* (Lewis & Brooks-Gunn, 1979) - self and other distinction - recognition of self, through contingency - self, located in space
Seven to Nine Months	*Subjective Self* (Stern, 1985) - awareness of separate needs that also interface - share subjective experiences (e.g., affective states)
Eight to Twelve Months	*Emergence: self permanence, self categories* (Lewis & Brooks-Gunn, 1979) - recognition of self through contingencies - feature recognition
The First Year	*Procedural knowledge vis a vis The Moral Self* (Emde et al, 1991) - prerepresentational affective core - affective, perceptual, behavioral procedures: to act, react - perceptual, knowledge systems for distinguishing self from others
Eight to Eighteen Months	*Sensorimotor Substages* (Case, 1991) - personal agency - build model of own capabilities

TABLE 2 Continued

The Second Year	
Fifteen + months	*Verbal Self* (Stern, 1985) - verbal labels - gender identity - self recognition *Agentic self* (Watson & Fischer, 1977)
12 to 24 months	*Categorical Self* (Lewis & Brooks-Gunn, 1979) - consolidation, basic self categories (age, gender) - feature recognition, without contingency *Evaluative Self* (Kagan, 1984) - recognition of standards - comparison, self with others *Separate self* (Sroufe, 1990)
18 to 24 months	*Self Concept: Autonomous Self* (Sroufe, 1979) - sense of self as actor (e.g., coping, self evaluation, shame) - sense of separateness (e.g., affection, ambivalence, defiance)
24 months	*Authorial Self* (Wolf, 1982, 1990)
Third and Fourth Years	
3 years	*Moral Self: Executive "we"* (Emde et al, 1991) - narratives, internalized rules, reciprocity - work with simple forms of moral dilemmas
3 to 4 years	*Evaluative Self* (Kagan, 1984) - evaluate actions, relative to self - evaluate self, relative to others
3 years	*Extended Self* (Neisser, 1988) - personal memories, anticipations
4 years	*Private Self* - knowledge, one's own unique experiences *Conceptual Self* - network of theories, assumptions (social roles, conventions)
5 years	*Self-monitoring Self* (Stroufe, 1990)

elements (see Table 3). Language is not listed as a separate category because comprehension and/or speech is intrinsic to all of the categories.

Social Precursors and Maintainers. Irrespective of one's philosophical/theoretical orientation, there is consensus that the earliest forms of selfhood originate in interactions of infants and their caregivers (e.g., Bretherton, 1990; Case, 1991; Emde, et al, 1991; Mahler, Pine, & Bergman, 1975). Emde and colleagues (Emde et al, 1991) suggest that infants possess inborn tendencies such as activity, self-regulation (e.g., physiological regulation, vital developmental functions), social fittedness, affective monitoring, and cognitive assimilation that facilitate social interactions. The infant and caregiver relationship

Table 3 A categorizing strategy: Themes in the early self system

Social interaction precursors/maintainers of the self system
Refers to the importance of caregiver-infant/toddler interactions such that the infant gathers emotional strength from others, learns to trust others' actions, and becomes tuned into others' wishes, desires, values, and affective states.

Physical elements
Refers to the young child's recognition and knowledge of own body parts and body schema; awareness of own actions on objects and with other people.

Cognitive aspects
Refers to the young child's elemental beliefs about the self (e.g., gender), memories of one's own self activities, roles (e.g., a child, a sibling) that the self is involved in, and knowledge of rules/routines that one is supposed to follow.

Evaluative/Motivational
Refers to *good* and *bad* feelings the young child has about his/her actions, the way he/she looks, or an event in which he/she participated. Feelings presumably influence the child's desire to re-engage with others or in an activity.

then ". . . provides the context in which the basic motives become activated" (p. 257), often through emotional attunement. Out of this emerges the affective core of self and in time the core develops into a moral self.

Others use different terms to describe the quality of relationships which serves as a springboard for so many developmental competencies. Hobson (1989, 1990) uses the term affective relatedness, and Wellman (1993) talks about connections in that child and others are engaged in joint attention, use of gestures in pointing and showing, and visually checking another's gaze. The infant gathers emotional strength from these kinds of exchanges but is also building an understanding of self in relation to others (Brownell & Kopp, 1991).

Although the social interactions of developmentally delayed children have been studied (e.g., Down syndrome, Cicchetti & Ganiban, 1990), the social relationships have not been studied for the implications to the self system. Indeed, children with autism are the only nonnormal group of children whose social relationships have been analyzed in this regard. Research with autistic children indicate they have problems in social interactions that involve pointing and joint attention (Baron-Cohen, 1989; Mundy & Sigman, 1989; Mundy, Sigman, Kasari, 1990)[3]. Hobson (1990) suggests that interpersonal development among autistic children includes problems with sharing and exchanging thoughts, inability to ask questions when appropriate, little understanding of people as agents, and difficulty in imitating others. These children, Hobson

[3] Children with Down syndrome have often been used as comparison groups in these studies; the problem is that a cohesive data set vis a vis interactions and the self system is not available for this group of children.

continues, also lack underlying abilities to engage in affectively patterned experiences. Taken together, the data make a compelling case for disorders of self among children with autism.

Prudence is warranted before making generalizations to other groups of delayed children. First, we know little of autistic children's infancy; the reported data are typically obtained from older children who are functioning at relatively low developmental ages. One can only wonder if affective attunement and general parent child interactions were distorted in infancy among those children who were later diagnosed as autistic. Similarly, one can ask if the general disintegration that marks the autistic child's social interactions has a counterpart in decomposing a self that was in the making. Second, the developmental path for autism involves a great deal of regression and deviance, and less delay at least in early life. This pattern is not commonly found among other children who have developmental delays.

Physical. The physical side of self is elemental in that it represents perceptual and procedural knowledge of the body, that is, *recognition* of: one's own body parts and the constellation of same (a body image), and *awareness* of one's own physical actions. Self-recognition, awareness of physical agency, gender recognition, and James's (1890) *me* are illustrative examples the physical self. The physical side of selfhood is one of the earliest indications that an independent self system is forming.

Seminal studies by Lewis and Brooks-Gunn (1979), extended by others (e.g., Watson & Fischer, 1977), and subsequently replicated numerous times, indicate that mid-point in the second year children begin to recognize when their own faces are "marred" temporarily by a chalk mark. Rubbing the chalk mark, mild distress, even a form of embarassment are common responses. Butterworth (1990) has summarized mirror and video self-recognition tasks during infancy: at 3 to 8 months babies show an unlearned attraction to images of others, at 8 to 12 months they begin to see themselves as permanent objects, at 12 to 15 months months self-other differentiation occurs, and then between 15 and 24 months there is facial feature detection.

The self and mirror recognition tasks make up the bulk of research on physical and categorical self in infants and young children. Of importance, self recognition is not a uniquely human response as was demonstrated by Gallup's seminal studies with non human primates (1970). Thus there may be an evolutionary-biological underpinning that partially contributes to self-recognition. By extension, it would seem that only the most severe biological or social stresses could distort or do away with the response. In fact, most children with autism, Down syndrome, and other forms of developmental delay achieve self-recognition when their developmental age is relatively commensurate with the developmental ages of normal toddlers. (Unfortunately a number of investigators have not provided developmental age data.)

Representative findings have recently been detailed in Cicchetti, Beeghly, Carlson, & Toth (1990), and thus only general findings are mentioned here. Generally speaking, children and pre-adolescents who have been diagnosed as autistic show self-recognition if their developmental age is approximately two years or older. Baron-Cohen (1993) noted that when autistic children show self-recognition, they often do not show embarrassment or shyness. Failure in self-recognition has been correlated with language impairment with problems with object permanence tasks. Among children with Down syndrome, similar trends have been noted. As with children with autism, there are subtle group differences in terms of interest in the mirror as a stimulus, per se. Children with generalized developmental delay have also been studied. Developmental age is age a critical factor in self-recognition. Children who are seriously impaired and functioning at very young developental ages tend to show little interest in the task.

In terms of gender identification, normally developing children at about 18 months or so identify several body parts and a few months later use the terms me, mine, and I. Hobson (1990) suggests autistic individuals have difficulty recognizing the age and sex related characteristics of themselves and others. They also show difficulties in use of personal and other pronouns.

In sum, there is evidence that developmentally delayed children do develop an awareness of the physical side of selfhood, at least as manifested by self-recognition tasks. Those children who have difficulty with self-recognition appear to be quite impaired, and inferentially, seem not to have reached the appropriate developmental age. The interface between physical characteristics and the language children come to use to describe those characteristics are problematic for individuals with autism. Whether this holds for other groups is not known; however, given the language problems often found children who have other kinds of developmental delays it is likely.

Cognitive. The cognitive component of early self reflects ideas (beliefs) about identity (e.g., I am a girl), memories of one's own experiences (e.g., yesterday was my birthday), roles that the self and others can assume (e.g., child, sibling, friend, mommy in play with dolls), and knowledge of standards for one's own behaviors. Often the cognitive dimensions of self become explicit through the use of language (e.g., Bates, 1990).

Neisser's (1988) discussion of the self system provides a useful taxonomy for considering the cognitive elements of self that are particularly relevant to early life. In his scheme, the *extended self* refers to the child's memory of past and future events in which he/she played or will play a role, script knowledge of events in which the child participates, and recall of particular events in the child's experiences. The *private self* refers to the fact that children begin to understand the privacy of their own mental lives at around four years of age. Stated another way, there is a realization that others are not privy to our thoughts unless we communicate those thoughts. The *conceptual self* refers to knowledge that the child acquires about particular people in particular roles. Recent years have seen a wealth of data potentially applicable to the theme of extended self (e.g., Bauer & Mandler, 1990; Fivush & Hudson, 1990; Nelson, 1986, 1989; Wolf, 1990) and similarly there is some work on children's understanding of roles (e.g., Shantz, 1983). The use of language in describing self activities has been reported (e.g., Wolf, Rygh, & Altshuler, 1984; Lee, 1992). Not surprisingly, the growth of spoken language and talking about the self are concurrent developments.

Going beyond Neisser's formulation, there is a body of research that shows that: a) children at first classify and categorize the self into multiple dimensions which initially are physical and later they classify with abstract qualities, and b) role categories become differentiated with age and often have a hierarchical structure (e.g., Bannister & Agnew, 1976; Glick & Zigler, 1985; Harter, 1983, 1986; L'Ecuyer, 1981, Norem-Heibeisen, 1981; Rosenberg, 1979).

Two groups of children, those with Down syndrome and those with autism, comprise the data base for developmentally delayed children vis a vis the cognitive aspects of selfhood. Cicchetti and colleagues (see summary, Cicchetti & Ganiban, 1990) examined self related language used in symbolic play. Their findings revealed children with Down syndrome showed the same, albeit delayed, developmental sequence when compared to normally developing children. However, only those children who were the most cognitively advanced were able to use language to represent their own selves and others in hypothetical situations. This finding suggests to us that non concrete aspects of the self (e.g., representation of roles, recognition of sense of responsibility, integration of knowledge about self) may be problematic for children with Down syndrome.

Other cognitive aspects related to the self system can be found in the *theory of mind* research in which autistic children (and some comparison samples, e.g., Down syndrome, Baron-Cohen, Leslie, & Frith, 1985) have primarily comprised the study samples. However, as Wellman (1993) points out it is only the children with autism who have difficulty with theory of mind tasks that other children (normal or delayed) can accomplish when they are about four years developmental age.[4]

Thus again, we find ourselves with a limited data base. There are rich and thoughtful ideas about cognitive contributors to selfhood in normally developing children and there is a burgeoning body of studies that are applicable. A small body of research is available about children with Down syndrome and a specialized (though fascinating) data base has been gathered from children who have autism. The data base is not comprehensive nor can we draw inferences about the cognitive aspects of selfhood with other groups of young developmentally delayed children. This is a research area that could and should be a high priority.

Evaluative/Motivational. There is ample evidence that mid point in the second year, toddlers can make judgements about the *goodness* or *badness* of events, objects, or even their own actions (e.g., Dunn, Bretherton, & Munn, 1987; Emde, et al, 1991; Kagan, 1981; Stipek, Gralinski, & Kopp, 1990). It appears though that an evaluation in which the child actually embeds him(her)self in a wrongdoing does not occur until about age three years (e.g., Stipek, McClintic, & Recchia, 1992). Stipek et al's (1990) study revealed a sequence of self-recognition, self-description and evaluation, and emotional response to wrongdoing and self-regulation among children who were between 14 to 40 months of age. To our knowledge, similar kinds of studies have not been done with developmentally delayed young children.

---

[4] As yet though, only a small subset of all developmentally delayed young children have been tested with this paradigm. There is a great deal of behavioral heterogeneity in this group of children.

In Sum. Our examination of the self system of normally developing young children has provided a view of a developmental system that is increasingly complex and operates in a feedback circuit where one *system* facilitates the growth of another. Quoting Connell (1990), ". . . the young child's emerging abilities to symbolically generate interpersonal goals, to hold in mind these goals, to communicate to the social surround the nature of these goals, and to use symbolic . . . information . . . . are all seen as function of social exchange. Thus, the dialectical relations between the young toddlers' needs for competence, autonomy, and relatedness and the matrix of social communications *produce* the cognitive advances manifested in verbal/reflective versions of self-system processes." (p 91).

In comparion, we can not define the self system among developmentally delayed children, nor can we definitively characterize its developmental and cognitive parameters. We do not know if it functions in ways that are similar to the patterns observed in normally developing children (see Brownell & Kopp, 1991). Moreover, at this point we can not even infer if disorders in the self system are partially responsible for difficulties with compliance and self-regulation. This comment by Samet (1993) reflects the way we might proceed—we would only add that it applies to non normally developing children as well.

> "We need to understand the sense of personal identity that enables normal individuals to tie their present self to the past and to the future, to care about themselves in a long-term way, to think about their existence as a life, and ultimately to identify other beings as the same in this regard. In ways we still do not understand very well, all this is implicated in the ability to build relationips with other selves, to feel guilt, pride, devotion, to have personal values, and to generally take oneself to be part of a social and moral community" (Samet, 1993, p 447).

Concluding Comments

In this chapter we often used research with normally developing young children as a springboard to examine the behavior and functioning of developmentally delayed children. This descriptive data base, that developmentalists have assiduously collected for decades, provides the architectural structure for our developmental knowledge. The structure has enabled us to build further—to examine origins, linkages, processes, pathways, and more.

It is unfortunate but true that accidents of nature—chromosomal anomalies, prenatal infections, early birth—have also allowed us to study developmental processes in other groups of children. These studies have added to our core of developmental knowledge (e.g., Cicchetti, in press). We now suggest that additional research,—in which we decompose processes involved in cognition, in the self system, in emotional life—, of young developmentally delayed children will potentially lead to more effective interventions and also allow better understanding of the nature of developmental processes. At the very least we ought to be able to precisely identify those within child factors that contribute to noncompliance and problematic self-regulation.

REFERENCES

Bannister, D., & Agnew, J. (1976). The child's construing of self. In J. Cole (Ed.), *Nebraska symposium on motivation* (pp 99–125). Lincoln: University of Nebraska Press.

Baron-Cohen, S. (1989). The autistic child's theory of mind: a case of specific developmental delay. *Journal of Child Psychology and Psychiatry,* 30, 285–297.

Baron-Cohen, S., Tager-Flusberg, H., & Cohen, D. J. (1993). *Understanding other minds: Perspectives from Autism.* Oxford: Oxford University Press.

Bates, E. (1990). Language about me and you: Pronominal reference and the emerging concept of self. In D. Cicchetti & M. Beeghly (Eds.), *The self in transition: Infancy to childhood,* (pp.165–182). Chicago: University of Chicago Press.

Bauer, P. J., & Mandler, J. M. (1990). One- to two-year-olds' recall of events. In R. Fivush, & J. A. Hudson, J. A. (Eds.), *Knowing and remembering in young children,* (pp.). Cambridge: Cambridge University Press.

Bretherton, I. (1985). Attachment theory: Retrospect and prospect. In I. Bretherton & E. Waters (Eds.), Growing points of attachment theory and research. *Monographs of the Society for Research in Child Development,* 50 (1–2, Serial No. 209) (pp. 3–35).

Bretherton, I. (1990). Open communication and internal working models: Their role in the development of attachment relationships. In R. Thompson (Ed.), *Nebraska Symposium on Motivation, 1988: Socioemotional development,* (pp 57–114). Lincoln, NE: University of Nebraska Press.

Brownell, C. A., & Kopp, C. B. (1991). Common threads, diverse solutions: Concluding commentary. *Developmental Review,* 11, 288–303.

Butterworth, G. (1990). Self perception in infancy. In D. Cicchetti & M. Beeghly (Eds.), *The self in transition: Infancy to childhood,* (pp. 119–138). Chicago: University of Chicago Press.

Camp, B. W. (1980). Two psychoeducational treatment programs for young aggressive boys. In C. K. Whalen & B. Henker (Eds.), *Hyperactive children: The social ecology of identification and treatment,* (pp.). New York: Academic.

Campbell, S. B., Szumowski, E. K., Ewing, L. J., Gluck, D. S., & Breaux, A. M. (1982). A multidimensional assessment of parent-identified behavior problem toddlers. *Journal of Abnormal Child Psychology,* 10, 569–592.

Campos, J. J., Kermoian, R., & Zumbahlen, M. R. (in press). Socioemotional transformations in the family system following infant crawling. *New directions in child development.*

Case, R. (1991). Stages in the development of the young child's first sense of self. *Developmental Review,* 11, 210–230.

Cicchetti, D. (in press). Developmental theory: Lessons from the study of risk and psychopathology. In S. Matthysse, D. Levy, J. Kagan, & F. Benes (Eds.), *Psychopathology: The evolving science of mental disorder.* New York: Cambridge.

Cicchetti, D., & Beeghly, M. (1990). *Children with Down syndrome: A developmental perspective.* Cambridge: Cambridge.

Cicchetti, D., & Ganiban, J. (1990). The organization and coherence of developmental processes in infants and children with Down syndrome. In R. M. Hodapp, J. Burack, & E. Zigler (Eds.), *Issues in the developmental approach to mental retardation,* (pp. 169–225). New York: Cambridge.

Cicchetti, D., Beeghly, M., Carlson, V., Toth, S. L. (1990). The emergence of the self in atypical populations. In D. Cicchetti & M. Beeghly (Eds.), *The self in transition: Infancy to childhood,* (pp. 309–344). Chicago: University of Chicago Press.

Connell, J. (1990). Context, self, and action: A motivational analysis of self-system processes across the life span. In D. Cicchetti & M. Beeghly (Eds.), *The self in transition: Infancy to childhood*, (pp. 61–98). Chicago: University of Chicago Press.
Crockenberg, S., & Litman, C. (1990). Autonomy as competence in 2-year-olds: Maternal correlates of child defiance, compliance, and self-assertion. *Developmental Psychology*, 26, 961–971.
Damon, W., & Hart, D. (1982). The development of self-understanding from infancy through adolescence. *Child Development*, 53, 841–864.
Douglas, V. I. (1980). Treatment and training approaches to hyperactivity: Establishing internal or external control. In C. K. Whalen & B. Henker (Eds.), *Hyperactive children: The social ecology of identification and treatment*, (pp. 283–318). New York: Academic.
Dunn, J., Bretherton, I., & Munn, P. (1987). Conversations about feeling states between mothers and their young children. *Developmental Psychology*, 23, 132–139.
Emde, R. N., Biringen, Z., Clyman, R. B., & Oppenheim, D. (1991). The self of infancy: Affective core and procedural knowledge. *Developmental Review*, 11, 251–270.
Erikson, E. (1950). *Childhood and society*. New York: Norton.
Escalona, S. K. (1963). Patterns of infantile experience and the developmental process. *Psychoanalytic Study of the Child*, 18, 197–244.
Fivush, R., & Hudson, J. A. (1990). *Knowing and remembering in young children*. Cambridge: Cambridge University Press.
Freud, A. (1966). *Writings of Anna Freud: Normality and pathology in childhood*. New York: International Universities Press.
Gallup, G. G. (1970). Chimpanzees: Self-recognition. *Science*, 167, 86–87.
Glick, M., & Zigler, E. (1985). Self-image: A cognitive-developmental approach. In R. L. Leahy (Ed.), *The development of the self*. New York: Academic Press.
Gralinski, J. H., & Kopp, C. B. (1993). Everyday rules for behavior: Mothers' requests to young children. *Developmental Psychology*, 29, 573–584.
Harris, R. I. (1978). Impulse control in deaf children: Research and clinical issues. In L. S. Liben (Ed.), *Deaf children: Developmental perspectives*, (pp. 137–156). New York: Academic.
Harter, S. (1983). Developmental perspectives on the self-system. In E. M. Hetherington (Ed.), *Socialization, personality, and social development*, Vol. 4. In P. Mussen (Ed.), Handbook of child psychology. New York: Wiley.
Harter, S. (1986). Cognitive-developmental processes in the integration of concepts about emotions and the self. *Social Cognition*, 4, 119–151.
Hobson, R. P. (1989). On sharing experiences. *Development and Psychopathology*, 1, 197–203.
Hobson, R. P. (1990). On the origins of self and the case of autism. *Development and Psychopathology*, 2, 163–181.
Hobson, R. P. (1993). Understanding persons: the role of affect. In S. Baron-Cohen, H., Tager-Flusberg, & D. J. Cohen, (Eds.), *Understanding other minds: Perspectives from Autism*, (pp. 204–227). Oxford: Oxford University Press.
James, W. (1890). *The principles of psychology*. New York:Holt.
Kagan, J. (1981). *The second year: The emergence of self-awareness*. Cambridge: Harvard University Press.
Kaler, S. R., & Kopp, C. B. (1990). Compliance and comprehension in very young toddlers. *Child Development*, 61, 1997–2003.
Kendall, P. C., & Braswell, L. (1985). *Cognitive-behavioral therapy for impulsive children*. New York: Guilford.
Kilstrom, J. F., Cantor, N., Albright, J. S., Chew, B. R., Klein, S. B., & Niedenthal, P. M. (1988). Information processing and the study of self. In L. Berkowitz (Ed.),

Advances in experimental social psychology (Vol. 21, pp. 145–188). Orlando, FL: Academic Press.

Klimes-Dougan, B. (1992). *The development of negotiation in young children.* Unpublished doctoral dissertation, University of Florida.

Kochanska, G. (1991). Socialization and temperament in the development of guilt and conscience. *Child Development,* 62, 1379–1392.

Kochanska, G. (1993). Toward a synthesis of parental socialization and child temperament in early development of conscience. *Child Development,* 64, 325–347.

Kopp, C. B. (1982). The antecedents of self-regulation: A developmental perspective. *Developmental Psychology,* 18, 199–214.

Kopp, C. B. (1987). The growth of self-regulation: Caregivers and children. In N. Eisenberg (Ed.), *New directions in developmental psychology,* (pp.). New York:Wiley.

Kopp, C. B. (1991). Young children's progression to self-regulation. In M. Bullock (Ed.), The development of intentional actions: Cognitive, motivational, and interactive processes. *Human Development,* 22, 38–54.

Kopp, C. B., Klimes-Dougan, B., & Matheson, C. (in preparation). *Developmentally delayed preschoolers: Behavioral compliance to everyday rules and cognitive correlates.*

Kopp, C. B., Krakow, J. B., & Johnson, K. (1983). Strategy production by young Down syndrome children. *American Journal of Mental Deficiency,* 88, 164–169.

Kopp, C. B., Krakow, J. B., & Vaughn, B. E. (1983). Patterns of self-control in young handicapped children. In M. Perlmutter (Ed.), *Development and policy concerning children with special needs. The Minnesota Symposia on Child Psychology,* 16., . Hillsdale, NJ: Erlbaum.

Kopp, C. B., & Parmelee, A. H. (1979). Prenatal and perinatal influences on behavior. In J. Osofsky (Ed.), *Handbook of infant development,* (pp. New York: Wiley.

Krakow, J. B., & Kopp, C. B. (1983). The effects of developmental delay on sustained attention in young children. *Child Development,* 54, 1143–1155.

Kuczynski, L. (1984).Socialization goals and mother-child interaction: Strategies for long-term and short-term compliance. *Developmental Psychology,* 20, 1061–1073.

Kuczynski, L., Kochanska, G., Radke-Yarrow, M., & Girnius-Brown, O. (1987). A developmental interpretation of young children's noncompliance. *Developmental Psychology,* 23, 799–806.

Lange, MacKinnon, & Nida (1989). Knowledge, strategy, & motivational contributions to preschool childrens' object recall. Developmental Psychology, 25, 772–779.

L'Ecuyer, R. (1981). The development of the self-concept through the life span. In M.D. Lynch, A. A. Norem-Hebeisen, K. Gergen (Eds.), *Self-concept: Advances in theory and research* (pp. 203–218). Cambridge, MA: Ballinger.

Lewis, M. (1991). Ways of knowing the self. *Developmental Review,* 11, 231–242.

Lewis, M., & Brooks-Gunn, J. (1979). *Social cognition and the acquisition of self.* New York: Plenum.

Maccoby, E. E., & Martin, J. (1983). Socialization in the context of the family: Parent-child interaction. In E. M. Hetherington (Ed.), P. H. Mussen (Series Ed.), *Handbook of child psychology: Vol. 4 Socialization, personality, and social development,* (pp.). New York: Wiley.

Mahler, M. S., Pine, F., & Bergman, A. (1975). *The psychological birth of the infant.* New York: Basic Books.

Mandler, J. (1990). Recall and its verbal expression. In R. Fivush, & J. A. Hudson (Eds.), *Knowing and remembering in young children,* (pp.). Cambridge: Cambridge University Press.

Markus, H. (1980). The self in thought and memory. In D. M. Wegner, & R. R. Vallacher (Eds.), *The self in social psychology* (pp. 102–130). New York: Oxford University Press.

Masten, A. S., Best, K. M., & Garmezy, N. (1990). Resilience and development: Contributions from the study of children who overcome adversity. *Development and Psychopathology,* 2, 425–444.

Mischel, W. (1983). The role of knowledge and ideation in the development of delay capacity. In L. Liben (Ed.), *Piaget and the foundations of knowledge,* (pp. 201–229). Hillsdale, NJ: Erlbaum.

Mundy, P., & Sigman, M. (1989). The theoretical implications of joint attention deficits in autism. *Development and Psychopathology,* 1, 173–183.

Mundy, P., Sigman, M., & Kasari, C. (1990). A longitudinal study of joint attention and language development in autistic children. *Journal of Autism and Developmental Disorders,* 20, 115–23.

Neisser, U. (1988). Five kinds of self knowledge. *Philosophical Psychology,* 1, 35–59.

Neisser, U. (1991). Perceptually given aspects of the self. *Developmental Review,* 11, 197–209.

Nelson, K. (1986). Event knowledge: Structure and function in development. Hillsdale, NJ: Erlbaum.

Nelson, K. (1990). Remembering, forgetting, and childhood amnesia. In R. Fivush, & J. A. Hudson (Eds.), *Knowing and remembering in young children,* (pp.). Cambridge: Cambridge University Press.

Rogers, T. B. (1981). A model of the self as an aspect of the human information processing system. In N. Cantor & J. Kilstrom (Eds.), *Personality, cognition, and social interaction.* Hillsdale, N.J.: Lawrence Erlbaum.

Rogoff, B., Sellers, M. J., Pirrotta, S., Fox, N., & White, S. (1975). Age of assignment of roles and responsibilities to children. *Human Development,* 18, 353–369.

Rosenberg, M. (1979). *Conceiving the self.* New York: Basic Books.

Rumsfeld, S. (1989). Undergraduate research project, UCLA, unpublished.

Samet, J. Autism and theory of mind: some philosophical perspectives. In S. Baron-Cohen, H., Tager-Flusberg, & D. J. Cohen, (Eds.), *Understanding other minds: Perspectives from Autism,* (pp. 427–449). Oxford: Oxford University Press.

Schaffer, R., & Crook, C. (1979). Maternal control techniques in a directed play situation. *Child Development,* 50, 989–996.

Schaffer, R., & Crook, C. (1980). Child compliance and maternal control techniques. *Developmental Psychology,* 16, 54–61.

Shantz, C. (1983). Social cognition. In J. Flavell & E. Markman (Eds.) Cognitive development. In P. H. Mussen (Series Ed.), *Handbook of child psychology (Vol. 3).* (pp. 841–889). New York: Wiley.

Schneider-Rosen, K., & Wenz-Gross, M. (1990). Patterns of compliance from eighteen to thirty months of age. *Child Development,* 61, 85–98.

Spitz, R. (1959). *A genetic field theory of ego formation.* New York: International Universities Press.

Stern, D. (1985). *The interpersonal world of the infant.* New York: Basic Books.

Stipek, D. J., Gralinski, J. H., & Kopp, C. B. (1990). Self-concept development in the toddler years. *Developmental Psychology,* 26, 972–977.

Stipek, D., Recchia, S., & McClintic, S. (1992). Self-concept development in young children. *Monographs of the Society for Research in Child Development,* 57(1, Serial No. 226).

Vaughn, B. E., Kopp, C. B., & Krakow, J. B. (1984). The emergence and consolidation of self-control from 18- to 30-months of age: Normative trends and individual differences. *Child Development,* 55, 990–1004.

Vaughn, B. E., Kopp, C. B., Krakow, J. B., Johnson, K., & Schwartz, S. S. (1986). Process analysis of the behavior of very young children in delay tasks. *Developmental Psychology,* 22, 752–759.

Watson, M. W., & Fischer, K. W. (1977). A developmental sequence of agent use in late infancy. *Child Development*, 48, 828–836.

Weisz, J., & Zigler, E. (1979). Cognitive development in retarded and nonretarded persons: Piagetian tests of the similar sequence hypothesis. *Psychological Bulletin*, 86, 831–851.

Wellman, H. (1993). Early understanding of mind: the normal case. In S. Baron-Cohen, H., Tager-Flusberg, & D. J. Cohen, (Eds.), *Understanding other minds: Perspectives from Autism*, (pp. 10–39). Oxford: Oxford University Press.

Wolf, D. P. (1990). Being of several minds: Voices and versions of the self in early childhood 183–212.

Wolf, D., Rygh, J, Altshuler, J. (1984). Agency and experience: Actions and states in play narratives. In I. Bretherton (Ed.), *Symbolic play: The development of social understanding*, (pp.). Orlando, FL:Academic

Zigler, E. (1968). Developmental versus difference theories of mental retardation and the problem of motivation. *American Journal of Mental Deficiency*, 73, 536–556.

III The Development of the Will: A Neuropsychological Analysis of Gilles de la Tourette Syndrome.

Simon Baron Cohen*, Mary M. Robertson#, and John Moriarty#.

"No wise fish would go anywhere without a porpoise . . . Why, if a fish came to *me*, and told me he was going on a journey, I should say, "With what porpoise?" (The Mock Turtle, in *Alice in Wonderland*. Quoted by Boden, 1987, p.664).

In a volume concerned with the development of a concept of self and its dysfunction, it is important to begin with some key conceptual distinctions, so as to confine the discussion to specific mechanisms and processes. The concept of self is otherwise just too nebulous, too slippery, and in danger of being scientifically worthless. To this end, along with other contributors to this volume, we distinguish several different levels of self concept, namely, self-esteem, self-recognition, self-identity, self-consciousness, and self-control. In this chapter we restrict our discussion to a consideration of the last of these levels, self-control. Other chapters in this volume take up the various levels of self-concept that we do not address (see for example, Chandler, Harter and Marold, and Marold, this volume). Regarding terminology, we use the term self-control synonymously with the terms volition, or the will, and for brevity opt to use the last of these in most instances.

In the first part of the chapter, we discuss the development of the will, and the problems in defining this. We consider various criteria for identifying an act as volitional, and summarize some of the evidence from infancy research in relation to these different criteria. In the second part of this chapter we then consider the development of a specific neurocognitive mechanism, the *Intention Editor* (Baron-Cohen, Cross, Crowson, and Robertson, 1993), which we suggest begins to function in early childhood. We go on to review its status as a possible

---

We are indebted to Michael Trimble and Donald Cohen for their support and guidance in this work. Parts of this chapter are reprinted from Baron-Cohen, Cross, Crowson, and Robertson, 1993.

sub-system with the *Supervisory Attentional System* (Shallice, 1988), a mechanism that controls planning in general. The Intention Editor is examined as one key mechanism that underlies the will. We then turn to consider the hypothesis that a dysfunction in the development of the Intention Editor plays a significant role in the problems of children with Gilles de la Tourette Syndrome (GTS), and argue that experimental neuropsychological research in this area may be fruitful not only for learning about this disorder, but also for casting light on the development of this aspect of the self.

The Development of the Will in Infancy

Willed action has often been thought to be a quality unique to human beings. Young (1987, p. 147) argues that this view is mistaken, and that equivalent but simpler behaviours can be found in other organisms. But what is meant by the will? Libet (1985) defines an act as voluntary, and a function of the subject's will, "when (a) it arises endogenously, not in direct response to an external stimulus or cue; (b) there are no externally imposed restrictions or compulsions that directly or immediately control subjects' initiation and performance of the act; and (c) subjects *feel* introspectively that they are performing the act on their own initiative and that they are *free* to start or not start the act as they wish" (*ibid*, p.529–530). This definition works reasonably well for adults with language, who can act as informants. However, to make any headway in this area as regards infants, we are forced into identifying *behavioural criteria* for an infant's act being under self-control, or volition. We begin by examining some possibilities.

Criterion 1: Distinguishing Reflexive vs Flexible Behaviour

The traditional view is that willed action is behaviour that is *not reflexive*. This begs the question as to what a reflex is. This has been a major concern in the history of neurology and neuropsychology (Sherrington, 1906; see also Merton, 1987). In general, reflexes are "the automatic reactions of the nervous system to stimuli impinging on the body or arising within it" (*ibid*, p. 676).[1] Using this definition, it is clear that human babies manifest a range of reflexes (Prechtl, 1974, 1986). For example, infants show the pupil reflex to light, the knee jerk reflex, the startle reflex (involving arm flexion triggered by a loud noise), the Moro reflex (elicited by allowing the baby's head to drop slightly, which results in a sequence of arm-extension and fist clenching), and the stepping reflex (elicited when the infant is supported in an upright posture over a surface so

[1] Some reflexes do clearly come under a degree of voluntary control (e.g., coughing can be inhibited until the intermission of concerts; urination can be controlled by the second year of life, etc).

that pressure is exerted on the sole of the foot). Bremner (1988, p.35) provides a good review of these neonatal reflexes, and these seem relatively straight forward to identify. However, an important question to ask is what would count as examples of infant behaviour that are *not* reflexive, and may therefore be signs of early (volitional) self-control?

As Merton (1987, p. 677) writes, "The point at which an animal's responses to stimuli cease to be regarded as a reflex and are called deliberate or voluntary, or by some similar term, is ill-defined". In thinking about infancy, however, one candidate behaviour for being non-reflexive might be visual tracking. Whilst infants seem poor at controlling their limbs, they seem precociously in control of their eye movements. Neonates, for example, fixate interesting stationary objects and follow moving objects (Banks and Salapatek, 1983). Bremner (1988, p. 39) characterizes this as follows: "While their eye movements are rather sluggish and, in the case of tracking, very much less smooth than those of adults, we are quite definitely dealing with behaviours that are visually guided. Rather than running off in a fixed pattern after the initiating stimulus, these eye movements are altered more or less continuously in response to information about object position". Such *flexibility in response to an object* seems a plausible criterion in identifying non-reflexive behaviour. Of course, under a strict analysis, flexibility by itself need not imply a behaviour is volitional. It might simply be evidence of a reflex that is "wired" for flexibility. However, given the inflexibility of most reflexes, flexibility may be a *liberal* index of volition.

Criterion 2: Expressing Interest and Preferences

One important tool for investigating infant cognition is the preferential looking paradigm. In this method, the infant is presented with two stimulus displays simultaneously, and the duration of the infant's looking time to each display is measured. A longer looking time is taken as a measure of the infant's ability to discriminate the two stimulus sets, as well as their preference for one stimulus over the other. There is now a wealth of infancy data using this technique. A good review of this can be found in Karmiloff-Smith (1992). For example, Johnson and Morton (1991) presented infants with 2D stimuli on a head-shaped board. The stimuli included a "face" with normal configuration of the eyes, nose and mouth, and a "face" with a scrambled configuration of these features. The studies showed that neonates looked for longer periods at, and tracked further using both head and eye movements, the stimuli with face-like arrangements. Such experiments not only give us a clue about the starting state of the infant's perceptual system, to what it is pre-programmed to attend, but also what the infant "prefers".

If we accept the argument that longer looking time, i.e., preference, is an index of what the infant is *interested in,* can we extend the argument further to propose that interest is itself a sign of volition? There are problems in this argument, since a preference could simply be a "drive" to prefer stimulus A over stimulus B. Intuitively, it might seem that we *choose* to look at what we are interested in. Such intuitions may however be misleading.

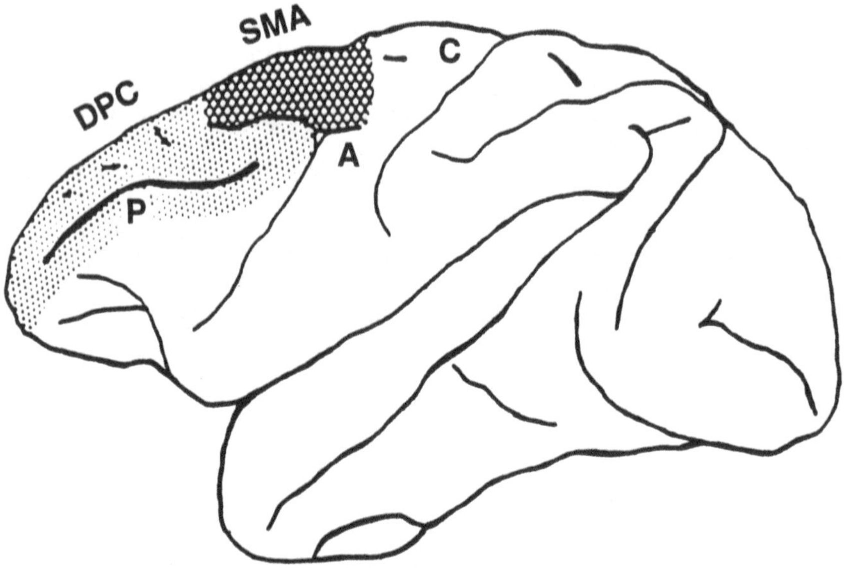

FIGURE 1 A lateral view of the rhesus monkey (*macaca mulatta*) brain, showing supplementary motor area (SMA) as hatched lines (SMA extends further down the midline than can be shown in this diagram), and dorsolateral prefrontal cortex (DPC) as dotted lines. C = central sulcus; A = arcuate sulcus; P = principal sulcus. Reproduced from Diamond (1991), with permission.

Criterion 3: Inhibition

Clearly, one crucial achievement in the early development of self-control must be *inhibition*. Diamond (1991) discusses the growth of inhibition as essentially the inhibition of action tendencies. The importance of motor inhibition has a relatively long history (e.g., Twitchell, 1965, 1970). Inhibition of action tendencies begin, on Diamond's account, around 8–12 months, and depends crucially on the maturation of the the dorsolateral prefrontal cortex (DPC: see Figure 1). An action response tendency she defines as the strongest response of the moment—e.g., reaching straight for a visible goal.

Diamond's notion of inhibition is in many ways synonymous with the notion of self-control, or the will. Thus, inhibition (or absence) of a routine response to a stimulus may count as a useful index of willed action.

Criterion 4: Identifying Intentions

Within philosophy of mind the problem of defining volition has been tackled by employing a different conceptual distinction, namely, identifying when behaviour is intentional versus non-intentional. Frye (1991) discusses some of the applications of the philosophical arguments to the analysis of infant behaviour. He highlights the work of the British philosopher, Anscombe (1957). In Anscombe's model, an act is intentional if it is performed to bring about a future state of affairs. Another way of putting this is to say that an act is intentional if the act is composed of both a goal and a means to that goal. Thus, an act is intentional if the actor did x in order to bring about y. This analysis allows one to distinguish an intentional act from non-intentional acts, such as accidents, coincidences, mistakes, or cases of "fortuitous success". Ascombe's criterion seems conceptually tighter than the previous criteria. However, without a way of identifying what the person's goal is, and whether their action was carried out as a means to that goal, we are left with the same problem of how to decide that their act was intentional. This is particularly troublesome in the case of infants, who have no language to inform us of their reasons for acting.

Frye (1991) argues that to some extent these problems are surmountable. His solution has been to carry out experiments in which the consequences of an infant's action are changed, and then observe if the infant shows a surprise reaction. The idea of using the surprise reaction as an index of cognition is discussed in detail elsewhere (Charlesworth, 1969). Frye reports the results of experiments of this nature, with infants age 8, 16, and 24 months. These found that even children in the youngest of these age groups were able to pull a cloth (the means) in order to bring a toy into reach (the goal), and showed surprise (as independently rated by blind observers) following the changed goal manipulations, when the toy went backwards or remained standing still when the cloth was pulled. Such studies suggest that intentional actions are probably present in 8 month olds. Naturally, such tests may underestimate intentionality in younger infants, since the tasks depend on motor skills such as pulling cloths, etc.

We are attracted by Frye's approach to the problem of defining volition, in that it places at centre stage the notion of *intentions* driving action.[2] In the next section, we extend this idea to argue that in the first 5 or 6 years of life, normal children develop the capacity to edit simultaneously competing intentions.

---

[2] Note Boden (1987) on this notion: "Some psychologists refuse point blank to admit the concept of purpose into their theories, regarding it as not merely unhelpful but positively mystifying. Others are content to use it as convenient shorthand, but believe that purposive explanations of behaviour could in principle be replaced by complicated stimulus-response or neurophysiological explanations in which the concept of purpose would not appear. Yet others insist that psychology must give a central role to purpose, that action and experience cannot possibly be explained without it." (p. 664). We fall into this latter group, but hold the assumption—along with many these days—that intentions, purposes, etc, are representations that are instantiated on a cerebral level, and are therefore not pure "mind-stuff", nor are they mysterious. Positing intentions in no way entails dualism.

The Intention Editor

Our notion is that in early childhood, a qualitatively new stage of self-control emerges: the ability to edit simultaneously competing intentions. We suggest this reflects the maturation of a neurocognitive mechanism, which we call the Intention Editor (Baron-Cohen et al, 1993). For the purposes of explicating this idea, we need to clarify certain assumptions that we make. First, we assume that at one level of description, *intentions* drive action. They not only drive our motor action, but also our speech, and even some of our thought. Here, we define intentions as representations of future action, speech or thought. In Figure 2, which is a functional diagram of our model, intentions are shown as housed in a Store, and can be activated by either perceptual stimuli, or by each other, or by other cognitions (Frith and Done, 1989). As was noted in Frye's (1991) account earlier, such intentions contain information specifying not only the goal-state of a future action, utterance, or thought, but also information about how to implement or reach that goal state. This notion is consistent with the classical theories of volition (see Kimble and Perlmuter, 1970, for a review), such as that by William James (1890)[3].

Secondly, we assume that even after intentions have been accessed and activated, there is a point at which they can be inhibited. In Figure 2, we depict this by showing an Inhibitor, the function of which is simply to change the activation weight of a particular intention from positive to negative. The Inhibitor is held to be a very simple mechanism in that it can only act on one intention at a time. The notion of an Inhibitor of course reminds us that intentions are separable from the actions they drive.

However, what happens when *several* intentions have been activated? Here, the Inhibitor cannot deactivate these, because (as stated above) it can only operate on one intention at at time. Here we need to introduce the second mechanism, the Intention Editor, which is only triggered when there are *two or more competing intentions* that have been simultaneously activated, only one of which can actually be executed. The others are then deactivated, and are thus not executed.

So, when given a task such as **Do x** (e.g., push the blue button), this may entail just one intention being activated. We call this a *Single Intention Task.* Many of the examples of volitional behaviour in infancy described earlier would be examples of Single Intention actions. Here the Inhibitor would be able to control action versus inaction. Given a task which requires the subject to perform a sequence of actions, one at a time, such as **Do x, then do y** (e.g., push the blue button, then the red button), this, too, may entail just *one* intention being activated and executed *at a time.* We call this a (short) *Serial Intention*

---

[3] In James' theory, an action is caused by an *image.* In Miller, Gallanter and Pribam's (1960) theory an action is caused by a *plan.* In Luria's (1966) theory, an action is caused by a *motor plan.* The term *plan* would do equally well in our model, but we opt for the term *intention.*

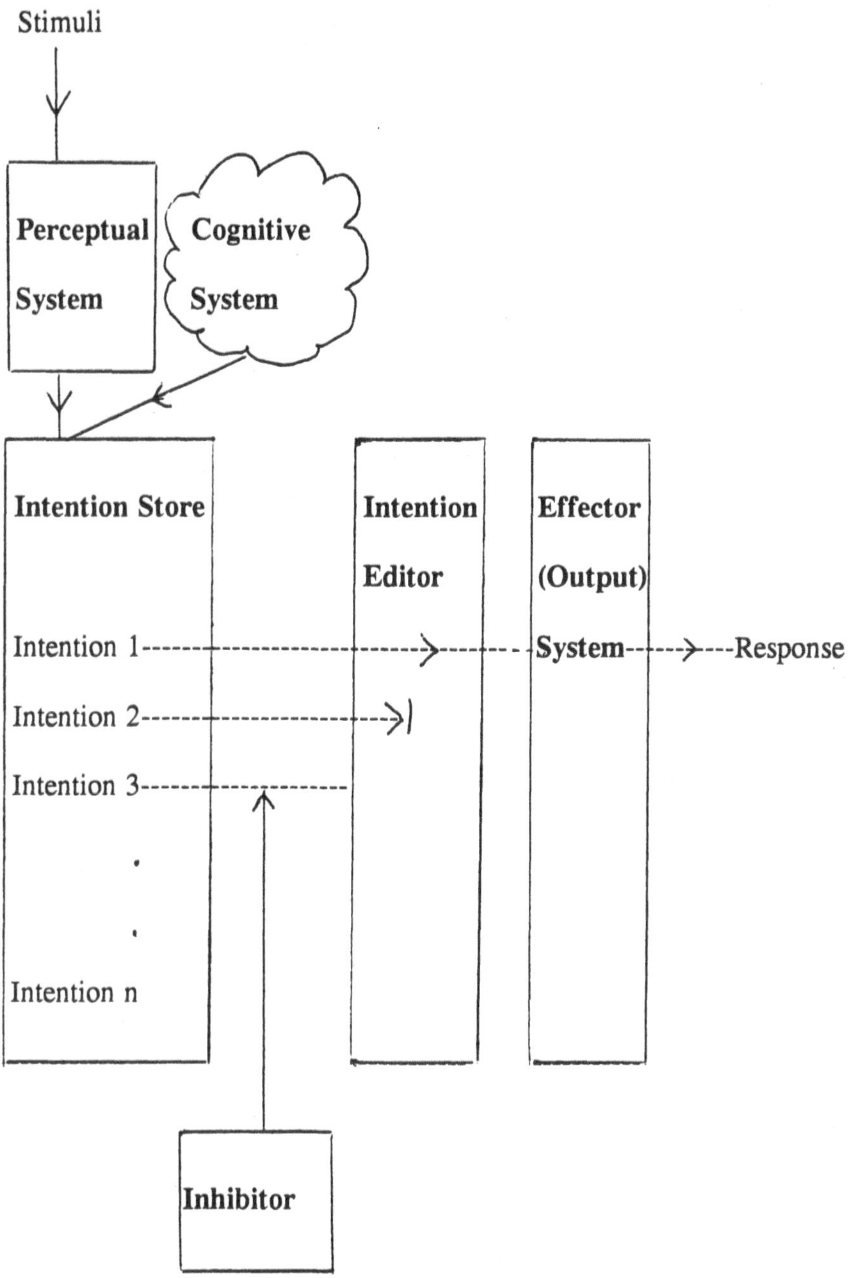

FIGURE 2 A functional model of intentional control. The Inhibitor changes the activation of an intention from +ive to −ive, but only acts on one intention at a time. (Here it is shown acting on Intention 3). The Intention Editor is triggered when several intentions are activated simultaneously. (Here, Intentions 1–3 are simultaneously activated). The Intention Editor passes one (here Intention 1) on to an Effector system, whilst deactivating the other(s: here Intention 2). In GTS, the Intention Editor is hypothesized to be impaired, whilst the Inhibitor is intact.

TABLE 1 Different Task Types

	Task Description	Intention Analysis of each Task
Simple Intention Task:	Do x.	Activate intention x, then execute intention x.
(Short) Serial Intention Task:	Do x; then do y.	Activate intention x, then execute intention x; then activate intention y, then execute intention y.
(Long) Serial Intention Task:	Do x; then do y; then do z.	Activate intention x, then execute intention x; then activate intention y, then execute intention y; then activate intention z, then execute intention z.
Parallel Intention Task:	Do x and y simultaneously.	Activate *both* intention x and intention y *simultaneously*, then edit one, then execute the other.

Task. It is what, in Diamond's (1991) earlier account, was called a "relational" ability. Similarly, if the task is **Do x, then do y, then do z** (e.g., push the red button, then the blue button, then the green button), this may still only entail *one* intention being activated and executed *at a time*, even though the sequence has lengthened. We call this a (long) Serial Intention Task. This would still come within Diamond's category of "relational" actions.

In contrast, the Intention Editor is *necessarily* triggered in *Parallel Intention Tasks*, in which the subject has to do two different things simultaneously. An clear example of a Parallel Intention Task, in our view, is the Stroop Test (Stroop, 1935), in which the intention to read the word is activated by the stimulus, yet an alternative intention (to name the colour of the ink) is activated by the Experimenter's instruction. These different Task Types are summarized in Table 1, along with analyses of each Task Type in terms of the number of intentions that are *minimally* activated in each.

We assume that intentions vary in terms of their potential for triggering the Editor. That is, some intentions are dangerous (e.g., the intention to hit, etc) and/or are socially disapproved of (e.g., the intention to swear in formal, public settings, etc). In our model, these sort of intentions are therefore tagged with high values. Other intentions are relatively harmless (e.g., the intention to fiddle with one's hair) and/or are socially acceptable (e.g., the intention to whistle a tune whilst walking in public). In our model, these are therefore tagged with low values. The Intention Editor is triggered more readily by intentions with higher values. The value tagged to an intention is presumably derived from both learning (e.g., a social rule) and biology (e.g., avoiding pain).

We conceive of the Intention Editor as part of our *central* processes. It does not operate on any one output system (motor, speech or thought), but rather it operates on the intentions themselves. For this last assumption to be correct, one would expect, for example, that once this mechanism had developed in the normal child, it should operate over the range of output systems. Later in this chapter, we review some preliminary evidence both for the gradual development of this mechanism in the normal case, and for its place in central processes. But first we turn to consider two key questions from the perspective of developmental psychopathology (Cicchetti, 1984): Might this framework for understanding the normal development of the will help make sense of a clinical phenomenon? If so, what light might this shed on the underlying processes? We have begun to explore the developmental psychopathology of the will by testing the hypothesis that children with GTS have an abnormality in the development of the Intention Editor (but not in the Inhibitor). Before considering our evidence relevant to this hypothesis, we first describe what GTS is.

Gilles de la Tourette Syndrome (GTS)

The first clear description of this syndrome was made by Itard (1825). Georges Gilles de la Tourette (1885) went on to describe 8 more similar cases, emphasizing a *triad* of symptoms: multiple tics, coprolalia (unprovoked swearing) and echolalia (repetitive speech). Current diagnostic criteria for GTS require the presence of multiple motor tics, and at least one vocal tic, both of which must exceed a year's duration and begin before the age of 21 years (American Psychiatric Association, 1987). The location, number, frequency, complexity and severity of the tics characteristically change over time.

Although the exact prevalence of GTS is unknown, a currently accepted figure is 1 in 1000 males, and 1 in 10,000 females (Leckman, Knorr, Rassmusson, and Cohen, 1991). The mean onset of the symptoms is seven years old. It is found in all social classes and across cultures (Robertson, 1989). Excellent and up to date reviews of the disorder can be found in Cohen (1991) or Roberston and Yakeley (1993).

As Gilles de la Tourette (1885) suggested, a triad of symptoms tends to cluster in these patients, justifying the use of the term 'syndrome'. In the light of more recent research, many authors have suggested that the triad be conceptualised in terms of (a) motor tics, (b) vocal tics, and (c) obsessive thinking, since different patients manifest all or any combination of these three symptoms. We briefly summarise these three areas of abnormality:

Motor tics: The most frequent initial motor tics involve the eyes (such as eye blinking), head nodding and facial grimacing. Patients also often exhibit movements such as touching, hitting, jumping, spitting, kicking and stamping, as well as abnormalities of gait (Robertson, 1989). Finally, motor tics with specific *content* (such as echopraxia [or the tendency to copy seen gestures involuntarily], and copropraxia [involuntary obscene gestures]) may also be present.

Vocal tics: These are either non-verbal (e.g., throat-clearing, barking, sniffing, hissing and clicking) or are word-related (e.g., palilalia [involuntary syllable repetition] and jargon), or are clearly verbal (e.g., explosive utterances, coprolalia, word-tics and echolalia).

Obsessive thoughts: Many patients with GTS also show Obsessive-Compulsive Behaviour (Frankel, Cummings, Robertson, Trimble, Hill, and Benson, 1986; Montgomery, Clayton, and Friedhoff, 1982; Robertson, Trimble, and Lees, 1988; Robertson, Channon, Baker, and Flynn, 1993). In addition, many relatives of patients with GTS also report obsessive thoughts and compulsive actions, in the absence of tics (Kurlan, Behr, J, Medved, L, Shoulson, I, Pauls, D, Kidd, J, & Kidd, K, 1986; Pauls, Leckman, Towbin, Zahner, and Cohen, 1986; Robertson & Gourdie, 1990).

GTS: An Abnormality in the Development of the Intention Editor?

Having briefly described the disorder of GTS, we move next to consider it in relation to the model described earlier. We suggest that the triad of motor tics, vocal tics and obsessive thoughts may all arise as a result of an abnormality in the Intention Editor, whilst the Inhibitor is intact. In our first empirical studies of this (Baron-Cohen et al, 1993), we reported two experimental tests of this hypothesis. The hypothesis seems plausible in that a failure of the Intention Editor would result in actions being performed involuntarily, words and sounds being uttered involuntarily, and a difficulty in "getting rid" of unwanted, intrusive thoughts - that is, the triad of symptoms in GTS. Moreover, we predicted this deficit would be seen only when the task involved several competing, simultaneously activated intentions (Parallel Intention Tasks), but would not be seen in control conditions (Simple or Serial Intention Tasks), in which the Inhibitor would be sufficient.

The Luria Hand Alternation Task

This task was first described by Luria (1966), and which he attributes to Ozeretskii (1930). The task involves *alternation* of different hand positions. The subject is shown how to do it and then asked to try it. The hand positions are simple: opening one hand while closing the other, then switching these *simultaneously.* This pattern must then be repeated over a series of trials. In formal terms, the task can be described as follows: **Do x and y simultaneously. Then switch to the opposite pattern.** This formal description meets the task requirements for the Intention Editor to be triggered (minimally a Parallel Intention Task). Luria's illustration of the task is shown in Figure 3.

McCarthy and Warrington (1990) discuss this task in relation to a pattern of errors Luria and other neurologists and neuropsychologists saw in patients with bilateral brain damage to the premotor cortex. These errors fell into 3 types: (a) non-fluent alternating, (b) non-simultaneous alternating, and (c) failure to alternate. The second and third of these error patterns are illus-

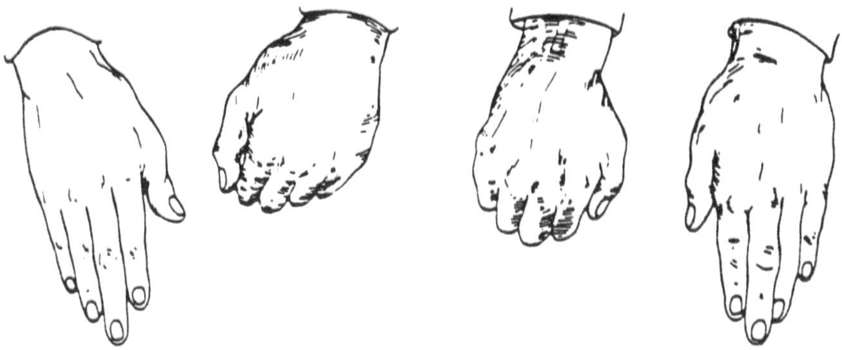

FIGURE 3 The Hand Alternation Task (reproduced from Luria, 1966, with permission).

trated in Figure 4 (reproduced from McCarthy and Warrington, 1990, with permission).

We predicted that if children with GTS were unable to edit intentions, then they would show errors on this task. In addition, we predicted that such errors would not occur in a normal control group of children. Our subjects were a group of 15 children with GTS, ranging from 6–18 years of age, with a mean of 12.31 years. They were all attending a specialist clinic at the National Hospital for Neurology and Neurosurgery in London, and had a clear diagnosis based on DSM-IIIR criteria. In order to collect data with this task from normal children, we assessed 15 normal children in each of 4 different age groups: 3, 4, 5, and 6 year olds. Finally, we predicted that children with GTS would not show errors on two different control tasks, which would only require the Inhibitor. The first control task was a (short) Serial Intention Task and therefore did not necessarily involve the Intention Editor. This task was as follows: open hands, then close hands, both hands performing the same action at the same time. In formal terms, it falls under the description **Do x, then do y.** The second control task was a (long) Serial Intention Task. This task was one of Luria's (1966) sequential movement tasks, the "fist-edge-palm" test: Using one hand, first make a fist, then hold out the hand in a rigid and vertical position, then turn the hand so that the palm faces upwards. In formal terms, it falls under the description **Do x, then do y, then do z.** In fact, all subjects with GTS achieved perfect performance (10 repetitions) on these control tasks, providing there was no pressure of time.

Figure 5 shows the mean best score for each group, on the experimental task. As can be seen, there is a clear progression among the normal groups, from 3 years through to 6 years of age. 3 year olds were significantly worse than 4 year olds and 4 year olds significantly worse than 5 year olds, though the 5 and 6 year olds did not differ. The five year olds were the youngest normal group to show ceiling performance (10 fluent, simultaneous alternations in a row), although this was not attained on the first trial by the majority of 5 year olds. In contrast, all but 3 of the 6 year olds were able to produce 10 correct alternations on the

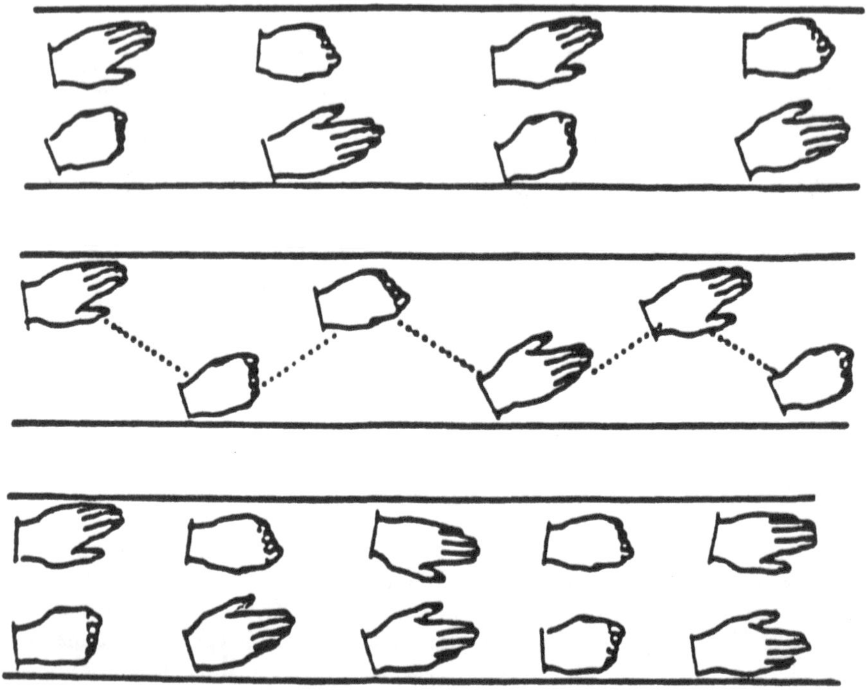

FIGURE 4 Correct and incorrect responses on the Hand-Alternation Task (reproduced from McCarthy and Warrington, 1990, with permission). Top line = correct; Middle line = Error 1 (Non-simultaneous alternating); Bottom line = Error 2 (Failure to alternate).

first trial, the other 3 doing so on the second trial. As predicted, the children with GTS made more errors than either the 5 or the 6 year olds.

On Luria's Hand Alternation Task, then, normal 5 and 6 year olds showed ceiling performance, after a relatively protracted development of this skill in the preceding two years. Llamas and Diamond (1991) report similar results. In contrast, we found that children with GTS, despite being considerably older, made significantly more errors than the 5 and 6 year olds. Given the similar deficits on this task by Luria's patients with damage to the frontal cortex, this would implicate a role for frontal pathology in children with GTS. There is some evidence for frontal abnormalities in GTS, from neuroimaging studies (Chase, Foster, Fedio, Brooks, Mansi, Kessler, and Dichiri, 1984; Chase, Geoffrey, Gillespie, and Burrows, 1986; Hall, Costa, Shields, Heavens, Robertson, and Ell, 1990).

The results from the Hand Alternation Task therefore constitute preliminary evidence in support of the hypothesis that these children have an abnormality in the development of the Intention Editor. However, by itself this might simply indicate a motor deficit, not a *central* impairment. This is particularly important because the task is quite complex in motor terms. We therefore employed an equivalent non-motor task, described next.

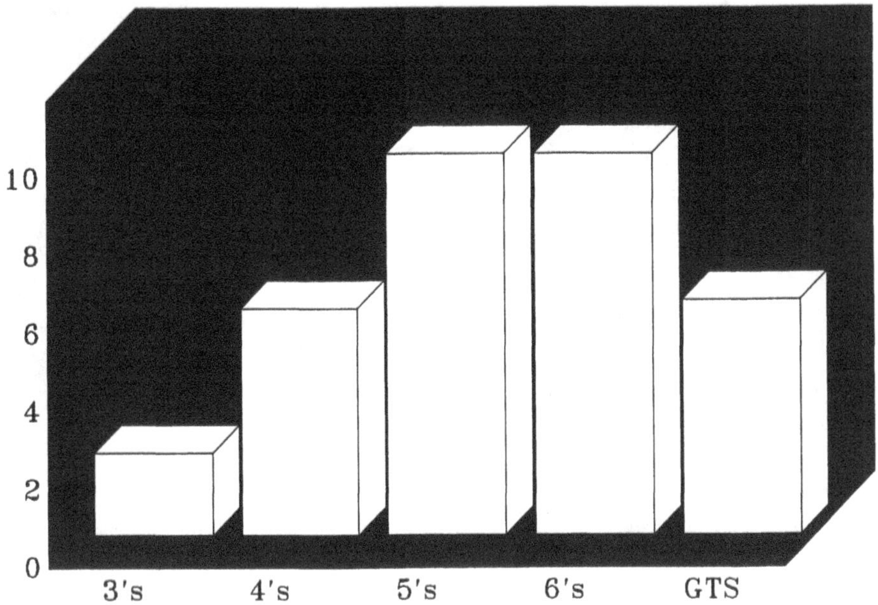

FIGURE 5 Results on the Luria Hand Alternation Test, expressed as mean best score (maximum = 10).

The Yes and No Game

Whereas in the Hand Alternation Task the subject had to execute one intention whilst inhibiting another in the motor domain, in the Yes and No Game we tested the subject's ability to do the same in the domain of speech. We used a well-known British game that is seen in parent-child play as well as child-child interaction, but which had not been used as a formal experimental procedure before, to the best of our knowledge. In this game, the subject is told that to win the game he or she must not say "Yes" or "No" in response to anything the experimenter might ask. Since these words are the usual ways of answering closed questions, the subject has to inhibit the strongly activated intention to say these words, and instead think of alternative ways to word their answer. For example, the experimenter might ask a subject called Michael "Is your name Michael?", to which the subject could reply "It is", or "That's right", etc. Whilst this task does not parallel the Luria Hand Alternation Task in all of its overt respects (e.g., in speech it is impossible to produce two observable responses simultaneously, whilst in movement this is possible), they are nevertheless similar in one key respect: They are both Parallel Intention Tasks, in that they both involve two intentions being activated simultaneously, one of which is edited and the other of which is translated into action.

In addition, the subjects with GTS were given a control task in which they simply had to say Yes, No, 10 times in a row. This is a (short) Serial Intention

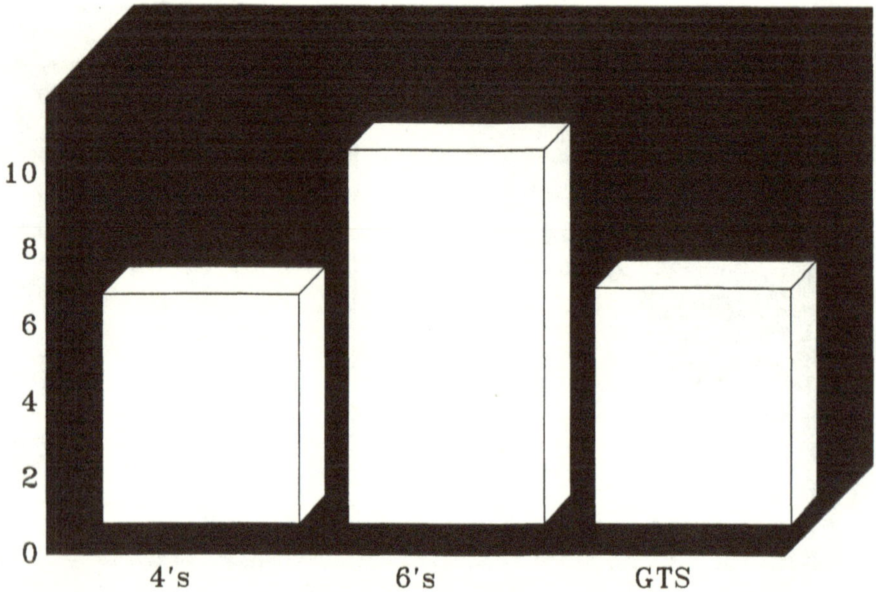

FIGURE 6 Results on the Yes and No Game, expressed as mean best score (maximum = 10).

Task, since in formal terms it falls under the description **Do x, then do y.** There were 10 trials, in random order. Any errors made were recorded. It was chosen in order to test the prediction that this would not present any difficulty for subjects with GTS, given that it could be carried out without having to activate two different intentions *simultaneously*, i.e., only involving the Inhibitor, but not the Intention Editor.

All of the subjects with GTS were at ceiling on the control task. Figure 6 shows the mean best score on the Experimental Task for each group. As can be seen, there is again a clear progression among the normal groups, from 4 to 6 years of age. 4 year olds were significantly worse than 6 year olds. All but 4 of the 6 year olds were able to produce 10 correct alternations on the first trial, the others doing so on the second or third trial. We assume that 6 year olds reflect the adult level of competence on this task. Again, as predicted, the children with GTS made more errors than the 6 year olds. The 4 year olds did not differ from the children with GTS.

Once again, then, both developmental change and pathology were identified on this task. There was an improvement between ages 4 and 6 in the normal groups, paralleling changes observed on the Luria Hand Alternation Task. Children with GTS, despite their chronological age advantage (to recap: they had a mean age of 12 years old), were significantly worse than normal 6 year olds at inhibiting an intention to say one thing (e.g., "Yes") whilst executing an intention to say something else (e.g., "That's right"). This was not due to failure to understand the rules of the game, as subjects always showed their awareness that they had made an error, by laughing and expressing 'annoyance' at their mistakes. Nor was it due to either perseveration, or an inability to follow simple instructions, or an inability to participate in a game, as their almost perfect performance on the control task demonstrated. It was only the Parallel Intention Task, which activates two different intentions *simultaneously*, and which is therefore held to require the Intention Editor, that elicited the deficit in subjects with GTS. These results are consistent with the hypothesis that the deficit detected in the Hand Alternation Task is not specifically motor in nature, but reflects a central system which operates on a range of output systems. We discuss the specificity of this mechanism next, by turning to a related mechanism.

The Supervisory Attention System

A related system is Shallice's (1988) *Supervisory Attentional System* (the SAS). To understand the SAS, we must first mention what Shallice calls the *Contention Scheduling System* (the CSS) which responds to external stimuli and repeats relevant, routine actions. For example, if a traffic light turns red when you are at a certain distance from it, you start braking. As Shallice (*ibid*, p.333) says, the "default option" is to brake. Another example he gives is reaching out to pull the light cord on entering a familiar room (Shallice, *ibid*, p.328). Both of these examples are routine action programs, or schemas, triggered simply by the situation. Shallice calls this process of routine selection between routine actions or thought operations "contention scheduling". This process sacrifices flexibility for speed of operation. The SAS, on the other hand, "has access to a representation of the environment and of the organism's intentions and cognitive capacities" (Shallice, *ibid*, p.335) and can oversee the CSS by activating or inhibiting alternative schemata. The primary function of the SAS therefore is to respond to novelty. Thus, in the A not B error (Diamond, 1991; Piaget, 1952), the SAS would be crucial in enabling the subject to switch responses appropriately. It is also seen as playing an essential part in decision-making. Shallice (1988) proposes that the SAS is impaired in patients with frontal lobe syndrome, resulting in disinhibition of actions.

We doubt that children with GTS are *generally* impaired in the SAS, in that they appear to be able to switch to new actions in an action sequence, and they do not appear to be simply stimulus-driven in their actions. For example, utilization behaviour (L'Hermitte, 1984), that is, being unable to resist grasping and using objects that are in sight, has not been documented in these patients (though systematic research in this area is largely lacking), and yet utilization behaviour is "how contention scheduling should operate when it is not subject to Supervisory System control" (Shallice, *ibid*, p.343). Nor do children with GTS seem unable to shift response in novel ways, which again would be predicted by a *global* SAS deficit. A relevant test of this would be the Wisconsin Card Sorting Test (Grant and Berg, 1948), which as far as we are aware has not been used with this group. Our prediction would be however that patients with GTS would be able to sort the cards according to novel rules when so instructed, rather than showing classic, "frontal" perseveration. If this is correct, this would suggest that in the case of children with GTS, the SAS is in general intact. One related test of the SAS that has been used with patients with GTS is the Go-No Go task, which found no specific impairment in this group (Sally Ozonoff, personal communication, 1993). However, it seems plausible that the Intention Editor is a specific component *within* the SAS, dedicated to editing out one of several intentions that are competing in *parallel*. This notion is compatible with Shallice's (*ibid*, p.352) proposal that the SAS is not internally equipotential, but may have modular sub-processes. In his later work (Shallice and Burgess, 1992) he addresses this issue directly, in discussing the possible fractionation of the SAS (p. 133).

The SAS is often discussed as a cognitive model of the "executive function" (Lezak, 1983; Milner and Petrides, 1984). By executive function is meant "the ability to maintain an appropriate problem-solving set for attainment of a future goal. (It includes) planning, impulse control, inhibition of prepotent but incorrect responses, set maintainance, organized search, and flexibility of thought and action" (Ozonoff, in press, p. 5, MS). It is clearly a broad concept. Executive function has been studied more often in relation to the adult system, but has become an area of inquiry in developmental neuropsychology recently too (Dennis, 1991; Stuss, 1992). Following adult neuropsychological research, there is now little doubt that executive function relies on the frontal lobes or, a little more precisely, the frontal system. Damage to this results in what Baddeley and Wilson (1988) call the "dysexecutive sydrome" - broad deficits in planning skills. Impairments in executive function as measured by classical frontal neuropsychological tests (the Wisconsin Cart Sorting Test, the Go-No Go Test, and others) have been documented in children with Attention Deficit Hyperactivity Disorder (Shue and Douglas, 1992), suggesting they may indeed suffer from a global SAS deficit.

In summary, the claim that children with GTS are impaired in the development of the Intention Editor is more specific than the claim that they have generalized frontal problems, or generalized executive system problems, or generalized SAS problems. Nevertheless, the relationship between the SAS and the Intention Editor remains to be investigated more fully.

Conclusions

In this chapter we have considered the development of one aspect of the self, namely self-control. We have reviewed our model that in early childhood self-control undergoes a qualitative change with the maturation of a new mechanism, the Intention Editor. We have presented some preliminary evidence that children with GTS have a deficit in the Intention Editor, and propose that this might underlie the key symptoms in their behaviour. In this respect, we have extended and narrowed down previous accounts of the psychology of GTS

(Cohen, 1991). To date, we have reported how the Intention Editor normally comes into operation in laboratory tasks involving simultaneously competing intentions. In the real world, such tasks might include talking politely to someone whom you think little of (editing a competing intention to use impolite language), or sitting quietly whilst working (editing intentions to jump up or move around). The motor and vocal tics, as well as coprolalia and copropraxia, that are features of GTS, can be seen as exactly the kinds of behaviours one would expect to see if this mechanism failed.

Characterizing the early development of this mechanism will require further experimental studies. Its study in clinical populations will allow us to address the question of whether different psychological processes that are held to be 'frontal' are independent of one another. For example, Baron-Cohen and Ring (in press) argue that the orbito-frontal region is particularly involved in the ability to attribute mental states, or what is often called a "theory of mind". This claim is consistent with the models developed by Stuss (1992) and Dennis (1991). One prediction would be that whilst children with GTS are impaired in the development of the Intention Editor, they are unimpaired in the development of a theory of mind. In contrast, we would expect children with autism to show the opposite pattern, given previous evidence (Baron-Cohen, Leslie and Frith, 1985; Baron-Cohen, 1990, 1993).

Secondly, clinical populations force us to make explicit how a postulated cognitive deficit relates to symptomatology. To say that an executive function deficit explains an observed behaviour pattern is clearly inadequate if such deficits are found in populations as diverse as schizophrenia (Frith, 1992), hyperactivity (Shue and Douglas, 1992), and autism (Ozonoff, Pennington, and Rogers, 1991). On the other hand, demonstrating deficits that are *specific* to different clinical populations does move us forward in understanding the relation between cognition and behaviour. In this respect, it will be important to test the functioning of the Intention Editor in a range of disorders, to establish the specificity of this deficit.

Finally, clinical groups afford us the opportunity to understand the interface between brain and cognition. Thus, recent neuroimaging studies of patients with GTS using SPECT suggest abnormalities in both the anterior cingulate (Chase et al, 1986; Moriarty, et al, 1993) and in the basal ganglia (Hall et al, 1990). This is consistent with GTS being caused by abnormalities in the basal ganglia-frontal circuitry, as Singer (1993) has argued. We are interested to explore the relationship between the Intention Editor and these neural structures in future studies.

The study of processes such as the Intention Editor in the normal case allow us to pursue a different set of questions. For example, it is not clear if "action slips" (Norman, 1981) in the normal individual are due to transient (non-pathological) changes in the functioning in the Intention Editor, or are the result of different processes altogether. Similarly, when we swear involuntarily, or in any other way "lose" our self-control, in what way is the Intention Editor involved in such behaviour? Indeed, if our model is correct, is it the case that we would all have GTS, but for the normal development of the Intention Editor?

REFERENCES

American Psychiatric Association (1987) *Diagnostic and Statistical Manual of Mental Disorders* (3rd edn, revised). Washington DC.

Anscombe, G, (1957) *Intention.* London: Blackwell.

Baddeley, A, & Wilson, B, (1988) Frontal amnesia and the dysexecutive syndrome. *Brain and Cognition,* **7,** 212–230.

Baron-Cohen, S, Leslie, A. M., & Frith, U, (1985) Does the autistic child have a 'theory of mind'? *Cognition,* **21,** 37–46.

Baron-Cohen, S, (1990) Autism: a specific cognitive disorder of "mind-blindness". *International Review of Psychiatry,* **2,** 79–88.

Baron-Cohen, S, (1993) From attention-goal psychology to belief-desire psychology: the development of a theory of mind and its dysfunction. pp. 59–82. In Baron-Cohen, S, Tager-Flusberg, H, & Cohen, D. J. (eds) *Understanding other minds: perspectives from autism.* Oxford University Press.

Baron-Cohen, S, Cross, P, Crowson, M, & Robertson, M, (1993) Can children with Gilles de la Tourette's Syndrome edit their intentions? *Psychological Medicine.*

Baron-Cohen, S, & Ring, H, (in press) The relationship between **EDD** and **ToMM:** neuropsychological and neurobiological perspectives. In Mitchell, P, & Lewis, C, (eds) *Origins of an understanding of mind.* Lawrence Erlbaum Associates.

Boden, M, (1987) Purpose. pp. 664–665. In Gregory, R, (ed) *The Oxford Companion to the Mind.* Oxford University Press.

Bremner, J. G. (1988) *Infancy.* Oxford: Basil Blackwell.

Caine, E, (1985) Gilles de la Tourette's syndrome: a review of clinical and research studies and consideration of future directions for investigation. *Archives of Neurology,* 42, 393–397.

Channon, S, Flynn, D, & Robertson, M, (1992) Attentional deficits in Gilles de la Tourette Syndrome. *Journal of Neuropsychiatry, Neurology, and Behavioural Neurology,* **5,** 170–177.

Chase, T, Foster, N, Fedio, P, Brooks, R, Mansi, L, Kessler, R, & Dichiri, G (1984) Gilles de la Tourette syndrome: studies with the fluorine-18-labelled fluorodeoxyglucose positron emission tomographic method. *Annals of Neurology,* 15 (Suppl.), S175.

Chase, T, Geoffrey, V, Gillespie, M, & Burrows, G, (1986) Structural and functional studies of Gilles de la Tourette syndrome. *Revue Neurologique* (Paris), 142, 851–855.

Cicchetti, D, (1984) The emergence of developmental psychopathology. *Child Development,* **55,** 1–7.

Cohen, D, (1991) Tourette's Syndrome: developmental psychopathology of a model neuropsychiatric disorder of childhood. *Strecker Monograph Series XXVII,* Institute of Pennsylvania Hospital, 111 N. 49th St, Philadelphia, PA 19139, USA.

Cohen, D, Bruun, R, & Leckman, J, (1988, eds) *Tourette Syndrome and Tic Disorders.* New York: John Wiley and Sons.

Cohen, D, Young, J, Nathanson, J, & Shaywitz, B, (1979) Clonidine in Tourette's Syndrome. *Lancet,* **2,** 551–553.

Dennis, M, (1991) Frontal lobe function in childhood and adolescence: a heuristic for assessing attention regulation, executive control, and intentional states important for social discourse. *Developmental Neuropsychology,* **7,** 327–358.

Diamond, A, (1991) Neuropsychological insights into the meaning of object concept development. pp. 67–110. In Carey, S, & Gelman, R, (eds) *The epigenesis of mind.* Lawrence Erlbaum Associates.

Dunn, L, Dunn, L, Whetton, C, & Pintilie, D (1982) *British Picture Vocabulary Scale,* Windsor, Berks: NFER: Nelson.

Frankel, M, Cummings, J, Robertson, M, Trimble, M, Hill, M, & Benson, D, (1986) Obsessions and compulsions in Gilles de la Tourette's syndrome. *Neurology*, 36, 378–382.

Frith, C, (1987) The positive and negative symptoms of schizophrenia reflect impairments in the perception and initiation of action. *Psychological Medicine*, **17**, 631–648.

Frith, C, (1992) *The cognitive neuropsychology of schizophrenia.* London: Lawrence Erlbaum Associates.

Frith, C, & Done, J, (1989) Experiences of alien control in schizophrenia reflect a disorder in the central monitoring of action. *Psychological Medicine*, **19**, 359–363.

Frith, U, Morton, J, & Leslie, A, (1991) The cognitive basis of a biological disorder: autism. *Trends in Neuroscience*, **14**, 433–438.

Frye, D, (1991) The origins of intention in infancy. pp. 15–38. In Frye, D, & Moore, C, (eds) *Children's theories of mind.* Hillsdale, New Jersey: Lawrence Erlbaum Associates.

Gilles de La Tourette, G, (1885) Etude sur une affection nerveuse caracterisee par de l'incoordination motrice accompagnee d'echolalie et de copralalie. *Archives of Neurology*, 9, 19–42, 158–200.

Grant, D, & Berg, E, (1948) A behavioral analysis of degree of reinforcement and ease of shifting to new responses in a Weigl-type card-sorting problem. *Journal of Experimental Psychology*, **38**, 404–411.

Gray, J, Feldon, J, Rawlins, J, Hemsley, D, & Smith, A, (1991) The neuropsychology of schizophrenia. *Behavioural and Brain Sciences*, **14**, 1–84.

Hall, M, Costa, D, Shields, J, Heavens, J, Robertson, M, & Ell, P, (1990) Brain perfusion patterns with 99Tcm-HMPAO/SPECT in patients with Gilles de la Tourette Syndrome: short report. *Nuclear Medicine*, supplement **27**, 243–245.

Incagnoli, T, & Kane, R, (1981) Neuropsychological functioning in Gilles de la Tourette's Syndrome. *Journal of Clinical Neuropsychology*, 3, 165–169.

Itard, J, (1825) Memoire sur quelques fonctions involuntaires des appareils de la locomotion de la prehension et de la voix. *Archives of General Medicine*, 8, 385–407.

James, W, (1890) *Principles of psychology.* New York: Holt.

Johnson, M, & Morton, J, (1991) *Biology and cognitive development: the case of face recognition.* Oxford: Blackwell.

Karmiloff-Smith, A, (1992) *Beyond modularity.* Bradford Books: MIT Press.

Kelso, J, (1984) Phase transitions and critical behaviour in human bimanual coordination. *American Journal of Physiology: Regulatory, Integrative, and Comparative*, **246**, R1000–R1004.

Kidd, K, Prusoff, B, & Cohen, D, (1980) The familial pattern of Gilles de la Tourette's Syndrome. *Archives of General Psychiatry*, **37**, 1336–1339.

Kimble, G, & Perlmuter, L, (1970) The problem of volition. *Psychological Review*, **77**, 361–384.

Kurlan, R, Behr, J, Medved, L, Shoulson, I, Pauls, D, Kidd, J, & Kidd, K, (1986) Familial Tourette's syndrome: report of a large pedigree and potential for linkage analysis. *Neurology*, 36, 772–776.

Libet, B, (1985) Unconscious cerebral initiative and the role of conscious will in voluntary action. *The Behavioral and Brain Sciences*, **8**, 529–566.

Llamas, C, & Diamond, A, (1991) Development of frontal cortex abilities in children between 3–8 years. *Abstracts of the Society for Research in Child Development*, **8**, 347.

Leckman, J, Knorr, A, Rassmusson, A, & Cohen, D, (1991) Basal ganglia research and Tourette's Syndrome. *Trends in Neuroscience*, **14**, 94.

Lezak, M, (1983) *Neuropsychological assessment.* New York: Oxford University Press.

L'Hermitte, F, (1984) 'Utilization behaviour' and its relation to lesions of the frontal lobes. *Brain*, **106**, 237–255.

Luria, A, (1966) *The higher cortical functions of man.* New York: Basic Books.

McCarthy, R, & Warrington, E, (1990) *Cognitive Neuropsychology.* Academic Press.
Merton, P, (1987) Reflex action. pp. 676–677. In Gregory, R, (ed) *The Oxford Companion to the Mind.* Oxford University Press.
Miller, G, Gallanter, E, & Pribram, K, (1960) *Plans and the structure of behaviour.* New York: Holt, Rinehart & Winston.
Milner, B, & Petrides, M, (1984) Behavioural effects of frontal lobe lesions in man. *Trends in Neurosciences,* **7,** 403–407.
Montgomery, M, Clayton, P, & Friedhoff, A, (1982) Psychiatric illness in Tourette syndrome patients and first-degree relatives. In Friedhoff, A, & Chase, T, (eds) *Advances in Neurology,* Vol 35, New York, Raven Press.
Moriarty, J, Costa, D, Schmitz, B, Trimble, M, Robertson, M, & Ell, P, (1993) A study of Gilles de la Tourette Syndrome using HMPO SPECT. *Nuclear Medicine Communications,* **14,** 266–267.
Norman, D, (1981) Categorization of action slips. *Psychological Review,* **88,** 1–15.
Ozeretskii, N, (1930) Technique of investigating motor function: In M. Gurevich and N. Ozeretskii (eds) *Psychomotor functions.* Medgiz: Moscow.
Ozonoff, S, Pennington, B, & Rogers, S, (1991) Executive function deficits in high-functioning autistic children: relationship to theory of mind. *Journal of Child Psychology and Psychiatry,* **32,** 1081–1106.
Ozonoff, S, (in press) Executive functions in autism. In Schopler, E, & Mesibov, G, (eds) *Learning and cognition in autism.* New York: Plenum Press.
Pauls, D, & Leckman, J, (1986) The inheritance of Gilles de la Tourette's Syndrome and associated behaviours: evidence for autosomal dominant transmission. *New England Journal of Medicine,* **315,** 993–997.
Pauls, D, Leckman, J, Towbin, K, Zahner, G, & Cohen, D, (1986) A possible genetic relationship exists between Tourette's syndrome and obsessive-compulsive disorder. *Psychopharmacology Bulletin,* 22, 730–733.
Piaget, J, (1952) *The origins of intelligence in children.* (M. Cook, Trans.). New York: Basic Books. (Original published 1936).
Prechtl, H, (1974) The behavioural states of the newborn infant (a review). *Brain Research,* **76,** 1304–1311.
Prechtl, H, (1986) Prenatal motor development. In Wade, M, & Whiting, H, (eds), *Motor Development in Children: aspects of coordination and control.* Dordrecht: Nijhoff.
Rabbitt, P, (1966) Error correction time without external error signals. *Nature,* 212, 438.
Rachman, S, & Hodgson, R, (1980) *Obsessions and Compulsions.* Englewood Cliffs, NJ: Academic Press.
Rachman, S, de Silva, P, & Roper, G, (1976) The spontaneous decay of compulsive urges. *Behaviour Research and Therapy,* **14,** 445–453.
Robertson, M, (1989) The Gilles de la Tourette Syndrome: The Current Status. *British Journal of Psychiatry,* 154, 147–169.
Robertson, M, and Baron-Cohen, S, (in press) The neuropsychiatry and neuropsychology of Gilles de la Tourette's Syndrome. In Adams, K & Grant, I (eds) *Neuropsychological assessment of neuromedical disorders.* New York: Oxford University Press.
Robertson, M, Channon, S, Baker, J, & Flynn, D, (1993) The psychopathology of Gilles de la Tourette Syndrome: a controlled study. *British Journal of Psychiatry,* **162,** 114–117.
Robertson, M, and Gourdie, A, (1990) Familial Tourette's syndrome in a large British pedigree: Associated Psychopathology, Severity of Tourette's and Potential for Linkage Analysis. *British Journal of Psychiatry,* 156, 515–521.
Robertson, M, Trimble, M, & Lees, A, (1988) The psychopathology of the Gilles de la Tourette Syndrome: a phenomenological analysis. *British Journal of Psychiatry,* **152,** 383–390.

Robertson, M, & Yakeley, J, (1993) Obsessive-compulsive disorder and self-injurious behaviour. pp. 45–87. In Kurlan, R, (ed) *Handbook of Tourette's Syndrome and Related Tic and Behavioural Disorders.* New York: Marcel Dekker, Inc.

Shallice, T, (1988) *From neuropsychology to neural structure.* Cambridge: Cambridge University Press.

Shallice, T, & Burgess, P (1992) Higher-order cognitive impairments and frontal lobe lesions in man. pp. 125–138. In Levin, H, Eisenberg, H, & Benton, A, (eds) *Frontal lobe function and injury.* Oxford: Oxford University Press.

Shapiro, A, Shapiro, E, & Clarkin, J, (1974) Clinical psychological testing in Tourette's Syndrome. *Journal of Personality Assessment,* 38, 464–478.

Shapiro, A, Shapiro, E, Young, J, & Feinberg, J, (1988) *Gilles de la Tourette Syndrome.* New York: Raven Press.

Sherrington, C, (1906) *The integrative action of the nervous system.* New edition: 1947. Cambridge: Cambridge University Press.

Shue, K, & Douglas, V, (1992) Attention deficit hyperactivity disorder and the frontal lobe syndrome. *Brain and Cognition,* , **20,** 104–124.

Singer, H, (1993) Pathobiology. pp. 267–287. In Kurlan, R, (ed) *Handbook of Tourette's Syndrome and Related Tic and Behavioural Disorders.* New York: Marcel Dekker, Inc.

Stroop, J, (1935) Studies in interference in serial verbal reactions. *Journal of Experimental Psychology,* **18,** 643–661.

Stuss, D, (1992) Biological and psychological development of executive functions. *Brain and Cognition,* **20,** 8–23.

Twitchell, T, (1965) The automatic grasping responses of infants. *Neuropsychologia,* **3,** 247–259.

Twitchell, T, (1970) Reflex mechanisms and the development of prehension. pp. 25–45. In Connolly, K, (ed) *Mechanisms of motor skill development.* New York: Academic Press.

Young, J. Z. (1987) Choice, Biological. pp. 147–148. In Gregory, R, (ed) *The Oxford Companion to the Mind.* Oxford University Press.

IV Peering into the Black Box: An Exploratory Treatise on the Development of Self in Young Children*

Patricia M. Crittenden

Introduction

No human is identical to any other and yet all develop in accordance with the same principles regulating the interaction of biology and circumstance. Explaining this phenomenon, the development of an infinite variety of unique selves, is the business of developmental psychology. In this chapter, I undertake the ambitious task of attempting to explain the early development of self and individual differences in self in terms of the functioning of the human mind. To do so I draw on a set of principles imbedded in a diversity of psychological theories. From them, I attempt to synthesize new theory regarding patterns of mental functioning and to apply that theory to the healthy and psychopathological development of self in the first seven years of life.

Because we cannot yet directly explore the functioning of the mind, it is treated here as a 'black box' whose functions can be observed in the form of behavior. This behavior is then used as a means for inferring structural differences. Unlike empirical hypothesis testing, there is no presumption that these structures are 'real'. Rather they are employed to generate explanations for patterns of observed phenomena and hypotheses that can be tested. Although the theory itself exceeds the power of empirical science to prove, it, nevertheless, remains an essential framework, i.e., representational model, from which to attribute meaning to the more limited findings of empirical studies (Hermans, Kempden, & van Loon, 1992).

Plan of the Chapter. The chapter begins with a brief theoretical overview of several concepts that are central to this paper: a) mind and self, b) affect and

*Work on this chapter was supported by grant #5-T32-MH15161 from the National Institutes of Health. It is a pleasure to acknowledge the assistance and support of Angelika H. Claussen, A. Sharon Heller, Sandra Pipp, David Sugarman, and Maria von Salish in the revisions of earlier drafts.

cognition, c) internal representational models and memory systems, and d) patterns of attachment. Next the development of self is considered in terms of developmental processes and individual differences in developmental processes in each of three age periods: infancy, the preschool years, and the early school years. At each age period, central developmental tasks are used to highlight developmental processes and individual differences, particularly differences tied to vulnerability to psychopathology. The chapter concludes with a brief summary of each age period; this summary may provide a useful initial overview as well.

Theory and Constructs

1. A Theoretical Perspective

Although attachment theory is not a theory of self, contained within it, in the notion of internal representational models, is the basis for such a theory. In this chapter the concept of internal representational models is applied to the development of self. The underlying notion is that Bowlby's ideas regarding mental processing of information, together with Ainsworth's (1979) tripartite categories of individual differences in quality of attachment (i.e., secure, anxious/avoidant, and anxious/ambivalent) can explain major patterns of functioning, personality, and motivation as well as provide a framework through which to understand aspects of mental health and psychopathology.

Mind and Self. Before looking directly at this topic, some attention needs to be given to the words 'mind' and 'self' as used in this chapter. Viewed historically, Western thinking tends to focus on differences and distinctions. Eastern thought, on the other hand, focuses on similarities and unities (Geertz, 1984; Markus & Kitayama, 1990; Roland, 1988; Shweder & Bourne, 1982). This is reflected in the common usage of the terms 'mind' and 'self.'

The term 'mind' carries cognitive associations, in spite of the fact that its physical counterpart, the brain, regulates both affect and cognition. Indeed, so strong is the focus on cognition that I could find no English term that uneqivocably referred to the integration of affect and cognition. Their integration, i.e., their joint contribution to mental functioning, is, however, an important process. Consequently, in this chapter the word 'mind' is appropriated for that use as is the word 'mental' (Freud, 1923; Izard, 1982). When pure cognition or affect are meant, those words are used.

Similarly, the use of the term 'self' commonly implies differentiating self from others, i.e., that which makes the self unique. Indeed, most theories of development describe the self as emerging from a state of jointness/diffusion with others and moving toward a state of independence/autonomy and differentiation (Damon & Hart, 1988; Erikson, 1950; Freud, 1966; Mahler, Pine, & Bergman, 1975; Neisser, 1991). A different, more culturally neutral, perspective is offered here based on the assumption that the self exists only in the context of 'the other' and that at all ages it functions to both join and differentiate. If in Western cultures this leads to more information about separateness and differentiation than about jointness and integration, possibly that is a finding to be evaluated rather than a defining feature of the self. Put another way, discussion of the development of 'self' in this chapter focuses on the experience of self in relationships (Emde & Buchsbaum, 1990; Stern, 1985). Particularly with regard to young children, this may be an essential context for understanding the development of self (Bretherton, 1987; Emde, 1983; Harter, 1983; Kegan, 1982; Kernberg, 1976; Pipp, 1990; Snow, 1990; Sroufe, 1990).

2. Internal Representational Models

Bowlby proposed that individuals construct mental representations of attachment relationships (Bowlby, 1980). This idea itself is not new. The notion that there are *several* such models, each tied to a different memory system, is, however, an elegant integration of cognitive theory and research with learning theory and the psychoanalytic roots of attachment theory. This integration is then cast in a developmental framework.

Structure, Function, and Content

According to Bowlby, an internal representational model is a mental structure consisting of an individual's representation of 1) him- or herself (in the context of a specific attachment relationship), 2) the attachment figure (in the context of the relationship with the self), and, importantly, 3) the affect associated with the relationship. Thus, an internal representational model is, in fact, an integrated *pair* of models containing both cognitive and affective information. Affect is especially important because, according to Bowlby, affect ties certain kinds of situations (which give rise to feelings) with certain kinds of responses (which increase the probability of safety, health, etc.). Affect, in other words, functions as a primitive, rapid, and efficient appraisal system (Campos, Campos, & Barrett, 1989; Darwin, 1872/1965; Zajonc, 1980.) Cognition functions to mediate the relations among perception, affect, and behavior. In addition, cognitive maturation permits the development of mental structures for perceiving and storing new types of information, including affective information. This, in turn, paves the way for children to learn new ways with which to use these structures, i.e., new functions to be applied to the structures.

Although Bowlby focused most directly upon the mental structures, i.e., memory systems and internal representational models, implied in his clinical discussions are the notions of content, i.e., what is remembered, and mental functions, i.e., how the memory systems are used. In the discussion to follow, the roles of affect and cognition in the construction of the three components of the self, i.e., structure, function, and content, are considered. These are conceptualized as aspects of a concatenated system (Bowlby, 1969/1982) in which familiar material is repeatedly abstracted into internal representational models as new material from the zone of proximal development is absorbed and structured by the mind. The result is both greater simplicity in mental functioning as detailed information is repeatedly stripped of detail and abstracted into internal representational models and also greater complexity as new distinctions are perceived, new structures created, and new functions employed.

Memory Systems and Internal Representational Models

Based on Tulving's work on semantic and episodic memory systems (Tulving, 1972), Bowlby hypothesized that individuals construct at least two types of internal representational models of the self for each relationship (Bowlby, 1980). Tulving's more recent work, however, describes a third memory system, procedural memory, based on sensorimotor representation (Tulving, 1985).

Procedural Memory and Internal Representational Models. Because infants do not have language, it becomes important to identify their means of encoding and retrieving information. According to Tulving (1985), the first memory system to develop is procedural memory which consists of enacted patterns of behavior that are generalized. In the context of repeated experiences with their attachment figures, infants come to expect *behaviorally* (and without consciousness) their caregivers' and their own familiar patterns of behavior.

The notion of procedural memory is closely related to the Piagetian concept of sensorimotor schemata (Piaget, 1952) as well as to the notions of enactive representation (Bruner, Olver, & Greenfield, 1966), RIGs, i.e., representations of interactions that have been internalized (Stern, 1985), generalized event structures (Pipp, 1990), and perceptual sets (Basch, 1977). Procedural models, as I conceptualize them, are generalized schemata; it is the 'working' function of the model to attune behavior to the constraints of specific occasions (Crittenden, 1990).

I have proposed that infants develop procedural models of attachment relationships (Crittenden, 1990, 1992b). These models exist only as patterns of self and other behavior, together with the affect associated with their enactment. Furthermore, based on studies of the organization of infant behavior (Sroufe, 1990), I have suggested that the encoded behaviors are functional organizations of behavior rather than patterns of specific behaviors. For example, an infant might encode "When I signal how I feel, my mother behaves in ways that are comforting", rather than "When I cry, my mother picks me up." Under less auspicious conditions, an infant might encode the more complex and discouraging information that "When I signal, my mother rejects me" or "When I am quiet, she does not bother me." These examples show how behaviors can be perceived and encoded in procedural models as functional classes rather than reflexive links between specific self and other behaviors. The evidence suggests that by the last quarter of the first year of life infants combine stimulus-response patterns flexibly into organized patterns of behavior in which any of a number of behaviors may be used to fulfill the function of the pattern.

Viewed from this perspective, it appears that it is individual differences in procedural models of the self and the attachment figure that Ainsworth is tapping in the Strange Situation (Ainsworth, Blehar, Waters, & Wall, 1978.) Moreover, as Tulving concluded, it is this system of preconscious memory that guides most of our daily behavior across our life span. Put another way, preconscious procedural thinking continues uninterrupted until one perceives a discrepancy between what one expects and what one experiences. Only at that point will mental processes become conscious (Lashley, 1958/60). Consequently, perception of self-relevant discrepancies of outcomes with expectations becomes a key feature in the process of developing a sense of self. Such perception creates the opportunity for change in the development of models of the self.

Semantic Memory and Internal Representational Models. Semantic memory consists of verbally encoded, context-free (i.e., generalized) information. Associated with semantic memory are semantic internal representational models, in this case, models of the self and the attachment figure. According to Bowlby, early semantic memory is 'borrowed' from parents. That is, parents give children both the language and meanings with which to describe themselves and others.

For example, a securely attached child might have the paired generalizations that "My mother loves and understands me" and "I am loveable and capable of being understood". The associated feelings might be satisfaction and comfort. An anxiously attached child, on the other hand, might have the paired representations that "My mother is powerful and angry" and "I am demanding and bad." The associated feelings might be anxiety, fear, and shame. This example highlights the potential of children to recognize the feeling state of the attachment figure while failing to perceive their own feelings and instead attributing their behavior to traits. These traits, and not the behavior of the attachment figure, may become associated with the child's distress. Elsewhere, I have suggested that this memory system and representational model function to regulate behavior when individuals consciously attempt to solve problems (Crittenden, 1992b.)

Episodic Memory and Internal Representational Models. Episodic memory consists of chronologically organized experiences, i.e., the things we usually refer to when we speak of having 'memories'. Such memories contain both many types of information, e.g., visual, auditory, kinetic, and also their organization in time and space. They also contain the affect experienced by the individual. With regard to the self, this memory system is generally referred to as autobiographical memory (Hudson, 1990b; Snow, 1990) or personal narrative memory (Eisenberg, 1985; Nelson, 1986).

For example, a securely attached child might remember the night her parents planned to go out, but then canceled their plans when they realized that she was sick and worried about being left with a babysitter. In the same situation, an anxiously attached child is more likely to have memories of her parents not recognizing the intensity of her desire for them or of their disapproving of her feelings. Thus, the content of the episodic memory system differs as a function of children's experience. Elsewhere, I have suggested that this memory system regulates behavior when individuals are too affectively aroused to engage in the cognitive task of problem-solving (Crittenden, 1992b.)

Internal Representational Models. Several points are important here. First, Bowlby proposes that there is a real difference in the experiences of children who develop different representational models. In each of the examples above, one set of parents was responsive, the other rejecting. Second, the content of the three models (procedural, semantic, and episodic) may not be identical. In fact, the models may be in conflict. The child who remembered her parents leaving her with the babysitter may come to *act* (procedurally) very independent, to *think* (semantically) of herself as demanding, 'too sensitive', and incompetent (which is what her parents told her), and to *feel* (episodically) herself to be rejected, unloved, and hurt. Serious discrepancies in the information in different internal representational models are hypothesized to characterize pathological outcomes (Bowlby, 1980.) In terms of models of self, they reflect cases of incompatible self models that are not recognized or used as the basis for further exploration of the true nature of self. Third, both the semantic and episodic memory systems (and their associated internal representational models) use language to encode and retrieve information. Developmentally, semantic memory is thought to first develop around the second year of life with the advent of children's early verbal self-descriptions (Engel, 1986; Kihlstrom, 1982; Pillemer & White, 1989).

3. Affect and Cognition

The development of cognition has been the focus of extensive theory development and empirical investigation (Case, 1985; Fischer, 1980; Flavell & Markman, 1983). As a result, in spite of on-going inquiry regarding specific processes, there is wide agreement regarding the overall progress of cognitive development in childhood. Specifically, it is clear that the pace of maturation is uneven with periods of rapid change alternating with periods of relative stability. Development of self is necessarily influenced by these patterns.

Much less attention has been paid to the development of affect. Instead, there are isolated bodies of research and theory that do not readily coalesce to form a complete theory of the development of affect. Such a theory is, however, an essential component for understanding the development of self. Consequently, a perspective is offered here which, simplistic as it is, may facilitate exploration of the development of self in young children.

The heart of the perspective taken is that humans are born with the rudiments of both affect (Ekman, 1982; Izard, 1982; Tompkins, 1962–3) and cognition (Bower, 1974; Fischer, 1980; Piaget, 1952). Furthermore, it is in the context of maturation and experience that humans generate new feelings, new cognitions, and integrations of affect with cognition (Zajonc, Pietromonaco, Bargh, 1982). Such a perspective, however, leaves unaddressed two issues that have been the focus of considerable theory and empirical research.

Maturation. The first is the role of maturation. Because cognitive development clearly has a strong maturational component, the integration of cognition with affect must be an on-going process of reorganization leading to successively more complex organizations (Fischer, 1980). Whether there is also a maturational component underlying the development of affect is less clear although there is increasing evidence that some affects are associated with known periods of neurological change (Emde, Gaensbauer, & Harmon, 1976). For example, the appearance of smiles at 3–4 weeks (Emde, et al, 1976) and wariness at 7–9 months (Lewis & Rosenblum, 1974) may both reflect maturational processes. Later changes in affect, such as the emergence of coy behavior at about two years and sexual desire at puberty, suggest the on-going influence of maturation on the development of affect. Regardless of the basis of any specific affective change, the notion that underlies the perspective on self presented here is that maturation during periods of rapid neurological change results in both new cognitive capabilities and also new affective capabilities. The developing mind functions to integrate these in ways that yield increasingly well organized (and reorganized) representations of reality.

Which Leads - Affect or Cognition?. The second issue is the relative influence of affect and cognition. Put another way, does cognition drive affect or affect drive cognition? Although recent study has emphasized the "executive" role of cognition (Damon & Hart, 1988; Plutchik, 1980; Scheier & Carver, 1982), there are those who hold that affect is the overriding influence on cognition, especially in early development (Brownell & Kopp, 1991; Ekman, 1984; Izard, 1982; Zajonc, 1980; Zajonc, et al., 1982). The arguments underlying each perspective are persuasive and coherent. Moreover, empirical (though not definitive) data can be marshalled to support each position. This suggests the validity of each.

A possible resolution of this apparent incompatibility is that each pattern of effects exists, but to different extents in different individuals. In other words, some individuals may depend upon the organizing influence of cognition to moderate affect. Such individuals would be expected to have both representational models of the self that contained a predominance of cognitive information and also learned patterns of mental processing that depended more heavily on cognition than on affect. Other individuals might show the opposite pattern. In still other individuals, representations might be neither predominantly cognitive nor predominantly affective and the mental processes might depend equally upon affectively-derived and cognitively-derived information.

It is a central thesis of this treatise that this tripartite division of individual differences a) is relevant to the self, b) explains the predictive power of Ainsworth's three patterns of attachment, and c) can account for many of the findings of disparate theoretical approaches. Consequently, it is hypothesized that, when there is a balance between affect and cognition and an integration of the information derived from each, mental functioning and representational models of the self will consist of a seamless blend of the two sources of information with relative proportions varied in response to variations in situations. Individuals who display this balance, integration, and flexibility are expected to exhibit adaptation under the widest range of circumstances; in other words, they display mental health. From this perspective, unhealthy functioning and risk for psychopathology will be associated with the emphasis on either affect or cognition at the expense of the other. The concern of this chapter is with the implications of such differences for the functioning of the self.

4. Ainsworth's Patterns of Attachment

In her studies of infants, Ainsworth described three patterns of attachment, i.e., three ways in which infants organize their behavior with regard to their attachment figures. These patterns have been related to prior differences in mothers' responsiveness to infant signals and to later developmental outcomes, particularly with social-emotional behavior (Ainsworth, et al, 1978; Belsky, Rovine, & Taylor, 1984; Grossmann, Grossmann, & Swann, 1986; Matas, Arend, & Sroufe, 1978). In addition, these patterns have been applied to older children, adolescents, and adults. In most studies, however, the linkage is clearest for secure and avoidant patterns. Indeed, little is understood about the ambivalent pattern between infancy and adulthood (Bretherton, 1988).

Elsewhere I have suggested that the reason for the power of these infant-derived patterns across the life-span and across various areas of social-emotional functioning is that they represent three patterns of processing information (Crittenden, 1992b). That is, secure individuals integrate affect and cognition and use information from all memory systems. They learn to do this in the context of reciprocal interactions with supportive attachment figures who regulate the challenge of the environment such that children are both often successful and often challenged to stretch their skills just a little bit (Vygotskii, 1987). Type A individuals (who are labeled anxious-avoidant in infancy) emphasize cognition and avoid awareness of affect. Consequently, they often have limited awareness of affectively generated procedures and hold affectively arousing episodes in unconscious episodic memory. Instead of integrating information from all three memory systems, Type A individuals tend to depend excessively upon parentally-derived semantic memory. In the context of attachment figures who reject them when they express a desire for closeness, such individuals learn to inhibit display of distress and desire, thus, seeming more independent than other groups of children. Type C individuals (who are labeled anxious-ambivalent in infancy) tend to emphasize affect and to distrust cognition; they depend more upon procedural and episodic models than upon semantic models to regulate their behavior. Their attachment figures tend to be inconsistently responsive. This pattern of intermittent reinforcement of affect functions to teach infants to demand contact constantly and with intense affect. In addition, both Crittenden and Radke-Yarrow and her colleagues have identified an A/C pattern that combines the characteristics of the two patterns, but without the balance and integration of the secure Type B pattern (Crittenden, 1985b; Radke-Yarrow, Cummings, Kuczinski, & Chapman, 1985). See Figure 1.

Perception and Self in Infancy

1. Developmental Processes in Early Infancy

Although infants are born into a world as complex as that of adults, they perceive only limited portions of it. Indeed, they become perceptually aware of salient features of the environment in a predictable and functional sequence (Bower, 1974). In addition, as Vygotskii (1987) proposed, parents actively manage their children's access to the world so as to ensure that children are not confronted with greater complexity than they can manage.

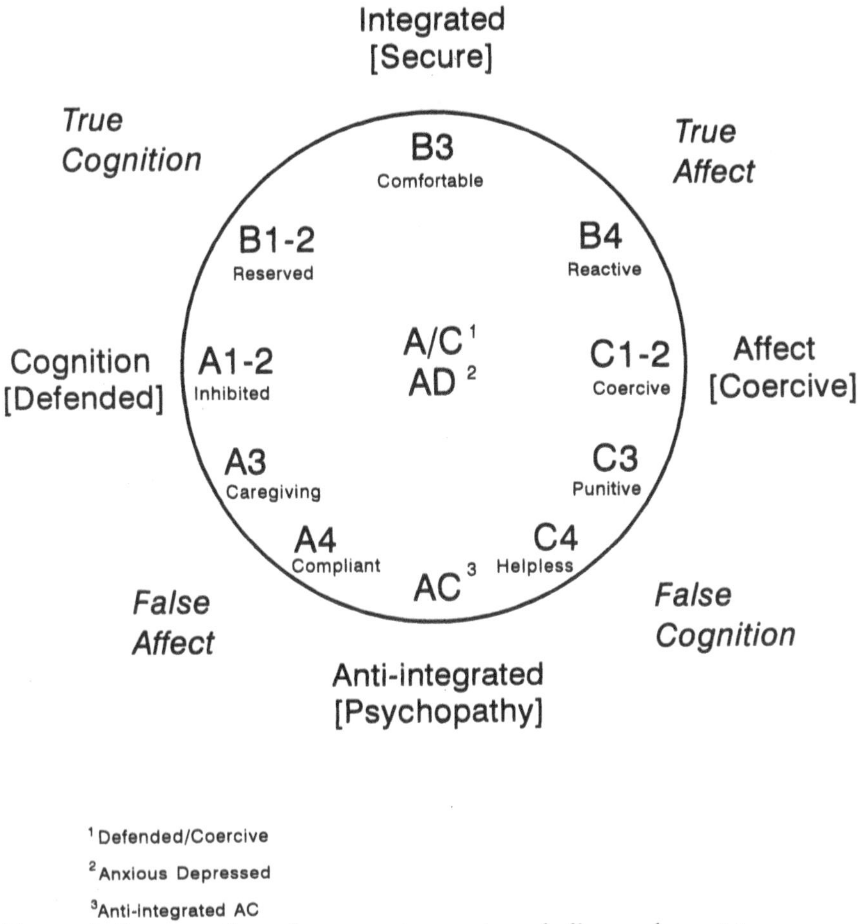

FIGURE 1 Patterns of attachment as integration of affect and cognition.

Species-Specific Behavior

Early in infancy, feeling states occupy infants' attention. Work by Izard (1977), Ekman (1973), Emde (1980), and Tompkins (1972/3) has identified a small number of innate feelings displayed by human infants. Although there is not entire agreement regarding the exact assortment of feelings or their time of onset, by one year of age they include pleasure, interest, surprise, distress, anger/rage, and distaste. These feelings are expressed in predictable ways under predictable kinds of conditions, for example, distress to internal perceptions is associated with hunger. Infants, however, have no awareness of the eliciting conditions or of their responses (Emde, et al., 1976; Redican, 1982).

These behaviors tend to be affectively arousing to adults with the affect leading to predictable patterns of adult behavior (Bowlby, 1969/82; Lorenz, 1966; Tinbergen, 1951). In other words, caregivers interpret and respond to these behaviors, using species-specific patterns of infant-elicited behavior (Papousek & Papousek, 1979). By doing so, parents help their infants to regulate transitions between affectively different states (Stern, 1985; Tronick, 1989). Most of this caregiver behavior is also preconscious. It has, however, been uniquely shaped by each adult's prior experience.

Through this process of feeling and behaving, infant states are communicated to caregivers; the actions of caregivers provide infants with feedback regarding the functional meaning of their behavior and the responsiveness of the caregivers. Out of these experiences, infants and caregivers construct unique, relationship-specific meaning systems. These become the basis for individual differences in the early development of self.

An Example

The creation of this meaning system that caregiver and infant construct can be described using an example from an abusive mother whom I once knew. Vicki had an infant whom Vicki felt was unusually irritable and colicky. During a visit to Vicki's home, I observed her infant begin to make little fussing sounds, to squirm, and to open her eyes widely, then slowly let them droop shut before she stretched them wide again, fussed, and squirmed, and so on. Both Vicki and I, being typical adult members of our species, alerted to this behavior, engaged in a mental process of interpreting the meaning of the behavior, and, in Vicki's case, responded actively. Vicki first shook a rattle in front of her infant and then picked her up and put her in an infant seat on the table near where we spoke. Needless to say, her baby cried more.

Startled by Vicki's response, I asked her why she did that. She told me that when her baby acted that way, she was bored. So Vicki had offered her stimulation. I, on the other hand, had interpreted the infant's behavior as meaning she was sleepy and I would have responded quite differently.

Vicki and I would each have constructed with her daughter different meanings for the behavior that her infant had shown. Over time with her mother, Vicki's infant could be expected to learn to inhibit the described behavior when she was sleepy and, possibly, to display it when she was bored. In other words, the innate bias toward an association between certain feeling states and behaviors was being shaped, in the context of specific interactants, to have a relationship-specific meaning.

Moreover, Vicki's infant would develop a very different model of herself in the relationship with her mother as opposed to that with me. Assuming that I was correct about the infant's actual feeling state, with me, her behavior and my response would have led to smooth changes in feeling states, a sense that experiencing and expressing feeling was tied to feeling comfortable, and the sense of being in synchrony with others (Brazelton, Koslowski, & Main, 1974; Tronick, 1989.) In her actual situation, her behavior led to exacerbation of her feeling states and the feeling of being stranded in a frightening morass of intensifying emotion. Moreover, my experience with Vicki's baby would have been one of interacting with an easy to read and easy to soothe infant. From Vicki's perspective, however, her baby would seem to be a demanding, colicky infant.

It is important to note that it is of little consequence for predicting the nature of the model of self being developed whether Vicki's infant was actually (temperamentally) more irritable than most infants, or even more lethargic than most. It is only important that, when her infant acted, Vicki responded with a meaning that intensified her infant's distress. If her baby had been difficult and she had responded with behavior that reduced the child's distress, her daughter's developing model of self would have been quite different.

Individual Differences in Procedural Models in Early Infancy

There are three important aspects to this interpretation. First, behavior is the means of communication between infant and caregiver. Furthermore, it is the caregiver who interprets the behavior and gives it dyadic meaning. In Stern's terms, this attunement enables the infant to feel comfortable with feelings and competent to move among feeling states as well as to enjoy the intimate sharing of feelings with attachment figures (Stern, 1985). Conversely, lack of attunement, that is, the misconstruing of the meaning of the infant's behavior by the caregiver (or the caregiver's enmeshment in the infant's feeling states) leads to fear of feelings and a functional lack of competence to resolve feelings as well as discomfort with intimacy.

Second, the functions used by infants consist of perceiving, feeling, and acting, together with the ability to recognize increasingly complex associations among these. All other functions are carried out for infants by adults. If adults successfully carry out these functions, infants are freed from unrelieved periods of intense affective arousal and, consequently, are more able to attend to, and engage with, their environment. Their experience of self, therefore, will include not only their expression and resolution of feelings, but also their competence to interact with objects and people. Infants who often experience intense and unremitting distress are likely to fear affective arousal and to experience themselves as painfully emotional, disorganized, and ineffective.

Third, infants' way of "knowing" the nature of these experiences is through feeling/action schemata. The feelings experienced and actions taken most frequently become defining features of the emerging self. In addition, when interactants misconstrue infants' actual states, a dysynchrony results which cannot be understood by infants. The discomfort of this dysynchrony becomes the content of the experience of the self. Meaning and self, therefore, are inextricably tied to both feeling and action in early infancy.

Motivational States

Toward the end of the first year of life, infants associate affective aspects of their experience with the behavior of specific individuals. Out of this integration of affect and cognition, there emerge the early forms of two emotions[1] that

---

[1] Selecting a term for these integrated states has been difficult. I have chosen to use 'affect' when cognition is not implied and emotion when the integration of cognition with affect is meant.

will occupy human attention across the life-span. One of these, aggression, has received a great deal of attention in the psychological literature whereas the other, love, has been startlingly overlooked (Thompson & Borrello, 1992).

Aggression. A fundamental problem in the extensive literature on aggression is the definition of aggression. A central question is the role of cognition (Bandura, 1973; Buss, 1961; Dollard, Doob, Miller, Mowrer, and Sears, 1939). Depending upon the answer, aggression is hypothesized to result from operant conditioning (Patterson, 1976), classical conditioning (Berkowitz, 1974), modeling (Bandura, 1973), social information processing (Dodge, 1986), or innate drives (Lorenz, 1966, Strepansky, 1977; Tinbergen, 1951). Most of these perspectives have been tested empirically in a developmental framework, with no theory being refuted sufficiently for rejection and none being supported sufficiently for general acceptance. Two reasons for this seem most likely. The first has to do with overlooking the role of affect. Given the affective salience of being aggressive, being the victim of aggression, or even observing aggression, it is startling how much more attention is paid by all of these theories, except psychoanalytic theory, to the role of cognition than to that of affect. This omission may explain some of the inadequacy of the theories to adequately predict aggression and precursors of aggression.

The second reason has to do with development. Most studies of aggression have samples of children in whom aggression has already developed. Consequently, researchers may miss the origins of aggression. In addition, theories have not included systemic analysis of how aggressive behavior functions between individuals. Patterson's work is the notable exception and, as such, is most compatible with the perspective presented here (Patterson, 1982, 1991).

The one theory that has received little empirical support is psychoanalytic theory. Although there is little evidence for an aggression drive (Lore & Schultz, 1993), the notion that aggression can be inhibited and/or displaced through unconscious processes may prove useful in understanding those individual differences in aggression that are tied to disorders of the self (Neuman, 1987).

A developmental perspective indicates that young infants display behavior associated with anger/rage (Oster & Ekman, 1978). Moreover, in that state they exhibit behavior associated with aggression, i.e., they flail their arms, kick their legs, and scream. Few observers or parents, however, consider this behavior in young infants to be aggressive. Indeed, the class of parents who most frequently makes this false attribution is abusive parents.

Following the seven to nine month neurological shift (Emde, et al., 1976), this changes. Infants' ability to associate their feelings with the behavior of others leads to focused anger. That is, when infants feel anger or distress and can attribute this condition to something a caregiver did or did not do, they express their anger as aggressive behavior, e.g., hitting, kicking, *directed* toward the caregiver (Fabes, Eisenberg, McCormick, & Wilson, 1988.) It is this directed anger that Bowlby identifies as resulting from caregiver unresponsiveness and as functioning to promote caregiver availability (Bowlby, 1969/82, 1973). The manner in which infants learn to incorporate aggression and suppression of aggression into strategies for managing relationships is a function of their experience, especially experience with attachment figures.

Needless to say, defining aggression in this manner does not address the full range of behavior identified as aggressive in adult humans. It may, however, provide a perspective on the roots of aggression prior to its complex display in older children and adults.

Love. In a similar manner, infants who experience pleasure from their caregivers' attentions come to focus their feelings of pleasure on the person responsible for them. For example, the anxiety felt by infants who are left alone is diminished by the approach of attachment figures. This, it seems to me, is the beginning of love. Although the large literature on attachment rarely refers specifically to 'love', the development in children of an 'affectional bond' is, as Bowlby says, surely the beginning of love (Bowlby, 1958; 1969/82). Indeed, love is so intrinsic to the notion of attachment that its near absence as a word in the psychological literature is nothing less than astounding.

From the perspective outlined here, both aggression and love are 'synthesized' emotions generated out of more basic affective states that are integrated with cognitive information learned from experience with caregivers. Moreover, both appear following a major neurological shift that has known influence on both cognitive and emotional functioning. In addition, both are tied to the parent-infant relationship and function to intensify the relationship. Finally, it should be noted that love and aggression are not mutually exclusive; most infants (and older humans as well) feel both love and aggression for the same attachment figure. Because these emotions are tied to relationships of the self with important others, their organization and expression with regard to the relationship has implications for how infants perceive themselves.

2. Individual Differences in Early Infancy

Infants exhibit individual differences in the sense of self that emerges from their relationships with caregivers. That is, in the context of their caregivers' response to them, infants experience some feelings more often and more intensely than others and, more importantly, come to feel more or less competent to move from one feeling state to another without experiencing disorganizing periods of distress. Depending upon the responsiveness of their care-givers, they also feel more or less comfortable with their feeling states, more or less recognized by their caregivers, and more or less competent to communicate with their caregivers. Infants who are left to cope alone with distress may come both to fear feelings and also to dislike the self that has such feelings.

3. Developmental Processes in Later Infancy: Attachment

By twelve months of age, feelings and behaviors that represent the experiences of infants with their caregivers become organized, as procedural models of self and attachment figure, around the goal of maintaining access to the attachment figure (Bowlby, 1969/82). Essentially all children form a goal-corrected attachment to a primary caregiver. In the context of this relationship, feelings and behaviors function so as to enable children to maximize *both* protection from the attachment figure *and* exploration of the environment. That is, the attachment relationship functions to foster closeness and separation.

4. Individual Differences in Later Infancy

Quality of Attachment

Although every child is unique, Ainsworth has demonstrated that two patterns, security and avoidance, can differentiate the majority of infants in terms of the previous degree of attunement of caregivers to their infants (Ainsworth, 1979.) A third pattern, ambivalence, typifies a small percentage of infants.

Secure Attachment. Infants whose caregivers are sensitively responsive to their signals are considered securely attached. Such infants develop procedural models of themselves as competent to communicate with attachment figures and to regulate, with their caregivers' help, their feeling states so that they feel comfortable most of the time. In social learning theory terms, they are positively reinforced for expressing their feelings.

Anxious-Avoidant Attachment. Avoidant infants who have experienced rejection or unresponsiveness when they signal distress, learn to inhibit behavior indicative of both distress and anger (Main, 1981). That is, they are punished for expressing their feelings. Early on, they inhibit affective behavior by actively avoiding the perceptions that elicit feelings. For example, in the Strange Situation, 12 month old infants refuse to look at their mother, thus, avoiding activation of the attachment behavior system and feelings of distress and anger associated with rejection by an attachment figure. In extreme cases, maltreated children as young as one year of age not only inhibit accurate information about their feeling states, but also display falsely positive affect which does not match their true feelings (Crittenden, 1988a,b; Crittenden & DiLalla, 1988). Doing so represents an accomplishment that has many benefits for children. It also contains the basis for great confusion regarding the true nature of the self. When one considers that in infancy memory is encoded only through behavioral procedures tied to perception and feeling states, behaving in ways that belie how one truly feels must create serious and unresolvable incongruencies in the infant's experience of self. When resolution of this incongruency is accomplished by learning not to perceive conditions tied to distress, infants (and the children and adults that they become) may both exclude accurate information about themselves from their mental functioning and also fail to behave in ways that enable others to know and respond to their felt self.

Anxious-ambivalent attachment. The third group of infants, ambivalently attached infants, experience inconsistently responsive attachment figures. In social learning terms, they have experienced both random and intermittant positive reinforcement of intense displays of affectively arousing behavior. Such a reinforcement schedule may be too complex to enable infants to learn, in a sensorimotor manner, the contingencies upon their behavior.

Based on work with preschool children, I would now describe these infants as not yet having an organized pattern of behavior (Crittenden, 1992a). That is, they have not been able to establish a meaning system of communication with their caregivers that functions to allow them to predict caregivers' behavior.

With sensorimotor intelligence, infants can 'understand' only caregivers' responsiveness or lack of responsiveness. Consequently, they organize their perceptions and responses to fit one of these two constructions. In other words, they mentally dichotomize reality so as to respond to it in an organized manner. Although this argument is not typical among attachment researchers, it is in line with thinking about children's way of mentally organizing experience as good or bad (Fischer, Shaver, & Carnochan, 1990; Russell & Ridgeway, 1983).

The few infants whose reality is so evenly divided between parental sensitivity and insensitivity that they cannot organize as either secure or avoidant experience the anguish of unresolvable arousal in which desire for the attachment figure, distress at her absence, and aggression toward her are all felt concurrently. Without an organization of behavior that functions to change the probabilities on parental behavior, such infants cannot resolve their intense and mixed feelings. Although their feelings include anxiety, anger, and desire for their attachment figures, their lack of a strategy for resolving these feelings leads to escalating distress and, frequently, self-defeating aggressiveness. Their model of self, therefore, carries both an unorganized mixture of competing affects and a functional lack of communicative and coping competence.

Mind and Self in Infancy

Processes. The functional achievement of infancy with regard to the self is the modification of patterns of innate behavior to fit more closely the unique aspects of each infant's environment. Structurally, this can be described as an elaborated network of perception-response bonds that are generalized into pairs of procedural representational models of self and attachment figures. With these structures, infants can respond adaptively to most of the situations in which they find themselves. Because they cannot represent information abstractly, however, they cannot think about, or communicate about, this process, nor can they recover previous experience for reconsideration in the light of new understandings. Without these skills, infants cannot intentionally influence the direction of their own development. Consequently, they remain rooted in the behavioral here and now. Their emerging ability to identify the causal agents of their experiences, however, enables them to focus their anger and pleasure as aggression and love, in ways that more effectively achieve their desires.

Risk for Psychopathology. Although risk for psychopathology is associated with anxious attachment, neither risk nor anxious attachment is equivalent to psychopathology. Indeed, most anxiously attached children are not disturbed (Fagot & Kavanaugh, 1990). Nevertheless, to the extent that early experience with attachment figures teaches children to distort the way they process cognitive and affective information, anxiously attached children experience greater risk that they will encounter situations in which the excluded information is essential for an adaptive response. When such situations are critical to functioning or recur frequently, psychopathology may be an outcome.

Infants whose experience consists of a) reduced perception of conditions that lead to distress, b) an inability to achieve a behavioral organization that enables them to predictably influence their attachment figures, and/or c) predominantly negative information about themselves as participants in relationships are at greater risk for psychopathology than securely attached infants. Reduced perception creates risk of generating future distortions because it limits both infants' experience with others and also their potential to receive positive information about themselves. This is true regardless of whether the excluded information is cognition or affect. The inability to organize creates the risk that children will conceptualize reality as chaotic and will develop the belief that they are ineffective and helpless. Conversely, they may attribute to themselves responsibility for managing the attachment figure's angry behavior. This may lead to both cognitive limitations and affective distortions. The procedural expectation of a negative self in relationships may become a self-fulfilling prophesy through both the absence of disconfirming information and also infants' reluctance to engage in intimate relationships. In addition, when children accurately reflect their internal states, parents are best able to regulate their own behavior so as to assist children's self-regulation.

The Self in the Preschool Years

In the preschool years, mental development with regard to the self consists of 1) several functional changes in perception, b) the development of two new structures, semantic and episodic memory, and c) the development of new 'self-conscious' emotions. In addition, the relationship with attachment figures is reorganized on the basis of preoperational mental functioning. Individual differences in self are expressed in terms of quality of attachment - as it becomes organized in the preschool years.

1. Quality of Attachment

Reorganization of Infant Attachment Into a Goal-corrected Partnership

To understand individual differences among preschool-aged children, the notion of attachment needs to be extended to preoperational functioning and the goal-corrected partnership (Bowlby, 1969/82; Marvin, 1977). Children's new mental competencies of a) symbolic representation of daily routines, b) memory of the past and a concept of future, and c) language with which to communicate these understandings enable children to take on some responsibility for managing access to their attachment figures. Through verbal and non-verbal communication, children and attachment figures plan their access to one another and share information about their experiences when apart - thus, bridging physical separation with psychological connection.

Based on these new skills, I have described patterns of individual differences in the organization of attachment in the preschool years (Crittenden, 1992a). These patterns were conceptualized not only in terms of behavior patterns and behavioral strategies, but also in terms of patterns of negotiation and, most important for this discussion, regulation of feeling states, regulation of display of affect, and attributions of responsibility for feeling states.

Quality of Attachment in the Preschool Years

Secure Attachment. From the perspective of this new classificatory system, secure children are those who display their true feelings directly and who share with others responsibility for resolving uncomfortable feelings. Stated in terms of the self, secure children have learned that their self is acceptable and will be nurtured by others. Furthermore, their attachment figures are particularly competent at coaching them regarding how to use self-coping skills such as organized toy play (a cognitive skill) and verbal self-reassurances (an affective skill). These skills are employed by the children in their mothers' absence.

Defended Attachment. Defended children, who represent the outgrowth of the infant avoidant group, inhibit display of their true feelings and sometimes falsely display positive affect that does not match their feelings. Their strategy is to monitor attachment figures so as to remain close enough for protection without behaving so as to elicit approach or intimacy. The strategy is regulatory in that defended children approach when the attachment figure withdraws (physically or psychologically) and withdraw when the attachment figure approaches, thus remaining "close, but not too close." In addition, they take upon themselves the entire responsibility for regulating their feeling states. Because they cannot actually carry out such regulation, they must engage in defensive processes, i.e., functions through which they can deny the true feelings with which they are unable to cope. At the pathological extreme, having learned that their true affective self is unacceptable, such children may construct and present a false self (Winnicott, 1958) showing only those feelings desired by caregivers (Crittenden, 1992b.)

Coercive Attachment. The developmental extension of the ambivalent pattern is the coercive strategy of the preschool years. This strategy represents the transformation of the angry and passive behavior of infants into aggressive and coy behavior. These are organized around coercion of the attachment figure. That is, preoperational children recognize the power of angry behavior to threaten others into compliance with their wishes and the power of coy, helpless behavior to disarm aggression against them and to elicit nurturance (in compliance with their wishes.) The strategy is regulatory in that children show anger and aggression until attachment figures themselves show anger. Then the angry child suddenly shows disarming, coy behavior. This continues until the parent is fed up with the feigned helplessness and becomes angry. The child switches again to the threatening behavior pattern, thus, maintaining the coercive strategy.

For coercive children, communication of feelings in infancy has failed to elicit support from attachment figures. This is often combined with parental use of verbal put-offs, e.g., bribing the child with a treat that never appears; telling the child to get something, then sneaking away when the child turns to get it. Because such cognitive explanations not only do not lead to comfort, but also are misleading, children often abandon effort to integrate emerging cognitive and linguistic competencies with affect and, instead, focus on coordinating intense affective displays of aggression or helplessness to coerce attachment figures. Intuitive recognition of the power of the alternation of intensely displayed affects enables preoperational children to construct procedural representational models that both reflect their complex reality and also function to use affective arousal to coerce attachment figures into attending to them. From the perspective of social learning theory, such children have learned that they can change the contingencies on their attachment figure's behavior by displaying heightened affect, especially negative affect. Because their attachment figures respond with an intermittant schedule of positive reinforcement, their children tend to become increasingly impervious to occassional negative consequences.

In this process, coercive children learn to inhibit selectively the display of a portion of their feelings and to regulate their affective displays so as to alternately use angry (i.e., threatening) displays or coy/disarming (i.e., bribing) displays. In either case, they convey to caregivers that the caregivers alone hold the responsibility for resolving their feelings. At the pathological extreme, children who separate their awareness and presentation of feeling states may become stuck in one half of the strategy (and, thus, unable to regulate their behavior) or unable to construct a coherent self from the splits between affect and cognition and between distressed vulnerability and angry aggression.

Because the coercive strategy represents an adaptive response to parents who are neither predominantly sensitive nor predominantly rejecting/unresponsive, many children who were classified as secure or avoidant in infancy may be expected to shift to this strategy. This will result in a change in the proportions of Type A, Type B, and Type C children. Indeed, initially, many toddlers may try out the new strategy with some finding it successful and others later shifting back to secure and defensive patterns. Therefore, it seems likely that, as maturation opens new pathways, there will be shifts in children's functioning. Because periods of transition and increased flexibility accentuate the influence of attachment figures on children, intervention that changes attachment figures' behavior might be most effective during periods of reorganization.

Upon the base of procedural representational models of self and attachment figure with associated affect that were developed in infancy, five aspects of changed perception in the preschool years are considered: 1) perceptual perspective-taking, 2) the social construction of self, 3) exclusion of self, 4) the development of self-conscious emotions, and 5) linguistic representation of self. Each is tied to important aspects of the development of the self and involves individual differences in the way the self is constructed. Moreover, each is dependent upon the intuitive intelligence which characterizes the intellectual functioning of preoperational children.

2. Perceptual Perspective-taking

Developmental Change in Awareness of Self

In the preschool years, children become aware that others observe them. This awareness creates affective responses in children. Infants, of course, can be decorated. Moreover, they are individual and delightful in their presentation. They are not, however, aware of themselves as being viewed by others (Lewis & Brooks-Gunn, 1979). Similarly, individuals from other mammalian species have unique and delightful personalities. Nevertheless, these animals are not self aware. Only humans beyond infancy (and possibly some other primates) have this capacity to use perceptual perspective-taking.

That preschoolers have this self-awareness seems indisputable. The nature of the self of which they are aware is, however, less clear. Certainly, preschool-aged children have the capacity for visual self-recognition (Lewis & Brooks-Gunn; 1979; Schneider-Rosen & Cicchetti, 1991). This capacity, however, seems to be neither a necessary, nor a logical outcome of the development of self in infancy. Moreover, it is not a likely form of self experience during the long period of our evolution as a species, prior to the last century or two. Rather, it may be the pattern of feelings, unique to each individual but relatively stable across time, that forms the content of preschoolers' emerging self-awareness (Emde, Birigen, Clyman, & Oppenheim, 1991; Izard, 1982; Schneider-Rosen & Cicchetti, 1991). By this is meant that the child is aware of feeling "like himself" (or herself) or "not like himself." He (or she) *feels* how he presents himself to others. It is striking how our everyday use of language implies this same notion. When someone seems different, we say, "You don't look like yourself today" or "He isn't acting like himself today." But with reference to ourselves, we say "I don't feel like myself today."

Individual Differences in Preschooler's Feelings of Self

There is a range of ways that preschool-aged children feel about being observed. An example may best describe this. Four year old Yiota and her two year old brother Demitri were both told that I was coming the next day to take a picture of them wearing different hats. Yiota arose early and chose her clothing with care. It was feminine and matched, down to her lavender socks and shoes. She then awaited my arrival expectantly. When I knocked on the door, she ran part way to it, then stood back watching me shyly, but with eager anticipation.

Her brother Demitri also looked forward to my arrival. He, however, did not arrange his clothing. Instead, dressed still in his pajamas, he ran all the way to the door, stared at me for a moment, then turned his attention to the pile of hats I set on the floor. It took no encouragement to get him to try on several hats and to parade around in them. Wearing the hats made him feel exuberantly self-conscious. Yiota was slower to try on a hat. Her coy smile, however, made it clear that she too felt pleasure in the new self that she created and displayed by wearing the hat.

Both children were self-conscious. That is, they were aware of being observed and could equally have been described as having 'mastered' the task of perceptual perspective-taking. The differences were in affect. In this case, both children appeared to associate positive affects with themselves, although not the same affects. Both expressed confidence that they could manage the situation although individual differences appeared there, too. Yiota's coy response had a disarming and engaging quality. Demitri's response was robust and enthusiastic.

Qualitative Differences in the "Valence" Attached to the Affective Self

In fact, every child develops a unique affective self. This self can be described in terms of predominant feelings, preferred feelings, style of managing shifts among feeling states, and conditions associated with feelings. These aspects of self are unique to each child, but not inherently desirable or undesirable. For example, there is no reason to expect more or less successful developmental outcomes from children as different as Yiota and Demitri.

On the other hand, important people in each child's environment will have an affective response to the child's affective self. These responses can be thought of as adding a qualitative "valence" to the child's experience of self. That is, if others are delighted by him (or her), or appreciate him, or respond sensitively to him, the child is likely to feel comfortable with himself (or herself) and to value himself - as others do. Conversely, if others ignore, reject, misconstrue, or mock his (or her) expression of his affective self, the child is likely to feel angry, hurt, and vulnerable or worthless, embarrassed, and ashamed, etc. It is this qualitative difference in children's intuitive perception of how they are perceived by others which defines one type of important individual difference in the development of self.

Again, attachment provides a useful paradigm through which to cluster qualitative differences in the valence attached to children's sense of self. A study of Greek children who had been institutionalized from early infancy under (relatively) auspicious conditions provides an example (Crittenden, et al., 1992). During play interactions with their caregiver, the institutionalized children focused entirely on reciprocal patterns of formatted play (for example, repetitive naming games, shape sorting, puzzle completion) and avoided spontaneous affective games. Their caregivers, unlike most mothers, used pseudo-affectionate behaviors that have been associated with covert hostility and avoidance of intimacy (Crittenden & DiLalla, 1988). Overall, these caregivers were described as treating the children in a kindly, but generic, manner that precluded intimacy or the elicitation of unique characteristics in the children. In the Strange Situation coded using the Miami procedure (Crittenden, 1992a), almost half of the children were classified as defended/coercive (Type A/C), with an additional 31% being defended and 10% each secure and coercive. In three assessments of self development (the rouge-on-nose mirror procedure for assessing self recognition, an imitation task that required looking at the caregiver's face, and a hat wearing procedure to assess perceptual perspective-taking) the results were striking. Many of the institutionalized children as old as 24 months failed to touch the red spot on their noses; however, unlike younger children without visual self-recognition, they did not show interest in the mirror image. Instead, the younger children looked in an unfocussed manner at the image of themselves. The older children actively turned away in distress in a manner similar to the maltreated children observed by Schneider-Rosen and Cicchetti (1991). Moreover, children who could readily imitate activities with the toys refused to look at the faces of their attachment figures' in order to put the hat on. Finally, when the attachment figure placed the hat on the child's head and said brightly, "Look at me!", the institutionalized children turned away with expressions best described as shame, while pulling the hats off their heads. In response to all three measures, the institutionalized children's behavior suggested that discomfort and shame were associated with the self. Moreover, the children acted so as to reduce their own and others' experience of them as individuals.

In conclusion, the perspective offered here focuses less on *when* the self develops and instead finds evidence that some form of self is present in all young children. Its quality, however, varies greatly as a function of the way in which children have experienced and mentally organized the relationship with attachment figures. This follows closely the argument of Bowlby that psychopathology is less a matter of developmental rate, fixation, or regression and more a matter of differentiated developmental pathways, all of which progress forward and all of which represent the integration of maturation with experience and constitution (Bowlby, 1979). For inconsistently reared children, the affect associated with self is indicative of angry resentment of the other's unpredictable availability. For institutionalized children, the self appears to be experienced as unlovable and inconsolable - even when the overt physical experiences associated with love and comfort are provided. For these children, exclusion from uniquely intimate interactions seems to be a critical indicator of potentially irreversible psychopathology. Their greater composure in the regular playroom when given little individual attention suggests that their only feeling of security may lie in highly structured, invariant surroundings in which interpersonal interactions are protected from spontaneity by rigid role formats numbly carried out in the absence of unique differentiation of selves.

3. The Self in a Social Context

A second way in which the preschool-aged child's perception of self is different from infants' is that preschoolers become aware of important people other than their parents. That is, as Lewis pointed out, preschoolers develop social networks (Lewis & Brooks-Gunn, 1979.)

Developmental Processes

From the perspective of attachment theory, development of self through relationships is an on-going process that begins at birth. Infants are not only physically vulnerable when alone, but also they have no caregiver from whom they can experience response to, and regulation of, their feeling states. Metaphorically speaking, they are tossed about in a sea of emotion. Possibly for this reason children are exceptionally alert to signals of psychological unavailability. Even when, as toddlers, they embark on exploration away from the attachment figure, they remain connected through shared goals and joint plans (Marvin, 1977). Thus, in the safe context of one or two parental attachment figures, they explore without fearing being overwhelmed by either events or feelings.

As preschoolers, however, children become perceptually alert to a larger world. Whereas infants had only one or two figures to reflect to them the nature of their affective selves and to provide valence, preschoolers have enlarging networks. First, additional family relationships become important. Later, a network of friends, relatives, and neighbors becomes salient.

One way to conceptualize the process that is underway is to think of each relationship as a mirror. This perspective has its roots in the work of symbolic interactionalists such as Mead (1934) and Cooley (1909/1962). I propose, however, that each mirror be thought of as being uniquely warped by the reflecting individuals' own distorted social perceptions, interpretations, and behavior, i.e., by internal representational models of the mirroring persons. From these mirrors, children have the opportunity to extract information about themselves. As more mirrors, each with a unique reflection of the child, are added, children's self perception will change in two ways.

First, the new relationships create the potential for new experiences, new feelings, and new integrations of feeling with experience. New information, thus, is created and reflected to the child. This information can be used to update, change, or elaborate existing internal representations of self and others (Bowlby, 1980; Bretherton, 1985, 1988; Crittenden, 1992a, 1992b). Because the relationships are both new and among the first few relationships that children experience, they may have more impact than later developing relationships.

Second, the increasing array of differently warped mirrors permits the extraction of invariants from the multiple images. In other words, the skew in self-perception provided by any one or two caregivers' relationships with the child may be modified, and potentially corrected, as the child experiences additional relationships. Given the resistance of schema to change, individual differences in the probability of children's modifying their models are relevant to adaptive development.

This line of thinking does not imply that all relationships are of equal importance. Far from it, it appears quite certain that the emotional salience of attachment relationships has a powerful impact on what children perceive and on how they affect others. Nevertheless, opportunities for variation and comparison are presented by the enlarging social network of the preschool-aged child.

Neither does this line of thinking imply that the child consciously sifts through the available information seeking variation and constancy among the reflections of self. Rather, it is presumed that the mind functions so as to organize perception and experience (Lashley, 1958/60) and that an outcome of this process is change in the child's intuitive recognition of self. Two types of change are explored here. One is cultural, the other qualitative.

Individual Differences in the Social Reflection of Self

Cultural Variability. In the preschool years, adults are less attuned to each child's unique features than are adults to infants. Instead, culturally normative expectations begin to influence the response of adults to children. Some cultural expectations are obvious (although hotly debated) such as gender and age expectations. Others are more subtle. It may be that as children move among relationships, they come intuitively to recognize a) aspects of themselves that they hold in common with other people, b) aspects that make them unique, and c) aspects that are unique to specific relationships. Of course, this does not imply that there is any conscious or purposeful activity underway. But in the preoperational sense of intuitive intelligence, children may both experience these congruities and incongruities and also organize their behavior on the basis of them. Moreover, these aspects of self, together with the degree of synchrony experienced procedurally, may influence the content of internal representational models of themselves that children construct.

The nature and distribution of felt congruities and incongruities is probably less a function of the nature of children than of the culture in which children develop (Cushman, 1990; Heelas & Lock, 1981; Heiddeger, 1962/1977; Shweder & LeVine, 1984). That is, cultures can emphasize the commonality among members by placing a positive valence on feelings and behavior which are shared by, or compatible with, those of other group members (Rosaldo, 1984). Or they can emphasize and support children's individuality and self-expression. Neither is inherently a more accurate reflection of the human self and, in fact, both seem to be essential components. This is, however, one dimension, with implications for the development of self, upon which cultures vary.

The range of that variability is of interest. Humans are a highly plastic species. Consequently, it is probable that a wide range of variability on the dimension of commonality-individuality is entirely tolerable for human development. Nevertheless, when the relative proportions of common versus individual personality become extreme, there may be danger for both the culture and individuals within it. For example, if young children receive approval for acting in concert with their peers and are punished, however subtly, for imposing their individuality on others, a society is created which emphasizes commonality among humans and (by implication) their interchangeability. Individuality may be lost. At this extreme, individuals may become unhappy, angry, and ultimately depressed.

On the other hand, if the culture urges its children to assert their individuality, to self-actualize, if you will, without attention to social commitments, the opposite process leading to the same state of affective discontent may occur (Sampson, 1988). Without a sense of commonality, individuals feel isolated. The inability to establish long-term, intimate, mutually satisfying relationships based on joint feeling states becomes more difficult. Without shared intimacy, humans become unhappy, irritable, and angry, and, if even the anger does not draw important others to them, ultimately depressed. Under such conditions, cultural groups may become characterized by geographic instability, divorce, job changes, and violence. In such cases, even crowds become lonely and the risks of individual pathology become greater.

Qualitative Differences in the Social Perception of Self. Moving back to individual development, differences in network density may result in qualitative differences in the self. Dense networks are those in which most members know each other. The networks of preschool children may be more or less dense. That is, the network may constitute a closed society in which everyone knows everyone. At the other extreme, children's relationships may be entirely unrelated. Both extremes carry risk to children's developing sense of self.

A highly dense (or very limited) network may provide little variability among the reflections of self as well as little opportunity to experiment with new patterns of behavior. Especially when the network itself is atypical, this may increase the risk of constricted, distorted, and/or inflexible models of self. My own study of continuity of style of relationship across attachment, spousal, and network relationships suggests that this process occurs in many maltreating families, particularly those in which neglect is prominent (Crittenden, 1985, 1988a). In such cases, the content of the models of self across the various relationships appeared to be essentially identical.

On the other hand, a large, but highly disengaged, network, in which there are many members, few of whom know one another, may make it difficult for children to perceive continuity of self. Although many mirrors, each with its own distortion, reflect images of themselves, there is little opportunity for children to view the mirrors without viewing themselves concurrently. That is, because they cannot observe network members interacting with each other, children may not be able to differentiate self contributions to their interactions from contributions of other persons.

The risk when such comparisons are infrequent is two-fold: 1) children may experience themselves as many different selves rather than perceiving themselves as a unified self viewed from different perspectives and 2) children may misattribute characteristics of the interactions. Specifically, defended children may accept responsibility for the behavior of others, thus, over-attributing the characteristics of the interaction to themselves whereas coercive children may under-attribute characteristics to themselves, thus, giving responsibility for the interaction to the other person. Abusive families may represent the former condition. Chaotic marginally maltreating families may provide the latter type of fragmenting experience (Crittenden, 1988a.) In such cases, multiple unrelated models of the self may be constructed (Crittenden, 1990, 1992b).

4. Exclusion of Self

Developmental Processes

A third perceptual change in the development of the self in the preschool years is children's awareness of being excluded from important relationships. Infants are unaware of relationships and people who are not involved directly with them. In such a state, jealousy is not a possible emotion. Comfortable as that is, the preschool years bring this state to an end.

Again, it is the wider perceptual frame of older children together with their awareness of person permanence which unsettles their models of themselves and relationships. The classic example is children's inadvertent viewing of the primal scene. Although the sexual import of this has generally been emphasized, its significance may lie in children's new awareness of being excluded.

This seems reasonable because few preschool-aged children have a basis from which to interpret or react to the sexual aspects of their parents' behavior. They do, however, have the emerging ability to realize that the two central people in their lives are present, are affectively involved, and are unaware of them. Moreover, if children manage to attract their parents' attention, their parents are likely to react with distress and to send them away. This presents young children with a most uncomfortable challenge to their sense of self.

The challenge is not, however, tied to the specific activity of their parents. A hug, an involving argument, an evening with guests, a concentrated conversation, or an afternoon nap for two will all produce the same awareness that others have involving and satisfying experiences that do not, and cannot, include oneself. This painful experience, however, opens at least two doors to opportunity. Resolving the challenge of exclusion pushes children to develop coping strategies. It also enables them to begin to conceptualize others as whole people engaged in activities in which they display a range of characteristics - just as children themselves do.

Qualitative Differences in Coping with the Challenge of Exclusion

Universal as the experience of exclusion is, its meaning for children varies as will children's ability to institute effective strategies to cope with their feelings. Again, Ainsworth's patterns of attachment and their associated patterns of processing information provide a useful paradigm for considering individual differences in how children handle the challenge of exclusion.

Secure Children. When children have models of themselves as highly valued and have experienced synchrony in their interactions with attachment figures, their reactions to exclusion may well resemble those of securely attached infants whose mothers have unexpectedly left them alone. They will be uneasy, they may protest, but they will, nevertheless, feel secure in the ultimate availability and responsivity of their attachment figures. In addition, they will implement productive coping strategies such as seeking a playmate (who will reflect to them their value) or playing with toys (that foster cognitive development and self-reliance.) Moreover, many securely attached children, upon regaining the parent's attention, will be able to express verbally their feelings and receive both comfort and explanations from the parent.

Defended Children. If, on the other hand, children have experienced frequent rejection or parental unavailability, their representational models of themselves and their attachment figures will suggest different interpretations for this new experience. When rejection and/or withdrawal have more frequently been their experience, children's already well developed defensive strategy is likely to serve them again. A silent retreat, attention to displacement activities, and in some cases, later caregiving to parents are likely outcomes. Unfortunately, this solution provides no opportunity for children to reassess their worth from new perspectives. When such models are applied to newly developing relationships, it increases the probability that children will not test the potential for more satisfying interactions.

Coercive Children. In the case of inconsistent availability, children may engage in a coercive strategy, the predictable outcome of which is that they will attract their attachment figures' attention and demand some form of caregiving. In other words, their feelings and behavior will function to enable children to end their state of exclusion, even if the cost is parental anger. Often, however, attachment figures collude in their children's effort to avoid exclusion. Doing so denies children necessary opportunities for learning self-reliance. Moreover, such parents reinforce a model of self in which children are unable to balance their feelings and desires with those of others. In a very basic sense, there is the risk that such children may become unfit for human society.

5. New 'Self-conscious' Feelings

Maturational and Developmental Changes

In the preschool years, the integration of cognition with affect produces major changes in the social-emotional functioning of children. The ability to experience and respond to a newly widened range of feeling states creates breadth in the models of self and other. The discussion here will center on three types of cognitive-affective states: 1) disgust, for its relevance to defining the boundaries of self, 2) coyness, for its relevance to the coercive strategy, and 3) embarrassment/shame, for its relevance to self-evaluation.

Affective-Cognitive Structures

Disgust. Disgust is rarely considered as a emotion with implications for the self. Nevertheless, as Rozin and Fallon (1987) point out, it provides one means of defining the boundaries of self. According to Rozin and Fallon, disgust does not appear as a fully developed emotion until approximately the eighth year of life even though the facial display associated with it is present in neonates (Rosenstein & Oster, 1988). Only after children have the cognitive concepts of incorporation and contamination can they feel disgust (as opposed to the 'distaste' of infancy.) Rozin and Fallon argue that the mouth and, especially, the lips are the physical boundary between self and not-self. This border is highly charged with affect. Viewed from this perspective, that which we ingest is or becomes a part of ourselves (although not necessarily considered to *be* ourselves) whereas that which we reject is not. Our strongest reactions of disgust are to bodily substances, e.g., feces, saliva. Not only are these substances contaminated once they leave our bodies, they contaminate anything they touch. Thus, we are disgusted by drinking from another person's glass (and, conversely, convey social connectedness by sharing a cup.)

Two points are of interest. First, infants are not capable of the cognitive understandings necessary for the emotion of disgust. These concepts develop during the preoperational period and become integrated with the feeling of distaste with the advent of concrete operations. Thus, disgust is best considered a cognitive-affective structure, i.e., an emotion. Second, the distinction between self and other that appears to be so clearly demarcated by disgust is actually quite permeable under specific affective conditions. Specifically, among those who are intimate, disgust is not shown for bodily substances. Indeed, the opposite may be true; they may be valued and eagerly incorporated. For example, infants nurse, mothers eat their children's food, lovers kiss and have sexual intercourse. Thus, in a physical, affective, and cognitive manner, disgust provides a model for defining the self as both separate from, and connected to, others.

Coyness. In infancy, the emerging cognitive ability to associate feelings with the behavior of others was associated with the development of the emotions of aggression and love. This occurred at the time of a neurological shift in cognitive and affective functioning. A similar maturational process, occurring in the latter half on the second year of life, may underlie the development of a cluster of emotions that reflect self-consciousness. In this case, the underlying cognitive advance is the mastery of perceptual perspective-taking. The affective change associated with this period of maturational quickening may be the appearance of coy behavior. Although the roots of coy behavior have been less fully explored that those of other affective displays, there is reason to believe that their appearance may be universal and unrelated to experience, i.e., not learned through shaping or modeling. Once present, however, coy behaviors undergo a number of transformations based on 1) mental integration of associated feelings with cognitive awareness of others' perspective with regard to the self and 2) shaping in accord with familial and cultural display rules.

Morphologically, coyness includes oblique peeking out to look at another person, opening the mouth but covering the teeth with lips or tongue, tilting the head to one side, lifting the shoulders (as though cringing), and standing with the tummy protruding and/or bared. Often, coy behavior also includes 'soft' self- stimulating behavior, e.g., twiddling with the hair, putting fingers in the mouth. One of the functions of the behaviors associated with coyness is that, among animals, they signal submission in the context of a fight that the signaling animal is loosing. By displaying these behaviors which increase vulnerability (e.g., exposing the abdomen and neck), the submissive animal terminates the aggression. Thus, by making the self more vulnerable, the animal protects itself. Presuming the animal to be a human, it seems likely that the accompanying feelings are fear and anger - fear of destruction and anger at having to make oneself vulnerable to protect oneself.

Coy behavior also signals desire for continued social contact. By glancing obliquely at the dominant person, children attract attention without the risk of prolonged, and potentially threatening, eye contact. By quickly looking away, children communicate both desire for relationship and submission. Coy behavior, in other words, functions as a non-verbal apology and communicates acceptance of a place in a dominance hierarchy.

From an ethological perspective, coy behavior in children may represent a very adaptive and flexible behavior. It combines elements of invitation with elements of submission. This characteristic may function to protect children during a period when they are embarking on exploration of the social world outside the family and when adults begin to expect self-regulation of desires from children. That is, children are coming in contact with numerous adults and older children, all of whom are far more socially skilled than they. Coy behavior signals the child's interest in the new person while concurrently signaling the child's feeling of vulnerability. The effect is to slow the approach and to give the young child the power to regulate its pace. In the context of infractions of household rules, coy behavior functions to signal submission and a desire for mercy; it disarms parental anger. In both cases, coy behavior is non-threatening, disarms the other's aggression, and elicits nurturance.

The coercive pattern of attachment that I have described above and elsewhere (Crittenden, 1992a,b) uses the alternation of coy behaviors that disarm aggression and aggressive behaviors that threaten. Essentially all preschool-aged children discover and try out the coercive strategy as a new means of getting their way. Hence, the 'terrible twos'. Some preschool-aged children ultimately settle on this strategy as the best way of increasing the probability that their attachment figures will respond more nearly as they wish. Their anger at not being able to predict or influence their attachment figures' nurturance is expressed openly as angry/aggressive threats that function to motivate attachment figures to end the display. When children push attachment figures too far and elicit anger, children switch to coy/disarming behavior. Doing so hides their own anger and displays instead their vulnerability. It also tends to terminate adults' aggression toward them and elicits nurturance. It is easy to see that, by splitting their affective displays, children are failing to display all their feelings. Consequently, aggressive children may be presumed to feel fearful and vulnerable whereas disarming children may be presumed to feel angry.

As Patterson (1976, 1991) has pointed out, parents participate in this strategy. Indeed, our observations of attachment figures in the Strange Situation indicate that they use submissive behavior in response to child aggression, i.e., they comply with child demands in an effort to appease pouty and disruptive children. In response to disarming behavior, attachment figures first offer nurturant assistance, but, if that fails, often become frustrated and, eventually, angry. In most cases, the parent finally gives in and does what the child appears to want. Unfortunately, as Patterson has shown, this rarely resolves the on-going angry struggle. The irony is that coercive children do not really want what they seem to be demanding, i.e., to have their way, to be given a treat, etc. This becomes clear when coercive children throw out their ultimate, hurtful, and desperate threat, "Then I don't love you any more!" More than anything, coercive children want to be able to communicate their desires in an open and direct manner with the confidence that their attachment figure will understand and respond in a satisfying and predictable manner most of the time. This, of course, is what inconsistent parents are least able to do.

The 'Shame' Group of Emotions. Because they are able to take the perspective of someone viewing them, preschool-aged children become self-conscious. Consequently, they not only experience their own feelings, they become aware of how others feel about them. Darwin (1872/1965) referred to the set of emotions that we experience when we perceive affective responses to ourselves as the 'Shame group' of states of mind. However one labels them, there is wide agreement that they represent an integration of cognition and affect (Izard, 1982; Lewis, 1992; Zahn-Waxler & Kochanska, 1990; Zajonc, 1980). There is little consensus, however, regarding their differentiation and development.

A review of the many perspectives on these emotions exceeds the province of this chapter. Consequently, two are selected because they have implications for the self, are related to one another, and fit the perspective on the integration of affect and cognition offered here. These are embarrassment and shame. Although guilt and pride naturally belong with these, these require a degree of cognitive competence not possible until concrete operations and, consequently, are not discussed here.

Both embarrassment and shame result from recognition that one has behaved in an inappropriate manner. Moreover, both have been hypothesized by paleoarcheologists to have evolved in our species as a means of facilitating group cohesion in early human communities (Leakey & Lewin, 1983). In older children and adults, *self*-awareness of not living up to a standard is sufficient to elicit embarrassment and shame (Duval and Wicklund, 1972; Harter, 1988). In the preschool years, however, the standard is just being learned and is not yet internalized. Preoperational children, however, are becoming aware of standards and of failing to meet standards (Cicchetti & Aber, 1986; Kagan, 1981). This awareness is the result of seeing the effect of their behavior on observers.

Often the effect is pleasure and even delight on the observing adult's part; indeed, awareness of this pleasure is probably the impetus to the delightful 'show-off' quality of toddlers whose antics are displayed to anyone who will watch (Stechler, 1990). When children carry this too far, adult pleasure changes to disapproval. Most children act a bit confused at the turn of events, retreat a bit, and offer coy behavior that signals both submission and the desire to be accepted. This pattern is what we call embarrassment. It functions to repair the rift in the relationship. The confusion may be an indication that the child both recognizes that something is amiss and yet does not know exactly what it is, i.e., there is a global, non-specific awareness of unsuitability.

Some parents, on the other hand, are substantially more displeased by their toddler's behavior. Instead of displeasure that turns to tenderness and forgiveness, their expressions become those of disgust. Their children cringe as though hit. No reinstatement of the relationship occurs. A comparison with a nonhuman species might be useful. To protect itself when losing a fight, a rat must show submission. If complete submission is displayed, the rat will be ejected from the group and will ultimately die. To survive, the submissive rat must find a way to establish a working relationship with the dominant rat; this relationship must fall between complete submission and challenging threats or anger (Barnett, 1975). Embarrassment in humans may accomplish this purpose. It uses many of the coy behaviors associated with disarming anger and terminating aggression as well as those that elicit nurturance.

When, however, the adults response is one of disgust, the child feels rejected as a person. Because preoperational children are not yet capable of differentiating their actions from their selves, they cannot understand that although what they did was wrong, they are good. This is simply too complex. Instead, their perception is of the adults' response to their entire being. If the rebuke is gentle and is accompanied by forgiveness and reestablishment of a loving relationship, children can learn to inhibit certain behaviors. If, however, the expression of disgust conveys that others want no part of them, the outcome may be like that of submissive rats. The head drops, the chest caves in, and the child cringes away as though struck by blows (Lewis, 1992). Moreover, because the unworthiness cannot be focused, it cannot be corrected. Consequently, children who are shamed frequently may incorporate shame as an undefined, unchanging, and unfocussed aspect of self to be displayed in submissive withdrawal or denied in the presentation of a false self. Its appearance so early in development and before cognitive and language skills are sufficient to explain either the child's or the parent's behavior may explain its impact on later development (Erikson, 1950).

Other parents frequently fail to respond at all to their children. Especially when the child has been seeking their attention, offering affection, or showing-off, the experience of being seen through, of failing to elicit any response, leaves even the best aspects of themselves shamed. This is analogous to constant repetition of the occasional experience of greeting a person who fails to recognize us and passes by obliviously; our reaction is to feel shamed and wish to hide. For some children, this is experience is frequent with their attachment figures and leads to intense, often unresolvable, feelings of shame.

Individual Differences in the Self-conscious Emotions. Although every child experiences each of these emotions some of the time, there are individual differences in the expression of embarrassment and shame. Defended children are the most likely to be told they should be ashamed of themselves; moreover, they are most likely to have elicited this response by behaving in a manner that displayed feelings. In other words, defended children are the most likely to be rejected as individuals and to associate the rejection displayed feelings. Their perception, therefore, is of being shameful. Coercive children are the most likely to be encouraged in their charged affective display - to be egged on in their cute behavior - and then, suddenly punished for it. Their response is likely to be one of either placating the accusing parent or blaming the accuser who encouraged them. Compared to defended children, coercive children are relatively unlikely to themselves feel shame. Indeed, they are more likely to discover intuitively the power of blame to induce shame and submissiveness in their parents. Coercive children, in other words, may tend to be shameless.

6. Language and the Development of Self

The final perceptual change that affects the development of self in the preschool years is children's awareness of, and attention to, denotative aspects of verbal communication. Although human speech is perceived, attended to, interpreted meaningfully, and responded to even by neonates (Bruner, 1975; Bullowa, 1979; Stern, 1974), its denotative meaning is not perceived until late in infancy and does not become a major avenue for growth until the preoperational period. Comprehension of the meanings of words and meaningful use of words enable children to represent knowledge of self and other abstractly. This, in turn, allows children to experience the self in the present, past, and future. It also enables them to organize their knowledge of self flexibly and adaptively. On the other hand, abstraction of the uniqueness of each experience into words that represent it necessarily implies loss of information. That is, to gain access to more information, humans must give up some information. The preoperational period is important not only for the information about self that is gained and lost, but even more for what is learned about how to select what to generalize, what to keep as accurately as possible, and what to discard altogether.

Developmental Processes

In late infancy, a few words are acquired and used. During the preschool years, these few words become a rapidly enlarging vocabulary which is organized meaningfully in simple grammatical constructions. This new competence influences the development of self not only through the information obtained about themselves, but also as the basis for three structural changes in the mental organization of information. These structures modify information in ways that permit children to represent and access information efficiently. Each structure, however, distorts information in predictable ways. That is, each is biased in terms of the kind of information represented, the accuracy of the information, and the means of accessing and using the information. Attachment figures play a particularly important role in the nature of these biases.

Semantic Models of Self. The first of the structural changes is the development of semantic memory and representational models. Young children learn many semantic generalizations for the experiences in their daily lives. Two are discussed here in terms of their relevance to the development of self: self-descriptors and emotion words.

First, as young children learn labels for human characteristics and hear such labels applied to themselves, semantic memory and models of self are created. With verbally encoded information about themselves, children can call back aspects of self that they are not currently feeling or enacting. With time and further cognitive development, this will enable children to consider their own nature consciously. In the preoperational period, however, it simply enables them to become perceptually conscious of features of themselves of which formerly they had been aware only in the preconscious sense of feeling and action. Because these labels are provided by others, they are biased in favor of others' perspectives. Nevertheless, they constitute the language and meaning out of which children construct their first semantic representational models of themselves.

Second, language is used to refer to feeling states. Words that refer to feeling states enable children to talk with others about feelings, to share interpretations regarding the motivation and effects of behavior, and to clarify misinterpretations about these (Bretherton, Fritz, Zahn-Waxler, & Ridgeway, 1986; Stern, 1985). By about one and a half years of age, children use words that refer to affect and emotion (Bretherton, Fritz, Zahn-Waxler, & Ridgeway, 1986; Bretherton, McNew, & Beeghly-Smith, 1981) and by three years are able to converse about their own and others' feeling states and the causes and consequences of feelings (Bretherton & Beeghly, 1982; Dunn, Bretherton, & Munn, 1987). There is considerable variation in the types of occasions that elicit feeling language with such talk being concentrated in disputes (Dunn, Brown, & Beardsall, 1991). Of particular interest to this discussion is evidence of children's ability, as early as 21 months of age, to fake verbal and non-verbal emotion displays (Dunn, Bretherton, & Munn, 1987). That is, even before the age of two years, children can knowingly pretend to have a feeling and talk about having the feeling in ways that do not accurately reflect their actual feelings. Finally, as would be expected from the Vygotskiian theory of joint construction of developmental progress, the evidence indicates that mothers' verbal behavior changes over time in ways that guide and prepare for children's mastery of these communicative skills (Beeghly, Bretherton, & Mervis, 1986; Dunn, Bretherton, & Munn, 1987).

Episodic Models of Self. The second structural change in the preoperational period is the development of autobiographical episodic memory. The brief stories which children tell of themselves and their experiences constitute, at the time, their perceptions of the salient aspects of their lives. These stories are, however, quite ephemeral. The story told to a child's mother immediately after the event is likely to be forgotten by the time the father returns home. Even fewer stories will be available by the time of grandma's visit a few weeks later. By adulthood only a select few of these early episodic memories will remain.

The basis for their selection is unclear although I have proposed elsewhere that intense affective arousal may typify episodes retained in episodic memory as opposed to those absorbed into generalized forms of internal representational models, e.g., procedural and semantic models or scripts (Crittenden, 1992b). There is support for this position in empirical studies indicating that emotional events may be remembered better than non-emotional events (Christianson & Loftus, 1987; Goodman, Hirshman, Hepps, & Rudy, 1991) and that stress enhances memory (Gold, 1987) and reduces suggestibility (Goodman, et al., 1991). Regardless of the veracity of the episodes, affective valence may be critical to which episodes will be retained in long-term storage (Fivush, Gray, Fromhoff, 1987) as well as to which memories are evoked (Blaney, 1986).

Retention is not, however, an all or nothing proposition. There is strong evidence that children retain memories that they cannot always access. Sometimes the failure to tell is voluntary as when the child considers the memory to be a secret (Pipe & Goodman, 1991). At other times, however, the child has the information, but without the appropriate prompt, cannot access it (Fivush & Hamond, 1990; Hudson, 1990). In other cases, the child may not remember episodes which create unpleasant feelings when remembered. For example, as safeguard against parental disapproval and unresolvable emotional arousal, defended children may hold experiences and feelings that counter parental perspectives 'out of consciousness'. Coercive children, on the other hand, may 'forget' evidence of competence or of their own intolerable behavior. This type of memory has been labeled 'unconscious' and is, of course, of considerable interest in cases of disordered development (Bowlby, 1980; Freud, 1968/1900; Miller, 1992).

Other biases also influence episodic models. Parents are an important influence not only on the content of episodes, but also on children's ability to articulate episodes, their understanding of which episodes to select for presentation and storage, and what aspects of experience are worthy of retention (Snow, 1990). In guiding children into the construction of an autobiography, parents pass on cultural values; for example, Western parents may emphasize episodes of individuality whereas Oriental parents may encourage recall of experiences of collaborative accomplishment. Subtle signals may also alert children to episodes that cannot be retold, that are best 'forgotten' (Dunn, Brown, & Beardsall, 1991). In addition, episodes that are told to parents or other adults may be corrected by adults. These corrections may be accurate or may modify the memory to fit parental perceptions and/or preferences (Bowlby, 1980). For example, a child might relate an instance in which his parent spanked him. In his version, the child may not mention doing anything to elicit the spanking. His parent, however, may remind him of this important feature of the incident, thus, correcting his memory such that it becomes more accurate and useful for regulating his future behavior. On the other hand, he may have reported his parent's anger accurately, but the parent 'corrects' the memory so as to seem righteous. In this case, the parent's bias may be encoded as the child's memory.

Although most people have some episodic memories from the preschool years, differentiation of these memories from wishes, 'made-up' memories, dreams, and parental stories can be difficult. Indeed, most preschool-aged children occasionally relate 'memories' that could not possibly have occurred (Johnson & Foley, 1984.) For example, the two-year old son of a colleague told her, in a wise and knowing tone, how he remembered when she had been a little boy and had fallen off her riding toy. Children also relate 'memories' that express unfulfilled desires (e.g., "We went to the zoo and I had lots and lots and lots of candy!") or unrealized fears ("and the lion tried to eat me.") Conversely, when asked to produce make-believe stories, most four and five year old children relate personal episodes (Gruendel, 1980; Hudson & Shapiro, in press). In other words, preschool-aged children understand the form of narrative episodes and the scripts typical of 'true' experiences, but they do not differentiate well between things that actually happened and things that they can imagine happening.

Episodic memory, consequently, may contain not only actual episodes but also transformed episodes, dreamed episodes, parentally-corrected episodes, etc. Some of the episodes may be transformed by children who distort memories of their behavior and feelings so as to protect themselves from unfavorable attributions. For example, in the situation described earlier of a sick child who wanted her parents to stay home, the child whose parents went out anyway might 'forget' her fearfulness (a shameful emotion) and focus solely on her parents' stated righteousness. A coercive child in such a situation might exaggerate both the extent of the illness and that of her parents' disregard of her wishes.

Transformed episodes, however, do not necessarily degrade or confuse children's mental functioning. Through permitting children to rearrange old content into new scenarios, they enable children to imagine themselves in varied roles (Markus & Nurius, 1986; Wolf, 1990). Thus, children's selves can expand beyond the confines of bodily experience. In many ways this is similar to daydreaming in older children. It differs, however, in that young children may not be able to tell, when recalling an episode, how it came to be a memory, i.e., whether it was real or imagined (Loftus, 1989).

Scripts. The procedural models that represented the daily, recurring events of their lives for infants can be expressed only as patterns of sensorimotor behavior. They are, however, representable in linguistic form. Toddlers learn to use language in precisely this manner to describe context-free regularities in daily routines, e.g., bedtime routines. Others have referred to these as verbalized procedural models, generic personal memory, or generic event memories (Conway, 1990). Following the trend in developmental psychology, they are referred to here as scripts (Bretherton, 1988; Fivush, 1987; Nelson, 1986; Schank & Abelson, 1977). Such scripts bear a relation to both procedures and episodes. They differ from procedural memory in being represented symbolically and, thus, freed from enaction. They differ from episodes in not representing specific occasions. As such, they may be considered a subcategory of semantic models of self. The point, however, is not what label is used nor how scripts are categorized. What is important is that language takes on a new function that requires access to more than one memory system.

With regard to scripts, one function is to facilitate children's differentiation of familiar and unique experiences (Fivush & Hamond, 1990; Hudson, 1990b). That is, because so much experience is new to young children, attention to similarities - to typical routines - enables children to more quickly make them familiar and, thus, to reduce the complexity of information. This, in turn, enables children to process more information. This has been described as a change from young children's attention to the typical to older children's (3–4 year olds) attention to the unique (Fivush & Hamond, 1990; Nelson, 1988). From a Vygotskiian perspective, however, the only change may be the placement of the boundary between familiar and unfamiliar. The increasing number and complexity of scripts constitute not only an enlarging fund of information about the familiar, but also an efficient method for remembering, organizing, and interpreting information. Children can use this fund of self-and-other information to organize their behavior in future similar situations as well as to focus their attention on the unexpected and novel. A second function of scripts may be to enhance children's feeling of jointness with others. Although Garvey (1984) and Grice (1975) emphasize the constraints against repeating oneself and reporting shared knowledge, these conventions may not apply to all situations. Repetition of jointly shared information may express shared aspects of self (Edwards & Middleton, 1988). That is, children (and adults) may repeat familiar stories not because they have new details, insights, or perspectives to offer but because, by repeating the familiar, they share perspectives with others. This sharing of self through shared history and jointly held information may both confirm and solidify relationships with others and also provide a context for defining the jointly held aspects of self. Knowing that they are accepted members of groups, especially family groups, may be as important for children as knowing how they differ from others.

Reliance on scripts, however, can also distort recall. When asked to recall specific experiences that are similar to other experiences, children tend to confuse the details of individual occasions and are more susceptible to misleading information (Farrar & Goodman, 1992; Hudson, 1990a). It appears from these studies that the script is used to recreate episodes and, in the process, is open to distortion (Barclay & DeCooke, 1988).

Attachment Figures and Other Important Adults. Although Piagetian thinking presents children as interacting directly with the world and, on the basis of their experience, constructing a cognitive framework to explain their experience, Vygotskiian theory allocates an important role to parents. Studies of language development suggest that parents' coaching and shaping of children's experience in their (changing) zone of proximal development is critical to children's learning *how* to remember and converse about memories (Fivush & Hamond, 1990). Indeed, without guidance, children seem unable to relate events that they do, in fact, remember (Fivush & Hamond, 1990). Moreover, mothers' style of eliciting memories influences the extent to which children will be able to converse about memories, with elaborative mothers having children who converse with greater detail and organization than children of pragmatic/repetitive mothers (Engel, 1986; Hudson, 1990b).

In addition, mothers, as representatives of family and culture, teach children what counts as information (White & Epston, 1990). Indeed, children may 'prune out' information which does not fit dominant narratives as expressed by mothers' comments and questions. These pruned experiences may remain as inchoate memories, material out of which new stories can potentially be constructed, if and when the memories are accessed.

Individual Differences in Models of Self

These new linguistic competencies are a double-edged sword. For children developing comfortably in a supportive environment, these competencies enable them more rapidly and accurately to fine-tune their relations with other people and with the environment. For children whose experiences are painful, the new linguistic/cognitive tools may either create opportunities for change or solidify distortions already developed in procedural memory. In other words, language opens doors to new aspects of development for some children while it closes doors to change for others (Dunn, Bretherton, & Munn, 1987).

Individual Differences in Semantic Memory. Considering first the more felicitous outcome, access to language as a verbal means of encoding information permits preschool-aged children to become conscious of themselves and to experience aspects of themselves mentally and without behavioral enactment. When the words, meanings, and stories supplied by others are generally positive and accurate, they provide the basis for a positive self image. In addition, they create a climate in which thoughtful exploration of the self can be undertaken enthusiastically and with expectation of pleasure (Gersten, Coster, Schneider-Rosen, Carlson, & Cicchetti, 1986). Although such exploration will not occur until children become intellectually more sophisticated, nevertheless, the preschool-aged child is gathering the set of skills and tools necessary for later self-consideration and is developing the motivation to engage in that process.

For children who develop in less advantageous circumstances, however, language may either function to create opportunities for self-correction or, alternatively, to reduce the possibility of change in the direction of their development. Although individual differences in children's use of feeling words have been related to maternal input, less is known about the significance of these differences than about developmental progressions in their occurrence (Dunn, Brown, & Beardsall, 1991). Implicit in the discussions of them, however, has been the assumption that more talk about feelings is desirable and that, when such talk is limited, it may be associated with defensive strategies. The perspective offered here would suggest that either too little or too much emphasis on affect could be harmful.

Within procedural memory and models of self and other, defended children already have discrepancies between what they feel and what they do. Moreover, the primary figures in their lives reject their 'felt self' (Winnicott, 1963) and approve of the falsely presented self. In other words, the language which defended children learn often describes them as they act and not as they feel

(Cicchetti & Beeghly, 1987; Gersten, et al. 1986). In such cases, emotion words may be used to separate feelings from experiences (Dunn, Bretherton, & Munn, 1987). Similarly, recognition of others' feeling states may be helpful if it leads to empathy, but less healthy if it reduces children's awareness of their own feelings or if it enables children compulsively to organize their behavior so as to sooth others' feelings (Crittenden, 1992a; Crittenden & DiLalla, 1988).

Exaggerated affect may be used coercively. The examples of faked affect noted by Dunn, Bretherton, & Munn (1987) in which children pretended to feel emotions to get a treat suggest use of the coercive strategy of exaggerating affect to induce compliance from adults. The point is that the amount of use of language referring to feelings may be less important than how the language is used. Identifying these inversions may require observation of atypical samples, such as maltreated children (Cicchetti, 1991; Cicchetti & Toth, 1991; Crittenden, 1992b; Lynch & Cicchetti, 1991).

Individual Differences in Episodic Memory. Episodic memories vary in the extent to which they reflect children's actual experience and in the positiveness of that reflection on the child. These variations can be clustered in terms of how affect and cognition are integrated.

Defended children may find, when they act in accord with parental wishes (and not in accord with their own feelings), that their parents are pleased and supportive (or at least not hostile). On the other hand, when they act in accord with their feelings, they may be labeled as 'bad'. Because both situations contain conflict, memories of both are likely to be encoded to episodic memory. The memories, however, reflect either a bad "felt" self (who acted solely out of self-interest and in disregard for others) or a good "acted" self (who acted in accord with others and with disregard for self). Conscious episodic memory may reflect the false positive images of self whereas unconscious episodic memory may contain banished memories of disheartening experiences of the felt self being abused, rejected, humiliated, etc. If, as is often the case, the parents also portray their child in incompatible ways - an idealized perfect child and a rejected bad child who must be socialized to be tolerated - the child may come increasingly to split awareness of self into separate, unintegrated models.

Thus, verbally encoded episodes can come to define a self that is either bad or false. Under these conditions, it is unlikely that children will have a desire to explore their personal history in detail. The loss to development of such a response is great. Children who cannot successfully communicate with their caregivers about their feelings often fail to receive nurturance, are confirmed in their belief that they are bad and a source of others' trouble and pain, and learn that not acting on their feelings reduces the both threat from others and also their own distress. In sum, such children learn that distorting their view of themselves by ignoring affective information and using others' distorted view to regulate their behavior is in their best interest.

For some defended children, their privately experienced selves may become a treasured, sustaining source of nurturance and pleasure. Imagined stories of their desires being fulfilled may become more satisfying than their meager and bitter realities. Such children may be highly motivated to deceive themselves by constructing a false episodic memory. Doing so can make each day easier for children in very difficult circumstances while, concurrently, interfering with the ability of their minds to provide accurate information. The risk is that this enhanced episodic memory may become more attractive than real life. This is a particular risk in the preschool years because every child has some made-up memories and few can differentiate them from real memories.

It is ironic that when distortions and omissions borrowed from parents are encoded as children's models of self, they limit or skew children's developing selves while, nevertheless, increasing the synchrony between children's perspectives and those of their caregivers. That synchrony may be advantageous and, especially in cases of severe distortion, may provide protection to children. For example, the tendency of maltreated children to believe that they are to blame for their mistreatment (Amsterdam, Brill, Bell, and Edwards, 1979) may 1) reduce the likelihood of their eliciting further abuse through protests or challenges, 2) increase the probability that they will exert the effort to behave in compliance with caregiver expectations, and 3) preserve their mental health by enabling them to maintain the illusion of control rather than perceiving themselves to be helplessly victimized by irrational and malevolent caregivers. Thus, defended children protect themselves both physically and psychologically by distorting their mental functioning (Cassidy & Kobak, 1988). It is this paradoxical outcome that creates the potential for mental disorder.

A similar process may be hypothesized for coercive children. In this case, however, the identification and labeling of good and bad self are likely to be applied to the same behavior with the same associated feelings. The labels, in other words, may be used in confusing ways. An aggressive young boy may be valued and praised for his masculine feistiness. Nevertheless, the same adults may also laugh at his childish pretense of power. Indeed, they may tease and taunt him to elicit aggressive displays for their enjoyment. Then, when his escalating frustration, anger, and fear of abandonment result in intolerable behavior, his parents may suddenly themselves become angry, punish him, and label him as "bad." Similarly, a little girl may charm adults with her shy coyness, but her pleasure may turn to distress when adults mock her to elicit her shyness for their amusement. When she becomes totally distraught, they may become disgusted with her incompetence, call her a "baby", and refuse to let her join their activities.

In both cases, children must yield to escalating affect to attract the attention of important adults. When they do so, however, they receive the irrational and painful feedback that that which is attractive and desired by adults is also prohibited. Indeed, their behavior and feelings, which are elicited gleefully by adults, are then punished. The attributions to themselves are equally irrational. Rather than developing two selves, one good and the other bad, coercive children may develop an incoherent self that is at once good and bad depending upon the whim of the accuser.

Correction of these biases is sometimes possible if children perceive the discrepancy and present their puzzlement verbally to attachment figures. Under such circumstances, there is the possibility that attachment figures may understand children's perspective and actively help them to sort out the problem. If, on the other hand, attachment figures are offended or hurt by children's real feelings or stories of their feelings, children's words and stories may be ignored, criticized, or 'corrected'. In that case, children will learn to use parentally accepted language and to tell approved stories. The language and self-narratives of how they really felt may remain unspoken.

Individual Differences in Scripts. Because scripts typify one's experience in social relationships, individual differences in routine experience may have a powerful impact on children's self. For example, frequent and routine experience of incestuous sexuality may become a part of sexually abused children's unscrutininzed, taken-for-granted understanding of the nature of relationships. Unlike unusual, traumatic episodes of sexual abuse that stand out in their affront to expectations (to scripts), recurrent patterns of behavior, including patterns of unpleasant behavior, may no longer be represented as autobiographical episodes. Such memories may not merely be hard to recover, they may not exist as occasion-specific episodes. If, in addition, children are told that their generalized scripts must be kept secret or themselves perceive that the scripts are in conflict with openly stated semantic generalizations, the scripts, too, may be very difficult to recover. Moreover, without occasion-specific detail, the scripts may not be believed by others.

Under these conditions, the clearest evidence of their existence may be their use to guide behavior in the present. Thus, one interpretation (but definitely not the only interpretation) of certain kinds of inappropriate sexual behavior may be that procedural models and/or scripts are being accessed to regulate behavior. The power of unarticulated, but verbally representable scripts is, therefore, potentially very great.

The effect can reflect either a defended pattern of not integrating affect with cognition or a coercive pattern of instrumental use of heightened affective display. Continuing to use sexual abuse as an example, a defended girl who has been repeatedly abused may be inexplicably unable to experience feelings in relationships. This may include both the failure to experience pleasure in receiving affection and lack of anger when others misuse her. On the other hand, a sexually abused girl with a coercive strategy may carry the enactment even further. As a young child, she may have learned that coyness can be used flirtatiously to gain not only attention, but also favors. Later, when she is no longer a vulnerable little child, her response when sexual contact is required may be the outrage of the threatening half of the coercive strategy.

Mind and Self in the Preschool Years

Processes. During the preschool years, children develop new mental functions based on new perceptions, generate the self-conscious emotions, and begin to encode two new kinds of information, i.e., semantic generalizations and autobiographical episodes. All of these integrate affect and cognition, although the way in which they are integrated is affected by biases associated with each memory system. Moreover, although the uniqueness of each child's experience results in differences in content, the power of individual differences is primarily in how children learn to select information for encoding and under what conditions it can be retrieved. In the context of mental reorganization, other people may have more influence on development of self models than during periods of developmental stability (Pillemer, Rhinehart, & White, 1986; Trzebinska, 1992). Moreover, because the models of self that are created are a joint function of children and others, especially attachment figures, the models are open to distortion. Thus, the advantage of guidance from an experienced older person is balanced against the potential for distortion that cannot be detected by the child. Consequently, models of the self may never be 'true' in the veridical, literal sense. Nevertheless, they may accurately represent the personal meaning of experience (Conway, 1990). Indeed, in a world that constantly changes, veridical representation might not only be relatively unimportant, it might be less advantageous than memories that live and change with us (Bartlett, 1932). The accumulation of these memories, true or biased, in different memory systems constitutes a primary achievement of the construction of self in the preschool years. Thus, by the end of the preschool years, children know a lot about themselves. They could not yet, however, be said to know themselves.

Risk for Psychopathology. With access to three memory systems, children have several guides to behavior. Procedural models reflect children's current enacted understanding. Semantic models contain parentally-given information that usually exceeds children's maturity. Episodic models, on the other hand, are relatively immature, i.e., they contain information from children's past when they were less experienced and mature than they are at the time of retrieval. Because preschool-aged children cannot yet integrate information from these memory systems, their ability to regulate their feeling states is critical to their being able to function on the basis of semantic or procedural memory.

Defended children signal relatively little regarding their feelings and appear to be comfortable and competent. Unfortunately, this provides their parents, who tend to be under-responsive to affect, misleading information. The risk is that during periods of intense arousal, defended children will be unable to manage their intensifying (but undisplayed) feelings. Without parental assistance, defended children may find themselves accessing episodic models without awareness. As a consequence, they may act on the basis of patterns developed when they were younger. This, of course, can explain the observation that under stress some children 'regress.' Integration of this behavior into the child's emerging 'false self' will prove difficult and may result in feelings of shame. Under these conditions, current experience may also be encoded to unconscious memory. In other words, the primary risk to defended children in the preschool years is based on negative evaluations of self by others that leads to reification of perceptual biases.

There are two risks to coercive children. First, children's distrust of cognition may come to include distrust of language. Instead, they may depend upon the power of affect to achieve their desires. In doing so, children reduce their resources for self-regulation of their behavior. Second, children may not be able to construct a single, coherent self model that is not tied to changes in affective state. Without such a unified self around which to organize their further development, the process of becoming self-reliant and responsible, that was already awry in infancy, is likely to be further jeopardized.

For both defended and coercive children, however, encoding information linguistically often reduces access to true affect and recall of actual behavior, thus, amplifying the individual differences developed in infancy. Moreover, as work by Cicchetti and his colleagues suggests, disturbed preschoolers seem to have little inclination to engage in verbal self-exploration (Cicchetti & Beeghly, 1987; Coster, Gersten, Beeghly, & Cicchetti, 1989). Such limitations may be expected to function to reduce the probability that troubled children will spontaneously recognize improvements in their environment, reorganize their models of themselves and others, or modify their behavior in ways that facilitate relationships and the development of positive self-concepts.

The Transition to the School Years

Although it is beyond the scope of this chapter to describe fully the development of self in children capable of thinking using concrete logical operations, aspects of the transition to the mental functioning of school-aged children are directly related to processes begun in the preschool years. Some of these are considered here. Whereas preschool-aged children created the mental structures necessary for conscious awareness of self, school-aged children learn to use those structures. Four examples of situations that imply new functional competencies are offered. School-aged children are expected to: 1) generate semantic generalizations of their own; 2) explain why they behaved as they did, 3) focus on goals of achievement and mastery, and 4) generate self-evaluative emotions. Each task depends upon children being able to access and integrate information from separate memory systems and to use that integration to induce logical conclusions from which new and more adaptive responses can be deduced.

Put another way, the major advance associated with the shift to concrete operations is the ability of the mind to generate new functions for existing structures. These functions include a) using information from procedural, semantic, and episodic models to regulate behavior, b) recognizing that semantic generalizations about self do not necessarily describe every behavior of the self (i.e., a 'good' boy can do 'bad' things), and, ultimately, c) creating a model of self that combines and integrates, in a logical and coherent way, information from procedural, semantic, and episodic memory. In addition, school-aged children develop several self-evaluative emotions. Two of these, pride and guilt, are discussed here.

1. Explaining One's Own Behavior

Self-explanations as Emerging Self-narratives

Preschool-aged children spend a lot of time asking "Why?" and answering with illogical "Becauses." Although they have the words of causation, they have no understanding of either their meaning or the actual reasons for things. The competencies gained in the preschool years coalesce in a major task of the school years - being able to explain why one did what one did, especially when one should not have done it. In other words, children are expected to be able to account for their own behavior, to answer the question "Why did you do that?"

The answer must have special, quite restrictive properties. It must be both rational and acceptable to the questioner, usually the child's parents or teachers. In addition, children are expected to tie their behavior in current situations to their previous behavior, such that current behavior becomes a logical extension of what is already known about them. That is, children are expected to present coherent selves. Finally, it is presumed that the answer will be true. In other words, children are asked to construct and articulate coherent and meaningful mini-self-narratives.

Although being able to say why one did something may seem simple and obvious, it represents a major advance in children's construction of self. Given that behavior is regulated by (at least) three memory systems, each of which processes information differently, asking a child to explain why he (or she) did something demands considerable self awareness. If the theory presented above regarding differences in the value placed by children on affective and cognitive information is accurate, then some children will find it extremely difficult to explain their behavior, especially when they behave in ways that are forbidden.

This task is important for two reasons. First, children's relations with adults improve when they can explain their behavior satisfactorily. This may seem too pragmatic to be worth mentioning in a paper on mental functioning. To children, however, it may be the only relevant reason for accomplishing this relatively unpleasant and difficult task. Second, structuring a narrative life history that is coherent and explanatory over time appears to be essential for healthy mental functioning (Allport, 1961; Basch, 1976; Erikson, 1959; Kohut, 1977). Integration of the unexpected, illogical, and forbidden constitutes a special challenge to the development of a consistent self (Cohler, 1982; Gergen, 1980). Again, Ainsworth's patterns of attachment define important distinctions.

Individual Differences in Emerging Self Narratives

Secure Children. Securely attached children can flexibly access all memory systems, view themselves and others from several perspectives, integrate affect and cognition, and accept both desirable and undesirable aspects of themselves. Consequently, they are likely to be best able to explain why they have acted as they have. In addition, they are unlikely to have acted frequently in highly unacceptable ways, so that painful explanations will not be needed frequently. Moreover, they are likely to presume their ultimate acceptability, in spite of misdeeds and unkind feelings, to others. Finally, they know (intuitively) from prior experience that others are not threatened by attributions of shared responsibility. The outcome is that they can learn to explain, with reasonable accuracy, the interactive effects among their selves, others, and contexts.

The benefits of this process are inestimable. Explaining one's behavior is an initial step toward the later task of constructing a self narrative, a story of who one is, how one feels, thinks, and acts, and what one is becoming. Toward the end of the preschool years and into the school years, children undertake this task. The beginning consists of simple event narratives - why one ate the cookies before dinner, why one took the money off the dresser, why one didn't come home on time. Being able to explain these things in an honest, accurate, and acceptable manner is critical not only to being able to explain one's self, but also to being willing to engage in the self examination needed to do so.

Defended Children. Some children find it difficult to explain their behavior. Among these are defended children whose early development has led to 1) inhibition of feelings and actions that are not acceptable, 2) semantic representations of self that are negative when they are accurate and positive when they result from inhibition, and 3) episodic memories that are 'corrected' or held out of awareness. Compared to securely attached children, such children will have little access to the affect that underlies their behavior and will, instead, be consciously aware of what they should do as well as the necessity of meeting that standard. The inhibited feelings of anger, hurt, jealousy, etc., however, provide the motivation for behavior that is, indeed, forbidden.

How does a child explain misbehavior, for example, stealing, when both the behavior and the displaced feeling of desire that motivated it are forbidden? When, in addition, one has developed a persona of being especially 'good' and never having 'bad' feelings, how does a child explain that the persona is false? How does a child *know* that the persona is false when the mind functions so as to keep affect and forbidden behavior out of awareness?

On the other hand, an answer must be given. The task of the defended child is to construct a rationale for their behavior that satisfactorily 'explains' it. If negative feelings (to which the child has no conscious access) actually motivated the behavior, the child may have to rummage through semantic memory for some scrap of logical explanation. Often something can be found that is consistent with the conscious, semantic self: "I was just borrowing the money and was going to tell you". With age, children become better at both concealing their behavior and creating ingenious explanations for it, thus, protecting their self and maintaining its false veneer.

In extreme cases, however, defended children's feelings may be so intense and so forbidden that the resulting behavior is beyond explanation in terms of the acceptable self. In such cases, regardless of the validity of the evidence, the behavior must be denied - both to one's self and to all others. For example, a withdrawn, defended child with an image of being a very good, even perfect, little girl may desire to assert herself, to make her mark. So she carves her name - in capital letters - in the expensive mahogany dining room table at which she is forbidden to eat.

The behavior is explicable, but outrageous. It and the feelings that motivated it are entirely unacceptable and incompatible with her parentally-given semantic model of self. She denies the act. The evidence, however, is unmistakable. Yet there is no acceptable explanation. She stands, in her most disarming and appealing way, denying to herself and to her parents the obvious truth.

Truth, however, is more subjective than this presentation would suggest. Yes, she carved her name in the table. Admitting to it, however, might define her as aggressively disobedient. If her behavior was motivated by a desire to be recognized as a whole self, a child with many feelings and desires including the feelings of anger and the desire to be recognized for whom she is and accepted into the family unit, her truth may be different from, and incompatible with, her parents'. This truth, however, exceeds the ability of a child to articulate or understand, even though it may influence her behavior. In an inversion of the experience of securely attached children, she copes with the effects of her feelings and the conflict between her truth and her parents' by retreating further from awareness of the feelings and the conflicts. In so doing, she becomes both less able to account for herself and also more dependent upon others for information about herself.

Because defended children depend upon others for explanations of their behavior, they become vulnerable to self-doubt and to explanations that define their character negatively. For example, a child who fights repeatedly with siblings (whom he perceives to be favored by his parents) may, when he cannot explain his behavior in ways acceptable to his parents, be told that he is "mean." Such explanations, ingrained in semantic memory, become part of defended children's parentally-defined personality. In accepting such explanations, defended children become both solely responsible for their behavior and, concurrently, not responsible - after all, who can be expected to change what they are? Instead, they feel ashamed of, and try to hide, their true selves. Ultimately, the lack of an explanation that reflects the actual interaction of self and context in producing behavior places defended children at risk for both grandiose and morosely negative views of themselves. Moreover, being dependent upon others for information about the self functions to promote continued distortions of self.

Coercive Children. Coercive children explain misbehavior in the opposite manner from defended children. A coercive child caught fighting with his siblings might use his emerging concrete logic to respond, "But he started it!" or "You didn't punish Johnny when he hit me!" The effect is both to blame someone else for the problem and to turn the focus of the discussion away from the self. Using such strategy, the child may, indeed, avoid punishment, but he will have lost an opportunity to learn to integrate aspects of self, in this case, representations from different memory systems and different perspectives. Instead, the child's new logical capacity is being used to obscure the self.

Other coercive children learn to use the irrational logic that their parents use with them. For example, Gina's abusive mother had returned after leaving her alone for a few minutes. Gina, in a pouty tone, posed the issue directly, "Why'd you leave me?" Her mother responded, "I didn't leave you." "You did, too!" "No, I didn't; I was right there (pointing to the door)." After a pause during which she appeared to be thinking, Gina pointed to the microphone hanging from the ceiling and told her mother to "Get it." Her mother explained that it was out of reach. Gina demanded, "Try, Mom!" This continued several rounds as Gina insisted that her mother attempt the obviously impossible. Reluctantly and with embarrassment, her mother finally stood up, arms hanging at her side, and said, "See, I can't reach it." Gina countered, "But you didn't try!" Suddenly, her mother turned the tables by taunting, "Then you get it!" Looking totally exasperated, Gina said, "You know I can't; I'm too little." Astoundingly, her mother replied, "No, you're not. You get it."

This discussion is linguistically mature and has clear reciprocal qualities. But the logic is bizarre. Gina's mother has refused to accept reality as the senses perceive it. To cope, Gina must learn not only to speak the language, but also to use distortions of logic to converse about relationships. Although this clearly distorts her understanding of self (and other), it also demands, and even fosters, considerable intellectual competence.

On the basis of such experience, coercive children continue to fail to apply controls to the behavior elicited by their emotions. If they are also anxious about relationships (and, thus, demanding of attention) and unable to focus for extended periods of time on independent activities, then they may be seen as having attention deficit disorder and/or hyperactivity. For some this may also become academic deficit; for others, intellectual functioning may be challenged enough to be fostered. A few may so frustrate others with their outbursts and obstenancy that they put themselves at risk for becoming both perpetrators and victims of violence.

2. Inducing Semantic Generalizations From Episodic Memory

Communication Between Memory Systems

Although children's earliest episodic memories are probably validated in terms of parentally-derived semantic models (Bowlby, 1980), this order of influence changes as children develop the ability to deduce for themselves logical generalizations (Crittenden, 1992b.) By the early school years, children who have accumulated a store of episodic memories begin to draw their own (semantic) conclusions regarding their own nature and that of important others.

Because the episodes are experienced from children's own perspectives, these generalizations more closely reflect their own experience than parentally-derived generalizations from the preschool years. This tends to make the associated representational models more accurate to children's experience. Concurrently, it limits children's understandings to that of which they are mentally capable at the time of forming the generalization.

For example, children using concrete operations find it difficult to accept 'shades of grey'. Consequently, child-derived generalizations are likely to overstate reality and to discard some discrepant information. In other words, the 'goodness' or 'badness' of their selves and others will appear more starkly than they exist in reality. Moreover, because children, even more than adults, are influenced by the perceptual proximity of recent occurrences (Pynoos & Nader, 1989), these exert a distorting influence upon children's emerging semantic memories and models. On the other hand, the perceptual biases imbedded in existing models tend to distort reality to fit past models. The outcome of these two influences, the first for change and the second for stability, may differ for children whose contexts differ in their supportiveness.

Individual Differences in the Construction of Semantic Representational Models

Secure children. Children whose experience of reality has been supported by parents who a) validate their child's perceptions, b) tolerate negative affect (especially when directed toward themselves), and c) help children to tie experiences to generalizations may be expected to freely generate conclusions, to compare them to parentally-derived conclusions, and to puzzle openly over observed discrepancies. With help from adults, they can construct hierarchical models that reasonably account for variations in their own and others' behavior (Crittenden, 1990; Milbrath, Horowitz, & Wordlaw, 1992). For example, a girl who is normally easy-going may, when she is getting sick, find herself scrapping with her mother. If she can be clear about her confusion, her mother can help her to understand that, when they are sick or tired, even nice people can behave unpleasantly. Her semantic model of herself can be reorganized to reflect her being usually nice, but under some conditions, grouchy.

Similarly, a child whose friends suddenly exclude him from play can be helped to understand that they are mostly nice, and will be nice to him again, but sometimes children are unfair and mean. Thus, such children not only develop increasingly accurate models of themselves and others, they also gain experience in using different sources of information, i.e., procedural/semantic/episodic and parent-/child-derived, to reach balanced conclusions.

Defended Children. Defended children, whose emerging episodic memories have resulted in parental disapproval, may have both a depleted store of episodes from which to generalize and reservations about doing so. Indeed, the more harsh the parents' rejection of children's experience and conclusions, the more likely it is that children will find it more comfortable to continue to depend consciously upon parents' generalizations. Such children are likely to screen experience in terms of its congruence with existing parental semantic conclusions and to discard (or set out of consciousness) experiences that cannot be interpreted from that perspective. Their modeling of discrepant experiences regarding themselves is likely to result in multiple unintegrated models of themselves, e.g., one model will be positive and another negative. The child will use one or the other to regulate behavior with neither awareness of having more than one model, nor the means to integrate them into a single model. Failure to create an integrated model reduces the conflict children experience when their own view of themselves is discrepant with their parents'. In addition, however, it gives children both a distorted and negative view of themselves and also little experience with cross-validating information from different sources.

Coercive Children. Coercive children who have found little resolution of their feelings of anger and resentment are likely to derive semantic models of others as unpredictable, desired, and powerful whereas they will view themselves as misunderstood, vulnerable, and mistreated. Such models will reflect coercive children's perception of themselves as innocent and of others as responsible for their problems. In addition, they will lead coercive children to maintain a vigilant alertness for any evidence of future insults, thus, increasing their already distorted perceptual bias toward identifying threatening behavior in others. The outcome, in terms of development of self, will be to perceive one's self as blameless but vulnerable, and others as responsible and inordinately powerful. Their behavior, consequently, will be organized to gain control over others' behavior through failure to exercise control over their own feelings. For a discussion of this process among maltreating families, see Crittenden (1988a).

3. Achievement and Mastery

School-aged children are expected to be able to focus their attention on achievement and mastery in several spheres including school, peer relationships, physical competencies, and moral development. Dweck and her colleagues have produced an impressive body of research showing that differences how two groups of children conceptualize this challenge are critical for their performance (Dweck, 1990; Dweck & Legget, 1988). It is startling how closely these two groups, that Dweck labels "Mastery-oriented' and 'Helpless,'[2] resemble secure and defended functioning, respectively, in terms of how they use semantic internal representational models of themselves to organize their behavior in problem-solving situations.

Dweck's work shows that mastery-oriented children interpret difficult tasks on which they experience failure as challenges to be solved through effort. They redouble their effort, engage in effective problem-solving strategies, instruct themselves to try harder, and manage their feelings by giving themselves self-encouragement. Dweck concluded that they interpret the task as an opportunity to improve their ability. Their goals, in other words, are learning goals. Helpless children, on the other hand, seem to perceive difficult tasks as tests of their abilities, i.e., traits. In the face of set-backs, they become discouraged quickly. They report negative self-attributions and prognoses regarding their ultimate success accompanied by statements that the task is inappropriate or unfair. In other words, they offer excuses. Finally, they make frequent self-aggrandizing statements that are unrelated to their immediate performance (Cassidy, 1988). From the perspective offered here, these children appear to feel threatened by failure and to be searching in semantic memory for explanations that could invalidate the challenge. The generalizations that they find are not helpful because they are overstated and contradictory.

Dweck tied the learning and performance goals of these groups of children to their implicit beliefs regarding the nature of intelligence. Mastery-oriented children were described as viewing ability as incremental (changing) whereas helpless children saw it as a self trait (and, therefore, unchangeable). She also applied these (semantic) beliefs and associated styles of problem-solving to the social and moral domains and found evidence of continuity. She concluded that these beliefs may be the root of adaptive and maladaptive behavior.

Underlying these beliefs, however, is the developmental history that led them. That history is, I think, well described by attachment theory and research. Certainly, it is easy to propose that defended children would both view the self as incompetent and also dismiss the value of the tests. Moreover, instead of focussing on the opportunity to learn, and thus improve their selves, defended children would be expected to fear loss of a previously-established 'good' self, and the exposure of their hidden 'bad' self.

The attachment literature also suggests the presence of a third, coercive, group of children. Dweck's focus on cognitive-social aspects of development may

---

[2] Dweck's 'Helpless' group is not the same as my 'Helpless' subgroup of the Coercive (Type C) pattern.

explain the absence in her scheme of coercive children who regulate their behavior more on the basis of affectively generated information than semantic attributions. Were coercive children to be added to Dweck's model, it is my expectation that they would seek challenges as a context in which to draw attention to their need for help from others. With the addition of the coercive group of children, greater attention to other memory systems, and conceptualization of affect as coordinate with (rather than subordinate to) cognition, Dweck's theory could be expanded to account for a greater proportion of school-aged children's normal and psychopathological behavior.

4. Self-evaluative Emotions

In the preschool years, children used perceptual perspective-taking to discern others' evaluations of themselves. Although these evaluations were often in response to specific acts of children, preschool-aged children perceived them globally as reflections on self. When the reflections were negative, children felt embarrassment or shame. By the school years, children begin to differentiate self from behavior, thus, coming to understand that a 'good' person can do 'bad' things (Fischer, et al., 1990). In addition, school-aged children internalize, i.e., apply to themselves, adults' standards of behavior. These two accomplishments coalesce in the development of pride and guilt.

In both cases, these emotions attribute responsibility for children's behavior to the child. When the behavior is approved, the feeling is pride; when the behavior is unacceptable, the feeling is guilt. Guilt differs from shame in that it is specific, one is guilty of an act, whereas shame refers to the whole self. That is, one is guilty of doing something, but ashamed of oneself. The difference between behavior and self is very important because it protects the self. Even a person who is guilty of doing something quite awful that reflects very poorly upon the self is, nevertheless, only guilty of doing something, not of being something (Zahn-Waxler & Kochanska, 1990). Similarly, pride reflects specific accomplishments that reflect well on one's self.

Experience of these feelings provides an affective signal of the probable effect of action as well as reinforcement for actions taken. Thus, emotions developed in part from cognitive information come to regulate behavior, just as innate feelings in early infancy do (Bowlby, 1969/82). Guilt, in other words, functions to build conscience and, with reparation, enables one to rejoin one's social group, whereas shame leaves one publically outcast (Izard, 1977).

Risk for Psychopathology

There are two major risks in the school years. First, children with models of distorted relationships constructed on the basis of excluded information may be unable to construct meta-models that reduce the distortions by combining information from all models. Such children will be forced to regulate their behavior on the basis of less information than other children and may have less control over which model regulates behavior at any given time. Because their behavior will frequently be inappropriate, they will experience the very kinds of disapproving reactions that caused them to distort their processing of information initially. The second risk is that children's models of early relationships will be applied without modification to new relationships. This will reduce greatly the potential of such children to experience alternate attachment figures who could nurture their development. The application of models based on anxious relationships is often described as the inability of children to trust others; its resolution is sought in the trustworthy behavior of the new figure. From the perspective outlined here, trustworthiness would seem not to be the issue. Even abusive parents are safe and trustworthy most of the time. The issue is the small, but real, probability of being let down; extremely anxious children fear that enough to forgo connecting with others.

Consequently, some seriously abused children learn to mentally organize reality so as to reduce uncertainty in ways that elicit as little risk of violence as possible. By perceiving everything in terms of potential threats, they increase the probability of responding so as to prevent the threat from being realized (Bradbury & Fincham, 1990). Rieder and Cicchetti (1989) provide empirical evidence of abused children applying exactly such a perceptual set to both threatening and non-threatening experiences. As a result, these children may experience fewer incompatibilities which, in turn, will lead to fewer integrations and a more rigid model of self and others. Mental development will be hampered such that children do not live up to their genotypic potential. In other words, some children may distort their mental functioning so as to reduce the probability of parental violence. If, however, mental functioning depends upon recognition of discrepancies (Kagan, 1971; Lashley, 1958/1960), then these children may be protecting their physical selves at the expense of their psychological selves.

Other abused children may find that careful attention to discrepancies enables them to make astute evaluations of conditions and probabilities of parental violence. Such children may become extremely sensitive to nuances of behavior and learn to respond with equally subtle variations. For these children who experience extreme environmental challenge, even a slight advantage in genotype may become magnified into a substantial difference in phenotype.

In addition, there are risks when much mental functioning is unconscious. To be used to regulate behavior under emotionally arousing conditions, information in episodic memory needs to be evaluated in terms of semantic logic and procedural experience. This implies conscious evaluation of episodic memories in the light of current circumstances and newer understandings. The tendency of defended children to hold some memories out of consciousness greatly impedes this process.

Summary and Conclusions

It is ironic that, by the time humans have the mental competence to consider their own functioning and the language with which to articulate their observations, so much development has occurred that few, if any, can report accurately on the process that has culminated in their present selves. Thus, the roots of the supremely human achievement of an infinite variety of uniquely adapted selves are hidden in the mystery of early human development (Fraiberg, 1959). While awaiting the closing of the chasm between neuroscience and psychology, developmental psychologists and psychopathologists must, like researchers in all of the sciences, be content to assemble theoretical explanations with which to explain and predict the functioning of fundamental 'black boxes' (von Baeyer, 1992). In this chapter, the functioning, structure, and content of one such black box, the immature human mind, are explored with regard to the development of self. Observations of the behavior of infants and young children, i.e., the outcome of the functioning of the black box, are used to support theoretical propositions drawn from attachment theory regarding the structure and content of the developing human mind's representation of self. Because mental functioning integrates affect and cognition, individual differences in how children learn to use affect and cognition to guide their behavior may make children more or less vulnerable to psychopathology.

1. Summary of Developmental Processes

The Self in Infancy

In infancy the developmental task is to transform species-specific, innate, perceptual-response patterns into elaborated and contextually-adapted patterns of behavior. The work of Stern and Tronick is central to understanding the functions of the emerging infant self whereas theory proposed by Bowlby, together with Tulving's notion of procedural memory, is central to understanding the structure of the infant self. Vygotskii's dialectical theory of the social generation of mental development was combined with Piaget's theory of periodic transformation during periods of rapid neurological change to identify both periods of change and also periods during which the influence of attachment figures would be greatest. Ainsworth's three patterns of attachment are employed to describe individual differences in how children learn to use their minds.

The conclusions are that infants construct preconscious procedural models of self and other behavior and that they experience their selves in terms of familiar patterns of shifts among affective states. Moreover, through the integration of cognition and affect, infants generate new affective states, love and aggression. In terms of individual differences, secure infants learn to integrate affectively-derived information with cognitively-derived information and to seek assistance, support, and clarification from attachment figures. Avoidant infants learn that use of affective information leads to incongruent and unpleasant results; consequently, they learn to discard (defensively exclude) affective information in favor of cognitive information and to depend as little as possible upon attachment figures for assistance and support. Ambivalent infants are unable to find a mental or behavioral strategy, i.e., procedural representational model, around which to organize their behavior and, consequently, express their distress at being unable to predict or influence their environment. It is proposed that procedural models that exclude important information, including use of attachment figures as sources of information, leave children vulnerable to maladaptive patterns of mental activity and overt behavior.

The Preschool Years

For the preschool years, the focus is on the widening perceptual experience of preoperational children and their ability, as a function of maturation, to generate new functions for procedural models and to construct new mental structures. As a function of maturation and in the context of interaction with attachment figures, preschool-aged children transform their procedural models. Secure children use their new skills to establish a goal-corrected partnership with their attachment figures. For defended children, this involves more elaborate defensive patterns based on both the inhibition and falsification of affect. Coercive children develop a strategy of selectively inhibiting one set of feelings (anger/aggression or vulnerability/fearfulness) while displaying the other in exaggerated form and then reversing the displays. In an inversion of the defended strategy, coercive children defensively exclude cognitive information and, sometimes, use false cognitions to coerce others. All three procedural patterns are clearly regulatory, i.e., they are based on feedback.

The major perceptual change in the preschool years is children's awareness of others' perception of them, i.e., perceptual perspective-taking. Five contexts in which perceptual perspective-taking influences the development of self were considered: 1) others' view of children, 2) a network of relationships from which to draw information about the self, 3) relationships that exclude the self, 4) the development of self-conscious emotions, especially embarrassment, and shame, and 5) the denotative meaning of language used to describe the self. The power of others' perceptions of children derives in part from the affective valence of others' response to them. The validity of that response, however, cannot yet be evaluated independently by children.

The second major change occurring in the preschool years is the development of new mental structures with which children organize information about themselves and their environment in potentially more flexible ways. The development of semantic memory/models, episodic memory/models, and scripts (treated as a subcategory of semantic memory) enable preschool-aged children to encode new types of information. Semantic models are biased to reflect what parents tell children. Even if the message is inaccurate, children's semantic models may reflect the misinformation as truth; if the message is incoherent, children may be unable to construct coherent semantic models of themselves and others. As a result, some children organize their behavior in problem-solving situations on the basis of false and misleading premises, whereas others abandon the process of trying to make sense of the senseless and continue to depend upon procedural models for guidance. Autobiographical episodic models are biased in two ways. When children's experiences are deviant, models of these experiences reflect that deviance. In addition, if children's experiences are more painful than they can tolerate, memories of the experiences may be held either out of awareness (where the pain can be avoided) or constantly in consciousness (where they can motivate the individual to resolve the issue). Because episodic models are hypothesized to regulate behavior under high affective arousal, unconscious storage and retrieval may result in unexpected and inappropriate behavior. Preoccupying conscious awareness of the affect associated with troubling experiences, on the other hand, may lead to mistaken perceptions of threats, resentful behavior, and the failure to tackle new developmental challenges until their increasing urgency imposes them upon children. Such situations deprive children of the leisure to experiment with new and varied solutions to challenges. Finally, scripts provide a short-hand way to access recurrent episodic experience. When that experience is deviant and/or maladaptive, the development of scripts to represent it can reduce the possibility of children becoming conscious of the source of maladaptive behavior.

In sum, the preschool years contribute to an enlarging store of information about the self as well as to the construction of new structures with which to organize and (later) manipulate information. Behavior, however, still defines the self, which remains rooted in the present. Moreover, although this self is more varied than the dichotomously-defined self of infancy, new self-attributes are not considered as a whole. That is, at one moment children may define themselves as naughty and at another as very good. They are not, however, able to conceptualize themselves as having both qualities, nor to relate these qualities hierarchically. Nor can they integrate information encoded in different ways. Thus, although all three memory systems operate and encode information about the same experiences, preoperational children cannot integrate these sources of information. Consequently, the 'self' varies considerably from occasion to occasion.

The Transition to the School Years

Following the shift to concrete operations, children learn to integrate information from different memory systems into a single, increasingly coherent, hierarchically organized model of self. Because information is derived from different sources, each vulnerable to different distortions, preschool-aged children accumulate, in both content and structure, the basis for a multi-method test of the nature of the self and others. By analogy, it is as though children create several lenses through which to view the world. Each lens, however, is warped differently from the others. By peering first through one and then another, school-aged children construct images that are relatively free of distortion. Developing procedures (functions) to carry out this test, i.e., using and integrating information from different memory systems to construct more accurate models of reality, is a major developmental task. The focus, then, in the shift to concrete operations is on the development of mental functions with which to operate upon existing content and structures. The task is to create and articulate a coherent self from an integration of information from each of the memory systems/models. This integrated self can be articulated as having antithetical qualities, e.g., sometimes one is good, sometimes bad (Fischer, et al, 1990). Patterns of access to, and use of, this information to regulate perception, interpretation, and behavior are learned in the context of support from attachment figures and other important adults. The self, then, becomes the both typical pattern of mental functioning and also the sum of the information held.

When children identify incongruencies in the ways that they think and feel about situations, they have the potential to examine the information and correct existing biases. When the discrepancies are slight, children can themselves manage the task and, in doing so, improve their mental functioning. Parents' support of this activity, especially when discrepancies are great, is critical to children's ability to learn to use their minds to correct distortions and to synthesize new and more accurate meta-models of themselves and others. If parents function as guides to the process as well as safe havens of support and encouragement, children are able to resolve many of the discrepancies they experience. Mental health, then, may be associated with establishing relationships that enable one to learn to integrate sources of information in ways that create a more flexible, less biased self.

If, on the other hand, discrepancies are great or support is limited, then the task is more daunting. Because children develop distortions to protect themselves from pain, there is, in many cases, a continuing need for the distortion. As any therapist will attest, the task of changing distorted models and ways of accessing models is extremely difficult. Nevertheless, failure to develop meta-models that integrate memory systems in ways that reduce distortions may be a reasonable basis for differentiating vulnerability to psychopathology from psychopathology. Such a hypothesis can account for the more tenacious quality of disturbance in the school years as opposed to the preschool years and also the higher number of referrals for treatment of school-aged children (Achenbach, 1984).

2. Psychopathology

Development, through the interaction of maturation and experience, provides children with increasingly complex mental structures with which to discern, organize, and respond to reality. This does not, however, assure that the representations will be accurate or that mental processes will be used to explore reality (Crittenden, 1992b; Fischer & Pipp, 1984). The opposite may be true. The representations may be distorted and mental processes may reify the distortions. In this section that concludes an already speculative paper, I will venture a few guesses regarding the relation of extremes of individual differences in the development of self to psychopathology.

Problems Tied to Type C Mental Processing of Information: Exaggeration of Affect and Inhibition of Cognition

Because their behavior more frequently causes adults problems, coercive children are likely to be identified in early childhood and the school years as needing treatment. Among coercive children, there is likely to be a gender bias in the display of subpatterns with threatening children more often being boys and disarming children more often girls. Such a bias is consistent with differences in behavior and referral rates of school-aged children (Achenbach, 1984).

Children using the threatening pattern appear poised toward conduct disorders. When combined with failure to focus on cognitive tasks, their provocative efforts to secure attention and their angry behavior fit the predominantly male pattern of learning disabilities and attention deficit disorder. Their behavior, however, may actually express both an intensified focus on relationships and also learned strategies of gaining positive reinforcement from attachment figures by hightening displays of affectively arousing behavior. Their risk taking and imperviousness to punishment both follow from interrmittant schedules of positive reinforcement from attachment figures. In other words, threatening children may be quite focussed, although the focus of their attention is not that of teachers, parents, or even peers. The disarming half of the coercive pattern can, however, enable such children to be perceived as engaging, charming, and delightful companions. Indeed, they are often able to so charm and disarm others that they are forgiven or tolerated when others would be censured severely. It should be remembered, however, that even when children have been enculturated to display gender-congruent patterns, the coercive strategy only works when both patterns are used in alternation. Moreover, it can only be maintained in the context of a cooperating interactive partner, i.e., one who uses threats and bribes in alternation with the child.

Other threatening coercive children are sufficiently intelligent that they become skilled at dealing with the irrational. These children use the appearance of logic to coerce others into satisfying their affective desires. Such individuals are often perceived by others with mixed feelings; they are seen as being both manipulatively powerful and potentially dangerous and also charmingly attractive. In the extreme, their intelligence combined with refusal to accept responsibility for their behavior and a lack of feelings of shame can lead to cunningly aggressive behavior displayed without remorse. Their disarming pattern of behavior functions as the key that enables them to attract and falsely reassure others of their trustworthiness.

Children who use the disarming pattern experience the same mental (cognitive-affective) problems as threatening children. However, they display their plight more often as coy, submissive, helpless behavior. Moreover, they tend to be girls. Like boys, when girls focus exclusively on relationships and fail to find logic in cognition, they show very limited academic achievement. However, because their behavior is less obstreperous and functions to elicit help from caregivers, teachers may both nurture such children more (thus failing to identify their academic failure) and attend less to their interpersonal problems. This perspective suggests that there may be a group of girls suffering from the same learning deficits as boys who, nevertheless, remain unidentified because their behavior is less noxious, elicits caregiving, and is congruent with the lower standards demanded by teachers of girls.

Nevertheless, because anger underlies their disarming/submissive behavior, some will develop passive-aggressive personalities. In relationships, this might be expressed as resentful submission to the power of aggressive partners (who attract them through coy/flirtatious behavior). Because coercive individuals rarely understand their own role in relationships and instead blame others, there is the risk of self-righteous explosions of violence that are justified as being out-of-character and necessary for self-defense. The perspective offered here would suggest that the explosions were in character, but rarely displayed.

Problems Tied to Type A Mental Processing of Information: Inhibition of Affect and Exaggeration of Cognition

Defended children's problems have to do with the recognition and expression of affect, discomfort with intimacy, and dependence upon others for guidance as to their selves. In childhood, this may be manifested as withdrawal, over-achievement, and over-compliance with authority. These problems, however, are more painful to children than to the adults around them. Consequently, defended children are more likely to be identified as troubled in adolescence when they will be expected to establish stable and intimate peer relationships and to create personal value systems that integrate internal desires with external constraints (Erikson, 1950). Without access to information regarding both their own and others' feelings, these tasks will be very difficult for defended adolescents. Expression of these difficulties by withdrawal from intimate relationships, promiscuity, and covert defiance of community standards are likely to result in diagnoses of mental or emotional disturbance. Lack of affect and self-blame may be associated with diagnoses of low-grade, chronic depression. In addition, because they cannot trust their minds to provide accurate information, defended children are at risk for obsessive/compulsive disorders. Moreover, because affect can trigger unconscious memories, this may include impulsively aggressive behavior, particularly, displaced aggression. In extreme cases, in which the feelings of shame are too intense to be tolerated, defended individuals may act on the basis of a falsely created ideal, powerful, and righteous self. Although this, too, can lead to anti-social behavior, underlying it is a reserve of self-condemnation that may be expressed self-destructively.

Internalizing and Externalizing Problems

Although at first glance, it appears that defended children are likely to experience internalizing problems and coercive children externalizing problems, the reality is not, I think, so clear. Defended children do inhibit affect and internalize adults' standards. They may also, however, unconsciously access episodic models of their true feelings and act on those feelings. This is especially true when they perceive themselves to be more powerful than others, e.g., the teacher's pet may bully other children. Similarly, coercive children may appear to be externalizers although disarming children effectively hide their anger, thus, being 'internal.' The point is that this distinction does not map directly onto the model of developmental disorders being offered here.

A Perspective on Depression

There are, of course, many different perspectives one can take on depression. One that I find particularly provocative is that of Gut (1989) who hypothesizes that there is an evolutionarily derived 'basic depressed response' that has adaptive value. Specifically, when an important and intractable problem must be resolved before one can move on, the basic depressed response is evoked. In this depressed state, individuals become increasingly impervious to distractions as they focus on resolution of the problem. As all the individual's resources, waking and sleeping, are directed toward the one issue, the probability of novel juxtapositions of ideas that may yield new and productive solutions increases. Eventually, a resolution is indeed discovered and the individual is released to again pursue the range of interests and activities that engage humans. The outcome, however, is not only the solution, but also the generation of new mental processes in the context of a transformed understanding of self. For example, after the death of a spouse, survivors become depressed and only recover once they begin to construct a new model of 'self-without-partner'.

I find it exciting to contemplate depression as a productive state of focussed mental activity. What is painfully clear, however, from the developmental course that I have outlined here is that the capacity to function mentally has been progressively reduced in defended and coercive individuals. Without access to both thoughts and feelings and without integrative mental functions, novel juxtapositions are less likely.

The defended and coercive patterns represent both patterns of behavior and also patterns of mental processing of information. Although they are opposites, they have much in common. Both are skewed patterns developed to assist children to adapt to skewed environments. Furthermore, in both cases, children must 'give up' some of their selves in order to make this adaptation. Specifically, defended children lose access to affect and, as a result, cannot use strategies based on affect or the integration of affect and cognition. Coercive children, on the other hand, have limited access to strategies involving cognition. In addition, carried to their limits, both patterns can lock children into skewed patterns of perception, interpretation, and action.

When experience becomes so distorted that even their skewed strategies no longer work or when children become locked into these patterns in spite of changes in circumstances, the outcome may be complete inability to resolve problems. The pervasive experience of such failure combined with the inability to self-correct mental and behavioral patterns may be a basis for depression.

In one sense this formulation is very similar to Seligman's learned helplessness (Seligman, 1975). It is, however, based on a history of certain mental and physical adaptations that now fail to function and also fail to permit alteration of functioning. This perspective suggests that children who deny affect and then find cognition useless will have one route into the cognitive-affective disorder of depression whereas children who deny cognition only to find that affect misleads them will have taken the reverse route.

Although this analysis emphasizes the risk for depression of individuals using the defended and coercive patterns of mentally processing information, it does not preclude the possibility of secure individuals becoming depressed (cf. Cicchetti & Schneider-Rosen, 1986; Cummings & Cicchetti, 1990). It does, however, reduce the range of circumstances under which this is expected to occur. Because secure individuals have balanced patterns of mental functioning, they can respond flexibly to changes in circumstances (Sroufe, 1989). This includes using the defended and coercive behavioral strategies when they are the most likely to be effective. It does not, however, involve using mental processing of information in an unconscious and inflexible manner.

Unrestrained Behavior

Impulsive and impetuous behavior are hallmarks of childhood maladjustment. The perspective offered here suggests that there may be two roots to such behavior. Defended children may act impulsively without awareness of the motivation behind their actions. Without awareness, they have little potential to regulate, or even, delay their behavior. Neither are they able to avoid activating situations because they do not recognize the critical features of such situations. Impetuous children, on the other hand, are likely to be coercive children. They know how they feel ('why' they are acting as they are), but they have such underdeveloped and poorly integrated semantic understandings that they see no reason for regulating their behavior. Again, this perspective suggests the need for differential diagnoses and treatments.

3. Issues

Affect and Cognition

Much discussion in psychology has centered around the relative influence of affect and cognition on human behavior. The approach taken here is relatively simple and straight-forward. Developmentally, both affect and cognition are thought to be present at birth in the form of a few basic feeling states and reflexive responses to common environmental stimuli. These are presumed to interact in ways that result in both more integrated use of information and also more differentiated responses to variations in the environment. In infancy, this results in new cognitively based emotions, for example, the focussed feelings of love and aggression. In the preschool years, affect and cognition interact with social experiences to generate even more complex emotions, such as embarrassment and shame, based on awareness of others' emotional responses to the self. Finally, in the transition to concrete operations, cultural norms influence children's affective interpretation of social relationships, thus, adding yet another component to emerging affects such as guilt and pride.

At any given age, the relative influence of affect and cognition on behavior is best conceptualized in terms of individual differences in adaptation. In the attachment frame used here to describe these differences, secure children have access to both affectively-generated information and cognitively-generated information and integrate these sources of information with increasing flexibility to fit the constraints of varied situations. They use cognition to moderate affect and affect to inform cognition. Defended children, on the other hand, come to fear and distrust affectively-based information and to depend increasingly on cognitively-generated information. Coercive children engage in the opposite process, i.e., they distrust cognitively-generated information and function on the basis of unmoderated affect. Thus, in terms of individual differences, both affect and cognition are important with their balance being the ultimate outcome of a sound organism developing in a supportive environment.

The Organization of Self

One of the issues treated by many researchers studying the self is whether the self should be conceptualized as a single or multiple entity (Brownell & Kopp, 1991). It is possible that much of the disagreement is semantic, rather than substantive. I doubt that anyone would dispute that children (and other people) can have more than one perspective on situations (including themselves), competing affective reactions, or both consciously participate in events and mentally view those events before and after their occurrence. Whether these types of differentiations are best conceptualized as multiple selves or as different sources of information, different functions, and different aspects of a unified self is in part a matter of preference regarding semantics.

There is, however, an important underlying issue with theoretical and practical implications. To function adequately, the developing self must both allow for variation in the self and others and also find continuity across time and situations. The alternatives, a rigid, unchanging self or a fragmented, unconnected self, are indicative of malfunction and psychopathology.

For this reason, I like the notion of a single self that develops from several sources of information (memory systems) and with age serves an increasing number of functions, such as imagining, evaluating, planning, and explaining. Such a self ultimately becomes organized hierarchically such that behavior under different conditions and in different relationships can be represented (Crittenden, 1990; Kagan, 1991; Milbrath, et al, 1992). By labeling these common components this way, differentiation can be made between the multiple selves, fragmented selves, and split selves that typify pathological conditions in which mental processing of information is incomplete or distorted. The point, however, is not to let differences in semantic preferences obscure the important under-lying meanings about which there is often more agreement than about the slicing of 'self space' into constructs or the labels applied to those constructs.

Independence and Connectedness

Most of the literature on the development of self presumes that the self moves toward greater independence and autonomy. Indeed, only the studies of the self in infancy or with pathological outcomes mention parents in any detail (Snow, 1990). Nevertheless, there seems to be no doubt that the early development of self is integrally tied to relationships with attachment figures.

The perspective of attachment theory is very helpful in this context by reminding us how important, throughout our life, are our ties to others. Indeed, it becomes difficult to find meaning in any of the functions of the self if there are no other people. Attributes as simple as rating oneself on characteristics such as appearance, preferences, and skills all contain an inherent comparison to some reference person or group. Our cogno-affective emotions (aggression, love, shame, guilt, pride, etc.) all presume the presence of important others. Indeed, rather than enabling us to survive alone, it could well be argued that, with development, the self enables us to function ever more smoothly within our social context and increasingly intimately with a selected few people. Thus, even as we differentiate ourselves from others, we are concurrently identifying our similarities, associating ourselves with groups, and building bridges to others that reduce our differences and maintain the ties of even our physical well-being to important others (Hofer, 1984). Failure to connect ourselves to others, i.e., failure to manage adequately social and intimate relationships (both spousal and parent-child), is an indicator of dysfunction and is tied to psychopathology.

Possibly a way to reconcile the obvious pattern of becoming increasingly self-reliant with the continued importance of relationships is to think of the self as being active in the zone of proximal development. Because this zone constantly moves forward, the appearance is one of increasing independence. Because this zone always exists in growing individuals, the need for exchange with and support from others remains constant.

Developmental Pathways

Bowlby's notion of developmental pathways has been used implicitly throughout this chapter (Bowlby, 1969/82, 1973). In this section, explicit consideration is given to the notions of continuity and change in the self. In agreement with Bowlby's theory, the perspective offered here presumes that development is both coherent and changing. Thus, early development sets children on alternate pathways while, nevertheless, leaving the course of future development indeterminate (Gergen, 1980). Instead of fixing children on certain tracks, the process of development might better be conceptualized as changing patterns of probabilities associated with alternate pathways.

Opportunities for change derive from several sources. Maturation, including the timed activation of a variety of personality-relevant genes, imposes periodic disorganization on existing patterns of mental functioning. Particularly during periods of rapid neurological change, new cognitive and affective capabilities must be integrated with existing patterns mental functioning. The outcome may be substantial changes in the processing of information as well as in the construction of self.

In addition, mental functioning itself operates to identify important new information that requires attention and, possibly, accommodation. Although at the extremes, mental functioning may exclude entirely either affect or cognition, in the great majority of individuals, functioning is a matter of bias in the treatment of information rather than complete exclusion. Consequently, the mind itself may discover the need to attend to new information and to reorganize both models of self/other and patterns of mental functioning. Self-guided change is, therefore, a possibility.

The most frequently noted impetus to change is the occurrence of events that are highly discrepant with existing models. When these events have significant relevance to oneself, they may force a reorganization of models and patterns of mental functioning. Events such as the death of an attachment figure, a family move, or divorce can function in this manner. Similarly, the availability of new and potentially helpful attachment figures may result in shifts from one developmental pathway to another.

Given all of this, is there any continuity? Is there any way to predict change? Some degree of continuity appears to be favored by the bias at any given point in time toward mental processing repeating itself. The concatenations of reorganization are more likely to reflect current functioning than otherwise. Moreover, the more abstract the representation of prior experience, the less open to reinterpretation it is. On the other hand, change does occur in ways that are better conceptualized as coherence (Crittenden, Partridge, & Claussen, 1991; Sroufe, 1990) than continuity. Thus, predictions of later relationships that are defined predominantly by patterning in infancy may be misleading; coherent change may be a relatively more ubiquitous phenomenon.

Prediction is a more difficult problem. Although the scientific method of developmental psychology is based on testing of a priori hypotheses regarding effects, individual development may be too varied and random to permit accurate prediction. Instead, the operation of main effects and interactions upon groups of individuals may accurately identify important influences upon development without predicting any given individual's course of development. Even with complete specification of variables, powerful forms of path analysis, and longitudinally gathered data, individual outcomes may escape prediction.

The explanation, of course, is that, even with the unrealistic presumption of full knowledge of individuals' unique genetic heritage and complete understanding of the interrelations among aspects of functioning, many events are random and entirely unrelated to the functioning of affected individuals. To take my favorite example, Hurricane Andrew changed dramatically the lives of several hundred thousand people. Even immediately prior to the hurricane, it was impossible to predict who would be affected or in what way. Nor was there any association between individual characteristics and the presence of the hurricane. Moreover, even though general trends (such as the occurrence of intense anxiety) can be identified, there remains a wide range of types and severities of effects. Nevertheless, the hurricane changed the lives of its victims - forever. They (their selves) will never be the same again.

Accepting that many important *events* are random and unpredictable, however, does not presume that their *effects* are random. To the contrary, their effects may be entirely lawful. That is, given knowledge of the unique conditions surrounding each individual's experience of unpredictable events, the outcome may, in theory, be entirely explainable. For example, using again the example of Hurricane Andrew, knowledge of prior functioning, together with information about the event and its context (for each individual), may enable researchers to explain, in terms of lawful processes, why some individuals recovered quickly whereas others remain mired in bitterness, confusion, or depression (Cicchetti, 1984; Sroufe & Rutter, 1984).

This perspective is consistent with both an understanding of the indeterminacy and equifinality of systems (von Bertalanffy, 1950) and with current thinking regarding the functioning of large and complex systems over many cases and long periods of time (Gleick, 1988). From this perspective, although principles of functioning derived from hypothesis testing on groups may provide a road-map of general trends, for any given life, the uncertainty of future events imposes unpredictability on development (McCown, Johnson, & Shure, in press). Consequently, all that one can reasonably expect is to predict group main effects and explain post hoc individual pathways of development. These pathways can, nevertheless, be lawful even if they are neither predictable, nor linear (Thelen, 1992). Thus, on a case by case basis, we may be able to explain with relative completeness the process by which individuals arrived at their present selves. Predictions, however, may be limited to group effects with a substantial proportion of variance left unaccounted for.

In cases of smooth and untroubled functioning, this complex argument may be largely unnecessary. For cases of personal challenge, especially cases of psychopathology, however, it suggests the need to add new research techniques to our present repertoire of hypothesis testing tools. Without new techniques based on lawful outcomes of unpredictable events, we may find it difficult to understand and respond therapeutically to cases of distorted development.

4. Conclusion

In conclusion, this chapter has described a process through which the species-specific preconscious patterns of behavior of neonates are gradually transformed to become a human self, unique to each individual, that at its best is varied in its functions and elegantly flexible in its structure. Early in this chapter, I defined the focus as exploring the function of the self to regulate individuals' behavior, to answer the following questions: What kind of person am I? What can such a person do? What should they do? What are they expected to do? How shall incompatibilities in the answers to these questions be resolved? The process through which this occurs is identified as an interaction between maturation and experience, with maturation creating the potential for new structures and functions and experience creating the need and occasion for their expression.

The theory offered here is at heart very simple. In a process that reflects biological trends of increasing complexity in simpler organisms yielding to a balance of complexity and simplicity in higher organisms, infants generate both functions and structures. Preschool-aged children add new functions and structures while concurrently abstracting more knowledge into existing structures. By the school years, simplification (abstraction) nears a balance with increasing complexity as construction of meta-models, based on all memory systems, becomes a dominant task. Ainsworth's three patterns of attachment, reframed as patterns of processing information based predominantly on affect, cognition, and the integration of affect and cognition, interact with maturation and environmental circumstances to generate the variety of unique selves that are the hallmark of our species. Because many events are random, the specific display of self cannot be predicted in a linear fashion for any individual. Nevertheless, response to both predictable and unpredictable circumstances can be studied from the perspective of lawful interactions of mental patterns of processing information with existing competencies, maturation, and genetic endowment (Smith & Sera, 1992). Across repeated interactions, each slightly different from the others, these simple notions can result in a complex array of unique outcomes (Thelen, 1990).

It is clear that children have many and varied sources of information, none of which is sufficient or even entirely accurate. Resolving discrepancies depends upon the ability of the mind to the perceive discrepancies, especially internal discrepancies, that suggest that the model of reality is not consistent, coherent, or functional. When models are inconsistent, children must determine the errors and correct them, often by synthesizing a higher understanding at which the information becomes consistent. The alternative is to discard the information. Defended and coercive children are similar in that to greater or lessor extents they resolve inconsistency by discarding information. They differ in that defended children discard affectively-derived information whereas coercive children discard cognitively-derived information. Secure children retain most information and, with the help of their attachment figures, correct misunderstood information and synthesize higher level understandings, i.e., meta-models. The achievement is not only more accurate and flexible models, it is also the learned patterns of using the mind to accomplish this function.

This chapter has offered an integrative theory, based on notions of quality of attachment and information processing, regarding the development of self in young children. Little or none of this theory, however, is intended to be interpreted in an absolute or literal manner. Instead, it is offered more as a metaphor with which to describe behavior and from which to draw testable hypotheses. Above all, it should be conceptualized as an open model - one that is open to modification as new information, functions, or structures yield new and informative insights.

REFERENCES

Achenbach, T. M. (1984). The status of research related to psychopathology. In W. A. Collins (Ed.), *Development during middle childhood: The years from six to twelve* (370–397). Washington, D.C.: National Academy Press.

Ainsworth, M. D. S. (1979). Infant-mother attachment. *American Psychologist, 34*, 932–937.

Ainsworth, M. D. S., Blehar, M., Waters, E., & Wall, S. (1978). *Patterns of attachment: A psychological study of the Strange Situation.* Hillsdale, NJ: Lawrence Erlbaum Associates.

Allport, G. W. (1961). *Pattern and growth in personality.* New York: Holt, Rinehart, & Winston.

Amsterdam, J. L., Brill, M., Bell, N. W., & Edwards, D. (1979). Coping with abuse: Adolescents' views. *Victimology, 4*, 278–284.

Bandura, A. (1973). *Aggression: A social learning analysis.* Englewood Cliffs, NJ: Prentice-Hall.

Barclay, C. R., & DeCooke, P. A. (1988). Ordinary everyday memories: Some of the things of which selves are made. In U. Neisser & E. Winograd (Eds.), *Remembering reconsidered: Ecological and traditional approaches to the study of memory* (pp. 91–125). New York: Cambridge University Press.

Barnett, S. A. (1975). *The rat: A study in behavior* (2nd edition). Chicago: University of Chicago Press.

Bartlett, F. C. (1932). *Remembering: A study in experimental and social psychology.* Cambridge: Cambridge University Press.

Basch, M. F. (1976). Psychoanalysis and communication science. *Annual or Psychoanalysis, 4,* 385–422.

Basch, M. F. (1977). Developmental psychology and explanatory theory in psychoanalysis. *The Annals of Psychoanalysis, 5,* 229–263.

Beeghly, M., Bretherton, I., & Mervis, C. (1986). Mothers' internal state language to toddlers: The socialization of psychological understanding. *British Journal of Developmental Psychology, 4,* 247–260.

Belsky, J., Rovine, M., & Taylor, D. (1984). The Pennsylvania Infant and Family Development Project III: The origins of individual differences in infant-mother attachment: Maternal and infant contributions. *Child Development, 55,* 718–728.

Berkowitz, L. (1974). Some determinants of impulsive aggression: Role of mediated associations with reinforcement for aggression. *Psychological Review 81,* 165–176.

Blaney, P. H. (1986). Affect and memory: A review. *Psychological Bulletin, 99,* 229–246.

Bower, T. (1974). *Development in infancy.* San Francisco: W. H. Freeman.

Bowlby, J. (1958). The nature of the child's tie to its mother. *International Journal of Psycho-Analysis,* XXXIX, 1–23.

Bowlby, J. (1969/1982). *Attachment and loss. Vol. I: Attachment.* New York: Basic Books.

Bowlby, J. (1973). *Attachment and loss. Vol. II: Separation.* New York: Basic Books.

Bowlby, J. (1979). *The making and breaking of affectional bonds.* London: Tavistock Publications.

Bowlby, J. (1980). *Attachment and loss. Vol. III: Loss.* New York: Basic Books.

Bradbury, T. N., & Fincham, F. D. (1990). Attributions in marriage: Review and critique. *Psychological Bulletin, 107,* 3–33.

Brazelton, T. G., & Koslowski, B., & Main, M. (1974). The origins of reciprocity. In M. Lewis & L. A. Rosenblum (Eds.), *The effect of the infant on its caregiver.* New York: Wiley.

Bretherton, I. (1985). Attachment theory: Retrospect and prospect. In I. Bretherton and E. Waters (Eds.), Growing points in attachment theory and research. *Monographs of the Society for Research in Child Development, 50,* (1–2, Serial No. 209), 3–35.

Bretherton, I. (1987). New perspectives on attachment relations: Security, communication, and internal working models. In J. Osofsky (Ed.), *Handbook of infant development* (pp.1061–1100). New York: Wiley.

Bretherton, I. (1988). Open communication and internal working models: Their role in the development of attachment relationships. In R. A. Thompson (Ed.), *Nebraska Symposium on motivation: Socio-emotional development* (pp. 57–113). Lincoln, NE: University of Nebraska Press.

Bretherton, I., & Beeghly, M. (1982). Talking about internal states: The acquisition of an explicit theory of mind. *Developmental Psychology, 18,* 906–921.

Bretherton, I., Fritz, J., Zahn-Waxler, C., & Ridgeway, D. (1986). Learning to talk about emotions: A functionalist perspective. *Child Development, 57,* 529–548.

Bretherton, I., NcNew, S., & Beeghly-Smith, M. (1981). Early person knowledge as expressed in gestural and verbal communication: When do infants acquire a "theory of mind"? In M. E. Lamb & L. R. Sherrod (Eds.), *Infant social cognition* (pp. 333–373). Hillsdale, NJ: Lawrence Erlbaum Associates.

Brownell, C. A., & Kopp, C. B. (1991). Common threads, diverse solutions: Concluding commentary. *Developmental Review, 11,* 288–303.

Bruner, J. S. (1975). The ontogenesis of speech acts. *Journal of Child Language, 2,* 1–19.
Bruner, J. S., Olver, R. R., & Greenfield, P. M. (1966). *Studies in cognitive growth.* New York, Wiley.
Bullowa, M. (Ed.), (1979). *Before speech: The beginning of interpersonal communication.* New York: Cambridge University Press.
Buss, A. H. (1961). *The psychology of aggression.* New York: John Wiley.
Campos, J. J., Campos, R. G.., & Barrett, K. C. (1989). Emergent themes in the study of emotional development and emotion regulation. *Developmental Psychology, 25,* 394–402.
Camras, L. (1989, April). Maternal facial behavior and recognition of emotional expression by abused and non-abused children. Paper presented at the biennial meeting of the Society for Research in Child Development. Kansas City, MO.
Case, R. (1985). *Intellectual development: Birth to adulthood.* New York: Academic Press.
Cassidy, J. (1988). Child-mother attachment and the self in six-year olds. *Child Development, 59,* 121–134.
Cassidy, J., & Kobak, R. R. (1988). Avoidance and its relationship to other defensive processes. In J. Belsky & T. Nezworski (Eds.), *Clinical implications of attachment* (pp. 300–323). Hillsdale, NJ: Lawrence Erlbaum Associates.
Christianson, S., & Loftus, E. F. (1987). Memory for traumatic events. *Applied Cognitive Psychology, 1,* 435–443.
Cicchetti, D. (1984). The emergence of developmental psychopathology. *Child Development, 55,* 1–7.
Cicchetti, D. (1991). Fractures in the crystal: Developmental Psychopathology and the emergence of the self. *Developmental Review, 11,* 271–287.
Cicchetti, D., & Aber, J. L. (1986). Early precursors to later depression: An organizational perspective. In L. Lipsitt & C. Rovee-Collier (Eds.), *Advances in infancy,* vol. 4 (pp. 87–137).Norwood, NJ: Ablex.
Cicchetti, D., & Beeghly, M. (1987). Symbolic Development in Maltreated Youngsters: An Organizational Perspective. *New Directions for Child Development, 36,* 47–68.
Cicchetti, D. & Beeghly, M. (1990). Perspectives on the study of the self in transition. In D. Cicchetti & M. Beeghly (Eds.), *The self in transition: Infancy to childhood* (pp. 1–15). Chicago: University of Chicago Press.
Cicchetti, D., & Schneider-Rosen, K. (1986). An Organizational Approach to Childhood Depression. In M. Rutter, C. Izard, & P. Read (Eds.), *Depression in Young People, Clinical and Developmental Perspectives.* (pp 71–134). New York: Guilford.
Cicchetti, D., & Toth, S. (1991). The making of a developmental psychopathologist. In J. Cantor, C. Spieker, and L. Lipsitt (Eds.), *Child behavior and development: Training for diversity,* (pp 34–72). Norwood, NJ: Ablex.
Cohler, B. J. (1982). Personal narrative and life course. In P. B. Baltes & O. G. Brim (Eds.), *Life-span development and behavior,* Vol.4 (pp. 205–241). New York: Academic Press.
Conway, M. A. (1990). *Autobiographical memory: An introduction.* Philadelphia: Open University Press.
Cooley, C. H. (1962). *Social organization: A study of the larger mind.* New York: Schocken. (Originally published in 1909).
Coster, W. J., Gersten, M. S., Beeghly, M., & Cicchetti, D. (1989). Communicative functioning in maltreated toddlers. *Developmental Psychology, 25,* 1020–1029.
Crittenden, P. M. (1985). Social networks, quality of parenting, and child development. *Child Development, 56,* 1299–1313.
Crittenden, P. M. (1988a). Distorted patterns of relationship in maltreating families: The role of internal representational models. *Journal of Reproductive and Infant Psychology, 6,* 183–199.

Crittenden, P. M. (1988b). Relationships at risk. In J. Belsky & T. Nezworski (Eds.), *Clinical implications of attachment* (pp. 136–174). Hillsdale, NJ: Lawrence Erlbaum Associates.

Crittenden, P. M. (1990). Internal representational models of attachment relationships. *Infant Mental Health Journal, 11*, 259–277.

Crittenden, P. M. (1992a). Quality of attachment in the preschool years. *Development and Psychopathology, 4*, 209–241.

Crittenden, P. M. (1992b). Treatment of anxious attachment in infancy and early childhood. *Development and Psychopathology, 4*, 575–602.

Crittenden, P. M., & DiLalla, D. (1988). Compulsive compliance: The development of an inhibitory coping strategy in infancy. *Journal of Abnormal Child Psychology, 16*, 585–599.

Crittenden, P. M., Partridge, M. F., & Claussen, A. H. (1991). Family patterns of relationship in normative and dysfunctional families. *Development and Psychopathology, 3*, 491–512.

Crittenden, P. M., P. Vorria, P. Kakitsis, Z. Denegri, Z. Papaligoura, A. Claussen, & E. Poleomarkaki. (1992, September). Comparison of Mother-Child Relationship of Greek Children Raised in Institutional Care with Those Raised at Home. Fifth European Conference on Developmental Psychology, Sevilla, Spain.

Cummings, E. M., & Cicchetti, D. (1990). Attachment, Depression, and the Transmission of Depression. In M. T. Greenberg, D. Cicchetti, & E. M. Cummings (Eds.), *Attachment in the preschool years*, (pp 339–372). Chicago, IL: University of Chicago Press.

Cushman, P. (1990). Why the self is empty: Toward a historically situated psychology. *American Psychologist, 45*, 599–611.

Damon, W., & Hart, D. (1988). *Self understanding in childhood and adolescence.* New York: Cambridge University Press.

Darwin, C. (1872/1965). *The expression of emotions in man and animals.* Chicago: University of Chicago Press.

Davitz, J. R. (1969). *The language of emotion.* New York: Academic Press.

Dodge, D. A. (1986). A social information processing model of social competence in children. In M. Perlmutter (Ed.), *Minnesota symposia on child psychology* (Vol. 18, pp. 77–125). Hillsdale, NJ: Lawrence Erlbaum Associates.

Dollard, J., Doob, L., Miller, N. E., Mowrer, O. H., & Sears, R. R. (1939). *Frustration and aggression.* New Haven: Yale University Press.

Dunn, J., Bretherton, I., & Munn, P. (1987). Conversations about feeling states between mothers and their young children. *Developmental Psychology, 23*, 132–139.

Dunn, J., Brown, J., & Beardsall, L. (1991). Family talk about feeling states and children's later understanding of others' emotions. *Developmental Psychology, 27*, 448–445.

Duval, S., & Wicklund, R. A. (1972). *A theory of objective self-awareness.* New York: Academic Press.

Dweck, C. S. (1990). Self-theories and goals: Their role in motivation, personality, and development. In R. A. Dienstbier (Ed.), *Nebraska symposium on motivation: Perspectives on motivation: Current theory and research on motivation* (pp. 199–235). Lincoln, NE: University of Nebraska Press.

Dweck, C. S., & Legget, E. L. (1988). A social-cognitive approach to motivation and personality. *American Psychologist, 48*, 256–273.

Edwards, D. & Middleton, D. (1988). Conversational remembering and family relationships: How children learn to remember. *Journal of Social and Personal Relationships, 5*, 3–25.

Egeland, B., & Farber, E. A. (1984). Infant-mother attachment: Factors related to its development and changes over time. *Child Development, 55*, 753–771.

Eisenberg, A. (1985). Learning to describe past experiences in conversation. *Discourse Processes, 8,* 177–204.

Ekman, P. (Ed.) (1973). *Darwin and facial expression.* New York: Academic Press.

Ekman, P. (1984). Expression and the nature of emotion. In K. R. Scherer and P. Ekman (Eds.), *Approaches to emotion (pp. 319–343).* Hillsdale, NJ: Lawrence Erlbaum Associates.

Emde, R. M. (1980). Levels of meaning for infant emotions: A biosocial view. In W. A. Collins (Ed.), *Development of cognition, affect, and social relations: Minnesota Symposium on Child Psychology* (Vol. 13) pp. 1–37. Hillsdale, NJ: Lawrence Earlbaum.

Emde, R. N. (1983). The prerepresentational self and its affective core. *The Psychoanalytic Study of the Child, 38,* 165–192.

Emde, R. N., Biringen, Z., Clyman, R. B., & Oppenheim, D. (1991). The moral self in infancy: Affective core and procedural knowledge. *Developmental Review, 11,* 251–270.

Emde, R. M., & Buchsbaum (1990). "Didn't You Hear My Mommy?" Autonomy with Connectedness in Moral Self Emergence. In D. Cicchetti & M. Beeghly (Eds.), *The self in transition: Infancy to childhood* (pp. 35–60). Chicago: University of Chicago Press.

Emde, R. N., Gaensbauer, T. J., & Harmon, R. J. (1976). *Emotional expression in infancy: A biobehavioral study.* New York: International Universities Press.

Engel, S. (1986). Learning to reminisce: A developmental study of how children talk about the past. Ph.D. Thesis, City University of New York.

Erikson, E. H. (1950). *Childhood and society.* New York: Norton.

Erikson, E. H. (1959). Identity and the life-cycle. *Psychological Issues, 1*(1, Whole No. 1).

Fabes, R. A., Eisenberg, N., McCormick, S. E., & Wilson, M. S. (1988). Preschoolers' attribution of situational determinants of others' naturally occurring emotions. *Developmental Psychology, 24,* 376–385.

Fagot, B. I., & Kavanagh, K. (1990). The prediction of anti-social behavior from avoidant attachment classifications. *Child Development, 61,* 864–873.

Farrar, M. J., & Goodman, G. S. (1992). Developmental changes in event memory. *Child Development, 63,* 173–187.

Fischer, K. W. (1980). A theory of cognitive development: The control and construction of hierarchies of skills. *Psychological Review, 87,* 477–531.

Fischer, K. W., & Pipp, S. (1984). Development of the structures of unconscious thought. In K. Bowers and K. Meichenbaum (eds.), *he unconscious reconsidered* (pp. 88–148). New York: Wiley.

Fischer. K. W., Shaver, P. R., & Carnochan, P. (1990). How emotions develop and how they organize development. *Cognition and Emotion, 4,* 81–127.

Fivush, R. (1987). Scripts and categories: Interrelationships in development. In U. Neisser (Ed.), *Concepts and conceptual development: Ecological and intellectual factors in categorization.* Cambridge: University of Cambridge Press.

Fivush, R., Gray, J. T., & Fromhoff, F. A. (1987). Two year olds talk about the past. *Cognitive Development, 2,* 393–410. emotional tone and salience of early memories)

Fivush, R. & Hamond, N. R. (1990). Autobiographical memory across the preschool years: Toward reconceptualizing childhood amnesia. In R. Fivush & J. A. Hudson (Eds.), *Knowing and remembering in young children* (pp. 223–248). New York: Cambridge University Press.

Flavell, J. H., & Markman, E. M. (1983). *Handbook of child psychology, Vol. 3. Cognitive development.* New York: Wiley.

Fraiberg, S. (1959). *The magic years: Understanding and handling the problems of early childhood.* New York: Scribner.

Freud, A. (1966). *Writings of Anna Freud: Normality and pathology in childhood.* New York: International University Press.

Freud, S. (1923). *The Ego and the Id.* In Strachey (1966–74), Vol. 19, pp. 12–66.

Freud, S. (1968/1900). The interpretation of dreams. In *The standard edition of the complete psychological works of Sigmund Freud* (Vols. 4 and 5). London: Hogarth Press.

Garvey, C. (1977). *Children's talk.* Cambridge, MA: Harvard University Press.

Geertz, C. (1984). On the nature of anthropological understanding. In R. A. Schweder & R. A. Levine (Eds.), *Cultural theory: Essays on mind, self, and emotion.* Cambridge, MA: Cambridge University Press.

Gergen, K. (1980). The emerging crisis in theory of life-span development. In P. Baltes & O. Brim, Jr. (Eds.), *Life-span development and behavior* (Vol. 3). New York: Academic Press.

Gersten, M., Coster, W., Schneider-Rosen, K., Carlson, V., & Cicchetti, D. (1986). The social-emotional bases of communicative functioning: Quality of attachment, language development, and early maltreatment. In M. E. Lamb, A. L. Brown, & B. Rogott (Eds.), *Advances in developmental psychology* Vol.4 (pp. 105–151). Hillsdale, NJ: Lawrence Erlbaum Associates.

Gleick, J. (1988). *Chaos: Making of a new science.* New York: Penguin.

Gold, P. E. (1987). Sweet memories. *American Scientist, 75,* 151–155.

Goodman, G. S., Hirshman, J. E., Hepps, D., & Rudy, L. (1991). Children's memory for stressful events. *Merrill-Palmer Quarterly, 37,* 109–158.

Grice, H. P. (1975). Logic and conversation. In P. Cole & J. L. Morgan (Eds.), *Syntax and semantics: Vol. 3. Speech acts* (pp.41–58). New York: Academic Press.

Grossmann, K. E., Grossmann, K. A., & Swann, A. (1986). Capturing the wider view of attachment: A reanalysis of Ainsworth's Strange Situation. In C. E. Izard, & P. B. Reeves (Eds.), *Measuring emotions in children, Vol. 2.* (pp. 124–171). New York: Cambridge University Press.

Gruendel, J. M. (1980). *Scripts and stories: A study of children's event narratives.* Unpublished doctoral dissertation, Yale University.

Gut, E. (1989). *Productive and unproductive depression: Success or failure of a vital process.* New York: Basic Books.

Harter, S. (1983). Developmental perspectives on the self-system. In P. H. Mussen (Ed.), *Handbook of child psychology. Vol. 4, Socialization, personality, and social development* (pp. 275–385). New York: Wiley.

Harter, S. (1988). Developmental processes in the construction of self. In T. D. Yawkey & J. E. Johnson (Eds.), *Integrative processes and socialization: Early to middle childhood* (pp. 45–78). Hillsdale, NJ: Lawrence Erlbaum Associates.

Heelas, P., & Lock, A. (Eds.) (1981). *Indigenous psychologies: The anthropology of the self.* London: Academic Press.

Heiddeger, M. (1977). *The question concerning technology and other essays. New York: Harper and Row.*

Hermans, J. M., Kempden, J. G., & van Loon, R. J. P., 1992). *American Psychologist, 47,* 23–33.

Hofer, M. A. (1984). Relationships as regulators: A psychobiologic perspective on bereavement. *Psychosomatic Medicine,* 46, 183–97.

Hudson, J. A. (1990a). Constructive processes in children's autobiographical memory. *Developmental Psychology, 26,* 180–187.

Hudson, J. A. (1990b). The emergence of autobiographical memory in mother-child conversation. In R. Fivush & J. A. Hudson (Eds.), *Knowing and remembering in young children.* New York: Cambridge University Press.

Hudson, J. A., & Shapiro, L. R. (in press). From knowing to telling: The development of children's of children's scripts, stories, and personal narratives. In A.

McCabe & C. Peterson (Eds.), *New directions in narrative structure.* Hillsdale, NJ: Earlbaum.

Izard, C. E. (1977). *Human Emotions.* New York: Plenum Press.

Izard, C. E. (1982). Comments on emotion and cognition: Can there be a working relationship? In M. S. Clark & S. T. Fiske (Eds.), *Affect and Cognition* (pp. 229–240). Hillsdale, NJ: Lawrence Erlbaum Associates.

Kagan, J. (1981). *The second year: The emergence of self-awareness.* Cambridge, MA: Harvard University Press.

Kagan, J. (1991). The theoretical utility for constructs for self. *Developmental Review, 11,* 244–250.

Kegan, R. (1982). *The evolving self.* Cambridge, MA: Harvard University Press.

Kernberg, O. (1976). *Object relations theory and clinical psychoanalysis.* New York: Aronson.

Kihlstrom, J. (1982). On personality and memory. In N. Cantos & J. Kihlstrom (Eds.), *Personality, cognition, and social interaction* (pp. 123–152). Hillsdale, NJ: Lawrence Earlbaum.

Kohut, H. (1977). *The restoration of the self.* New York: International Universities Press.

Lashley, K. S. (1958/60). Cerebral organization and behavior. In F. A. Beach, D. O. Hebb, C. T. Morgan, H. W. Nissen (Eds.), *The neuropsychology of Lashley* (pp. 529–543). New York: McGraw-Hill.

Leakey, R. & Lewin, R. (1983). *People of the lake.* New York: Avon.

Lewis, M. (1992). *Shame: The exposed self.* New York: The Free Press.

Lewis, M. & Brooks-Gunn, J. (1978). Self-knowledge and emotional development. In M. Lewis and L. A. Rosenblum (Eds.), *The development of affect* (pp. 205–226). New York: Plenum Press.

Lewis, M., & Brooks-Gunn, J. (1979). *Social cognition and the acquisition of self.* New York: Plenum Press.

Lewis. M., & Rosenblum, L. A. (Eds.) (1974). *The origins of fear.* New York: Wiley.

Loftus, E., & Hoffman, H. G. (1989). Misinformation and memory: The creation of new memories. *Journal of Experimental Psychology, 118,* 100–104.

Lore, R. K., & Schultz, L. A. (1993). Control of human aggression: A comparative perspective. *American Psychologist, 48,* 16–25.

Lorenz, K.Z. (1966). *On aggression.* New York: Harcourt, Brace, Jovanovitch.

Lynch, M., & Cicchetti, D. (1991). Patterns of relatedness in maltreated and nonmaltreated children: Connections among multiple representational models. *Development and Psychopathology, 3,* 207–226.

Mahler, M., Pine, F., & Bergman, A. (1975). *The psychological birth of the human infant.* New York: Basic Books.

Main, M. (1981). Avoidance in the service of attachment: A working paper. In K. Immelmann, G. Barlow, L. Petrinovich, and M. Main (Eds.), *Behavioral development: The Bielfeld interdisciplinary project* (pp. 651–693). New York: Cambridge University Press.

Markus, H., & Kitayama, S. (1990). *Culture and the self: Implications for cognition, emotion, and motivation.* Unpublished paper.

Markus, H. & Nurius, P. (1986). Possible selves. *American Psychologist, 41,* 954–969.

Marvin, R. S. (1977). An ethological-cognitive model for attenuation of mother-child attachment behavior. In T. M. Alloway, L. Kramer, & P. Pliner (Eds.), *Advances in the study of communication and affect* (Vol. 3): *The development of social attachments* (pp. 25–60). New York: Plenum.

Matas, L, Arend, R. A., & Sroufe, L. A. (1978). Continuity of adaptation in the second year of life: The relationship between quality of attachment and later competence. *Child Development, 49,* 547–556.

McCown, W., Johnson, J., & Shure, M. (in press). *The impulsive client: Theory, research, and practice.* Washington, D.C.: American Psychological Society.

Mead, G. H. (1934). *Mind, self, and society.* Chicago: University of Chicago Press.

Milbrath, C., Horowitz, L., & Wordlaw, M. (1992, August). Attachment patterns and self and other schemas in pathological mourning. Paper presented as a part of the symposium "Representations of self and other in well-being and psychopathology," Chair, N. Field, at the meeting of the American Psychological Association, Washington, D.C.

Neisser, U. (1991). Two perceptually given aspects of the self and their development. *Developmental Review, 11,* 197–209.

Nelson, K. (1986). *Event knowledge: Structure and function in development.* Hillsdale, NJ: Lawrence Erlbaum Associates.

Nelson, K. (1988). The ontogeny of memory for real events. In U. Neisser & E. Winograd (Eds.), *Remembering reconsidered: Ecological and traditional approaches to the study of memory* (pp. 244–277). New York: Cambridge University Press.

Neuman, G. G. (1987). Past and present thinking on aggression: An introductory overview. In G. G. Neuman (Ed.), *Origins of human aggression.* New York: Human Sciences Press.

Oster, H., & Ekman, P. (1978). Facial behavior in child development. *Minnesota Symposium in Child Psychology,* (Vol. 11, pp. 231–276). Minneapolis: University of Minnesota Press.

Miller, N. E. (1992). Some examples of psychophysiology and the unconscious. *Biofeedback and self-regulation, 17,* 3–16.

Papousek, H., & Papousek, M. (1979). Early ontogeny of human social interaction: Its biological roots and social dimensions. In K. Foppa, W. Lepenies, & D. Ploog (Eds.), *Human ethology: Claims and limits of a new discipline* (pp. 456–489). New York: Cambridge University Press.

Patterson, G. R. (1976). *The aggressive child: Victim and architect of a coercive system.* In L. A. Hamerlynk, L. C. Handy, & E. J. Mash (Eds.), *Behavior modification and families. I. Theory and research* (pp.267–316). New York: Bruner-Mazel.

Patterson, G. (1982). *Coercive families,* Eugene, OR: Castalia Publishing Company.

Patterson, G. R. (1991). Antisocial parents: Unskilled and vulnerable. In P. A. Cowan & E. M. Hetherington (Eds.), *Family transitions. Advances in family research series* (pp.195–218). Hillsdale, NJ: Lawrence Erlbaum Associates.

Piaget, J. (1952). *The origins of intelligence.* New York: International Universities Press.

Pillemer, D. B., Rhinehart, E. D. & White, S. H. (1988). Very long-term memories of the first year in college. *Journal of Experimental Psychology: Learning, Memory, and Cognition, 14,* 709–15.

Pillemer, D. B., & White, S. H. (1989). Childhood events recalled by children and adults. In H. W. Reese (Ed.), *Advances in child development and behavior* (Vol. 21, pp. 297–340). New York: Academic Press.

Pipe, M. E., & Goodman, G. S. (1991). Elements of secrecy: Implications for children's testimony. *Behavioral Sciences and the Law,* 9, 33–41.

Pipp, S. (1990). Sensorimotor and representational internal representational working models of self, other, and relationship: Mechanisms of connection and separation. In D. Cicchetti & M. Beeghly (Eds.), *The self in transition: Infancy to childhood* (pp. 243–264). Chicago: University of Chicago Press.

Plutchik, R. (1980). *Emotion: A psychoevolutionary synthesis.* New York: Harper & Row.

Pynoos, R. S., & Nader, K. (1989). Children's memory and proximity to violence. *Journal of the American Academy of Child and Adolescent Psychiatry,* 28, 236–241.

Radke-Yarrow, M., Cummings, E. M., Kuczynski, L. & Chapman, M. (1985). Patterns of attachment in two and three-year-olds in normal families and families with parental depression. *Child Development, 56,* 884–893.

Redican, W. K. (1982). An evolutionary perspective on human facial displays. In P. Ekman (Ed.), *Emotion in the human face* (pp.212–280). Cambridge: Cambridge University Press.

Rieder, C. & Cicchetti, D. (1989). An organizational perspective on cognitive control functioning and cognitive-affective balance in maltreated children. *Developmental Psychology, 25,* 482–493.

Roland, A. (1988). *In search of self in India and Japan.* Princeton, NJ: Princeton University Press.

Rosaldo, M. (1984). Toward an anthropology of self and feeling. In R. Shweder & R, LeVine (Eds.), *Culture theory: Essays on mind, self, and emotion,* (pp.137–157). New York: Cambridge University Press.

Rosenstein, D. & Oster, H. (1988). Differential facial responses to four basic tastes in newborns. *Child Development, 59,* 1555–1568.

Rozin, P., & Fallon, A. E. (1987). A perspective on disgust. *Psychological Review, 94,* 23–41.

Russell, J. A. & Ridgeway, D. (1983). Dimensions underlying children's emotion concepts. *Developmental Psychology, 19,* 795–804.

Sampson, E. E. (1988). The debate on individualism: Ingenious psychologies of the individual and their role in interpersonal and societal functioning. *American Psychologist, 43,* 15–22.

Schank, R. C., & Abelson, R. P. (1977). *Scripts, plans, goals, and understanding.* Hillsdale, NJ: Lawrence Erlbaum Associates.

Scheier, M. F., & Carver, C. S. (1982). Cognition, affect, and self-regulation. In M. S. Clark and S. T. Fiske (Eds.), *Affect and Cognition* (pp. 157–184). Hillsdale, NJ: Lawrence Erlbaum Associates.

Schneider-Rosen, K. & Cicchetti, D. (1991). Early self-knowledge and emotional development: Visual self-recognition and affective reactions to mirror self images in maltreated and non-maltreated toddlers. *Developmental Psychology. 27,* 471–478.

Seligman, M. E. P. (1975). *Helplessness: On depression, development, and death.* San Francisco: Freeman.

Shweder, R., & Bourne, E. (1982). Does the concept of person vary cross-culturally? In R. Shweder & R, LeVine (Eds.), *Culture theory: Essays on mind, self, and emotion,* (pp. 158–199). New York: Cambridge University Press.

Shweder, R., & LeVine, R. (Eds.) (1984). *Culture theory: Essays on mind, self, and emotion.* New York: Cambridge University Press.

Smith, L. B., & Sera, M. D. (1992). A developmental analysis of the polar structure of dimensions. *Cognitive Psychology, 24,* 99–142.

Snow, K. (1990). Building memories: The ontogeny of autobiography. In D. Cicchetti & M. Beeghly (Eds.), *The self in transition: Infancy to childhood,* (pp. 213–242). Chicago: University of Chicago Press.

Sroufe, L. A. (1989). Relationships, self, and individual adaptation. In A. J. Sameroff & R. N. Emde (Eds.). *Relationship disturbances in early development* (pp. 70–94). New York: Basic Books.

Sroufe, L. A. (1990). An organizational perspective on the self. In D. Cicchetti & M. Beeghly (Eds.), *The self in transition: Infancy to childhood* (pp. 281–307). Chicago: University of Chicago Press.

Sroufe, L. A., & Rutter, M. (1984). The domain of developmental psychopathology. *Child Development, 55,* 317–325.

Stechler, G. (1990). Psychoanalytic perspectives on self during the transitional period. In D. Cicchetti & M. Beeghly (Eds.), *The self in transition: Infancy to childhood* (pp. 17–33). Chicago: University of Chicago Press.

Stern, D. N. (1974). The goal and structure of mother-infant play. *Journal of the American Academy of Child Psychiatry, 13,* 402–421.

Stern, D. (1985). *The interpersonal world of the infant.* New York: Basic Books.

Strepansky, P. E. (1977). *A history of aggression in Freud.* New York: International Universities Press.

Thelen, E. (1990). Dynamical systems and the generation of individual differences. In J. Colombo & J. W. Fagan (Eds.), *Individual differences in infancy: Reliability, stability, and prediction* (pp.19–43). Hillsdale, NJ: Lawrence Erlbaum Associates.

Thelen, E. (1992). Development as a dynamic system. *Current Directions, 1,* 189–193.

Thompson, B., & Borrello, G. M. (1992). Different views of love: Deductive and inductive lines of inquiry. *Current Directions in Psychological Science, 1,* 154–156.

Tinbergen, N. (1951). *The study of instinct.* London: Oxford University Press.

Tompkins, S. S. (1962–3). *Affect, imagery, and consciousness, Vols. I & II.* New York: Springer.

Tronick, E. Z. (1989). Emotions and emotional communication in infants. *American Psychologist, 44,* 112–119.

Trzebinska, E. (1992). Development of the self in family interactions. *Pezeglad Psychologiczny,* 2, *12–21.*

Tulving, E. (1972). Episodic and semantic memory. In E. Tulving & W. Donaldson (Eds.), *Organization of memory.* New York: Academic Press.

Tulving, E. (1985). How many memory systems are there? *American Psychologist, 40,* 385–398.

Tversky, A., & Kahneman, D. (1982). Judgment under uncertainty: Heuristics and biases. In D. Kahneman & A. Tversky (Eds.), *Judgment under uncertainty: Heuristics and biases* (pp. 3–20). Cambridge, England: Cambridge University Press.

White, M., & Epston, D. (1990). *Narrative means to therapeutic ends.* New York: Norton.

Von Baeyer, H. C. (1992). Physika: Close the black boxes. *The Sciences.* July–August, 8–11.

Vygotskii, L. S. (1987). The collected works of L. S. Vygotskii. R. W. Rieber & A. S. Carlton (Eds.), translated by N. Minick. New York: Plenum Press.

Winnicott, D. W. (1958). *Collected papers.* New York: Basic Books.

Wolf, D. P. (1990). Being of several minds: Voices and version of the self in early childhood. In D. Cicchetti & M. Beeghly (Eds.), *The self in transition: Infancy to childhood* (pp. 183–212). Chicago: University of Chicago Press.

Zajonc, R. B.(1980). Feeling and thinking: Preferences need no inferences. *American Psychologist. 35,* 151–175.

Zajonc, R. B., Pietromonaco, P., Bargh, J. (1982). Independence and interaction of affect and cognition. In M. S. Clark and S. T. Fiske (Eds.), *Affect and Cognition* (pp. 211–227). Hillsdale, NJ: Lawrence Erlbaum Associates.

Zahn-Waxler, C. ,& Kochanska, (1990). The origins of guilt. In R. A. Thompson (Ed.), *Nebraska Symposium on motivation: Socio-emotional development* (pp.183–258). Lincoln, NE: University of Nebraska Press.

V Affective Splitting and Dissociation in Normal and Maltreated Children: Developmental Pathways for Self in Relationships

KURT W. FISCHER AND CATHERINE AYOUB

People organize their worlds in terms of positive and negative splits—good and bad, right and wrong, heaven and hell, friends and enemies, good guys and bad guys, virtue and sin. Research over the last century has shown consistently that in people's organization of concepts, emotions, perceptions of self and others, and most other things, this split defines the first, most fundamental dimension organizing human experience and conception, an evaluation dimension involving positive and negative or approach and avoidance (Mahler, Pine, & Bergman, 1975; Osgood, Suci, & Tannenbaum, 1957; Shaver, Schwartz, Kirson, & O'Connor, 1987; Stern, 1985; Sullivan, 1953; Wundt, 1905/1907).

Despite the importance of this dimension, scholars have largely neglected it in analyzing the forces shaping developmental pathways. Studies of emotional development have mostly focused on a particular emotion such as anxiety or love or a small set of basic emotions, but not on the dimension of positive and negative evaluation (Campos, Barrett, Lamb, Goldsmith, & Stenberg, 1983; Izard, 1977; Malatesta, 1988; Sroufe, 1979). We hypothesize that positive and

Note: This paper is based in part on presentations given at the Rochester Symposium on Developmental Psychopathology, October 1991, the meetings of the Society for Research in Child Development, March 1991, and the meetings of the Jean Piaget Society, May, 1992. Sources of support for the work reported include the MacArthur Foundation, Harvard University, and the Center for Advanced Study in the Behavioral Sciences. We thank Thomas Bidell, Joseph Campos, Nancy Cole, Donna Elmendorf, Jane Haltiwanger, Helen Hand, Susan Harter, Susie Lamborn, Donna Marold, Michael Mascolo, Sandra Pipp, Elaine Rotenberg, Phillip Shaver, Louise Silvern, and Michael Westerman for their general contributions to the work reported here. We especially thank Gil Noam, Rosemary Calverley, Rebecca Hencke, and Pamela Raya for their important contributions to our developmental analyses of maltreated children.

negative valence are fundamental organizers of development and that both normal development and psychopathology are centrally molded by positive and negative experiences.

Biases or constraints growing from positive and negative experiences organize action and thought from birth and thus shape development (Fischer, Shaver, & Carnochan, 1990). One of the most obvious ways that the evaluation dimension organizes behavior is affective splitting, in which a person separates two events, people, objects, or aspects of a situation into positive and negative, even though to another observer the things are neither truly separate nor simply positive and negative (Fischer & Pipp, 1984; Harter & Buddin, 1987). Examples of splitting from our observations illustrate how splitting occurs naturally in young children. A 2-year-old boy split his mother into good and bad. She had left him at his grandparents' for a few days so that mother and father could have a brief vacation. When she called him on the telephone, he spoke to her affectionately, but he also told her that there was a "bad Mommy" who had left him at his grandparents. A 4-year-old girl, asked if she can be happy and sad at the same time, split her emotions: "No way! I've only got one head." A 5-year-old boy split a social encounter as he described an interaction he had observed in which two children were simultaneously mean and nice to each other. He split the one interaction into two: "First, Jason was mean to Kyle. He hit him, and Kyle wouldn't play with him. Then a long time later, Jason and Kyle played together and were nice." Another 5-year-old portrayed the same interaction by simply dropping the nice part and acting out how the children were mean to each other.

These examples illustrate normal affective splitting in young children, but splitting is also important for development of psychopathology, and in cases of abuse and other trauma it can pervade an individual's personality organization. Recent work in the area of trauma and psychopathology supports a connection between the repeated trauma of abuse and a pervasive array of changes in thinking and emotion that produce serious disturbance (Cole & Putnam, 1992; Herman, 1992; Terr, 1991). Symptoms include basic fragmentations in a person's sense of self and malignant feelings of inner badness at the core of beliefs about self and world. The case of Marilyn van Derbur illustrates one type of fragmentation.

A young girl living in a proper middle class family, Marilyn was sexually abused by her father at night for a number of years during grade school and early adolescence (Van Derbur Atler, 1991). During this period she acted like a different person during the day and at night, splitting herself into a day child and a night child. Here is her description:

> In order to survive, I split into a day child, who giggled and smiled, and a night child, who lay awake in a fetal position, only to be pried apart by my father. Until I was 24, the day child had no conscious knowledge of the night child. During the day, no embarrassing or angry glances ever passed between my father and me . . . because I had no conscious knowledge of what he was doing to me.
>
> . . . The more degraded the night child became, the more the day child needed to excel . . . from skiing on the University of Colorado's ski team, to

> being a debutante, to graduating with Phi Beta Kappa Honors, to being named Miss America. I believed I was the happiest person who ever lived. I truly believed that.

The day child was bright and socially skilled, a good student with lots of friends. The night child was anxious and panicky, experiencing frequent night terrors and numbing. The abuse stopped when she went away to preparatory school, and she did not remember it for years. At age 18 she began to experience disturbing dreams and periods of sudden anxiety "for no reason," especially at night and on dates. At 24 years, she remembered the abuse and the night child and gradually brought together her split experiences.

Our developmental analysis of these kinds of splitting builds upon a broader framework, dynamic skills theory. In the course of the chapter we will describe key aspects of skills theory that explicate development of splitting in normal and maltreated children. More extensive elaborations of the theory are available elsewhere (Fischer, 1980; Fischer, Bullock, Rotenberg, & Raya, 1993; Fischer & Farrar, 1987; Fischer, et al., 1990). Within the skills framework, development involves a person's construction of progressively more complex control systems called skills. A skill is a property of not just the person but the person and situation together, because it is literally composed of both the person's activities and the context or situation in which the activities occur. Action and thought occur in situations composed of tasks, events, other people, and culture; and all these situational factors are part of the skill. Cognitive and emotional development flow together from these changing control systems. Emotions are more than internal experiences (feelings); they are adaptive reactions arising from the control systems: People evaluate how a situation relates to their goals and concerns, and they react emotionally based on that evaluation (Barrett & Campos, 1987; Frijda, 1986; Lazarus, 1991; Shaver, et al., 1987). These emotional reactions bias or constrain activity to certain action tendencies or scripts for the particular emotion. In this way they mold both immediate activity and long-term development, as when short-term anger produces immediate aggression and efforts to dominate, and recurrent, long-term anger produces emphasis on power, dominance, and assignment of blame.

Development moves through successively more complex levels of control systems (skills), thus producing more complex cognition, emotion, and psychopathology. Unlike traditional views of development, however, there is no simple progression up a uniform ladder of stages. Instead, skills develop through richly varied, diverse pathways, molded powerfully by emotions as well as many other dynamically interacting influences (Fischer, Knight, & Van Parys, 1993). Unlike traditional views of psychopathology, most mental illness does not involve either fixation at an early stage or regression to that stage. Instead, psychopathology develops increasing complexity with age or time, in a manner similar to more ordinary skills. The complexity creates new, more sophisticated skills that are usually adaptive in the person's particular world, where they are based in experience. Outside that world, these same skills can produce sophisticated forms of difficulty rather than straightforward adaptations (Fischer & Pipp, 1984; Holt, 1976; Noam, 1990; Silvern, 1984).

The Web of Development

People develop simultaneously along many strands, building a developmental web like that shown in Figure 1 (Bidell & Fischer, 1992). Each strand involves distinct control systems that progress to higher levels of complexity but are largely independent of the other strands. Dynamic skills theory provides tools for analyzing the complexity of control systems and thus predicting the sequence along a strand and comparing complexity across strands, as we will demonstrate later for several pathways. Many factors interact dynamically to affect what strands a person constructs and how he or she constructs each one. In the affective organization of social interaction, for example, strands commonly include nice interactions, mean interactions, and those that are both mean and nice. The forms of these strands vary with context too, so that for example mean interactions with adults take a different form from mean interactions with peers. One goal of this chapter is to describe several strands for development of psychopathology arising from maltreatment, especially repeated physical assault (physical abuse) or sexual exploitation (sexual abuse). These several strands provide examples of the diversity of development that we believe is commonplace in normality as well as psychopathology, although most prior cognitive developmental research has used methods that precluded the detection of such diversity in pathways (Case & Edelstein, 1993).

Within the weblike structure, there is an additional characteristic not specified in Figure 1: As people develop along each strand, their activities do not occupy one point or step on the strand but instead vary across a range (Brown & Reeve, 1987; Fischer, et al., 1993). That is, a person acts in ways that vary in complexity and so occupy a section of a strand, as illustrated in Table 1. In stories about mean social interactions, a 7-year-old girl tells or acts out stories that differ in complexity, varying across steps in a section of a strand. She does not tell all her stories at the same step or point on the strand. In one set of conditions, for example, she tells or acts out stories at Step 4 and all the lower steps in Table 1. There is presumably order in this variation, but until recently there has been little research to uncover the order.

One principle of order that we have found in the variation is what we call *developmental range,* defined by the difference between optimal and functional levels in Table 1. Both optimal and functional levels specify systematic limits on activities, but they differ in degree of contextual support, often controlled or provided by another person. When a child is trying to tell a mean story and an adult or skilled peer provides support for the child by explaining an appropriately high-level story, then the support helps the child to act at her *optimal level,* the upper limit on her performance under optimal conditions, such as Step 8 in Table 1. When the same child is trying to tell a mean story but has no such support, she acts at her *functional level,* the upper limit on her spontaneous performance, such as Step 4 in Table 1. A child's functional level is usually much lower than her optimal level. These limits are consistent and reliable for a particular domain. Also, optimal and functional levels show different growth curves. Functional levels typically show slow, continuous growth. Optimal lev-

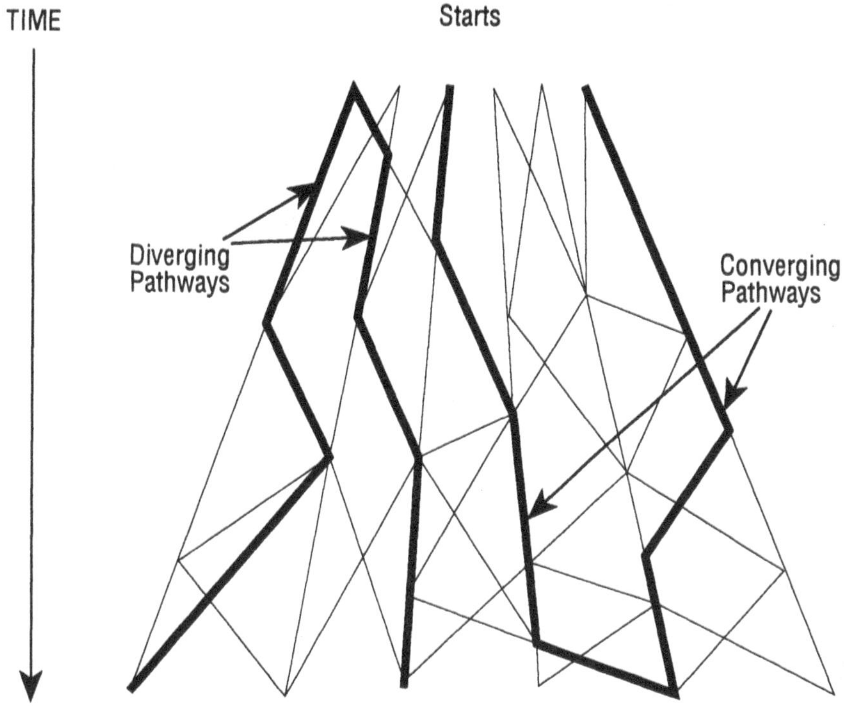

FIGURE 1 Web of Development

els, on the other hand, show consistent periods of discontinuity, sharp spurts in growth when a new type of skill structure is emerging. Steps where these discontinuities typically occur are labeled with numerals I to III in Table 1.

The Natural Fractionation of the Mind

As the many strands in the developmental web imply, the mind is naturally fractionated, with many distinct control systems that are not strongly connected with each other, not coordinated or integrated (Fischer & Pipp, 1984). Contrary to the assumptions of many models of the mind, including Piaget's (1957; 1975), people do not have integrated, fundamentally logical minds. Instead, we have many control systems that are naturally separate, although potentially we can develop coordination and integration of many of them.

Task and domain differences are an especially well documented source of fractionation, with hundreds of studies demonstrating that distinct tasks intended to measure the "same" ability produce different behaviors at different developmental levels. In the study of cognitive development, these findings are summed up in the conclusion that décalage (unevenness) is the rule in development (Biggs & Collis, 1982; Flavell, 1982). For example, many 7-year-olds

TABLE 1 Developmental Range of a 7-Year-Old

Level	Step	
I	1	
	2	
	3	
II	4	FUNCTIONAL LEVEL (low support)
	5	
	6	
	7	
III	8	OPTIMAL LEVEL (high support)
	9	

understand conservation of liquid amount—that when a liquid such as orange juice is poured into a container of a different shape or size, the amount of liquid remains the same. The same children asked about conservation of area, such as the amount of field covered by a set of farm buildings in varying locations, will not generalize the liquid conservation skill to this new task. The notion of conservation begins not as a general concept but as a particular one tied to the task and domain where it is learned. Consequently, there are separate developmental strands for conservation of liquid and conservation of area.

Many other factors produce separate developmental strands too, including context, emotion, and meaning, with the result that fractionation is inevitable and pervasive. Differences in context lead to separate strands. In the classroom, children learn one skill for addition, while in trading marbles on the playground, they learn a different skill for addition (Rogoff, 1990). Emotions produce distinct strands, as already illustrated for affective splitting. Even meaning leads to fractionation: When a child treats an event as an instance of one concept, such as conceiving of pouring a glass of orange juice in terms of conservation of amount of liquid, she will seldom integrate that event with a virtually identical one treated as an instance of another concept, such as pouring another glass of orange juice as a way to help a thirsty friend. These two instances can be related, but the coordination is not automatic and requires a specific effort.

Because of the pervasiveness of fractionation, people often do not even recognize elements that go together in the world. When we encounter a task that is complex or confusing for us, we simplify it by dropping out components or splitting it into separate tasks. The examples of affective splitting described earlier demonstrate this process. When a 2-year-old was upset with his mother, he split her into two separate mothers, one good and one bad. When two 5-year-olds attempted to explain a story in which people acted simultaneously nice and mean to each other, they showed different kinds of simplification and splitting. One child split the story into two separate pieces, one story about a nice interaction and a separate story about a mean one. The other child omitted the nice part of the story, portraying the interaction as simply mean.

Splitting is not limited to emotion. A process analogous to affective splitting occurs in many situations with no powerful positive and negative emotions when people separate related components of a task. In conservation of amount of liquid, for example, children split amount into two separate quantities—height and width (Piaget & Szeminska, 1941/1952). Sometimes they respond in terms of just height, sometimes in terms of just width, and sometimes they vacillate between the two.

Although splitting and other forms of fractionation are pervasive, they need not be permanent. People develop from fractionation *toward integration* in particular domains, constructing specific coordinations among previously separate skills. Coordination is one of the most important processes in development and the foundation for more complex, sophisticated control systems (Bidell & Fischer, 1994; Fischer & Rose, 1993b). Vacillation or co-occurrence of separate skills is often a sign of developmental progress, a step along the path to integration. When a child vacillates between two skills or shows them both in tandem, a process called shift of focus in skills theory, he or she is often in transition to a new coordination. Research from various laboratories shows that the capacity to activate two related skills in parallel or in alternation is often a sign of transition to a new understanding, a new coordination (Goldin-Meadow, Alibali, & Church, 1993; Gottlieb, Taylor, & Ruderman, 1977; Roberts, 1981). For example, splitting an integrated nice/mean story into two sequential stories, one about being nice and one about being mean, demonstrates the shift-of-focus capacity and indicates progress away from total splitting toward integration.

Passive and Active Splitting and Dissociation

Splitting is a special case of the more general category of dissociation, in which elements are separated even though according to some external criterion they should be coordinated. Affective splitting involves separation along the positive/negative evaluation dimension, or more generally between opposites. Dissociation refers to separation of elements along some dimension(s), including ones other than positive/negative evaluation. The natural fractionation of the mind means that splitting and other forms of dissociation are pervasive in human activity and experience.

In work on psychopathology, the terms *dissociation* and *splitting* are often used more narrowly to refer to motivated separation, such as dissociating a feeling from the thought where it originated, dissociating the self into multiple personalities, or splitting family and friends into good and bad people (Breuer & Freud, 1895/1955; Kernberg, 1976; Noam, Powers, Kilkenny, & Beedy, 1991; Putnam, 1989; Putnam, Helmers, & Trickett, in press). Clinical analyses, especially those based in Freud (Freud, 1917; Freud, 1923/1961), typically assume that dissociation and splitting are actively controlled, usually in some unconscious way. If a person does not connect two skills or experiences that the psychologist sees as related, then he or she is assumed to be striving to separate them through an unconscious motive. Yet if the mind is naturally fractionated, this assumption must be questioned: Splitting and dissociation occur normally, and they occur routinely simply because a person has not coordinated skills or experiences that are naturally separate (Feffer, 1982). Often they are not driven by any specific motive.

On the other hand, splitting and dissociation can be motivated. Motivated dissociation and splitting are like many of the other mental phenomena Freud postulated, such as unconscious processing of information and mental conflicts leading to slips of the tongue: They are special cases of more general characteristics that are not usually motivated (Marcel, 1983; Motley, 1985; Weiss, 1990).

Understanding the development of splitting and dissociation requires distinguishing between the frequent separation that comes from natural fractionation and the controlled separation in motivated dissociation and splitting. The reaction of 8-year-old Shirley to sexual abuse illustrates how dissociation can be motivated and controlled, as well as adaptive (Canadian Broadcasting Corporation, 1990). Shirley was repeatedly raped by her father in her bed in the basement of her home, and when she resisted his advances, he beat her up. To cope with being raped, she focused on a small hole in the wall above her bed, concentrating so intensely on the hole that she felt that she put herself into it. When she was in the hole, she dissociated her experience from the ongoing rape, and she could get through the trauma without major distress. One day when her mother was out shopping, her father raped her upstairs instead of in the basement. Without the normal context, especially the hole in the wall, she could not dissociate, and she began screaming and fighting her father. He became enraged and knocked her unconscious and then continued with the rape. This sort of situation in abuse and other kinds of trauma leads children to develop skills of dissociation (Cole & Putnam, 1992; Famularo, Kinscherff, Fenton, & Ayoub, in press; McCann & Pearlman, 1992; Terr, 1991; van der Kolk, 1987).

In this way, people can develop controlled dissociation and splitting, in addition to the natural, passive fractionation produced by tasks, contexts, emotions, meaning incompatibility, and other organizing influences. Dissociation and splitting thus vary along a dimension from active to passive (Fischer & Pipp, 1984). In *active dissociation*, people purposely (consciously or unconsciously) keep two experiences, activities, or characteristics separated. Some disorders, such as multiple personality, are founded in active dissociation. Many defense mechanisms are types of active dissociation, such as repression, where one part of the mind acts to keep a thought or feeling out of awareness of another part of the mind. Besides many cases described in the psychopathology literature, experimental research has clearly established that repression and other forms of active dissociation occur, not only in pathology but also normally, especially for hypnosis, dreaming, and religious spirit possession (Erdelyi, 1985; Foulkes, 1982; Hilgard, 1977; Mischel & Mischel, 1958; Orne, 1959; Vaillant, 1986).

Active dissociation is a developmental "accomplishment" when viewed from a dynamic skills perspective. *A person must create a coordination in order to actively dissociate*, coordinating several skills so as to keep at least two components separated. By 4 to 6 years of age, children first become able actively to dissociate a few components from one another, as when Shirley put herself in the hole in the wall in order to separate her experience from what was happening to her body during rape. With development, people can construct more and more complex and sophisticated types of dissociative coordination, separating multiple components in complex relations (Freud, 1936/1966; Haan, 1977; Noam, et al., 1991; Vaillant, 1977). We hypothesize that the strong forms of active dissociation that are often described in psychopathology first develop during adolescence, with the capacity to build complex abstract skills coordinating many components of action, thought, and feeling.

In this chapter, we will describe three developmental pathways that vary along the dimension from passive to active dissociation. *Normal affective splitting* is based primarily in passive dissociation, developing from a state of uncontrolled splitting induced by an emotional bias: Older children and adults can construct skills to coordinate across the affective split, but the splitting tendency remains throughout life. It can be limited but not eliminated. In contrast, people who develop *multiple personality* use a strong form of active dissociation, *co-conscious dissociation,* in which co-conscious mental agents, usually called "personalities," are kept separate from each other and can act upon each other. These active dissociations seem to arise from severe trauma, such as repeated sexual abuse, which leads children to learn dissociative skills for coping. Active and passive dissociation are interwoven in situations of *hidden family violence,* where parents rigidly separate the physically and emotionally abusive private world of the home from the well behaved public world of school, church, and community. In this situation, children develop *isolating dissociation,* in which development moves along two dissociated pathways, one for public, "good" self in more conventional and distant interactions and a second for private, "bad" self in intimate interactions within the family. This dissociation is originally based on environmentally supported, passive dissociations tied to children's experiences in public and private contexts. With time, it develops toward more active dissociation, in which older children and adults seek to keep their private and public worlds completely separated.

Development of Normal Affective Splitting

Normal affective splitting arises from the natural fractionation induced by positive and negative emotions, and it moves through a developmental course toward integration as children become able to see beyond the immediate limitations of their emotional biases. At the same time, developmental pathways for splitting vary as a function of emotional experience, with different experiences biasing development in different directions.

Positive versus Negative

Affective splitting is pervasive in human activity and experience because emotions are such potent forces for fractionation, acting as biases or constraints

TABLE 2 Prototypic Script for Adult Anger

Antecedents: Illegitimate Interruption, Violation, or Harm
Something or someone violates the person's wishes or expectations, obstructs or interferes with the person's freedom of movement or goal-attainment, hurts or insults the person, ignores or demeans the person's status.
This interference or harm is perceived as illegitimate, as something that should not happen and should not be allowed to happen.

Responses: Vigorous Protest, Attack, Retaliation
The person becomes energized, and mentally and behaviorally organized, to protest or fight or retaliate, thereby restoring justice, freedom of movement or passage, proper recognition, etc.
The person looks and sounds angry (e.g., face red, brows furled, voice raised) and moves in an emphatic, threatening, or exaggerated way.
The person is preoccupied with the anger-inducing situation and repeatedly insists that he or she is right, deserves better treatment, etc.

Self-Control Procedures: Suppression and Redefinition
The person may try to suppress or hide the anger or redefine or remove the situation so that anger is no longer called for.

Fischer et al. (1990); simplified version of results reported by Shaver et al. (1987)

that organize action and thought into particular social-emotional scripts (Fischer, et al., 1990; Lazarus, 1991; Malatesta, 1988; Shaver, et al., 1987). Under the influence of one emotion, such as anger, a person naturally follows a given script, perceiving events as unfair or illegitimate, becoming energized, and tending toward aggression or verbal attack, as shown in Table 2, which portrays a prototypical anger sequence for interactions of self and other. Under the influence of another emotion, such as joy, the person naturally follows a different script, interpreting events optimistically, becoming energized, and relishing other people's company, as in Table 3. There are, of course, many emotion scripts besides anger and joy, and among them all, the bias toward fractionation is especially potent when one script is negative and the other positive. Moving beyond the split requires construction of a higher order skill to coordinate them.

In research to investigate the development of positive and negative splitting in interactions, we have used new, sensitive research methods for analyzing how activities order developmentally and how emotions constrain these orderings. The studies involved children's stories, actions, and explanations about positive/negative splits, such as nice/mean and good/bad interactions, as well as adolescents' characterizations of themselves in close relationships as depicted in interviews (Calverley, 1993; Elmendorf, 1992; Fischer & Elmendorf, 1986; Fischer, Hand, Watson, Van Parys, & Tucker, 1984b; Harter & Buddin, 1987; Hencke, 1991; Kennedy, 1991; Raya, 1993). With new scaling techniques for detecting developmental webs (Fischer & Rose, 1993a) and with both cross-sectional and longitudinal data, these studies have produced maps of develop-

TABLE 3 Prototypic Script for Adult Joy

Antecedents: Desirable Outcome, Achievement, Affection, Esteem
The person receives or attains something wished or strived for; receives esteem, praise, or affection (is accepted, liked, loved); has surprisingly good fortune or receives a benefit that exceeds expectations.

Responses: Smiling, Laughing, Communicating Good Feelings, Positive Outlook
The person smiles, laughs, is warm and sociable, communicates and shares the good news and good feelings, is optimistic and less vulnerable to worry, feels and acts energized or excited, jumps up and down, hugs others, is kind and generous toward others.

Self-Control Procedures: Not a Salient Issue
(Although suppression of joy in the interest of decorum or avoidance of envy is possible, such self-control efforts are not prototypical.)

Fischer et al. (1990); simplified version of results reported by Shaver et al. (1987).

mental pathways for positive and negative interactions from 1 to 20 years of age. Subjects have included volunteer middle class participants and maltreated children and adolescents.

A number of the studies have involved the development of mean and nice interactions, which are closely related to the scripts for anger and joy. Many children followed the model developmental pathway (web) diagrammed in Figure 2, which shows developmental orderings based on complexity and positiive/negative splitting for a series of stories for mean and/or nice interactions. The tasks on the left of the web involve nice interactions, those on the right involve mean interactions, and those in the middle coordinate nice and mean. Table 4 provides definitions and examples of the tasks in Figure 2, as well as additional tasks tested in the research. (The tasks in Table 4 and Figure 2 also represent the steps shown earlier in Table 1.)

Development of affective splitting starts with a basic separation of positive and negative, as shown at the top of Figure 2, where nice and mean are independent (no developmental ordering and no coordination). Throughout the web, positive and negative strands continue to be partly independent.

Levels of Coordination of Positive and Negative

As children build more complex control systems, they move gradually toward integration across the positive and negative split. In general, children start with the developmentally primitive state of splitting into mean and nice or good and bad, and they move gradually toward integrating these opposite emotional valences. The integrations range from a primitive coordination by shifting early in the sequence (Task 3) to a partial integration (Tasks 4 and 7) and finally a strong integration (Tasks 8 and beyond).

The main developmental levels in this progression are shown in Table 5 for the period from 2 years to early adulthood for nice-mean stories. (Earlier levels

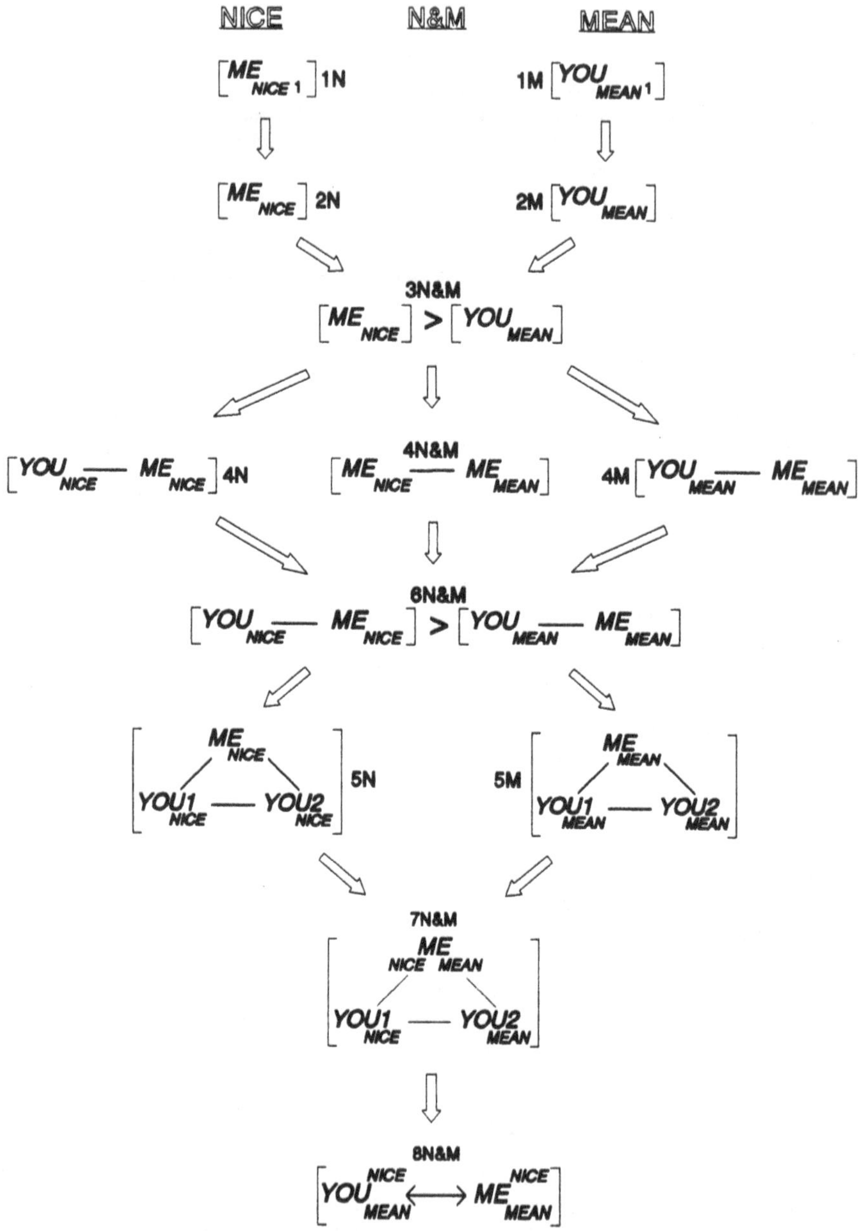

FIGURE 2 Developmental Sequence of Mean and Nice Social Interactions Based on Complexity and No Affective Bias

Note: Conventions for the skill formulas are described in Table 5. In Tasks 1 and 2, the number 1 after the words ***NICE*** or ***MEAN*** indicates that there is only one action or characteristic in the category—one instance of nice or mean behavior. The absence of any number indicates that the category includes multiple, flexible actions or characteristics.

TABLE 4 Tasks for Assessing Development of Understanding Mean and Nice Social Interactions

Level	Task[1]	Skill	Examples
Rp1: Single Representations	1 N; M	*Active agent*: A person performs at least one action fitting a social-interaction category of mean or nice.	Child pretends that one doll hits another doll ("mean") or gives another doll candy ("nice").
	2 N; M	*Behavioral category*: A person performs at least two actions fitting an interaction category of mean or nice.	Child has one doll act mean to another doll, hitting it and saying, "I don't like you." The second doll can be passive.
	3 N & M	*Shifting behavioral categories*: One person performs at least two actions fitting the category nice, as in Task 2, and then a second person performs at least two actions fitting the category mean.	Child has one doll act nice to a second doll, giving it candy and saying, "Let's play." A third doll enters and acts mean to the second one, hitting it and saying, "Give me your ball!" In both cases, the second doll can be passive.
Rp2: Representational Mappings	4 N; M	*One-dimensional social influence*: The mean actions of one person produce reciprocal mean actions in a second person. The same contingency can occur for nice actions.	Child has one doll say mean things and hit another doll, who responds by hitting and expressing dislike for the first one. The second one's action is clearly produced by the first one's action.
	4 N & M	*Combination of opposite categories in a single person*: One person performs actions fitting two specified opposing categories, such as nice and mean.	Child has one doll act nice to a second doll, saying "Let's be friends," but at the same time, the first doll shoves the second and takes away his blocks, saying that he wants to build something for the second one. The second doll can be passive throughout.

Table 4 Continued

Level	Task[1]	Skill	Examples
	5 N; M	*One-dimensional social influence with three characters behaving in similar ways*: Same as Task 4 N or 4 M, but with three people interacting reciprocally in a mean way (or alternatively, in a nice way).	With three dolls, child has one tease the others, while a second one hits the others. The third doll rejects both of the first because they are mean.
	6 N & M	*Shifting one-dimensional social influence*: The nice actions of one person produce reciprocal nice actions in a second person. Then, in a separate story, the mean actions of a third person produce reciprocal mean actions in the second person. (Or a reciprocal mean interaction can occur first, and then a reciprocal nice interaction).	With three dolls, child has one act friendly to a second one, who responds nicely. Then, a third doll hits the second one, who responds meanly.
	7 N & M	*One-dimensional social influence with three characters behaving in opposite ways*: The nice actions of one person and the mean actions of a second person produce reciprocal nice and mean actions in the third person.	With three dolls, child has one act friendly to a second, while a third one hits the second. The second doll responds nicely to the first doll and meanly to the third.
Rp3: Representational Systems	8 N & M	*Two-dimensional social influence*: Two people interact in ways fitting opposite categories, such that the first one acts both nice and mean, and the second one responds with reciprocal actions in the same categories.	Child has one doll initiate friendship with a second doll but in a mean way. The second one, confused about the discrepancy, declines the friendship because of the meanness. The first then apologizes and makes another friendly gesture, to which the second one responds positively.

	9 N & M	*Two-dimensional social influence with three characters*: Same as Task 8 but with three people interacting reciprocally according to opposite categories.	With three dolls, child has one doll act friendly to a second one, while a third initiates play in a mean way. The second doll acts friendly to the first one and rejects the third, pointing out the the latter's meaness. The third then apologizes for being mean, while the first does something new that is mean. The second doll accepts the third one's apology and rejects the first one, pointing out the change in his or her action.
Rp4/A1: Systems of Representational Systems, Which Are Single Abstractions	10 N & M	*Single abstraction integrating opposite actions*: Two instances of interactions involving opposite actions take place as in Task 8, and the relations between the two interactions are explained in terms of some general abstraction, such as that intentions matter more actions.	With three characters, child has one act friendly to a second, while a third initiates play in a mean way. The second character responds to each accordingly, but then learns that the nice one had mean intentions while the mean one had nice intentions. The second character then changes his or her action to each of the others to match their intentions and explains that he or she cares more about people's intentions than their actions.
	11 N & M	*Shifting abstractions, each integrating opposite actions*: First, two instances of interactions involving opposite actions are explained in terms of an abstraction such as intention (as in Task 10). Then two other instances of interactions involving opposite actions are explained in terms of a different abstraction, such as responsibility. What matters is whether people take responsibility for the harm they do.	First, child performs a story like that in Task 10. Then child shifts to a second different story, such as the following: With three characters, child has two of them act mean to a third. The first one takes responsibility for the action by admitting his or her blame and accepting the consequences. The second one takes no such responsibility. The third one forgives the one who took responsibility and refuses to forgive the one who did not take responsibility, because she cares about whether people take responsibility for the harm they do.

TABLE 4 Continued

Level	Task[1]	Skill	Examples
A2: Abstract Mappings	12 N & M	*Relation of two abstractions integrating opposite actions*: Two instances of interactions involving opposite actions are explained in terms of the relation of two abstractions, such as intention and responsibility: People who have a deceitful intention can be forgiven if they take responsibility in a way that undoes the deceit.	With three dolls, child has two of them act nice on the surface to a third, both with the intention of deceiving him into doing their homework. When the deceit is discovered by the third character, the first one takes responsibility for his or her deceit by admitting the intention and thus re-establishing his or her honesty. But the second one does not show such responsibility. The third character forgives the first, but not the second, because he or she cares about whether people take responsibility for deceitful intentions and undo the deceit.

Note: The designations for skill level follow the standard forms from dynamic skills theory (Fischer & Farrar, 1987).

[1]The letters following the number indicate different versions of the task: N for a task about nice interactions, M for one about mean interactions, and N & M for one about both nice and mean interactions.

are described elsewhere; see Fischer and Hogan, 1989.) Each level produces a qualitatively new type of skill for controlling nice and mean interactions, marked by a period of discontinuities (abrupt changes) in activity under optimal conditions (Fischer & Farrar, 1987). Although there are no general skills allowing a level to be instantly applied broadly, the levels do apply to children's movement along any strand in the developmental web as they construct successive skills in a context or domain. The steps between levels are constructed by microdevelopmental transformation rules for building skills within a level, as illustrated by the majority of steps in Figure 2. In addition, the levels themselves show a higher order, called tiers, in which they cycle through structures from single sets to mappings to systems to systems of systems, which start a new tier. This structure is evident in the representational and abstract tiers in Table 5.

The general pattern of progressive coordination with development is evident in the diagrams in Table 5, with each level showing a new type of relation of component skills. Because skills progress through the levels in each domain, development in any domain can be predicted and analyzed in terms of skill structures like those in Table 5. We will illustrate the levels and tiers for coordination across an affective split, and later we will describe other pathways that show levels for types of dissociation arising from maltreatment.

Early in the nice/mean pathway, 2- and 3-year-old children organize behavior in terms of single concrete representations for *agents*, people or animate objects that carry out concrete actions and have concrete characteristics (Level Rp1, Tasks 1 to 3). At this level, splitting is pervasive. Children represent a doll or person doing nice things, as in $\boldsymbol{ME_{NICE}}$, or separately they represent a doll or person doing mean things, as in $\boldsymbol{YOU_{MEAN}}$. At this level there is no real coordination of nice and mean, but at best sequential co-occurrence, first one representation and then the other (Task 3), which is called shift of focus in dynamic skills theory:

$$[\boldsymbol{ME_{NICE}}] > [\boldsymbol{YOU_{MEAN}}] \quad (1)$$

Most 2- and 3-year-olds can do no better than this type of juxtaposition, which involves elementary splitting of me and you. They also can shift between positive and negative representations of one person, including themselves:

$$[\boldsymbol{ME_{MEAN}}] > [\boldsymbol{ME_{NICE}}] \quad (2)$$

Because of the phenomena of developmental range (Table 1) this level continues to be prominent for several more years, at least until age 5 or 6. An example is the 4-year-old girl who said that she could not be happy and sad at the same time: "No way! I've only got one head."

Gradually, children build more complex control systems that integrate components, including positive and negative, in higher level skills. At about age 4, representational mappings emerge, in which children coordinate a few representations in a single skill (Level Rp2, Tasks 4 to 7). At this point, most coordinations maintain splitting, coordinating components that have the same valence. For example, they relate $\boldsymbol{YOU_{MEAN}}$ with $\boldsymbol{ME_{MEAN}}$ to produce an un-

Table 5 Levels of Skill Development

Level	Tier[1]: Representational	Tier[1]: Abstract	Examples of Skills	Age[2]
S4/Rp1: Single Representations[3]	$[YOU_{MEAN}]^{OR} [ME_{NICE}]$		**Relations of sensorimotor action systems to produce concrete representations of objects, people (agents), or events:** Child pretends that doll is hitting someone. Child says, "Doll mean."	18–24 mos.
Rp2: Representational Mappings	$[YOU_{MEAN} — ME_{MEAN}]$		**Simple relations of representations:** Child makes one doll's mean actions produce reciprocal mean actions in the other doll. Child makes two dolls act as Mom and Dad in parental roles. Child understands that self knows a secret and the teacher does not know it.	3.5–4.5 yr
Rp3: Representational Systems	$\left[YOU^{NICE}_{MEAN} \leftrightarrow ME^{NICE}_{MEAN}\right]$		**Complex relations of subsets of representations:** Child makes two dolls interact in reciprocally nice and mean ways. Child makes two dolls act as Mom and Dad as well as doctor and teacher simultaneously (two reciprocal roles). Child understands that to prevent teacher from learning a secret, he or she must hide signs of it in own actions.	6–7

Level	Formula	Description	Age
Single Abstractions	$\begin{bmatrix} YOU1_{MEAN} \leftrightarrow ME_{MEAN} \\ \Updownarrow \\ YOU2^{NICE}_{MEAN} \leftrightarrow ME^{NICE}_{MEAN} \end{bmatrix}$	**tems to produce abstractions (intangible concepts) about objects, events, or people (personalties):** Person explains that intentions matter more than actions: In dealing with others, intention is more important than action, so that positive intention is not only better than negative intention but also overrides negative action. Person sees Dad as having general personality characteristics, such as conformity, emotionality, or secretiveness.	
A2: Abstract Mappings	$[INTE_{NEG} — RESP_{POS}]$	**Simple relations of abstractions:** Person relates intention to responsibility, indicating how a particular intention such as deceit behind a harmful act determines the responsibility for remedying the harm. Person sees a personality characteristic of Dad and a characteristic of Mom as complementary (or as incompatible). Similar for self and friend.	14–16
A3: Abstract Systems	$\begin{bmatrix} INTE^{DECEIT}_{HARM} \leftrightarrow RESP^{FLAW}_{HELP} \end{bmatrix}$	**Complex relations of subsets of abstractions:** When harm is inflicted on someone, two types of intention (deceit and unintentional harm) are related to two types of responsibility (dealing with the flaw in one's character and helping the person harmed) so that one's specific intention determines the nature of one's responsibility.	18–20

Table 5 Continued

Level	Tier[1]		Examples of Skills	Age[2]
	Representational	Abstract		
			Person sees several personality characteristics of Mom and Dad as complementary (or as incompatible), defining their special relationship. Similar for Self with friend or lover.	
A4: Systems of Abstract Systems: Principles[4]		$\begin{bmatrix} \text{INTE } A^{DECEIT}_{HARM} & \leftrightarrow & \text{RESP } A^{FLAW}_{HELP} \\ & \Updownarrow & \\ \text{INTE } B^{R}_{S} & \leftrightarrow & \text{RESP } B^{R}_{S} \end{bmatrix}$	**General principles for integrating systems of abstractions**: Person understands moral principle of justice, integrating several types of relations between intention and responsibility. Person uses a general principle to integrate characteristics of Mom's and Dad's relationship as it changes across situations or over time. Similar for Self with friend or lover.	23–25

[1]The specific formulas shown are for the first example at each level, which involves nice and mean interactions. Formulas for the other examples at each level follow the same general format.

[2]Ages given are modal ages at which a level first appears based on research with middle-class American or European children. They may differ across cultures and other social groups.

[3]Representations grow from coordinations of sensorimotor systems, but for simplicity that relation has been omitted from this table.

[4]The skill structure shown for Level A4 is a system of abstract systems, which is also a principle. The principle that emerges from this structure could be designated by a separate structure, such as P, but because there is no evidence for later levels beyond A4, we have not included the separate structure for P.

Note: In skill structures, each word or letter denotes a skill component, with each large word or letter designating a main component (set) and each subscript or superscript designating a subset of the main component. Italics designate representations, and outline letters designate abstractions. Lines connecting sets designate relations forming a mapping, single-line arrows designate relations forming a system, and double-line arrows designate relations forming a system of systems. Examples of additional representational skills and their components are elaborated in Table 4 and Figure 2.

derstanding of negative social influence or contingency—I will be mean to you because you were mean to me (Task 4M):

$$[\boldsymbol{YOU_{MEAN}} \overline{\qquad} \boldsymbol{ME_{MEAN}}] \tag{3}$$

Or they can construct a similar skill for nice contingency—I will be nice to you because you were nice to me (Task 4N):

$$[\boldsymbol{YOU_{NICE}} \overline{\qquad} \boldsymbol{ME_{NICE}}] \tag{4}$$

Real integration begins with a few mappings coordinating opposite-valence components for the same person or context. For example, a 4-year-old girl relates $\boldsymbol{ME_{NICE}}$ with $\boldsymbol{ME_{MEAN}}$ to understand that she can be nice and mean at the same time (Task 4 N&M):

$$[\boldsymbol{ME_{NICE}} \overline{\qquad} \boldsymbol{ME_{MEAN}}] \tag{5}$$

Similarly, 4-year-old Seth explained to his father one day, "You know, Daddy, I'm mostly happy, but right here [pointing to a place on his head] I'm a little bit sad." This coordination of opposite emotions occurred several years earlier than reported in most other research (Donaldson & Westerman, 1986; Harris, 1985; Harter & Buddin, 1987; Stein & Levine, 1989). Assessments in those studies have used complex tasks rather than the very simple tasks that we have administered, and in addition, the studies usually have not included high-support assessment conditions to elicit optimal-level performance (Fischer, et al., 1993; Fischer, et al., 1984b; Lamborn, Fischer, & Pipp, 1994).

At 6 or 7 years, integration becomes more powerful with the development of representational systems, control systems relating multiple representations in a single skill (Level Rp3, Tasks 8 and 9). Children coordinate two mappings to produce a skill where two or more people interacting can both show related positive and negative activities, as in two-dimensional social influence—I will be nice to you because you were nice to me and at the same time mean to you because you were mean to me:

$$[\boldsymbol{YOU^{NICE}_{MEAN}} \leftrightarrow \boldsymbol{ME^{NICE}_{MEAN}}] \tag{6}$$

By 9 or 10 years, as these skills are gradually consolidated and made routine, children can commonly integrate across an affective split, which is why most research finds evidence for integration by this age. On the other hand, when children have strong positive or negative feelings, they still show splitting most of the time, using skills that maintain the split instead of those that integrate across it.

According to dynamic skills theory, development moves not only through levels but also through large-scale reorganizations called tiers, at which new combinations of components are consolidated to produce a new kind of unit or chunk. A new tier emerges at 10 or 12 years, when children coordinate their skills in a new way that moves them from representations to abstractions. They coordinate several representational systems to form a system of systems, which in its consolidated form is a single abstraction, simultaneously Level Rp4 and Level A1 (Task 10 in Table 4). In Table 5, the coordination of representational systems is diagrammed in the column for representations, and the abstraction emerging from that coordination is indicated in the column for abstractions.

For example, to coordinate several systems for combining positive and negative in social interactions, an adolescent constructs an abstraction such as intentionality or responsibility (Fischer, Hand, & Russell, 1984). For positive intentionality, a 12-year-old girl evaluates how two other people have interacted with her, indicating that whether each of them actually harmed her (were mean) is less important than whether they intended to be helpful or nice: Intentions matter more than actions.

$$\begin{bmatrix} YOU1\,{}^{NICE}_{MEAN} \leftrightarrow ME^{NICE}_{MEAN} \\ \Updownarrow \\ YOU2\,{}^{NICE}_{MEAN} \leftrightarrow ME^{NICE}_{MEAN} \end{bmatrix} = [\mathbb{INTE}_{POS}] \qquad \text{(7 and 8)}$$

For negative responsibility, a girl evaluates how two people have taken responsibility for problems they cause for other people, coordinating the two interactions so as to judge negatively the one who did not take responsibility. The coordination of two systems for interactions thus results in a new abstraction for negative responsibility:

$$[\mathbb{RESP}_{NEG}] \qquad \text{(9)}$$

In both of these cases, the abstraction moves beyond the specifics of representing concrete actions to the less tangible generalities of abstract characterizations of the "real" meaning underlying actions. Put simply, adolescents move *from conceiving people as agents to conceiving them as personalities.*

The emergence of abstractions provides the potential for new, more powerful and less concrete types of evaluation, including sophisticated splitting. The intentionality example shows how with single abstractions the positive/negative dimension continues to organize people's actions, producing more refined splitting and coordination of positive and negative. Different nice and mean aspects of actions are compared, and the ultimate evaluation of the person is made in terms of the aspect judged to be more important—who was truly nice and who was truly mean. In this way, the new capacity for abstraction produces a new kind of splitting, with nice versus mean or good versus bad replaced by less tangible splits, such as benevolent versus malevolent or intended good versus intended evil. The limitations of early levels of abstraction are similar in many ways to those of early levels of representation: Young adolescents cannot yet coordinate multiple abstractions just as young preschool children cannot yet coordinate multiple representations. Adolescents are therefore prone to affective splitting of abstractions, as in shifting between treating someone with a negative intention as "really" bad or malevolent and treating someone with a positive intention as "really" good or benevolent:

$$[\mathrm{INTE}_{\mathrm{NEG}}] > [\mathrm{INTE}_{\mathrm{POS}}] \tag{10}$$

Abstractions develop in many different domains, in which children move from representing things in terms of their concrete characteristics to conceiving them in less tangible terms based on more subtle properties—abstractions. In personality, adolescents move from construing people as concrete agents to conceiving them as personalities, with complex, hidden or inferred characteristics, such as conformity, inconsistency, emotionality, conservatism, partnership, secretiveness (Harter, 1983; Kennedy, 1991; Lamborn, et al., 1994; Nucci, 1993; Rosenberg, 1979; Selman & Schultz, 1990). Even the concept of personality itself requires an abstract conception of a person. Other domains where the development of abstractions have been described include law, morality, mathematics, and epistemology (Adelson, Green, & O'Neil, 1969; Colby, Kohlberg, Gibbs, & Lieberman, 1983; Fischer, et al., 1984a; Kitchener, Lynch, Fischer, & Wood, 1993). Later in the chapter, we will show some of the shapes that abstractions take in the development of active dissociation.

Adolescents develop abstract mappings at about age 15, in which they coordinate two single abstractions in a single skill (Level A2, Task 12). In the example in Tables 4 and 5, negative intentionality, is coordinated with positive responsibility, to produce a judgment that a negative intention can be undone by taking positive responsibility for the bad intention:

$$[\mathrm{INTE}_{\mathrm{NEG}} \text{ — } \mathrm{RESP}_{\mathrm{POS}}] \tag{11}$$

A skill example that is especially important in social-emotional development is coordinating one personality conception or identity with another, as people often do in close relationships. Two adolescent best friends or romantic partners will spend many hours getting to know each other so that they can each map some part of their two personalities together. For example, 16-year-old high school students Paul and Elaine met in their church's youth group and became good friends, spending many hours talking about their religious beliefs and how they bring religion into their everyday lives. They found important differences in the specific activities they did but a common concern with altruism—helping less fortunate people in their community, each in an arena where they had special interests. Paul volunteered to help serve dinner to the homeless once every week, while Elaine preferred being a Big Sister to a younger girl from a poor family. Their shared understanding involved a mapping of their conceptions of their two personal altruistic commitments:

$$[\mathrm{ELAINE}_{\mathrm{ALTR'M\ E}} \text{ — } \mathrm{PAUL}_{\mathrm{ALTR'M\ P}}] \tag{12}$$

Similarly, adolescents use mappings to make other personality comparisons. They analyze how some personality characteristics of their parents are complementary (or perhaps incompatible). They apply these analytic skills to themselves, comparing and evaluating their own internal personality characteristics. With this capacity to compare comes an emotional consequence—an upsurge in perceived conflicts in their own personalities as well as conflicts with their parents (Harter & Monsour, 1992; Kennedy, 1991; Lamborn, 1986).

At approximately 20 years, young adults develop abstract systems, in which they coordinate several abstract mappings to form a system combining multiple abstractions in a single skill. For example, they can relate several types of intention and responsibility to each other simultaneously, specifying how one type of intention requires taking responsibility in one way while another type of intention requires taking responsibility in a different way:

$$\left[\mathrm{INTE}_{\mathrm{HARM}}^{\mathrm{DECEIT}} \leftrightarrow \mathrm{RESP}_{\mathrm{HELP}}^{\mathrm{FLAW}} \right] \tag{13}$$

In social relationships, two friends or lovers can coordinate several aspects of each other's personalities or identities in a single skill, relating for example professional and parental identities of both partners. Paul and Elaine continued their relationship as well as their religious commitments, and by age 21 they had fallen in love and built mutual understandings about how their individual conceptions of their future professions and parenting shared their altruistic commitment:

$$\left[\mathrm{ELAINE}_{\mathrm{PROF'N\ E}}^{\mathrm{PARENT\ E}} \overset{\mathrm{altr'm}}{\leftrightarrow} \mathrm{PAUL}_{\mathrm{PROF'N\ P}}^{\mathrm{PARENT\ P}} \right] \tag{14}$$

Or a person can analyze how several characteristics of his or her parents fit together to define their special relationship.

Finally, the highest documented level of skill development emerges at about age 25 with the development of systems of abstract systems, which are principles (Level A4). Since we first postulated this level, several studies have supported its existence (Fischer, Kenny, & Pipp, 1990; Kitchener, et al., 1993). By their mid-20s, many people develop coordinations of diverse perspectives about knowledge through the principle of reflective judgment. Some people develop coordinations of diverse moral interests through the principle of justice (Colby, et al., 1983), which can involve relations between different types of intention and responsibility:

$$\begin{bmatrix} \mathrm{INTE\ A}_{\mathrm{HARM}}^{\mathrm{DECEIT}} & \leftrightarrow & \mathrm{RESP\ A}_{\mathrm{HELP}}^{\mathrm{FLAW}} \\ & \updownarrow & \\ \mathrm{INTE\ B}_{\mathrm{S}}^{\mathrm{R}} & \leftrightarrow & \mathrm{RESP\ B}_{\mathrm{S}}^{\mathrm{R}} \end{bmatrix} \tag{15}$$

In close relationships, a person can explicate changes in the relationship over time or situation, understanding how at different times it has involved distinct but related connections between the partners' personal characteristics.

Note that even with the great complexity and sophistication of this highest stage, the evaluative dimension behind splitting continues to potently organize action and thought. Evaluations about what is right or wrong, good or bad, healthy or sick pervade human activity at every level.

In summary, splitting of positive and negative emotions is a powerful force in development. Positive and negative pathways are partly independent, and as children advance cognitively, they usually became capable of coordinating positive and negative under progressively more circumstances. Splitting does not disappear suddenly in development, but it comes and goes as factors such as contextual support and emotional state push an individual up or down a developmental sequence (strand). While splitting may become less common with development, it remains prevalent even in adults, especially when they are emotional or when they have little contextual support for integration across a split.

Diversity in Normal Development of Splitting

The developmental web in Figure 2, complex as it is, is only one of the pathways for normal splitting. There is great diversity in development both between and within individuals. That is, different children show different pathways in the same assessment situation, and a given child shows different pathways with variations in context or emotional state.

One source of variation is degree of social-contextual support for integration of positive and negative, which causes a child to move up or down in her developmental range in a matter of minutes. As a result, splitting comes and goes in the same child. When the immediate context provides social priming for, say, a story integrating mean and nice behavior, a 7-year-old girl can control a high-level skill integrating mean and nice, as in Tasks 8 or 9. A few minutes later, without such social-contextual support, the same girl typically shows splitting, as in Task 4 (N or M version). In this kind of variation, the general shape of the web may remain the same, but the child's location in the web varies with context.

Webs of different shapes are produced by variations in emotional state. Anger facilitates control of complex mean interactions, and happiness facilitates control of complex nice ones. Each emotion evokes a preemptive social script that biases the person toward a certain kind of interaction during the emotion, including a certain interpretation of other people's behavior. An anger script biases the individual toward taking offense at another person's actions, and therefore toward seeing someone else as mean and in turn acting mean. On the other hand, a joy script produces the opposite effect, a bias toward the positive, imcluding a tendency to interpret actions as nice and in turn to act nice.

Children who are shy or behaviorally inhibited (as Kagan, 1989, calls them) show such a bias toward the positive in the mean and nice stories. In an ongoing longitudinal study of inhibited and outgoing children, highly inhibited children have shown a bias toward nice and an avoidance of mean, especially when the stories involved a self character acting mean (Hencke & Raya, 1993; Hencke, 1991). This avoidance occurred even when the children were specifically asked to imitate a story about mean interaction. It was evident both in the children's emotional reactions and in their relatively slow development of understanding of mean stories (including those integrating mean and nice). The delay was specific to negative stories and was not present in other developomental measures. In other words, shyness seemed to lead to increased affective splitting, with a predominance of the positive, especially in representing the self. In terms of developmental pathway, the shy children showed a shift in the web in Figure 2 that favored the positive (left) and delayed the negative (right). Figure 3 gives our best estimate of the shifted developmental pathway that these shy children show. The shift is predicted to be especially evident for representations of self, where negative evaluations are rigidly shunned; this bias in self development may relate to what Block (1980) has called ego overcontrol.

Indeed, there are probably few individual children who exhibit the developmental balance between positive and negative represented in Figure 2, which shows no differences between relative positions and orderings for positive and negative. Figure 2 represents the form development would take if children were influenced by only splitting and task complexity, with no general bias toward positive or negative. Many studies contradict this assumption, suggesting that most children evidence a general bias toward positive (Connell, 1991; Harter, 1983; Harter & Monsour, 1992; Ruble, 1983).

Even the hypothesis of a uniform positivity bias probably does not hold, however. At early ages, negative may develop ahead of positive (Elmendorf, 1992; Hand & Fischer, 1989; Hencke, 1991). For most children with no known history of maltreatment, stories about social interactions seem to show a bias of negative over positive until at least 3 years, and then somewhere between 4 and 6 years the pattern seems to reverse. Of course, this negativity bias does not hold for shy children, who show the positivity bias in Figure 3 from an early age. Young children who are not shy seem to enjoy negative stories acted out in the safe environment of the preschool classroom or laboratory playroom. They prefer mean stories and understand them better. By 4 to 6 years, most children shift toward a positivity bias, especially for stories about the self. According to the social-perception research literature, this positivity bias is pervasive in adulthood (Greenwald, 1980). Most children and adults prefer primarily positive interactions, demonstrate a richer understanding of positive interactions, and characterize themselves in predominantly positive terms. This positivity bias can be considered a relatively mature form of affective splitting, based in the natural tendency toward positive representation of self: There is a positive/negative split, with emphasis on positive and deemphasis on negative; but there is also consideration of both positive and negative, at least some of the time.

Experience seems to play a major role in producing these diverse developmental pathways, even with temperamental characteristics such as shyness (Kagan, 1989). A shy emotional makeup appears to lead to recurrent experience of strong emotional reactions to mildly negative interactions or attributions about the child, producing an emotionally mediated positivity bias. We expect that many other kinds of emotional experiences affect developmental pathways. One of the most potent is recurrent maltreatment, which seems to radically shift the shape of development.

Growing Up Abused

A thesis of this paper is that recurring, extreme emotional experiences caused by maltreatment can fundamentally alter social-emotional development, inducing changes in how people organize themselves, especially along the positive/

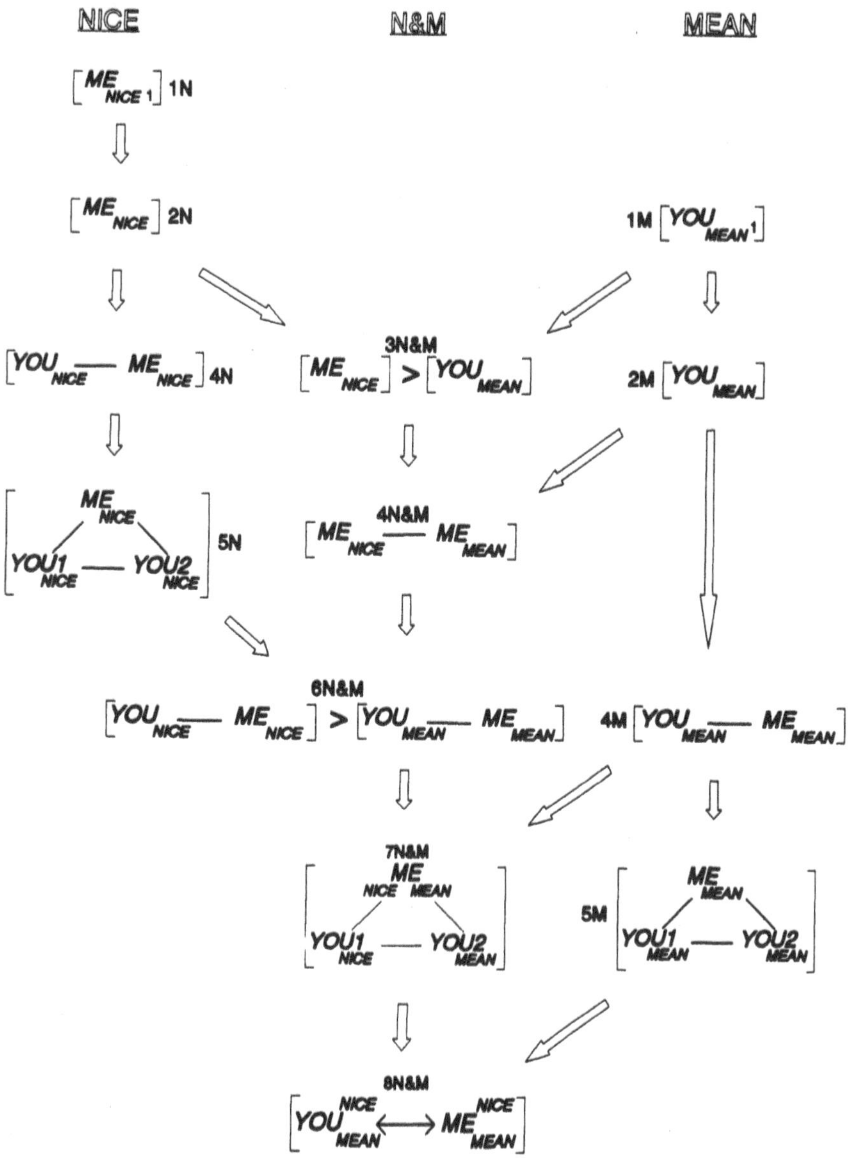

FIGURE 3 Developmental Sequence of Mean and Nice Social Interactions with Positive Affective Bias

Note: Conventions for the skill formulas are described in Table 5. In Tasks 1 and 2, the number 1 after the words ***NICE*** or ***MEAN*** indicates that there is only one action or characteristic in the category—one instance of nice or mean behavior. The absence of any number indicates that the category includes multiple, flexible actions or characteristics.

negative dimension and in terms of social-emotional dissociation. Among the most important changes are a predominant negativity in representing self and social relationships and an elaborate, sophisticated splitting and dissociation of self and others. Research indicates that the repeated traumas of maltreatment often produce a cluster of fundamental changes in personality that include malignant feelings of inner badness and basic fragmentations in self (Breuer & Freud, 1895/1955; Buchsbaum, Toth, Clyman, Cicchetti, & Emde, 1992; Cole & Putnam, 1992; Famularo, et al., in press; George & Main, 1979; Herman, 1992; Putnam, 1993; Terr, 1991; Westen & Cohen, 1992). The most psychologically destructive patterns of maltreatment seem to be both ongoing sexual abuse and physical abuse coupled with emotional maltreatment.

Our approach to analysis of development of maltreated children is based in the new interdisciplinary science of developmental psychopathology, which has crystalized over the last two decades. This approach is grounded in the belief that an integrative theory of development across the life-span encompasses both normative and clinical populations, with the body of knowledge about one population informing that about the other. Of particular importance is the relation of normative and pathological developmental pathways, understanding of which we hope to enhance through our work with maltreated children.

Developmental psychopathology assumes a dynamic, organizational perspective, in which many factors in children's lives interact in dynamic ways to determine the etiology and intergenerational transmission of child maltreatment (Cicchetti, 1989; Cicchetti & Schneider-Rosen, 1984). Factors such as parent history and characteristics, family organization, child attributes, social stressors, and community environment all mutually interact to influence children and determine occurrence and effects of maltreatment. From this perspective, Cicchetti and Rizley (1981) define four types of risk factors in maltreatment: vulnerability factors, challengers, protective factors, and buffers. Vulnerability factors are long-term, enduring influences that increase the likelihood of maltreatment and so affect the child's developmental pathway. Challengers are short-term conditions and stresses that confront families and may increase the likelihood of maltreatment in the predisposed parent. Protective factors are enduring attributes that contribute to decreasing the risk of maltreatment or its transmission across generations. Buffers are transient compensatory factors that may protect a family from stress, such as a good job, improved financial conditions, or a child's move to a new developmental level.

The developmental trajectories of negativity and dissociation described in this chapter are set in motion by severe, short-term challengers or long-term vulnerability factors producing child maltreatment. As children attempt to cope with the extreme dangers of repeated sexual, physical, or emotional abuse, they organize their thought and action in ways that are adaptive in dealing with the abuses, helping them to survive. These patterns can become integrated into the fabric of a child's personality, and then they often prove to be maladaptive for coping with more benign, day-to-day interactions. Although the maladaptive patterns generally share the characteristics of negativity bias and predominance of dissociation and splitting, they vary in important ways with type and severity of maltreatment, as well as with the timing of the trauma, its recurrence, and a child's emotional reactions to maltreatment. Consequently abusive experiences produce diverse developmental pathways, including the two that we are focusing on—multiple personality and hidden family violence—as well as borderline and narcissistic personality disorder and psychopathy.

Two Key Characteristics: Negativity Bias and Dissociation

Although research is only beginning on the developmental pathways of abused children, there are data available to guide an initial sketch of the pathways produced by abuse, some of which we have already reviewed briefly. In our own research in progress, we are assessing abused children's constructions about positive and negative interactions, relationships, and self-representations (Ayoub, Willett, & Robinson, 1993; Calverley, 1993; Fischer, 1991; Raya, 1993), and other researchers have collected relevant data as well.

Research to date indicates that in severely maltreated children and adolescents, the normal positivity bias in representations disappears at a very young age and is replaced by a reverse affective split, a negativity bias. Instead of biasing their representations of self and important social relationships towards the positive, maltreated children bias them toward the negative: Their emotions are often dominated by the negative, and they endlessly act out and talk about predominantly negative representations of events and interactions. From an early age, when maltreated children focus on positive interactions, they seem to represent relationships in a conventionalized, rigid, stereotyped manner. Representations of negative interactions, on the other hand, tend to be rich, dynamic, involving, and often frightening for people around the children and sometimes even for the children themselves. As the children grow older, they often make an effort to inhibit negative expression in certain contexts, particularly when they sense danger from a powerful adult or older child (Ayoub, Raya, & Fischer, 1993).

In addition to this major transformation to a negativity bias, abuse seems to produce increased splitting and dissociation in representation of self and others. Patients with dissociative pathologies such as multiple personality and borderline personality show a remarkably high incidence of severe maltreatment (Fagan & McMahon, 1984; Putnam, 1989; Westen & Cohen, 1992). Diverse research with preschoolers and older children suggests that maltreatment leads to prominent dissociation and splitting at an early age, which seem to develop from the foundations of abusive relationships (Calverley, 1993; Raya, 1993). Crittenden (1988) reported that some maltreated toddlers displayed "false positive affect." Vondra, Barnett, and Cicchetti (1989) found that young school-age children who had been maltreated tended to overrate their competence. Cicchetti and Beeghly (1987) noted that maltreated children used proportionally fewer words about internal states, attributed their internal states to fewer social agents, and were more context-bound than their counterparts who were not maltreated. Cicchetti (in press) proposes that maltreated children attempt to control their anxiety and fear by modifying their language to exclude certain aspects and contexts associated with maltreatment: They do not talk about certain topics or use certain kinds of language. This specific affective splitting enhances unrealistic views of self and others, leading eventually to adult characterological disorders such as narcissistic and borderline personality (Kernberg, 1975; Kohut, 1971).

In reacting to the recurrent trauma from maltreatment, children experience an intense struggle for control and competence. Judith Herman (1992) points out that the traumas "destroy the belief that one can be oneself in relation to others." Previous research suggests that the trauma of maltreatment is associated with delay in the development of self and in the ability to get along with and understand others (Aber, Allen, Carlson, & Cicchetti, 1989; Mueller & Silverman, 1989), but we will show how maltreatment often produces not simple developmental delay but a shift to a different developmental pathway characterized by a negativity bias and the use of splitting and dissociation to organize self and relationships.

These results do *not* mean that only abused children show emotional splitting. Splitting and dissociation are normal processes shown in all children and adults under many circumstances, as we illustrated earlier. But abuse leads to new kinds of dissociation and splitting, such as a negativity bias, a positive-conventional versus negative-dynamic split, and a sharp dissociation between different parts of close relationships.

Abusive Relationships

We assume that the developing organization of action and thought is shaped fundamentally by close relationships in the family, so that child and adult come to relate to other people (and social organizations) in ways based in their family relationships (Shapiro & Carr, 1991; Stern, 1985; Sullivan, 1953). Close relationships are fundamental to the child's personality development (Ainsworth, Blehar, Waters, & Wall, 1978; Bretherton & Waters, 1985; Crittenden, 1993; Vondra, Barnett, & Cicchetti, 1990) and may be the primary source of environmental influences on personality development (Waller & Shaver, 1993). From the start, a child's organization of these interactions is naturally split into positive and negative, including good and bad self, good and bad parent, nice and mean peers, and good and evil forces in the world.

Severe, continued maltreatment in the family or other close relationships dramatically alters the ways that children organize positive and negative in close relationships and interactions and thus transforms their developmental pathways. From the initial bias toward splitting the world into good and bad based on affect, children who are not maltreated gradually move toward integrating these opposite emotional valences and often focusing on the positive. Maltreated children, on the other hand, develop different pathways in which relationships and experiences are severely split and dissociated and the direction of organization is shifted to predominance of negative over positive. By adolescence and adulthood, many of these children have constructed fundamentally negative views of themselves and their worlds, what Westen (1992) calls malevolent self-concepts instead of benevolent ones; and they have developed advanced, sophisticated ways of dissociating events, people, and experiences.

Some fortunate children find healthy relationships that help them grow out of abusive pathways, but even they seem to show consequences of the abuse (Cicchetti, 1989).

The conflict for children in close, abusive relationships is fundamental—between attachment to a caregiver and experience of that caregiver as a dangerous power without mercy (Herman, 1992). Child victims are caught between their need to protect attachments amd their regular experience of injury, malice, threat, or other kinds of maltreatment. Instead of developing the usual core self, with a positivity bias and a tendency to gradually integrate self and others across emotional splits, maltreated children learn to split themselves along emotional lines, to react in terms of the shifting affective tones set by the adults they are close to.

Different patterns of maltreatment coupled with the child's ways of adapting to abuse appear to lead to different developmental pathways involving distinct types of splitting and dissociation, such as multiple personality disorder and hidden family violence. Both pathways include a negativity bias and a predominance of dissociation and splitting, but the pathways are otherwise very different. In hidden family violence, children grow up in a family that rigidly separates a private, violent world from a public, benevolent one. They gradually internalize or appropriate this separation and construct their own dissociation based in it (Fischer, et al., 1984b; Rogoff, 1990; Vygotsky, 1978). In multiple personality, children grow up in a less predictable world, in which they are subjected to severe, repeated, uncontrollable abuse, often of multiple varieties. Instead of dissociating their world into private and public, they dissociate themselves into different agents organized around distinct emotional experiences, especially those arising from the abuse. In this way, they develop the capacity to form multiple distinctive, dissociated "personalities."

We have used three sources of data in inferring these two pathways: clinical case studies from our own experience, case studies and research findings from the published literature, and our ongoing research with abused preschoolers and adolescents (Ayoub, et al., 1993b; Calverley, Fischer, & Ayoub, in press; Raya, 1993). In portraying pathways for multiple personality and hidden family violence, we will provide clinical descriptions based on real cases to illustrate developmental levels in each pathway, including both adult and child cases.

Multiple Personality Disorder: Development of Co-conscious Dissociation

In multiple personality disorder a person constructs distinctive agencies or co-consciousnesses (usually termed "personalities") for organizing different affective realms of his or her life, thus producing one of the most extreme and complex dissociative skills. The extremity and clarity of the dissociation, as well as its genesis from severe maltreatment in childhood, make the disorder a natural for developmental analysis. For many years, multiple personality disorder was in disrepute as a diagnostic category and was often confused with schizophrenia and schizoid disorders (Bliss, 1980; Rosenbaum, 1980). Recent research has demonstrated both that it is a distinct disorder and that it is closely tied to childhood trauma, especially abuse (Fagan & McMahon, 1984; Putnam, 1989). The disorder is also remarkable for the distinctness of the dissociated personalities, with not only different emotional responses and personality profiles but even different physiological reactions, handedness, and other biological indicators of personality (Henninger, 1992; Putnam, 1989). Although the co-consciousnesses are not fully separate personalities, they are separated in many ways, and their separation develops through a specific pathway, usually linked to trauma and maltreatment in childhood.

Skills for Co-conscious Dissociation

In our model of development of multiple personality, the multiple agencies are built through co-conscious dissociation (Fischer & Pipp, 1984). The natural dissociation that arises from intense emotional experiences during trauma produces the beginnings of two or more co-conscious agencies that have different dominant emotions and function independently without affective coordination or interference, at least some of the time. With development a person builds a dissociative coordination between the agencies, so that he or she can switch between two (or more) largely incompatible self-organizations, with only one in dominant control at a time. Because of the agencies' independent functioning, they can develop separate skills to high levels of complexity. Once this dissociative strategy for dealing with stress is established, it can lead to a proliferation of co-consciousnesses to deal with different situations. In fact, often the multiple personalities are not stable over long periods but change systematically.

The agencies are not truly independent, of course. They have three kinds of connections, each of which requires a set of skills that need to be constructed. First, they are actively dissociated—not only defined in contrast to each other but actively kept separate. Second, the person can switch from one agency to another, which requires a skill relating the two. Third, in limited ways they can act on each other, with one affecting activity, memory, or experience in the other. At any moment, one co-conscious agency controls the body (or most of it, at least), yet at some point in development another one becomes able to affect the experience of the one in control, preventing or inducing an activity or feeling. This co-conscious repression and induction often relate to fears that the co-consciousness in the background will somehow be harmed by a particular experience or action of the co-consciousness in control. For example, in the famous case of *The Three Faces of Eve,* the co-conscious agency Eve Black had access to many of the memories of Eve White and sometimes interfered with Eve White's activity and experience, preventing her from remembering something or inserting a thought or feeling into her awareness. These kinds of repressive and inductive connections lead to dissociative experiences such as depersonalization and hearing voices.

Here is a clinical case that illustrates some of these properties of multiple personality, including the foundation in trauma and the existence of independent co-consciousnesses:

> At age 30, Ms. L came to therapy complaining of anxiety attacks and headaches. She worked adeptly as a computer programmer, but she had difficulty talking with the people for whom she worked. She indicated that she found herself unable to remember some periods of time, she sometimes found herself in unusual and embarrassing dress, and she occasionally experienced feelings of depersonalization. As a child, Ms. L. had been physically abused in a sadistic way by a stepfather and an older brother, and the brother had also subjected her to sadistic sexual activity.
>
> After 2 years, she was diagnosed as having multiple personality disorder, with an elaborated system of co-conscious personalities. In her therapy, at least four separate co-conscious agencies have presented to her therapist: (a) Lois, the host personality, who is depressed and isolated and has low-self-esteem, (b) Helen, a stern mother of three children who insists that she be obeyed, (c) Joyce, a sexy 27-year-old, and (d) Samantha, a 6-year-old girl. The three women agencies each appeared to function as adults, with adequate understanding of high-level abstractions such as personality conceptions. The child agency seemed to function cognitively like a child of age 6 or 8, showing at least a beginning understanding of two-dimensional social influence (Task 7 or 8 in Table 4 and Figure 2).

The capacity to produce separate co-conscious agencies is a developmental accomplishment, one that takes many years to construct and consolidate to the degree evident in Ms. L. This high-level dissociative capacity seems to be similar in some ways to the more ordinary adolescent and adult capacity to relate one's own personality to someone else's (as described in Table 5). The central difference is that the relation of agencies in multiple personality in Ms. L is dissociative within a person, while the more ordinary relation of personalities in different people is often integrating across people. According to this analysis, construction of the full array of multiple-personality skills requires at least abstract mappings (Level A2 in Table 5), in which several abstractions are dissociatively coordinated:

$$[\text{PERS'Y } \mathbb{A}_{V} \;—\!\blacksquare\!—\; \text{PERS'Y } \mathbb{B}_{W}] \qquad (16)$$

With specific skills of this kind, the person can keep several co-conscious agencies separate, switch between them, and have one act on or influence the other (the three types of connections among co-conscious agencies).

Also, each co-conscious personality can develop separately along its own pathway, constructing relations among personality traits, motives, and the like in a manner partly analogous to the way a person without multiple personality develops his or her personality. However, co-conscious personalities are often fluid, changing so much with differing life circumstances that one personality disappears over time and is replaced by others. A single, long-term, continuous pathway for each personality cannot be assumed, but we do posit a long-term, continuous pathway for the development of the dissociative skills in multiple personality.

In our model, multiple personalities emerge in adolescence and develop further into adulthood. But that is only part of the story. Dissociation of full-blown "personalities" may await adolescence, but simpler forms of dissociation—concrete co-conscious agents—develop at a much earlier age. They define the beginnings of the developmental pathway for co-conscious dissociation in multiple personality.

First Tier of Dissociation: Co-conscious Agents

In the development of dissociative coordination, children show a much simpler type of skill than adults. Their dissociative skills coordinate representations rather than abstractions, and so they have *co-conscious agents* rather than *co-conscious personalities*. Throughout this chapter, we use the term co-conscious agen*cies* to include both agents and personalities. Agents control concrete actions or characteristics, while personalities control intangible motives or personality traits. Gradually, the co-conscious agents of children become the co-conscious personalities of adolescents and adults (Table 6).

Fluent control of independent agents first appears in normal development at about 2 to 2½ years, when children can pretend that a doll is walking, talking, playing, or hitting, and can speak sentences that describe the same actions in dolls, people, and other agents. The representations of nice or mean actions shown in the stories for Level Rp1 of Table 4 are one set of examples, and there are many others in the research literature (Bretherton & Beeghly, 1989; Fischer, et al., 1984b; Piaget, 1946/1951; Rubin, Fein, & Vandenberg, 1983; Watson & Fischer, 1980; Wolf, 1982). At this point children can shift between mean and nice representations, as described earlier:

$$[\boldsymbol{ME}_{\boldsymbol{MEAN}}] > [\boldsymbol{ME}_{\boldsymbol{NICE}}] \tag{17}$$

They can also use this capacity to shift in order to build their first crude skill for dissociation. For example, if they perceive being mean as dangerous, then when they think of being mean, they can try to deny that state and shift instead to the opposite, being nice.

$$\frac{\underline{\boldsymbol{not}}}{[\boldsymbol{ME}_{\boldsymbol{MEAN}}]} \not> [\boldsymbol{ME}_{\boldsymbol{NICE}}] \tag{18}$$

The shift symbol with a thick line through it indicates a dissociative relation; the skill to the left is the one defended against, as indicated by the ***not***, and the one to the right is shifted to as the desired state. This dissociative strategy can only be used easily when the context supports the representation that is being shifted to, in this case $\boldsymbol{ME_{NICE}}$. If the context supports the opposite representation, $\boldsymbol{ME_{MEAN}}$, children will have great difficulty sustaining the shift. They need the stronger dissociative structures that develop at higher levels to impose dissociations successfully without strong contextual support.

A couple more years are required for the child to build fluent relations between two agents in representational mappings (Level Rp2) at about 3½ to 4 years. According to our model of multiple personality, the emergence of mappings brings the first development of genuine (but simple) dissociative coordination. For two agents to actively dissociate from each other requires at least a simple mapping between two representations. The process is similar to the mapping of two agents in one-dimensional social influence (Tasks 4N and 4M in Table 4) and the mapping of opposite emotions in a single agent (Task 4N & M). This first co-conscious dissociative coordination is essentially a mapping of two agents with different defining emotional states. The thick line in the middle of the mapping relation indicates dissociation.

$$[\textbf{AGENT 1}_{\textbf{MEAN}} \text{ —▮— } \textbf{AGENT 2}_{\textbf{NICE}}] \tag{19}$$

The limited evidence on development of multiple personality indicates that it does indeed emerge at about 4 years of age (Bliss, 1980; Fagan & McMahon, 1984; Kluft, 1985). In addition, clinical evidence indicates that repression (a defensive mechanism using active dissociation) also first appears at about this same age (Freud, 1936/1966; Vaillant, 1977).

The case of Carrie Smith, a severely abused young girl, illustrates the early development of co-conscious agents in the preschool years, starting before full dissociative coordination has appeared:

> At age 3, Carrie Smith was removed from her home because of allegations of physical abuse, neglect, and sexual abuse by her mother and two "fathers" who lived in their home. She and her two siblings were locked in a dark bedroom for a month, repeatedly sexually abused by all three adults, and physically abused by one of the "fathers."
>
> When Carrie Smith arrived in her foster home, she was prone to lengthy tantrums and periods of crying, did not talk in sentences, often screamed in her sleep, and was both self-destructive and aggressive to others. At age 4, after a year in this new home, she functioned with less anxiety, had developed basic routines for eating and sleeping, and was much more controllable.
>
> Along with the improved general behavior, however, came dramatic changes in her personality organization. According to her foster mother, she began to have night terrors in which she seemed to reenact her abuse in her dreams, particularly the sexual abuse by adults. She did not remember these terrors and activities the next morning.
>
> At the same time, her daytime behavior also changed. She began to switch her mood and behavior quickly in ways that showed consistent patterns of affect, food preference, and activity—patterns that seemed to reflect separate agencies. For each pattern, there was one dominant affect, and during different episodes Carrie sometimes called herself by different names. For example, she would suddenly assert that her name was Carla (her mother's name) and that she was pregnant (as her mother was at the time of Carrie's removal). She did

Table 6 Levels of Development of Dissociative Coordination in Multiple Personality

Level	Dissociative Skills[1]: Representational Tier	Dissociative Skills[1]: Abstract Tier	Examples of Dissociative and Non-dissociative Skills	Age[2]
S4/Rp1: Single Representations[3]	<u>*not*</u> $\left[AGENT\ 1_{M} \right] \nLeftrightarrow \left[AGENT\ 2_{N} \right]$		**Single concrete representations of people as agents:** When child is expected to be nice and she thinks of being mean, she shifts abruptly to a nice representation, to avoid being mean (active dissociation). Child pretends that she is her mother Carla hitting someone and saying mean things, and then she shifts to pretending that she is Carrie hugging a baby and saying nice things (not active dissociation).	18–24 mos.
Rp2: Representational Mappings	$\left[AGENT\ 1_{M} \nleftrightarrow AGENT\ 2_{N} \right]$		**Simple relations of representations:** When she feels threatened, child switches from agent nice Carrie to agent mean Carla. and she switches back when she feels comfortable again (act. dissoc). As Carla, child acts mean in response to actions by someone else (not act. dissoc).	3.5–4.5 yr

Level	Skill Structure	Description	Age
Rp3: Representational Systems	$\left[AGENT\ 1_{M}^{J} \leftrightarrow AGENT\ 2_{N}^{K} \right]$	**Complex relations of subsets of representations:** Child switches from agent Carrie to agent Carla, with each agent having several key concrete characteristics that determine when switching will occur (act. dissoc.). As Carla, child acts both tough (mean) and seductive with a man, whom she expects to be tough and sexual in return (not act. dissoc.).	6–7
Rp4/A1: Single Abstractions	$\left[\begin{array}{c} AGENT\ 1_{M}^{J} \leftrightarrow AGENT\ 2_{N}^{K} \\ \Updownarrow \\ AGENT\ 1_{G}^{E} \leftrightarrow AGENT\ 3_{H}^{F} \end{array} \right] = [PERS'Y\ A_{V}]$	**Relations of representational systems to produce abstractions (intangible concepts) about people (personalties):** For one agent (#1), person coordinates several specific relations with other agents (#2 and #3) in terms of an intangible characteristic, motive, or the like, thus forming a co-conscious personality (Personality A) with that characteristic (act. dissoc.).	10–12

		Within each agency, person develops abstract personality concepts and motives, thus beginning to form separate "personalities" instead of mere agents. No coordination of agencies as personalities, only as concrete agents (not act. dissoc).	
A2: Abstract Mappings	[PERS'Y A_V —+— PERS'Y B_W]	**Simple relations of abstractions**: Person relates two personalities, not just concrete agents, so that Personality A can influence the activity or experience of Personality B (act. dissoc).	14–16

Table 6 Continued

Level	Dissociative Skills[1] Representational Tier	Abstract Tier	Examples of Dissociative and Non-dissociative Skills	Age[2]
			Within each personality, person relates several abstract personal characteristics, such as moral concern and need for obedience from children in Ms. L's Helen (not act. dissoc.).	
A3: Abstract Systems		[PERS'Y A_{V}^{X} ↔ PERS'Y B_{W}^{Y}]	**Complex relations of subsets of abstractions**: Person relates two personalities so that Personality A can influence the activity or experience of Personality B along several dimensions simultaneously (act. dissoc.). Within each personality, person relates complex set of personal characteristics in multiple dimensions, such as several types of intentionality and several types of responsibility as part of agency Helen's concern for morality and obedience (not act. dissoc.).	18–20

A4: Systems of Abstract Systems: Principles[4]	[PERS'Y A^X_V ↔ PERS'Y B^Y_W ↕ PERS'Y C^R_T ↔ PERS'Y D^S_U]	**General principles for integrating systems of abstractions:** Dissociative strategies can be remarkably sophisticated, with switches and influences between personalities being determined by subtle relations reflective of some system-wide organization (act. dissoc.). However, effects of dissociation may mean that this level often produces only the capacity for facile switching and influence among many personalities, as opposed to systematic integration. Within each personality, person can understand general principles, such as moral principle of justice, integrating relations between types of intention and responsibility (not act. dissoc.).	23–25

[1]The skill structures in the diagrams are examples of skills showing the simplest general form of a dissociative structure for a given level and are described in the first example, which in each case involves active dissociation. The second example is an instance of a more ordinary skill at this level and therefore does *not* fit the dissociative structure in the diagram; instead it shows a type of structure that is characteristic of the level but lacks the dissociation. In general, at least three kinds of dissociative skills can be built: After Level Rp1, children can build skills for keeping the agencies separate and distinct and skills for switching from one agency to another. Skills whereby one agency intervenes in another's ongoing activity or experience require higher levels, probably level A2 abstract mappings and beyond. Examples of other dissociative skills are descirbed in the text of the chapter.

[2]Ages given are estimates of modal ages at which a level first appears based on cognitive developmental research described elsewhere (Fischer & Farrar, 1987; Fischer et al., 1993; Kitchener et al., 1993). They may differ across cultures and other social groups.

[3]Representations grow from coordinations of sensorimotor systems, but for simplicity that relation has been omitted from this table.

[4]The skill structure shown for Level A4 is a system of abstract systems, which is also a principle. The principle that emerges from this structure could be designated by a separate structure, such as **P**, but because there is no evidence for later levels beyond A4, we have not included the separate structure for **P**.

Note: In skill structures, each word or letter denotes a skill component, with each large word or letter designating a main component (set) and each subscript or superscript designating a subset of the main component. Italics designate representations, and outline letters designate abstractions. Lines connecting sets designate relations forming a mapping, single-line arrows designate relations forming a system, and double-line arrows designate relations forming a system of systems. An arrowhead without a line (>) designates a shift of focus between two skills. A dark rectangle in the middle of a line or arrow indicates that the relation is dissociative.

> not say that she was acting like Carla but that she was Carla. In this pattern, she was highly seductive as well as mean and angry at everyone. She was verbally abusive to her foster mother, speaking in an adult tone and swearing frequently. She also engaged in sexually explicit behavior.
>
> Carrie would then abruptly change to a different pattern, in which she called herself Carrie, who was a good, parentified girl. Now, when asked about Carla, she said that Carla was her mother and denied acting like Carla. In this pattern, she was obedient and concerned over the young children in the foster home. She liked to care for babies and worried about their diapers.

To keep our referents clear, we use "Carrie Smith" for the patient, "Carrie" for the (nice) girl agent, and "Carla" for the (mean) woman agent.

Carrie Smith demonstrates concretely how the early development of dissociative skills can occur. Our hypothesis is that when she began to act as the two agents, mean Carla and nice Carrie, she was showing the beginnings of active dissociation: She kept the two agents separate and changed from one to the other as a defense when she was frightened or in some other way motivated to be in a different emotional state. This capacity to switch between agents and keep them separate even without a clearly supportive context involves a representational mapping for dissociation.

At age 3, when she was in her mother's home and then first entered her foster home, she had separate representations for her mother Carla and herself (Level Rp1). When her mother was mean (a common state) 3-year-old Carrie Smith represented her as another person (a you, not a me) who was mean: **YOU-CARLA**$_{MEAN}$. When Carrie Smith was playing or fantasizing, she sometimes represented herself as mean Carla, and other times as nice Carrie, but she could not coordinate these two agents except by shift of focus:

$$[\textbf{ME-CARLA}_{MEAN}] > [\textbf{ME-CARRIE}_{NICE}] \quad (20)$$

As Carrie Smith developed dissociative skills in order to cope with her trauma and anxiety, she gradually constructed a representational mapping for dissociative coordination of herself as both Carla and Carrie (Level Rp2):[1]

$$[\textbf{ME-CARLA}_{MEAN} \text{ —▮— } \textbf{ME-CARRIE}_{NICE}] \quad (21)$$

By age 4 she could often control whether she was Carrie or Carla, keeping the two agencies dissociated and switching to whichever one she needed affectively

---

[1] The designation of who is "me" and who is "you" in these dissociative skills is tricky. From an observer's viewpoint, both Carla and Carrie are organizations of the same person ("me," Carrie Smith), but from the viewpoint of one of the agents the other one is "you." By this argument, each dissociative skill diagram could readily be changed to two (or more) separate skills, one relating **ME-CARLA** to **YOU-CARRIE** and a second relating **ME-CARRIE** to **YOU-CARLA.** There are parallel differences in process too: When Carrie Smith is organized as agent Carla, she would seem to use a different skill for dissociating from agent Carrie than she uses when she is organized as agent Carrie and dissociating from agent Carla. Nevertheless, for simplicity, we have diagrammed only one dissociative skill for these relationships.

at the moment. She mapped mean Carla and nice Carrie together, in a manner similar to the normal mapping of two agents with different affects in children's pretend play (Task 4 in Table 4). By 5 and 6 years, she had become skilled at making such switches and could even describe her experience of switching:

> At age 6 years Carrie Smith reported that "the girl inside of me" called Carla would take her to another place to get away from things that scared her. When asked by the therapist how Carla got Carrie Smith to another place, she replied, "She hears someone yell at me and then she would do something. I'd be saying, 'I'm scared, and I can't move', but I'd be running because that's Carla's legs doing that, but I couldn't stop it. I couldn't feel it when my Mom grabbed my arm, not until after when Carla goes back in and then my arm is my own arm. Then it starts hurting."

Besides dissociative skills, Carrie Smith also developed more ordinary mappings for social contingencies based within only one agent, with no obvious dissociation. For example, she could have Carrie act nice to someone who was nice to her,

$$\left[\textbf{ME-CARRIE}_{\textbf{NICE}} \text{———} \textbf{YOU}_{\textbf{NICE}}\right] \qquad (22)$$

or have Carla act mean to someone who was mean to her,

$$\left[\textbf{ME-CARLA}_{\textbf{MEAN}} \text{———} \textbf{YOU}_{\textbf{MEAN}}\right] \qquad (23)$$

Note, however, that when Carrie Smith was actually using the dissociative skill, her optimal level would set a limit on the complexity of skill she could use at that moment, according to our skills model. If the dissociative skill (formula 21) was at her optimal level, then her developmental limit while using that skill would prevent her from controlling a social contingency (formula 22 or 23) at the same time: When she was using her mapping capacity to control the dissociative skill, she would have no capacity left over to simultaneously control a social contingency. Doing both dissociation and social contingency simultaneously would require developing a more complex mapping or a skill at the next level, representational systems.

As Carrie Smith continued on the pathway of development of dissociative coordination, her next major advance involved representational systems (Level Rp3), where she moved beyond the limits of mappings to relate several aspects of the agents Carla and Carrie in the same dissociative skill. As a result, the two co-conscious agencies became much more textured and flexible—two-dimensional instead of one-dimensional—because her new optimal-level limits allowed her to expand each agent beyond one dimension during dissociation. For example, Carla could be simultaneously mean and seductive, while Carrie was simultaneously nice (pleasant) and parental, taking care of a baby:

$$\left[\textbf{ME-CARLA}^{\textbf{SEDUCTIVE}}_{\textbf{MEAN}} \leftrightarrow\!\blacksquare\!\rightarrow \textbf{ME-CARRIE}^{\textbf{CAREGIVING}}_{\textbf{NICE}}\right] \qquad (24)$$

Besides shifting between agents, another common skill of co-conscious dissociation is removing oneself from the body that is being abused, as described earlier for Shirley, who put herself into a hole in the wall whenever her father raped her. A co-conscious agent removes her experience from the body, which she treats as another person, a "you." Carrie Smith described how her agent Carrie removed herself from her body, which became an object of observation:

> At 11 years of age, Carrie Smith talked about a recent episode of abuse by her mother that occurred during a visit home. She said that her mother put her on a table, tied her up, and left her there for hours. She described herself as "not minding" because she "wasn't really there." When asked what she meant, she said that she felt herself (Carrie) looking down from the ceiling onto the child Carrie Smith tied up on the table. Although she acknowledged that she was that child, she also stated that during the experience she was not the child. Instead, she was looking at the child on the table, thinking "Poor girl, she must be scared and small." When asked the identity of the person looking down, Carrie Smith said, "Why, the one who takes care of me when I get scared or afraid," which is the agent Carrie.

This dissociative coordination required at least a representational system, with which Carrie could build a complex concrete relation between co-conscious agent Carrie and the child herself Carrie Smith (or at least her body):

$$\left[\underset{SCARED}{\overset{SMALL}{YOU\text{-}CARRIE\ S.}} \;\leftrightarrow\; \underset{NICE}{\overset{CAREGIVING}{ME\text{-}CARRIE}} \qquad \right] \qquad (25)$$

Consolidating these representational systems relating a number of characteristics of concrete agents requires several years. Then, children can build on the consolidated systems to begin development beyond co-conscious concrete agents, to build dissociative skills involving coconscious personalities.

Second Tier of Dissociation: Co-conscious Personalities

Table 6 sketches the developmental pathway that we propose for dissociative coordination in multiple personality, starting with development of concrete agents like Carla and Carrie. This general outline portrays the general form of skills for co-conscious dissociative coordination that are common to many individual pathways. Of course, the outline does not capture the rich variations that individual people show in their specific pathways, but the case examples provide some examples of that variation.

At about age 10 to 12, the emergence of abstractions produces the developmental transition from agencies to personalities. Just as a young person can integrate two representational systems to produce a moral abstraction such as intentionality or a personality concept such as conformity, he or she can dissociatively coordinate two representational systems like those in formulas 24 and 25 to produce a co-conscious personality. For example, a person can coordinate a system for switching between two given agents with a second system for switching between one of them and a third agent, as shown in Table 6 (Level

Rp4/A1). This coordination produces a new type of agency, a "personality" based in the coordination.

Carrie Smith built an abstract skill for the co-conscious personality Carla, through which Carla could enact her wish to control other people—in this case two other co-conscious agents, Carrie and Mom. She could coordinate a representational system for switching between Carla and Carrie with a second system for switching between Carla and another agent that she had developed, Mom. The co-conscious agent Mom occupied the role she was named for: She was good at dealing with children and giving people advice about them. When Carla wanted a nice, conventional person, she could call upon Carrie. When she wanted someone to deal with a child, she could call upon Mom. This coordination produced a skill that subsumed how agent Carla (Agent 1 in Table 6) controlled and switched to both nice Carrie and child-expert Mom (Agents 2 and 3):

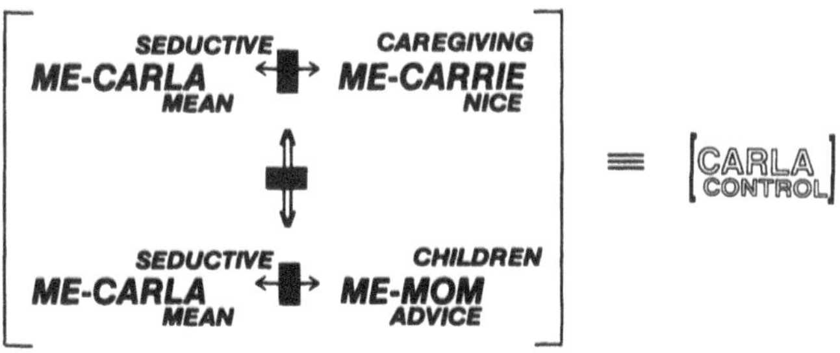

(26 and 27)

In this way Carla became a co-conscious personality with a specific motive structure, a wish to control others. Through her coordinations with other agents, concrete agent Carla became motivated co-conscious personality Carla. This process is analogous to the way that an abstract personality characteristic or value such as intentionality or conformity develops from the coordination of interactions among concrete agents (Table 5). Of course, motives are present at earlier ages, but they are not coordinated and controlled the way they can be with an abstraction.

A new skill level not only leads to new dissociative skills, but it also improves the flexibility and generalizability of skills from the previous level (Fischer & Farrar, 1987). When Carrie Smith described her observation of her own body being tied to the table, for example, she was 11 years of age, old enough to be capable of single abstractions. From our case material, it is difficult to tell whether she was using a representational system or a single abstraction. But if she were using an abstraction, she would have been able to coordinate a representational system for agent Carrie with another system for the body of Carrie Smith, thus producing a more fluid and better controlled version of the dissociated observing skill than with a single representational system. A detailed skill analysis of her actions could discriminate whether she was using a representational system or an abstraction (Granott, 1993; Kitchener, et al., 1993).

The skill for an (abstract) co-conscious personality produced by this new developmental level is still severely limited, however, because the young person cannot yet control relations among personalities except by reducing them to concrete agents (representational systems within an abstraction). For both Carla and Carrie to be dissociatively coordinated as co-conscious personalities instead of as concrete agents, Carrie Smith must build an abstract mapping (Level A2), which 10- to 12-year-olds are generally not capable of.

At about age 15, when abstract mappings begin to emerge, people can coordinate one abstraction with another, and thereby one co-conscious personality with another. This coordination of personalities allows intangible personal characteristics to be dissociatively related in the two personalities. One co-consciousness (Personality A in Table 6) can evaluate what is occurring in the activity or experience of another and intervene to change an activity or thought in the other (characteristic W in Personality B in Table 6), as when Eve Black intervened in Eve White's activity while Eve White had primary control of the body. This sort of complex relation between agencies is probably not possible with anything less than a mapping, which is why earlier we described multiple personality as requiring at least abstract mappings (as in the cases of Ms. L and *The Three Faces of Eve*).

Carrie Smith illustrated this kind of relation in her description of the relation between Carrie and the co-conscious personality Mom:

> After Carrie Smith had a child (a boy named John), her co-conscious personality "Mom" took responsibility for most childrearing decisions and gave advice whenever Carrie was anxious about how to care for son John or needed guidance with him. For example, Mom told Carrie what to do for John when he was crying or needed to be fed or have his diaper changed. At times, Mom directly took over taking care of John instead of just advising Carrie. Carrie described Mom as a motherly woman in her 40s who "knows all about children."

The personalities Mom and Carrie relate to each other, apparently even having conversations. The relationship is well defined in terms of one dimension of personality, Mom's skill at parenting and Carrie's naive need for help at parenting:

$$[\text{CARRIE}_{\text{NEED}} \overset{\text{parenting}}{\longleftrightarrow} \text{MOM}_{\text{SKILL}}] \qquad (28)$$

Within each co-conscious personality, a person using abstract mappings can also build non-dissociative personality skills involving several related abstractions, as described for normal development in Table 5. For example, Carrie could build an understanding of how intention relates to responsibility in a mapping, so that a negative intention could be corrected by a positive act of responsibility:

$$[\text{INTE}_{\text{NEG}} \text{ --- } \text{RESP}_{\text{POS}}] \qquad (29)$$

Such a skill built by one personality, such as Carrie, may not function with other personalities, such as Carla or Mom.

Level A3 abstract systems begin to emerge at about age 20, when young adults can coordinate several abstract mappings together to produce complex relations among multiple abstractions. This sort of capacity produces a new power in relating co-conscious personalities, including more fluid skills by which one personality can influence several aspects of ongoing activity or experience in another (Personality A influencing characteristics W and Y in Personality B in Table 6). Here are examples of how these skills functioned in the case of Carrie Smith:

> By her early 20s Carrie Smith had developed a number of complex co-conscious personalities. Carrie, her core personality, shared conscious access to some other personalities, but she did not know about others. An example is the co-conscious agency Carla, who had developed into a seductive, self-centered party-girl personality who used drugs and was seductive with men. Carla sometimes spoke to Carrie and baited her about her abstinence from drugs and her prudishness about sex. One New Year's Eve when Carrie Smith went to a party, Carrie remembered that Carla had been speaking to her, but then she remembered nothing else until she woke up in the room of a man she did not know. Carla took control unbeknownst to Carrie and drank lots of alcohol, used cocaine, and went with a man to his room. Carla began to seduce the man and then "left," baiting Carrie by returning control to her. Carrie screamed and tried to run away. Later she reported that she had been raped and did not know how she got to her assailant's room.

These fluid connections among co-conscious personalities Carrie and Carla are much more complex than the earlier connections between Carrie and Mom, with not only changes in who is in control but also complex conversations at some points and blacking out at others. This sort of activity requires the complexity of Level A3 abstract systems, in which several aspects of the two personalities can be coordinated, such as Carla's and Carrie's attitudes about sex and drugs. Carla is sexually promiscuous and freely uses drugs, and she baits Carrie about her sexual prudishness and her abstinence from drug use.

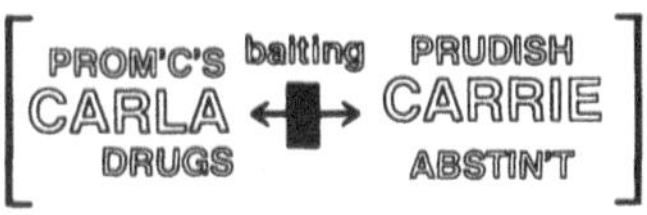

(30)

Finally, systems of abstract systems begin to appear at about age 25, when adults can coordinate several abstract systems in terms of a general principle. With such a structure, dissociative strategies can be remarkably sophisticated. Because the coordinations are based in dissociation, however, the sophistication may show itself primarily as a remarkable facility at switching among co-conscious personalities and having them influence each other. Here is an example expressed in terms of general personalities instead of the specific agencies of Carrie Smith.

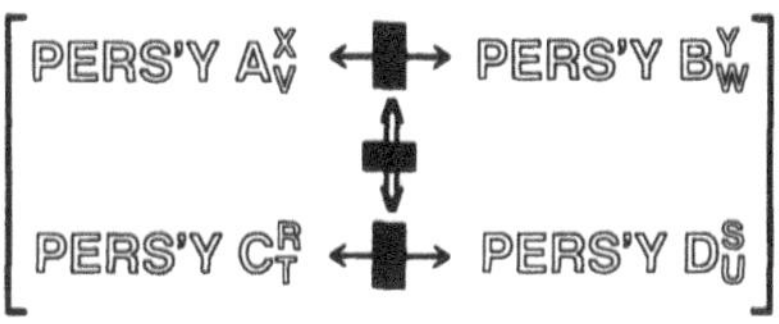

(31)

This skill uses coordination to enact sophisticated co-conscious dissociation, but the same sort of skill without the dissociative blocks is used to produce powerful integrations across roles and contexts in normal personality development, such as coordination of moral or epistemological activities around a general principle (Colby, et al., 1983; Kitchener, et al., 1993). The focus on dissociative coordination in multiple personality may preclude or minimize these sorts of integrations. Carrie Smith's experience illustrates how the coordination process can be used to move toward replacing dissociative coordination with integration:

> By her late twenties Carrie Smith had entered treatment, where she began work on identifying and integrating her personalities. As she became more comfortable with her diagnosis and her therapist, she developed a process of "talking" to Mom, Carla, and several other adult and child personalities. Her therapist focused on a technique called "talking through," talking to the personality system as a whole. Carrie Smith began to be able to assemble some whole memories from fragments and in this way consciously began to integrate material from the past held by a number of separate personalities. She also learned more about who "came out" when she was frightened, tired, or in a parenting role. As she learned to anticipate these happenings, she was also more able to integrate them and stay in consciousness as the host while she heard other personalities talk to her and even argue over taking control. The new integrations helped her to gain flexibility from combining the complementary strengths of the various personalities and compensating for their individual weaknesses.

Of course, integration is also possible at much earlier ages in simpler forms.

In summary, in the development of multiple personality, co-conscious dissociation and splitting grow out of abuse or other types of trauma and develop into remarkably sophisticated, complex levels of dissociative coordination. The intense, uncontrollable affective experiences arising from maltreatment and trauma induce dissociation at an early age, and some children then pursue dissociative coordination as a means of coping with the strains and demands of their stressful social lives. Multiple personality does not primarily involve developmental delay or arrest but instead involves a type of dissociative coordination that produces an unusual developmental pathway.

Hidden Family Violence: Development of Isolating Dissociation

Another pattern of maltreatment, which we call "hidden family violence," produces a second unusual developmental pathway based in a different kind of dissociation, grounded in isolation more than coordination. In our experience a number of abusive families follow this pattern, sharply splitting their public and private lives in a way that encapsulates violence in their private relationships while maintaining strongly positive public relationships (Ayoub, Grace, Paradise, & Newberger, 1991). Children growing up in these families develop along two dissociated and split pathways—the benevolent self in public relationships and the malevolent (abusive or abused) one in private relationships. There is little or no integration between these two domains, which are kept isolated from each other.

A cluster of contextual and emotional factors produces these split pathways, starting with passive dissociation of public and private from early childhood. With time and development, the dissociation becomes more active as children internalize the separation and become motivated to maintain it. The mechanism they use is largely isolating dissociation, which occurs through shifting from public to private or vice versa, supported by contextual and emotional factors promoting passive dissociation. By adulthood, people developing along this pathway can have great skill at sustaining the separation.

In public settings, such as on the job, in the shopping mall, or at church, people in these families are well behaved, even outstanding citizens. There is no public sign of abuse or violence at home. In fact, many of these adults are champions of moral causes and are often highly critical of anyone who does not conform to their norms and beliefs. Often times they search out strong, specific, and concrete rules of conduct, such as devout religious belief or intense commitment to a social or ethnic group or club.

When these people are asked about maltreatment, they strongly reject it. In many cases, the denial does not seem to be simple lying: The adult appears to believe it and is highly consistent in maintaining it in the public setting. According to our model, these adults maintain such a powerful split between public and private truths that in public they seem to have no access to knowledge about the malevolent world they perpetuate at home. In many maltreating families, simple lying undoubtedly occurs, but we are not describing them.

The distinction between public and private is not limited to maltreating families, of course, but is pervasive in human cultures. Families everywhere clearly distinguish between what is appropriate in public and in private. In some nations such as Japan, the distinction is remarkably strong and sharp, while in others it is more flexible; but the distinction seems to be universal (Heider, 1991; Kantor & Lehr, 1984; Morsbach & Tyler, 1986; Wallbott & Scherer, 1994). What distinguishes hidden family violence is not the distinction itself, but the way the distinction is defined emotionally, including isolating dissociation. In these families, the private world is marked by abuse, tyranny, and a focus on power. The public world is marked by a prosocial stance, stereotyped positive images that are often prescribed by strong external value systems, and an inability to talk about or publicly acknowledge the nature of the private world.

Skills for Isolating Dissociation

Both multiple personality and hidden family violence begin with dissociations caused by affective experiences associated with trauma, usually in important relationships. In contrast to multiple personality, however, hidden family violence is built around a rigid social-situational structure that maintains a sharp dissociation between public and private domains. As a result, the child growing up in this situation develops not dissociative coordination between separate, related co-conscious agencies but instead *isolating dissociation,* in which public and private worlds are kept separate without coordination. The support of the many contextual and emotional factors marking public versus private leads to a natural passive dissociation that isolates the domains from each other. Children learn mostly to shift from one domain to the other based on these factors, and they do not coordinate the domains. They use the mechanism of shift of focus, the simplest kind of association between two skills, requiring no true coordination (Bidell & Fischer, 1994; Fischer, 1980).

In our own research with toddlers and preschool children, a number of the children show affective splitting as an adaptation to their maltreatment as early as the first half of the second year. The splitting is especially pronounced in children who have been not only physically threatened and abused but also emotionally berated. These toddlers begin to actively inhibit or avoid some negative emotional expressions, particularly involving activities or characteristics of their caregiving parent. They display conventional but faked (ingenuine) positive affect, or they adopt a caretaking or parentified stance that expresses their negativity bias but with them in control or with the negativity sublimated (Ayoub, et al., 1993a). Other studies describe similar avoidance and false positive displays in young maltreated children (Cicchetti & Beeghly, 1987; Crittenden, 1988) as well as sequelae in adulthood (Main & Hesse, 1990).

These toddlers and preschoolers also show another kind of splitting that is based on their perceptions of the power of others. With adults whom they perceive as powerful and threatening, they often defer and inhibit negative affect; but with peers and adults whom they perceive as less powerful, they are often aggressive.

In early development the several factors that conspire to produce and reinforce this public/private dissociation include context, task, secrecy, helplessness, punishment, emotional experience, and affective splitting. Children experience sexual, physical, or severe emotional abuse at home and not in school or other public places, so context produces passive dissociation. Also, at home the tasks or activities that children do are typically different from those done in schools, stores, churches, or other public places. Parents in hidden-violence families reinforce this separation by being secretive about their life at home and forbidding their children from talking about it, especially with outsiders. Violating this prescription can lead to severe punishment. In addition, children's emotional experience with their family in public is distinctly different from that in private, which promotes affective splitting: Outside the home, the parents are polite and overtly kind to their children, while inside the home they are often abusive tyrants.

The case of Marilyn van Derbur mentioned in the introduction illustrates the pattern, although the abuse in her case was primarily sexual and not physical. Her father abused her secretly at home at night. During the day and in public he was a prominent, respected citizen and showed no signs of being abusive. The result was that Ms. van Derbur developed two dissociated worlds—that of the successful, respected, good public child of the day and that of the secret, ashamed, bad private child of the night.

The kind of hidden family violence that we have encountered most frequently is characterized by private physical and emotional abuse. Our developmental model will focus on that pattern, which is illustrated by the case of Mr. M:

> Mr. M was a 37-year-old successful businessman, a church elder, and a respected community leader in a small New England town. In his business he owned a fleet of ice cream trucks, which drove through family neighborhoods ringing their bells to bring children and adults to buy ice cream. Mr. M said that he did not have any close friends, but his family was what was important to him and it was good, close, and widely respected in the community. He talked a lot about his successful business, its role in making children happy, his family's regular attendance at church, his children's consistent school attendance, and his position in the church. He told everyone that his marriage was wonderful and his wife was the perfect woman for him. In public he appeared to be the model husband and father, gracious and attentive to his wife and children.
>
> At home Mr. M was dominant, ruling with an iron fist and needing to be correct in all things. He was routinely degrading and physically abusive to his wife. He would read her the Bible, selecting passages that according to his interpretation, admonished her that she was "a whore" and should repent. He would then physically assault her, telling her that she must obey him as the scripture demands. He was often sadistic in his punishment of the children as well. It was this physical abuse of the children that his wife, under great stress, eventually reported, thus bringing him to the attention of the Department of Social Services.
>
> When asked about his own childhood, Mr. M described it in idyllic terms, but with no recollection of details. He said that his father was a good provider and a respected citizen. Other evidence from family friends indicated that his father was a stern disciplinarian who was harsh with all his children, including the young Mr. M.
>
> Mr. M consistently denied that he was violent or tyrannical at home. His children also denied that he abused them and claimed that their injuries came from accidents at home, on the playground, or in sports, although the evidence was strong that they had been physically abused. When Mr. M's wife and children were able to "escape" from their home and felt safe in a shelter, they were able to relate information about their private abuse. Even after allegations were made and confirmed with physical evidence, Mr. M denied them.
>
> Mr. M kept his public and private worlds completely separate. In the public world, he was an outstanding citizen and community leader, but at home he was a tyrant and expected his children and wife to obey his every command. In his conversations with community members and social workers, there was not a hint of his negative private life. When the question of abuse was raised, he denied it, and when questioning persisted, he became indignant. It seemed that in the public realm he truly believed that he was not an abusive man.

Mr. M's was a strong case of isolating dissociation between public and private worlds. The developmental "accomplishment" here is very different from multiple personality, in that there is no sophisticated coordination of the two "personalities." Yet there is still advanced development. In hidden family violence, the two worlds can each develop to high skill levels with remarkably little connection: In the public world, the person is conforming and respected, and in the private world, he or she is bad and tyrannical (like Mr. M) or victimized (like his wife and children). Along with the isolating dissociation of public and private, there are some minimal coordinations between the worlds, but these mostly seem to involve ways of maintaining the dissociation, such as skills for shifting to the private domain when one is in a public place. As we describe the development of isolating dissociation in hidden family violence, we will illustrate the coordinations along with the dissociations.

Just as with normal affective splitting and multiple personality, dissociation in hidden family violence develops through a series of levels, moving from representations of concrete agents in social interactions to abstractions of intangible personality and motivational characteristics. Early in this development, the public/private split in young children is maintained by the contextual supports provided by their family's separation of public and private worlds and by the distinctive organizing emotions in the two worlds. These supports for splitting are not enough, however, for them to keep the worlds apart consistently. Here is an example of young Johnny's early struggles with hidden family violence:

> While he was alone in a corner of the daycare classroom, 2½-year-old Johnny enacted a story about his father being mean to him. First, he said, "Johnny, you bothered me, come here you little brat!" He then dropped the father doll and grabbed the boy doll directly, shaking his fist and saying, "Don't you be bad, you dumb boy! How many times have I told you? Don't bother me!" He then hit the doll in the face and threw it across the room.
>
> Later, when Johnny went to preschool, his teacher became concerned because he picked on other children, particularly when he thought she was not watching. She called a conference with his parents, at which the father became upset when he heard that his son was disruptive. He told the teacher that he would take care of the problem at home. For the next few days at school, Johnny was very quiet and withdrawn and would not play with anyone.

These child victims of hidden family violence, caught between their need to protect attachments and their regular experience of physical injury, malice, and threat, become performers who do not know they are performing. Instead of developing an integration of public and private, they live like chameleons, learning to shift colors based on the demands of the adults around them. As the children grow, they incorporate a sense of badness based on their private lives, and at the same time they begin to identify with the aggressor to meet his or her needs and eventually, in many cases, to take on his or her role as they grow up. This is an etiology for an abuser who portrays a good face to the public while being sadistic, controlling, and abusive in private.

First Tier of Dissociation: Isolating Agents

This pattern of hidden family violence develops through a sequence of levels of isolating dissociation, according to our model, as outlined in Table 7. First, children develop *isolating agents*, which are coordinated within each domain, public or private, but not across domains. Gradually the isolating agents of children become the *isolating personalities* of adolescents and adults, and the dissociation becomes highly skilled.

When fluent control of individual agents first develops at 2 to 2½ years, isolating dissociation starts with the shift-of-focus process described for the beginnings of multiple personality (Table 6, Level Rp1). Children become anxious when, for example, they see their father getting angry in a way that reminds them of previous abuse. Because they typically attribute negativity to themselves, $\mathbf{ME}_{MEAN}$, they attempt to shift from that negative representation to what they believe their father wants instead, $\mathbf{ME}_{NICE}$. This sort of shift of focus occurs normally in most children when their caregivers become upset. For example, when 2½-year-old Jonathan heard his mother sounding grumpy, he started to jump around, laughing and trying to get her to play. He attempted to shift the polarity of affect from negative to positive:

$$[\mathbf{ME}_{MEAN}] > [\mathbf{ME}_{NICE}] \qquad (32)$$

But when parental upset leads to abuse, children often dissociate the two poles, maintaining vigilance for the slightest hint of negativity and then shifting unconsciously to the positive, such as $\mathbf{ME}_{GOOD}$, and so avoiding the negative, $\mathbf{ME}_{BAD}$.

$$\overset{\text{not}}{\overline{[\mathbf{ME}_{BAD}]}} \not> [\mathbf{ME}_{GOOD}] \qquad (33)$$

In this first crude skill for dissociation, a child defends against $\mathbf{ME}_{BAD}$ and unconsciously shifts to $\mathbf{ME}_{GOOD}$, provided that the context supports the latter. If the context supports the opposite representation, $\mathbf{ME}_{BAD}$, children will have great difficulty sustaining the shift at this level.

Normal children at this age also begin to distinguish between how to act in private and in public—between, for example, dealing with their family at home and visiting a neighbor's house or playing on the community playground. They thus learn to shift between representations of the two worlds and so begin to appropriate or internalize differences in their private and public worlds. In public, they try to maintain a focus on $\mathbf{ME}_{GOOD}$, reserving $\mathbf{ME}_{BAD}$ mostly for private settings (as parents can attest), although they are still able to shift back and forth.

$$[\mathbf{ME\text{-}PRIVATE}_{BAD}] > [\mathbf{ME\text{-}PUBLIC}_{GOOD}] \qquad (34)$$

When maltreated children can distinguish private and public, they begin to dissociate the two. For example, when they are on the playground, they must not act in terms of their private world, but instead must be good and proper, not acting out the private **ME**s that relate to abusive interactions at home.

$$\overset{\text{not}}{\overline{[\mathbf{ME\text{-}PRIVATE}_{BAD}]}} \not> [\mathbf{ME\text{-}PUBLIC}_{GOOD}] \qquad (35)$$

Table 7 Levels of Development of Isolating Dissociation in Hidden Family Violence

Level	Dissociative Skills[1]: Representational Tier	Dissociative Skills[1]: Abstract Tier	Examples of Dissociative and Non-dissociative Skills	Age[2]
S4/Rp1: Single Representations[3]	not $\left[\mathit{ME\text{-}PRIVATE}_{BAD} \right] \nrightarrow \left[\mathit{ME\text{-}PUBLIC}_{GOOD} \right]$		**Single concrete representations of people as agents:** When child is expected to be good and he thinks of being bad, he shifts abruptly to a good representation to avoid being bad [active dissociation]. Child pretends that he is his father hitting someone and saying mean things, and then he shifts to pretending that he is a good boy, playing nicely by himself (not active dissociation).	18–24 mos.
Rp2: Representational Mappings	$\left[\mathit{ME}_{BAD} \overset{private}{\longleftrightarrow} \mathit{YOU}_{BOSS} \right] \nrightarrow \left[\mathit{ME}_{GOOD} \overset{public}{\longleftrightarrow} \mathit{YOU}_{GOOD} \right]$		**Simple relations of representations:** When child is in a public setting, he avoids acting out his private family role of being bad with an adult, shifting instead to his public role of acting good with an adult (act. diss.). When child sees his mother beginning to act mean, he tries to move her attention to something she likes, such as a present he made for her (not act. diss.).	3.5–4.5 yr

Rp3: Representational Systems	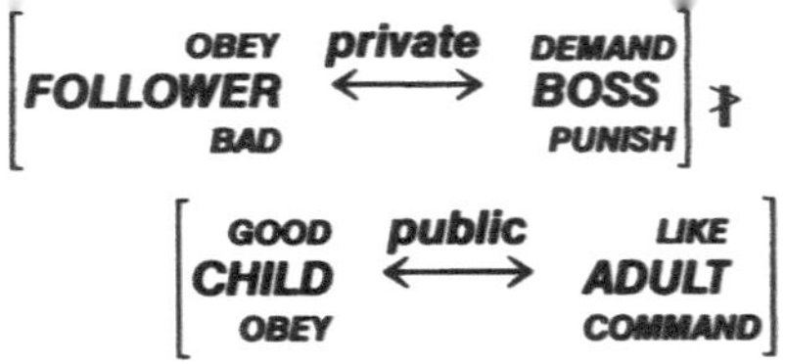	**Complex relations of subsets of representations:** Child shifts between two dissociated role relationships: In private, he is usually the obedient follower who is punished when bad; but sometimes he takes on the demanding, punishing boss role. In public, he is usually the good obedient child; but sometimes he may take on the commanding, friendly adult role (act. diss.). In lying, child coordinates the lie with his knowledge of the other person's information and beliefs so as to deceive more effectively (not act. diss.).	6–7
Rp4/A1: Single Abstractions	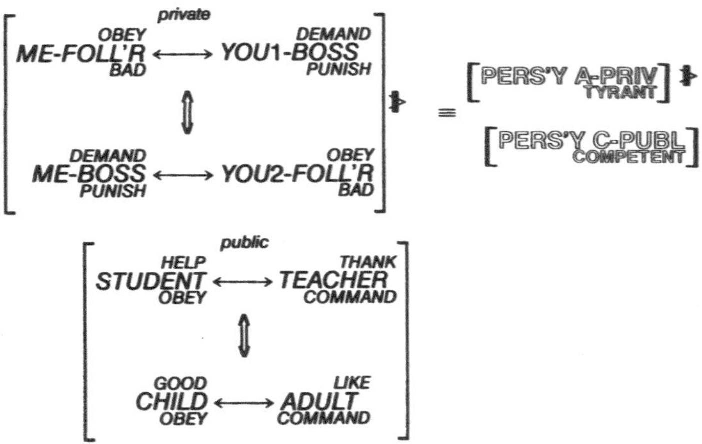	**Relations of representational systems to produce abstractions (intangible concepts) about people (personalities):** Person coordinates several concrete role relationships in terms of intangible personality characteristics to form dissociated personalities by domain. He shifts between tyrant (or victim) for the private domain and competent person for the public (act. diss.). Within each domain, person coordinates concrete behaviors and characteristics to form various abstract personality concepts and motives, thus establishing separate public and private personalities instead of mere agents (not act. diss.).	10–12

Table 7 (continued)

Level	Dissociative Skills[1] Representational Tier	Abstract Tier	Examples of Dissociative and Non-dissociative Skills	Age[2]
A2: Abstract Mappings		[PERS'Y A (TYRANT) —private— PERS'Y B (VICTIM)] ⇹ [PERS'Y C (COMPETENT) —public— PERS'Y D (IMPRESSED)]	**Simple relations of abstractions:** Person shifts between coordinations of personalities in dissociated private and public domains, relating (for example) tyrant and victim personalities in private and separately, competent and satisfied personalities in public (act. diss.). Within each domain, person relates several abstract personal characteristics, such as public moral concern with need for obedience from followers and children (not act. diss.).	14–16
A3: Abstract Systems		[LOVER PERS'Y A TYRANT ←private→ LOVED PERS'Y B VICTIM] ⇹ [PROSOCIAL PERS'Y C COMPETENT ←public→ GRATIFIED PERS'Y D IMPRESSED]	**Complex relations of subsets of abstractions:** In dissociated private and public domains, person coordinates personalities along several dimensions simultaneously. In private, lover/loved one is coordinated with tyrant/victim; in public, prosocial/gratified with competent/impressed (act. diss.). Within each domain, person relates complex set of personal characteristics along several dimensions, such as two types of intentionality and responsibility as part of public concern for morality and obedience (not act. diss.).	18–20

A4: Systems of Abstract Systems: Principles[4]	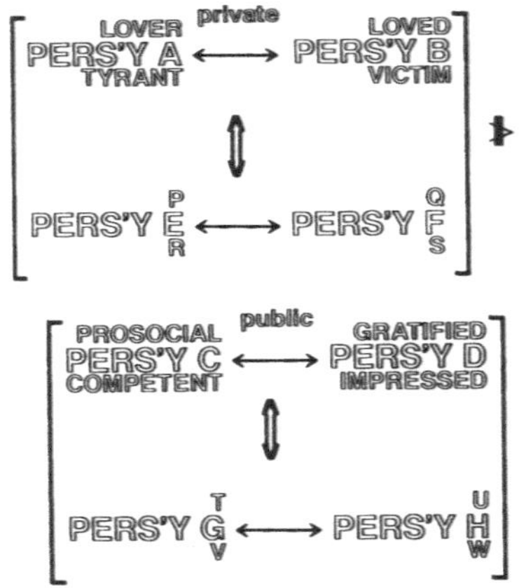	**General principles for integrating systems of abstractions:** Dissociative strategies can be sophisticated, but they are still based in maintaining strong separation of private and public domains rather than coordinating them. Within each domain, person shows full-fledged, complex adult personalities, but simultaneously the dissociations produce rigidities and stupidities at times because of the inability to integrate across domains (act. diss.). Within each domain, person can understand general principles, such as moral principle of justice, integrating relations between types of intention and responsibility (not act. diss.).	23–25

[1]The skill structures in the diagrams are examples of skills showing the simplest general form of a dissociative structure for a given level and are described in the first example, which in each case involves active dissociation. The second example is an instance of a more ordinary skill at this level and therefore does *not* fit the dissociative structure in the diagram; instead it shows a type of structure that is characteristic of the level and of the hidden-family-violence pattern but lacks the dissociation. The text of the chapter describes examples of other skills as well.

[2]Ages given are estimates of modal ages at which a level first appears based on cognitive developmental research described elsewhere (Fischer & Farrar, 1987; Fischer et al., 1993; Kitchener et al., 1993). They may differ across cultures and other social groups.

[3]Representations grow from coordinations of sensorimotor systems, but for simplicity that relation has been omitted from this table.

[4]The skill structure shown for Level A4 is a system of abstract systems, which is also a principle. The principle that emerges from this structure could be designated by a separate structure, such as **P**, but because there is no evidence for later levels beyond A4, we have not included the separate structure for **P**.

Note: In skill structures, each word or letter denotes a skill component, with each large word or letter designating a main component (set) and each subscript or superscript designating a subset of the main component. Italics designate representations, and outline letters designate abstractions. Lines connecting sets designate relations forming a mapping, single-line arrows designate relations forming a system, and double-line arrows designate relations forming a system of systems. An arrowhead without a line (>) designates a shift of focus between two skills. A dark rectangle in the middle of the arrowhead indicates that the relation is dissociative.

This isolating-dissociation mechanism allows ***ME-PUBLIC*** to be sustained over ***ME-PRIVATE*** only if the context generally supports the public representation. The same limit was present for the simpler isolating shift from $\boldsymbol{ME_{BAD}}$ to $\boldsymbol{ME_{GOOD}}$ (formula 33). Single representations provide little power to overcome strong context effects and are therefore not very effective. It is relations between representations that give children the capacity to direct their own activities effectively. Firmer dissociation requires the stronger structures that develop with coordination of representations into mappings and beyond. Recall the case of Carrie Smith, who showed only unstable dissociation until age 4, when she developed the ability to coordinate two co-conscious agencies in a mapping and switch between them.

Normally the development of mappings at about 4 years and older leads to all kinds of new social skills involving other people (Fischer, et al., 1984b). Children subject to hidden family violence use these skills extensively in their private lives. For instance, social contingencies (Table 4, Task 4 and beyond) help children to cope with negative emotions in their families and friends. When 4-year-old Jason's mother started scolding his father at the dinner table, the boy began to draw attention energetically to the nice drawing he had done earlier that day (which was taped on the wall near the table). The switch to a positive topic was so abrupt and obvious that his parents immediately recognized his attempt to change their interaction to positive. This is not merely a shift of focus (like formula 32) because the child was not only trying to do something positive with Mom; instead, he was attempting to move her attention to something that she was happy about:

$$[\boldsymbol{MOM_{MEAN}} \overline{\quad\quad} \boldsymbol{MOM_{NICE}}] \tag{36}$$

At the same time, children begin to understand many common social role relationships, such as mother to father, mother to child, and doctor to patient (Fischer, et al., 1984b; Fischer & Watson, 1981; Watson, 1984; Watson & Getz, 1991). These new understandings allow children in abusive families to start to develop clear separation of public and private roles, which is necessary for strong isolating dissociation of public and private. For example, they can sometimes maintain a public style of interaction even in situations that do not provide strong contextual support for it, such as acting out ***ME-PUBLIC*** when playing on a playground with their father, with whom their private relationship is one of abusive boss interacting with bad child:

$$\frac{\textbf{not}}{[\boldsymbol{ME_{BAD}} \xrightarrow{\textit{private}} \mathbf{DAD_{BOSS}}]} \nrightarrow [\boldsymbol{ME_{GOOD}} \xrightarrow{\textit{public}} \boldsymbol{DAD_{GOOD}}] \tag{37}$$

By 6 or 7 years children begin to construct representational systems (Level Rp3), which give them more flexible control over public and private dissociations. For example, on the playground or at school, they can shift between public and private interactions depending on who is present and who is more powerful. The case of Roger illustrates this developmental step: In his behavior, Roger showed a sharp distinction in both affect and action between public and private modes of interaction, and he attempted to impose the private mode on other children whom he thought he could dominate. The emotional tone of the interaction shifted abruptly when he changed between public and private modes.

> At age 9 Roger was a boy of average intelligence who made a conscious effort to please his teacher and participate in class in order to obtain her approval. He often succeeded in being charming. When being watched by adults in the classroom, Roger was a model student. He also helped certain teachers by preparing materials for them or offering to monitor class when they had to leave the room for a short time. However, when out of sight of the teacher and other adults, he was a ruthless bully, frequently threatening other children to get their possessions or to force them to help him with his homework. Roger was also overtly condescending to the girls in his class. Roger's relations with his peers were based on his assessment of power and status. When approached by an older, stronger boy, Roger yielded in deference. If the boy threatened him, he would often begin crying and begging not to be harmed.
>
> When asked about his family, Roger stated that they were a good family and listed his father's virtues—a business, money, and respect within the community. He did not mention that his father, Mr. S, was a strict and unpredictable man, and his mother was passive, distant, and visibly sad. The father expected the children to respond quickly to his every request. Mr. S's anger was often triggered by what outsiders would have seen as unimportant acts, although of course outsiders did not witness them. In private Mr. S often told his children that they were worthless and would grow up to be misfits. He also routinely degraded his wife, criticizing her ethnic background and physically abusing her. She often cried in silence.

From these examples, it is clear both that Roger's home environment followed the hidden family violence pattern and that his dissociation of public and private was already pervasive. It appeared not only in distinctions between public and private settings but also in his relationships at school. In public at school (with teachers watching), he was a good boy who obeyed the teacher and sought her approval. In private at home he was a submissive child (a follower or victim) who obeyed his father's demands and was punished when he was bad. At school, the private domain also came to the fore when there were no teachers watching: Roger would take either the follower or the bully role, depending on his assessment of the other child's power. These relatively complex social relationships involved (a) both public and private representational systems (Level Rp3) coordinating several roles and (b) an isolating shift of focus between public and private systems:

$$\left[\text{ME-FOLL'R}^{\text{OBEY}}_{\text{BAD}} \overset{\text{private}}{\longleftrightarrow} \text{YOU-BOSS}^{\text{DEMAND}}_{\text{PUNISH}} \right] \nrightarrow \qquad (38)$$

$$\left[\text{ME-STUD'T}^{\text{GOOD}}_{\text{OBEY}} \overset{\text{public}}{\longleftrightarrow} \text{YOU-TEAC'R}^{\text{LIKE}}_{\text{COMMAND}} \right]$$

In this skill, Roger took the roles of follower and student, ***ME-FOLLOWER*** and ***ME-STUDENT,*** but in appropriate contexts he also could switch which role he adopted, acting as boss or teacher (***ME-BOSS*** or ***ME-TEACHER***) to someone else as follower or student (***YOU-FOLLOWER*** or ***YOU-STUDENT***), respectively. Depending upon the context and affective tone, he could be either follower or boss, student or teacher.

Presumably when Roger was younger—or still now when he was functioning low in his developmental range—he also used simpler versions of this skill, such as mappings of the same relationships with one dimension deleted from each (Level Rp2):

$$\left[\mathit{ME\text{-}FOLL'R}_{BAD} \overset{private}{\text{———}} \mathit{YOU\text{-}BOSS}_{PUNISH}\right] \nrightarrow \tag{39}$$

$$\left[\mathit{ME\text{-}STUD'T}_{GOOD} \overset{public}{\text{———}} \mathit{YOU\text{-}TEAC'R}_{LIKE}\right]$$

At Roger's age, most children become skilled at deception and lying (Lamborn, et al., 1994; Saarni, 1984; Saarni & Lewis, 1993). Of course, deception is central in hidden family violence because individuals lie to both others and themselves. Purposeful lies require relating at least two representations to each other, the truth and the falsehood. To understand that they are lying, children must coordinate the two representations in their own minds:

$$\left[\mathit{TRUTH} \text{———} \mathit{LIE}\right] \tag{40}$$

Children thus develop purposeful lies by using representational mappings and then go on to master them with the next level of skills, representational systems. For example, Roger stole a toy from another student named James and then "helped" James by telling him that the least popular child in the class, Colin, had stolen it. This kind of lie required coordinating at least several potential states of James' knowledge (such as about Roger helping and Colin stealing) with several potential claims or actions on Roger's part (such as Roger stealing the toy and blaming Colin):

$$\left[\underset{BLAME\ COL.}{\overset{STOLE}{ROGER}} \overset{lie}{\leftrightarrow} \underset{COL.\ STOLE}{\overset{ROG\ HELP}{JAMES}}\right] \tag{41}$$

Second Tier of Dissociation: Isolating Personalities

Over the next several years, Roger made the transition to the next developmental tier, moving from representational systems relating concrete agents to abstractions for people as personalities. His isolating dissociation became much more effective, because his new understanding of motivation and personality made him more skilled at both deceiving people and maintaining the separation of public and private relationships. By coordinating representational systems into abstractions as described earlier (Level Rp4/A1), he moved beyond complex concrete interactions to build abstractions for his general characteristics in either public or private (separately). For example, in private, he coordinated two representational systems for abusive bossiness, one in which he acted as boss to some other victim and a separate one in which he acted as victim to some other boss. We call the resulting general personality characteristic "tyranny" because his goal was to be the tyrant:

$$\left.\begin{array}{ccc} \underset{\text{BAD}}{\overset{\text{OBEY}}{\text{ME-FOLL'R}}} & \overset{\text{private}}{\leftrightarrow} & \underset{\text{PUNISH}}{\overset{\text{DEMAND}}{\text{YOU1-BOSS}}} \\ & \Updownarrow & \\ \underset{\text{PUNISH}}{\overset{\text{DEMAND}}{\text{ME-BOSS}}} & \leftrightarrow & \underset{\text{BAD}}{\overset{\text{OBEY}}{\text{YOU2-FOLL'R}}} \end{array}\right] \equiv \left[\underset{\text{TYRANT}}{\text{ROGER-PRIV}}\right] \qquad \text{(42 and 43)}$$

Separately in public and private domains, he built such abstract personality characteristics and continued to use isolating dissociation to keep them separate:

$$\left[\underset{\text{TYRANT}}{\text{ROGER-PRIV}}\right] \nrightarrow \left[\underset{\text{COMPETENT}}{\text{ROGER-PUBL}}\right] \qquad (44)$$

With this new level of skill, his isolating dissociation of his two worlds became stronger. By age 16, when he had consolidated his single abstractions and was beginning to construct abstract mappings (Level A2), his public personality was much in evidence at school, and he used it skillfully, as illustrated by the following:

> At 16 years Roger was an apparently successful sophomore in high school. He was on the student council and the track team, although he did not have any close friends. He spent a good deal of time attempting to gain the attention of older student council members. He also helped the vice principal, whom he saw as the person in the school with the power to set the rules. Roger was a force in school politics, presenting himself as someone who knew the answers and could handle issues better than other students, particularly those his age or younger. He ignored or was openly cruel to younger students. He was condescending to girls in general and to boys he saw as weaker than himself.
>
> At home Roger was quiet and withdrawn with his father, who remained rigid and cold. When his father confronted him about something, Roger whined and hung his head. With his mother, on the other hand, he was verbally abusive when his father was not at home, and during one argument he pushed her into a door. He also used threats of harm to force his younger brother to do many of his chores for him.

Roger seems to be constructing abstract mappings that coordinate the personality characteristics of victim and tyrant in the private domain and those of competent student leader and impressed or satisfied authority in the public domain:

$$\left[\underset{\text{VICTIM}}{\text{ROGER}} \overset{\text{private}}{\text{——}} \underset{\text{TYRANT}}{\text{FATHER}}\right] \nrightarrow \qquad (45)$$

$$\left[\underset{\text{COMPETENT}}{\text{ROGER}} \overset{\text{public}}{\text{——}} \underset{\text{IMPRESSED}}{\text{AUTH'TY}}\right]$$

This skill structure puts Roger in the roles of victim and competent student leader, but he is also able to reverse the relationship to take the role of tyrant in relation to someone else as victim, as illustrated by his treatment of girls, younger students, and his mother:

$$\left[\underset{\text{TYRANT}}{\text{ROGER}} \overset{\text{private}}{\text{——}} \underset{\text{VICTIM}}{\text{MOTHER}}\right] \qquad (46)$$

It is unclear whether he could reverse the public relationship so as to take on the role of satisfied authority, since he tended to be bossy and tyrannical.

As Roger moved into adulthood, he developed these skills further and used them to begin to establish himself in his community. At the same time, he also began to look for a wife. His affective splitting became especially evident in the way that he treated the young woman he courted.

> At age 24, Roger was continuing to show his competence and good qualities in public. He joined the local church and was asked to be on the church board. He became a member of the Young Republican Club and attended anti-abortion rallies at the Community Center. He offered to do volunteer work promoting his town's business for the Chamber of Commerce. He started to build his own real-estate business.
>
> A few months earlier, he began to date a 17-year-old young woman named June, who had just completed high school. They met when she came to work for him as a temporary secretary. Roger was most attentive to her, sending flowers to her almost daily and buying her expensive gifts including a sapphire ring and diamond earrings. He repeatedly told her how special she was and denied that she could have a single fault.
>
> As their relationship developed, Roger became exceedingly possessive, controlling, and domineering. He insisted on accompanying her to the hair stylist "to help the stylist know how I like your hair". He told June to throw away the clothes in her closet and accompanied her to pick out new clothes. When they were alone, Roger repeatedly needed to show superior knowledge in all areas. He also insinuated that June was not a good cook, did not know how to dress, and could not be out alone because of her naivete.

Roger was building more complex skills in both private and public domains, perpetuating his split between positive competence in public and negative tyranny in private. In his relationship with June, where he was attempting to build his own family, he showed an unhappy combination of love with tyranny. His efforts were directed at bringing her into his isolating dissociation, placing her in his private world and not letting her be part of his public one except as a stereotype (the perfect wife). In his public world, on the other hand, he combined his general competence with a prosocial orientation, doing good for the community through church and Chamber of Commerce. In these ways, he constructed abstract systems (Level A3) for continuing his isolating dissociation of these two worlds:

[LOVER ROGER TYRANT —private↔— LOVED JUNE VICTIM] ⇻
[PROSOCIAL ROGER COMPETENT —public↔— GRATIFIED AUTH'Y IMPRESSED] (47)

Eventually Roger will construct still more sophisticated skills of isolating dissociation, separating his private and public worlds into separate systems organized by principles for integrating abstractions, as diagramed in Table 7 (Level A4). The sophistication and complexity of these skills is clear, even while they are also obviously pathological and dangerous.

Unfortunately Roger is establishing a pattern of hidden violence in the family he is planning, as evidenced by his actions with June. His developmental pathway resembles that shown by Mr. M, as described earlier. Here is a description of Mr. M's outrageous efforts to control his wife, which can be seen as an extreme extension of the way Roger treated June.

> Mr. M, a 37-year-old successful businessman and respected community leader, married his wife when she was only 18 and he was 35. He initially lavished her with gifts and said she was the perfect woman for him.
>
> As the marriage progressed, he found that she often did not do what he told her to do: He wanted her to stay at home, and she wanted to continue working. In public, he continued to be the model husband, and at work he continued to tell his fellow workers how wonderful his marriage was. But at home he became angry and critical and attempted to control more and more of her life. He began buying all her clothes and make-up and would not let her go grocery shopping. Eventually he locked her in their home, and when she became pregnant, he attempted to control her even more. He insisted on taking graphic pictures of every stage of labor and delivery, despite her protest. After delivery he tried to breastfeed the baby himself, despite the biological impossibility.
>
> During the time of these bizarre behaviors, he maintained his highly respectable roles in the community as church board member, respected businessman, and community leader.

The bizarreness of Mr. M's behaviors did not preclude his continuing skill at maintaining separation of public and private. He had so mastered and extended isolating dissociation throughout his activities that overlap between domains was rare. Here are some of the ways that he maintained the isolation:

> Mr. M was a deacon in his church and the treasurer of the church board. The other parishioners saw him as a good business man who could also organize events. He was also seen as generous because he made many donations to the church. He ruled over the church budget with an iron fist, maintaining complete control over the finances, including the exclusive right to handle the money and disperse funds. When challenged about church financial matters, he became indignant and rigid, but his role was not often questioned because of his skill at handling the finances and his confidence in his abilities.
>
> In his food business, Mr. M showed similar skills, including sophisticated wholesale purchasing practices, effective business management techniques, and successful sales activities (such as using ice-cream trucks and drivers that

> were very appealing to children and their families and so led to strong sales in family neighborhoods).
>
> The parishioners at his church and the employees at his business knew little about his family interactions. Although his wife and children attended church with him regularly, they did not offer their opinions nor did they independently attend functions or participate in church activities. He and his family were widely admired.

The parallels are remarkable between the cases of Mr. M and Roger—and among many others in our experience. That is why we have given the pattern its own name, "hidden family violence," and outlined a model of its development. The pattern begins with a maltreating family that sharply dissociates their public, proper world from their private, tyrannical one. Children growing up in this family are abused physically and emotionally, and sometimes sexually as well. From this contextual and affective splitting, the children develop contextual dissociation that isolates public from private, and eventually their maltreatment promotes more complex dissociation as well. Children learn to dissociatively shift away from one world into the other one, depending on context and affective state. In the extreme children come to be literally unable to coordinate their two worlds, not only treating them as distinct but being unable to psychologically access one world while they are in the other. Isolating dissociation thus produces a different developmental pathway from co-conscious dissociation, because the latter involves dissociative coordination rather than isolation. On the other hand, the two developmental pathways are similar in that they both produce not developmental delay or arrest but instead movement to advanced developmental levels involving skills of great complexity in dissociation.

Conclusion: Psychopathology Is Not Developmental Immaturity

In conclusion, our dynamic analysis of development of normal affective splitting and abnormal co-conscious and isolating dissociation calls into question the traditional view that psychopathology typically involves developmental immaturity or regression. Development does bring the potential for integrating across splits and dissociations, but it also brings the potential for construction of more and more powerful types of splitting and dissociation. Much psychopathology is characterized by advanced skills for splitting and dissociation, not simply by immature or regressed development.

On the one hand, splitting of positive and negative emotions is a powerful force in development, leading to affective splitting and dissociation that is especially strong in early childhood. With development, normal children and adults become capable of integrating positive and negative in many arenas and more generally of integrating many activities that are naturally dissociated as a result of context, affect, and other organizing influences.

On the other hand, splitting and dissociation can take advanced forms, based on the sophisticated capacities that develop naturally in human beings. Maltreatment in childhood often produces such advanced forms of dissociation and splitting. It promotes severe active splitting and dissociation and reverses the polarity of affective organization so that the negative (malevolent) becomes central to important parts of self and others in relationships. With development, maltreated children develop increasingly sophisticated skills for adapting to their abusive relationships.

Multiple personality disorder and hidden family violence are two patterns of dissociative development arising from maltreatment (and often perpetuating it in the next generation). In multiple personality, children develop dissociated co-conscious agents and then personalities that are organized around the affects from maltreatment as well as the children's adaptive needs. In hidden family violence, children develop dissociatively isolated agents and then personalities that are separated into two distinct worlds—a negative, tyrannical private world and a positive, altruistic public one. The skills that people eventually construct as they develop along these pathways are remarkably complex and sophisticated, easily paralleling the complexities of normal development.

The main reason that most scholars and practitioners studying psychopathology have failed to see this complexity is that they have not analyzed development from the viewpoint of their patients. Analyses of normal development have often suffered from a similar limitation, with the observer often forcing his or her viewpoint on the subjects of study (Bidell & Fischer, 1992; Bronfenbrenner, 1993; Cole & Scribner, 1974; Fischer, et al., 1993; Noam, 1988). In addition, patients are often observed in situations that minimize their level of functioning because of stress and absence of contextual support.

For both multiple personality and hidden family violence, observers can easily classify people as developmentally immature by using frameworks that assume "normal" developmental pathways instead of the strange pathways that these people actually follow. To conclude, we will illustrate *how a sophisticated dissociative skill can easily be made to seem developmentally immature* when it is subjected to this kind of misguided analysis.

In developing multiple personality, Carrie Smith constructed a number of complex, sophisticated skills for co-conscious dissociation among her various "personalities." For example, in early adulthood she constructed a complex abstract skill (Level A3) relating Carla and Carrie, evidenced by Carla's acting in ways specifically designed to bait Carrie by offending her sensibilities. This kind of skill does not develop until about age 20 at the earliest in normal development (Fischer, et al., 1990).

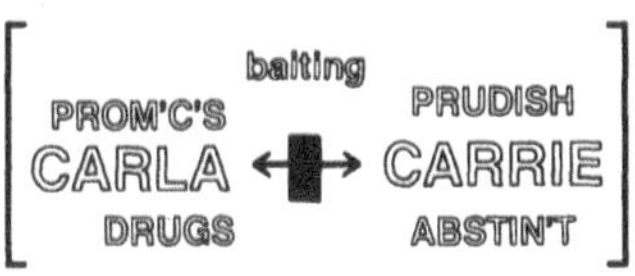

(48)

Recall how Carla used drugs and began to have sex with a man at a party and then withdrew, leaving Carrie to find herself in a dangerous and objectionable situation, which included what Carrie experienced as rape. If this scenario is analyzed not in terms of the sophisticated adaptations of multiple personality but instead in terms of the simplistic descriptions given by the confused, upset

Carrie, the skill involved seems minimal: Carla had talked to Carrie at the party, tempting her to be promiscuous, and then she suddenly found herself being raped. All that is required for these simple descriptions is a representational mapping relating simple concrete actions, a skill that is characteristic of 4-year-olds:

$$\left[\textit{ME-CARLA}_{\textit{TEMPT}} \;\text{——}\; \textit{ME-CARRIE}_{\textit{RAPED}}\right] \qquad (49)$$

Similarly for hidden family violence, Mr. M and Roger built the sophisticated skills required to dissociate their public and private worlds, acting as highly skilled businessmen and community members in one world and tyrants or victims in the other. Here is the kind of abstract system (Level A3) that they constructed for coordinating personalities in each world and isolating the two worlds from each other.

$$\left[\begin{array}{c} \text{LOVER} \\ \text{PERS'Y A1} \\ \text{TYRANT} \end{array} \overset{\text{private}}{\longleftrightarrow} \begin{array}{c} \text{LOVED} \\ \text{PERS'Y B} \\ \text{VICTIM} \end{array}\right] \nleftrightarrow \qquad (50)$$
$$\left[\begin{array}{c} \text{PROSOCIAL} \\ \text{PERS'Y A2} \\ \text{COMPETENT} \end{array} \overset{\text{public}}{\longleftrightarrow} \begin{array}{c} \text{GRATIFIED} \\ \text{PERS'Y C} \\ \text{IMPRESSED} \end{array}\right]$$

At the same time, when a public person such as a church member or a social worker asked them to describe their private world, none of this complexity was evident. Instead they gave impoverished answers demonstrating only minimal skills. Roger stated simply that he was a good man and that he loved June, at best a representational mapping that could have been produced by a 4-year-old:

$$\left[\textit{ME}_{\textit{GOOD}} \;\text{——}\; \textit{JUNE}_{\textit{LOVED}}\right] \qquad (51)$$

Mr. M provided an even more vivid case of impoverished descriptions of his family. When asked about his daughter, he gave only stereotyped, simple, concrete descriptions, even though he showed no overt signs of anxiety or distress. He said that his daughter was "a good girl," and when asked to elaborate, he said, "She does the sorts of things that good girls do. She goes to school. She wears pretty clothes." Throughout the discussion, he never once used her name. This response required only a single representation, a cluster of characteristics of a good girl, an answer that many 2- and 3-year-olds could produce:

$$\left[\textit{GIRL}_{\textit{GOOD}}\right] \qquad (52)$$

The impoverishment of Carrie's, Roger's, and Mr. M's descriptions of their close relationships was certainly real and should not be ignored. At the same time, these low-level descriptions do not demonstrate developmental delay or regression. Everyone shows low-level responses some of the time, especially when dealing with dissociated, split topics in difficult situations. Scholars and therapists make a serious error when they take these impoverished descriptions to reflect a generally low level of development.

Understanding the development of troubled people like these requires analyzing their adaptations to the strange, abusive worlds where they live. In those worlds, they develop remarkably sophisticated skills that generally parallel the skills of normal development, but that are built on the devastating dissociations that arise from their unfortunate lives. They do not fail to develop, but they develop strangely, in the ways demanded for adaptation to abusive relationships.

REFERENCES

Aber, J. L., Allen, J. P., Carlson, V., & Cicchetti, D. (1989). The effects of maltreatment on development during early childhood: Recent studies and their theoretical, clinical, and policy implications. In D. Cicchetti & V. Carlson (Ed.), *Child maltreatment: Theory and research on the causes and consequences of child abuse and neglect* (pp. 579–619). Cambridge, U.K.: Cambridge University Press.

Adelson, J., Green, B., & O'Neil, R. P. (1969). The growth of the idea of law in adolescence. *Developmental Psychology, 1*, 327–332.

Ainsworth, M. D., Blehar, M., Waters, E., & Wall, S. (1978). *Patterns of attachment: A psychological study of the strange situation.* Hillsdale, N.J.: Erlbaum.

Ayoub, C., Grace, P., Paradise, J., & Newberger, E. (1991). Alleging psychological impairment of the accuser to defend oneself against a child abuse allegation: A manifestation of wife battering and false accusation. *Child and Youth Services, 15*(2), 191–208.

Ayoub, C., Raya, P., & Fischer, K. W. (1993a). Social interactions in young maltreated toddlers: The development of self in relationships. Paper presented at the meetings of the Society for Research in Child Development. New Orleans.

Ayoub, C., Willett, J. B., & Robinson, D. (1993b). Families at risk of child maltreatment: Entry-level characteristics and growth in family functioning. *Child Abuse and Neglect, 16*, 495–511.

Barrett, K. C., & Campos, J. J. (1987). Perspectives on emotional development II: A functionalist approach to emotions. In J. Osofsky (Ed.), *Handbook of infant development* (2nd ed., pp. 555–578). New York: Wiley.

Bidell, T. R., & Fischer, K. W. (1992). Beyond the stage debate: Action, structure, and variability in Piagetian theory and research. In R. Sternberg & C. Berg (Ed.), *Intellectual development* (pp. 100–140). New York: Cambridge University Press.

Bidell, T. R., & Fischer, K. W. (1994). Developmental transitions in children's early on-line planning. In M. M. Haith, J. B. Benson, R. J. Roberts Jr., & B. F. Pennington (Ed.), *Development of future-oriented processes* (in press). Chicago: University of Chicago Press.

Biggs, J., & Collis, K. (1982). *Evaluating the quality of learning: The SOLO taxonomy (structure of the observed learning outcome).* New York: Academic Press.

Bliss, E. L. (1980). Multiple personalities. *Archives of General Psychiatry, 37*, 1388–1397.

Block, J. H., & Block, J. (1980). The role of ego-control and ego-resiliency in the organization of behavior. In W. A. Collins (Ed.), *Minnesota Symposium on Child Psychology, 13.* Hillsdale, N.J.: Erlbaum.

Bretherton, I., & Beeghly, M. (1989). Pretense: Acting "as if". In J. Lockman & N. Hazan (Ed.), *Action in social context: Perspectives on early development.* New York: Plenum.

Bretherton, I., & Waters, E. (1985). *Growing points of attachment theory and research. Monographs of the Society for Research in Child Development, 50*(1–2, Serial No. 209).

Breuer, J., & Freud, S. (1955). *Studies on hysteria* (A. Strachey & J. Strachey, Trans.). In J. Strachey (Ed.), *Standard Edition of the Complete Psychological Works of Sigmund Freud* (Vol. 2). London: Hogarth Press. (Originally published, 1895).

Bronfenbrenner, U. (1993). The ecology of cognitive development. In R. H. Wozniak & K. W. Fischer (Ed.), *Development in context: Acting and thinking in specific environments* (pp. 3–44). Hillsdale, N.J.: Erlbaum.

Brown, A. L., & Reeve, R. (1987). Bandwidths of competence: The role of supportive contexts in learning and development. In L. S. Liben (Ed.), *Development and learning: Conflict or congruence?* Hillsdale, N.J.: Erlbaum.

Buchsbaum, H. K., Toth, S. L., Clyman, R. B., Cicchetti, D., & Emde, R. N. (1992). The use of a narrative story stem technique with maltreated children: Implications for theory and practice. *Development and Psychopathology,* 4, 603–625.

Calverley, R., Fischer, K. W., & Ayoub, C. (in press). Complex affective splitting in sexually abused adolescent girls. *Development and Psychopathology,* in press.

Calverley, R. M. (1993). *Differentiation and integration in the self-understanding of sexually abused adolescent girls.* Unpublished qualifying paper, Harvard University.

Campos, J. J., Barrett, K. C., Lamb, M. E., Goldsmith, H. H., & Stenberg, C. (1983). Socioemotional development. In M. M. Haith & J. J. Campos (Ed.), & P. H. Mussen (Series Ed.), *Handbook of child psychology: Vol. 2. Infancy and developmental psychobiology* (pp. 783–915). New York: Wiley.

Canadian Broadcasting Corporation (1990). *To a safer place.*

Case, R., & Edelstein, W. (1993). *The new structuralism in cognitive development: Theory and research on individual pathways. Contributions to Human Development, 23.* Basel, Switzerland: Karger.

Cicchetti, D. (1989). How research on child maltreatment has informed the study of child development: Perspectives from developmental psychopathology. In D. Cicchetti & V. Carlson (Ed.), *Child maltreatment: Theory and research on the causes and consequences of child abuse and neglect* (pp. 377–431). Cambridge, U.K.: Cambridge University Press.

Cicchetti, D. (in press). Developmental theory: Lessons from the study of risk and psychopathology. In S. Matthysse, D. Levy, J. Kagan, & F. Benes (Ed.), *Psychopathology: The evolving science of mental disorder.* New York: Cambridge University Press.

Cicchetti, D., & Beeghly, M. (1987). Symbolic development in maltreated youngsters: An organizational perspective. In D. Cicchetti & M. Beeghly (Ed.), *Atypical symbolic development. New Directions for Child Development, 36,* 5–29. San Francisco: Jossey-Bass.

Cicchetti, D., & Rizley, R. (1981). Developmental perspectives on the etiology, intergenerational transmission, and sequelae of child maltreatment. In R. Rizley & D. Cicchetti (Ed.), *Developmental perspectives on child maltreatment. New Directions for Child Development, 11,* 31–55. San Francisco: Jossey-Bass.

Colby, A., Kohlberg, L., Gibbs, J., & Lieberman, M. (1983). *A longitudinal study of moral judgement. Monographs of the Society for Research in Child Development, 48* (1, Serial no. 200).

Cole, M., & Scribner, S. (1974). *Culture and thought: A psychological introduction.* New York: Wiley.

Cole, P. M., & Putnam, F. W. (1992). Effect of incest on self and social functioning: A developmental psychopathology perspective. *Journal of Consulting and Clinical Psychology,* 60, 174–184.

Connell, J. P. (1991). Context, self, and action: A motivational analysis of self-system processes across the life span. In D. Cicchetti & M. Beeghly (Ed.), *The self in transition: Infancy to childhood* (pp. 61–97). Chicago: University of Chicago Press.

Crittenden, P. M. (1988). Relationships at risk. In J. Belsky & T. Nezworski (Ed.), *Clinical implications of attachment theory* (pp. 136–174). Hillsdale, N.J.: Erlbaum.
Crittenden, P. M. (1993). Peering into the black box: An exploratory treatise on the development of self in young children. In D. Cicchetti & S. L. Toth (Ed.), *Rochester Symposium on Development and Psychopathology: Vol. 5. The self and its disorders*. Rochester, N.Y.: University of Rochester Press.
Donaldson, S. K., & Westerman, M. A. (1986). Development of children's understanding of ambivalence and causal theories of emotions. *Developmental Psychology, 22*, 655–622.
Elmendorf, D. (1992). *Preschool children's interpretations of the intentions behind physically harmful acts: Developmental changes in understanding, misunderstanding, and distortion.* Unpublished doctoral dissertation, University of Denver.
Erdelyi, M. H. (1985). *Psychoanalysis: Freud's cognitive psychology.* New York: W. H. Freeman.
Fagan, J., & McMahon, P. P. (1984). Incipient multiple personality in children: Four cases. *Journal of Nervous and Mental Disease, 172*, 26–36.
Famularo, R., Kinscherff, R., Fenton, T., & Ayoub, C. (in press). Maternal and child post-traumatic stress disorder in cases of child maltreatment. *Child Abuse and Neglect.*
Feffer, M. (1982). *The structure of Freudian thought.* New York: International Universities Press.
Fischer, K. W. (1980). A theory of cognitive development: The control and construction of hierarchies of skills. *Psychological Review, 87*, 477–531.
Fischer, K. W. (1991). Emotional splitting as an organizer of functional and dysfunctional development. *Newsletter of the International Society for the Study of Behavioral Development, 19*, 4.
Fischer, K. W., Bullock, D., Rotenberg, E. J., & Raya, P. (1993). The dynamics of competence: How context contributes directly to skill. In R. H. Wozniak & K. W. Fischer (Ed.), *Development in context: Acting and thinking in specific environments* (pp. 93–117). Hillsdale, N.J.: Erlbaum.
Fischer, K. W., & Elmendorf, D. (1986). Becoming a different person: Transformations in personality and social behavior. In M. Perlmutter (Ed.), *Cognitive perspectives on children's social development. Minnesota Symposium on Child Psychology, 18*, 137–178. Hillsdale, N.J.: Erlbaum.
Fischer, K. W., & Farrar, M. J. (1987). Generalizations about generalization: How a theory of skill development explains both generality and specificity. *International Journal of Psychology, 22*, 643–677.
Fischer, K. W., Hand, H. H., & Russell, S. L. (1984a). The development of abstractions in adolescence and adulthood. In M. Commons, F. A. Richards, & C. Armon (Ed.), *Beyond formal operations* (pp. 43–73). New York: Praeger.
Fischer, K. W., Hand, H. H., Watson, M. W., Van Parys, M., & Tucker, J. (1984b). Putting the child into socialization: The development of social categories in preschool children. In L. Katz (Ed.), *Current topics in early childhood education* (Vol. 5, pp. 27–72). Norwood, N.J.: Ablex.
Fischer, K. W., & Hogan, A. (1989). The big picture for infant development: Levels and variations. In J. Lockman & N. Hazen (Ed.), *Action in social context: Perspectives on early development* (pp. 275–305). New York: Plenum.
Fischer, K. W., Kenny, S. L., & Pipp, S. L. (1990). How cognitive processes and environmental conditions organize discontinuities in the development of abstractions. In C. N. Alexander, E. J. Langer, & R. M. Oetzel (Ed.), *Higher stages of development* (pp. 162–187). New York: Oxford University Press.
Fischer, K. W., Knight, C. C., & Van Parys, M. (1993). Analyzing diversity in developmental pathways: Methods and concepts. In W. Edelstein & R. Case (Ed.), *Con-*

structivist approaches to development. Contributions to Human Development, 23, 33–56. Basel, Switzerland: S. Karger.

Fischer, K. W., & Pipp, S. L. (1984). Development of the structures of unconscious thought. In K. Bowers & D. Meichenbaum (Ed.), *The unconscious reconsidered* (pp. 88–148). New York: Wiley.

Fischer, K. W., & Rose, S. P. (1993a). *Analyzing patterns of development: How to do research using developmental task analysis. A book on methods and concepts for dynamic-skill development research.* Cambridge, MA: Harvard University Cognitive Development Laboratory, in preparation.

Fischer, K. W., & Rose, S. P. (1993b). Development of coordination of components in brain and behavior: A framework for theory and research. In G. Dawson & K. W. Fischer (Ed.), *Human behavior and the developing brain.* New York: Guilford.

Fischer, K. W., Shaver, P., & Carnochan, P. G. (1990). How emotions develop and how they organize development. *Cognition and Emotion, 4,* 81–127.

Fischer, K. W., & Watson, M. W. (1981). Explaining the Oedipus conflict. In K. W. Fischer (Ed.), *Cognitive development. New Directions for Child Development, 12,* 79–92. San Francisco: Jossey-Bass.

Flavell, J. (1982). On cognitive development. *Child Development, 53,* 1–10.

Foulkes, D. (1982). *Children's dreams: Longitudinal studies.* New York: Wiley.

Freud, A. (1966). *The ego and the mechanisms of defense* (C. Baines, Trans.). New York: International Universities Press. (Originally published, 1936).

Freud, S. *Introductory lectures on psychoanalysis,* also titled *A general introduction to psychoanalysis* (J. Strachey, Trans.). In J. Strachey (Ed.), *Standard edition of the psychological works of Sigmund Freud* (Vol. 15 & 16). London: Hogarth Press, 1961 & 1963. (Originally published, 1917).

Freud, S. (1961). *The ego and the id* (J. Riviere & J. Strachey, Trans.). In J. Strachey (Ed.), *Standard edition of the complete psychological works of Sigmund Freud* (Vol. 19). London: Hogarth Press. (Originally published, 1923).

Frijda, N. H. (1986). *The emotions.* Cambridge, England: Cambridge University Press.

George, C., & Main, M. (1979). Social interactions of young abused children: Approach, avoidance, and aggression. *Child Development, 50,* 306–318.

Goldin-Meadow, S., Alibali, M., & Church, R. B. (1993). Transitions in concept acquisition: Using the hand to read the mind. *Psychological Review,* in press.

Gottlieb, D. E., Taylor, S. E., & Ruderman, A. (1977). Cognitive bases of children's moral judgments. *Developmental Psychology, 13,* 547–556.

Granott, N. (1993). *Microdevelopment of co-construction of knowledge during problem-solving: Puzzled minds, weird creatures, and wuggles.* Unpublished doctoral dissertation, M.I.T.

Greenwald, A. G. (1980). The totalitarian ego: Fabrication and revision of personal history. *American Psychologist, 35,* 603–618.

Haan, N. (1977). *Coping and defending.* New York: Academic Press.

Hand, H. H., & Fischer, K. W. (1989). *Development of understanding mean and nice and other opposites in social interaction.* Cognitive Development Laboratory Report. Cambridge, MA: Harvard University.

Harris, P. L. (1985). What children know about the situations that provoke emotion. In M. Lewis & C. Saarni (Ed.), *The socialization of emotions* (pp. 161–186). New York: Plenum Press.

Harter, S. (1983). Developmental perspectives on the self-system. In E. M. Hetherington (Ed.), & P. H. Mussen (Series Ed.), *Handbook of child psychology: Vol. 4. Socialization, personality, and social development* (pp. 275–385). New York: Wiley.

Harter, S., & Buddin, B. (1987). Children's understanding of the simultaneity of two emotions: A five-stage developmental sequence. *Developmental Psychology, 23,* 388–399.

Harter, S., & Monsour, A. (1992). Developmental analysis of conflict caused by opposing attributes in the adolescent self-portrait. *Developmental Psychology, 28*, 251–260.

Heider, K. (1991). *Landscapes of emotion: Mapping three cultures of emotion in Indonesia.* New York: Cambridge University Press.

Hencke, R., & Raya, P. (1993). You're mean! Individual differences between three-year-old boys and girls in narratives about nice and mean social interactions. Paper presented at the meetings of the Society for Research in Child Development. New Orleans.

Hencke, R. W. (1991). Who me? Individual differences in preschool children's understandings of nice and mean attributes in the self. Paper presented at the meetings of the Society for Research in Child Development. Seattle, Washington.

Henninger, P. (1992). Conditional handedness: Handedness changes in multiple personality disordered subject reflect shift in hemispheric dominance. *Consciousness and Cognition, 1*, 265–287.

Herman, J. (1992). *Trauma and Recovery.* New York: Basic Books.

Hilgard, E. R. (1977). *Divided consciousness.* New York: Wiley.

Holt, R. R. (1976). Freud's theory of the primary process. *Psychoanalysis and Contemporary Science, 5*, 61–99.

Izard, C. E. (1977). *Human emotions.* New York: Plenum.

Kagan, J. (1989). Temperamental contributions to social behavior. *American Psychologist, 44*, 668–674.

Kantor, D., & Lehr, W. (1984). *Inside the family.* San Francisco: Jossey-Bass.

Kennedy, B. (1991). *The development of self-understanding in adolescence.* Unpublished qualifying paper, Harvard University.

Kernberg, O. (1975). *Borderline conditions and pathological narcissism.* New York: Aronson.

Kernberg, O. (1976). *Object relations theory and psychoanalysis.* New York: Aronson.

Kitchener, K. S., Lynch, C. L., Fischer, K. W., & Wood, P. K. (1993). Developmental range of reflective judgment: The effect of contextual support and practice on developmental stage. *Developmental Psychology, 29*, 893–906.

Kluft, R. P. (Ed.) (1985). *Childhood antecedents of multiple personality.* Washington, D.C.: American Psychiatric Press.

Kohut, H. (1971). *The analysis of the self.* New York: International Universities Press.

Lamborn, S. (1986). Relations between social-cognitive development and personal experience: Understanding honesty and kindness in relationships. *Dissertation Abstracts International, 47*(8), 2959A. (University Microfilms No. DA8626347). (Doctoral dissertation, University of Denver).

Lamborn, S. D., Fischer, K. W., & Pipp, S. L. (1994). Constructive criticism and social lies: A developmental sequence for understanding honesty and kindness. *Developmental Psychology,* in press.

Lazarus, R. S. (1991). *Emotion and adaptation.* New York: Oxford University Press.

Mahler, M. S., Pine, F., & Bergman, A. (1975). *The psychological birth of the human infant: Symbiosis and individuation.* New York: Basic Books.

Main, M., & Hesse, E. (1990). Parents' unresolved traumatic experiences are related to infant disorganized attachment status: Is frightened and/or frightening parental behavior the linking mechanism? In M. T. Greenberg, D. Cicchetti, & E. M. Cummings (Ed.), *Attachment in the preschool years* (pp. 161–182). Chicago: University of Chicago Press.

Malatesta, C. Z. (1988). The role of emotions in the development and organization of personality. In R. A. Thompson & R. A. Dienstbier (Ed.), *Socioemotional development. Nebraska Symposium on Motivation, 36.* Lincoln, NE: University of Nebraska Press.

Marcel, A. J. (1983). Conscious and unconscious perception: Experiments on visual masking and word recognition. *Cognitive Psychology, 15*, 197–237.

McCann, L., & Pearlman, L. A. (1992). Constructivist self-development theory: A theoretical model of psychological adaptation to severe trauma. In D. Sakheim & S. Devine (Ed.), *Out of darkness* (pp. 185–206). New York: Lexington Books.

Mischel, W., & Mischel, F. (1958). Psychological aspects of spirit possession. *American Anthropologist, 60*, 249–260.

Morsbach, H., & Tyler, W. J. (1986). A Japanese emotion: Amae. In R. Harré (Ed.), *The social construction of emotions* (pp. 289–307). Oxford, England: Basil Blackwell.

Motley, M. T. (1985). Slips of the tongue. *Scientific American, 253*(3), 116–127.

Noam, G. G. (1988). A constructivist approach to developmental psychopathology. In E. D. Nannis & P. A. Cowan (Ed.), *Developmental psychopathology and its treatment. New Directons for Child Development, 39*. San Francisco: Jossey-Bass.

Noam, G. G. (1990). Beyond Freud and Piaget: Biographical world—Interpersonal self. In T. E. Wren (Ed.), *The moral domain* (pp. 360–399). Cambridge, MA: MIT Press.

Noam, G. G., Powers, S. J., Kilkenny, R., & Beedy, J. (1991). The interpersonal self in life-span developmental perspective: Theory, measurement, and longitudinal case analyses. *Lifespan Development and Behavior, 10*, 59–104. Hillsdale, N.J.: Erlbaum.

Nucci, L. (1993). Personal freedom and moral development. Paper presented at the meetings of the Jean Piaget Society: Values and Knowledge. Philadelphia, PA.

Orne, M. T. (1959). The nature of hypnosis: Artifact and essence. *Journal of Abnormal and Social Psychology, 58*, 277–299.

Osgood, C. E., Suci, G. J., & Tannenbaum, P. (1957). *The measurement of meaning*. Urbana, IL: University of Illinois Press.

Piaget, J. (1951). *Play, dreams, and imitation in childhood* (C. Gattegno & F. M. Hodgson, Trans.). New York: Harcourt Brace. (Originally published, 1946).

Piaget, J. (1957). Logique et équilibre dans les comportements du sujet. *Études d'Épistémologie Génétique, 2*, 27–118.

Piaget, J. (1975). L'équilibration des structures cognitives: Problème central du développement. *Études d'Épistémologie Génétique, 33*.

Piaget, J., & Szeminska, A. (1952). *The child's conception of number* (C. Gattegno & F. M. Hodgson, Trans.). London: Routledge & Kegan Paul. (Originally published, 1941).

Putnam, F. W. (1989). *Diagnosis and treatment of multiple personality disorder.* New York: Guilford.

Putnam, F. W. (1993). Dissociative disorders in children: Behavioral profiles and problems. *Child Abuse and Neglect, 17*, 39–45.

Putnam, F. W., Helmers, K., & Trickett, P. K. (in press). Development, reliability, and validity of a child dissociation scale. *Child Abuse & Neglect*, in press.

Raya, P. (1993). *The relationship between empathic responses in a young neglected child and maternal values, goals, and child-rearing practices: A case study.* Unpublished qualifying paper, Harvard University.

Roberts, R. J., Jr. (1981). Errors and the assessment of cognitive development. In K. W. Fischer (Ed.), *Cognitive development. New Directions for Child Development, 12*, 69–78. San Francisco: Jossey-Bass.

Rogoff, B. (1990). *Apprenticeship in thinking: Cognitive development in social context.* New York: Oxford University Press.

Rosenbaum, M. (1980). The role of the term schizophrenia in the decline of diagnoses of multiple personality. *Archives of General Psychiatry, 37*, 1383–1385.

Rosenberg, M. (1979). *Conceiving the self.* New York: Basic Books.

Rubin, K. H., Fein, G., & Vandenberg, B. (1983). Play. In E. M. Hetherington (Ed.), & P. H. Mussen (Series Ed.), *Handbook of child psychology: Vol. 4. Socialization, personality, and social behavior* (pp. 693–774). New York: Wiley.

Ruble, D. N. (1983). The development of social comparison processes and their role in achievement-related self-socialization. In E. T. Higgins, D. N. Ruble, & W. W. Hartup (Ed.), *Social cognition and social development: A socio-cultural perspective* (pp. 134–157). New York: Cambridge University Press.

Saarni, C. (1984). An observational study of children's attempts to monitor their expressive behavior. *Child Development, 55,* 1504–1513.

Selman, R. L., & Schultz, L. H. (1990). *Making a friend in youth.* Chicago: University of Chicago Press.

Shapiro, E. R., & Carr, A. W. (1991). *Lost in familiar places: Creating new connections between the individual and society.* New Haven, CN: Yale University Press.

Shaver, P. R., Schwartz, J., Kirson, D., & O'Connor, C. (1987). Emotion knowledge: Further exploration of a prototype approach. *Journal of Personality and Social Psychology, 52,* 1061–1086.

Silvern, L. (1984). Traditional descriptions of childhood emotional-behavioral disorders and an alternative: Disorder as a failure of system functions. In G. Gollin (Ed.), *Developmental plasticity* (pp. 95–102). New York: Academic Press.

Sroufe, L. A. (1979). Socioemotional development. In J. Osofsky (Ed.), *Handbook of infant development* (1st ed., pp. 462–516). New York: Wiley.

Stein, N. L., & Levine, L. J. (1989). The causal organization of emotional knowledge: A developmental study. *Cognition and Emotion, 3,* 343–378.

Stern, D. N. (1985). *The interpersonal world of the infant: A view from psychoanalysis and developmental psychology.* New York: Basic Books.

Sullivan, H. S. (1953). *The interpersonal theory of psychiatry.* New York: Norton.

Terr, L. C. (1991). Childhood traumas: An outline and overview. *American Journal of Psychiatry, 148*(1), 10–20.

Vaillant, G. E. (1977). *Adaptation to life.* Boston: Little, Brown.

Vaillant, G. E. (Ed.) (1986). *Empirical studies of ego mechanisms of defense.* Washington, D.C.: American Psychiatric Press.

van der Kolk, B. A. (1987). *Psychological trauma.* Washington, D.C.: American Psychiatric Press.

Van Derbur Atler, M. (1991). Address presented at the Kempe National Center for Prevention and Treatment of Child Abuse and Neglect. Denver, CO.

Vondra, J. I., Barnett, D., & Cicchetti, D. (1989). Perceived competence and actual competence among maltreated and comparison school children. *Development and Psychopathology, 1,* 237–255.

Vondra, J. I., Barnett, D., & Cicchetti, D. (1990). Self-concept, motivation, and competence among preschoolers from maltreating and comparison families. *Child Abuse and Neglect, 14,* 525–540.

Vygotsky, L. (1978). *Mind in society: The development of higher psychological processes* (M. Cole & V. John-Steiner & S. Scribner & E. Souberman, Trans.). Cambridge, Massachusetts: Harvard University Press.

Wallbott, H. G., & Scherer, K. R. (1994). Cultural differences in experiencing shame and guilt. In J. P. Tangney & K. W. Fischer (Ed.), *The self-conscious emotions: Pride, shame, and guilt.* New York: Guilford.

Waller, N. G., & Shaver, P. R. (1993). *The biological and cultural transmission of romantic love styles: A twin-family study.* Unpublished manuscript, University of California, Davis.

Watson, M. W. (1984). Development of social role understanding. *Developmental Review, 4,* 192–213.

Watson, M. W., & Fischer, K. W. (1980). Development of social roles in elicited and spontaneous behavior during the preschool years. *Developmental Psychology, 16*, 484–494.

Watson, M. W., & Getz, K. (1991). The relationship between Oedipal behaviors and children's family role concepts. *Merrill-Palmer Quarterly, 36*, 487–505.

Weiss, J. (1990). Unconscious mental functioning. *Scientific American, 262*(3), 103–109.

Westen, D., & Cohen, R. (1992). The self in borderline personality disorder: A psychodynamic perspective. In Z. Segal & S. Blatt (Ed.), *Self-representation and emotional disorder: Cognitive and psychodynamic perspectives.* New York: Guilford Press.

Wolf, D. (1982). Understanding others: A longitudinal case study of the concept of independent agency. In G. Forman (Ed.), *Action and thought: From sensorimotor schemes to symbolic operations.* New York: Academic Press.

Wundt, W. (1907). *Outlines of psychology* (Judd, C. H., Trans.). New York: Stechert. (Originally published, 1905).

VI The Impact of Sexual Abuse on Self Structure

Drew Westen

Sexual abuse in childhood is now recognized to be widespread in our society (Herman, 1992; Newberger, 1990; Russell, 1986; Terr, 1991) and is probably increasing in prevalence as traditional family structures continue to erode. Childhood sexual abuse is known to have a number of potential longterm sequelae, including symptoms of post-traumatic stress disorder such as intrusive thoughts and anxiety symptoms, as well as other difficulties such as sexual inhibition or promiscuity, vulnerability to depression, and generalized interpersonal distrust (Browne & Finkelhor, 1986; Gelinas, 1983; Kendall-Tackett, Williams, & Finkelhor, 1993; Wyatt & Powell, 1988).

Perhaps surprisingly, no systematic program of research has explored the ramifications of sexual abuse on the experience and representation of self, although the literature cited above has produced findings regarding particular symptoms such as dissociative experiences and low self-esteem. This chapter will draw upon existing research and clinical observation to begin to chart this domain. To do so, however, first requires that one carefully distinguish various dimensions of self, and then consider the impact of sexual abuse on each of these dimensions.

Dimensions of "Self"

Assessing the impact of sexual abuse or any other experience on "the self" first requires that one specify precisely what the self is. In the history of psychology, this has been more easily said than done: Often the notion of self has been so broad as to be redundant with terms such as personality, or theorists have rejected the self entirely. What follows is a brief distinction of a number of dimensions of self (see Westen, 1985, 1991, 1992; for related conceptualizations relevant to these issues, see Epstein, 1990, 1991; Stern, 1985).

The author would like to thank Mary Harvey, Carolyn Newberger, Eli Newberger, Susan Roth, and the editors of this volume for their comments on an earlier draft of the manuscript.

Self versus Self-Concept

The first distinction that needs to be drawn is between *self* and *self-representation, self-concept,* or *self-schema.* Many self theorists have used these terms interchangeably. Rogers (1959) used "self" and "self-concept" as synonyms, as do contemporary cognitive theorists such as Markus, who defines the self as "what one takes oneself to be" (Markus and Cross, 1990). This is a rather peculiar state of affairs, because the self-concept or self-schema must be a person's concept or schema of *something,* presumably of the self, rendering the definition tautological.

The distinction between self and self-concept is actually quite important. Characterologically depressed patients will often agree with their therapists that they have a negative self-concept, but they are frequently unwilling to alter that representation until they have changed what they believe is the badness of the *actual* self—the person they are representing. In other words, while the therapist may conceptualize the problem as a negative self-schema or self-representation, the patient may view the negative self-representation as an accurate portrayal of a negative reality: "*I* am the problem, not my view of myself."

The only coherent way to define "self," then, is as in colloquial speech: The *self* is the person, as when one says "myself," "himself", or "herself." Thus, when people say, "I gave myself a talking to," they do not mean, "I had a chat with my self-schemas"; or when they assert, "I'll do it myself," they do not mean, "leave it to my self-representations, they'll take care of it." If "self" refers to the person—the whole psychophysiological organism—then various hyphenated terms make sense: Self-concept refers to the person's concept of the self, self-esteem refers to the extent to which the person likes or respects the self, etc.

Self as Subject and Self as Object

This leads to a second distinction, drawn by William James (1890), between self as subject and self as object. The self as subject or "I"—or what one might call the *sense of self*—is the subjective experience of oneself as agent of one's actions, thinker of one's thoughts, and feeler of one's feelings. That is, the self as subject refers to the experience of self at the center of one's consciousness. It also includes a sense of continuity of consciousness over time. The self as object or "me," in contrast, includes the variety of ways in which the person represents himself or herself. Although this distinction appears categorical, sense of self and representations of self probably form a continuum, with the sense of self largely incapable of conscious rendering but including some relatively undifferentiated representational elements.

Defining the sense of self requires some clarity about the concept of consciousness, which is no easy task. For James, consciousness was a constantly moving stream of thoughts, feelings, and perceptions. Consciousness has at least two related functions: monitoring the self and the environment, and controlling thought and behavior (Kihlstrom, 1984). By focusing particular attention on aspects of reality, consciousness allows people to initiate and terminate thought and action related to need-states and goals. Disruptions in consciousness are likely to affect these functions as well as the sense of self as the subject or author of consciousness.

With respect to self as object, self-representations (or self-schemas in cognitive language) may be conscious or unconscious. A growing body of cognitive research now supports the notion that much of mental life is unconscious (Kihlstrom, Barnhardt, & Tataryn, 1992; Uleman & Bargh, 1989). If representations can be unconscious, then surely this must be true of self-representations. Both contemporary psychoanalytic theory (Brenner, 1982) and parallel distributed processing models in cognitive science (Rumelhart, McClelland, and the PDP Group, 1986) suggest that conscious representations are synthesized from a multitude of unconscious component processes that may collaborate, conflict, or compete for access to consciousness. From a psychoanalytic perspective, self-representations, like other aspects of mental life, are compromise-formations—that is, products of compromise among multiple psychological processes, including wishes, fears, efforts at veridical information processing, and defenses against unpleasant emotions. From a cognitive perspective, conscious representations are synthesized from a multitude of competing and collaborating neural modules or circuits. Most of these circuits have no conscious component even when activated; only their product is conscious.

One can thus distinguish *working self-representations*—that is, representations that are to some degree activated—from *conscious self-representations*. Working representations of the self, like the internal working models postulated by attachment theorists (Bowlby, 1969; Bretherton, 1990; Crittenden, 1990; Main, 1990), include both conscious and unconscious, avowed and disavowed, components. They are patterned networks of processing information about the self that influence conscious thought, feeling, or behavior, whether or not these components themselves attain consciousness.

Working representations are the joint product of current environmental events and cognitions as well as enduring representations of self that comprise the *self-system* in longterm memory. Research on internal working models of attachment suggests that infants, children, and adults have multiple models of attachment relationships, each associated with different representations of self, although these models are also likely to generalize into broader, prototypic representations (Crittenden, 1990; Lynch & Cicchetti, 1991). Recent research on the development of representations of the self documents progressive differentiation in children's views of themselves in different relationships (Harter & Monsour, 1992). Younger children tend to see themselves as basically the same across all roles and relationships. As they get older, particularly as they move into adolescence, they recognize that they behave differently with different people or in various roles (e.g., as sister versus as daughter, or at school versus with friends), and begin to try to integrate these various representations.

Many cognitive theorists (see Kihlstrom et al, 1992) have tried to avoid the notion that mental contents can be kept from awareness because of their affective consequences (such as anxiety). However, the available data are quite clear that the consciousness of representations, including representations of self, depends on at least two variables. One is level of cognitive activation, as in spreading activation models (Collins & Loftus, 1975) which propose that the more activation spreads to a node on a network of associations, the more likely it is to become conscious. Thus, a situation such as rejection by a lover is likely to activate not only highly relevant representations of self as rejected by previous lovers but also, potentially, representations of self rejected in other circumstances, such as parental or peer rejection, because of their associative connections. In individuals who are vulnerable to feelings of rejection because of their attachment history, the associations between different types of rejection may be particularly dense, leading to strong activation of representations of parental rejection and its attendant self-representations in this circumstance.

The second variable is more affective and motivational—namely, whether representations are connected to needs and goals, and whether they feel good or bad. The person with a history of parental rejection may have minimal conscious access to self-as-rejected schemas (or to wishes for closeness connected with representations of self-being-held or self-being-loved) because these have been defensively blocked from consciousness. Aside from a century of clinical data, an accumulating body of experimental evidence documents that what people betray about their self-representations with their physiology and behavior may differ substantially from what they consciously believe about themselves (see McClelland, Koestner, & Weinberger, 1989; Pennebaker, 1989; Shedler, Mayman, & Manis, in press; Westen, 1990). Conscious representations can, in fact, be polar opposites of activated unconscious working representations, as when a person who feels guilty about an action convinces himself that he does not (despite telltale physiological or behavioral signs, such as increased electrodermal activity or stammering). In this case, the conscious self-representation ("I am innocent") is a defensive transformation of the unconsciously activated schema, and is constructed because of its affect-regulatory properties (minimization of guilt).

Cognitive and behavioral theorists over the past decades have argued that such processes are too complex to be carried out unconsciously (e.g., Greenwald, 1992); however, these mechanisms may be no more complex than other forms of information processing that occur unconsciously. Cognitive processes that inhibit or distort representations that attain consciousness can be conditioned through their association with affect: Just as a behavior that averts a punishing experience will be reinforced, so, too, will a cognitive operation that minimizes conscious experience of an unpleasant emotion such as shame or anxiety be likely to be maintained or used again in analogous situations (Westen, 1985). Essentially, the mental process is encoded as a successful affect-regulation strategy, and the minimization of negative affect (or maximization of positive affect, which can also occur with idealization or grandiosity) motivates its future activation.

Investigations of adult attachment have provided evidence for the inhibition of conscious access to representations of the self, others, and relationships based on their affective qualities. Adults with secure attachment styles speak freely and openly about their relationships with their parents. People with ambivalent styles appear preoccupied with, and ambivalent about their parents. Avoidant adults dismiss the importance of attachment relationships or offer idealized generalizations about their parents while being unable to back them up with specific examples (Main, Kaplan, & Cassidy, 1985). Researchers have argued that these avoidant adults, like avoidant infants, deactivate or shut off attachment-related feelings as a way of coping with them.

Physiological evidence of this deactivation comes from a recent study that monitored electrodermal response (a measure of anxiety or conflict) while subjects were asked to recall memories involving separation, rejection, and threat from their parents (Dozier & Kobak, in press). The extent to which a Q-sort of the individual's responses on the Adult Attachment Interview matched a prototype of secure attachment was slightly inversely correlated with electrodermal response; that is, the more security, the less physiological reactivity. The picture was quite different with avoidance, where the correlation was strongly positive (in the range of .40): The more individuals showed avoidant, deactivating strategies, the more physiological reactivity they manifest while answering affectively evocative questions about separations, rejections, and parental threats. This disjunction between reported concerns and physiologically expressed affect appeared only while subjects responded to probes that were theoretically expected to draw this kind of defensive strategy (such as rejections) and did not emerge on affectively neutral items. Similar research finds that people who believe themselves to be psychologically healthy and emotionally stable, but whose early memories manifest signs of psychopathology, show psychophysiological patterns associated with heart disease. They also show considerable physiological reactivity while claiming to be emotionally unperturbed (Shedler, Mayman, & Manis, in press).

Representations of self, like other schemas, probably have aspects of hierarchical organization. Nested within a "self as academic" schema may be a "self as writer of chapters" subschema, which itself subsumes several specific incidents of writing chapters. Each level of the hierarchy is likely to include different semantic, sensory, and affective components. For example, my "self as academic schema" is generally associated with positive affect, which contributes to my self-esteem. (This probably exemplifies one of those defensive representations described above.) My "self as writer of chapters" schema is associated with positive and negative affects, such as pride and retrospective dismay at previous published papers, as well as anxiety about commitments I have made for the future. At the bottom level of the hierarchy are episodic memores involving the self, which are also typically affectively charged (such as "self almost holding up publication of this volume by turning in the manuscript so late").

Other Dimensions of Self

Self-representations are densely connected with other schemas. Of special importance in this respect are *self-with-other* or *relationship schemas* that include self-representations. These have been described variously by researchers as representations of interaction that have been generalized or RIGs (Stern, 1985), relationship schemas (Baldwin, 1993; Horowitz, 1987), core conflictual relationship themes (Luborsky & Crits-Christoph, 1990), internal working models (Bretherton, 1990; Main, 1990), and self-with-other representations (Ogilvie & Ashmore, 1991).

Other self-related phenomena include *self-esteem,* which refers to the individual's momentary and enduring affective valuations of the self; *wished-for, feared,* and *ideal self-representations* which guide thought, feeling, and behavior; and *self-presentation,* the aim of which is to influence others' representations of oneself. Finally, the most inclusive concept related to self is *identity* (Erikson, 1968), which includes a sense of personal history, a coherent and integrated prototypic representation of the self, an affective weighting of various self-representations (e.g., an investment in being a man, a woman, an academic, a clinician, a baker, etc.), commitment to values and beliefs that endure over time, and a recognition by the community that one is who what one believes oneself to be.

The Impact of Sexual Abuse on Aspects of Self: Some Complexities and Caveats

The point to making these distinctions is that sexual abuse may not uniformly affect all of these dimensions of self, and the various components of the abuse experience may differentially impact diverse aspects of self. Finkelhor and Brown (1985) distinguish several toxic aspects of sexual abuse. These include betrayal, traumatic sexualization, stigmatization, and powerlessness. Betrayal may lead to pervasive distrust and malevolent self-with-other schemas. Our research with psychiatric patients does, in fact, suggest that a childhood history of sexual abuse is associated with malevolent representations of relationships that emerge in the Thematic Apperception Test (TAT) responses and early memories of adolescents and adults (Nigg, Silk, Westen, et al, 1992; Westen, Lohr, Silk, et al, 1990; Westen, Ludolph, Block, Wixom, and Wiss, 1990). Betrayal is unlikely, however, to produce the kind of disrupted *sense of self* that violence or helplessness in the face of physical danger do. The sense of self as consistent over time and as the feeler and thinker of one's conscious experience is likely to break down as a result of dissociative efforts to escape from pain and helplessness. Traumatic sexualization has a direct impact on motives, many of which include representations of feared or wished-for self. Stigmatization directly influences the content of self-representations.

The aim in the remainder of this chapter is briefly to describe the impact child sexual abuse can have on the aspects of self outlined above. Before doing so, however, several caveats and complexities need to be addressed.

Individual Differences in the Response to Sexual Abuse

First, not all sexual abuse victims are alike. Some will manifest few or none of the disturbances in aspects of self described below (Kendall-Tackett et al, 1993; Mannarino & Cohen, 1986). Sexual abuse experiences vary tremendously in ways that are likely to influence the impact of sexual abuse on aspects of self. These include the type of abuse experienced (e.g., fondling versus penetration), the familial closeness of the perpetrator (e.g., father or stepfather versus neighbor), the duration of abuse, the number of perpetrators, and the degree of violence involved. These variables are known to influence severity of psychiatric symptomatology secondary to abuse (see, e.g., Browne & Finkelhor, 1986; Kendall-Tackett et al, 1993; Wyatt & Newcomb, 1990), and all of them are similarly likely to influence the extent of pathology or health in various domains of self.

Another important variable is whether the trauma was disclosed, whether caretakers validated and supported the disclosure, and the results of professional action following disclosure. Some children live with a secret that no one else knows, the reality of which they may grow to doubt or repress over the years. They may come to distrust their own thoughts and memories, or believe that significant others know about the abuse but are choosing to do nothing, with implications for feelings about both the self and other people. Other children disclose the abuse, only to be punished or disbelieved, or to see their mothers struggle with a decision about whether to break up the family. These are generally no-win situations for the child. The best-case scenario, if the mother believes her child and takes appropriate action, may be for the child to live with a parent who is now herself seriously stressed if not clinically depressed or traumatized by the disclosure and its aftermath (Newberger, Gremy, Waternaux, & Newberger, in press). The mother may now be economically stressed because of the loss of her husband's or lover's income, struggle with her own feelings of betrayed by her lover, or be resentful of the child who "forced" her to give up an attachment figure of her own. This may only intensify the child's feelings of guilt around the abuse.

Children also differ in the way they respond to sexual abuse, varying tremendously in their resiliency in the face of traumatic experiences. The way sexual abuse experiences disrupt aspects of self depends on the meanings the individual attributes to the abuse. The plural, "meanings," is important here, because children simultaneously and sequentially make sense of abuse in many ways and have differential conscious access to these meanings. Perhaps the most common way that children construct a reality of the experience is to view themselves as bad and to blame. At other levels, however, they may see the world as malevolent, may view the experience as their most intimate relationship, or may not conceive of the relationship as particularly problematic until years later.

Developmental Differences in Response to Sexual Abuse

Another key variable is the developmental period in childhood during which the abuse took place. Data are somewhat conflicting on the impact of sexual abuse at different ages, although several studies find that the later the abuse, the more pervasive the effects (Kendall-Tackett et al, 1993; Newberger, Newberger, & Gremy (1991). This is a somewhat paradoxical finding, as developmental psychopathologists have tended to presume that the earlier a pathogenic experience occurs, particularly if it is continuous over a period of time, the more damaging.

In many domains of social development this appears to be true, particularly with attachment. Although the data are surprisingly sparse on this question, research supports the observations of Bowlby (1969) and other psychoanalytic theorists of the 1940s and 1950s that early disruptions in the attachment relationship tend to have far-reaching consequences in later development (see, e.g., Tizard and Hodges, 1986; Westen, Ludolph, et al, 1990). This would make sense from an ethological perspective, in that the first few years appear to be a sensitive period for the development of attachment, and from a psychoanalytic perspective, which emphasizes the lasting impact of early experiences. It also may make sense from a cognitive-developmental viewpoint, in that earlier schemas are far less differentiated than the schemas that develop later, so that fundamentally shaping them in one direction or another may impact a whole network of schemas that later differentiate out of them. A child who develops a global assumption about the self as bad, for example, may later have difficulty anchoring any enduring positive self-schemas in particular domains because of the lack of a cognitive "grounding" for them. This line of reasoning might add a developmental component to adult theory and research on the assumptive worlds of trauma survivors, who generally have less secure, comforting, and positive underlying assumptions about themselves, the world, and people than their nontraumatized peers (Epstein, 1990, 1991; Janoff-Bulman, 1992; McCann & Pearlman, 1990).

With sexual abuse, however, matters are likely to be more complicated, as the meaning of sexual abuse can be quite different at different developmental epochs. A two-year-old who is penetrated by an adult will probably find the experience terrifying and painful, will attach pain and fears about body damage to developing schemas about sexuality, and will have little way to understand what is happening and why. A fourteen-year-old who is molested by her step-father already has notions about sexuality, about right and wrong, and about incest, and has a body that is more mature. Depending on the degree of coercion and sadism, then, her experience of abuse may be fraught as much with guilt as with fear and pain, and the impact on her experience of herself may be quite different. In contrast, a brief episode of abuse that occurred to a seven-year-old and has been repressed may have delayed effects that emerge in adolescence, as the child starts to explore sexuality, begin to recall what happened, and attach guilt-laden meanings and self-blaming attributions to the experience. The meaning of the abuse may change with development, as the child wrestles with a new understanding of what has happened, setting off a new round of psychological consequences.

Distinguishing the Impact of Sexual Abuse from Problematic Attachment Patterns

One of the major difficulties in establishing empirically the relation between sexual abuse and disruptions of various aspects of self is that problematic attachment patterns as early as the first year of life can produce similar psychological sequelae, presumably mediated through internal working models of the self, others, and relationships. Although temperament plays at least a modest role in influencing patterns of attachment in infancy (Vaughn et al, 1992), the variable that appears to have the biggest impact on security of attachment is the mother's sensitivity to her baby's signals (Ainsworth, 1979; Sroufe & Fleeson, 1986). When mothers are responsive to their children's communications, are psychologically accessible, enjoy their babies, and convey a sense of acceptance, infants are more likely to feel secure. In contrast, infants whose mothers do not respond to their needs will not form secure attachment bonds and will display more anger, fear, or avoidance behaviors (Bretherton, 1985; Ricks, 1985; Erickson, Sroufe & Egelund, 1985; Pederson et al, 1990). (Similarly, the extent to which fathers feel positively about their infant and their role in its development at 3 months correlates .54 with the later attachment security of the infant-father pair; Cox et al, 1992.)

Of particular relevance is a recently-discovered form of insecure attachment called *disorganized-disoriented* (Main & Solomon, 1986). Disorganized children perform contradictory actions, such as approaching the mother while simultaneously averting their heads or gazing away. They also appear disoriented, as manifest in stereotyped rocking and dazed facial expressions suggesting the simultaneous activation of mutually contradictory behavioral tendencies. Researchers have theorized that these children have extreme difficulty forming coherent representations of their attachment relationships because their caregivers are so unpredictable. This pattern of attachment is of special relevance to the understanding of abuse victims of various kinds because it has been observed to be the predominant attachment pattern in high-risk and maltreated samples (see Cicchetti, 1991; Lyons-Ruth et al, 1990). Mothers whose children manifest a disorganized pattern of attachment in infancy often suffer unresolved loss or abuse from their own childhoods (Main, Kaplan, & Cassidy, 1985). Their children show signs of extreme vulnerability—or other forms of maltreatment—long before they themselves may become victims of sexual abuse, and many of these resemble symptoms of abuse (such as low self-esteem and depression).

Prior patterns of attachment presumably play a key role in moderating the impact of sexual abuse on many aspects of psychological functioning, including dimensions of self. Early insecure attachment could create a diathesis that leaves the child vulnerable in a number of ways. A child who constructs a view of the self as bad or unlovable in the context of primary attachment relationships may readily view herself as bad and blameworthy in the context of sexual abuse. She may also harbor disavowed destructive fantasies toward her mother that become activated in secret, if frightening, liasons with a man who avers to love her mother, and hence may be especially prone to guilt and self-blame. Abuse experiences may also amplify disorganized cognitive structures and activate dissociative processes. Children whose early attachment history leaves them prone to have difficulty making sense of why people act as they do may have even more trouble integrating abuse events than children whose prior relationships are more secure and whose mental representations are more coherent. In our own research we have found that a history of sexual abuse and a history of difficulties in the first five years of life (such as disrupted attachment, maternal separation, and neglect) both predict the tendency of adolescents to provide peculiar, unorganized, or preoperational attributions of the causes of people's behavior as expressed in TAT stories (Westen, Ludolph, et al, 1990).

The way specific internal working models may generalize to broad assumptions about the world or the self may be of importance in the way traumatic experiences are later integrated. Several theorists have focused on shattered assumptions caused by traumatic events (Janoff-Bulman, 1992) or the difficulty of assimilating abuse experiences into existing schemas (Horowitz, 1986). If early models lead the child to expect abuse or misattunement, then abuse experiences are not cognitively discrepant, and no assumptions are shattered. The roots of later difficulties may thus lie elsewhere in survivors who suffered chronic and continuous maltreatment or misattunement from childhood, who all too readily assimilate abusive experiences as adults. For these individuals, the aim of treatment may be to *shatter* assumptions and to *create* discrepancies, as in a therapeutic relationship that is unexpectedly benign, caring, bounded, and focused on meeting the patient's and not the therapist's needs.

Distinguishing The Impact of Sexual Abuse from Other Forms of Maltreatment and Family Dysfunction

Another caveat is that distinguishing the effects of sexual abuse per se from other experiences with which it frequently covaries is difficult. Children who are sexually abused are frequently physically abused or neglected. These other forms of maltreatment produce some similar symptoms (such as anxiety, depression, poor peer relations, and aggression) and can disrupt aspects of self (see Cicchetti, 1991). For example, maltreated toddlers show less positive affect in visual self-recognition tasks, and refer less to their internal states, than toddlers who are not similarly at risk. Once again this may have an impact on their later ability to make sense of their own and others' actions, as internal states mediate most interpersonal behavior, and people who cannot make sophisticated and accurate inferences about other people's mental states are likely to have difficulty understanding them. This lack of attention to internal processes also appears in the responses of mothers of maltreated infants (Cicchetti, 1991). Developing a sense of agency is difficult when one focuses little attention on one's internal goals and intentions. Maltreated children also frequently offer defensively idealized, confused portraits of their relationships, particularly with their abusive parents (Lynch & Cicchetti, 1991), which the investigators have analogized to disorganized internal working models in infancy.

Sexual abuse victims often undergo other toxic experiences. Although sexual abuse occurs in all strata, socioeconomic status is related to various forms of abuse and neglect (see Crittenden et al, 1991; Trickett et al, 1991), so that poor inner city children are particularly at risk for multiple and severe forms of abuse. Further, the way the system responds to children is itself frequently pathogenic. In a longitudinal study, Widom (1991) found that children removed from their homes for various forms of abuse who were sent from placement to placement were much more likely to be arrested as adolescents or adults or to commit a violent crime than their abused peers who had two or less placements. The current foster care system in the United States tends to maximize the damage abusive parents have done to their children's capacity to attach.

A growing body of research suggests that a generally pathological family environment may be as or more important than sexual abuse in generating many of the symptoms ascribed to sexual abuse (Claussen & Crittenden, 1991; Conte & Schuerman, 1987; Nash, Hulsey, Sexton, Harralson, & Lambert, 1993).

Methodologically, far too many studies have used sexual abuse as an independent variable while failing to control for obvious confounds such as parental psychopathology or family dysfunction. Nash et al (1993) administered a family functioning self-report instrument to abused and nonabused subjects to assess the relation between family dysfunction and symptoms assessed from the MMPI and the Rorschach Inkblot Test. They found that sexual abuse and family dysfunction were both associated with psychopathology, but that covariation for perceived family pathology eliminated most of the differences between the abused and nonabused samples. Notable exceptions were the Hypochondriasis and Paranoia scales of the MMPI and a Self-Perception cluster on the Rorschach indicative of a sense of self as damaged. Although other researchers dispute such findings (Briere & Elliott, 1993), the evidence suggests that sexual abuse and broader family dysfunction are not independent, may produce similar effects (with exceptions such as sexualized behavior), and may interact (see Kendall-Tackett et al, 1993). Sexual abuse in the context of a chaotic, dangerous, or unpredictable home life is likely to have more far-reaching effects than sexual abuse that is anomalous in the context of family experience.

Part of the controversy over the relative roles of family pathology and sexual abuse stems from a political concern, namely that this enterprise will revert to the mother-blaming characteristic of a previous era of psychiatry. Sexual abuse is, after all, a crime perpetrated primarily by men, who deserve the full blame for their actions. At the same time, however, maternal denial, insensitivity, unconscious collusion, and victim-blaming are not uncommon, and the presence of poorly socialized and sexually abusive men in the household may reflect in part a maternal pathology of object relations or a repetition of her own abuse experiences.

Indeed, an emerging body of evidence implicates maternal object-relational disturbance and post-traumatic stress disorder in the creation of homes vulnerable to sexually predatory men. Newberger et al (1991) found that one-third of the mothers of a group of severely sexually abused children had abuse histories themselves, the vast majority being quite severe (anal or vaginal penetration). The longer the duration of the mother's own abuse as a child, the greater the force used by the perpetrator against her child; the authors concluded that severely abused women were vulnerable to developing relationships with violent, coersive men. Sexually abused mothers tended to lead chaotic, stressful lives, and to have men living in the home with them at the time of their child's abuse and beyond.

The role of such men, and the link to maternal object-relational pathology, are suggested by other investigations. Nash et al (1993) found stepfathers to be particularly prevalent in the homes of patients with an abuse history (defined stringently in terms of relatively serious abuse). Sirles and Frank (1989) found that mothers were most likely to disbelieve their children's accounts of abuse when the perpetrator was a step-father or live-in partner. Gomes-Schwartz et al (1990) found that many such mothers punished, scolded, or expressed hostility toward the child victim, and the vast majority allowed the perpetrator to stay in the home if given the choice. Another study comparing adolescents who experienced neglect, physical abuse, and sexual abuse with normal adolescents found that psychopathology in the mothers (as assessed by the SCL-90-R) was highest in the sexually abuse group (Williamson, Borduin, & Howe, 1991).

Once again, none of this is to suggest that men who victimize children are not responsible for their actions, or that maternal object-relational pathology is endemic to all or most cases of sexual abuse. From an empirical perspective, however, the presence of victimizing men is not independent of the pathology of a subgroup of mothers, many of them severely traumatized themselves, who cannot form stable and adaptive attachments. Their own problematic style of attachment contributes to the vulnerabilities of their children in two ways, one direct and one indirect. First, it undermines the attachment security of their children, and hence generates a pre-abuse diathesis. Second, it contributes to the creation of home environments that render their children vulnerable to male aggression. Their own experience of childhood abuse may create a compulsion to repeat that leads them to deny, or to tolerate, ongoing victimization of themselves and their children.[1]

Whether familial dysfunction accounts for some of the effects normally attributed to sexual abuse is not simply a political or even an empirical question. It has profound clinical implications as well. As Lebowitz, Harvey, & Herman (in press) note, "failure to identify or address the trauma remains at present the most common therapeutic error in the treatment of survivors," and they observe that "premature or over-zealous uncovering work is probably the second most common error. . ." A third may be the failure to address the continuous pathogenic experiences such as neglect, indifference, and empathic failures that do not stand out as readily or elicit our horror and indignation the way sexual abuse does, but that may account for some of the ongoing difficulties of survivors of sexual abuse. Clinicians also need to be sensitive not to invalidate the firmly-held and sometimes valid belief of their patients that their mothers should have but in fact did not intervene to protect them, which may feel like as traumatic a betrayal as that of the abuser. The patient's experience, and not the therapist's ideological commitments, should determine the appropriate empathic response and should give rise to exploration of material whose meaning may or may not change upon reexamination.

The Role of Culture

Another caveat is that little is known about the role of culture in mediating or moderating the relation between sexual abuse experiences and dimensions of self. What complicates matters is that cultural variables are important on both sides of the equation. Conceptions of self differ tremendously across cultures and historical epochs (Baumeister, 1987; Geertz, 1983; Markus & Kitayama, 1991; Shweder & Bourne, 1984; Westen, 1985, 1991). The bounded, individualistic view of self in contemporary Western industrial societies contrasts with a more

[1]An analogy to Munchausen's syndrome may be relevant here, although the latter requires a more active role of the mother and does not depend upon the presence of an abusive man.

contextualized notion of selfhood in other cultures and in the West prior to the Industrial Revolution. If the structure and content of self-representations vary cross-culturally, then the impact of sexual abuse on these representations is likely to vary as well.

Definitions of abusive parenting also differ widely across (and within) cultures (see Korbin, 1981). To what extent particular acts are experienced as traumatic depends in part on cultural norms and expectations (Giovannoni, 1979). In some Asian cultures, parents masturbate their infants to sleep. In other cultures, girls are initiated into sex by age-mates of their fathers. In many societies marriage (and hence sexual intercourse) in the early teenage years is arranged rather than based on personal desire and would be tantamount to rape in our own culture. Precisely how cultural constructions of appropriate and inappropriate sexual activity shape the meaning, and subsequent sequelae, of childhood sexual contacts with adults is unknown.

A Final Caveat: Data Would be a Plus

A chapter such as this should ideally come at the end of a research program, or at least in the middle. Instead, this one comes at the beginning. Most of the claims to be made are relatively unsubstantiated hypotheses, based on clinical observation, available research, and data from pilot interviewing Robert Cohen and I conducted at the University of Michigan with inpatients with abuse histories, borderline personality disorder, or both. In addition, the views presented here were shaped primarily by work with adolescents and adults who have been abused, not with children in the midst of abuse. This clearly imposes limitations which others with more experience will hopefully transcend.

Nevertheless, speculation is, at this point, the state of the art. Colleagues and I at The Cambridge Hospital in the Victims of Violence Program are currently piloting an interview and developing a scoring procedure for assessing aspects of self in sexual abuse victims in the context of studying criteria for treatment outcome. This research is based on Mary Harvey's conceptualization of domains of recovery, such as authority over memory, integration of memory with emotion, affect tolerance, safe attachment, self-esteem, and self-coherence (Harvey & Herman, 1992; Lebowitz, Harvey, & Herman, in press).

The Sense of Self

The experience of childhood sexual abuse can disrupt all of the aspects of the sense of self described earlier: the sense of continuity in time, the sense of self as feeler and thinker, and the sense of agency. The extreme case, of course, is multiple personality disorder, in which different alters may actually assume ownership of different feelings, memories, motives, and states of consciousness (see Putnam, 1991, this volume). Dissociative experiences stemming from abuse play a particularly important role in abuse-related disruptions in the sense of self, whether this disruption is mild or severe. The sense of continuity is severed by amnesic episodes and altered states of consciousness that feel like "not me" and cannot be woven into the fabric of consciousness over time. One survivor of sexual abuse, for example, literally could not recall the events of the prior day, leaving her with an experience of self as disjointed and temporally disconnected.

Depersonalization, particularly the experience of feelings or thoughts occurring outside the body, also disrupts the normal sense of self as subject. One severe abuse victim in her thirties who had been involved in prostitution reported quitting the trade because she could not afford to spend the hours outside of her body that occurred each time she "turned a trick."

Sexual abuse survivors, like other sufferers of post-traumatic stress disorder (Horowitz, 1986), may also experience massive disruptions in affective experience and cognitive control, such as numbing, flooding with overwhelming affects, and alternations of intrusive memories and loss of memory. Maintaining a sense of the self as the author of one's thoughts and feelings becomes extremely difficult when thoughts and feelings come and go from awareness without the degree of executive control that most nontraumatized individuals experience. This is not, of course, absolute: We are all, to some degree, captive to the stimuli and unconscious processes that determine the focus of our attention, but most of the time the contents of consciousness are tied to consciously recognizable goals and circumstances that provide a sense of ownership and control, to whatever degree illusory.

Sexual abuse can also distort the sense of agency. In part, this may result from the splitting off of motivational systems, particularly around sexual impulses, that cannot be owned as one's own. A psychotherapy patient was describing an incident in which she was getting involved with a man but presented the account with a peculiar lack of agency, as if the ship was sailing but no one was at the helm. When asked if she was attracted to him, she shook her head and said "no," but followed this a second later with, "yes, uh-huh." She then responded, astonished at her own dual communication, "I don't know where either of those came from." The tendency to experience extreme and overwhelming affects can also prevent a sense of agency, as it may result in impulsive actions such as suicide attempts and gestures that may then appear to have come "out of the blue." Once again the extreme case is multiple personality disorder, in which different personalities may be unaware of the actions of the others, let alone the intentions or motives (see Putnam, 1989).

Self-Representations

Childhood sexual abuse can affect self-representations in multiple ways. First, abuse shrouds some of the most fundamental representations of self in emotional pain and conflict: bodily representations. Freud and other psychoanalysts have stressed that among the first representations of self are tactile and visual representations (see Fisher, 1990). Sexual abuse often leaves its victims unsure of the relation between pleasure and pain, fear and arousal, and hence distorts some of the most primary representations of bodily experience. Recent investigations have documented discrete neurophysiological patterns underlying different emotions (Levenson, 1992). Nevertheless, social psychological research documented many years ago that feelings such as fear, anger, and sexual arousal can often be difficult to distinguish subjectively, and that people often use contextual cues to try to define and attribute their own feelings (e.g., Dutton & Aron, 1975; Zillman, 1978). This is likely to be a developmental process, which can be complicated by intense affective states combining pain and fear with genital manipulation. Residual conflicts in adolescence involving the normative desire to be attractive coupled with the desperate wish to be ugly to avoid inciting sexual interest or abuse can lead to substantial distortions in body image. One patient who had developed physically in early adolescence became anorexic—with the attendant distortion in body image—in an apparent effort to defeminize her body. At normal weight, she saw her body as fat, which served the function of protecting her from fear of unwanted sexual attention and desirability.

Sexual abuse can have a substantial impact on bodily self-representations in other ways. As Nash et al (1993) showed, it often leaves victims feeling fundamentally damaged or preoccupied with bodily experiences or body damage. This may reflect both the experience of being physically invaded as well as actual tissue damage, as when an immature body is traumatized by penetration that leads to observable scarring, which may serve as a daily reminder of the experience. Sexually abused children also may contract venereal diseases from their abusers (Newberger, 1990). This may lead to the association of pain and illness with sexuality and with the genitals. In older children and adolescents who understand what venereal diseases are and who have heard cultural messages about their origins and meanings, contraction of venereal diseases may intensify shameful feelings about the body and a general sense of stigmatization.

Second, sexual abuse can lead to a disruption of episodic memories, as in the substantial periods of amnesia that characterize many abuse victims, and of the links between episodic and semantic knowledge (see also Crittenden, 1990). Semantic memory refers to general knowledge or facts, while episodic memory consists of memories of particular episodes or events from personal experience (Tulving, 1972). Sexual abuse often leads to ablation from memory of entire periods of the individual's past. One research subject described looking at childhood pictures of herself and having no sense of recognition of either herself or the objects around her in the photographs. She had no memories before age 14, and the repression was so complete that even visual self-recognition of her physiognomy during that period was eliminated. In cases such as this, episodic memories appear to be completely blocked because either the abuse was so frequent that no memory is safe, or because nonabuse memories are densely interconnected with abuse memories, rendering all memories potentially anxiety-provoking—that is, all roads lead to abuse.

Sexual abuse also sometimes leads to a severing of the link between generalized self-knowledge and particular episodes. One patient, while beginning to recover some of her childhood memories in psychotherapy, would often speak fluently, offering a generalization such as, "My mother used to beat us until we bled." If asked for details, however, she would be at a loss to explain its basis, and would be shocked that it had come out of her mouth. Researchers studying adults who are "dismissing" of attachment, who often have avoidantly attached children, similarly find a discrepancy between verbal generalizations ("My mother and I had a great relationship") and absent or conflicting episodic memories (Main, Kaplan, & Cassidy, 1985). Following Bowlby (1969), theorists have explained this in terms of the defensive processing of information designed to minimize anxiety (Bretherton, 1990). Crittenden (1990) has argued that semantic memory may serve as a "gate keeper" to episodic memory, and that closing the gates may be one strategy for managing discomfort. Interestingly, despite numerous controversies in academic psychological literature abut the concept of repression, no one who works in this field—including theorists whose orientation is primarily cognitive (e.g., McCann & Pearlman, 1990)—questions the existence of repressive mechanisms in sexual abuse victims.

When sexual victimization occurs during the preschool or toddler years, so that the child lacks the representational capacity to encode the experiences semantically at the time of the event, the link between semantic and episodic memory may never be forged. Terr (1991) describes a 5-year-old child who was, unbeknownst to her parents, sexually misused by child pornographers when she was in daycare from 15 to 18 months:

> While playing in my office, this child told me that a baby she had just drawn was "all naked" and "a bad girl. . ." Despite the fact that the little girl's only verbal memory of the events was "I think there was a grave danger at a lady—MaryBeth's—house," her volumes of drawings [of nude adults when she had first begun to draw] represented strongly visualized elements that she had retained and had needed to recreate from these very early, nonverbal experiences (p. 12).

A third potential impact of sexual abuse on self-representations is the rendering of many currently active schemas or representations inaccessible to consciousness. Activation can spread to schemas that cannot be consciously accessed because their content is too painful or terrifying, leading to thoughts, emotions, or actions that the person cannot understand or acknowledge. A woman in her early thirties came to a clinic because of panic attacks and depression. She did not recognize the relation between the onset of these symptoms and a significant event in her life: the beginnings of her first consensual sexual relation. The therapist suspected sexual abuse in the first session because of a contradictory pattern of behavior: A flicker of fear crossed her face as he flipped the "Do not Disturb" sign on the door, yet she behaved in a flirtatious way throughout the session. The patient was unaware of her sexual abuse history until active memories began to influence her dreams. In one dream, her mother was a pimp and she was a prostitute. Her associations led to the recognition that she had felt that her mother had "pimped" her as a way of keeping the mother's lover from leaving; they also brought to our attention a profoundly repressed view of herself as a "whore." One could hypothesize, as well, that the symptoms that brought her to the clinic—depression and panic—stemmed from activation of representations associated with sexual activity by her incipient sexual relationship. These representations thus appeared to influence both her emotional state and her dream content despite their inaccessibility to consciousness.

This example raises an important point about the relation between conscious and unconscious representations of self in sexual abuse victims. Before treatment, the patient would never have acknowledged the presence of a "self as whore" schema, which is prevalent in some survivors, who construct this view of self at a time during which they do not understand concepts of responsibility. They frequently present themselves and others with a very different representation of self as either nonsexual or naive, which defends against the unconscious representation. Similarly, some sexual abuse victims conceptualize themselves as liking or getting along with only men or only women, masking unconscious hatred toward men they view as abusers or women as failed protectors or rivals.

Fourth, sexual abuse can affect self-attributional processes which normally contribute to the development of self-representations. As in other forms of post-traumatic stress (van der Kolk, 1987), but perhaps to a greater degree, sexual abuse victims may demonstrate a cognitive constriction that applies particularly to introspection and to attributions aobut the self. One might call this a "metacognitive shutdown," in that it entails a shutting down of the normal metacognitive processes—thinking about one's own thought and behavior—that normally develop substantially through adolescence and beyond. A woman who was molested by her grandfather actively avoided driving down the street next to her house because an old man on that street reminded her of him. Before exploring this in psychotherapy, however, she did not know why she avoided the street, and, more remarkably, she had never even wondered about it. Sexual abuse victims sometimes perform seemingly peculiar behaviors, such as barricading themselves in their bedrooms at night, and often actively constrict attributional activity so that they can avoid coming upon the reasons for their behavior. The active nature of this constriction—the fact that it does not simply reflect an "oversight" or inattention to a seemingly meaningless detail—is clear when the person is repeatedly asked about it by others and shrugs it off as uninteresting or a personal quirk.

Constriction of self-attributional and metacognitive activity may be required in order to carry out motives shaped by abuse that would otherwise be impossible to execute. Abuse victims who engage in promiscuous activity, prostitution, or other forms of sexual exploitation without economic necessity often appear unaware of the connection between their history (even when this is not repressed) and their current actions. Without active inhibition of cognitive processes, victims undoubtedly tend to recognize that such behavior is related to the trauma and should be avoided at all costs, particularly when it is accompanied by unpleasant consequences, painful emotional states, or dissociative episodes. Indeed, simple operant conditioning would put a stop to behaviors of this sort if they did not serve some psychological function.

Disruptions in cognitive functioning of relevance to self-understanding are not limited to sexual abuse victims. Several studies have found an impact of physical abuse on children's IQ and particularly on their use of language (Newberger, 1990). A study of physically abused and nonabused children combining data from two samples found lower scores on a test of verbal ability (the Peabody Picture Vocabulary Test) among the abused children (Trickett et al, 1991). Other investigations have documented generalized problems with memory and attention in severe abuse victims in adulthood (Sutker et al, 1990). The impact of specifically sexual abuse, however, is unclear. In a sample of adolescent inpatients, sexual abuse victims in particular had significantly lower verbal IQ scores than comparison subjects (Westen, Ludolph, Misle, et al, 1990).[2] Presumably the problems with language seen in children who were maltreated that cannot be attributed to socioeconomic status, including children who were sexually molested, reflect a combination of factors: Defensive shutting down of associational and attributional processes, shifting of cognitive resources away from exploration and toward establishing security and safety, and interaction with parents who may themselves be less comfortable with words.

Fifth, sexual abuse experiences may disrupt normal developmental processes associated with self-representation. In the normal course of events, children's representations become more abstract, differentiated, subtle, and focused on internal states and qualities as they develop (see Damon & Hart, 1988). Children tend to view themselves in absolute terms—as nice or mean, dumb or smart—until social comparison processes begin to give them a sense of their relative position on various evaluative domains. As Harter and Monsour (1992) have documented, teenagers begin thinking about the way seemingly opposite traits (such as being cheerful with friends but depressed with parents) may be integrated (for example, into a generalization such as "I'm moody"). For individuals who lack access to salient aspects of themselves, especially aspects that are affectively highly charged, such integration is difficult.

Self-with-Other, Wished-for, Feared, and Ideal Self Schemas

As noted earlier, a salient feature of the self-with-other or relationship schemas of sexual abuse victims documented in research is their malevolence. The theme of victimization and a generalized distrust of relationships are common in adults who were abused as children. Interestingly, in research to date this has been more true of victims of sexual than physical abuse, suggesting that these victim-victimizer schemas are not simply learned expectancies about the probability of physical harm (Nigg et al, 1992). Rather, they appear to reflect the individual's attempt to construct a reality that makes sense of betrayal and exploitation, as well as frequently sadism, at the hands of presumed protectors. A sense of trust can be shattered in other forms of trauma as well (Janoff-Bulman, 1992).

The impact on wished-for, feared, and ideal self schemas is highly variable, and moves into issues of motivation that are beyond the scope of the present chapter.[3] These forms of representations become motivationally significant when activated in tandem with representations of actual self, leading to affects

---

[2]Clinically, when I suspect sexual abuse, I now generally ask whether the person had trouble writing papers in school, achieving on standardized tests of verbal ability, interpreting literature for English classes, etc. This is not, of course, always diagnostic—some sexual abuse victims may even show the opposite pattern, with intrusions of violent but elaborate imagery—but it has proven useful on more than one occasion.

[3]The same is true of the representations of *others'* representations of the self that people attempt to alter with self-presentation strategies.

and subsequent attempts at affect regulation (see Higgins, 1990; Westen, 1985). For example, a child with a feared-self-representation of self-as-rejected-by-mother will likely be highly vigilant for any indication that this representation is being actualized. In response, he may deactivate his conscious desire for contact with her, or he may step up his efforts to maximize contact and respond to her needs. The aim of these responses is to quell a disquieting affective state.

Because of realistic concerns about victim blaming, theorists sometimes offer the untenable view that abuse experiences affect more strictly cognitive processes such as expectancies while leaving motivational structures intact. This leads, for example, to explanations of revictimization in terms of skills deficits, such as lack of knowledge of danger situations to be avoided, or as a preference for the familiar.

Although these more cognitive phenomena may be part of the picture, a more parsimonious explanation is that sexual abuse in childhood can distort representations of wished-for and feared states, including states of the self, just as it can more strictly cognitive representations. For example, sexual excitement may become associated with coercion, either of the self or others, leading to sexualized behavior or perpetration on other children. Sexualization is, indeed, one of the most pronounced symptoms in sexually abused children (Beitchman, Zuckkerr, Hood, daCosta, & Akman, 1991).

In adolescence and adulthood these motivational distortions may be expressed as promiscuity (Kendall-Tackett et al, 1993), victimization of others, or self-victimization such as body piercing or participation in abusive relationships. Males convicted of sexual offenses and violent crimes such as murder have elevated incidence of sexual abuse in their own histories (see Becker, 1988; Groth & Birnbaum, 1979); women who were victimized as children are disproportionately represented among adult rape victims (Koss & Dinero, 1989). Abuse victims may not wish for pain per se (except, perhaps, as compensation for guilt), but they may wish for experiences highly associated with pain or victimization. Our contemporary understanding of the compulsion to repeat remains as incomplete as Freud's, although careful study of representations of desired and feared states may offer some insights.

Clinically, the failure to deal with distorted motivational processes of this sort, motivated by a well-intentioned but nonetheless countertransferential unwillingness to explore current problematic motives and childhood constructions of culpability, can, paradoxically, be harmful to the patients it is intended to protect. Clinician-guided denial of this sort both invalidates survivors' experience of themselves as efficacious and responsible for their actions, and renders them less likely to alter self-destructive patterns. The important point is to validate their experience—for example, to acknowledge their deep-seated belief that they are responsible for the abuse perpetrated on them as children—without accepting it. The aim is to offer another way of construing the past and to help disentangle current and future circumstances in which they have control from those in which they do not. Victims of sexual abuse need the freedom to explore their childhood views of responsibility and, over time, to recast these in an adult understanding of the limits of childhood motives and intentions in the face of unequal power relationships.

Self-Esteem

Investigations of self-esteem in sexual abuse victims have produced variable results (see Kendall-Tackett et al, 1993), although many studies find lowered self-esteem among abuse victims (e.g., Jehu, 1989). This can entail a generalized lowering of self-regard, a deep sense of inner badness or contamination, or pervasive guilt and shame. As Cohen (1992) has pointed out, guilt in the face of traumas of various sorts is a common symptom that is seldom explained by theories of post-traumatic stress, particularly cognitively oriented theories that emphasize feelings of helplessness.

Abuse in childhood, and sexual abuse in particular, likely has several qualities that render it particularly evocative of guilt and low self-esteem (for a review of relevant research on the links between child maltreatment and adult depression, see Bemporad & Romano, 1992). The tendency of children to focus on deeds instead of intentions (Piaget, 1932; Shantz, 1983), as well as the propensity of children to think in egocentric ways about causality, render them more likely to take responsibility for what happened. Abusers often exhort or threaten children not to disclose the abuse, or bribe them to perform certain activities, leading to the feeling of choice that is then morally evaluated. In roughly forty to sixty percent of cases, perpetrators use rewards such as candy, money, or closeness to influence their victims, or they misrepresent to the child what is happening as a game or something normal between men and their children (Burgess, Holmstrom, & McCausland, 1977; Silver, Boon, & Stone, 1983). Further, the lack of mature concepts of responsibility and authority play a role, particularly as sexual abuse experiences become repressed and hence inaccessible to conscious revision with development.

Children who are sexually abused, particularly when this is accompanied by physical abuse and is perpetrated by a caretaker, also face a bitter dilemma that can have a substantial impact on self-esteem. They can either attribute the abuse to themselves, and hence see themselves as bad or evil, or they can attribute the blame to the abuser, and conclude that the world is unsafe and malevolent. Many children would prefer to opt for self-blame, because it allows a sense of control over future events (see Janoff-Bulman, 1992), permits some sense of safety, and maintains the hope of redemption through changing one's behaviors or through self-punishment as a form of penance. Often one sees the alternation of these constellations in abuse victims—profound self-hate and profound distrust.

A final factor that contributes to guilt and low self-esteem in survivors of sexual abuse is their conscious or unconscious condemnation of their own behavior in adolescence and adulthood. Having sexual feelings *at all* may feel grossly immoral when sex is associated with abuse and when sexual feelings are not experienced as volitional (as when they are denied or dissociated). Sexual abuse victims who repetitively act out their abuse through promiscuous behavior, prostitution, pornography, or sexual activities laced with aggression or masochism may condemn themselves for their impulses and actions. They may also reason backwards about causality, believing that their "badness" (seductiveness, promiscuity, etc.) led to the abuse, rather than vice versa.

Identity

Finally, childhood sexual abuse can generally impair the sense of historical and cross-situational coherence that contributes to identity. Amnesic periods, grossly inconsistent behavior across situations (such as religiosity coupled with casual sexual activity), and emotions that seem to come and go inexplicably can create difficulty piecing together a coherent and organized view of the self. Identity also includes a commitment to values and assumptions about the world, which can be disrupted by abuse (Epstein, 1990; Janoff-Bulman, 1992).

Identity is also in part socially bestowed. The way victims and their families handle sexual abuse can thus affect identity. Families may validate or invalidate aspects of the identity of survivors of abuse, recognizing why certain family members display certain characteristics or now interact guardedly with one another, or creating pseudo-interactions that deny the realities of what transpired. This can lead to an experience of unreality that undermines both identity and certainty of one's own thoughts.

Methodological Issues and Directions for Future Research

My aim in this chapter was to tackle a conceptual task, delineating multiple domains of self and examining the impact of abuse on each of them. In concluding, I will briefly note a corresponding methodological task, namely how to operationalize these different domains. On the face of it, finding measures of "self" should not be difficult; entire volumes have been devoted simply to summarizing the plethora of measures of self-concept, self-esteem, and the like (Wylie, 1979). The traditional way of studying dimensions of self has been self-report.

For some dimensions of self this is a reasonable strategy, but different domains require different methods. For example, assessing the sense of self as continuous through time is relatively straightforward and can be accomplished by questionnaire. People are generally quite adept at answering questions such as, "Can you remember what you did yesterday?" or "Do you often find that you have lost hours or days that you cannot account for?"

For other dimensions self-report is highly problematic for a number of reasons (for a more thorough discussion of these issues and of methods for accessing self-representations, see Westen, 1991, and Westen & Cohen, 1992). People lack access to many cognitive processes (Nisbett & Wilson, 1977), among them representational processes, so that asking them to describe these processes or mental contents through introspection is not a valid method of assessment. The only representations of self that are conscious are conscious representations, but they constitute only a small subset of the working representations that affect thought, motivation, feeling, and behavior. Further, the relation between the representations that people report when self-reflecting on questionnaires and the actual working representations activated in intimate relationships is entirely unknown. Additionally, the fact that some sexual abuse victims have no memory of the abuse, have minimal access to highly charged representations of self, and may have highly contradictory representations at different levels of awareness poses an extreme challenge to investigators who want to assess self-representations by self-report.

Researchers studying dimensions of self in sexual abuse will thus need to rely upon multiple measures, and to tailor their measures to different domains. Several strategies could be useful in circumventing the problems of self-report in assessing self-representations. One that we have been pursuing is to ask people to describe relationship episodes with significant others (that is, interactions that were meaningful, problematic, typical, or salient), and to code implicit representations of self from these episode descriptions. This approach is similar in certain respects to procedures used by Luborsky & Crits-Christoph (1990). Several dimensions can be coded from these responses. One is the complexity of self-understanding implicit in the response: To what degree does the individual recognize the impact of her enduring personality dispositions or attributes on the interpersonal events she encounters? Similarly, people vary on their attention to their internal states and the complexity with which they describe their subjective experience. Another important variable is the self-with-other schemas, or relationship themes, that people express repetitively in their narratives. Themes of particular relevance to sexual abuse victims may include representations of victimization, sexual victimization, neglect, feeling misunderstood, betrayal, self-victimization, and safety. These themes can be reliably assessed by Q-sort.

Other strategies might employ experimental procedures used in cognitive and psychophysiological research. Priming procedures, which activate a network of semantic knowledge by presenting a member of the network, may be useful in assessing unconscious schematic processes that may be disavowed. For example, a priming procedure could be used to assess the frequency of repressed representations such as the "self as whore" schema described earlier in sexual abuse victims. In semantic priming studies, subjects who have been exposed to a word like "chair" are likely to respond more quickly when faced with a lexical decision task, such as deciding whether the word "table" is a word, if the two words are semantically related. The reason is that presentation of the prime (chair) presumably spreads activation to related concepts along networks of association, so that the target word (table) is more readily recognized, manifest in reduced response latency (reaction time). Using a similar procedure, subjects could be primed with words that they have described as self-referent. Subsequent recognition of words like "whore" or "seduce" should then be facilitated if these words are indeed self-referent, even if disavowed.

An alternative procedure would be to assess psychophysiological variables such as electrodermal activity, blood pulse volume, or brain activity while presenting subjects with words hypothesized to be related to unconscious self-schemas but consciously disavowed. A similar strategy was employed in the study of deactivating strategies by Dozier and Kobak (in press) described earlier using electrodermal response. Wong, Shevrin, & Williams, (in press) have recently obtained results using subliminal and supraliminal presentations of words specifically chosen to reflect the conflicts of individual subjects by a team of clinicians, using brain activity as the dependent variable.

This chapter has attempted to set an agenda for future research. Instead of asking the question, "How does sexual abuse affect the self?" it suggests a more potentially fruitful question: "How do the multiple aspects of sexual abuse affect different dimensions of self, and under what circumstances will alterations or disruptions in aspects of self occur?" This is a much more complex question, but one befitting a complex set of phenomena.

REFERENCES

Ainsworth, M. (1979). Infant-mother. *American Psychologist, 34*, 932–937.

Baumeister, R. (1987). How the self became a problem: A psychological review of historical research. *Journal of Personality and Social Psychology, 52*, 163–176.

Becker, J. (1988). The effects of child sexual abuse on adolescent sexual offenders. In G. Wyatt & G. Powell (Eds.), *The lasting effects of child sexual abuse* (pp. 193–207). Beverly Hills, CA: Sage.

Beitchman, J., Zuckkerr, K., Hood, J., DaCosta, G., & Akman, D. (1991). A review of the short-term effects of child sexual abuse. *Child Abuse & Neglect, 15*, 537–556.

Bemporad, J., & Romano, S. (1992). Childhood maltreatment and adult depression: A review of research. In D. Cicchetti & S. Toth (Eds.), *Development perspectives on depression. Rochester Symposium on Developmental Psychopathology*, Vol. 4 (pp. 351–376). Rochester: University of Rochester Press.

Block, M. J. (1990). *Mothers of females adolescents with borderline personality disorder: Intrapsychic and social functioning.* Unpublished dictoral dissertation, University of Michigan.

Bowlby, J. (1969). *Attachment and loss*, Vol. 1, *Attachment*. New York: Basic Books.

Brenner, C. (1982) *The Mind in Conflict*. New York: International Universities Press.

Bretherton, I. (1985). Attachment theory: Retrospect and prospects. In I. Bretherton & E. Waters (Eds.), *Growing points of attachment theory and research. Monographs of the Society for Research in Child Development*, 50 (1–2, Serial No. 209), pp. 3–35.

Bretherton, I. (1990). Communication patterns, internal working models, and the integenerational transmission of attachment relationships. *Infant Mental Health Journal, 11*, 237–252.

Briere, J., & Elliott, D. (1993). Sexual abuse, family environment, and psychological symptoms: On the validity of statistical control. *Journal of Consulting and Clinical Psychology, 61*, 284–288.

Browne, A. & Finkelhor, D. (1986). Impact of child sexual abuse: A review of the research. *Psychological Bulletin*, 99, 66–77.

Bruyer, R. (1991). Covert face recognition in prosopagnosisa: A review. *Brain and Cognition, 15*, 223–235.

Burgess, A., Holstrom, L., & McCausland, M. (1977). Child sexual assault by a family member: Decisions following disclosure. *Victimology, 2*, 236–250.

Capaldi, D., & Patterson, G. R. (1991). Relation of parental transitions to boys' adjustment problems: I. A linear hypothesis. II. Mothers at risk for transitions and unskilled parenting. *Developmental Psychology*, 27, 489–504.

Cicchetti, D. (1991). Fractures in the crystal: Developmental psychopathology and the emergence of self. *Developmental Review*, 11, 271–287.

Cicchetti, D., & Schneider-Rosen, K. (1986). An organizational approach to childhood depression. In M. Rutter, C. Izard, & P. Read (Eds.), *Depression in young people: Developmental, and clinical perspectives* (pp. 71–134). New York: Guilford Press.

Clausen, A., & Crittenden, P. (1991). Physical and psychological maltreatment: Relations among types of maltreatment. *Child Abuse & Neglect, 15,* 5–18.

Cohen, (1992). *The role of self-continuity in Vietnam combat veterans.* Unpublished doctoral dissertation, University of Michigan, Ann Harbor, Michigan.

Collins, A., & Loftus, E. (1975). A spreading-activation theory of semantic processing. *Psychological Review,* 82, 407–428.

Conte, J., & Schuerman, J. (1987). The effects of sexual abuse on children: A multidimensional view. *Journal of Interpersonal Violence, 2,* 380–390.

Crittenden, P. (1990). Internal representational models of attachment relationships. *Infant Mental Health Journal, 11,* 259–277.

Crittenden, P., Partridge, M., & Claussen, A. (1991). Family patterns of relationship in normative and dysfunctional families. *Development & Psychopathology,* 3, 491–512.

Damon, W., & Hart, D. (1988). *Self-understanding in childhood and adolescence.* New York: Cambridge University Press.

Dutton, D, & Aron, A. (1974). Some evidence for heightened sexual attraction under conditions of high anxiety. *Journal of Personality and Social Psychology,* 30, 510–517.

Epstein, S. (1990). Cognitive-experiential self theory. In L. Pervin (Ed.), *Handbook of personality: Theory and research* (pp. 165–192). New York: Guilford Press.

Epstein, S. (1991). The self-concept, the traumatic neurosis, and the structure of personality. In D. Ozer, J. Healy, and A. Stewart (Eds.), *Perspectives in personality,* Vol.3, pp. 63–98). London: Jessica Kingsley Publishers.

Finkelhor, D., & Brown, A. (1985). The traumatic impact of child sexual abuse: A conceptualization. *American Journal of Orthopsychiatry,* 55, 530–541.

Fisher, S. (1990). The evolution of psychological concepts about the body. In T. Cash & T. Pruzinsky (Eds.), *Body images: Development, deviance, and change* (pp. 3–20). New York: Guilford Press.

Fitzgerald, H., Sullivan, L., Ham, H., Zucker, R., Bruckel, S., Schneider, A., & Noll, R. (1993). Predictors of behavior problems in three-year old sons of alcoholics: Early evidence of the onset of risk. *Child Development,* 64, 110–123.

Geertz, C. (1983). *Local knowledge: Further essays in interpretive anthropology.* New York: Basic Books.

Gelinas, D. J. (1983). The persisting negative effects of incest. *Psychiatry,* 46, 312–332.

Gomes-Schwartz, B., Horowitz, J., & Cardarelli, A. (1990). *Child sexual abuse: The initial effects.* Beverly Hills, CA: Sage.

Greenwald, A. (1992). New look 3: Unconscious cognition reclaimed. *American Psychologist,* 47, 766–779.

Groth, A., & Birnbaum, J. (1979). *Men who rape: A psychology of the offender.* New York: Plenum.

Harter, S., & Monsour, A. (1992). Developmental analysis of conflict caused by opposing attributes in the adolescent self-portrait. *Development Psychology,* 28, 251–260.

Harvey, M., & Herman, J. (1992). The trauma of sexual victimization: Feminist contributions to theory, research, and practice. *PTSD Research Quarterly,* 3, 1–8.

Herman, J. (1992). *Trauma and recovery.* New York: Basic Books.

Higgins, E. T. (1990). Personality, social psychology, and person-situation relations: Standards and knowledge activation as a common language. In L. Pervin (Ed.), *Handbook of personality: Theory and research* (pp. 301–338). New York: Guilford Press.

Horowitz, M. (1986). *Stress response syndromes.* New York: Jason Aronson.

Horowitz, M. J. (1987). *States of mind: Configurational analysis of individual psychology,* 2nd ed. New York: Plenum.

James, W. (1890). *The principles of psychology.* New York: Henry Hold.

Janoff-Bulman, R. (1992). *Shattered assumptions: Towards a new psychology of trauma.* New York: Free Press.

Jehu, D. (1989). Mood disturbances among women clients sexually abused in childhood. *Journal of Interpersonal Violence, 4,* 164–184.

Kendall-Tackett, K., Williams, L., & Finkelhor, D. (in press). The impact of sexual abuse on children: A review and synthesis of recent empirical studies. *Psychological Bulletin, 113,* 164–180.

Kihlstrom, J. (1984). Conscious, subconscious, unconscious: A cognitive perspective. In K. Bowers & D. Meichenbaum (Eds.), *The unconscious reconsidered* (pp. 149–211). New York: Academic.

Kihlstrom, J., Barnhardt, T., & Tataryn, D. (1992). The psychological unconscious: Found, lost, and regained. *American Psychologist, 47,* 788–791.

Korbin, J., Ed. (1981). *Child abuse and neglect: Cross-cultural perspectives.* Berkeley: University of California Press.

Koss, M., & Dinero, T. (1989). Discriminant analysis of risk factors for sexual victimization among a national sample of college women. *Journal of Consulting and Clinical Psychology, 57,* 242–250.

Lebowitz, L., Harvey, M., & Herman, J. (in press). A stage by dimension model of recovery from sexual trauma. *Journal of Interpersonal Violence.*

Levenson, R. W. (1992). Autonomic nervous system differences among emotions. *Psychological Science,* 3, 23–27.

Luborsky, L., & Crits-Christoph, P. (1990). *Understanding transference: The core conflictual relationship theme method.* New York: Basic Books.

Lynch, M., & Cicchetti, D. (1991). Patterns of relatedness in maltreated and nonmaltreated children: Connections among multiple representational models. *Development and Psychopathology, 3,* 207–226.

Lyons-Ruth, K., Connell, D., Grunebaum, H., & Botein, S. (1990). Infants at social risk: Maternal depression and family support services as mediators of infant development and security of attachment. *Child Development,* 61, 85–98.

Main, M. (1990). Cross-cultural studies of attachment organization: Recent studies, changing methodologies, and the concept of conditional strategies. *Human Development,* 33, 48–61.

Main, M., Kaplan, N., & Cassidy, J. (1985). Security in infancy, childhood, and adulthood: A move to the level of representation. In I Bretherton & E. Waters (Eds.), *Growing points of attachment theory and research.* Monographs of the Society for Research in Child Development, Vol. 50, Nos. 1–2, pp. 67–104.

Main, M., & Solomon, J. (1986). Discovery of a new, insecure-disorganized/disoriented attachment pattern. In T. Brazelton & M. Yogman (Eds.), *Affective development in infancy* (pp. 95–124). Norwood, N.J.: Ablex.

Mannarino, A., & Cohen, J. (1986). A clinical-demographic study of sexually abused children. *Child Abuse & Neglect, 10,* 17–23.

Markus, H., & Cross, S. (1990). The interpersonal self. In L. Pervin (Ed.), *Handbook of personality: Theory and research* (pp. 576–608). New York: Guilford Press.

Markus, H. R. & Kitayama, S. (1991). Culture and the self: Implications for cognition, emotion, and motivation. *Psychological Review,* 98, 224–253.

McCann, I. L., & Pearlman, L. A. (1990). *Psychological trauma and the adult survivor: Theory, therapy, and transformation.* New York: Brunner/Mazel.

McClelland, D. C., Koestner, R., & Weinberger, J. (1989). How do self-attributed and implicit motives differ? *Psychological Bulletin,* 96, 690–702.

Morrow, K. (1991). Attributions of female adolescent incest victims regarding their molestation. *Child Abuse & Neglect, 15,* 477–483.

Mueller, N., & Silverman, N. (1989). Peer relations in maltreated children. In D. Cicchetti & V. Carlson (Eds.), *Child maltreatment: Theory and research on the causes and consequences of child abuse and neglect* (pp. 529–578). New York: Cambridge University Press.

Nash, M., Hulsey, T., Sexton, M., Harralson, T., & Lambert, W. (1993). Long-term sequelae of childhood sexual abuse: Perceived family environment, psychopathology, and dissociation. *Journal of Consulting and Clinical Psychology, 61,* 276–283.

Newberger, E. (1990). Child abuse. In M. Rosenberg (Ed.), *Violence: A public health approach* (pp. 51–78). Oxford: Oxford University Press.

Newberger, E., Newberger, C., & Gremy, I. (1991). *Dual vulnerability of sexually victimized mothers and sexually victimized children: A longitudinal study.* Presented at the 7th Annual Convention of the International Society for Traumatic Stress Studies, Washington, D.C., October.

Nigg, J. T., Silk, K. R., Westen, D., Lohr, N., Gold, L. J., Ogata, S., & Goodrich, S. (1991). Object representations in the early memories of sexually abused borderline patients. *American Journal of Psychiatry, 148,* 864–869.

Nisbett, R., & Wilson, T. (1977). Telling more than we can know: Verbal reports on mental processes. *Psychological Review*, 84, 231–259.

Ogilvie, D., & Ashmore, R. (1991). Self-with-other representations as a unit of analysis in self-concept research. In R. Curtis (Ed.), *The relational self* (pp.). New York: Guilford Press.

Patterson, C. J., Kupersmidt, J. B., & Griesler, P. (1990). Children's perceptions of self and of relationships with others as a function of sociometric status. *Child Development, 61,* 1335–1349.

Pennebaker, J. W. (1990). Stream of consciousness and stress: Levels of thinking. In J.S. Uleman and J.A. Bargh (eds.), *Unintended thought* (pp. 327–350). N.Y.: Guilford Press.

Piaget, J. (1932/1965). *The moral judgment of the child.* New York: Free Press.

Putnam, F. (1990). *Diagnosis and treatment of multiple personality disorder.* New York: Guilford Press.

Putnam. F. (1991). Recent research on multiple personality disorder. *Psychiatric Clinics of North America, 14,* 489–502.

Ricks, M. (1985). The social transmission of parental behavior: Attachment across generations. In I. Bretherton & E. Waters (Eds.), *Growing points of attachment theory and research. Monographs of the Society for Research in Child Development*, 50, (1–2, Serial No. 209), 211–227.

Rogers, C. (1959). A theory of therapy, personality, and interpersonal relationships, as developed in the client-centered framework. In S. Koch (Ed.), *Psychology: A study of a science,* Vol. 3, *Formulations of the personal and the social context* (184–255). New York: McGraw-Hill.

Roth, S., & Newman, E. (in press). The process of coping with incest for adult survivors: Measurement and implications for treatment and research. *Journal of Interpersonal Violence.*

Rumelhart, D., McClelland, J., & the PDP Research Group. (1986). *Parellel distributed processing: Explorations in the microstructures of cognition*, Vol.1, *Foundations.* Cambridge: MIT Press.

Russell, D. E. (1986). *The secret trauma: Incest in the lives of girls and women.* New York: Basic Books.

Salzinger, S., Feldman, R., & Hammer, M. (1993). The effects of physical abuse on children's social relationships. *Child Development, 64,* 169–187.

Shantz, C. (1983). Social cognition. In J. Flavell & E. Markman (Eds.), *Handbook of child psychology,* Vol. 3: Cognitive Development (pp. 495–555). New York: Wiley. 83.

Shedler, J., Mayman, M., & Manis, M. (in press). The illusion of mental health. *American Psychologist.*

Shweder, R., & Bourne, E. (1984). Does the concept of the person vary cross-culturally? In R. Shweder & R. LeVine (Eds.), *Culture theory: Essays on mind, self, and emotion* (pp. 158–199). New York: Cambridge University Press.
Silver, R., Boon, C., & Stones, M. (1983). Searching for meaning in misfortune: Making sense of incest. *Journal of Social Issues, 39,* 81–102.
Sirles, E., & Frank, P. (1989). Factors influencing mother's reactions to intrafamily sexual abuse. *Child Abuse and Neglect, 13,* 131–139.
Sroufe, L. A., & Fleeson, W. (1986). Attachment and the construction of relationships. In W. W. Hartup & Z. Rubin (Eds.), *Relationships and development.* Hillsdale, N.J.: Erlbaum.
Stern, D. (1985). *The interpersonal world of the infant: A view from psychoanalysis and developmental psychology.* New York: Basic Books.
Sutker, P., Galina, H., West, J. A., & Allain, A. N. (1990). Trauma-induced weight loss and cognitive deficits among former prisoners of war. *Journal of Consulting and Clinical Psychology, 58,* 323–328.
Terr, L. (1991). Childhood traumas: An outline and overview. *American Journal of Psychiatry, 148,* 10–20.
Tizard, B., & Hodges, J. (1978). The effects of early institutional rearing on the development of eight-year-old children. *Journal of Child Psychology and Psychotherapy,* 19, 99–108.
Trickett, P., Aber, J. L., Carlson, V., & Cicchetti, D. (1991). Relationship of socioeconomic status to the etiology and developmental sequelae of physical child abuse. *Developmental Psychology, 27,* 148–158.
Tulving, E. (1972). Episodic and semantic memory. In E. Tulving & W. Donaldson (Eds.), *Organization of memory* (pp. 381–403). New York: Academic.
Uleman, J. S., & Bargh, J. A. (1989). *Unintended thought.* New York: Guilford Press.
van der Kolk, B., Ed. (1987). *Psychological trauma.* Washington, D.C.: American Psychiatric Press.
Weinberger, D. A. (1990). The construct validity of the repressive coping style. In J. Singer (Ed.), *Repression and dissociation.* Chicago: University of Chicago Press.
Westen, D. (1985). *Self and society: Narcissism, collectivism, and the development of morals.* New York: Cambridge University Press.
Westen, D. (1990). Psychoanalytic approaches to personality. In L. Pervin (Ed.), *Handbook of personality: Theory and research* (pp. 21–65). New York: Guilford.
Westen, D. (1991). Cultural, emotional, and unconscious aspects of self. In R. C. Curtis (Ed.), *The relational self: Theoretical convergences in psychoanalysis and social psychology* (pp. 181–210). New York: Guilford Press.
Westen, D. (1992). The cognitive self and the psychoanalytic self: Can we put our selves together? *Psychological Inquiry, 3,* 1–13.
Westen, D. and Cohen, R. (1992). "The self" in borderline personality disorder. In Z. Segal and S. Blatt (Eds.), *The self in emotional distress: Cognitive and psychodynamic perspectives* (pp. 334–360). N.Y.: Guilford Press.
Westen, D., Lohr, N., Silk, K., Gold, L., & Kerber, K. (1990). Object relations and social cognition in borderlines, major depressives, and normals: A TAT analysis. *Psychological Assessment: A Journal of Consulting and Clinical Psychology,* 2, 355–364.
Westen, D., Ludolph, P., Block, J., Wixom, J., Wiss, F. C. (1990) Developmental history and object relations in psychiatrically disturbed adolescent females. *American Journal of Psychiatry, 147,* 1061–1068.
Westen, D., Ludolph, P., Misle, B., Ruffins, S., & Block, M. J. (1990). Physical and sexual abuse in female adolescents with borderline personality disorder. *American Journal of Orthopsychiatry, 60,* 55–66.

Widom, C. (1991). The role of placement experiences in mediating the criminal consequences of early childhood victimization. *American Journal of Orthopsychiatry, 61*, 195–209.

Williamson, J. M., Borduin, C. M., & Howe, B. A. (1991). The ecology of adolescent maltreatment: A multilevel examination of adolescent physical abuse, sexual abuse, and neglect. *Journal of Consulting and Clinical Psychology,* 59, 449–457.

Wiss, F. C. (1991). *Aspects of the self.* Unpublished doctoral dissertation, University of Michigan, Ann Arbor.

Wong, P., Shevrin, H., & Williams, W. (in press). Conscious and nononscious processes: An ERP index of an anticipatory response in a conditioning paradigm using visually masked stimuli. *Psychophysiology*.

Wyatt, G. E., & Newcomb, M. (1990). Internal and external mediators of women's sexual abuse in childhood. *Journal of Consulting and Clinical Psychology,* 58, 758–767.

Wyatt, G. E., & Powell, G., Eds. (1988). *Lasting effects of child sexual abuse.* Beverly Hills, CA: Sage.

Zillman, D. (1978). Attribution and misattribution of excitatory reactions. In J. H. Harvey, W. Ickes, & R. F. Kidd (Eds.), *New directions in attribution research,* Vol. 2. Hillsdale, New Jersey: Lawrence Erlbaum.

VII Dissociation and Disturbances of Self

FRANK W. PUTNAM

Introduction

Definitions and Dimensions of Dissociation

Dissociation is a complex psychophysiological process that produces alterations in sense of self, accessibility of memory and knowledge and integration of behavior (Putnam, 1991b). Dissociation exists on a continuum with most individuals manifesting short, often situation-dependent, episodes of normative dissociation such as day-dreaming (Putnam, 1991b). Some individuals may experience prolonged or frequent episodes of dissociation that interfere with their functioning and significantly alter their sense of self. In extreme cases, individuals may develop a dissociative disorder such as multiple personality disorder (MPD) that produces profound disturbances in the psychological organization and representation of self and in the availability of information and memories. Although most definitions of dissociation focus on the failure of the individual to integrate information in a normal way, research suggests that dissociation has several underlying dimensions. These include alterations in memory, disturbances of identity, passive influence experiences and trance/absorption phenomena.

Clinically the memory dysfunctions are quite complicated and interconnected but they can be experimentally dissected to some degree in laboratory studies (Putnam, 1991c). Memory dysfunctions include: 1) deficits in retrieval of implicit knowledge across behavioral state; 2) deficits in retrieval of autobiographical memory; 3) deficits in retrieval of explicit information on free recall tests across behavioral state (cued recall appears to be less disrupted by dissociation—at least in laboratory settings); 4) intermittent and disruptive intrusions of traumatic memories into awareness and 5) difficulty in determining whether a given memory reflects an actual event or information acquired through a non-experiential source (e.g., reading or hearing about the event).

Disturbances of identity found in dissociative disorder patients include: 1) existence of alter "personalities" that exchange control over the individual's behavior and express a subjective sense of individuality and separateness; 2) depersonalization - in which the individual feels as if he or she is dead, unreal or detached from their surroundings and situation; and 3) psychogenic amnesia in which the individual forgets important highly personal information, e.g., his/her name. The alter personality states of MPD patients are often incorrectly portrayed as if they were separate and distinct individuals. In actuality, these psychological structures exhibit narrow ranges of functioning and affect and are best conceptualized as discrete behavioral states (Kluft, 1991; Putnam, 1991c; Putnam, 1992).

Passive influence experiences, especially prominent in MPD, involve the individual feeling as if he or she were controlled by a force within them (Kluft, 1987). Intensely dysphoric, passive influence experiences may include a sense of being made to do against one's will something that is loathsome or that is harmful to the individual or others. At times the dissociating individual may feel as if he or she loses control over part of his or her body so that it has "a mind of its own". For example, patients with MPD may experience "automatic writing", in which they subjectively do not feel as if they are in control of the writing hand and are surprised by what is written.

Auditory hallucinations, another form of dissociative passive influence experience, take a distinct form in the dissociative disorders that helps to differentiate them from hallucinations found in psychotic disorders (Coons, 1984; Goff, Brotman, Kindlon, Waites, & Amico, 1991; Putnam, 1989). Dissociative hallucinations are most likely to be experienced as internalized voices rather than externalized voices. The voices are heard distinctly, often have distinctive attributes such as gender, age and affect, and may be pejorative and berating or supportive and comforting (Putnam, 1989). Specific hallucinated voices are frequently associated with specific situations or experiences, e.g., when depressed, a dissociative patient hallucinated the voice of her incestuous stepfather commanding her to commit suicide. The dissociating individual is generally aware that the voice(s) is a hallucination, but for fear of being labeled "crazy" may not report the hallucinations until after a secure therapeutic alliance is established.

The fourth dimension of dissociation takes the form of experiences of intense absorption or enthrallment and spontaneous trance states. Spontaneous trance states, not uncommon in normal children and adolescents, are very frequent in adult dissociative disorder patients and interfere with the ongoing processing of information (Putnam, 1991a; Putnam, 1993). The trance and absorption experiences and symptoms in dissociative patients resemble phenomena seen in hypnosis and in individuals labeled as 'fantasy prone' (Barrett, 1992; Lynn, Rhue, & Green, 1988; Silva & Kirsch, 1992). The overlaps and interrelationships among hypnosis, fantasy, absorption and dissociation are poorly understood at present.

Psychophysiology of Dissociation

The psychophysiology of dissociation has been of interest to medical researchers since the turn of the century when Prince and Peterson conducted their first experiments using a crude version of a polygraph or "lie detector". Modern studies using a variety of measures, including electroencephalograms (EEG), single positron emission tomography (SPECT), regional cerebral blood flow (rCBF) and other brain imaging methodologies indicate that distinct central and autonomic nervous system changes do accompany changes in alter personality state (switching) (Putnam, 1991c). Preliminary research on the mechanisms of alter personality state switches suggests that these transitions resemble the changes found in transitions between the behavioral states of infants (Putnam, 1988; Wolff, 1987). One theory suggests that the childhood trauma associated with the development of dissociative disorders may interfere with the development of mature patterns of state modulation (Putnam, 1988).

Measurement of Dissociation

The measurement of dissociation has made great strides during the last decade. A number of adult self-report measures exist, the best validated of which is the Dissociative Experiences Scale (DES) developed by Bernstein and Putnam (Bernstein & Putnam, 1986). The DES has been used in over 80 published studies and included in national epidemiological research on posttraumatic stress disorder and other trauma-related conditions.[1] Investigations with the DES and other dissociation measures indicates that dissociation exists on a continuum in clinical and non-clinical samples (Albini & Pease, 1989; Bliss, 1986; Putnam, 1991b; Ross, Joshi, & Currie, 1990a). There are no gender differences in DES scores and, at least within U.S. samples, no evidence of significant cultural or ethnic differences; however, to date few studies have systematically examined cultural variables (Putnam, 1991b). A large sample, discriminant function analysis of the DES has been conducted and cutting scores for suspecting MPD empirically established (Carlson, Putnam, Ross, Torem, Coons, Dill, et al., 1993). Based on an analysis of the Receiver Operating Characteristics (ROC) of the DES, it exceeds the sensitivity and specificity of most psychiatric diagnostic tests.

Structured dissociative disorder psychiatric interviews yielding DSM-III/IIIR/IV diagnoses are available. The Dissociative Disorders Interview Schedule (DDIS) developed by Ross and colleagues is probably the most widely used measure (Ross, Heber, Norton, Anderson, Anderson, & Barchet, 1989). Our experience would suggest that the DDIS, though useful, over diagnoses MPD. The Structured Clinical Interview for DSM-III-R Dissociative Disorders (SCID-D) is a lengthy interview that has good validity and reliability and has been translated by a number of European investigators (Boon & Draijer, 1993; Steinberg, Rounsaville, & Cicchetti, 1990). Both diagnostic interviews are highly correlated with DES scores (Ross, Miller, Bjornson, Reagor, Fraser, & Anderson, 1990b; Steinberg, Rounsaville, & Cicchetti, 1991).

Measurement of dissociation in children and adolescents is just beginning to receive attention. A number of scales, questionnaires and "predictor lists" have been published (Evers-Szostak & Sanders, 1992; Putnam, Helmers, & Trickett, In press; Reagor, Kasten, & Morelli, 1992; Tyson, 1992). Of these, the Child

---

[1]The DES is a public domain document. A copy of the DES and scoring manual are available for $1 from: Eve B. Carlson, Ph.D., Department of Psychology, Beloit College, 700 College Street, Beloit, WI 53511.

Dissociative Checklist (CDC), an observer-report measure patterned on the Child Behavior Checklist (CBCL) (Achenbach & Edelbrock, 1981), is the best validated (Hornstein & Putnam, 1992; Putnam et al., In press).[2] For a variety of reasons, self-report measures of dissociation have poor validity with young children (Putnam, 1991a; Putnam, 1993). An adolescent self-report measure, the Adolescent Dissociative Experiences Scale (ADDES), is being fielded and should be ready for distribution in the near future.[3]

At this time, there are no definitive structured interviews, self-report scales or psychological tests for diagnosing dissociative disorders in children or adolescents. Dissociative disorder diagnoses can be very difficult to make in youth and are seriously confounded by the high levels of "normative" dissociation seen in some children and adolescents (Putnam, 1991a; Putnam, 1993). Unfortunately, some well-meaning child clinicians are mistaking normative dissociation for pathological dissociation in some cases. The diagnosis of childhood MPD or other dissociative disorder should only be made in a child or adolescent who has been clinically followed for some time and after repeated assessments of the degree of dissociation and its interference with the child's behavior and functioning have been made across a variety of contexts, e.g., at home, in school, with peers, etc. Dissociative disorder diagnoses should not be made without strong evidence that the child is experiencing a number of dimensions of pathological dissociation, e.g., extensive amnesias, depersonalization or other identity disturbance, frequent trance-like behavior and passive influence experiences.

Linkage of Dissociation to Traumatic Antecedents

One of the major findings to emerge from recent research with dissociation scales and structured interviews is the close linkage of high levels of dissociation with traumatic experiences. Although this relationship was intuitively known to many clinicians, recent research has confirmed and extended this finding, particularly in populations where traumatic antecedents were not previously considered to be important factors. Studies with dissociative and post-traumatic stress disorder patients have consistently linked increased DES scores to traumatic experiences (Putnam, 1991b). However, research with "non-traumatic" disorders, such as general psychiatric patients samples (Chu & Dill, 1990), borderline personality disorder patients (Herman, Perry, & van der Kolk, 1989); eating disorder patients (Demitrack, Putnam, Brewerton, Brandt, & Gold, 1990), and chronically psychotic patients (Goff et al., 1991) have also established that traumatic experiences increase an individual's propensity to dissociate (Putnam, 1985). Studies of non-clinical samples have similarly confirmed this relationship (Briere & Runtz, 1988; Cardena & Spiegel, 1993; Nash, Hul-

---

[2]For a free copy of the Child Dissociative Checklist (CDC) and supporting material contact: Frank W. Putnam, M.D., Bldg. 15K, NIMH, 9000 Rockville Pike, Bethesda, MD 20892.

[3]Contact Judy Armstrong, Ph.D., Sheppard Pratt Hospital, 6501 N. Charles Street, P.O. Box 6815, Baltimore, MD 21285–6815.

sey, Sexton, Harralson, & Lambert, In press; Sandberg & Lynn, 1992; Sanders, McRoberts, & Tollefson, 1989).

Little is known about which trauma-related factors, e.g., type of trauma, frequency, duration, relationship to perpetrator, loss of control, etc., influence the development of dissociative symptoms. However, several studies suggest that early childhood traumatic experiences are more likely than later traumatic experiences to produce increased dissociation. Studies by Chu and Dill and colleagues with adult psychiatric patients demonstrate a significant negative correlation between DES scores and the age of onset for traumatic experiences (Chu & Dill, 1990) (Kirby, Chu & Dill, 1993—see References). Adults with dissociative disorders generally have earlier onset for abuse and trauma than national averages. For example, several studies (Putnam, Guroff, Silberman, Barban, & Post, 1986; Ross, Miller, Bjornson, Reagor, Fraser, & Anderson, 1991; Schultz, Braun, & Kluft, 1989) have found an onset of sexual abuse between age 3–5 years in MPD patients compared to national averages of 7–9 years (Putnam & Trickett, 1993). Many authorities believe that patients who develop dissociative disorders experience more severe and more different types of abuse; however, only one study has systematically investigated this with a comparison group (Putnam et al., In press).

Normal Developmental Course of Dissociation over the Life Span

Little is known about the normative course of dissociation over the life span. Cross-sectional studies with adults demonstrate a gradual but significant decline in DES scores from adolescence through the seventh decade (Bernstein & Putnam, 1986; Putnam, 1991b; Ross et al., 1990a). Studies with adolescents suggest that the rate of decline in DES scores is greatest during early to middle adolescence (Sanders et al., 1989). Some authorities have extrapolated a life span trajectory of normative dissociation from research on hypnotizability. However, recent research suggests that clinical dissociation, as measured by the instruments discussed above, and hypnotizability, as measured by standard hypnosis scales, are only weak to moderate correlates and caution should be used in analogizing one form of dissociation with the other (Barrett, 1992; Frankel, 1990; Frischholz, Braun, Sachs, Schwartz, Lewis, Schaeffer, et al., In press; Lynn et al., 1988; Nash et al., In press; Sandberg & Lynn, 1992; Silva & Kirsch, 1992).

Based on cross-sectional research, it appears as if CDC scores are low and show little change from ages 6 to 16 years in non-traumatized control subjects (Putnam et al., In press). CDC scores for non-traumatized, non-clinical samples average (2.3 $\pm$ 2.7 SD) and show little variation with age. In a traumatized population there is often a marked heterogeneity of CDC scores and cross-sectional analyses suggest that dissociation declines with age. The abused children in our longitudinal study show a great deal of variability in their CDC scores, with about 20% of such a sample manifesting significant levels of dissociation (i.e., CDC scores of 12 or more) (Putnam et al., In press). The decline in CDC scores with age seen in our traumatized sample probably represents two factors. The first reflects a real decline in dissociative behavior with increasing age. The second reflects a deceased sensitivity of the CDC for dissociative behaviors in older children and adolescents. The ADDES, a self-report dissociation measure for adolescents, is being developed to span the age gap between the CDC and the DES.

Children meeting DSM-IIIR criteria for dissociative disorders are generally so pathologically dissociative that they score near the top of the CDC and no decline with age is seen in cross-sectional data (Hornstein & Putnam, 1992; Putnam et al., In press). Two studies have found that children and adolescents with MPD score about 25 ± 5.2 on the CDC (Hornstein & Putnam, 1992; Putnam et al., In press). Children with Dissociative Disorder Not Otherwise Specified (DDNOS) score around 16.5 ± 4.7 on the CDC. Further work on the validation of these instruments is progressing.

Dissociation and Psychopathology

Two lines of evidence connect dissociation with a broad spectrum of psychopathology. The first is the range of associated psychopathology found in patients with DSM-IIIR dissociative disorder diagnoses. A number of studies, using differing methodologies, have characterized the clinical profiles of these patients (Coons, Bowman, & Milstein, 1988; Putnam et al., 1986; Ross et al., 1990b; Ross, Norton, & Wozney, 1989; Schultz et al., 1989). A strikingly uniform set of clinical features emerges from a review of these data. Dissociative disorder patients, particularly patients with MPD, exhibit clinical profiles characterized by a plethora of psychiatric symptoms including: depression, anxiety, hallucinations, passive influence phenomena, drug and alcohol abuse, post-traumatic symptoms, obsessive-compulsive symptoms, eating problems, conversion and somatoform symptoms. Dissociative disorder patients are likely to be self-destructive (Ross & Norton, 1989). They are also likely to have acquired four or more non-dissociative psychiatric diagnoses and have long histories of psychiatric contact (Coons et al., 1988; Putnam et al., 1986; Ross et al., 1990b; Ross et al., 1989; Schultz et al., 1989).

Much has been made of this plethora of psychiatric symptoms and MPD has been called the great imitator (Putnam, 1989), a medical moniker previously bestowed on Syphilis, infamous for its varied clinical presentations. In fact, only a minority of dissociative disorder patients (about 15% in one series (Kluft, 1991)) present with classic dissociative symptoms. The well-replicated finding of polysymptomatology in dissociative disorder patients suggests that dissociation is diffusely related to psychopathology rather than being more directly related to specific symptoms.

The second source of information comes from the study of dissociation in non-dissociative disorder clinical and in non-clinical samples. Studies of the contributions of dissociation to the clinical phenomenology of eating disorder patients (Demitrack et al., 1990), chronically psychotic patients (Goff et al., 1991), and PTSD patients (Branscomb, 1991; Bremner, Southwick, Brett, Fontana, Rosenheck, & Charney, 1992), all suggest that within a given diagnostic category, increased levels of dissociation are associated with greater severity of symptoms and higher rates of self destructive behavior. In college student samples, several studies have linked elevated levels of dissociation with increased psychopathology (Briere, 1990; Nash et al., In press; Sandberg & Lynn, 1992; Sanders et al., 1989)

Although considerably fewer studies have been conducted, work with children and adolescents appears to replicate the diffuse relationship between dissociation and psychopathology described above for adults. Children with DSM-IIIR dissociative disorders also present with a plethora of psychiatric symptoms and generally receive several psychiatric diagnoses (Dell & Eisenhower, 1990; Hornstein & Putnam, 1992; Hornstein & Tyson, 1991; Putnam, 1993). In the largest sample published to date, the average child dissociative disorder case had received about 3 major psychiatric diagnoses and presented with an array of affective, anxiety, posttraumatic and conduct disorder symptoms (Hornstein & Putnam, 1992). Smaller sample studies and individual case reports also indicate that child and adolescent dissociative disorder cases are typically polysymptomatic with a variety of initial clinical presentations (Bowman, 1990; Bowman, Blix, & Coons, 1985; Dell & Eisenhower, 1990; Fagan & McMahon, 1984; Fine, 1988; Fink, 1988; Hornstein & Tyson, 1991; Kluft, 1984; Kluft, 1985; Malenbaum & Russel, 1987; McElroy, 1992; Tyson, 1992; Weiss, Sutton, & Utecht, 1985).

Research on the influence of dissociation on symptoms and behavior problems in both traumatized and non-traumatized child samples supports the notion that dissociation is diffusely related to psychopathology. Data from the Trickett and Putnam longitudinal study of sexually abused girls indicates that CDC scores are strongly correlated with overall and many of the subscale scores of the Child Behavior Checklist (CBCL) (Achenbach & Edelbrock, 1981) (Putnam and Trickett-unpublished data). The correlation coefficients between CDC scores and CBCL subscales for the non-traumatized comparison sample equal or exceed those coefficients for the abuse sample in many instances - indicating that strong relationships between dissociation and behavior problems are present in clinical and non-clinical samples. CDC scores are well correlated with a number of self-report measures in abused and comparison children including the Child Depression Inventory (CDI), levels of adrenal stress hormones, and with motor activity levels measured by computerized actometers (Putnam and Trickett - unpublished data). CDC scores are also significantly correlated with teacher assessments of academic performance and social skills (Trickett, McBride, & Putnam, 1993).

Impact of Dissociation on Developmental Processes

Preliminary research on the effects of dissociation on memory (see (Putnam, 1991c)) and on the relationship of dissociation to attachment, suggest that pathological levels of dissociation strongly impact developmental processes, especially those processes associated with the development of self, regulation of emotion and the integration of behavior. The following discussion, while largely speculative, is intended to suggest how dissociation may shift developmental processes toward abnormal trajectories.

Dissociative Alterations in the Development of Self

The dissociative disorders contain a set of disturbances in identity and other aspects of self. Clinically these disturbances of identity are manifest as: 1) psychogenic amnesia; 2) depersonalization; and 3) alternate identities. Underlying these alterations of identity are the dissociative disturbances of memory and psychophysiology discussed above.

Self is a complex construct with a long history in Western thought (Cicchetti & Beeghly, 1990). For the purposes of this paper, I will borrow a heuristic framework from the work of Daniel Stern (Stern, 1985) and focus on dissociative disruptions of his four core components of self: 1) self-agency; 2) self-coherence; 3) self-affectivity; and 4) self-continuity. David Fink (Fink, 1988), Daniel Seigel and others have also written or spoken about dissociative disturbances of self using Stern's framework.

Dissociative Disruptions of Self-Agency

Self-agency involves a sense of authorship of one's own behavior and actions and of nonauthorship of the actions of others (Stern, 1985). There is a sense of volition and control over one's self-generated actions which lead to expectable consequences. Self-agency is reinforced by feedback about one's actions both through perception and sensation and through the responses of others.

Significant levels of dissociation interfere with the development of an individual's sense of self agency on several levels. The person's sense of volition is undermined by dissociative process symptoms such as passive influence experiences and hallucinations. Passive influence experiences such as made thoughts, made affects, automatic writing and possession are subjectively experienced as if a force outside of the individual's conscious awareness is forcing him or her to do something against his or her will. The individual may be well-oriented to person, place, time and circumstance, but feels gripped by a powerful force that he or she cannot resist. At times, dissociating individuals may feel compelled to do or say something that is against their moral judgment or common sense.

Often passive influence experiences are accompanied by intense depersonalization, so that the person feels as if he or she is watching him/herself from a detached perspective. Many MPD patients recount suicide attempts as if they were internal homicides, with one alter personality state methodically attempting to kill another personality state while other dissociated aspects of self watch with detachment. Obviously such an experience does not foster an integrated sense of self or a coherent locus of self-agency.

At other times, the chronically dissociating individual simply discovers that they have done or said things that they cannot remember and cannot account for from a moral or rational perspective. This all-too-frequent experience is disturbing not only because the individual discovers that he/she has acted contrary to his/her moral values and better judgment, but also because the individual constantly worries about what else he/she may have done that has not yet been discovered.

Other key elements of self-agency, such as feedback and predictability of the consequences of one's actions are interrupted by dissociative switching and memory retrieval problems. Some times the individual experiences the consequences of an action that he/she does not remember doing; and at other times, the individual recalls the action but not the consequences. As a result, the dissociative individual has a great deal of difficulty learning from "past experience" and understanding "cause and effect" relationships.

Dissociative Disturbances of Self-Coherence

A stable sense of self as a single, coherent, bounded physical entity is central to Stern's notion of a core self (Stern, 1985). He identifies several subcomponents of self-coherence including: 1) unity of locus; 2) coherence of motion; and 3) coherence of temporal structure. Unity of locus implies that an individual is in one place at one time and that the individual's actions originate from that locus. The depersonalization, out-of-body experiences, and passive influence experiences described above all undermine the individual's sense of a unified locus of control from which his/her actions emanate. Coherence of motion and coherence of temporal structures depend upon a stability of perception and cognition which unfortunately is frequently interrupted by dissociative switching, intrusive memories, flashbacks, thought insertion, thought withdrawal and hallucinations. Similarly, the individual's experience of the coherence of his/her environment and others is hindered by switching, intrusions, alter personality state-dependent perception, and cognition and state-dependent memory retrieval problems.

Dissociative patients respond to these dissociative experiences by elaborating and representing (to themselves and others) alter personality states as separate entities capable of independent volitional activities. This is a concrete expression of their lack of a sense of unified self-coherence. Rather than defining and experiencing a self organized around a single locus of control, MPD patients represent self as a collection of autonomous agents, often in diametrical conflict with each other.

Disturbances of Self-Affectivity

Self-affectivity depends on internal invariant self events associated with specific states of emotion, e.g., joy, interest, distress, surprise and anger (Stern, 1985). Stern conceptualizes affects as discrete arousal states defined by a specific set of invariant self-events. A given constellation of emotional state-specific self-invariants includes: 1) a set of proprioceptive feedback patterns to/from facial display, respiratory rate and rhythm and vocal apparatus; 2) internal patterns of arousal and activation; and 3) emotion-specific qualities of feeling

(Stern, 1985). Citing the work of Izard (Izard, 1977) on the constancy of facial display over the life cycle, and preliminary work by Ekman and his colleagues (Ekman, Levenson, & Friesen, 1983) on the existence of specific physiological patterns characterizing different emotional states, Stern argues that the constancy of the internal experience of given emotional states across the life span makes them an excellent warrant of the stability of self over time.

As Fink (Fink, 1988) and others have noted, MPD patients frequently deny and distrust their emotional responses. The often overwhelming sensory and affective experiences associated with abusive experiences result in defensive patterns that serve to minimize, distort and constrict self-affectivity. A similar affective constriction is well-documented in combat veterans with post-traumatic stress disorder (Krystal, Kosten, Southwick, Mason, Perry, & Giller, 1989). It has long been recognized that the alter personality-states of MPD patients usually have a single predominating affect, e.g., anger, depression, fear. Most alter personality states are capable of experiencing only a limited range of affect. When an individual's affect changes, it is generally accompanied by a switch in personality state (Fink, 1988; Putnam, 1989). Different personality states may have very different affective responses to the same stimulus. Thus rather than contributing to the underlying constancy of self, in MPD patients affective responses restricted to specific alter personality states ultimately serve to define and reinforce the very different and separate senses of self associated with those alter personality states.

Other dissociative factors disrupt the predictability of affective responses in dissociative disorder patients. They find that they have inexplicable yet powerful affective shifts associated with social and environmental cues and triggers reminiscent of traumatic experiences. Passive influence experiences such as "made feelings", in which the individual is overcome by an affect that comes "out of the blue" and experientially does not seem to "belong" to him/her, disrupt the individual's sense of ownership of the affect. Flashbacks and the other intrusive affective experiences further contribute to affective turbulence and unpredictability.

Dissociative Interruptions in Self-Continuity

Self-continuity is the matrix that consolidates Stern's other aspects of self (agency, coherence and affectivity) into an integrated sense of self (Fink, 1988). Continuity of memory is central to self-continuity. Dissociative disturbances of memory, particularly compartmentalization, state-dependent retrieval and difficulty in determining whether a given memory is "real", seriously disrupts self-continuity. Time loss, amnesias, fugue episodes and switching all erode the individual's experience of continuity of self and behavior. Erratic access to fundamental autobiographical and other personal information undermines the individual's link to his or her life history and his or her experience of the continuity of self across time. Difficulty in determining whether a memory actually happened to oneself, to someone else, or was "incorporated" into memory from other sources, degrades the important self-referential qualities of autobiographical memory and creates doubt about the reality of what one remembers as his or her life. The extensive childhood amnesias suffered by dissociative patients further debase historical and autobiographical warrants of the continuity of self.

Summary of Dissociative Disturbances of Self

Pathological dissociation, which is highly associated with severe trauma, appears to disrupt the developmental processes required for the formation of a stable, "core" self. Dissociation disrupts the formation of self by directly interfering with critical underlying self subprocesses, e.g., self-agency, self-affectivity, and by interfering with the integration of these components of self into a coherent whole. Dissociative and traumatic symptoms such as depersonalization, switching, amnesias, flashbacks, hallucinations and passive influence symptoms interfere with the individual's sense of agency, ownership, predictability, coherence and continuity of behavior. A chronically dissociating individual may develop discrete states of consciousness with strongly held, individualized senses of identity; however, that individual fails in the larger developmental task of consolidating these states into a unified sense of self. It is likely that pathological dissociation makes a strong contribution to a variety of disturbances of self found in other trauma-related disorders, such as borderline personality disorder, eating disorders, somatization disorder and substance abuse disorders (Cole & Putnam, 1992; Putnam, 1990).

Impact of Pathological Dissociation on Other Developmental Processes

One of the exciting developments in the last few years has been the burgeoning interest of developmental psychopathologists in dissociation. Studies of the effects of dissociation on attachment are underway in a number of laboratories and the initial results appear to be promising (Barach, 1991; Main, 1993). These and other links between dissociation and developmental processes remain to be explored more fully. Because of it linkage with traumatic antecedents and its putative effects on the development of self, dissociation may prove to be a important window into the interactions between the developing child and his or her environment.

REFERENCES

Achenbach, T., & Edelbrock, C. (1981). Behavioral problems and competencies reported by parents of normal and disturbed children aged 4 through 16. *Monograph of the Society for Research in Child Development*, 46.

Albini, T. K., & Pease, T. E. (1989). Normal and pathological dissociations of early childhood. , *Dissociation*, 2(3), 144–150.

Barach, P. M. M. (1991). Multiple personality as an attachment disorder. *Dissociation*, 4, 117–123.

Barrett, D. (1992). Fantasizers and dissociators: Data on two distinct subgroups of deep trance subjects. *Psychological Reports, 71,* 1011–1014.

Bernstein, E., & Putnam, F. W. (1986). Development, reliability and validity of a dissociation scale. *Journal of Nervous and Mental Disease, 174,* 727–735.

Bliss, E. L. (1986). *Multiple personality, allied disorders and hypnosis.* New York: Oxford University Press.

Boon, S., & Draijer, N. (1993). Multiple personality disorder in the Netherlands: A clinical investigation of 71 patients. *American Journal of Psychiatry, 150,* 489–494.

Bowman, E. S. (1990). Adolescent multiple personality disorder in the nineteenth and early twentieth century. *Dissociation,* 3(4), 179–187.

Bowman, E. S., Blix, S., & Coons, P. M. (1985). Multiple personality in adolescence: Relationship to incestual experiences. *Journal of the American Academy of Child and Adolescent Psychiatry, 24*(1), 109–114.

Branscomb, L. (1991). Dissociation in combat-related posttraumatic stress disorder. *Dissociation, 4,* 13–20.

Bremner, J. D., Southwick, S., Brett, E., Fontana, A., Rosenheck, R., & Charney, D. S. (1992). Dissociation and posttraumatic stress disorder in Vietnam combat veterans. *American Journal of Psychiatry, 149,* 328–332.

Briere, J. (1990). Augmenting Hopkins SCL scales to measure dissociative symptoms. *Journal of Personality Assessment, 55,* 376–379.

Briere, J., & Runtz, M. (1988). Syptomatology associated with childhood sexual victimization in a nonclinical adult sample. *Child Abuse & Neglect, 12,* 51–59.

Cardena, E., & Spiegel, D. (1993). Dissociative reactions to the San Francisco Bay area earthquake of 1989. *American Journal of Psychiatry, 150,* 474–478.

Carlson, E. B., Putnam, F. W., Ross, C. A., Torem, M., Coons, P. M., Dill, D. L., Loewenstein, R. J., & Braun, B. G. (1993). Validity of the Dissociative Experiences Scale: A multicenter study. *American Journal of Psychiatry.* 150:1030–1036.

Chu, J. A., & Dill, D. L. (1990). Dissociative symptoms in relation to childhood physical and sexual abuse. *American Journal of Psychiatry, 147,* 887–892.

Cicchetti, D., & Beeghly, M. (1990). Perspectives on the study of the self in transition. In D. Cicchetti & M. Beeghly (Eds.), *The Self in Transition.* (pp. 1–15). Chicago: University of Chicago Press.

Cole, P. M., & Putnam, F. W. (1992). The effect of incest on self and social functioning: A developmental psychopathological perspective. *Journal of Clinical and Consulting Psychology, 60,* 174–184.

Coons, P. M. (1984). The differential diagnosis of multiple personality: A comprehensive review. *Psychiatric Clinics of North America., 7,* 51–65.

Coons, P. M., Bowman, E. S., & Milstein, V. (1988). Multiple personality disorder: A clinical investigation of 50 cases. *Journal of Nervous and Mental Disease., 176,* 519–527.

Dell, P. F., & Eisenhower, J. W. (1990). Adolescent multiple personality disorder. *Journal of the American Academy of Child and Adolscent Psychiatry, 29,* 359–366.

Demitrack, M. A., Putnam, F. W., Brewerton, T. D., Brandt, H. A., & Gold, P. W. (1990). Relation of clinical variables to dissociative phenomena in eating disorders. *American Journal of Psychiatry, 147,* 1184–1188.

Ekman, P., Levenson, R. W., & Friesen, W. V. (1983). Autonomic nervous system activity distinguishes among emotions. *Science, 221,* 1208–1210.

Evers-Szostak, M., & Sanders, S. (1992). The Children's Perceptual Alteration Scale (CPAS): A measure of children's dissociation. *Dissociation, 5,* 91–97.

Fagan, J., & McMahon, P. P. (1984). Incipent multiple personality in children: Four cases. *Journal of Nervous and Mental Disease, 172*(1), 26–36.

Fine, C. G. (1988). The work of Antoine Despine: The first scientific report on the diagnosis and treatment of a child with multiple personality disorder. *American Journal of Clinical Hypnosis, 31*(1), 33–39.
Fink, D. L. (1988). The core self: A developmental perspective on the dissociative disorders. *Dissociation, 1*(2), 43–47.
Frankel, F. H. (1990). Hypnotizability and dissociation. *American Journal of Psychiatry, 147*, 823–829.
Frischholz, E. J., Braun, B. G., Sachs, R. G., Schwartz, D. G., Lewis, J., Schaeffer, D., Westergaard, C., & Pasquotto, J. (In press). The relation between the DES and hypnotizability. *American Journal of Clinical Hypnosis.*
Goff, D. C., Brotman, A. W., Kindlon, D., Waites, M., & Amico, E. (1991). Self-reports of childhood abuse in chronically psychotic patients. *Psychiatry Research, 37*, 73–80.
Herman, J. L., Perry, J. C., & van der Kolk, B. A. (1989). Childhood trauma in borderline personality disorder. *American Journal of Psychiatry, 146*(4), 490–495.
Hornstein, N. L., & Putnam, F. W. (1992). Clinical phenomenology of child and adolescent dissociative disorders. *Journal of the American Academy of Child and Adolescent Psychiatry, 31*, 1077–1085.
Hornstein, N. L., & Tyson, S. (1991). Inpatient treatment of children with multiple personality/dissociative disorders and their families. *Psychiatric Clinics of North America, 14*(3), 631–648.
Izard, C. E. (1977). *Human emotions.* New York: Plenum Press.
Kirby, J. S., Chu J. A., Dill D. L. (1993). Correlates of Dissociative Symptomatology in patients with physical and sexual abuse histories. *Comprehensive Psychiatry* 34(4), 258–263.
Kluft, R. P. (1984). Multiple personality in childhood. *Psychiatric Clinics of North America, 7*(1), 121–134.
Kluft, R. P. (1985). Childhood multiple personality disorder: Predictors, clinical findings and treatment results. In R. P. Kluft (Eds.), *Childhood antecedents of multiple personality* Washington, D.C.: American Psychiatric Press.
Kluft, R. P. (1987). First-rank symptoms as a diagnostic clue to multiple personality disorder. *American Journal of Psychiatry, 144*, 293–298.
Kluft, R. P. (1991). Clinical presentations of multiple personality disorder. *Psychiatric Clinics of North America, 14*(3), 605–630.
Krystal, J. H., Kosten, T. R., Southwick, S., Mason, J. W., Perry, B. D., & Giller, E. L. (1989). Neurobiological aspects of PTSD: Review of clinical and preclinical studies. *Behavior Therapy, 20*, 177–198.
Lynn, S. J., Rhue, J. W., & Green, J. P. (1988). Multiple personality and fantasy proness: is there an association or dissociation? *British Journal of Experimental and Clinical Hypnosis, 5*, 138–142.
Main, M. (March, 1993). Unresolved attachment in adolescence: Highly predictable from the BLAAQ-U inventory, and related to dissociation and absorption. In Abstracts from the Bi-Annual Meeting of the *Society for Research in Child Development,* (p. 140). New Orleans.
Malenbaum, R., & Russel, A. J. (1987). Multiple personality disorder in an 11 year-old boy and his mother. *Journal of the American Academy of Child and Adolescent Psychiatry, 26*, 436–439.
McElroy, L. P. (1992). Early indicators of pathological dissociation in sexually abused children. *Child Abuse & Neglect, 16*, 833–846.
Nash, M. R., Hulsey, T. L., Sexton, M. C., Harralson, T. L., & Lambert, W. (In press). Long-term sequelae of childhood sexual abuse: Perceived family environment, psychopathology, and dissociation. *Journal of Clinical and Consulting Psychology.*

Putnam, F. W. (1985). Dissociation as a response to extreme trauma. In R. P. Kluft (Ed.), *Childhood antecedents of multiple personality* (pp. 66–97). Washington, D.C.: American Psychiatric Press.

Putnam, F. W. (1988). The switch process in multiple personality disorder and other state-change disorders. *Dissociation, 1*(1), 24–32.

Putnam, F. W. (1989). *Diagnosis and treatment of multiple personality disorder.* New York: Guilford Press.

Putnam, F. W. (1990). Disturbances of "self" in victims of childhood sexual abuse. In R. P. Kluft (Ed.), *Incest-related syndromes of adult psychopathology* (pp. 113–133). Washington, D.C.: American Psychiatric Press.

Putnam, F. W. (1991a). Dissociative disorders in children and adolescents: A developmental perspective. *Psychiatric Clinics of North America, 14*(3), 519–532.

Putnam, F. W. (1991b). Dissociative phenomena. In A. Tasman & S. M. Goldfinger (Eds.), *American psychiatric press review of psychiatry* (pp. 145–160). Washington, D.C.: American Psychiatric Press.

Putnam, F. W. (1991c). Recent research on multiple personality disorder. *Psychiatric Clinics of North America, 14,* 489–502.

Putnam, F. W. (1992). Are alter personalities fragments or figments? *Psychoanalytic Inquiry, 12,* 95–111.

Putnam, F. W. (1993). Dissociative disorders in children: Behavioral profiles and problems. *Child Abuse & Neglect, 17,* 39–45.

Putnam, F. W., Guroff, J. J., Silberman, E. K., Barban, L., & Post, R. M. (1986). The clinical phenomenology of multiple personality disorder: Review of 100 recent cases. *Journal of Clinical Psychiatry, 47*(6), 285–293.

Putnam, F. W., Helmers, K., & Trickett, P. K. (In press). Development, reliability, and validity of a child dissociation scale. *Child Abuse & Neglect.*

Putnam, F. W., & Trickett, P. K. (1993). Child sexual abuse: A model of chronic trauma. *Psychiatry, 56,* 82–95.

Reagor, P. A., Kasten, J. D., & Morelli, N. (1992). A checklist for screening dissociative disroders in children and adolescents. *Dissociation, 5,* 4–19.

Ross, C., Heber, S., Norton, G., Anderson, D., Anderson, G., & Barchet, P. (1989). The Dissociative Disorders Interview Schedule: A structured interview. *Dissociation, 2,* 169–189.

Ross, C. A., Joshi, S., & Currie, R. (1990a). Dissociative experiences in the general population. *American Journal of Psychiatry, 147,* 1547–1552.

Ross, C. A., Miller, S. D., Bjornson, L., Reagor, P., Fraser, G., & Anderson, G. (1990b). Structured interview data on 102 cases of multiple personality disorder from four centers. *American Journal of Psychiatry, 147,* 596–601.

Ross, C. A., Miller, S. D., Bjornson, L., Reagor, P., Fraser, G. A., & Anderson, G. (1991). Abuse histories in 102 cases of multiple personality disorder. *Canadian Journal of Psychiatry, 36,* 97–101.

Ross, C. A., & Norton, G. R. (1989). Suicide and parasuicide in multiple personality disorder. *Psychiatry, 52,* 365–371.

Ross, C. A., Norton, G. R., & Wozney, K. (1989). Multiple personality disorder: An analysis of 239 cases. *Canadian Journal of Psychiatry, 34,* 413–418.

Sandberg, D. A., & Lynn, S. J. (1992). Dissociative experiences, psychopathology and adjustment, and child and adolescent maltreatment in female college students. *Journal of Abnormal Psychology, 101,* 717–723.

Sanders, B., McRoberts, G., & Tollefson, C. (1989). Childhood stress and dissociation in a college population. *Dissociation, 2*(1), 17–23.

Schultz, R., Braun, B. G., & Kluft, R. P. (1989). Multiple personality disorder: Phenomenology of selected variables in comparison to major depression. *Dissociation, 2*(1), 45–51.

Silva, C. E., & Kirsch, I. (1992). Interpretive sets, expectency, fantasy proneness, and dissociation as predictors of hypnotic response. *Journal of Personality and Social Psychology, 63,* 847–856.

Steinberg, M., Rounsaville, B., & Cicchetti, D. (1990). The structured clinical interview for DSM-III-R dissociative disorders: Preliminary report on a new diagnostic instrument. *American Journal of Psychiatry, 147,* 76–82.

Steinberg, M., Rounsaville, B., & Cicchetti, D. (1991). Detection of dissociative disorders in psychiatric patients by a screening instrument and a structured interview. *American Journal of Psychiatry, 148,* 1050–1054.

Stern, D. N. (1985). *The interpersonal world of the infant.* New York: Basic Books.

Trickett, P. K., McBride, C., & Putnam, F. W. (March, 1993). Classroom performances and behavior of sexually abused girls: Relationships with verbal ability and level of dissociation. In Abstracts from the Bi-Annual Meeting of the *Society for Research in Child Development,* (p. 631). New Orleans.

Tyson, G. M. (1992). Childhood MPD/Dissociative Identity Disorder: Applying and extending current diagnostic checklists. *Dissociation, 5,* 20–27.

Weiss, M., Sutton, P. J., & Utecht, A. J. (1985). Multiple personality in a 10-year-old girl. *Journal of the American Academy of Child and Adolescent Psychiatry, 24*(4), 495–501.

Wolff, P. H. (1987). *The development of behavioral states and the expression of emotions in early infancy.* Chicago: University of Chicago Press.

VIII Attachment and Meta-Monitoring: Implications for Adolescent Autonomy and Psychopathology

Roger Kobak & Holland Cole

Attachment and Meta-Monitoring: Implications for Adolescent Autonomy and Psychopathology

Increased capacities for thinking about the self and parents are a hallmark of adolescent development (Hill & Holmbeck, 1986). Adolescent researchers have often commented on favorable and unfavorable manifestations of these new cognitive abilities. On the one hand, increased access to an internal world may result in excessive self-preoccupation (Harter, 1990), ego-centrism (Elkind, 1967) and a poignant disillusion with parents (Blos, 1979). On the other hand, these same abilities may enhance mutuality in parent-teen relationships (Youniss & Smollar, 1985), facilitate identity exploration (Harter, 1990) and increase teen's understanding and respect for parents (Blos, 1979). Attachment theory offers a fresh perspective on how these features of adolescent thinking create different pathways through adolescence. From this perspective, cognitive development increases adolescents' abilities to think about or *meta-monitor* internal models of self and parents. Yet, teens' capacity for meta-monitoring may be helped or hindered by their attachment relationships. Some teens may show an ease of access to personal experiences and tacit assumptions, while others may show very limited meta-monitoring abilities.

In the first part of this chapter, we consider ways in which cognitive growth creates new opportunities for adolescents to meta-monitor, update and revise models of self and parents. We then provide a theoretical sketch linking infant patterns for regulating attachment behavior to individual variation in the capacity for meta-monitoring. In the third section, we consider how George, Kaplan and Main's (1985) Attachment Interview (AAI) provides a context that tests adolescents' abilities to evaluate models of self and parents. To maintain coherent discourse with the interviewer, subjects must be capable of meta-monitoring models of self and parents. By assessing discourse coherence, Main and Goldwyn's (in press) "states of mind" provide researchers with a tool for assessing this capacity and its implications for adaptation and psychopathology in adolescent samples. We then consider how insecure attachment strategies and limited capacities for meta-monitoring may, in stressful circumstances, increase risk for depression and eating disorder.

Adolescent Social Cognition and the Capacity for Meta-Monitoring

Adolescence represents a period of dramatic change in teens' capacities for self-awareness and self-reflection. Formal operations provide teens with new abilities to think about thinking and to monitor and evaluate models of self and parents. This change fundamentally transforms adolescents' self-understanding and expectations for interactions with parents. The potential benefits of these new meta-monitoring capacities are apparent in this adolescent's reflection on her relationship with her father:

> It used to get on my nerves, the time with my family; like they do something that bugs me and it'd make me mad; like I'd be sitting and watching TV and someone would jump in front of me and that would make me real mad; now I still get mad but not that mad; a lot of my friends went off to school, so they're gone; but my family will be there; I think I accept them more; like my grandmother had a stroke a year or two ago, so she was real sick, so we spent a lot of time there, and when she talked to my father it was like he was a boy, and I never thought of him as growing up and being my age, so then I started to think about that and that he must have had a hard life, so I felt less selfish, and I don't get that mad at him when he asks me (to do things) . . . (Csikszentmihalyi & Larsen, 1985; p. 273)

This passage illustrates some of the cognitive changes required for monitoring and evaluating models of self and parents. First, this teen is able to think about and describe abstract aspects of self and parents such as personality and to access her inner world of feelings, thoughts, and memories. In discussing these features, she manages to articulate tacit attitudes toward her father that had previously structured her perceptions. Describing these attitudes provides her with cognitive perspective on previously unquestioned assumptions. Second, once models of self and parents become an object of thought, they can be contrasted with alternative possibilities. Comparing existing models with alternatives facilitates movement toward viewing models as constructions that are relative rather than absolute, and changeable rather than static. For instance, experiences with an insensitive father can be contrasted with observations of a father interacting with his sick mother. Third, considering alternative models allows existing models to be reevaluated and updated. This adolescent was able to incorporate new information into a model of her father as a person whom she could respect while allowing her to change her model of her self from a "selfish" to a more tolerant and forgiving person.

Many new cognitive capabilities for revising models of self and parents first emerge during adolescence. Self-reflection or the ability to take the self as an object of thought transforms the way that models of self and parents are updated and revised. Selman (1980) suggests that the acquisition of perspective-taking is essential for the development of self-reflection since one must first be aware that others are observing and evaluating the self. Whereas pre-adolescents generally operate at Level 2 self-reflective thinking characterized by recognizing the self as the possible target of others' perspectives, adolescents become capable of Level 3 thinking characterized by a mutual or third person perspective. In interpersonal situations, this type of thinking allows the individual to step outside a two person interaction to identify mutual interests or goals. In thinking about the self, Level 3 reasoning allows the individual to step outside or establish an autonomous perspective. This then creates the possibility of evaluating and integrating conflicting aspects of self.

To make the models an object of thought, the teen must access tacit experience to derive explicit descriptions of working models. This ability to distance from the immediacy of experience and to find appropriate generalizations about the self increases with cognitive development. Studies of children and adolescents point to fundamental shifts in self-understanding. In her review of literature on the self-system, Harter (1983) proposes a gradual transition from a self described in terms of physical attributes (size, appearance, gender), to descriptions of the self based on actions, to descriptions of the self based on psychological dimensions (moods, intentions, attitudes). Increasingly abstract self-descriptions allow individuals to integrate more concrete descriptions. For example, an abstract trait label such as "athletic" allows the child to integrate more concrete descriptions of self such as good in soccer, basketball, and gymnastics (Harter, 1988). Development toward abstract labels should also be apparent in how children describe attachment experience. For instance, the term "moody" could help the adolescent describe fluctuations in the parent-child relationship that had previously been experienced as mutually incompatible models of a loving and angry parent.

As adolescents' self-descriptions move from the concrete to the more abstract, they also shift from external to internal attributes. Damon and Hart (1988) describe a developmental progression in self-understanding moving from the physical self, to the social self, to the active self, to the psychological self. Thus, most adolescents describe the self with psychological labels such as "tolerant," "obnoxious," "empathic," or "sarcastic." This move toward psychological descriptions signals new access to the internal world of experience. Increasingly, adolescents will integrate internal cues involving feeling and memory in their self-descriptions. By articulating and differentiating internal cues, adolescents' gain new access to stored information in working models. Thus, while working models guide emotional appraisal and attachment behavior from infancy, adolescents may increase their skills for representing and articulating these models and making them available for review.

Representing and articulating tacit appraisals of self and parents provides a critical first step toward meta-monitoring working models. However, new capacities to operate on or evaluate models constitute the most dramatic cognitive advance during adolescence. These new abilities reflect changes in adolescents' reasoning. For example, increased reliance on logic gives adolescents a new freedom to reach conclusions that are at odds with empirical reality. Whereas pre-adolescents choose the correct conclusion from a set of premises only when it does not conflict with empirical reality, adolescents show improved ability to make valid inferences from propositions particularly when those conclusions conflict with empirical reality (Moshman & Franks, 1986). In other words, this shift in thinking allows adolescents to entertain possibilities that are different from the actual. For instance, our adolescent used this ability in observing the interaction between her father and his ailing mother. By following the logic of role relationships, she was able to reason beyond the immediate situation to imagine her father as a young child.

Information processing capabilities also show significant advances that enhance adolescents' ability to operate on and monitor models of self and parents. Case (1985) suggests that adolescents have more cognitive resources available that allow them to hold in mind several different aspects or representations of a topic or problem. Adolescents' abilities to reason about matters that are counterfactual and to attend to multiple aspects of a problem increase their ability to contrast what is actually the case with hypothetical situations and alternative possibilities. Thus, our adolescent was capable not only of imagining her father as a child (a counter-factual possibility), but also of contrasting that representation with her more immediate representation of her father as a parent. By holding both representations in mind, she was able to revise her previous representation into a more complex model of her father that diffused her sense of anger and resentment.

Increased information processing capacities and the ability to recognize alternative possibilities may initially disequilibrate the adolescent and his or her relationships with parents. In childhood, parents may appear to hold unquestionable truths and values. Thus, working models will be viewed as *the* model of self or parent, the only one that exists, and the only conceivable one. As adolescents come to recognize that alternative possibilities exist for how to relate to parents and that their parents' own knowledge about the world is fallible, parental injunctions may no longer appear binding, and parental flaws and shortcomings become increasingly salient. As a result, parents become "deidealized" and appear as more or less ordinary people possessing the usual uncertainties, problems, and idiosyncrasies (Steinberg & Silverberg, 1986). This implies a true "widening of the world," as adolescents can now grasp multiple aspects of reality that are different from those they personally experience (Guidano & Liotti, 1983).

The disequilibrating features of formal operational thinking have received considerable attention in the literature on adolescence (Chandler, 1987; Harter, 1990; Keating, 1990; Lapsley, 1990). Initially, when adolescents recognize that knowledge or belief is fallible, they may be prone to overextending this notion into generalized skepticism and doubt. For instance, when teens first perceive the limitations of previously questioned assumptions and recognize a plurality of alternative possibilities, they may conclude that there are no simple criteria for arbitrating between different perspectives. Studies of formal reasoning indicate that when early adolescents first begin to recognize limitations in their ability to draw conclusions, they overextend their "can't tell" response to syllogisms that in fact offer a valid conclusion (Overton, Ward, Noveck, Black, & O'Brien, 1987). As emerging skepticism and relativism destabilizes the world of adolescents and their parents, teens may seek ways of regaining a sense of certainty.

Chandler (1975) suggests that adolescents may respond to this period of uncertainty with a variety of "regressive solutions." He views stereotypy, cliquishness, and pressures toward conformity in adolescent peer groups as attempts to escape from uncertainties created by formal operational thinking.

Changes in thinking may also have a profound impact on behavior in parent-teen interactions. As the adolescent recognizes the relativism of knowledge, parental authority loses its unquestioned status. Parental knowledge may be as fallible as the teen's own knowledge. As a result, rules of conduct that were accepted in childhood lose much of their binding power. Smetana's (1988) research on parent-teen conflicts indicates a major shift in how adolescents reason about disagreement with their parents. Whereas pre-adolescents overwhelmingly accept parental rules as matters of convention, adolescents shift toward viewing rules as matters of personal jurisdiction to be arbitrated by the self. Thus, teens choose rules for personal conduct less in accord with parental authority and more in accord with the internal world of personal thoughts and feelings. This cognitive shift coincides with increased conflict between parents and teens during early adolescence (Steinberg, 1990).

Mature solutions to uncertainty and relativism require adolescents to identify values or criteria that allow them to arbitrate between different perspectives. Our adolescent was able to reconcile different views of her father by recognizing the value of her family as a source of stability in her life. By valuing her family relationships, she reordered her priorities and made pursuit of her own "selfish" goals less central. This shift in perspective helped her to decrease anger and frustration and gain new objectivity about herself and family. The search for values or criteria that may resolve multiple or conflicting perspectives may form a hallmark of mid-adolescence. Studies of the self-system highlight how adolescents become increasingly concerned with criteria of *consistency* in evaluating different aspects of the self (Harter, 1990). Harter reports that middle adolescents (ages 14 to 15) not only detect inconsistencies across their various role-related selves (with parents, friends, romantic partners), but are also extremely troubled and conflicted over these contradictions, much more so than younger (ages 11 and 12) or older (ages 17 to 18) teens.

Adolescents may also try to reconcile conflicting sources of information by evaluating the *validity* of different sources. While children can monitor the source of information about concrete events and memories (Main, 1991), adolescents can meta-monitor the validity of abstract propositions about self and parents. The ability to form abstract propositions about self and parents increases the potential for discrepancies and inconsistencies in attachment information. For instance, a teen may describe parents as loving and accepting and then recall memories of rejection by those parents. If the teen can meta-monitor his or her knowledge of self and parents, he or she might detect inconsistencies and start to evaluate the validity of conflicting models. Some teens may begin to search for the source of positive descriptions of parents and locate the source in the parents own statements. If such descriptions are at odds with the teen's own memories and experience, he or she may start to question the credibility of parental explanations. Such a situation could create a fertile context for updating or revising models of self and parents.

Increased access to the inner world of thought and feeling may facilitate the teen's evaluation of working models. Adolescents' ability to distinguish between true and false selves illustrates this use of emotional information. Harter (1990) found that most adolescents make a distinction between true and false self behavior and manage their self-presentation accordingly. Teens report that more false self behavior occurs in dating relationships, while true self behavior occurs more with close friends. Adolescents' ability to distinguish between true and false selves demonstrates a meta-monitoring capacity for comparing and contrasting different features of self. In addition, the distinction indicates an ability to weight different aspects of self in accordance with a validity criterion. In this case, the validity of the true self derives from teens' awareness of feelings of greater comfort and spontaneity that occur in their relationships with trusted companions (Winnicott, 1965). Thus, the truth value of different selves is determined not by external criteria but by access to the inner world of feeling.

Meta-monitoring models' consistency and validity creates the new possibilities for autonomy or self-direction. By reviewing models of self and parents, the adolescent can transform the self by integrating new experiences, memories, and feelings into models that are better attuned to current needs and circumstances. Updated models, in turn, allow the teen to regulate behavior in more adaptive ways. For instance, as adolescents come to value and accept attachment relationships, parent-teen interactions can be transformed from conflict to increased mutuality (Youniss & Smollar, 1985). Views of parents as obstacles to autonomy can be replaced by views of parents that emphasize acceptance of parents as human beings (Blos, 1962). Updated models that incorporate awareness of thoughts and feelings also play a critical role in identity formation. In thinking about self and parents, adolescents may identify attachment-related values such as support and trust that will serve as standards for future relationships. Finally, updated models may facilitate mature adult relationships in which the needs of the self are coordinated with those of relationship partners. Establishing greater mutuality in the parent-child relationship may coincide with adult relationships that require reciprocal coordination of support-giving and support-seeking (Weiss, 1982).

Attachment Strategies, Information Processing and Meta-Monitoring

Adolescents may vary in the extent to which they can update and revise their models of self and parents. Some may have difficulty tolerating disillusionment or integrating negative aspects of relationships with more positive features. The pathways that adolescents take in acquiring new cognitive abilities and renegotiating relationships with parents may be shaped by prior relationship history. Adolescents who have histories of secure relationships may be capable of flexibly revising models of self and parents, whereas adolescents with histories of insecure attachment may have difficulty identifying or revising problematic assumptions about self and parents. In this section, we will explore the possibility that individual differences in infant attachment security may influence rules for processing and organizing attachment information. These rules may in turn, organize adolescents' "states of mind" or capacity to meta-monitor models of self and parents in the Adult Attachment Interview (Main & Goldwyn, in press).

Bowlby (1969) conceived of attachment as a goal-corrected system that continually monitors the availability of the caregiver (Bretherton, 1980; Waters, & Deane, 1985). When an individual senses a discrepancy between desired availability and current circumstances, he or she will strive, through a variety of processes, to reduce this discrepancy. Such strivings form an action loop that is regulated appraisals of attachment figure availability and response. Figure I adapts Scheier and Carver's (1988) model of behavioral self-regulation to provide a schematic depiction of how different models of caregiver response result in different attachment strategies. When an individual perceives a situation as dangerous, challenging or as threatening access to the attachment figure (Kobak & Duehmler, in press), the attachment system is activated and a self-regulatory process begins.

If a child's working model forecasts effective caregiver response, then the child will actively engage in activities directed toward reestablishing contact with the attachment figure. Main (1990) labels this strategy *primary* because it allows the child to confidently gain access to the attachment figure and turn attention to other matters. Thus, by gaining confidence in the attachment figure's availability and in the effectiveness of attachment behaviors, the child can freely and flexibly coordinate attachment and exploration. Ainsworth observed this secure base phenomenon in both her home observations and in the Strange Situation (Ainsworth, et al., 1978). Thus, when access to the attachment figure is threatened, the infant attends to regaining access, but once access is achieved, attention moves back to exploration. However, if a child's model forecasts insensitive response, the attachment system remains in a state of continued activation. As a result, the child must not only continue to monitor the attachment figure's availability, but also must develop alternative strategies for regulating his or her own attachment behavior. Main (1990) labels such strategies *secondary* because they involve altering the normal output of the attachment system. From a control systems perspective, the two most general strategies for altering output involve either *deactivation* or *hyperactivation* of the attachment system.

The selection of secondary strategies hinges on the child's models of the attachment figures' response. If a child's model forecasts rejection, deactivation of attachment provides a viable secondary strategy that reduces the likelihood of experiencing painful rebuff from the attachment figure (Main, 1981). In the Strange Situation, the infant's avoidant behavior toward the attachment figure following separation indicates a deactivating strategy in which attention is diverted from the attachment figure to other aspects of the environment. Alternatively, if a working model forecasts inconsistent response, then the child may hyperactivate the attachment system. The child remains hypervigilant so as to maximize positive outcomes with the caregiver. In the Strange Situation, this strategy is associated with decreased exploration and increased contact-seeking mixed with anger toward the caregiver.

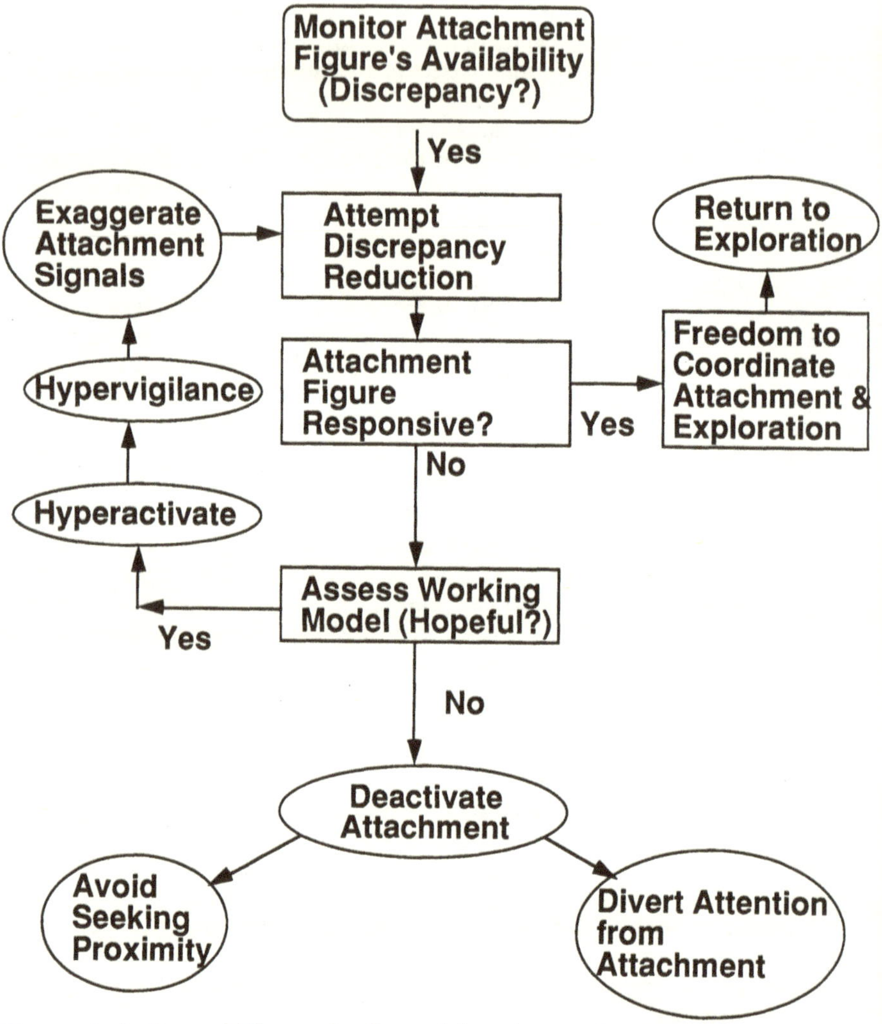

FIGURE 1 A Control Theory Analysis of Attachment Strategies

An important test of our control theory view of attachment strategies lies in the extent to which it provides a bridge between infant behavioral patterns and mental processes. This poses the problem of how to conceptualize mental process. In the third volume of his attachment trilogy, Bowlby (1980) provided an information processing account of mental processes to reformulate psychoanalytic conceptions of defense (see Erdelyi, 1985 and Peterfreund, 1983). In that volume, he linked "deactivation" of the attachment system to efforts to defensively exclude attachment information. Following his lead, we suggest that attachment strategies result in systematic differences in how individuals organize and process attachment information.

Attachment strategies may bias the individual in what information is attended to and what information is ignored. These rules or information processing biases (Bowlby, 1980; Main et al., 1985) are apparent in how individuals process emotional signals and think about attachment information. Secure strategies foster an *open/flexible style* of processing attachment information. This openness should increase the child's capacity to access and use attachment-related emotions (Kobak, Cole, Ferenz-Gillies, Fleming & Gamble, 1993). Thus, the child with a secure strategy can use feelings as appraisals of the environment, as clues about internal states, and as motivation for acting (Bowlby, 1969). This open and fluid use of emotional signals facilitates communication with the attachment figure (Bretherton, 1987) and provides the child with feedback for monitoring the effectiveness of different ways of maintaining access with the attachment figure.

A secure or open/flexible information processing style also should have important effects on the attentional and cognitive capacities needed to think about or *meta-monitor* attachment functioning. Meta-monitoring consists of the ability to step outside the "action loop" regulated by attainment of particular goals in order to evaluate alternative strategies and to redeploy or sustain attention (Scheier & Carver, 1990). Main (1983) identified an early form of meta-monitoring in toddler's capacities for self-directed speech. She observed that toddlers used speech while searching for an object in a manner that increased their ability to flexibly redirect or sustain attention when they met with difficulties in achieving their goals. To successfully meta-monitor, an individual must have access to emotional appraisals and the cognitive freedom or what Main (1991) terms *epistemic space* with which to review attachment functioning.

Our control theory model suggests that secure strategies may increase epistemic space required for meta-monitoring. Because a secure strategy develops from confidence in the attachment figure's availability and responsiveness, children employing this strategy spend *less* time monitoring the whereabouts of the parent. This frees the child to deploy attention to other matters including play, exploration and experimentation. At a more cognitive level, the freedom to deploy attention allows the individual to step outside the attachment action loop and to meta-monitor internal models of self and parents. With increasing cognitive development and adequate epistemic space, the individual may gain increasing sophistication in experimenting with, reviewing and evaluating internal models.

Secondary or insecure attachment strategies may limit epistemic space and bias processing of attachment information. Deactivating strategies foster a *closed/diversionary style* of processing attachment information. To deactivate the attachment system, an individual must carry on two activities simultaneously. First, he or she must continue to monitor the attachment figure. This restricts his or her ability to step-outside the action loop to meta-monitor the attachment system. Second, a deactivating strategy biases the individual toward diverting attention from attachment cues. Thus, when access to the attachment figure is jeopardized, this individual must actively engage in diversionary activities that result in avoiding the attachment figure. (Ainsworth, et al., 1978). Because emotional appraisals serve important signal functions for activating attachment behavior, restricting access to these appraisals may also maintain a deactivating strategy. Such defensive efforts may result in neutral or poker-faced expressions in situations that normally elicit sadness, anger, or disappointment (Cassidy & Kobak, 1988). The defensive effort required to maintain a deactivating strategy further reduces attention available for meta-monitoring attachment functioning.

Hyperactivating strategies foster a *closed/hypervigilant style* of processing attachment information. Individuals with hyperactivating strategies continue to monitor the attachment figure. As a result, they remain in a closed action loop that restricts meta-monitoring and cognitive exploration. Whereas the deactivating individual will attempt to divert attention from attachment-related information, the hyperactivating individual becomes preoccupied with attachment. This hypervigilance results in narrowed attention and decreased epistemic space that further inhibits cognitive exploration. Emotion regulation is also impaired. Although a hyperactivating strategy allows access to attachment-related emotions and signals, these signals fail to promote successful outcomes. As a result, an individual with such a strategy may be prone to excessive emotional displays that tend to dominate interactions and lead to poorly timed and ineffective attachment behavior.

These information processing styles may become apparent at times of change that require updating and revising models of self and parents. When the child has developed an open/flexible style that allows him or her to attend to and process attachment information, models are open to revision and updating occurs through a "continuous feeding in of small modifications, usually a process so gradual that it is hardly noticeable" (Bowlby, 1969, p. 82). However, if information processing is systematically restricted, models will be closed to updating and revision and thus resistant to change. For instance, if a previously unavailable parent were to become more responsive, the child might exclude this new information. As a result, models of self and parent would become outdated. Thus, the capacity for meta-monitoring may become increasingly important as the child copes with developmental challenges of adolescence.

Meta-Monitoring Models of Self and Parents in the Adult Attachment Interview

In this section, we consider how attachment strategies and information processing styles facilitate or hinder adolescents' capacities to meta-monitor, update, and revise models of self and parents. To successfully think about models, a teen must be capable of coordinating emotional, cognitive, and attentional processes. The Adult Attachment Interview (AAI) has provided researchers with a window on these processes. In this section, we will describe the interview as an assessment context, discuss Main and Goldwyn's use of discourse analysis to identify different "states of mind," and propose that attachment strategies organize adolescents' discourse or thinking about models of self and parents in the AAI.

George, Kaplan, and Main's (1985) Adult Attachment Interview creates a context for assessing how subjects think about models of self and parents. Interview questions direct the subject's attention toward different aspects of these models. Subjects are asked to provide general descriptions of relationships with parents and then support these propositions with memories from childhood. Access to stored information is further tested by asking subjects to recall personal experiences involving episodes of distress, illness, separations, and rejection by parents. To respond to interview questions, subjects must access memories and integrate this information with propositional or semantic knowledge about parents. This creates a context in which explicit knowledge of working models can be compared and contrasted with episodic information drawn from personal experience. Since memories are more concrete and emotionally charged, they tend to either support or contradict more abstract statements about parents. Thus, during the course of the interview, subjects may actively meta-monitor their own discourse for signs of consistency and validity. The interview also tests subjects' capacities for meta-monitoring models directly. For instance, subjects are asked to describe how relationships with parents have influenced their current personality and how these relationships have changed over time. Thus, the structured interview format creates a context that asks subjects to attend to internal models, generate information stored in those models, and examine this information for consistency and validity.

To successfully meta-monitor models, a teen must be capable of coordinating emotional, cognitive, and attentional processes. Access to relevant information is a prerequisite for reviewing models. For instance, teens must be comfortable forming general propositions fromtacitexperience and in accessing epsiodic memory. To access relevant information, attention must move flexibly from one source to another. Successful meta-monitoring requires something akin to the analyst's "evenly hovering" attention to new or unanticipated information (Peterfreund, 1983). At times, an individual must attend to unwelcome or painful information in order to update working models. Accepting parents as human beings often requires processing painful information about parental shortcomings or failings (Blos, 1978).

Because models operate as preverbal emotional appraisals, feeling often accompanies the processing of attachment information. From an ethological perspective, emotions serve critical signal functions that aid the individual in communicating with others and in monitoring his or her internal states (Bowlby, 1969). For emotions to serve a self-monitoring function, they must be "felt" by an individual. Thus, a teenager could describe his or her mother as loving with either considerable or very little accompanying feeling. When statements with emotional implications are felt, feeling and cognition are integrated. However, when feelings are absent, an observer might assume that propositions about self and parents may be split off from what may have actually been experienced. This dissociation suggests the presence of "multiple models" in which models based on propositional knowledge may be quite different from models based on episodic knowledge (Bowlby, 1973; Main, 1991).

Finally, to meta-monitor models of self and parents, the teen must have the cognitive freedom to experiment with possibility and to tolerate doubt. Main's

(1991) notion of epistemic space translates this freedom to tolerate uncertainty into terms more compatible with information processing. Confidence in the self or attachment figure creates epistemic space that allows the individual to contrast current models with alternative possibilities or to contrast the actual self with an ideal self. Thus, subjects' abilities to sustain attention to working models, tolerate uncertainty, and allow emotional appraisals to be felt all suggest the presence of epistemic space. When epistemic space is limited, models are less open to revision and change.

The AAI created new opportunities for researchers to assess individual differences in how adolescents and adults process and organize information about self and parents. Initially, Main and Goldwyn adopted an inductive approach describing how adult discourse in the AAI differed as a function of their infants' classifications in theStrange Situation.This approach allowed them to identify different "states of mind" that describe three major variations in the organization of subjects' discourse during the AAI. These states of mind, Free to Evaluate, Dismissing, and Preoccupied, parallel the infant classifications Secure, Anxious/Avoidant, and Anxious/Resistant, respectively. Main and Goldwyn (in press) have formalized their initial descriptions of AAI transcripts into an elaborated coding manual that borrows principles from discourse linguistics to rate and classify transcripts. This classification system makes discourse coherence the central marker of adult security or what we have termed subjects' ability to successfully meta-monitor models of self and parents.

Main and Goldwyn (in press) classify subjects as "Free to Evaluate" attachment models when their discourse is coherent or cooperative. The following illustration typifies this style of discourse:

> Interviewer: You said your mother was loving and caring. What are your memories of that?
>
> Subject: Well, when I broke my finger in a softball game, and nobody believed it was broken, my mom knew it was broken, and she took care of me. Whenever I fell down, she would always fix me up, and when I was sick, she would take off work or take me to work with her. Whenever I was upset about something, she would always come and talk to me and tell me that she was there. You know, I really admire my mother a lot. I think she did a good job, and I'd like to do that with my kids.

This subject demonstrates considerable flexibility in her response. Beginning with the proposition that her mother was loving and caring, she directs attention to memory and searches for episodes that support and further clarify her generalizations. She shows an ease of access to childhood experiences, and her discourse leaves the reader with the impression that her working model of her mother is consistent with and supported by her memories. Thus, she integrates stored information into a coherent and plausible model of her mother. She also demonstrates an ability to operate on her models by placing them in the larger context of valuing attachment relationships and thinking of the implications of these values for her own future as a parent.

Discourse in transcripts classified as Dismissing is marked by restricted access to childhood information, idealized descriptions of parents that lack plausibility, and devaluing of attachment relationships. The following illustration typifies this state of mind:

> Subject: I guess it would be your standard mother-daughter relationship.
>
> Interviewer: What adjectives might describe that?
>
> Subject: Oh, I don't know. Um . . . Oh, I don't even know. I mean, I wouldn't say she punished me any more or less than any other mother or whatever . . . My father had an office and it was located in the same like, it was like a mall kind of complex, and it had office buildings in it also, and he and my grandfather worked together, so we'd always go . . . My mother and I would go all the time to lunch and go see them, and I guess we were close in that way, like, but I . . . I don't know. I guess every mother and daughter do the same things.

This subject struggles in accessing information about her mother. She resorts to a stereotyped generalization about the relationship describing it as "standard" and then struggles to elaborate. She has difficulty staying on topic, and shifts unexpecetedly to discussing her father's office. When she returns to thinking about her mother, she shows extreme difficulty accessing relevant sources of information and again resorts to a vague generalization that is unsupported by personal experience. The excerpt conveys an impression that this subject has difficulty attending to her model of her mother and accessing attachment related information.

Subjects classified as Preoccupied show a different type of disturbance in meta-monitoring working models. Their transcripts are characterized by angry run-on sentences or passive speech that tends to wander (Main & Goldwyn, in press). For instance:

> Interviewer: So you said "secure but insecure." What are your memories of that?
>
> Subject: We were having this play for Christmas. Um . . . and um, I had practice that night, and for some reason I got my mom really upset. We were, um my sister and I were supposed to clean the kitchen up, and we emptied out the dishwasher, and we just threw the pots and pans underneath. We didn't stack them or anything, and she went up later to open the cupboard, and all the pots and pans came falling out, and she was really upset, so she got really mad at us . . . Well, she came out, and she says, "Alright. I've had it with you guys. I don't want to be your mother any more," and I was really upset. I cried for three days, and she, like, ran in her room. Then she came back out and she goes, "From now on you can call me Mrs. Smith."

In contrast to the Dismissing state of mind, this individual shows an ease of access to attachment information. However, her discourse oscillates between contradictory perspectives such as "secure but insecure." In an effort to support her general statement, the subject becomes involved in an excessively detailed account of an emotionally charged interaction that dominates her attention at the moment of the interview. This subject has difficulty articulating a clear model of her relationship with her mother that allows her to evaluate or gain an objective overview of the relationship. As a result, she presents contradictory experiences that are apparent to an outside reader but which she is unable to comment upon or integrate.

Our control theory analysis of attachment strategies and information processing can help us identify principles or biases that organize states of mind in the AAI (Kobak et al., 1993). A secure strategy fosters coordination of attention, feeling, behavior, and cognition in order to maintain access to the attachment figure. In the AAI, this strategy allows the subject to flexibly deploy attention and to access attachment memories as well as providing the freedom or epistemic space to evaluate models for consistency and validity. This open/flexible information processing style can be formally assessed from the coherence of interview discourse. In contrast, insecure information processing styles restrict adolescents' capacities for meta-monitoring and evaluating models of self and parents.

Features of a Dismissing state of mind are consistent with a strategy of *deactivating* the attachment system. This strategy develops in an attempt to exclude information that might normally activate the attachment system. In the AAI, subjects with such a strategy may divert attention from attachment related memories, restrict access to feeling, and as a result, show limited ability to evaluate models of self and parents. The task demands of the AAI should cause difficulty for these individuals. Processing restrictions resulting from a deactivating strategy will make it difficult to cooperate when the interviewer's questions direct attention to attachment information. For instance, by restricting access to attachment memories (i.e., remembering only non-attachment related information or not remembering at all), these subjects often do not provide adequate or believable responses to interview questions. Limited access to working models will also impair subjects' ability to revise or reevaluate models of self and parents. Often, subjects' indicate an unquestioning compliance with parental authority as they describe parents in an idealized or stereotyped manner. These subjects do not question or reevaluate parental practices for fear of somehow losing contact with the parent. Instead, they assume a stance that precludes meta-monitoring. Thus, closing models to revision.

A strategy of *hyperactivating* the attachment system accounts for the discourse features of a Preoccupied state of mind. Control theory suggests that hyperactivation results from repeated but only intermittently successful attempts to regain access to the attachment figure. As a result of the parent's inconsistent response, these individuals maintain the attachment system in a state of chronic activation reflected in hypervigilance toward the parent and exaggerated attachment signals and emotions. This strategy creates predictable biases in information processing. These subjects tend to focus excessive attention on parents, may be angry and resentful, and have difficulty integrating and organizing excessive amounts of attachment-related information. Consequently, they lack the epistemic space to cognitively explore or operate on models of either self or parents. These biases make it difficult for subjects to freely evaluate relationships with parents and lead to difficulty maintaining a balanced perspective or sense of the discourse context. Models of self may have an immature quality and remain poorly differentiated from parents.

Testing the Validity of AAI Assessments Among Adolescents

The AAI provides researchers with a valuable tool for studying ways in which attachment strategies influence discourse about self and parents in an interview setting. However, questions about the measurement and validity of attachment strategies must be addressed. In this section, we consider three aspects of the AAI's validity. First, we present a dimensional alternative to Main and Goldwyn's categorical system for measuring attachment strategies from interview discourse. Second, we consider convergent measures for ratings of interview discourse. In particular we examine non-verbal or psychophyiological indicators that accompany interview discourse. Finally, we evaluate the generalizability of AAI strategies. Does the teen's ability to communicate about models of self and parents in the AAI generalize to his or her ability to communicate within ongoing relationships with parents? For instance, does the capacity for meta-monitoring interview discourse influence the teen's ability to meta-monitor conversations between self and other during emotionally charged disagreements?

Measurement of AAI strategies from discourse processes poses a critical challenge to attachment researchers. Rating interview transcripts with Main and Goldwyn's system is a complex process that requires substantial training. Interview raters must make inferences about the subject's models for mother's and father's response, evaluate discourse coherence, and make inferences about the particular types of incoherence. Following this initial assessment, raters assign a major classification and sub-classification. Sub-classifications represent more subtle distinctions about the degree to which primary and secondary attachment strategies are evident in an interview transcript. For instance, subjects may demonstrate a primary secure strategy accompanied by mild deactivating or hyperactivating tendencies that lead to different sub-classifications within the secure group. Similarly, subjects may show extreme deactivating tendencies with virtually no memory of childhood or less extreme restrictions in feeling that result in different sub-classifications within the Dismissing group (Main & Goldwyn, in press). Due to limited sample sizes, these sub-categories are rarely used in data analysis and, as a result, important differences between sub-classifications are lost. By conceptualizing primary and secondary strategies as continuous variables, it may be possible to capture finer-grained distinctions between subjects that are amenable to statistical analysis.

In order to capture more variabilty in our measures of attachment strategies, we adopted Q-sort methodology. By translating descriptive features of Main and Goldwyn's classification system into items, a Q-sort gives raters considerable flexibility in describing interview transcripts. Interview descriptions can then be correlated with criterion sorts for security/anxiety and deactivation/hyperactivation to index attachment strategies as continuous variables. Q-methodology also offers several important psychometric features. By virtue of their forced distribution, Q-sorts are less subject to halo effects or artificially inflated interrater agreement than are rating scales (Block, 1971), and they allow raters to identify unreliable items. Q-methodology also provides a way to reduce rater error by compositing across multiple raters. Just as multiple-item scales are more reliable than single items, composites based on multiple raters are more reliable than single rater descriptions (Block & Block, 1980). Finally, Q-methodology allows greater flexibility in data analysis through use of criterion sorts, individual item analysis, clustering items into scale scores, or cluster analysis of subjects (Block, 1978; Waters & Deane, 1985).

One aspect of the Q-sort's validity centers on whether continuous variables can differentiate between Main and Goldwyn's classifications. In an initial study with a normal college population (Kobak, et al., 1993), independent raters Q-sorted interview transcripts that had been previously classified with Main and Goldwyn's system (Kobak & Sceery, 1988). Cut-off scores were established on the two major dimensions Secure/Anxious and Dismissing/Preoccupied in order to assign subjects to Dismissing, Preoccupied or Secure categories. This procedure produced a 79% (kappa = .65) agreement with independent classifications assigned using Main and Goldwyn's system. Borman (1992) also reports substantial convergence between categories derived fromt the Q-set and classifications done by Erik Hesse, a co-trainer for the AAI classification system. In a study with over 100 young adult subjects, half of whom had been hospitalized with psychiatric diagnoses during adolescence, Borman reports a 71% level of agreement (kappa = .54) between the two methods.

Reliable measures make it possible to investigate claims that discourse during the AAI is organized by particular strategies and rules for processing attachment information. If this claim is true, subjects who employ deactivating strategies should find the demands of the interview situation conflict with their tendency to deactivate the attachment system. At the level of discourse, subjects with this strategy describe the self as independent and somewhat neutral in attachment relationships and often report positive if somewhat vague relationships with parents. If these subjects' statements were accepted at face value, one might expect few apparent signs of conflict or difficulty. However, if such discourse is organized by a deactivating strategy that involves an active effort to defensively exclude and divert attention from attachment information, such a strategy should be accompanied by signs of an active inhibitory effort.

Dozier and Kobak (1992) tested this notion by gathering concurrent psychophysiology measures during the AAI. Work by Pennebaker and his colleagues (Pennebaker & Chew, 1985; Pennebaker, Hughes, & O'Heeron, 1987) provides evidence for the *specific* relationship between inhibition and skin conductance activity. Dozier and Kobak (1992) monitored skin conductance levels for 50 adolescents during a baseline period and throughout the Attachment Interview to test the hypothesized link between deactivating strategies and increased skin conductance activity. Adolescents employing deactivating strategies showed marked increases in skin conductance levels from baseline when asked to recall experiences of separation, rejection, and threat from parents. This finding supports our control theory notion that deactivating strategies are difficult to maintain in a context where questions continually direct subjects' attention to attachment information. In contrast and as expected, the interview context created less conflict for subjects with Secure or Hyperactivating strategies.

The extent to which information processing styles in the AAI generalize to other developmental tasks faced by adolescents remain unanswered. Examination of the changing parent-teen relationship provides an obvious starting point for addressing this question. Parent-teen relationships are often marked by increased conflict (Smetana, 1988) as adolescents assert their goals for increased autonomy in the face of parental constraints and concerns about the teens' well-being. At times, such conflicts may center around relatively minor issues such as completing homework or household chores, yet at other times they may center on more serious concerns such as sex, dating, or alcohol and drug use.

Although conflict may play a functional role in allowing the teen to move toward increased autonomy, it may also become dysfunctional if it escalates and undermines confidence in the parent's accessibility (Cooper, 1988). Attachment theory and research provide several useful guides for distinguishing functional from dysfunctional conflict. Children's growing linguistic and perspective-taking capabilities allow them to maintain the relationship with the parent as a "goal-corrected partnership" (Bowlby, 1973; Cicchetti, Cummings, Greenberg, & Marvin, 1990; Marvin, 1977)). As long as a cooperative sense of partnership is maintained, the parent-child relationship can accommodate differing goals that facilitate new arrangements and plans. However, if disagreements jeopardize cooperation, then the teen may perceive conflicts as potential threats to parental availability. Thus, conversations about disagreements provide critical clues to a teen's confidence in his or her parent's availability and responsiveness.

We expected that teens with secure strategies in the AAI would manage conversations about a goal conflicts more effectively in several ways (Kobak & Duehmler, in press). First, the child's confidence in the parent's availability and responsiveness motivates positive engagement in conversations. This engagement is apparent in the pre-verbal child's ability to directly signal attachment concerns to the parents (Bretherton, 1987) and to use the parent as a resource for problem-solving (Matas, Arend, & Sroufe, 1978). When working models forecast understanding and sensitive response, the teen learns that emotions can play a valuable communicative function (Bretherton, Ridgeway, & Cassidy, 1990). As a result, we expected that a secure AAI strategy would foster open assertion of the teen's goals.

A secure AAI strategy and the capacity for meta-monitoring may also increase the teen's perspective-taking capabilities. The link between secure working models and perspective-taking can be conceptualized in terms of the child's information processing capabilities. This link can be considered as a translation of the secure base phenomenon into information processing terms. That is the teen's confidence in the parent's availability reduces the amount of processing capacity required for focusing on attachment related concerns and frees the teen to attend to other matters (Main, 1991). As a result, the teen with a secure strategy has greater capacity to attend to the parent's signals and goals. In contrast, a teen who forecasts negative response from a parent may have to devote more attention to anticipating and preparing for possible negative responses, leaving him or her less free to attend to alternative points of view.

Finally, secure strategies contribute to the teen's capacity for accommodation and negotiation during conversation. Meta-monitoring or talking about feelings increases control over action tendencies and increases opportunities for decision-making. For instance, when the enthusiasm that motivates engagement, or anger that motivates increased assertion, or sadness that motivates withdrawal is verbalized, words may substitute for action. Expressing feelings in words allows action tendencies to be evaluated and reconsidered. Thus, anger associated with a goal conflict may be evaluated and expressed rather than taking the form of hostile actions (Furman, 1992). This capacity to verbalize feelings may greatly increase the teen's ability to discuss his or her goals without requiring that the parent immediately respond. As a result, new opportunities arise for finding compromise solutions. When the teen gains this capacity, conflicts can be resolved by forming joint plans. This increased capacity for self-control and modulation of goals introduces new flexibility into the teen's activities and makes cooperation and joint planning possible.

When an adolescent enters discussion of conflict with insecure AAI strategies, a variety of dysfunctional reactions may emerge. Teens using insecure strategies may have difficulty decoding their own emotional signals. If the teen is expending effort to deactivate or hyperactivate the attachment system, he or she will have less ability to process internal feeling cues and thus may have difficulty attending to or articulating emotional experience. As a result, emotional appraisals may be communicated through inappropriate nonverbal channels. For instance, a teen may perceive herself to be presenting a clear position to a parent and yet simultaneously communicate disgust through her voice tone or contempt through frustrated withdrawal from conversation. Similar limitations in decoding a parent's emotional signals may leave an insecure teen vulnerable to appraising an innocuous comment as a rejection or put down (Kobak, in press). Although all individuals are prone to inconsistent or unintended communications, teens with insecure strategies may be less capable of meta-monitoring their actions. As a result, they may be less able to acknowledge their own contribution or to repair relationship difficulties (Kobak & Duehmler, in press).

To test mothers' and teens' ability to maintain a cooperative partnership, we asked them into the laboratory to discuss a major area of disagreement in their relationship (Kobak et al., 1993). Grades, communication, and siblings were the most commonly identified problem topics. We then separately interviewed the mother and teen, audio-taped their statements of the problem, brought them back together, and replayed their tapes. After hearing each person's statement, mothers and teens were instructed to discuss the problem for 10 minutes and try to reach a mutually satisfying solution. To maintain cooperative conversation, teens and mothers had to directly communicate their goals, listen to their partner, and accommodate goals to allow for topic progression.

Videotapes of problem-solving conversations were rated on a series of scales assessing teens' and parents' communicative assertiveness, dysfunctional anger, avoidance of problem-solving, and support-validation. We expected that the security of teens' strategies in the AAI should facilitate cooperative conversation marked by assertive engagement, balanced discussion of both the mother's and teen's goals, greater support validation and less dysfunctional anger. Our results supported this hypothesis (Kobak, et al., 1993). More specifically, secure teens showed less dysfunctional anger, less avoidance of problem-solving and more balanced mother-teen dialogue. It should be noted, however, that interpretation of directions of effects in our findings is difficult. On the one hand, a secure discourse strategy in the AAI may emerge from a parent-child relationship characterized by cooperative discourse. On the other hand, the teen's discourse strategy may contribute to his or her ability to maintain cooperative conversation with the mother. The cross-sectional nature of our findings makes it impossible to resolve this ambiguity. However, we suspect that by adolescence, the child's way of conversing with parents and about parents has become organized and self-regulating in a manner that increases the teen's contribution to interactions with parents.

Allen and Hauser's (1991) prospective study of the transition from adolescence to adulthood provides compelling evidence linking cooperative parent-teen conversations about goal conflicts to security of young adults' AAI strategies assessed 10 years later. These investigators used a Kohlberg moral dilemma when teens were 16-years-old to elicit an issue that was a source of conflict or disagreement (Hauser et al., 1984). Transcripts of these conversations were scored with a coding system that rated each participant's "Autonomy-Relatedness" (Allen, Worrell, Borman, & Hauser, 1990). This scale consists of behaviors that are similar to the conversational skills that facilitate discourse coherency. Subjects' statements were rated for the extent to which they stated positions with clarity and confidence, elaborated positions in response to partners, and queried and validated their partners. Subjects' working models and "states of mind" with respect to attachment were assessed in the AAI when the subjects were 26 years old. Both mothers' and fathers' ratings of autonomy/relatedness or the extent to which they maintained cooperative conversation during a discussion of the moral dilemma were associated with teens' ratings of security 10 years later in the AAI (Allen & Hauser, 1991).

These initial studies point to the promise of our control theory analysis and suggest directions for future research. For instance, our speculations about emotional decoding deficits and cognitive perspective-taking during mother-teen problem-solving suggest processes that could be assessed and tested in future work. These findings also provide important clues about how security in the parent-teen relationship as assessed by parents' and teens' ability to maintain a cooperative goal-corrected partnership is related to teens' ability to meta-monitor models of self and parents in the AAI. Thus, open and cooperative communication within the parent-teen relationship is related to the developing adolescent's ability to meta-monitor or talk about the parent-teen relationship. Successful meta-monitoring as seen in the interview may also play an important role in facilitating teens' autonomous movement to relationships outside the family. In the next section, we consider how meta-monitoring capacities assessed in the AAI may help us understand resilience to adversity and risk for the emergence of psychopathology.

Attachment Strategies as Risk and Protective Factors for Psychopathology

The relation between attachment and psychopathology represents a promising direction within the emerging field of developmental psychopathology (Cicchetti, et al., 1990; Cicchetti & Greenberg, 1991; Sroufe & Rutter, 1984).

However, even at this early stage of bridging developmental with clinical psychology it is clear that insecure attachment relationships do not result in simple predictions of psychopathology (Sroufe, 1988). Our understanding of attachment and psychopathology, will most likely be advanced by developing more complex models that incorporate multiple risk factors and by conceptualizing the processes linking attachment relationships to personality functioning (Cicchetti & Schneider-Rosen, 1986; Cummings & Cicchetti, 1990). Our control theory analysis of attachment strategies and meta-monitoring represent a step in the direction of more explicit conceptualization. In this section, we will consider how these processes may possibly affect adolescents' capacities for managing stressful life events and transitions. This approach is consistent with a diathesis-stress model of psychopathology (Kobak, Sudler, & Gamble, 1991) that views attachment strategies and meta-monitoring as risk and protective factors for psychopathology.

The capacity for meta-monitoring working models can play a valuable protective or self-righting function for adolescents as they cope with a variety of transitions and stresses. As we have seen, the ability to meta-monitor working models in the AAI is associated with successful negotiation of parent-teen conflicts and movement toward autonomy. Similarly, teens who were free to evaluate models of self and parents showed more flexibility and resilience in coping with a normative transition such as entering college (Kobak & Sceery, 1988). Kobak and Sceery viewed the transition to college as a normative stress that would challenge teens' abilities to adapt to a new environment, form supportive relationships, and face challenging academic demands. Peer and self-report measures were collected over the course of the first year to assess adaptation. Students with secure strategies in the AAI were rated by peers as more ego-resilient, socially poised, dependable, productive, and warm in facing the demands of college life. In contrast, students with insecure AAI strategies were seen as withdrawing from frustration, tending to fall apart under stress, handling anxiety and stress by refusing to recognize their presence, and being uncomfortable with uncertainty or complexity. In sum, students with a secure information processing style mastered new challenges in the college environment, whereas students with insecure strategies were vulnerable to restricted, rigid, or maladaptive forms of coping.

The Kobak and Sceery (1988) study also revealed some differences between students with deactivating and hyperactivating strategies. Peers described students with deactivating strategies as more hostile and condescending, while describing students with hyperactivating strategies as more anxious, ruminating, and concerned about personal adequacy. In terms of self-report, students with hyperactivating strategies reported lower levels of social competence and higher levels of distress in a manner consistent with peer reports. However, those with deactivating strategies reported relatively few difficulties, even though their peers viewed them as less ego-resilient and more hostile.

Information processing styles in the AAI provide a potential explanation for these findings. Subjects with a strategy that allows them to process information openly in the AAI, successfully accommodate to the stresses and changes associated with entering college. Meta-monitoring may allow these subject greater flexibility in coping with changes in relationships with parents and in fostering successful relationships with college peers. In contrast, those with deactivating strategies were less resilient in coping with change, but acknowledged very little personal distress. This is consistent with the notion that these individuals may defensively exclude distressing information that would normally activate the attachment system. Finally, individuals with hyperactivating strategies not only showed difficulties in coping with the transitions but also reported these difficulties in terms of higher levels of personal distress. This is consistent with an information processing style involving excessive attention to and display of negative attachment-related emotions.

Limited information processing and impaired meta-monitoring may also lead to problems in identifying or successfully managing sources of interpersonal stress. For instance, a teen experiencing family conflict and turmoil may have difficulty acknowledging and processing feelings of anxiety, disappointment, and anger associated with decreased access to parents. To the extent that these feelings are not available for processing, the teen is likely to experience a great deal of undifferentiated negativity associated with models of an unlovable self or of rejecting parents. Although these models may not be available for conscious processing, they may continue to influence the teen's thoughts, feelings, and behavior. As a result, negative affect may take symptomatic forms rather than being available to adaptively guide decision-making and problem-solving (Guidano & Liotti, 1983). Deficits in self-understanding may also limit the teen's abilities to decode emotions in others. These difficulties increase the likelihood of dysfunction when the teen encounters stressful situations.

Theoretically, secondary strategies for deactivating or hyperactivating the attachment system involve attempts to alter the normal output of the attachment system (Main, 1990). Consequently, these strategies can never completely override the primary attachment system and may be prone to breaking down under stressful conditions. Even the best efforts to deactivate the attachment system require diversionary efforts that may falter when stress reaches high levels. For instance, the most avoidant or deactivating individual will seek proximity to an attachment figure when stress becomes intolerable. Similarly, hyperactivating strategies involving efforts to monitor attachment figures closely and to exaggerate signals of distress may not yield enough reassurance in high stress conditions. Thus, secondary strategies would become more rigid under stressful conditions. As a result, symptoms may reflect the individual's more extreme and consequently maladaptive attempts to maintain or reinstate a particular way of processing attachment information. For instance, by focusing attention on very narrow and specific domains of experience, symptoms could help to divert attention from attachment issues in a manner consistent with a deactivating strategy or represent an even more extreme expression of distress in a manner consistent with a hyperactivating strategy.

If this line of speculation is correct, different secondary strategies may predispose the individual toward attending to very different domains of experience and thus result in very different forms of symptom expression. Symptoms that would act to maintain a deactivating strategy must serve to divert attention from distress signals that would normally activate the attachment system. These symptoms must help to exclude internal signals of distress and help to direct a subject's attention away from attachment-related issues. A variety of diversionary activities could fulfill this function. For instance, a teen could adopt a defensive posture of compulsive self-reliance, or of not caring about family relationships as seen in conduct disorder. To avoid relying on others and to exclude unwelcome information about self and circumstances, these teens may be prone to diversionary pursuits involving drugs or alcohol, or engage in reckless behavior that occupies the teen's attention and excludes important information about potential dangers and consequences.

In contrast, symptoms that would serve to maintain a hyperactivating strategy must excessively focus attention toward attachment issues and internal signals of distress. As a result, teens with hyperactivating attachment strategies may be prone to inner-directed symptoms, including excessive self-focus. Thus, stressful life circumstances may lead to bouts of self-preoccupation accompanied by feelings of helplessness or inability to competently master developmental tasks and challenges. This preoccupied information processing style might also interfere with successful revision of models by overwhelming the individual with information that cannot be used for updating or revisions. This inner-directed focus may tend to perpetuate a negative model of self lacking in competence or autonomy. Thus, we would expect that while symptoms that maintain a deactivating strategy should be outer-directed, those consistent with a hyperactivating strategy should be inner-directed.

Those studies which have been able to examine the insecure groups separately have generally supported these hypotheses. In terms of the deactivating-outer directed link, Bowlby (1944) reported that avoidant personality was associated with antisocial tendencies or externally directed hostility in juvenile males. Using a longitudinal design, Renken, Egeland, Marvinney, Mangelsdorf, and Sroufe (1989) found that avoidant attachment predicted aggression in elementary school, although only in boys. The link between deactivating attachment and externally directed distress was also evident in a study of first year college students (Kobak & Sceery, 1988). In that study, students classified as Dismissing in the AAI were rated by their peers as being more hostile, while the Dismissing students themselves reported very little personal distress. Finally, Rosenstein and Horowitz (1993) found a strong correlation between Dismissing attachment in the AAI and conduct disorder and substance abuse in a sample of 60 adolscent psychiatric inpatients.

There is also empirical evidence in support of an association between hyperactiving attachment strategies and inner directed forms of distress. For instance, Renken, et al. (1989) found that boys (but not girls) with Anxious/Resistant attachment at 18 months were at increased risk for developing problems of passive-withdrawal in elementary school. DeMulder and Radke-Yarrow (1991) found that Anxious/Resistant children expressed more sadness (such as crying), and Berlin, Cassidy, and Belsky (1991), in a six-year follow-up of children assessed in the Strange Situation found that Anxious/Resistant children reported higher levels of loneliness than secure or avoidant children. Kobak and Sceery (1988) found that peers of Preoccupied college students rated them as more anxious. Finally, Rosenstein and Horowitz (1993) found a significant relationship between Preoccupation and affective disorders when subjects with a concurrent conduct disorder or substance abuse were removed from the analysis.

To further explore deactivating and hyperactivating strategies as risk factors for outer versus inner directed symptomatology, Cole and Kobak (1991) studied eating disordered and depressive symptoms among college women. By focusing exclusively on a female population we hoped to avoid gender confounds with internalizing and externalizing symptoms. Eating disorder may represent a form of symptomatology that is consistent with an outer-directed information processing style as these symptoms could help to maintain a diversionary focus for a teen's distress. By focusing on appearance and body weight to the exclusion of other concerns, these symptoms may divert attention away from internal signals of distress. Such a conceptualization is consistent with Bowlby's characterization of diversionary activities:

> (Such activities) give the impression, on the one hand, of being carried out under pressure and of absorbing an undue proportion of a person's attention, time and energy, perhaps in the form of overwork, and on the other, of being undertaken by him in some way at the expense of his giving his attention, time and energy to something else. They seem thus to be not merely alternatives but also to be playing a diversionary role; and this is probably what they do. (Bowlby, 1980, p. 66).

By focusing so much on body appearance and weight and adopting a compulsive concern with eating and dieting, the bulimic or anorexic restricts attention to a narrowly defined and seemingly controllable focus for negative feelings about self. Such a focus comes at the expense of being aware of or decoding internal signals or emotions.

Depressive symptoms may be consistent with an inner-directed information processing style. Among women, depressive symptoms are often associated with excessive self-focusing, rumination, and concern with personal adequacy (Block, Gjerde, & Block, 1991). Moreover, by focusing excessively on the self, being overwhelmed with negative emotions, and adopting a passive stance, depressive symptoms might serve to evoke care from an inconsistent caregiver. However, by ruminating excessively on the shortcomings of self and attachment figure, the preoccupied individual cannot attend to other activities requiring exploration and autonomy. Instead, this self-focused strategy may serve to maintain close contact with the attachment figure, but this contact is unsatisfactory because working models have not changed, and the same interaction patterns persist. This then may reinforce a sense of inefficacy and perpetuate feelings of helplessness and hopelessness (Pyszczynski & Greenberg, 1987). While self-focusing on negative self-cognitions, the individual with a hyperactivating strategy will have difficulty employing meta-monitoring to evaluate or disconfirm dysfunctional cognitions. Thus, without meta-monitoring, an individual may remain caught up in the preoccupied, self-focusing cycle and thus remain depressed. As a result, automatic thoughts arising from negative models of self are thus not under the control of meta-monitoring processes.

We tested these hypotheses about secondary attachment strategies and symptom expression in a study of college females (Cole & Kobak, 1991). Fifty-six

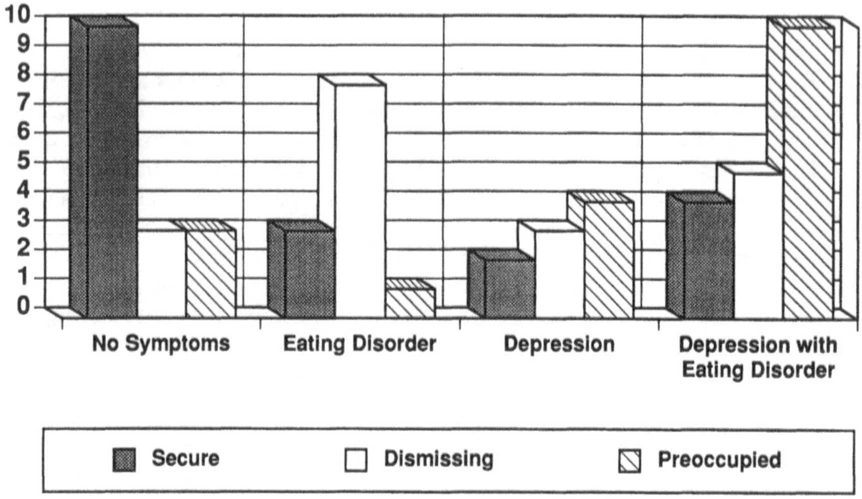

FIGURE 2 AAI Strategies and Depressive and Eating Disordered Symptoms

college women were selected who reported high or low levels of depressive and/or eating disordered symptoms. Subjects were administered the Adult Attachment Interview (AAI), and interview transcripts were rated with the Attachment Interview Q-sort (Kobak et al., 1993). The results indicated that women who reported elevated levels of depressive symptoms tended to use hyperactivating strategies, while women who reported elevated levels of eating disordered symptoms but not depressive symptoms tended to use deactivating strategies. When cut off scores on Q-sort dimensions were used to assign subjects to attachment classifications a similar pattern emerged. Figure 2 indicates that while women who were eating/disordered and depressed tended to be classified as Preoccupied, those with pure eating disordered symptoms tended to classified as Dismissing of attachment. These findings suggest that specific patterns of symptom reporting are associated with different attachment strategies.

Continuous measures were also consistent with our expectations. Hyperactivating strategies were associated with depressive tendencies even when reports of eating disorder were controlled. Thus, subjects reporting depressive symptoms were preoccupied with attachment experiences and played up personal feelings of hurt and anger in the AAI. Furthermore, when depressive tendencies were partialled out, deactivating strategies were associated with reports of eating disordered tendencies (i.e., deactivating strategies were found in subjects who reported high levels of eating disordered symptoms but low levels of depressive symptoms). These subjects reporting only eating disordered symptoms diverted attention from attachment topics by not cooperating in the interview, restricting access to attachment information, and playing down feelings of anger and vulnerability. Although these findings imply neither causality nor direction of effects, they do indicate that different types of symptom reporting are closely tied to particular AAI strategies.

Future Directions

We have argued that attachment strategies create systematic biases or rules for processing attachment information and meta-monitoring models of self and parents. The Adult Attachment Interview offers an assessment of these processing biases, and initial empirical results from this methodology are extremely promising. However, if the AAI measures a critical feature of adolescent personality, substantial new empirical work is required to successfully validate this construct and spell out the implications of this construct for adolescent health and psychopathology. It is important in moving the study of adolescent attachment forward that this construct be carefully articulated and that tests of this construct's convergent, discriminant, and predictive validity be carefully considered and conceptually guided. A number of themes and issues touched upon in this chapter require systematic investigation.

A first step in clarifying the nature of meta-monitoring in the AAI is to examine its relation to related constructs in the area of social cognitive development. Harter's assessments of the self-system during adolescence, Selman's stage model of interpersonal understanding, and Loevinger's model of ego development all offer promising avenues for future work. For instance, if our depiction of the growth of meta-monitoring capacities during adolescence is correct, we would anticipate that meta-monitoring in the AAI would be associated with higher levels of ego-development. In Loevinger's (1976) theory, the movement from lower to higher levels of ego development is premised on increases in cognitive differentiation and access to internal cues and emotional signals. For instance, movement from the Conformist to the Conscientious stage involves increased self-awareness and appreciation of multiple possibilities. These feelings become more differentiated in the Conscientious stage. The movement from Conscientious to Autonomous levels of functioning involve the individual's becoming more tolerant of him or herself and of others. Such a person can acknowledge inner conflict. Movement toward autonomous self-reflection involves a progressive increase in access to and processing of internal cues. Hauser's work linking ego development to family discourse processes may provide important points of convergence with meta-monitoring and emotion regulation in family interactions (Hauser, Powers, Jacobson, Noam, Weiss, & Follansbee, 1984; Hauser, Powers, & Noam, 1991).

If our view of the importance of meta-monitoring is correct, it should play a pivotal role in maintaining the adolescent on a healthy developmental pathway. Studies using such a model should begin with a consideration of the major developmental tasks faced by adolescents. Several such tasks present themselves. First, the way that meta-monitoring leads to transformation of the parent-teen relationship toward more mutuality is one potential avenue of study. Also, how does the capacity for meta-monitoring and the epistemic space required for revising the model of self also facilitate the cognitive exploration required for successful identity achievement during late adolescence? Finally, how does meta-monitoring lead adolescents to the identification of values that not only influence identity formation in occupational pursuits but also influence problem-solving capabilities in peer and romantic relationships? Do meta-monitoring abilities in the AAI translate into more careful planning and choice of relationship partners?

Our view of attachment strategies and information processing requires further exploration. Initial results linking meta-monitoring in the AAI to psychophysiology and communication during parent-teen conflict are promising. However, our notions of emotional decoding deficits that mediate information processing in the AAI and performance during parent-teen problem-solving remain speculative. Work on information processing deficits in conduct disordered boys and in maltreated children may provide valuable clues for how more precise assessment of information processing biases may be developed (Dodge, Pettit, McClaskey, & Brown, 1986; Rieder & Cicchetti, 1989). More generally, the link between meta-monitoring and interpersonal problem-solving capabilities needs to be addressed. The role of verbal IQ in facilitating the growth of meta-monitoring capacities must also be considered.

The association between meta-monitoring in the AAI and parent-teen communication suggests that adolescents' adaptation can be enhanced through either individually or family based interventions. On the one hand, treatment might focus on improving communication in the parent-teen dyad about conflict provoking issues (Kobak, in press) or alternatively, teens could benefit from revaluating models of self and parents in an individual or peer group context. In both individual and family based interventions, attachment-related fears may reduce the adolescent's capacity for meta-monitoring. As a result, attachment based approaches must initially focus on providing a supportive context that facilitates the teens' exploration of alternative viewpoints and negative appraisals of self and others (Kobak, Ruckdeschel, & Hazan, in press). Clinicians working with adolescents may also benefit from awareness of how the secondary deactivating or hyperactivating strategies effect the clients approach to treatment (Dozier, 1990). The clinician's ability to resist a deactivating clients' tendency to disengage from emotionally salient issues, or a hyperactivating client's tendency to become overinvolved, may itself be influenced by his or her own attachment security (Dozier, 1993). The clinician's capacity for meta-monitoring and balancing support and challenge in the therapeutic relationship also calls for further investigation.

Finally, our developmental pathways model of attachment and psychopathology has highlighted the need for careful conceptualization and assessment of the ecology of the developing adolescent. For adequate understanding of symptom formation, it is critical to understand the transitions and negative life events that are placing demands on the adolescent's processing capabilities. A developmental pathways model must also systematically examine how information processing biases influence adaptation over time. Thus, consideration of attachment strategies as risk and protective factors require prospective studies that determine whether these strategies predate the emergence of symptomatology. Further, questions of how information processing biases can themselves be changed hold critical import for treatment and clinical interventions. By examining attachment strategies over time and making use of clinical interventions designed to change these strategies, a developmental pathways model can guide future studies designed to answer fundamental questions about continuity and change in adolescent personality and adaptation.

REFERENCES

Ainsworth, M. D. S., Blehar, M. C., Waters, E., & Wall, S. (1978). *Patterns of attachment: A psychological study of the Strange Situation.* Hillsdale, NJ: Erlbaum.

Allen, J. P., Worrell, C. M., Borman, E. H., & Hauser, S. T. (1990). *Autonomy and relatedness coding system.* University of Virginia.

Allen, J. P. & Hauser, S. T. (1991). *Predictions of adult attachment representations, psychological distress, and competence from family interactions in adolescence.* Paper presented at the Society for Research on Child Development, Seattle, WA.

Berlin, L. J., Cassidy, J., & Belsky, J. (1991). *Loneliness in young children and infant-mother attachment.* Unpublished manuscript, Pennsylvania State University, University Park.

Block, J. (1971). *Lives through time.* Berkeley, CA: Bancroft.

Block, J. (1978). *The Q-sort method of personality assessment and psychiatric research.* Palo Alto, CA: Consulting Psychologists Press.

Block, J. H., & Block, J. (1980). The role of ego-control and ego-resiliency in the organization of behavior. In W. A. Collins (Ed.), *Minnesota symposium on child psychology* (Vol. 13, pp. 39–101). Hillsdale, NJ: Erlbaum.

Block, J. H., Gjerde, P. F., & Block, J. H. (1991). Personality antecedents of depressive tendencies in 18-year-olds: A prospective study. *Journal of Personality and Social Psychology, 60,* 726–738.

Blos, P. (1962). *On adolescence.* New York: Free Press.

Blos, P. (1979). *The adolescent passage.* New York: International Universities Press.

Borman, E. (1992). Assessing adult attachment. Masters thesis, Department of Psychology, Yale University.

Bowlby, J. (1944). Fourty-four juvenile thieves: Their characters and home life. *International Journal of Psychoanalysis, 25,* 19–52 & 107–127.

Bowlby, J. (1969). *Attachment and loss: Vol. 1 Attachment.* New York: Basic Books.

Bowlby, J. (1973). *Attachment and loss: Vol. 2 Separation, anxiety and anger.* New York: Basic Books.

Bowlby, J. (1980). *Attachment and loss: Vol. 3 Loss, sadness and depression.* New York: Basic Books.

Bretherton, I. (1980). Young children in stressful situations: The supporting role of attachment figures and unfamiliar caregivers. In B. G. Coelho & P. Ahmed (Eds.), *Uprooting and development* (pp. 179–210). New York: Plenum.

Bretherton, I. (1987). New perspectives on attachment relations: Security, communication, and internal working models. In J. Osofsky (Ed.), *Handbook of infant development* (pp. 1061–1100). New York: Wiley.

Bretherton, I., Ridgeway, D., & Cassidy, J. (1990). Assessing internal working models of the attachment relationship. In M. T. Greenberg, D. Cichetti, & E. M. Cummings (Ed.), *Attachment in the preschool years* (pp. 3–50). Chicago: University of Chicago Press.

Case, R. (1985). *Intellecutal development: Birth to adulthood.* New York: Academic Press.

Cassidy, J., & Kobak, R. (1988). Avoidance and its relation to other defensive processes. In J. Belsky & T. Neworski (Eds.), *Clinical implications of attachment* (pp. 300–323). Hillsdale, NJ: Erlbaum.

Chandler, M. (1975). Relativism and the problem of epistemological loneliness. *Human Development, 18,* 171–180.

Chandler, M. (1987). The Othello effect: Essay on the emergence and eclipse of skeptical doubt. *Human Development, 30,* 137–159.

Cicchetti, D., Cummings, M., Greenberg M., & Marvin, R. (1990). An organizational perspective on attachment theory beyond infancy: Implications for theory, measurement, and research. In M. Greenberg, D. Cicchetti, & E. M. Cummings (Eds.), *Attachment during the preschool years* (pp. 3–49). Chicago: University of Chicago Press.

Cicchetti, D. & Greenberg, M. T. (1991). Attachment and developmental psychopathology (Special Issue). *Development and Psychopathology, 3* (4).

Cicchetti, D. & Schneider-Rosen, K. (1986). An organizational approach to childhood depression. In M. Rutter, C. Izard, and P. Read (Eds.), *Depression in young people: Clinical and developmental perspectives* (pp. 71–134). New York: Guilford Press.

Cole, H., & Kobak, R. (1991). *Attachment and symptom reporting: Attentional processes in depression and eating disorder.* Unpublished manuscript, University of Delaware, Department of Psychology, Newark, DE.

Cooper, C. (1988). The role of conflict in parent-adolescent relationships. In M. Gunnar & W. A. Collins (Eds.), *Minnesota symposium on child psychology* (Vol. 21, pp. 181–187). Hillsdale, NJ: Erlbaum.

Csikszentmihalyi, M. & Larsen, R. (1985). *Being adolescent: Conflict and growth in the teenage years.* New York: Basic Books.

Cummings, E. M., & Cicchetti, D. (1990). Toward a transactional model of relations between attachment and depression. In M. Greenberg, D. Cicchetti, & M. Cummings (Ed.), *Attachment in the Preschool Years* (pp. 339–372). Chicago: University of Chicago Press.

Damon, W., & Hart, D. (1988). *Self-understanding in childhood and adolescence.* New York: Cambridge University Press.

DeMulder, E. K., & Radke-Yarrow, M. (1991). Attachment with affectively ill and well mothers: Concurrent behavioral correlates. *Development and Psychopathology, 3,* 227–242.

Dodge, K., Pettit, G. S., McClaskey, C. L., & Brown, M. M. (1986). Social competence in children. *Monographs of the Society for Research in Child Development, 51* (2, Serial No. 213).

Dozier, M., & Kobak, R. (1992). Psychophysiology in adolescent attachment interviews: Converging evidence for deactivating strategies. *Child Development, 63,* 1473–1480.

Dozier, M. (1990). Attachment organization and treatment use for adults with serious psychopathological disorders. *Development and Psychopathology, 2,* 47–60.

Dozier, M. (1993). Clinicians as caregivers: The role of attachment organization in treatment. Unpublished manuscript, Department of Psychology, Trinity University.

Elkind, D. (1967). Egocentricism in adolescence. *Child Development, 38,* 1025–1034.

Erdelyi, M. (1985). *Psychoanalysis: Freud's cognitive psychology.* New York: Freeman.

Furman, E. (1992). *Toddlers and their mothers: A study in early personality development.* Madison, CT: International Universities Press.

George, C., Kaplan, N., & Main, M. (1985). *The attachment interview for adults.* Unpublished manuscript, University of California, Berkeley, Department of Psychology.

Guidano, V. F., & Liotti, G. (1983). *Cognitive processes and emotional disorder: A structural approach to psychotherapy.* New York: Guilford.

Harter, S. (1990). Self and identity development. In. S. S. Feldman & G. Elliott (Eds.), *At the threshold: The developing adolescent* (pp. 352–387). Cambridge, MA: Harvard.

Harter, S. (1988). Developmental and dynamic changes in the nature of the self-concept: Implications for child psychotherapy. In S. Shirk (Ed.), *Cognitive development and child psychotherapy* (pp. 119–160). New York: Plenum.

Harter, S. (1983). Developmental perspectives on the self-system. In E. M. Hetherington, (Ed.) *Handbook of child psychology. Vol. 4. Socialization, personality and social development* (pp. 275–386). New York: Wiley.

Hauser, S. T., Powers, S. & Noam, G. (1991). *Adolescents and their families.* New York: Free Press.

Hauser, S. T., Powers, S., Jacobson, A., Noam, G., Weiss, B., & Follansbee, D. (1984). Family contexts of adolescent ego development. *Child Development, 55*, 195–213.

Hazan, C., & Shaver, P. (1987). Romantic love conceptualized as an attachment process. *Journal of Personality and Social Psychology, 52*, 511–524.

Hill, J. & Holmbeck, G. (1986). Attachment and autonomy during adolescence. In G. J. Whiterhurst, (Ed.), *Annals of child development.* Vol. 3 (pp. 145–189). Greenwich, CT: JAI Press.

Keating, D. (1990). Adolescent thinking. In. S. S. Feldman & G. Elliott (Eds.), *At the threshold: The developing adolescent* (pp. 54–90). Cambridge, MA: Harvard.

Kobak, R., Ruckdeschel, K., & Hazan, C. (in press). From symptom to signal: An attachment view of emotion in marital therapy. Chapter for S. Johnson and L. Greenberg (Eds.). *Emotions in Marital Therapy.* Brunner/Mazel.

Kobak, R. & Duehmler, S. (in press). Attachment and conversation: A discourse analysis of goal-corrected partnerships. Chapter for D. Perlman and K. Bartholomew (Eds.). *Advances in the Study of Personal Relationships, Vol. 5.*

Kobak, R. (in press). Attachment and the problem of coherence: Implications for the treatment of disturbed adolescents. *Adolescent Psychiatry.*

Kobak, R., Cole, H., Fleming, W., Ferenz-Gillies, R. & Gamble, W. (1993). Attachment and emotion regulation during mother-teen problem-solving: A control theory analysis. *Child Development, 64*, 231–245.

Kobak, R., Sudler, N., & Gamble, W. (1991). Attachment and depressive symptoms during adolescence: A developmental pathways analysis. *Development and Psychopathology, 3*, 461–474.

Kobak, R., & Sceery, A. (1988). Attachment in late adolescence: Working models, affect regulation, and representations of self and others. *Child Development, 59*, 135–146.

Lapsley, D. K. (1990). Continuity and discontinuity in adolescent social cognitive development. In R. Montemayor, G. Adams, & T. P. Gullotta (Eds.), *From childhood to adolescence: A transitional period?* (pp. 183–204). Newbury Park, Sage.

Loevinger, J. (1976). *Ego development: Conceptions and theories.* San Francisco: Jossey-Bass.

Main, M. (1991). Metacognitive knowledge, metacognitive monitoring, and singular (coherent) vs. multiple (incoherent) model of attachment: Findings and directions for future research. In J. S. Hinde, C. M. Parkes & P. Marris (Eds.), *Attachment across the lifecycle* (pp. 127–159). London: Routledge.

Main, M. (1990). Cross-cultural studies of attachment organization: Recent studies, changing methodologies, and the concept of conditional strategies. *Human Development, 33*, 48–61.

Main, M. (1983). Exploration, play and cognitive functioning as related to mother-infant attachment. *Infant Behavior and Development*, 6, 167–174.

Main, M. (1981). Avoidance in the service of proximity: A working paper. In K. Immelmann, G. Barlow, L. Petrinovitch, & M. Main (Ed.), *Behavioral development: The Bielefeld interdisciplinary project* (pp. 651–693). New York: Cambridge University Press.

Main, M., & Goldwyn, R. (in press). *Adult attachment classification system.* Unpublished manuscript, University of California, Berkeley, Department of Psychology.

Main, M., Kaplan, N., & Cassidy, J. (1985). Security in infancy, childhood and adulthood: A move to the level of representation. In I. Bretherton & E. Waters (Eds.), Growing points of attachment theory and research (pp. 66–106). *Monographs of the Society for Research in Child Development*, 50 (1–2, Serial No. 209).

Marvin, R. S. (1977). An ethological-cognitive model for the attenuation of mother-child attachment behavior. In T. M. Alloway, L. Krames, & P. Pliner (Ed.), *Advances in the study of communication and affect: Vol. 3. The development of social attachments* (pp. 25–60). New York: Plenum.

Matas, L., Arend, R. A., & Sroufe, L. A. (1978). Continuity and adaptation in the second year: The relationship between quality of attachment and later competence. *Child Development, 49*, 547–556.

Moshman, D., & Franks, B. A. (1986). Development of the concept of inferential validity. *Child Development, 57*, 153–165.

Overton, W. F; Ward, S. L.; Noveck, I. A.; Black, J.; & O'Brien, D. P. (1987). Form and content in the development of deductive reasoning. *Developmental psychology, 23*, 22–30.

Pennebaker, J. W., & Chew, C. H. (1985). Deception, electrodermal activity, and the inhibition of behavior. *Journal of Personality and Social Psychology, 49*, 1427–1433.

Pennebaker, J. W., Hughes, C. F., & O'Heeron, R. C. (1987). The psychophysiology of confession: Linking inhibitory and psychosomatic processes. *Journal of Personality and Social Psychology, 52*, 781–793.

Peterfreund, I. (1983). *The Process of Psychoanalytic Therapy: Models and Strategies.* Hillsdale, NJ: Erlbaum.

Pyszczynski, T., & Greenberg, J. (1987). Self-regulatory perseveration and the depressive self-focusing style: A self-awareness theory of reactive depression. *Psychological Bulletin, 102*, 122–138.

Renken, B., Egeland, B., Marvinney, D., Mangelsdorf, S., & Sroufe, L. A. (1989). Early childhood antecedents of aggression and passive-withdrawal in early elementary school. *Journal of Personality, 57*, 257–281.

Rieder, C., & Cicchetti, D. (1989). Organizational perspective on cognitive control functioning and cognitive-affective balance in maltreated children. *Developmental Psychology, 25*, 382–393.

Rosenstein, D. & Horowitz, H. (1993). Working models of attachment in psychiatrically hospitalized adolescents: Relations to psychopathology and personality. Presented SRCD, March, 1993.

Scheier, M. F., & Carver, C. S. (1988). A model of behavioral self-regulation: Translating intention into action. In L. Berkowitz (Ed.), *Advances in experimental social psychology* (Vol. 21, pp. 303–346). New York: Academic.

Scheier, M. F., & Carver, C. S. (1990). Origins and functions of positive and negative affect: A control-process view. *Psychological Review, 97*, 19–35.

Selman, R. (1980). *The growth of interpersonal understanding.* New York: Academic Press.

Smetana, J. (1988). Concepts of self and social convention: Adolescents' and parents' reasoning about hypothetical and actual family conflicts. In M. Gunnar & W. A. Collins (Eds.), *Minnesota symposium on child psychology* (Vol. 21, pp. 79–122). Hillsdale, NJ: Erlbaum.

Sroufe, A. (1988). The role of infant caregiver attachment in development. In J. Belsky, & T. Neworski (Ed.), *Clinical Implications of Attachment* (pp. pp. 18–40). Hillsdale, NJ: Erlbaum.

Sroufe, L. A., & Rutter, M. (1984). The domain of developmental psychopathology. *Child Development, 55*, 17–29.

Steinberg, L. & Silverberg, S. (1986). The vicissitudes of autonomy in early adolescence. *Child Development, 57*, 841–851.

Steinberg, L. (1990). Autonomy, conflict and harmony in the family relationship. In S. S. Feldman & G. Elliott (Eds.), *At the threshold: The developing adolescent* (pp. 255–276). Cambridge: Harvard University Press.

Waters, E., & Deane, K. E. (1985). Defining and assessing individual differences in attachment relationships: Q-methodology and the organization of behavior in infancy and early childhood. In I. Bretherton & E. Waters (Eds.), Growing points of attachment theory and research (pp. 41–65). *Monographs of the Society for Research in Child Development*, 50 (1–2, Serial No. 209).

Weiss, R. S. (1982). Attachment in adult life. In C. M. Parkes, & J. Stevenson-Hinde (Ed.), *The place of attachment in human behavior* (pp. pp. 171–184). New York: Basic Books.

Winnicott, D. (1965). *The maturational process and the facilitating environment*. New York: International Universities Press.

Youniss, J. & Smollar, J. (1985). *Adolescents relations with mothers, fathers, and friends*. Chicago: University of Chicago Press.

IX Clinical-Developmental Psychology in Developmental Psychopathology: Theory and Research of an Emerging Perspective

Gil G. Noam and Gayle Valiant

Developmental psychopathology has grown in the last ten years from a loose union of developmental and clinical pursuits to a full-fledged field of inquiry, encompassing broad issues of health, adaptation, and pathology. (Cicchetti, 1984b, 1989, 1990). Our own line of work, clinical-developmental psychology, has evolved during the same period, influenced by the many creative approaches that have emerged in developmental psychopathology. However, it has not been until recently that sufficient evidence has accumulated for the clinical-developmental perspective to gain momentum to help shape the study of dysfunction and recovery.

In order to provide a context for the constructivist, clinical-developmental perspective, we find it useful to highlight the influences of other research-based developmental psychopathology perspectives with their distinct methodological orientations and developmental foci. We will discuss the psychometric/epidemiological orientation, the natural history, resiliency, and attachment paradigms, drawing broad distinctions and pointing to important shifts that are presently occurring in each of these traditions. We argue that certain overarching developments point to advances in a constructivist and relational cognition orientation. After introducing the principles of clinical-developmental psychology, we discuss a variety of empirical findings from our laboratory and introduce evidence for an understanding of internalizing and externalizing dis-

We would like to thank the members of the research staff of the Laboratory of Developmental Psychology and Developmental Psychopathology at Harvard Medical School and McLean Hospital. In addition, we would like to acknowledge the clinical staff and the children, adolescents and families of the Child and Adolescent Program of McLean Hospital for facilitating our studies.

This work was also generously supported by the American Suicide Foundation, the Alden Trust, the Benton Trust, the Hall-Mercer Foundation, the Milton Fund of Harvard Medical School, and an NIMH Biomedical Support Grant. Dr. Noam's contribution was written during a fellowship year at the Center for Advanced Study Berlin.

orders as developmental phenomena. The chapter ends in a discussion of the implications of our findings for the study of recovery, social competency, and clinical application.

The Context for a Clinical-Developmental Psychology

Much of the present day research in developmental psychopathology has been conducted against the background of epidemiological and longitudinal studies that have generated information about prevalence and incidence of psychiatric disorders or problem behaviors (e.g., Rutter's Isle of Wright Study, Rutter, 1989). Because of this and other pioneering work, we now know the base rates of disorders in defined populations as well as their prevalences at different stages of development—an important counter balance against typical biases in clinical samples.

Given the scope of epidemiological and psychometric research, behavioral indices of maladaptation (symptoms and syndromes) have been fairly prominent, since they are least theory bound and provide a common denominator for research in many traditions. It is not surprising that within such an empirically and behaviorally based approach, age is frequently used as the central developmental "meter". But through developmental research, we know that chronological age is a very crude indicator, since many developmental processes are better understood in psychological terms defined independently of chronological age (Wohlwill, 1973). This observation has now been made by a number of investigators who are versed in the psychometric and epidemiological traditions. For example, Kazdin (1990) argued that because chronological age provides an insufficient developmental perspective on psychopathology, research efforts to use cognitive level and functioning as a developmental marker for troubled children and adolescents should be given far greater prominence.

Epidemiological research, however, is by definition based on a nomothetic approach to symptomatology. So while its focus is primarily on the identification of disorders and covariation of background variables with population outcomes, it does not address behavior at the level of the individual, nor can it elucidate a given individual's pathway of development and psychopathology. In addition, the large samples in epidemiological research do not easily lend themselves to an assessment of the meanings of symptoms. But without knowledge about such meanings our developmental explanations and interventions are handicapped. Stealing, for example, might always look the same, but it certainly plays a very different role in the "economy" of development and psychopatholgy. It is done to show off to a group of friends, as an act of revenge, or to help someone needy, to name only a few possibilities. In this vein, Achenbach (1982), one of the foremost contributors to the psychometric perspective, ends the first textbook in developmental psychopathology by providing a rationale for studying cognition and mental representations:

> "Many approaches to psychopathology neglect the children's capacities for constructive cognitive adaptation and reorganization. The child's mental rep-

resentations are end products of many organic and experiential factors, but these mental representations may yield a better prediction of behavior than all the separate determinants would. Modification of the mental representations may therefore be an important step in promoting more adaptive development" (p. 654–655).

Longitudinal research has enabled us to gain a perspective on the continuities and discontinuities associated with particular diagnoses and symptoms. A classic natural history study was Robins' longitudinal research of delinquent children and adolescents (Robins, 1966). This study made mental health professionals realize the surprisingly high continuities of conduct problems that begin in early adolescence and continue well into adulthood. Robins found that almost all antisocial adults began their 'delinquent career' in adolescence, and about half of delinquent adolescents end up antisocial adults.

For most other psychiatric problems of childhood and adolescence, continuity rates are far less impressive. For example, childhood depression and anxiety seem to be overcome at later points of development, often without any clinical intervention. This is not surprising, as many children suffer from serious anxiety and nightmares and end up not experiencing a life with chronic anxiety (Rutter & Garmezy, 1983). Similarly, earlier reviews suggested that depressive neurosis, as affective disorders used to be labeled, did not show a great deal of continuity. But the study of the natural history of depression can serve as an important example of how more precise definitions of disorders open the door to better follow-up of the evolution of disorders. Kovacs and Puig-Antich (1989) showed that early childhood depression was strongly correlated with serious depression well into middle childhood. This careful work challenged the earlier idea that childhood depression is easily reversible. Most likely, we are dealing with different depressive states or illnesses, some that signal a chronic course, and possibly a more biological base, and others that represent responses to situational stress, and are not necessarily of long-term consequence.

But how does one distinguish between these types? And, do these depressive problems follow different pathways because they are different depressive disorders or because of individual, personality, developmental, or cultural differences? Psychopathologists try to answer these questions mostly by defining the disorders as precisely as possible, but there are many essential factors that define the course disorders take. For example, what are the changes in psychosocial contexts, such as family, peer world, and school, that support or hinder coping strategies and resiliency (Cicchetti & Aber, 1986)? Again, delinquency serves as a good example. While some risk factors are located within the family environment, e.g., maternal psychiatric disorder, paternal delinquent behavior in the present or the past, overcrowding, etc., delinquent pathways are always related to psychosocial adaptational styles. The child often ends up in a delinquent peer group that changes the behavior and often escalates it. Many children, however, may only join these groups for short periods and find their way into more adaptive relationships, school, and work situations. Such developmental pathways are influenced by the type and severity of the conduct problems (e.g., isolates have a worse prognosis than social types), but many outcome variables are of a social nature and are quite unpredictable (e.g., a mentoring relationship with a juvenile officer).

Because of the complexity of variables and the unpredictable aspects of life, we continue to know little about the transfers from maladaptation to health that define so powerfully the natural history of disorders. In fact, the natural history of psychiatric disorder is simultaneously the natural history of recovery, for even those psychiatric disorders that show high continuity include many people who overcome or transform their problems. For that reason, Robins (1966) also argues that we know far too little about those dimensions that support healthy adaptation of the delinquent adolescents. She reminds us that half of her sample became well-functioning adults.

When we pursue this question of recovery—a creation of healthy adaptation—we are most in need of strong hypotheses and theories. Too many variables are involved to only observe and count. And too little is accomplished by focussing only on the disorder, rather than the adaptational repertoire, the relational context, and the meanings attributed to life circumstance.

Garmezy and his associates at the University of Minnesota understood the need to study the surprising ability many children demonstrate to resist stress and to avoid psychiatric problems despite great risks. Their creative theoretical and empirical work has had a significant influence on the emergence of developmental psychopathology.

In Garmezy's work, especially his work on stress and coping, we also find a strong trend to move beyond the study of behavioral adaptation. He states:

> "This new model radically alters the direction of the case-effect relationship between stress and coping. Coping is no longer simply a response to an event that has happened, but instead becomes an active force in shaping what is happening and what will happen" (Garmezy, 1981).

Coping is viewed as an interaction between the stressor and the individual who cognitively evaluates stressful events and judges the outcome which helps define how the stress is responded to. Thus Garmezy has become a strong proponent of a constructivist focus on stress and coping, the study of stressful life events that involve an understanding of the meanings these events hold for the child. He states:

> "The choice of the coping effort is seen as dependent upon the degree of uncertainty or ambiguity with regard to the posed threat, the severity of conflict . . . , and the magnitude of the individual's perceived helplessness vs. confidence in one's ability to control significant outcomes" (Garmezy, 1981).

Garmezy further describes how individuals attempt to reassess ongoing experiences and modify their internal experience to shape the course of events. Much work is needed, however, to bring the study of resiliency and coping from the general principles to explicitly longitudinal developmental terms. Such a focus will have to answer a number of difficult questions. For example, what are the new and typical vulnerabilities at each developmental stage or phase in the life span? What new capacities do these developmental transformations bring out that help people deal with adverse situations and support non-pathological adaptations? Although theory and data that answer these questions are still evolving, Garmezy's work and that by investigators in his tradition, have given us new and exciting insights. Most importantly, they have reframed the question about prevalence and continuities of psychopathology by placing the emphasis on strengths and coping in the face of pathogenic conditions. They provide an ideographic counterweight to the research traditions based on large scale normative data, focussing attention on the significance of interpersonal relationships, cognitive capacity and cognitive styles for psychological health and development.

The work of Garmezy and others leads to a consideration of the research into social competence. Researchers in this tradition have enumerated a number of definitions of competence ranging from a capacity for social intercourse (e.g., Dodge, 1986; Selman, 1985) to an operationalization of competence as some measure comprised of variables indicative of cognitive functioning, (e.g., I.Q. scores, and level of education), or interpersonal skills, (e.g., marital status, employment history) (Zigler & Glick, 1986) and number of friends, and school success (Achenbach & Edelbrock, 1987). Typically competence has been viewed as both an outcome variable, as for example when intervention studies attempt to modify the patterns of social intercourse (cf. Selman, Schwartz & Yeates, 1991), or as an independent variable which influences the outcome, as in studies which have demonstrated the relationship between pre-morbid competence and prognosis for recovery from psychopathology (Zigler & Glick, 1986) or illness (e.g., Heffner, Strauss & Grisell, 1975).

But as with stress and resiliency, the relationship between competence and psychopathology is not necessarily straightforward. For example, studies of adolescent suicide attemptors have found little difference between the social skills of suicide attemptors and non-attemptors (cf. Spirito, Brown, Overholser and Fritz, 1989 for a review). It is hard to reconcile this lack of difference except if we return to a meaning framework which states this may not be a salient feature for these youth, or alternatively, that social skills need to be seen in the context of other stressors, e.g. familial conflict. But we cannot know this unless we adopt a contextual, relational perspective which takes greater account of the individual.

In the majority of these studies however, the individual's perspective on competence has been ignored, arguing instead from some normative perspective of "healthy" or adaptive competence (cf. Oppenheimer, 1989 for a discussion of this issue). Hence while the research tradition of social competence has relevance for the study of psychopathology at the individual level, in its present approach, it largely denies the meaning of behaviors for the individual.

The constructive and relational perspective found a special proponent in John Bowlby's ethological-psychoanalytic perspective (Bowlby, 1952; 1960). Bowlby pointed our attention to the fact that resiliency and mental health, as well as disorder and psychopathology were anchored in early attachment relationships. In a variety of studies in the United States (e.g., Ainsworth, 1982; Main & Weston, 1981; 1982) and several other parts of the world (e.g., Grossmann & Grossmann, 1990) it has been shown that attachment patterns, once established, continue to persist and that they influence a variety of emotional states and problem behaviors such as separation anxiety, school failure, victimization, and bullying (Sroufe, 1983). Longitudinal research has further shown that children classified as avoidant demonstrate low self-worth, isolation, and rejection, feel more depression, and are rated less healthy by teachers and counselors than securely attached children (Urban, Carlson, Egeland, & Sroufe, 1991.

With these findings, building on Bowlby's theory, it has become more pressing to explain the mechanisms by which primary attachments shape later relationships and adaptations. Many investigators have used Bowlby's notion of the working model to describe the "missing link" to the process whereby primary dyadic relationships become part of the "self" over time. In this tradition it is assumed that with development, as social interaction increases, cognitive and emotional development become more differentiated, and internal working models must increase in complexity and be revised to fit new data and experiences.

This is reflected in assessment strategies. Early in childhood working models are assessed behaviorally. Later on language and representational capacities open new possibilities for exploring working models through play productions, retrospective interviews, etc. If the working model is also defined in cognitive and pre-representational terms, then one has to assume that cognitive, social, and emotional development can potentially transform the earlier "grammar of attachment." Cicchetti, Cummings, Greenberg, and Marvin (1990) explore the questions of continuities and discontinuities of attachment models in great detail. They view attachment as a central developmental line and espouse a view that movement from unproductive to productive attachment relationships and their internalizations can occur throughout the lifespan. Such a view is gaining prominence within the attachment paradigm (c.f. Main, Kaplan and Cassidy, 1985); however, a great deal more is needed to bridge the two traditions that attachment theory builds on, namely the psychoanalytically influenced view that early attachment patterns persist over time, and evidence from developmental psychology that relationships (including mental representations of relationships) undergo fundamental transformations throughout life. Despite significant progress in the past years, much thought and research is required to give the working model a truly developmental focus, by understanding the typical transformations in normal development. It is also important to trace changes in the working model in relationship to changes in symptoms and coping, to put Bowlby's hypotheses to a more rigorous test. A great deal of creative research in this direction is ongoing which includes developing bridges to clinical-developmental psychology.

Overarching Themes

Before introducing the clinical-developmental approach, we will summarize some important points which have emerged in this brief overview of other research traditions in developmental psychopathology. To begin with, most of the studies presently under way can be categorized in one or more of the above traditions. Many projects combine models and methods, integrating, for example, psychometric approaches with attachment research, or pursuing natural history of a disorder with measurement of stress and resiliency. But a young discipline can be helped by an "ideal type" categorization of approaches, with its own theoretical tradition, measurement strategies, and research community. The differences between these theories and methods lead to lively debate that parallels the paradigm debates in psychology, psychiatry, and other disciplines. This diversity is in contrast to other young disciplines, which at first had been unified by a general theory or model, such as Freudian psychoanalysis. While the diversity is productive, it sometimes poses the question whether developmental psychopathology is really a beginning discipline (cf. Cicchetti, 1984b, 1989) or rather a domain of application for existing developmental paradigms (cf. Achenbach, 1990).

A number of themes run through these different approaches, suggesting some convergence based on a common focus: the relationship between disorder and development with the help of longitudinal measurement. We have already pointed out a number of questions and themes as we introduced the different approaches. For example, many developmental psychopathology researchers have found limitations in a chronological approach. Age continues to be an important marker for development as it represents a shorthand for biological processes, life tasks, and vocational and professional status. But most developmentalists agree today that age is a crude indicator. For example, a great deal of variation exists regarding the onset of puberty and it is precisely the chronological differences that are of great interest (e.g., early onset of puberty in girls representing a risk factor for psychopathology). Similarly, cognitive, social cognitive, and emotional development are better understood from an evolving set of capacities or skills that are usually empirically correlated with chronological age, yet logically defined separately.

Another emerging consensus is the need to understand the role of relationships in the development and transformation of psychopathology and in fostering protective factors. The study of relationships has grown ever more sophisticated. Many differences exist between the attachment perspective that tends to emphasize early relationships and their continued power through the conservative nature of Bowlby's working model and Rutter's model that tends to stress the present-day conditions of intimate relationships. But even with these differences, Bowlby and more recent attachment researchers stress the possible changes of the working model through new attachment relationships. And Rutter points to the empirical evidence of the long-term and evolving potential problem of earlier loss. The communality, a more complex understanding of the long-term and evolving effects of childhood relationships across the life span, seems more important than the different ways of understanding relationships.

The focus on psychopathology, relationships and resiliency has led to another theme in much of developmental psychopathology research. While many investigators still believe that staying with observable symptoms is the most profitable research route to take, many developmentalists have found it essential to include an interpretive dimension, the self, or a notion of cognitive representation. Much clinical evidence has accumulated that indicates that behavior is changed most consistently and enduringly when meanings have been uncovered or cognitive representations have been altered. This idea is still controversial, and concepts used are quite diverse, but many researchers have become interested in the developing interpretations about self, relationships and psychopathology.

This shift toward a developmental, interactionist, and constructivist perspective in psychopathology research comes at a time when one further tradition in developmental psychopathology, clinical-developmental psychology, is gaining greater prominence building on exactly these basic premises. We do not suggest that this point of view has resolved all the problems. But a fruitful dialogue is possible which can help move the field forward.

Clinical-Developmental Psychology: A Necessary Approach in Developmental Psychopathology

Werner's theory and the studies in his tradition, (e.g., Bibace and Walsh, 1979) have originally been called a clinical-developmental approach and have given important impetus to the modern developmental psychopathology perspective (see, e.g., Cicchetti 1984b, 1990). In the past decade a number of investigators in the social-cognitive tradition (e.g., Kegan, 1982; Selman, Schwartz, & Yeates, 1991) have begun to relate the cognitive-conceptual development of self and relationships to risk and psychological disorder. Our use of the term clinical-developmental psychology incorporates Werner's ideas, but builds on a variety of other theoretical, clinical, and research traditions. In particular, our orientation combines concepts from cognitive-developmental theory with Erikson's (1968) work on the meaning of life tasks, as well as a variety of developmental models of the development of interpersonal relationships that have their origins in Sullivan's (1953) ideas. These sources provide building blocks for a theoretical and empirical line of work that derives its strength precisely where the other traditions have required most reworking. Researchers in clinical-developmental psychology pursue different developmental strands, explore a variety of disorders, and view the relationship between dysfunction and growth differently. But certain assumptions are shared and create important communalities. Even if the work of others is not best represented through this condensation of basic principles, our own evolving perspective is.

Mental Representations and Meaning Frames

For clinical-developmental psychologists, the transformation of mental representations of self and relationships has been a base on which to build a perspective of psychopathology. Many cross-sectional and longitudinal studies have shown that children, adolescents, and even adults shape and reshape their understanding of the social world. Piaget's early work on the moral judgment of the child (Piaget, 1932) was a milestone in uncovering developmental differences in how children construct and perceive social rules. Since then many Piagetian perspectives of the social world have been introduced, including the domains of social perspective-taking, moral development, conceptions of conventions, the self, etc. All of these studies about different domains of social development share in the idea that developmental levels are best understood in terms of the complexity of the representation of social reality. They also share, even after most researchers have given up the idea of a simple stagewise progression of cognitive function, in the idea that these representations develop in some logical sequence from less mature and differentiated to more complex and integrated.

While the initial work has been mostly on tracing the normative pathways in development, a great many implications are emerging for the study of dysfunction. Because we assume that the same events will be experienced differently depending on the developmental level of cognition, social cognition, and social-emotional development, clinical-developmental psychologists do not focus on behaviors and symptoms alone, but simultaneously on the meanings these problem behaviors hold for the individual. For example, running away from home can be a sign of an overly close and intrusive relationship with parents or a sign of neglect and abuse. It can be a part of a carefully planned and cognitively complex operation, or an impulsive decision, without consideration for the consequences of the behavior. But very little is still known about how the complexity of mental representations relate to the understanding, maintenance, and evolution of symptoms and syndromes. Uncovering connections between the better-explored world of social cognition and mental representations and the mostly unknown area of their relationship to dysfunctions make clinical-developmental psychology an exciting new area of inquiry.

Age Chronology

From these assumptions about development come significant questions about the usefulness of chronological age in the study of development and psychopathology. No doubt, today we know about interesting age trends in psychopathology. For example, certain phobias and anxieties, such as separation anxiety and nightmares are especially prevalent in early childhood and tend to decrease in middle childhood. Suicide rates rise dramatically in adolescence, and so do a number of other disorders such as obsessive-compulsive disorders, depression, and conduct problems. Age can serve as a simple organizer of many underlying processes. But the simplicity of an age approach is deceptive. When we study mental representations and meaning systems we quickly find that age is by no means a guarantor that basic cognitive and social cognitive processes have actually occurred. Many adolescents and adults, for example, do not ever reach formal-operational thought, even though most charts used in textbooks juxtapose this developmental level with adolescence. This, of course, is a common misapplication of the theory. The fact that many adolescents function at the formal operational level is empirically true. It is also correct that certain maturational capacities typically found in adolescence (in industrialized nations) are necessary for this cognitive level to appear. But the fact remains that these conditions by themselves do not precipitate a transformation in cognitive development. Many adolescents continue to function at concrete operational levels and use these capacities for the rest of their lives. If we use chronological age as our developmental psychopathology marker, we miss the fact that many of our subjects and patients within one age group use fundamentally different tools to construct their internal and interpersonal reality. For that reason, clinical-developmental psychology studies the complexity of meaning systems along cognitive, social, and emotional lines and in relation to symptoms, syndromes, or types of maladaptations. Paradoxically, from within such a perspective chronological age gains even greater importance than it does if we use it as a simple developmental marker. For any focus on mental representation has to deal with the question of when developmental capacities have 'fallen behind' and should be called delayed. In addition, one has to assume that different cognitive and social cognitive capacities, even when they have the same formal structure, will have a very different function at different ages in the life span.

This last point poses a great deal of problems to cognitive-developmentalists and provides a good example why clinical-developmental psychology cannot simply be the application of cognitive principles to clinical phenomena. It is quite typical for a person to reach, for example, a third-person perspective-taking position in early adolescence and to continue using the same basic structure of thought throughout adulthood. While on a formal level of analysis the thought patterns might be similar, a deeper analysis will reveal that form, functions, and content of thought and experience are quite different (e.g., Erikson, 1950; Vaillant, 1977). It is unlikely that the basic ways the seventy year old adult reflects on self and other, and is troubled by present, past and future events will be similar to the fifteen or forty year old (cf. Noam, Powers, Kilkenny, & Beedy, 1990) Thus, clinical-developmental psychology has to be an evolving set of principles that creates a broader perspective on the life span.

Relationships

Clinical-developmental psychology represents an interactionist perspective, placing a great deal of emphasis on relationships. While in traditional cognitive theories relationships were viewed in rather abstract ways (e.g., interactions with the "environment"), the clinical focus has brought an interest in relationships, especially relationships with significant others with whom the subject is intimately involved. This focus on persons and relationships came about at a time when social cognition as a field of study began to put forward many important distinctions about how people represent other people and relationships. Surprisingly, many ways in which children, adolescents and adults represent relationships differ throughout development. While the focus on relationships is shared with psychoanalysis and attachment theorists, the clinical-developmental perspective contributes to these approaches by tracing the transformations of how others and relationships are described and experienced. The fact that level of representation of relationships has something to do with types of symptoms and syndromes has created an important focus in clinical-developmental research.

Normative Development

We mentioned above that clinical-developmental psychology is not simply an application of cognitive psychology in the realm of psychological dysfunction. Instead it reformulates many traditionally held assumptions of normative theory. For example, the idea that higher stages of development are more adaptive, as claimed by Piaget and Kohlberg, requires serious reconsideration from a developmental psychopathology perspective. The same capacity that can produce more self-knowledge and adaptation, can also be used for more complex forms of self-deception and self-destruction. The conceptual problem—that complexity and maturity are built into one developmental model—is exposed when we study processes of dysfunction. Psychopathology can serve as a microscope as problems in developmental thinking become radicalized in clinical populations (Cicchetti, 1984b). In these populations complexity is often in stark contrast to maturity, integration, or adaptation. These issues, in a less extreme form, however, are part of normal life (Noam, 1993). In this context, the idea that overall psychological development occurs in neat and stepwise progression must be questioned as some capacities seem to be able to progress, or indeed regress, while others do not (cf. Noam, 1988 a,b,c). Again, this phenomenon of encapsulations and sequestered development was first most visible with disordered populations. But careful observations of so called normal development also reveals these phenomena, often in less extreme forms. Clinical-developmental psychology thus questions the normativeness of development as holistic, integrated and symptom-free. Instead, one needs to postulate normative vulnerabilities which are an outgrowth of typical forms of alienation and relational problems inherent in the institutional conflicts in complex societies (e.g., attachment needs in the family and work requirements; high rates of divorce, poverty, crime, etc. as normative life contexts for large parts of the population) (Noam, in press).

Adult Development

A very important aspect of clinical-developmental psychology is its ability to address issues of adult development. There is a great deal of evidence that representations of self and others can transform throughout the life span. Other clinical perspectives, such as psychoanalysis, have also focussed on intrapsychic and interpersonal representations and linked them to psychopathology. For example, ambivalent relationships to one's parents are viewed as the reason for self-destructive behavior to punish the self. But the representation of important "object relations" are usually viewed as early relationships. Adult psychopathology is thus connected to primitive internalizations of relationships, and is viewed as signifying uneven, or even primitive development. The clinical-developmental perspective put forward here is more focused on the continued transformations of the self and relationships. Throughout life, human beings have the capacity to create new forms of relationships to themselves and to others. Old relationships to parents and siblings also change throughout life, not only as a function of new interactions to these primary figures, but also because of new meanings given to the past (cf. Cicchetti, et al., 1990). This capacity for reframing relationships from birth to death can still imply that certain representations about past relationships remain unevolved and dysfunctional. In fact, attachment research has demonstrated the conservative nature of the internal working model. But, in principle, development—even fundamental transformations—can occur far beyond childhood and adolescence and can serve as an essential force toward recovery.

Transfers To Health

It is this last point, how continued development creates new opportunities for recovery, that we still know far too little about. Interestingly, this is the most important applied question for the developmental psychopathology approach: What developmental processes, if any, are at work when people transfer from dysfunction to adaptation? Most studies have been more interested in continuities of psychopathology and tracing the evolution of disorders. But we know from most clinical approaches, such as cognitive behavior therapy, client-centered psychotherapy, and psychoanalysis, that recovery is connected to relationships, self observation and reframing of experiences and attributions. Clinical-developmental psychology is concerned with tracing those cognitive, social and emotional capacities that are at work when people reflect on themselves and important relationships. Much research is needed to relate the developing capacities about the construction of the self and relationships to the problems of recovery.

Interpreting the evolution of cognitive functions as a progression to adaptation and health is inappropriate. To do so would represent a simple extrapolation of cognitive principles to the study of psychopathology. In fact, many people use their newly developing cognitive and social cognitive skills to create more complex forms of alienation, self-hate and psychopathology. It is an important aspect of clinical-developmental psychology to differentiate productive and destructive developmental pathways, and to learn to understand under what conditions the same capacities are used for very different purposes.

A Line of Research

Building on these principles we began to explore a variety of empirical questions about the relationship between development and psychopathology. The research involved herein has continuously defined and refined both our theoretical perspective and clinical approach. The character of clinical-developmental psychology has benefitted from this three-way interaction of theory, empirical study and clinical experience.

One model of development which has been employed in studies of both normative and pathological samples is Loevinger's theory of ego development (Loevinger, 1976). While our research involves a variety of models and methods, in the present chapter we will focus on Loevinger's model and measure of ego development. Loevinger defines the ego as the 'master trait' about which the personality develops. Consequently, her theory stresses the integrative nature of the ego. The theory builds on the assumption that each person has a customary orientation to the self and world, and that there are stages and transitions along which these 'frames of reference' may be grouped. Each of Loevinger's stages varies along dimensions of impulsivity, motivation, orientation, interpersonal and cognitive styles. While Loevinger's stages unite rather diverse developmental domains (i.e., moral, cognitive, interpersonal), they also address areas of relevance to maladaptation and pathology. For example, impulsivity and impulse control, manipulation and conformity are all defined as part of ego development as well as being areas traditionally addressed by clinicians in assessment of psychological adaptation and treatment.

At Loevinger's earliest stages of ego development individuals tend to be impulsive, dependent, and exploitive, demonstrating stereotypical cognitive styles. The 'pre-conformist' stages of ego development, I-2, Delta, and Delta/3, are all marked by these traits. The 'conformist' stages, I-3 and I-3/4, are marked by socio-centric concerns (e.g., acceptance by others), during which behaviors are often stereotyped and cliched. Individuals at the 'post-conformist' stages, I-4, I-4/5, I-5, I-6, demonstrate a high level of self-awareness and cognitive complexity, emphasizing mutuality and individuality in interpersonal relationships. These later stages occur primarily during late adolescence or adulthood (Redmore & Loevinger, 1979). Using psychological organization rather than age as a marker for development is one of the benchmarks of our approach to developmental psychopathology. A number of intriguing results have emerged using this approach.

All of the research cited below, except where otherwise stated, was conducted among an inpatient, consecutive admission, longitudinal sample of adolescents admitted for psychiatric services at McLean Hospital, Belmont, Massachusetts, a private Harvard Medical School affiliated psychiatric hospital. Data for this sample is being continually updated, hence different sample sizes in various studies will reflect particular datasets available for subsets of this group at given times. The adolescent group constitutes patients aged approximately 11–16 years. The patients are primarily white, from social classes one to five, with the largest group, from social class three, semi-professionals and small busi-

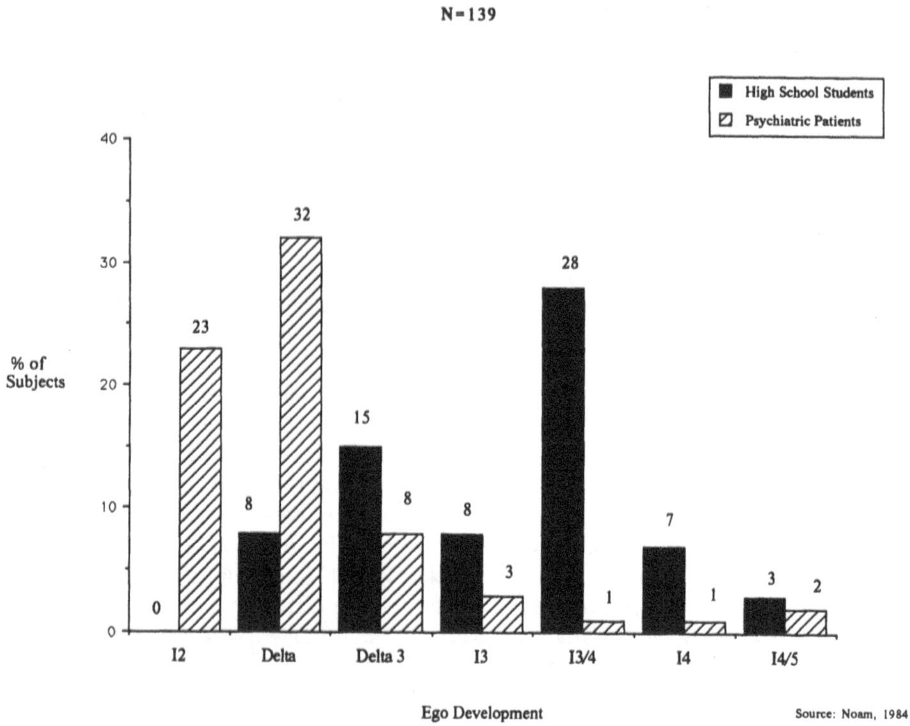

FIGURE 1 Distribution of Ego Stages of Adolescent Psychiatric Patients and High School Students

ness owners (cf. Hollingshead, 1957). Patients present with a wide variety of symptoms for which a full range of treatment services are available. In all of the research following, subjects with Wechsler Full Scale IQ levels below 85 have been eliminated from analyses.

An early collaborative study (Hauser, Jacobson, Noam & Powers, 1983) compared a sample of hospitalized inpatient youths with psychiatric disorders to a normative sample of non-hospitalized adolescents on a wide range of psychosocial measures. The majority of hospitalized adolescents were found to exhibit developmental delays when compared to the normative sample. In later research, growth indices in a variety of physical, social and cognitive domains were examined in relation to psychopathology (Noam, 1984). Figure 1 illustrates the distribution of adolescents at different developmental levels.

Approximately eighty percent of inpatient adolescents were found to be functioning at developmentally delayed positions. These developmentally delayed adolescents should not be viewed as a unitary group, however, as the three preconformist stages of ego development are marked by distinct cognitive and affective meaning systems. In addition, while this and other clinical samples were shown to be delayed in their ego development as a whole (cf. Browning, 1986), some individuals within these samples were functioning at more mature levels. We must be mindful here of the limitations of a nomothetic approach which may highlight generalizations about the overall relationship between development and psychopathology and the ideographic approach in which delays in ego development may provide only limited insight into individual psychopathology. Lastly, Figure 1 implies that we should not use a unitary view of adolescence, but instead should speak of different "adolescent worlds." This is illustrated in Noam, Powers, Kilkenny, and Beedy (1990), which found that adolescents conceptualize their important relationships with parents, peers, best friends, and role models differently, depending on the developmental level achieved. In a longitudinal study they noted the changes in perceptions of parents and in adolescents' relationships with parents that characterize the transition from the concretely focussed 'reciprocal-instrumental' stages of early adolescence to a self-other perspective enabled by a move to the 'mutual-inclusive' stages of late adolescence.

Another aspect of these perceptual and conceptual shifts which occur with increases in ego development is the way in which these shifts inform the adolescent's view of him/herself. We set out to examine this issue through a study of parent-child agreement about psychiatric symptoms and diagnoses (Noam & Valiant, under review). This study was based on a sample of 70 male and 73 female psychiatric inpatient adolescents and their parents or primary caretakers. In most cases (N = 134) the parent interview was completed by the mother or female guardian. We hypothesized that adolescents at higher stages of ego development would demonstrate greater self-awareness of symptoms and, with this, greater agreement with parental judgement of symptoms. We reasoned that at conformist stages a more socio-centric perspective develops, allowing the adolescent to better view themselves from another's point of view, thereby facilitating a more accurate assessment of their psychopathology. At the same time this socio-centric orientation would contribute to the desire to provide others with a better understanding of their inner psychological world. Typically researchers have found greatest parent-child agreement in areas of externalizing behaviors and symptoms, (e.g., conduct disorders and substance abuse); areas of internalizing/affective disorders have usually yielded low correspondences (see Achenbach, McConaughy, & Howell, 1987 for a review of these findings). Controlling for age and IQ differences, consistent trends were noted for higher parent-child agreement in areas of affective symptoms and depressive disorders among higher ego level adolescents when compared to lower ego level adolescents, in addition to higher agreement in externalizing symptoms and disorders. These findings suggest that adolescent treatment needs to take account of developmental capacity in cognitive organization. If treatment is to be effective the adolescent must be able to accept the judgement of pathology. This necessitates seeking to uncover the relationships between developmental levels and symptom patterns.

Ego Development, Symptoms, and Behavior.

With this goal in mind, a second set of studies investigated the associations between ego development and specific groups of maladaptive behaviors. We asked whether externalizing behaviors (e.g., aggression, delinquency) were significantly associated with immature ego development, and internalizing symptoms and behaviors more strongly associated with mature developmental levels. These questions are important both for exploring the relationship between social cognition and behavior, as well as to 'developmentalize' the distinction between internalizing and externalizing behaviors and problems found throughout the adolescent research literature (cf. Achenbach, 1982; Cicchetti & Toth, 1991). These studies extended the work of Phillips and Zigler (1964) conducted with adults using different methods and models of development. They found that symptoms are not arbitrary nor reducible to a specific disorder, but are "intimately related to maturational level attained" (Zigler & Glick, 1986, p.87).

Using the Child Behavior Checklist (Achenbach & Edelbrock, 1978), it was found that both internalizing and externalizing broad band symptom scales were significantly and negatively related to increases in ego development in a sample of 140 male and female adolescent inpatients (Noam, Hauser, Santostefano, Garrison, Jacobson, Powers, and Mead 1984). When partialling out effects of age, sex, and socio-economic background, ego level made a significant contribution to variance explained in externalizing scores, but not in internalizing scales.

This result was consistent with findings of other researchers which suggested a relationship between early stages of ego development and externalizing symptoms. Powitzky (1976), for example, found that among less socialized youthful offenders (bank robbers, drug offenders) lower ego levels were more prevalent. Frank and Quinlan (1976) had also found differences in ego stages when comparing delinquent and non-delinquent inner city adolescent females, with delinquents demonstrating lower ego levels. In a similar vein, Browning (1986) reported that youthful inpatients at lower stages of ego level demonstrated more assaultive behaviors and suicidal attempts. While the relationship between early stages of ego development and externalizing symptoms was demonstrated, a corresponding relationship between internalizing symptoms and higher stages of ego development was not found.

This led to further research which refined our measurement of symptoms and diagnoses. In Noam, et al., (1984) it was found that adolescents functioning at lower levels of ego development reported significantly more symptoms than higher stage adolescents. Using this finding, it was hypothesized that if number of symptoms were controlled, differences might begin to emerge in the topology of symptoms and diagnoses noted for adolescents at different ego levels. Using as a measure of symptomatology proportions of symptoms reported, Noam, Kilburn, and Ammen-Elkins (under review) found robust relationships between externalizing behaviors and lower ego levels, and internalizing symptoms with higher levels of ego development. The sample consisted of 320 adolescent psychiatric admissions (141 males and 179 females). The Achenbach Youth Self-Report was used as a measure of individual symptoms and behavior problems. Symptom proportions were measured by dividing the raw symptom factor score by the total raw symptom score. Correlations between proportion of externalizing symptoms and ego development were −.20, with delinquent symptoms correlating at −.25. Correlations between internalizing symptoms and ego-level

TABLE 1 Diagnostic Grouping by Ego Level

	Disorder					
	Adjustment	Anxiety	Conduct	Personality	Affective	Psychotic
EGO LEVEL	(N=25)	(N=8)	(N=51)	(N=21)	(N=22)	(N=12)
Preconformist (N=109)	54%	75%	82%	86%	77%	100%
Conformist/ Post Conformist (N=31)	46%	25%	18%	14%	23%	0%

Note: χ^2 (linear) = 9.38. df=1. p<.005 (all diagnoses): χ^2 (linear) = 13.87. df = 1. p<.001 (without affective disorder).

Source: Noam, G. G., & Houlihan, J. (1990).
Reprinted with permission from the American Journal of Orthopsychiatry.
Copyright 1990 by the American Orthopsychiatric Association, Inc.

were .25 and depressive subscale correlated .32 with ego-development; all probabilities were significant at $p \leq .001$.

Paget, Noam, Borst and Bartok (1990) grouped diagnoses into categories of conduct, affective, and mixed conduct/affective disorders. Using this typology conduct and mixed conduct/affective disorders were found to be more prevalent among pre-conformist stage adolescents. In their sample of 277 inpatient adolescents (124 males and 153 females), affective disorders were more commonly associated with female gender and conformist ego level stages (X^2 = 8.52, 2 d.f., $p \leq .014$).

The relationship between symptomatology and ego level was further explored in Noam and Houlihan (1990) among a sample of n = 140 adolescents, 74 males and 66 females. Arranging diagnostic categories in order of severity from adjustment to psychotic disorders, a consistent pattern emerged. With the exception of affective disorders, as severity of diagnosis increased, so did the percentage of subjects at pre-conformist levels, while the percentage of subjects at conformist/post-conformist stages decreased.

This same pattern was manifested in research conducted among adult psychiatric patients. Dill and Noam (1991) examined symptom severity and ego development in a sample of 86 adult outpatients with adverse symptoms. The sample consisted of 34 males and 52 females aged 19–71 with a median age of 30. Subjects ranged from social classes 1–5 with approximately ten percent of subjects evenly divided between the highest and lowest categories, and 36 percent in the middle category (i.e., social class 3). Correlations between ego development levels and symptom severity scores were uniformly negative across all but two symptom scales (obsessive-compulsive and interpersonal sensitivity). These results indicated that symptomatology generally decreases as ego level increases. One other possible interpretation raised by this finding was that while fewer symptoms might be associated with higher ego levels, this could be indicative of a movement toward more internalized symptomatology and pathology with higher stages of ego development.

What the research was beginning to highlight were patterns of symptoms and styles that covaried with levels of ego development. The relationship of externalizing symptoms with pre-conformist levels of ego development were fairly robust. So, too, were the relationships linking symptom severity to lower ego levels. These findings led to the discussion that if symptom expression was moderated by ego level, ego level might also shed light on the mechanisms linking cognitive maturity to symptom expression. To that end, studies were undertaken which examined the role of defenses in relation to ego level.

Ego Development and Defenses

Several studies using the Defense Mechanism Inventory (DMI: Ihilevich & Gleser, 1986) and Loevinger's measure in normal populations have demonstrated a relationship between ego development and defenses. In a study of normal adolescents, Levit (1989) reported that turning against others (TAO), (i.e., responding to conflict through attacking an external source), was inversely related to ego development. Labouvie-Vief, Hakim-Larson and Hobart (1987), in a study of normal subjects aged 10–77 years, found that turning against others (TAO) and projection (PRO), (i.e., attribution of negative characteristics as justification for aggression), were associated with lower ego development. Turning against self (TAS), (i.e., responding to conflict by directing aggression inwards), reversal (REV), (i.e., responding neutrally or positively toward frustration), and principalization (PRN), (i.e., coping with conflict by separating affect from the source of conflict through, for example, rationalization or isolation of affect), were positively linked to ego development. However, not all studies of defenses and ego development have found similar relationships (e.g., Vaillant & McCullough, 1987).

In a study of 291 adolescent inpatients, 122 males and 169 females, Recklitis and Noam (1990) examined the relationship between aggressive behavior, defenses and ego development. Using criteria of clinical restraints of adolescents and staff reports, the link between externalizing behaviors (assaultive behaviors) and lower ego levels was once again demonstrated. The correlations between ego development, defenses and symptom scales are shown in Table 2. A pattern linking externalizing behaviors to defenses of TAO, PRO, and REV was also demonstrated. Partialling subjects into assaultive and non-assaultive groups revealed significant differences between groups in ego level scores in the expected direction. The only defense in which these groups differed, however, was PRN, (i.e., coping with conflict through intellectualization, rationalization and isolation of affect). This suggests that the more psycho-socially mature adolescents, (i.e., those at conformist stages), were able to adopt a more cognitive approach to conflict resolution which serves as an inhibitor against impulsive action.

TABLE 2 Correlations Among Ego Development, Defenses and Symptom Scales

	TAO	PRO	PRN	TAS	REV	ISS
Ego Development (ISS)	−.29***	−.23***	.28***	.22***	.14*	----
Symptom Scales						
Delinquent	.39***	.21***	−.26***	−.12*	−.33***	−.30***
Aggressive	.29***	.27***	−.28***	−.03	−.30***	−.22***
Internalizing	.03	.10	−.21**	.31***	−.18**	−.04
Externalizing	.37***	.24***	−.30**	−.05	−.35***	−.27***
Total	.17**	.18**	−.27***	.18**	−.26***	−.15*

*p<.05. **p<.01. ***p<.001 two-tailed
Source: Recklitis & Noam (1990)

A second longitudinal study examined further the relationship between defenses and symptomatology, this time among a small sample of adolescents, 21 males and 16 females who were evaluated at admission to psychiatric hospital and again nine months later. Two ego pathway groups were defined in this study: progressors (subjects who progressed at least one-half stage in ego development) and non-progressors (subjects who regressed or stayed at the same ego level) (Noam, Recklitis, & Paget, 1991). While both groups showed significant reductions in symptoms in the nine months, ego progressors showed greater reductions in internalizing symptoms ($p=.03$), and a trend toward reductions in total ($p=.068$) and externalizing ($p=.058$) symptoms. While defenses remained virtually unchanged in the nine months for non-progressors, progressors demonstrated a decrease in the use of projection and reversal (see Figure 2).

The pattern of defenses demonstrated for the ego level progressors appeared once again to reinforce a cognitive approach to conflict resolution characterized by a level of ego maturity able to externalize conflict and rationalize instrumental aggression.

Both of these studies of defenses, however, indicated that while higher levels of ego development were characterized by distinct profiles of defenses and reductions in externalizing symptoms, there was no concomitant reduction in internalizing symptoms. In Recklitis and Noam (1990), for example, non-assaultive subjects were characterized as less aggressive; assaultive subjects, however, were found to exhibit similar levels of internalizing symptoms to non-assaultive patients.

While the relationship between externalizing behaviors and ego development emerged with each data set and each form of analysis, the internalizing results were less consistent and more ambiguous on the behavioral level. Thus, we began to study specific internalizing syndromes, particularly depression and suicidality in greater depth.

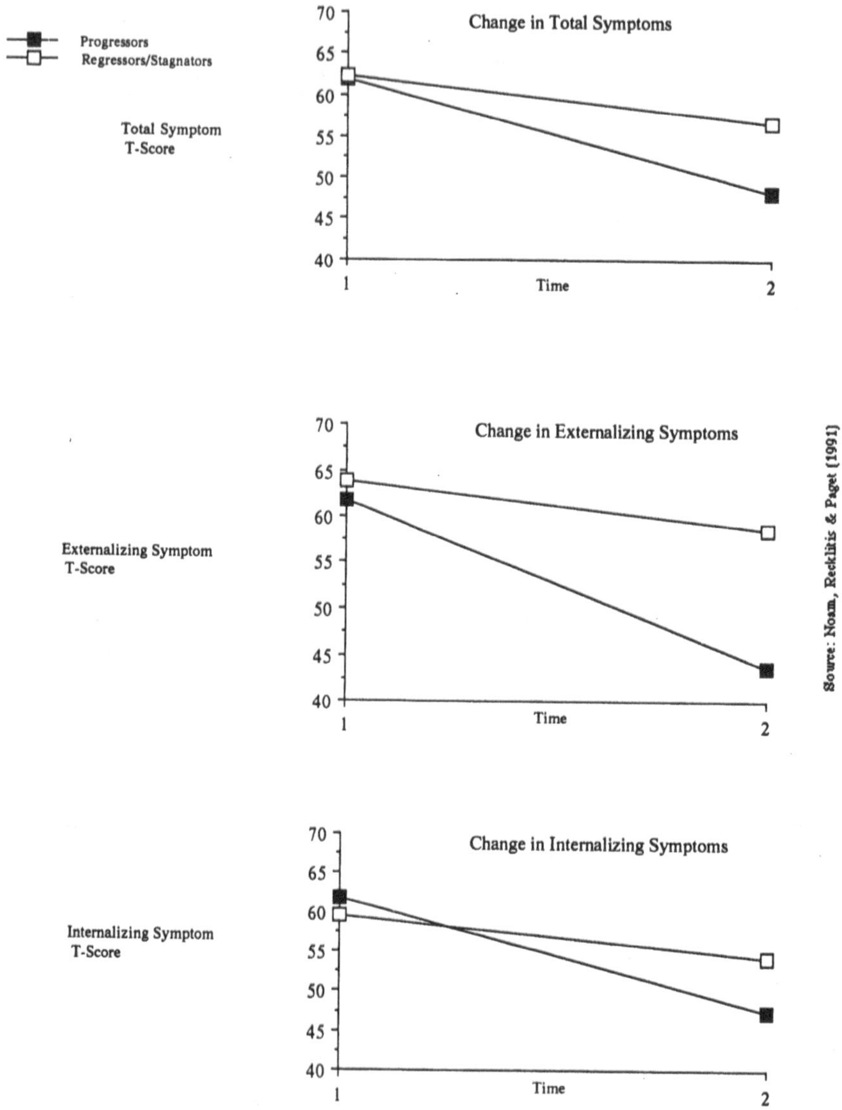

FIGURE 2 Changes in Defense Choice as a Function of Ego Pathway

Ego Development and Internalizing Disorders

Previous research has found that psychiatric disorders constitute one of the most important risk factors for adolescent suicidality. Retrospective studies of suicide completers have found that 95% were suffering from a DSMIII disorder (Shafii, Carrigan, Whittinghill, & Derrick, 1985). Depression has also been noted among youthful suicide attempters (Pfeffer, Newcorn, Kaplan, Mizruchi,

& Plutchik, 1988; Robbins & Alessi, 1985). Recent work has also found a significant proportion of suicidal adolescents who were not depressed, but rather sought treatment for conduct disorders or anti-social behaviors (Apter, Bleich, Plutchik, Mendelsohn, & Tyano, 1988). Comorbidity of psychiatric disorder has been found to enhance risk for suicidality (Brent, Perper, Goldstein, Kolko, Allan, Allman, & Zelenak, 1988; Kreitman, 1986). In a psychological autopsy of suicide completers, Shafii, Steltz-Lenarksy, Derrick, Beckner, and Whittinghill (1988) found that comorbidity, usually depression with substance abuse, conduct disorder or other mental disorder, was present in 81% of victims. It has been suggested (Blumenthal & Kupfer, 1988; Shaffer, 1974) that the comorbidity of conduct and affective disorders may be a potent precursor for suicidality.

The complex nature of suicidality suggested a more complex model than the single link between developmental level and suicidal behaviors. Borst, Noam and Bartok (1991) investigated the relationship of ego development, age, gender, and diagnosis to serious suicidal ideation and attempts among 219 inpatient adolescents, 96 males and 123 females. In addition to the established risk factors of gender and diagnosis, it was found that with increasing ego development adolescents became more prone to suicidal ideation and behaviors (see Table 3.). We concluded that the self-protective and externalizing qualities of the earlier developmental positions put a person at greater risk for impulsivity, conduct disorders or delinquency, but might shield the youth from directing aggression against the self, especially given the pattern of defenses which we had noted among these adolescents.

Although suicidal behavior was not expected to be an exclusive phenomenon of conformist stage youths, we assumed and found a higher proportion of suicide attempters within that group. However, while suicidality was more prevalent among conformist adolescents, the majority of adolescents studied were delayed in ego development, consistent with earlier findings about developmental delays among psychiatric adolescents (Noam, Hauser, Santostefano, Garrison, Jacobson, Powers, & Mead 1984). Hence, while 62% of conformist inpatients were found to be suicide attempters, the majority of attempters (79%) were at preconformist stages of ego development. This led to the proposal, following similar findings by Brent (1987), Pfeffer, Plutchick and Mizruchi (1983), and Shaffer (1974) that there may be two profiles of suicidality: the angry-defiant suicidal adolescents who are explicitly angry, impulsive, concrete, and often see suicide as revenge; and the self-blaming attempter who is more often depressed and concerned with socio-centric perspectives, who views suicide in terms of loss and abandonment.

The use of distinct profiles of suicidality to explicate the relationship between ego level, defenses, and psychiatric symptoms was explored further in Borst and Noam (1993). A sample of 139 inpatient psychiatric females, aged 13–16, were divided into four groups based on dimensions of suicidality (suicidal/non-suicidal) and stage of ego development (preconformist/conformist). Preconformist attempters were characterized by comorbidity of symptoms, both high internalizing and externalizing behaviors, as well as externalizing defenses. The conformist attempter presented with primarily internalizing symptoms (i.e., depressive), and scored highest on internalizing defenses (i.e., principalization).

TABLE 3 Suicidal Status by Age, Gender, Diagnostic Categories, and Ego Level (N = 219)

	Nonsuicidal Adolescents (N = 141)		Suicide Attempters (N = 78)	
Variables	N	%	N	%
Age				
12 and 13 years	41	67	19	33
14 years	45	54	35	46
15 and 16 years	55	68	29	32
Gender[a]				
Male	78	81	18	19
Female	63	51	60	49
Diagnostic Categories[b] (DISC)				
Conduct disorder	85	88	12	12
Affective disorder	19	49	20	51
Mixed conduct/affective	37	45	46	55
Diagnostic categories[c] (Clinician)				
Conduct disorder	77	81	18	19
Affective disorder	20	35	34	63
Mixed conduct/affective	16	60	10	38
"Other"	28	62	16	36
Ego development[d]				
Preconformist	131	68	62	32
Conformist	10	38	16	62

[a]Chi-square = 21.21; $df = 1$; $p < 0.0001$.
[b]Chi-square = 41.23; $df = 2$; $p < 0.0001$.
[c]Chi-square = 29.22; $df = 3$; $p < 0.0001$.
[d]Chi-square = 8.65; $df = 1$; $p < 0.003$.
Source: Borst, Noam, & Bartok (1991)

Using our three-pronged approach integrating theory, research and clinical practice, our view of the relationship between ego development and developmental psychopathology has been revised. Rather than viewing ego development as a marker for differences in types of psychopathologies, we now view ego development as shaping the expression of psychopathologies, noting the susceptibilities for different patterns of symptoms and defenses attendant at different stages of ego development.

Implications of a Clinical-Developmental Approach

When we create a new developmental psychopathology approach together with a line of research, we have to deal with a variety of new topics and questions. For that reason we will end this chapter by addressing issues which have benefitted from a clinical-developmental exploration and await further elaboration. In so doing we will discuss the complex relationship between developmental maturity, adaptation/maladaptation, and social competence.

Our research challenges the idea that higher ego stages are ipso facto more adaptive. We find in some studies that better adaptation is related to maturation in ego development, but in others that higher stages are related to more internalizing disorders. Loevinger stated early on that psychopathology can occur at any stage, and is "orthogonal" to ego development (Loevinger, 1976). But how are we to understand the concept of orthogonality? Does it mean that relationships between development and psychopathology are coincidental? Or are the constructs clearly distinct yet systematic relationships can be found empirically?

The problem we face with this essential question lies in the heterogeneity of the concepts of psychopathology and development. For example, with our present-day knowledge of schizophrenia, we have to assume that the biological factors are so strong, that the level of ego development would not play a large causal part. It remains an open, and interesting question, whether the level of development has something to do with the contents of the delusions and whether the process of recovery is aided by the skills inherent in development.

With certain types of delinquency we have to assume a very different relationship than with schizophrenia. Many dimensions that define early developmental stages of ego development (e.g., impulsivity, opportunism, self-protection, a focus on need-gratification, etc.) can influence an adolescent to 'choose' delinquent forms of adaptation. That does not mean that delinquency is explained by ego development, nor that they are the same constructs. Many adolescents and adults who function at early developmental levels are not delinquents; but most delinquents do not function at mature developmental positions. Similarly, the inability to cognitively experience the world from another's point of view is related to a lack of empathy and guilt, typical for early developmental positions. Lack of empathy and guilt are simultaneously related to conduct disorders and delinquency. However, not all forms of problems with empathy and guilt can be labelled delinquent, otherwise one would have to diagnose the majority of children at early stages of psycho-social development as psychopathological. Thus the constructs are not sufficiently separate to warrant the label of orthogonality.

At the mature levels of ego development, ego development and adaptation/maladaptation are also not entirely orthogonal. A conception of psychopathology is integrated into the sequence in its converse; compared to early ego development levels the higher stages read like definitions of psychological health. At the autonomous stage, for example, the person acknowledges and copes with conflict, transcends polarities, integrating complex ideas and relationships. Freed from oppressive demands from conscience, the person can act with tolerance and respect for others and "cherishes personal ties among his most precious values" (Loevinger 1976, p.23). It is hard to envision such a person as stealing or aggressively hurting another person. For these reasons, we should stop searching for a unitary relationship between psychopathology and development, but ask ourselves what developmental processes might be involved in which types of psychopathology?

This more complex view of developmental psychopathology which is beginning to take hold in other theory and research traditions as well (cf. Cicchetti, 1984a, 1989) is equally important for a more complex view of normative development. The study of psychopathology has opened our view to a conceptual problem in developmental psychology. We have found it problematic in so-called normal development to define developmental progression of social cognition (of which ego development is one example) simultaneously in terms of complexity of social understanding and mature adaptation. Complexity and quality of adaptation are not the same constructs. We face a dilemma: if we reconstruct development of cognition, especially social cognition without some ideal type of positive outcome (highest level), we return to a rather positivistic, seemingly value free position of description without prescription. However, combining a view of positive adaptation with developmental complexity creates an illusion of a unitary process, which while theoretically concise, is contradicted by reality. There are many people who are capable of developing complex understanding of themselves and others, but use these insights in the service of self-alienation and contempt for others. For them the adaptive quality of development has to be questioned, the formal complexity of their thoughts and feelings does not. In the study of psychopathology this neat combination of constructs, which should have been kept separate from the onset, breaks down. But in this case psychopathology serves only as a magnifying glass for processes that need to be separated even in non-pathological groups (cf. Cicchetti, 1984b, 1990).

This distinction is quite important for studying many phenomena. For example, evil actions are not only committed by those who are unevolved in cognitive and social development. Instead, many of those who participated in atrocities in Nazi Germany, or more recently in Argentina, Cambodia, or Yugoslavia, are often people who are very capable of complex understanding of social reality. It is this ability used for destructive purposes that is especially hard to accept: that those same individuals who are capable of understanding complex relationships and are "adapted" from a certain perspective, may be entirely pathological when it comes to values considered from a broader perspective.

The Milgram experiments (cf. Milgram, 1963; 1965) demonstrated the fragility of human resistance against destructive authority. Kohlberg's (1984) reconstructions also showed that those subjects who functioned at higher stages of moral development (and we can safely assume that their ego levels corresponded more or less to their moral levels) were less likely to "shock" a crying person in the next room to death. But level of development was by no means a guarantor for evolved behavior (defined as standing up to the authority and protecting the life of an unknown and 'suffering' human being).

This distinction between insight and pro-social behavior is usually framed as the difference between judgment and action. This distinction is useful as any researcher and clinician frequently encounters the gulf between insight, responsibility, and action. But already on the level of meanings and understanding represented here by the idea of ego development, one sees that concepts which are adaptive and maladaptive, truthful and defensive, self-supporting and self-alienating, complex and mature are in continuous interplay. Such interplay blurs the boundaries between health and pathology, and requires a new perspective on normative development as well. For that reason, our line of research has led to a reformulation of theory as well.

In our own redefinition of ego development in a theory of self (cf. Noam, 1991, 1992) each developmental advance in complexity produces the possibility for more complex and internalized self-destructive behavior, as well as for opportunities to transform vulnerabilities in order to create more mature adaptations. A new stage synthesis can be anything but integrative and holistic. Through continuous exchange between the organism and the environment, the person and the culture, the individual is challenged to establish increasingly more complex views about the self and others. These meaning systems are not purely related to thought, although their development is made possible by advances in the cognitive realm. At each new developmental position typical affects, meanings, and motivations emerge. From a clinical perspective, each position brings out new strengths and opportunities to rework past vulnerabilities. But each new system of self complexity can also lead to new weaknesses or to more complex forms of old dysfunctions. Instead of outlining the developmental positions shown in a number of other publications (e.g., Noam, 1988c; Noam, Powers, Kilkenny, & Beedy, 1990), we refer the reader to Table 4, Clinical-Developmental Interventions with Adolescents. This table briefly describes the strengths and weaknesses inherent in three adolescent-developmental positions and their implications for clinical interventions.

The model of separating self complexity from maturity and adaptation provides a link to research on social competence; for not only does development depend on maturity and complexity, but also on capacity to function in an environment conducive to actualization of growth potentials. Many psychopathology researchers have used social competence as a measure of actual competence in this domain. Achenbach and Edelbrock (1987), for example, in the Child Behavior Checklist and Youth Self Report include a section querying youth activities, friends, hobbies, and engagement in sports. Their Teacher Report Form also measures academic competence, i.e., grades, etc. Similarly, Zigler and Glick (1986) provide data linking pre-morbid social competence with symptomatology. Their scale consists of variables indicative of cognitive, interpersonal and social functioning, using age, IQ, education, marital status, occupation, and employment history as indices. The issue, however, is viewing social competence as a measure of both actual competence as well as an indicator of the potential (capacity) for significant social intercourse. While social competence is undoubtedly affected by psychopathology, we must begin to view competence as an interactive phenomenon influenced by and influencing development.

By focussing on the developmental dimensions, we can move beyond our tendencies to speak of adaptive competence in a general way and take account of the meanings of behaviors for individuals. Consistent with our view that higher is not necessarily better, (i.e., that higher levels of cognitive complexity may yield more complex self-deception), greater social competence is not necessarily

TABLE 4 Clinical-developmental interventions with adolescents

The Subjective-Physical Position	The Reciprocal-Instrumental Position	The Mutual-Overinclusive Position
Treatment focus		
• Interventions that focus on cognitive and emotional disorganization, impulsivity, attention problems, the constant need for physical presence of loved ones, and the lack of body control (e.g., supportive and behavioral-treatments in a structured environment, helping in creating a family structure, if possible).	• Milieu treatment with focus on issues of fairness and support for behavior that takes other people into consideration. • Central role for peer learning, as struggles with authority figures are typical (e.g., AA). • Activities with adult role models who work on skills and abilities (e.g., coaches).	• "Interpersonal therapy" with focus on depression and low self-esteem emerging in close relationships.
Setting		
• Usually long-term residential setting needed to contain serious impulsivity, depression, and potential for short psychotic episodes. Setting has to provide strong limits and rules that foster the learning of consequences of self's actions. • Predictable staff must be readily available.	• Containment in residential setting, often needed for a long period of time, especially when antisocial trends are strong. • But despite seeming disinterest in individual therapy, one-to-one relationships are important to create trust, but need to entail mutually satisfying activities (e.g., eating, sports, walks).	• Individual treatment (often in conjunction with family treatment) to help client express internalized feelings and, when necessary, short hospitalization (long, regressive hospitalizations to be avoided).
Support		
• Strong boundaries and limits with goal of internalizing external rules. Support with often enmeshed family system.	• Support in experience of unfairness of rules and situations and with the world that confronts externalizing stance. • Experience of nurturant relationship is critical as most patients have experienced trauma and neglect. • Confrontations to address manipulations.	• Strong commitment in every aspect of patients' experiences even when it seems more like friends talking. • Support for assertiveness needed. • Encouraging the expression of anger and frustration.

TABLE 4 (continued)

The Subjective-Physical Position	The Reciprocal-Instrumental Position	The Mutual-Overinclusive Position
Insight		
• Work with emerging ability to review behaviors, feelings, and thoughts. • Begin to recognize that multiple feelings can coexist about the same person or situation. • Learn about the fact that strategies are being used that are self-destructive.	• Emerging recognition that world can be influenced in productive ways and that rejections by others do not have to be addressed in terms of revenge and hostility. • Close relationships provide a possibility to begin to view the world through a sense of mutuality and community.	• Beginning reflection of what is occurring in the relationship as a pattern (e.g., "Everytime I am silent, I feel ashamed"). • Framing regression and low self-esteem in terms of a lack of inner agency. • Explore the problems of anger.
Typical therapeutic binds		
• Attempt by the therapist to interpret behavior in terms of symbolic meanings, when they are only understood in concrete and behavioral terms. Feeding into split between "good family, bad treatment staff" (or vice versa) often leads to a breakdown of the work.	• Patient confuses the therapist "being on my side" with jointly breaking rules (e.g., smoking in office before age). • Fear of consequences can lead to a style of nondisclosure. • Difficulty in talking about problems emerging in the relationship and past hurts because a biographical and transference focus has not yet developed.	• Silences in the treatment and feeling rejected by therapist require impossible proofs of acceptance (e.g., midnight phone calls). • Danger of fluctuation for therapist between demand for too much insight and self-observation and underestimating the capacity to observe relationship patterns and feeling states.

Source: Noam (1992)
Reprinted with permission from *Development and Psychopathology.*

more adaptive. Individuals who demonstrate higher social competence (e.g., good peer interaction, loyalty, etc.), may also be those who are involved in peer groups which are antithetical to established norms (e.g., street gangs, terrorist groups, etc.).

We described up to now that developmental complexity provides no guarantee that earlier problems become integrated into a new level of maturity. We have further argued that new skill levels reflected in ego development (e.g., perspective-taking, differentiating between different parts of the self, having a stronger sense of biography and trajectory into the future, etc.) can all be used in adaptive or maladaptive terms. In the development and application of natural sciences we are constantly confronted with this issue. Few would argue that understanding nuclear physics did not constitute scientific progress; however, the application of these insights to the creation and use of nuclear weaponry is far more controversial. New capacities are not good just because we define them as "developmental." Development has the great potential to create more insight, a greater ability for self reflection, and more understanding and thus a more tolerant perspective of others. But the skills that underly these processes can also turn old hurts and new alienations into ever more complex forms. Reflective powers can be used to create more alternatives making the self less able to chose and act. Similarly, understanding how others function does not necessarily lead to more tolerance or empathy. This same reflexivity can be applied to think out complex ploys to hurt others and to take revenge. We could continue with many more examples, but the basic principles should have become clear.

The idea is simple and straightforward, and one imagines most interventions encompassing aspects of this clinical-developmental idea, but this is not necessarily the case. Psychoanalysis views most forms of psychopathology as primitive, fixated, unevolved, and thus developmental transformations of dysfunctions to higher forms in adulthood have not received the necessary attention. In the cognitive-developmental tradition, development has been viewed as leading to greater adaptation; creating a context that fosters development was viewed as facilitating better adaptation. Most developmentalists thought maladaptation and dysfunction to be outside the purview of developmental psychology, thus leaving psychiatry unchallenged in the approach of creating entities rather than uncovering underlying developmental principles. With the establishment of developmental psychopathology and clinical-developmental psychology, new theoretical, clinical, and empirical bridges are now possible.

Conclusion

The work to date suggests that each new level in developmental complexity needs to be well-understood so tools for recovery can be created. Clinicians from all traditions have used ideas or implicit theories of development to create interventions. The psychoanalytic distinction of the pre-oedipal and oedipal era is, in fact, quite explicitly developmental and offers guidance on how to conduct treatment, even when the patient is an adult. But any intuitive analyst also gravitates to the present-day level of functioning. The assessment of that level will include many processes, such as verbal ability, impulse control, family relationships, ability to comprehend symbols and metaphors. These explorations are, of course, tied strongly to individual differences. No theory will, nor should, replace the intuitive abilities of therapists. The research findings and theoretical formulations of clinical-developmental psychopathology should, however, serve as an aid to therapists seeking to unify the strands of individual development with symptomatology in order to effect treatment.

REFERENCES

Achenbach, T. M. (1982). *Developmental Psychopathology.* (2nd ed.) New York: Wiley.

Achenbach, T. M. (1990). What is "developmental" about developmental psychopathology? In J. Rolf, A. Masten, D. Cicchetti, K. Nuechterlein, & S. Weintraub (Eds.), *Risk and protective fators in the development of psychopathology* (pp. 29–48). New York: Cambridge University Press.

Achenbach, T. M., & Edelbrock, C. (1978). The classification of child psychopathology: A review and analysis of empirical efforts. *Psychological Bulletin, 85,* 1275–1301.

Achenbach, T. M., & Edelbrock, C. (1983). *Manual for the Child Behavior Checklist.* Burlington, VT: University of Vermont Department of Psychiatry.

Achenbach, T. M., & Edelbrock, C. (1987). *Manual for the Youth Self Report and Profile.* Burlington, VT: University of Vermont Department of Psychiatry.

Achenbach, T. M., McConaughy, S. H., & Howell, C. T. (1987). Child/adolescent behavioral and emotional problems: Implications of cross-informant correlations for situational speciality. *Psychological Bulletin, 101,* 213–232.

Ainsworth, M. D. S. (1982). Attachment: Retrospect and Prospect. In C. M. Parkes & J. Stevenson-Hinde (Eds.), *The place of attachment in human behavior.* (pp. 3–30). Tavistock Press.

Apter, A., Bleich, A., Plutchik, R., Mendelsohn, S. & Tyano, S. (1988). Suicidal behavior, depression, and conduct disorder in hospitalized adolescents. *Journal of the American Academy of Child Adolescent Psychiatry, 27,* 696–699.

Bibace, R. & Walsh, M. (1979). Clinical-developmental psychologists in family practice setting. *Professional Psychology, 10,* 441–450.

Blumenthal, S. J. & Kupfer, D. J. (1988). Overview of early detection and treatment strategies for suicidal behavior in young people. *Journal of Youth and Adolescence,* 1–22.

Borst, S., & Noam, G. (1993). Developmental psychopathology in suicidal and nonsuicidal adolescent girls. *Journal of the American Academy of Child and Adolescent Psychiatry, 32,* 501–508.

Borst, S. R., Noam, G. G. & Bartok, J. (1991). Adolescent suicidality: A clinical-developmental approach. *Journal of the American Academy of Child and Adolescent Psychiatry, 30,* 796–803.

Bowlby, J. (1952). *Maternal care and mental health.* Geneva: Switzerland: World Health Organization.

Bowlby, J. (1960). Separation anxiety. *International Journal of Psychoanalysis, 41,* 89–113.

Brent, D. A. (1987). Correlates of medical lethality of suicide attempts in children and adolescents. *Journal of the American Academy of Child and Adolescent Psychiatry, 26,* 87–89.

Brent, D. A., Perper, J. A., Goldstein, C. E., Kolko, D. J., Allan, M. J., Allman, C. J., & Zelenak, J. P. (1988). Risk factors for adolescent suicide. A comparison of adolescent suicide with suicidal inpatients. *Archives of General Psychiatry, 45,* 581–88.

Browning, D. L. (1986). Psychiatric ward behavior and length of stay in adolescent and young adult inpatients: A developmental approach to prediction. *Journal of Consulting and Clinical Psychology, 54,* 227–230.

Cicchetti, D. (Ed.) (1984a). *Developmental Psychopathology.* Chicago, IL: University of Chicago Press.

Cicchetti, D. (1984b). The emergence of developmental psychopathology. *Child Development, 55,* 1–7.

Cicchetti, D. (Ed.) (1989). *Rochester Symposium on Developmental Psychopathology, Vol. 1: The Emergence of a Discipline.* Hillsdale, NJ: Lawrence Erlbaum Associates.

Cicchetti, D. (1990). A historical perspective of developmental psychopathology. In J. Rolf, A. Masten, D. Cicchetti, K. Nuechterlein, and S. Weintraub (Eds.), *Risk and Protective Factors in the Development of Psychopathology.* (pp. 2–28). New York: Cambridge University Press.

Cicchetti, D. & Aber, J. L. (1986). Early precursors to later depression: An organizational perspective. In L. Lipsitt and C. Rovee-Collier (Eds.), *Advances in Infancy, Vol. 4.* (pp. 87–137). Norwood, NJ: Ablex.

Cicchetti, D., Cummings, E. M., Greenberg, M. T., & Marvin, R. S. (1990). An organizational perspective on attachment beyond infancy. In M. Greenberg, D. Cicchetti, E. M. Cummings (Eds.), *Attachment in the Pre-School Years: Theory, Research, and Intervention.* (pp. 3–49). Chicago: The University of Chicago Press.

Cicchetti, D. & Toth, S. L. (Eds.) (1991). *Rochester Symposium on Developmental Psychopathology, Vol. 3: Models and Integrations.* Rochester, New York: University of Rochester Press.

Dill, D., & Noam, G. G. (1991) Adult development and symptomatology. *Psychiatry, 54,* 208–217.

Dodge, K. A. (1986). A social information processing theory of social competence in children. In M. Perlmutter (Ed.). *Minnesota Symposium on Child Psychology, 18,* 77–125.

Erikson, E. (1950) *Childhood and Society.* New York: Norton.

Erikson, E. (1968). *Identity, Youth and Crisis.* New York: Norton.

Frank, S., & Quinlan, D. (1976). Ego development and adjustment patterns in adolescence. *Journal of Abnormal Psychology, 85,* 505–510.

Garmezy, M. (1981). Children under stress: Perspectives on antecedents and correlates of vulnerability and resistance to psychopathology. In A. I. Rabin, J. Aronoff, A. M. Barclay, & R. A. Zuckers (Eds.). *Further explorations in personality.* (pp. 196–269). New York: Wiley Interscience.

Grossmann, K. E. & Grossmann, K. (1990). The wider concept of attachment in cross-cultural research. *Human Development, 33,* 31–47.

Hauser, S. T., Jacobson A., Noam, G., & Powers, S. (1983). Ego development and self-image complexity in early adolescence: Longitudinal studies of diabetic and psychiatric patients. *Archives of General Psychiatry, 40,* 325–332.

Heffner, P. A., Strauss, M. E., & Grisell, J. (1975). Rehospitalization of schizophrenics as a function of intelligence. *Journal of Abnormal Psychology,* 84, 745–736.

Hollingshead, A. (1957). *Two-factor index of social position.* Unpublished manuscript. Available from A. Hollingshead, Yale Station, New Haven, CT.

Ihilevich, D. & Gleser, G. C. (1986). *Defense Mechanisms.* Owosso, MI: DMI Associates.

Kazdin, A. E. (1990). Matchplay and firesetting in children: Relationship to parent, marital, and family dysfunction. *Journal of Clinical Child Psychology, 19,* 229–238.

Kegan, R. (1982). *The evolving self.* Cambridge, MA: Harvard University Press.

Kohlberg, L. (1984). Essays on moral development. Vol 2. *The Psychology of Moral Development.* San Francisco: Harper & Row.

Kovacs, M. & Puig-Antich, J. (1989). Major psychiatric disorders as risk factors in youth suicide. In: *Report of the Secretary's Task Force on Youth Suicide. Volume 2: Risk Factors for Youth Suicide.* (DHHS Pub. No. ADM 89–1622). (pp. 143–159). Washington, DC: Superintendent of Documents, U.S. Government Printing Office.

Kreitman, N. (1986). The clinical assessment, and management of the suicidal patient. In A. Roy (Ed.), *Suicide.* (pp. 181–195). Baltimore, MD: Williams & Williams.

Labouvie-Vief, G., Hakim-Larson, J., & Hobart, C. J. (1987). Age, ego level, and the life-span development of coping and defense processes. *Psychology and Aging, 2,* 286–293.

Levit, D. B. (1989). *A developmental study of ego defenses in adolescence.* Unpublished Doctoral Dissertation, Boston University.

Loevinger, J. (1976). *Ego Development.* San Francisco: Jossey-Bass.

Main, M. B., Kaplan, N., & Cassidy, J. (1985). Security in infancy, childhood and adulthood: A move to the level of representation. In I. Bretherton & E. Waters (Eds.) *Growing points of attachment theory and research, Monographs of the Society for Research in Child Development* 50 (1–2, Serial No. 209), 66–104.

Main, M. B. & Weston, D. R. (1981). Security of attachment to mother and father: Related to conflict behavior and the readiness to establish new relationships. *Child Development, 52,* 1064–1067.

Main, M. B. & Weston, D. R. (1982). Avoidance of the attachment figure in infancy: Descriptions and interpretations. In C. M. Parkes & J. Stevenson-Hinde (Eds.) *The Place of Attachment in Human Behavior.* London: Tavistock Press.

Milgram, S. (1963). Behavioral study of obedience. *Journal of Abnormal and Social Psychology, 67,* 371–78.

Milgram, S. (1965). Some conditions of obedience and disobedience to authority. *Human Relations, 18,* 57–76.

Noam, G. G. (1984). *Self, morality and biography: Studies in clinical-developmental psychology.* Unpublished doctoral dissertation. Harvard University.

Noam, G. G. (1988a). A constructivist approach to developmental psychopathology. In E.D. Nannis & P. A. Cowan (Eds..), *Developmental psychopathology and its treatment New directions for child development, 39,* 91–121. San Francisco: Jossey-Bass.

Noam, G. G. (1988b). The self, adult development and the theory of biography and transformation. In D. K. Lapsley & F. C. Power (Eds.), *Self, ego, and identity: Integrative approaches,* (pp. 3–29). New York: Springer

Noam, G. G. (1988c). The theory of biography and transformation: Foundation for clinical-developmental therapy. In S. R. Shirk (Ed.), *Cognitive development and child psychotherapy,* (pp. 273–317). New York: Plenum.

Noam, G. G. (1991) Beyond Freud and Piaget: Biographical worlds-interpersonal self. In T. Wren (Ed.) *The Moral Domain,* (pp. 360–399). Cambridge, MA.: MIT Press.

Noam, G. G. (1992). Development as the aim of clinical intervention. *Development and Psychopathology* 3, 679–696.

Noam, G. G. (1993) Ego development: True or False. *Psychological Inquiry* 4, 43–48.

Noam, G. G. (In press). Normative vulnerabilities of self-Moments of transformation in moral action. In G. Noam & T. Wren (Eds.) *The Moral Self.* Cambridge, MA: MIT Press.

Noam, G., Hauser, T., Santostefano, S., Garrison, W., Jacobson, A., Powers, S. I. & Mead, M. (1984). Ego development and psychopathology: a study of hospitalized adolescents. *Child Development,* 55, 184–194.

Noam, G., & Houlihan, J. (1990). Developmental dimensions of DSM-III diagnoses in adolescent psychiatric patients. *American Journal of Orthopsychiatry,* 60, 371–78.

Noam, G. G., Kilburn, D., & Ammen-Elkins, G. (under review). Adolescent Development and Psychiatric Symptomatology.

Noam, G. G., Powers, S., Kilkenny, R. & Beedy, J. (1990). The interpersonal self in lifespan developmental perspective: Theory, measurement and Longitudinal case analyses. *Lifespan-Developmental Psychology, 10,* , 59–104.

Noam, G., Recklitis, C., & Paget, K. (1991). Pathways of ego development: Contributions to maladaptation and adjustment. *Development and Psychopathology,* 3, 311–28.

Noam, G. G. & Valiant, G. (under review). The contribution of ego development to parent-child agreement on psychiatric symptoms and diagnoses.

Oppenheimer, L. (1989). The nature of social action: Social competence versus social conformist. In B. Schneider, G., Attili, J. Nadel, & R. P. Weissberg (Eds.), *Social competence in developmental perspective.* (pp. 41–69). NATO ASI Series, Vol. 51.

Paget, K. F., Noam, G. G., Borst, S., & Bartok, J. (June, 1990). *Ego Development, Psychiatric Diagnoses, and Gender in Adolescence: A Developmental Psychopathology Study.* Paper presented at the meeting of the American Psychological Society, Dallas.

Pfeffer, C. R., Newcorn, J., Kaplan, G., Mizruchi, M. S., & Plutchik, R. (1988). Suicidal behavior in adolescent psychiatric patients. *Journal of the American Academy of Child and Adolescent Psychiatry, 27,* 357–361.

Pfeffer, C. R., Plutchik, R., & Mizruchi, M. S. (1983). Suicidal and assaultive behavior in children: Classification, measurement and interrelations. *American Journal of Psychiatry, 140,* 154–57.

Phillips, L., & Zigler, E. (1964). Role orientation, the action-thought dimension, and outcome in psychiatric disorder. *Journal of Abnormal and Social Psychology, 68,* 381–389.

Piaget, J. (1932). *The moral judgement of the child.* New York: Harcourt, Brace and Company, Inc.

Powitzky, R. (1976). Ego levels and types of federal offenses. Unpublished doctoral dissertation, University of Texas Health Science Center, Dallas.

Recklitis, C. J., & Noam, G. G. (August 1990). *Aggression in Adolescent Psychopathology: Developmental and Personality Dimensions.* Presented at the annual meeting of the American Psychological Association, Boston, MA.

Redmore, C. & Loevinger, J. (1979). Ego development in adolescence: Longitudinal studies. *Journal of Youth and Adolescence, 8,* 1–20.

Robbins, D. R. & Alessi, N. E. (1985). Depressive symptoms and suicidal behavior in adolescents. *American Journal of Psychiatry, 142,* 588–592.

Robins, L. N. (1966). *Deviant children grown up.* Baltimore: Williams & Williams.

Rutter, M. (1989). Isle of Wright revisited: Twenty Five Years of child psychiatric epidemiology. *Journal of the American Academy of Child and Adolescent Psychiatry, 28,* 633–635.

Rutter, M. & Garmezy, N. (1983). Developmental psychopathology. In P. Mussen, *Handbook of child psychology. Vol 4: socialization.* (pp. 775–991). New York: Wiley.

Selman, R. L., Schwatz, L. H., & Yeates, K. O. (1991). Interpersonal understanding and action: A development and psychopathology perspective on research and prevention. In. D. Cicchetti & S. L. Toth (Eds.) *Rochester Symposium on developmental psychopathology, Vol. 3. Models and integrations.* (pp. 289–329). Rochester, NY: University of Rochester Press.

Shaffer, D. (1974). Suicide in Childhood and early adolescence. *Journal of Child Psychology and Psychiatry, 15,* 275–291.

Shafii, M., Carrigan, S., Whittinghill, J. R., & Derrick, A. (1985). Psychological autopsy of completed suicide in children and adolescents. *American Journal of Psychiatry, 142,* 1061–1064.

Shafii, M., Steltz-Lenarksy, J., Derrick, A. M., Beckner, C., & Whittinghill, J. R. (1988). Comorbidity of mental disorders in the postmortem diagnosis of completed suicide in children and adolescents. *Suicide and life-threatening behavior, 12,* 141–150.

Spirito, A., Brown, L., Overholser, J., & Fritz, G. (1989). Attempted suicide in adolescence: A review and critique of the literature. *Clinical Psychology Review, 9,* 335–363.

Sroufe, L. A. (1983). Infant-caregiver attachment and patterns of adaptation in preschool: The roots of maladaptation and competence. In M. Perlmutter (Ed.), *Minnesota Symposium in Child Psychology, No. 16,* (pp. 41–83). Minneapolis, MN: University of Minnesota Press.

Sullivan, H. S. (1953). The interpersonal theory of psychiatry. New York: Norton.

Urban, J., Carlson, E., Egeland, B., & Sroufe, L. A. (1991). Patterns of individual adaptation across childhood. *Development and Psychopathology, 3*, 445–460.

Vaillant, G. E. (1977). *Adaptation to Life.* Boston: Little Brown.

Vaillant, G. E., & McCullough, L. (1987). The Washington University Sentence Completion Test compared with other measures of adult ego development. *American Journal of Psychiatry, 144*, 1118–1194.

Wohlwill, J. F., (1973). The concept of experience: S or R? *Human Development, 16*, 90–107.

Zigler, E. & Glick, M. (1986). *A Developmental Approach to Adult Psychopathology.* Wiley Series on personality processes. New York: John Wiley & Sons, Inc.

X The Directionality of the Link Between Self-esteem and Affect: Beyond Causal Modeling

Susan Harter and Donna B. Marold

Global self-worth or self-esteem has emerged as a powerful construct within the fields of developmental, clinical, personality, cognitive, social, and educational psychology. Historically, efforts were primarily devoted to the identification of numerous *correlates* of self-esteem (Wylie, 1979), typically defined as the level of regard that one has for the self as a person (Epstein, 1973, 1991; Harter, 1986; Rosenberg, 1979, 1986). More recently, theorists have turned their attention to models that identify the causes as well as the consequences of one's level of self-esteem, addressing more compelling conceptual questions. What are the developmental precursors of an individual's level of self-eteem? Moreover, does one's self-esteem wield any psychological influence on other affective, cognitive, or behavioral outcomes that are critical to adaptive functioning? Our own work falls within this newer tradition. In the present chapter we would like to share the highlights of this programmatic effort, describing the evolution of a normative developmental model of self-esteem among adolescents that has powerful implications for the field of developmental psychopathology, in general, and depressive symptomatology, in particular. This evolutionary process has dictated that certain constructs be transformed into concepts that are more differentiated and elaborate, whereas others have necessarily undergone conceptual extinction.

The original model

Our original model relied heavily on the theoretical legacies of both James (1982) and Cooley (1902), each of whom offered insights into the precursors of

The research described here was supported by a grant from the W. T. Grant Foundation awarded to both authors. We would like to thank the personnel and adolescents at Flood Middle School, Rangeview High School, and Columbine Psychiatric Hospital, for their cooperation in making this research possible. Inquiries should be sent to the first author at the Department of Psychology, University of Denver, 2155 S. Race St., Denver, Colorado, 80208.

one's global sense of self-esteem. Both of these theorists were explicit on the point that one possesses a global concept of self, over and above more specific self-evaluations. However, their formulations took very divergent conceptual paths with regard to the specific determinants of one's global sense of worth as a person.

For James, global self-esteem was captured by the ratio of one's *successes* to one's *pretensions*. Accordingly, James contended that individuals do not scrutinize their every action or attribute. Rather one selectively attends to performance in domains of *importance*, arenas of one's life in which one has aspirations to succeed. Thus, if one evaluates oneself as competent in domains where one aspires to excel, high self-esteem will be conferred. Conversely, if one falls short of one's ideals, if one falters in domains where one aspires to success, low self-esteem will unfortunately ensue. It is critical to appreciate that from a Jamesian perspective, lack of competence in domains deemed *un*important to the self will *not* adversely affect self-esteem. For example, an individual may judge oneself to be unathletic; however, if athletic prowess is not an aspiration, such lack of competence will not erode one's self-esteem. The high self-esteem individual, therefore, is equipped with self-protective armor allowing one to *discount* the importance of domains in which one lacks ability. Conversely, the low self-esteem individual appears more defenseless in that he/she appears unable to devalue success in domains of demonstrated or perceived incompetence. For James, therefore, the individual's cognitive evaluation of his/her adequacy vis-a-vis one's aspirations was the cornerstone upon which self-esteem was constructed.

In contrast to James, Cooley (1902) postulated that the origins of self-esteem were primarily *social* in nature, adopting a mirror metaphor in describing his concept of the "looking glass self". For Cooley, the self was constructed by casting one's gaze into the social mirror to ascertain or devine the opinions of significant others toward the self. These characterizations, the reflected appraisals of others, were then incorporated or internalized as the self. Mead (1934) elaborated on this theme in his concept of the *generalized other,* which represented the pooled or collective judgments of the significant others in one's life. From such a perspective, if others hold the self in high regard, one's own sense of self-esteem will be high. Conversely, if others display little regard for the self, the incorporation of these negative opinions will have a crippling effect on self-esteem.

Findings in support of James' formulation

Our own model of the nature and psychological structure of self-evaluations in older children and adolescents (see Harter, 1986) lent itself to a Jamesian analysis. We had previously determined that children, beginning at approximately age eight, construct domain-specific evaluations of their competence or adequacy, as well as create a more global representation of their worth as a person, i.e., self-esteem (Harter, 1982, 1985a, 1986). The most salient domains, which were incorporated into our Self-Perception Profile for Children (Harter,

1985a), are Scholastic Competence, Athletic Competence, Social Acceptance, Physical Appearance, and Behavioral Conduct. Our instrument yields a *profile* of self-concept scores across the specific domains, as well as a separate index of the child's sense of global self-esteem or self-worth. In order to examine James' contention that competence or adequacy in domains of *importance* was the critical determinant of self-esteem, we constructed parallel importance items for each of the discrete domains.

Our findings have revealed precisely what James hypothesized, for older children, adolescents, college students, and adults in the world of work and family (Harter, 1990a). We have employed two data-analytic strategies, both of which tell the same story. One can construct actual discrepancy scores between importance ratings and competence judgments in each domain. Averaging these across domains, initially, we have determined that the larger the discrepancy, i.e., the more one's importance ratings exceed one's perceived adequacy or competence, the lower one's self-worth or self-esteem (terms that will be employed interchangeably). Across numerous studies, these correlations typically range from .60 to .72. Employing a second procedure, we have examined self-esteem as a function of the average absolute competence/adequacy judgments for *only* those domains rated important, and found a systematic, linear relationship emerges (see Harter, in press). Correlational approaches also reveal that the relationship between competence in domains deemed important and self-esteem ($r = .70$) far exceeds the correlation between competence in *un*important domains and self-esteem ($r = .30$).

This pattern of findings is not unique to our own data, but converges with other literature that has focused on the discrepancy between one's ideal and one's real self (see Glick & Zigler, 1985; Higgins, 1987, 1991; Markus & Nurius, 1986; Rosenberg, 1979; Tesser, 1988; Tesser & Campbell, 1983). As shall become evident in a subsequent section, such discrepancies are not only predictive of self-esteem, but of associated affects such as depression (see also Baumeister, 1990, Higgins, 1987, 1989).

From a developmental perspective, it should be noted that the these discrepancy models do not apply to younger children. Competence does not appear to be as critical to young children's self-esteem (Harter, 1990a), nor are young children cognitively able to simultaneously compare two concepts such as importance ratings and self-evaluations of their competence or adequacy (Fischer, 1980; Harter, 1990a; Higgins, 1991). Moreover, young children do not yet possess the cognitive capacity to construct a verbalizable representation of their overall worth as a person (Harter, 1987, 1990). They do, however, manifest or exude self-esteem in their behavior, allowing observers to reliably rate what we have conceptually and operationally identified as "presented self-esteem" (Haltiwanger & Harter, 1992).

Findings in support of Cooley's formulation

Recall that for Cooley (1902), self-esteem represented a *social* construction. According to his looking-glass self formulation, social support, in the form of positive regard from significant others, constituted the critical pychological building blocks of self-esteem. Thus approval or disapproval from others becomes incorporated into one's own esteem for the self. Developmentally, the internalization of *parental* approval or disapproval has been demonstrated to be particularlly critical to the self-esteem formation of young children (Harter, 1987, 1990).

In order to empirically examine Cooley's formulation among older children and adolescents, we identified four sources of potential support: parents, teachers, classmates, and close friends. We then created self-report items (see Social Support Scale for Children and Adolescents, Harter, 1985b) tapping the extent to which one feels that these others approve of or value the self. In creating such items we can then directly examine the link between the perceived regard from others and the perceived regard for the self, i.e., self-esteem.

Across numerous studies with older children and adolescents, college students, as well as adults in the world of work and family, we have demonstrated that the correlations between perceived support from significant others and self-esteem range from .50 to .65 (Harter, 1990a, 1990b). As anticipated from Cooley's model, those with the lowest levels of support report the lowest self-esteem; those with moderate support report correspondingly moderate levels of self-esteem, and those who garner the most support hold the self in the highest regard. Among the four sources of support that we have examined, we have repeatedly demonstrated that for older children and adolescents, classmate and parent approval constitute the best predictors of one's global worth as a person. Thus, Cooley's looking-glass self model on the origins of self-esteem appears to be clearly documented.

Moreover, our findings reveal that both James' and Cooley's formulations, taken together, provide a powerful explanation for the level of self-esteem displayed by older children and adolescents (Harter, 1987). As is evident in Figure 1, the effects of these two determinants are additive. At each level of social support (representing the average of classmate and parent approval), greater competence in domains of importance is associated with higher self-esteem. Similarly, at each level of competence in domains of importance, the more support one garners from classmates and parents, the higher one's self-esteem. Those individuals with the lowest self-esteem, therefore, are those who report both incompetence in domains of importance, and the absense of supportive approval from others.

Why should we care about self-esteem: The powerful link between self-esteem and depression.

During the past three decades, considerable attention has been devoted to an analysis of the determinants of self-esteem in the lives of children and adolescents (see Coopersmith, 1963; Harter, 1986, 1987,1990a; Rosenberg, 1979, 1986; Wylie, 1979). Yet why should we be concerned about self-esteem, unless

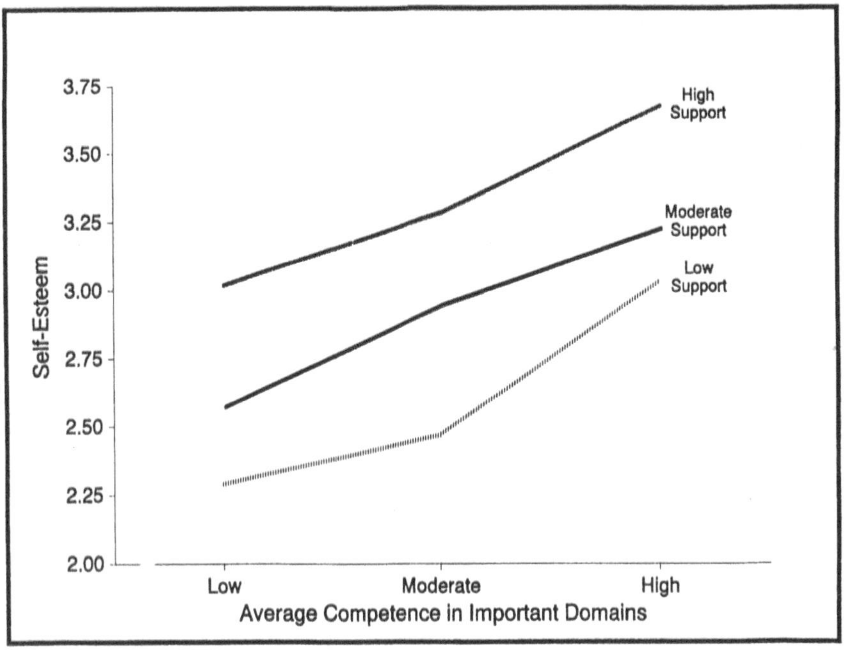

FIGURE 1. Additive influences of competence in domains of importance and social support on self-esteem.

we can demonstrate that it plays a vital role in individuals' lives, unless we can demonstrate that it performs some critical function? The efforts of numerous self-esteem researchers may well be misguided if self-esteem reduces to an epiphenomen that has little impact on the adaptiveness of one's everyday functioning.

It behooved us, therefore, to direct our attention to the potential *mediational* role of self-esteem, namely to identify constructs critical to the lives of individuals that self-esteem might impact. What are some likely candidates? What outcomes of any significance might self-esteem influence? A major candidate is one's *mood,* along the dimension of cheerful to depressed. Recent theory and research has placed increasing emphasis on cognitions that give rise to, or accompany, depression. Cognitions involving the *self* have found particular favor. There is clear historical precedent for including negative self-evaluations as one of a constellation of symptoms experienced in depression, beginning with Freud's (1968) observations of the low self-esteem displayed by adults suffering from depressive disorders. Those within the psychoanalytic tradition have continued to afford low self-esteem a central role in depression (Bibring, 1953; Blatt, 1974).

More recently a number of theorists who have addressed the manifestations of depression in children and adolescents, as well as in adults, have focused heavily on cognitive components involving the self. For example, attention has been drawn to the role of self-deprecatory ideation and hopelessness in depression (Abramson, Metalsky, & Alloy, 1989; Baumeister, 1990; Beck, 1975; Hammen

& Goodman-Brown, 1990; Kovacs & Beck, 1977, 1978, 1986), to attributional style (Abramson, Seligman, & Teasedale, 1986; Nolen-Hoeksema, Girgus, & Seligman, 1986; Seligman, 1975; Seligman & Peterson, 1986) and to cognitive and socio-cognitive influences as well as self-discrepancies (Baumeister, 1990; Higgins, 1987, 1989; Kaslow, Rehm, & Siegel, 1984; McCauley, Mitchell, Burke, & Moss, 1988; Pyszczynski & Greenberg, 1987). Higgins' work is particularly relevant since he finds that discrepancies between what one would *like* to be and what one *perceives* oneself to be produce dejection-related emotions such as depression.

In our own studies we consistently find that among older children and adolescents, self-esteem is highly related to affect, along a continuum of cheerful to depressed (with correlations ranging from .72 to .80). These findings are consistent with those of other investigators (Battle, 1987; Beck, 1975; Kaslow, Rehm, & Siegel, 1984). Of particular relevance to this chapter is our finding that older children and adolescents within our normative samples who report low self-esteem consistently report depressed affect (Renouf & Harter, 1990). Among a clinical sample of inpatient adolescents with psychiatric diagnoses of depression, we have also found a powerful link between self-esteem and self-reported depressed affect. Among those reporting depressed affect, 80% also report low self-esteem (Marold, Harter, and Whitesell, 1992).

Thus, in our original model, we concluded that the two causal constructs, competence in domains of importance and social support, served not only to impact one's level of self-esteem, but provoked a powerful emotional reaction which, for the low self-esteem child or adolescent, results in a chronic mood state of depression (see Figure 2). It should be noted this model is consistent with a number of sequential models to emerge in the 70's, models that have placed great emphasis on the mediational role of the self. The general character of these models involves the postulation of a chain of events in which self-observation leads to a cognitive self-evaluation, which in turn impacts other motivational, emotional, or behavioral systems. Such models have evolved from learning theory (Bandura, 1977, 1978), from social psychologists (Carver & Scheirer, 1981; Dweck & Elliot, 1983; Wicklynd, 1975; Wicklund & Frey, 1980), from clinicians with a cognitive-behavioral orientation (Kanfer, 1970, 1971, 1980; Kanfer & Phillips, 1970), and from personality psychologists emphasizing the primacy of cognitions over emotions (Lazarus, 1980, 1985; Weiner, 1985). However, we have begun to question the unidirectionality of such a sequence, an issue to which we shall return.

Major modifications in the original model

More recently, we have elaborated upon this basic model with regard to five particular issues, each of which will be dicussed below (see also Harter, Marold, & Whitesell, 1992). Rather than treating competence in domains of importance as but one construct, we have distinguished between two competence/

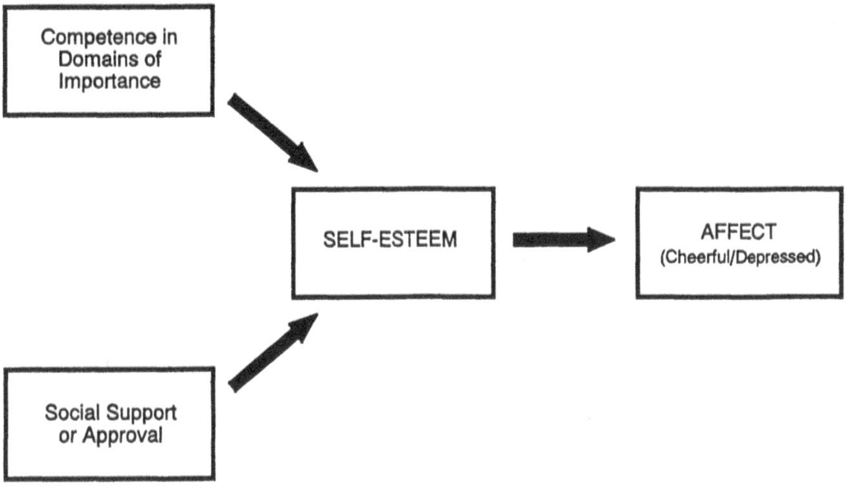

FIGURE 2. Original model of the determinants and consequences of self-esteem.

adequacy clusters of domains, (a) Physical Appearance, Peer Likability, and Athletic Competence, and (b) Scholastic Competence and Behavioral Conduct. Secondly, we have added direct paths from each of these clusters to the social support variables. Thirdly, we have added *hopelessness* to the model. A fourth modification required that we remove the hypothesized causal path between self-esteem and mood. This resulted in the creation of a *depression composite* comprised of self-esteem, depressed mood, and general hopelessness. Finally, we extended the model to include *suicidal ideation* as one potential outcome of depression, as defined by our composite. This most recent model is presented in Figure 3.

Distinction between two competence/adequacy clusters. Our findings have now revealed the existence of two distinct clusters of domains, given two empirical criteria. First, higher-order factoring of competence/adequacy subscale score reveals two discrete factors. Secondly, ratings of importance of each domain to self as well as to parents (see Harter, Marold, Whitesell, in press) for each cluster differ. The first cluster is comprised of Physical Appearance, Peer Likability, and Athletic Competence, and these domains, particularly Appearance and Likability, were judged to be more important to the self than to parents. The second cluster, comprised of Scholastic Competence and Behavior Conduct, formed a separate higher-order factor, and these two domains were judged to be more important to parents than to the self.

Links between these two clusters and social support. In our previous models designed to examine James' and Cooley's formulations (e.g., Harter, 1986, 1987, 1990), competence in domains of importance and social support were treated as independent contributors to self-esteem, and thus paths from the self-concept variables to social support were not included. However, a plausible hypothesis is

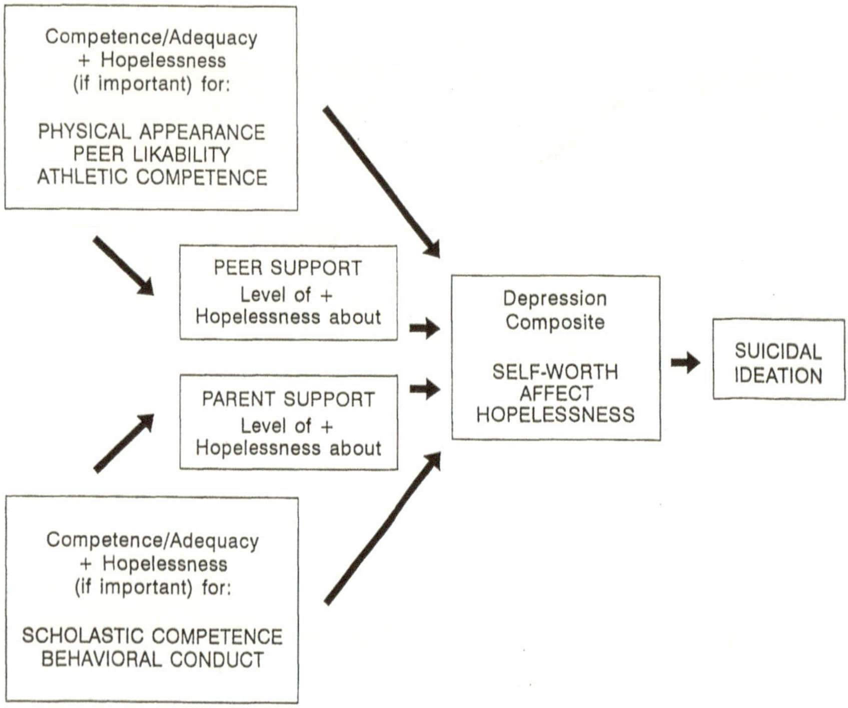

FIGURE 3. Revised model including determinants, depression composite, and suicidal ideation.

that one's level of competence or adequacy directly impacts the amount of support that one receives from significant others. More specifically, our findings demonstrate that the first cluster, comprised of Appearance, Likability, and Athletic Competence bears a stronger relationship to peer support than to parent support. As can be seen in the model (Figure 3), there is a direct path from this cluster to peer support reflecting the fact that the more good-looking, likable, and athletically competent one feels one is, the more one reports support, in the form of approval, from peers.

Not surprisingly, the cluster comprised of Scholastic Competence and Behavioral Conduct, judged more important to parents than the self, bears a stronger relationship to parent support than to peer support. Thus, if one evaluates the self positively in those arenas valued by parents, one also experiences greater parental approval.

Hopelessness. Following the lead of Beck (1967, 1975, 1987) and his colleagues (Kovacs & Beck, 1977, 1978), we further broadened our nomological network of constructs to include hopelessness, since hopelessness and helplessness have now been clearly implicated in depressive reactions (see also Seligman, 1975). We have included hopelessness at two levels, namely general hopelessness as well as feelings of hopelessness associated with each specific self-concept domain and source of social support. With regard to *general* hopelessness, namely the perception that one's overall future appears uncompromisingly bleak, we have discovered that such hopelessness is highly correlated (r's in the .70's) with global self-esteem as well as with depressed affect. As a result, we have combined these three constructs into what we have labelled the "depression composite".

With regard to *specific* feelings of hopelessness, our earlier research has revealed that perceptions of hopelessness for each of the domains and sources of support included in the model are highly correlated with self-reported levels of competence/adequacy and social support (Harter & Marold, 1990). Thus, if one evaluates the self as incompetent in domains where success is highly valued, or if one experiences low levels of social support, one is also highly likely to feel hopeless about the possibility of ever achieving competence or of obtaining support. For the purposes of statistical modeling, therefore, the constructs at the front end of the model were defined as a combination of level and hopelessness.

The introduction of the depression composite. In our earlier modeling efforts, a central feature was the inferred causal path from self-esteem to affect. As described above, we postulated, consistent with the prevailing models, that cognitions about the self directly impacted affect, such that if one was favored with high self-esteem, cheerfulness would constitute an affective consequence, whereas low self-esteem would provoke feelings of depression. The initial application of causal modeling techniques to our data revealed that such a model provided an excellent fit (Harter & Hogan, 1985; Harter, 1986). However, the mandate governing a thoughtful, comprehensive approach to the use of such statistical procedures requires that one test alternative models, particularly those in which the directionality of effects is reversed.

In our most recent modeling efforts, therefore, we have adopted this approach. In comparing such alternative models, we have discovered that if we reverse the order of self-esteem and affect, such that affect is treated as causally *prior* to self-esteem, this model fits the data just as well as our original model. This outcome should not be surprising, given that the correlation between self-esteem and affect has ranged from .70 to .80 across studies. Moreover, both self-esteem and affect correlate equally highly with the postulated antecedents in the model. Therefore, on balance, there were no compelling statistical grounds for asserting that the original directionality, although theoretically derived, truly captured the actual sequence of events.

In light of this discovery, it was incumbant upon us to remove the path from self-esteem to affect. As an alternative strategy, we created the Depression Composite, comprised of self-esteem, affect, and general hopelessness, given that hopelessness also correlates highly with both self-esteem and affect, as described above. The creation of the depression composite is not merely a statistical solution, given the multicolinearity of these constructs. Rather, the three constructs that comprise this composite appear to be critical to the identification of individuals at risk for depression. While there may be different antecedents or *pathways* to depression for different individuals, (a point to which we shall return), a low score on the depression composite for any individual constitutes a psychological red flag that may well be of diagnostic significance.

Suicidal ideation. Finally, we extended our model to one potential outcome, suicidal ideation. The incidence of suicide among adolescents has tripled in recent decades, leading to efforts to identify the determinants of this major mental health threat to our youth (see Maris, 1985; Pfeffer, 1986, 1988; ADAMHA's report from the Secretary's Task Force on Youth Suicide, 1989). Several broad classes of risk factors implicated in depression and suicidal behaviors have captured the attention of researchers, including biological precursors, epidemiological correlates, and social/psychological stressors. We have been particularly committed to an examination of the third class of risk factors. Evidence to date has revealed a constellation of social/psychological correlates that are predictive of suicidal behavior including depressed affect, poor self-concept in particular domains, real-ideal discrepancies, low self-esteem, hopelessness, and lack of social support (see Baumeister, 1990; Carlson & Cantwell, 1982; Cicchetti & Schneider-Rosen, 1986; Pfeffer, Conte, Plutchick & Jerrett, 1979; Marold, 1987; Pfeffer, 1986; Rutter, Izard & Read, 1985).

From a developmental perspective, these particular risk factors become increasingly salient as one moves into adolescence (see Emery, 1983). Self-awareness, self-consciousness, introspectiveness and preoccupation with one's self-image dramatically increase (see review by Harter, 1990). Self-esteem becomes more vulnerable (Rosenberg, 1986), and adolescents become more aware of the relationship between self-esteem, social support, and depressed affect (Harter, Marold & Jackson, 1991). With regard to the support system, the impact of peer support increases dramatically (Brown, 1990; Savin-Williams & Berndt, 1990). Although young adolescents are beginning to make bids for autonomy from parents, they are nevertheless struggling to remain connected (Cooper, Grotevant & Condon, 1983; Grotevant & Cooper, 1986; Steinberg, 1990), and thus parent support continues to be critical.

Depressive symptomatology itself increases in adolescence (see Carlson & Cantwell, 1982; Rutter, Izard, & Read, 1985; Sroufe & Rutter, 1985; Shaffer, 1985), and certain associated features such as hopelessness take on increasing importance since they require a level of cognitive functioning that is not completely developed in younger children (Carlson & Garber, 1986; Kendall, Cantwell & Kazdin, 1989; Rutter, 1988; Shaffer, 1985). Finally, suicidal behaviors themselves increase dramatically during adolescence (Carlson & Cantwell, 1982; Cantor, 1987; Hawton, 1986; Pfeffer, 1988; Shaffer, 1974, 1985; Shaffer & Fischer, 1981).

While there is a growing body of evidence on the *correlates* of suicidal behaviors, relatively little attention has been directed toward the development of theory-based *models* that identify risk factors representing the antecedents as well as mediators of suicidal behaviors. As Spirato, Brown, Overholser and Fritz (1989) have observed, we are particularly in need of models that consider antecedent stresses such as family, peer, and school problems, and that include emotional and cognitive states (e.g., depression and hopelessness) that may mediate outcomes such as suicidal behaviors.

Moreover, recently it has been urged that the field take seriously the study of suicidal behavior and its correlates in *normative* populations of young adolescents (Garrison, 1989). Historically, suicide research has focussed on clinical populations. More recently, investigators have demonstrated the fruitfulness of examining the prevalence and antecedents of suicidal behaviors among normative populations including college students (Bonner & Rich, 1987; Rudd, 1989), high school students (Smith & Crawford, 1986) and preadolescents (Pfeffer, Lipkins, Plutchick & Mizruchi, 1988; Pferrer, Zuckerman, Plutchick & Mizruchi, 1984). The period of early adolescence has received relatively little empirical attention. Thus, we sought to extend our efforts, with the goal of determining how the factors we had identified to date, namely domain specific self-concepts in areas deemed important, peer and parent social support, and the depression composite (self-esteem, depressed affect, and general hopelessness) might function as antecedents and mediators of suicidal ideation in young adolescents.

In extending our model to include suicidal ideation, we have begun to address the links between these constructs, asking the question of what provokes many among our youth to even consider terminating their lives. What cognitive and socio-emotional processes conspire to convince an adolescent that life is not worth living? What role do self-representations play in this intrapsychic plot that has such a potentially tragic outcome? What features of the adolescent's socialization history cause one to question one's worth as a person, and the worth of one's life?

The sequential model in Figure 3, which provides an excellent fit to the data (see Harter, Marold, & Whitesell, 1992) provides a number of clues. Self-evaluations of inadequacy with regard to one's appearance and one's likability, domains judged important to the self as well as to one's peers, appear to attenuate peer support, both of which impact the depression composite, i.e., both of which provoke the personally devastating combination of low self-esteem, depressed affect, and general hopelessness. Perceptions of scholastic incompetence as well as negative evaluations of one's behavioral conduct precipitate parental disapproval, and both feelings of inadequacy in conjunction with lack of parent support, in turn, impact the depression composite. The constellation of low self-esteem, depressed affect, and hopelessness, in turn, drives many to consider suicide as a solution, as a form of escape from the painful cognitions and affects concerning the self and the disapproving reactions of others (see also Baumeister, 1990).

The following poignant self-disclosure by one of the adolescents in our studies provides a personal cameo of the model that has evolved in our research:

"I look in the mirror and most days I don't like what I see, I don't like how I look, I don't like myself as a person. So I get depressed, bummed out. Plus, my family has rejected me and that makes me feel pretty lousy about myself. My mother is really on my case because I'm not living up to what she wants me to be. If I get A's in school, she's nice and is proud of me, but if I don't, she doesn't approve of me, you could say how she treats me is conditional on how I do. Mostly she tells me I'm a failure, and I'm beginning to believe it. Doing well in school has always been important to me, but now I feel like I'll never amount to anything. There's no way I'll ever be able to please her, its pretty hopeless. I don't get much support from other kids either. I probably never will because I'm an introvert, I don't even try to make friends. So a lot of the time I get depressed, really bummed out. When I'm depressed I feel sad, becaue other people have hurt me, but I'm also angry at them too, for not caring, for rejecting me. I feel so depressed that I often think about just killing myself. Life is worthless. But so is death. So what's the use."

Our adolescent narrator identifies each of the features in our sequential process model predisposing him to thoughts of suicide. He is dissatisfied with his appearance, his outer self, leading him to denigrate himself as a person, to question his essential worth as a human being. As an introvert, he questions his likability, acknowledging that he receives little support from peers. He is dissatisfied with his scholastic performance, a domain that he values, as does his mother who considers him a failure, a view that he has begun to internalize, leading him to devalue himself further. Interestingly, he labels her reactions as "conditional" (a concept to which we shall return), and such reactions further contribute to his feelings of worthlessness. This constellation of precursors ushers in very intense feelings of depression and hopelessness. The toll exacted is tortuous, as he wrestles with the question of whether to kill himself and with the uselessness of both his life and death.

Further insights gleaned from interviews with adolescents.

In our interviews with adolescents (from our normative samples) whom we have considered at risk, as defined by low scores on the depression composite, a number of intriguing new themes have emerged. The first, gleaned from self-disclosures such as the one just reported, involves the perceived *conditionality* of parent support. Such support is only forthcoming if the adolescent meets seemingly high performance standards set by the parents. A second theme, also identified in this same adolescent's account, makes reference to the experience of depression as not only profound sadness, but an emotion blend of sadness plus *anger.* Thirdly, these interviews have revealed that adolescents identify, as the primary causes of their depression, actions of *others against the self.*

Finally, adolescents' portrayals of the link between self-esteem and depressed affect reveal that in their phenomenological experience, one component does precede the other sequentially. More specifically, the revelation is that for some adolescents, self-esteem is reported to *precede* and provoke depressed affect, whereas for other adolescents the experience of depressed affect is the springboard to feelings of low self-esteem. For example, the youth whom we quoted above exemplifies the first orientation; when he looks in the mirror, he doesn't like how he looks, he doesn't like himself as a person, which in turn causes him to become depressed. In contrast, other adolescents gave vivid accounts of equally painful events in which significant others reject the self, leading them first to inevitable feelings of depression, followed by disdain for the self as a person. The next step, therefore, in our programmatic effort to better understand the causes and consequences of depression among adolescents was to empirically examine each of these themes more systematically. Moreover, we sought to determine the relationships among these constructs, in suggesting more differentiated models that would illuminate different pathways to depression. We explore these efforts next.

Conditionality of support.

In the detailed narrative cameo that was quoted earlier, this troubled adolescent complained that "if I get A's in school, my mother is nice and is proud of me, but if I don't, she doesn't approve of me, you could say how she treats me is conditional on how I do". In other interviews, adolescents also voiced their distress over the fact that parents only displayed their support if the adolecent met (typically high and seemingly unreasonable) parental standards of performance. In addition, adolescents identified the contingencies governing conditional *peer* support, namely that approval from age-mates would only be forthcoming if one met certain standards of behavior, attitudes, dress, etc. Thus, not only level but *type* of support emerged as a potential predictor in our network of constructs.

Following the descriptive lead of our adolescent interviewees, we first defined conditionality of support as the extent to which one feels that support is only forthcoming if one meets high parental or peer standards; we have contrasted it to unconditional positive regard (see Rogers & Dymond, 1954) in which one is loved or supported for who one is as a person, not for whether one fulfills the expectations of others. We operationally defined these constructs, writing items in our structured alternative format where we pitted conditional against unconditional support. Thus, a sample item would read: Some parents only support their kids if they do exactly what their parents want or expect BUT Other parents support their kids even if they don't do exactly what their parents want or expect. The respondent's task is to select which of these statements describes his/her own parents, after which they indicate whether that statement is Really True or Sort of True about one's parents.

Our findings (Harter, Marold, Whitesell, 1992) indicate that *level* of support and *conditionality* of support are correlated with one another, such that parents and peers who provide little support are also likely to to be perceived as only offering their support contingent upon the display of behaviors and attitudes that they demand. However, we have also demonstrated the damaging effects of conditionality on self-esteem, when level of support is controlled. In Figure 4, it can be observed that not only does level of support (high versus low) dramatically impact self-esteem, but that within each of these levels, the more conditional the perceived support, the lower one's self-esteem.

We are speculating that conditionality, even at relatively high levels of support, undermines self-esteem because it does *not* validate or signify approval of the self. That is, it does not communicate genuine support for who one is as a person. Rather, it serves to specify behavioral contingencies through which one

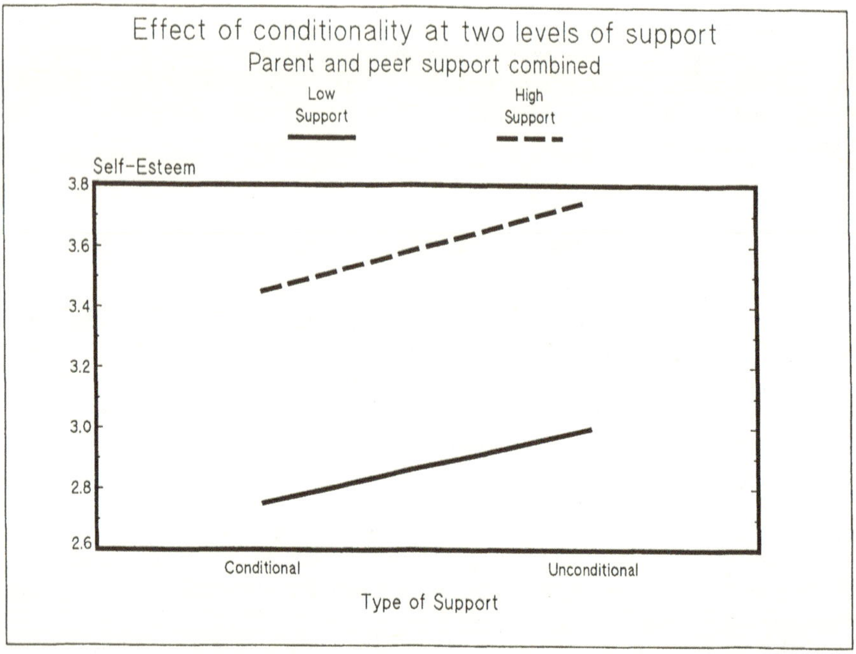

FIGURE 4. Impact of level and conditionality of support on self-esteem.

can please parents or peers. As such, it is undoubtedly interpreted as controlling, rather than enhancing (see Deci & Ryan, 1985). A similar pattern is obtained when we use *depression* composite scores as the dependent measure. Thus, conditionality of support not only undermines one's self-esteem but contributes to depressed mood as well as general hopelessness.

Depressed affect as a combination of sadness and anger.

The adolescent whom we quoted at length lamented that "when I am depressed I feel sad, because other people have hurt me, but I'm also angry at them too, for not caring, for rejecting me". Other adolescents voiced similar accounts of their emotional experience when depressed. In a pilot interview study of twelve adolescents from our normative sample who indicated that they frequently experienced depression, 11 of the 12 spontaneously mentioned that when they were in this emotional state, they felt angry or frustrated, in addition to feeling overwhelmingly sad (Harter & Whitesell, 1988).

According to Freudian (1968) theory, depression is experienced by adults as an affective combination of both sadness and anger. The primary emotion of sadness, typically over the loss of a significant other, is accompanied by anger or rage at being abandoned. However, since it is often impossible or inappropriate to direct such anger toward the lost other, it is defensively directed toward the self.

Within the more recent clinical literature, increasing attention has been paid to the co-occurrence of sadness and anger (see Curran, 1987; Gispert, Davis, Marsh, & Wheeler, 1987; Khan, 1987; Rutter, 1989). Moreover, the comorbidity of depressive features and conduct disorder symptoms among certain subgroups of children and adolescents also speaks to the combination of emotions reflecting both sadness and anger (see Puig-Antich, 1982; Shaffer, 1974; Withers & Kaplan, 1987).

Within the developmental literature, recent attention has been devoted to the experience of *mixed emotions* (Donaldson & Westerman, 1986; Harris, 1983; Harter & Buddin, 1987; Harter & Whitesell, 1988). These findings indicate that by middle childhood, children acknowledge the simultaneous occurrence of a variety of emotion combinations, including sadness and anger. Thus, it seemed fruitful to extend our inquiry to the phenomenological experience of depression as an emotion blend among young adolescents.

Based on these considerations, we anticipated that among a normative sample, most young adolescents would report that they experience depression as a mix of sadness and anger. With regard to the anger component, a critical question involves the particular target or object of anger. Is anger directed toward the *self*, as psychoanalytic formulations would imply (Asch, 1966; Bibring, 1953; Fenichel, 1945; Freud, 1968; Sandler & Joffe, 1965), or toward *others*? Recent clinical observations of adolescents by Cantor (1987) and Pfeffer (Pfeffer, 1986; Pfeffer, Zuckerman, Plutchick, & Mirzruchi, 1984) suggest that at this particular developmental level, depression is often manifest as anger toward others. Based on these observations, as well as on our own pilot studies, we predicted that, in describing the emotions they experience when depressed, the majority of young adolescents would report anger toward others, either as the primary target or in combination with anger directed toward the self.

Our first hypothesis, namely that the majority of adolescents would report anger, in addition to sadness, was supported. Eighty percent of the students sampled selected sadness and anger as the two emotions they most typically experienced when they were depressed. These findings suggest that depression in early adolescence is best characterized as an emotion blend, consistent with several theoretical approaches noted above, including the general psychoanalytic formulation (Freud, 1968), developmental theory emphasizing the emergence of the ability to experience two emotions simultaneously (Harter & Whitesell, 1988), and the recent emphasis on comorbidity (i.e., internalizing and externalizing symptoms or disorders, concurrently) within the clinical literature (Curran, 1987; Gispert et al., 1987; Khan, 1987; Rutter, 1989).

Of further interest was the particular target of anger. We hypothesized, based on the observations of Cantor (1987) and Pfeffer (1986) as well as on our own pilot work, that the majority of adolescents would report anger toward others, either as the primary target of this emotion, or in combination with anger directed toward the self. Consistent with these predictions, 39% of the adolescents in our sample reported anger toward others, whereas 40% reported anger toward both others and the self (Renouf & Harter, 1990). These results suggest that there may be at least two patterns of interest. In the first, profound sadness in consort with anger toward others, only, defines the experience of depression. In the second, sadness is accompanied by anger directed toward two targets, other as well as self. These two patterns may have implications for symptomatology and treatment. The first group, primarily experiencing anger toward others when depressed, may be more prone to conduct problems, including aggression toward others. The second group, who experience anger toward the self in addition to anger against others, may be more prone to self-injurious behaviors, including suicidal thoughts or attempts. Moreover, these different pattterns may bear links to the perceived causes of depression, as well as to the sequence in which self-esteem and depressed affect are experienced, both of which are discussed below.

The perceived causes of depression.

From a developmental perspective, it is noteworthy that adolescents within a normative sample do not report the emotional experience more predictable from the psychoanalytic perspective on adult depression, namely that anger would be primarily directed toward the self. In an attempt to unravel this seeming discrepancy, we next directed our empirical attention to the reported *causes* of depression among young adolescents.

We began with open-ended interviews, asking subjects to "think back to the most depressing thing that has happened to you in the past year" and then to decribe that event. The majority of adolescents' responses fell into the following eight categories:

(1) Psychological harm to the self by others, e.g., Someone made me feel bad. They hurt my feelings, teased me, or did something that made me feel bad.
(2) Physical harm to the self by others, e.g., Someone physically hurt me or did something to stuff that I own. They beat me up, hit me, broke or stole something that was mine.
(3) Death of someone close, e.g., Someone important to me died, for example, a family member, a friend, or a pet.
(4) Separation from someone close, e.g., Someone important to me went away. My parents got divorced, a friend moved away or a friend and I brok up with each other (this could also be a boy or girl friend).
(5) Conflict with someone close, e.g., I was not getting along with someone important to me. I was fighting with my parents, brothers or sisters, friends, boy or girl friend.
(6) Rejection by someone close, e.g., I felt rejected by someone important to me. Parents, brother or sister, a friend, a boy or girl friend, kids at school didn't want to be with me.
(7) Loneliness, e.g., I felt lonely and wished I had a friend or a boy or girl friend, or more friends than I had.

(8) Incompetence of the self, e.g., I did badly in something or messed up, or there was something I didn't like about myself. I got bad grades, did something dumb, messed up in sports, or didn't like something about the way I was.

Of interest is that the vast majority of causes generated by adolescents involve negative actions of *others toward the self*, i.e., various forms of psychological and physical harm or insult. (Only the last category explicitly makes reference to negative actions *by* the self.) Intuitively, therefore, it is plausible that adolescents would experience depression as anger toward others. To examine this issue empirically, we next asked a sample of young adolescents to report the level of anger toward others and anger toward the self that they would experience, for each of the eight causes (Renouf & Harter, 1990). Table 1 presents anger scores, where a 4 represents the highest, and a 1 the lowest, level of anger.

As would be expected, the first six causes, clearly representing actions of others against the self, provoked significantly more anger toward others than toward the self. (Loneliness produced only somewhat more anger toward others, and, as anticipated, incompetence by the self produced no differences in anger toward others and the self.) With regard to the first six categories, therefore, the majority of adolescents presumably view others as more responsible than the self for the outcomes of these events, provoking anger directed toward others. It is of interest, in this regard, that recent studies of clinical samples of depressed adolescents have revealed that at this particular developmental level, anger toward others is quite common (Cantor, 1987; Pfeffer, 1986). One could speculate that adolescents may not yet have developed the inhibitions or defenses that would prevent them from expressing their feelings toward the significant others whom they consider to be the cause of their depression-related anger.

In future research, it would be of interest to determine the primary causes of depression for an adult population, including the level of anger directed toward the self and others, in order to determine whether there is a developmental shift between adolescence and adulthood. Adults may well assume more responsibility for their role in negative social interactions and direct greater anger toward

TABLE 1 Anger at Others and at Self as a Function of the Particular Cause of Depression.

Cause	Anger/Other	Anger/Self
Psychological harm to self by others	3.04	1.81
Physical harm to self by others	3.54	2.45
Death of close significant other	3.03	2.45
Separation from significant other	3.19	2.29
Conflict with significant other	3.29	2.50
Rejection by significant other	3.00	2.47
Loneliness	3.12	2.75
Incompetence of self	2.89	2.78

the self, consistent with the psychoanalytic position. Alternatively, adults may *experience* anger toward others, but are less likely to *express* it. That is, adults may have developed stronger defenses or inhibitions against the display of angry or aggressive impulses toward others. For example, several researchers have reported suppressed anger and hostility in depressed adults (Biaggio & Godwin, 1987; Frank, Carpenter, & Kupfer, 1988; Riley, Treiber, & Woods, 1989). These issues deserve further study, however, since they suggest that the experience and/or the expression of the components of depression, particularly with regard to the target of anger, may well undergo developmental change between adolescence and adulthood.

Perceived directionality of self-esteem and depressed affect.

As described in an earlier section, in the initial model that provided the impetus for our work, we made the assumption, consistent with a variety of sequential models in the field, that the self-evaluative (cognitive) components *preceded* one's affective reactions. Thus, we postulated that self-esteem would be experienced prior to, and would therefore impact, one's emotional reaction of cheerfulness or depression. However, two sources of evidence have cautioned us against making the assumption that such a sequence describes the experiences of all individuals. As noted earlier, a comparison of alternative models through the application of structural equation techniques has demonstrated that a model in which there is a direct path from depressed affect to self-esteem fits the data just as well as the original model in which the path was defined as self-esteem to depressed affect. Moreover, interview data have revealed that many adolescents experience the depressive affective component prior to low self-esteem.

Our interest in this issue is paralleled, broadly, by recent trends with the field of emotion, where a new thrust has concerned links between cognition and affect (Frijda, 1986; Hoffman, 1986; Izard, 1983; Lazarus, 1980, 1984; Leventhal & Scherer, 1987; Weiner, 1985; Zajonc, 1980, 1984). A major debate has surrounded the primacy of these two systems. The most representative proponents of the two camps are Zajonc (1980, 1984) who has argued for the primacy of *affect*, and Lazarus (1980, 1984) whose position emphasizes the primacy of *cognition.* Weiner (1985) also represents the latter tradition, given his position that self-attributions give rise to distinct emotional states, depending on the specific nature of the attribution. We, too, fell victim to the mentality that one direction took precedence, initially espousing the view that the cognition judgments inherent in self-esteem preceded the affect of depression.

However, proponents of both positions have come to realize that the *directionality* of these links will vary, depending on the particular emotions and cognitions in question, e.g., primary versus secondary or socialized emotions, conscious versus unconscious cognitive processes, etc., as well as on particular developmental and individual difference factors (see Leventhal & Scherer, 1987). We concur with the revisionist stance. Our interview data, followed by a more systematic empirical inquiry described below, have required that we alter our position, acknowledging that the directionality of the link between self-esteem and depressed affect will differ across individuals. For some, low self-esteem will first be experienced, whereas for others, the depressive affect will occur prior to low self-esteem.

Recently, we have developed a methodology that holds promise for assessing this distinction (Harter & Jackson, 1993; Harter, Marold, & Jackson, 1991). Adolescents are given the task of deciding *Which Comes First.* They are initially provided with a description in which they are told that students their age often feel that "not liking yourself" and "feeling depressed" go together. However, some students feel that not liking yourself comes first, whereas other students first feel depressed. The subjects are asked to reflect upon whether they first feel that they do not like themselves or, alternatively, whether they first feel that they are depressed. Specifically, they are asked to pick one of the following two options: (1) I *first* feel *depressed* and *then* that makes me feel like I don't like myself or (2) I *first* feel like *I don't like myself* and *then* that makes me feel depressed. After they pick the option that best characterizes their own experience, they are asked to provide a brief written description of an event that represents an example of the sequence they selected.

The findings have been intriguing. First, with regard to the percentages of students endorsing each option, across several studies we have discovered that approximately half of a given sample indicates that the depression component is experienced first, whereas the remaining half indicate that the self-esteem component precedes their experience of depression. Moreover, in both normative as well as clinical samples of adolescents who report that they are depressed, approximately two-thirds of those in the low self-esteem to depressed affect directionality group are females, whereas the percentages reverse themselves in the depressed affect to low self-esteem group where two-thirds are males.

Content analyses have been illuminating, in that the experiences these adolescents describe directly match their choices, providing converging evidence for the meaningfulness of the directionality concept (Harter, Marold, & Jackson, 1991). There is little overlap in the content of causes or antecedents for each sequence, further suggesting that the distinction between each directionality orientation is very real. What particular causes are cited by members of each group?

Low self-esteem precedes depressed affect. Students identifying themselves as experiencing this directionality (Group A) cited examples in which they were dissatisfied with particular *self*-attributes. Three categories consistently emerge across samples: (1) *Physical appearance* heads the list, in that between two-thirds to three-fourths of subjects (typically more females than males) report that they are dissatisfied with some aspect of their looks, e.g., "When I try to do something with my face and hair and it doesn't work out and I think I'm ugly, then I get depressed." (2) Lack of *competence* is the next most prevalent category, e.g., "I watch the people in sports do what seems to be an easy sport and then when I try it, it doesn't even *look like* the sport so I get depressed." (3) Dissatisfaction with one's behavior or conduct in *social interactions* is the third most common category, e.g., "First I think I'm not a good friend, and then that makes me feel depressed." A more complete list of examples is provided in

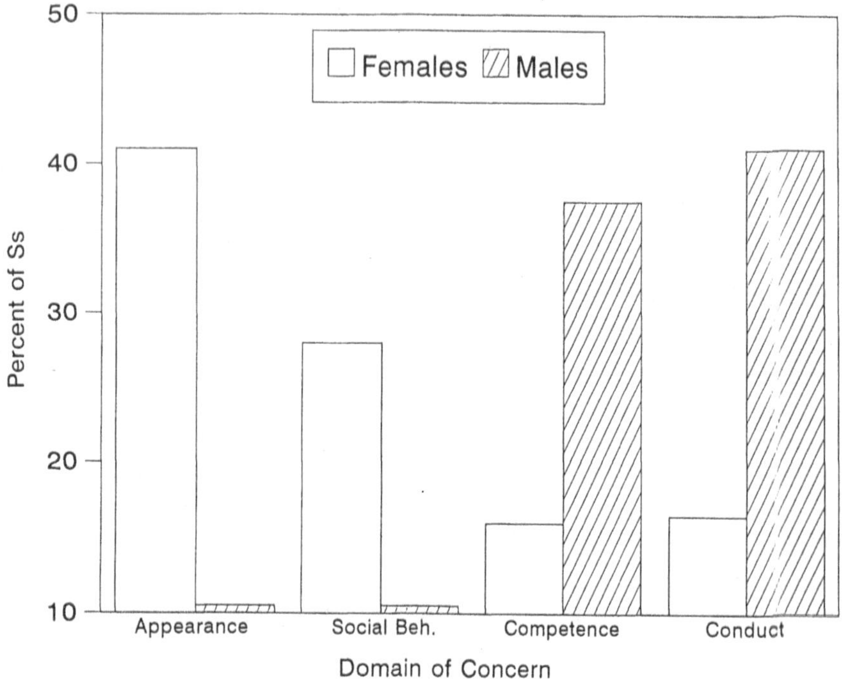

FIGURE 5. Gender differences in the particular concerns decribed by adolescents.

Table 2. Thus, the *causes* of depression for adolescents in this directionality group reside in an attribution that finds the self inadequate, incompetent or wanting.

Interestingly, we find gender differences in the particular themes or concerns that adolescents describe (see Figure 5). Girls are significantly more likely to find fault with their *appearance* and their *social behavior* (how they treat significant others with whom they have a relationship) than are boys, whereas the boys cite examples of *incompetence* (typically sports or scholastic performance) and *conduct* (behaving in ways that are not morally sanctioned, e.g., hitting, lying, stealing, acting out, etc.). These findings are consistent with the gender socialization literature revealing that females are particularly attuned to issues involving appearance (Allgood-Merton, Lewihsohn, & Hops, 1990; Harter, in press: Nolen-Hoeksema, 1987; Simmon & Blyth, 1987), as well as relationships and the ethics of caring (Chodorow, 1989) Gilligan, 1982; Huston, 1983; Miller, 1986). Males, on the other hand, are more concerned with achievement and related competencies (Huston, 1983; Miezdian, 1990) as well as more rule-bound principles of ethical conduct (Gilligan, 1982; Gilligan, Ward, & Taylor, 1988).

Depressed affect precedes low self-esteem. In contrast to the group above, adolescents for whom the experience of depressed affect comes first (Group B) invariably described actions performed by *others against the self.* The vast majority

TABLE 2 Examples of descriptions for each directionality orientation.

GROUP A. LOW SELF-ESTEEM PRECEDES DEPRESSED AFFECT

Appearance

When I try to do something with my face and hair and it doesn't work out and I think I'm ugly, then I get depressed.

I didn't like it that I was short, so I became depressed.

I don't like the way I look and then I get depressed because I think I can't change.

When I look in the mirror I think I am ugly and then I feel depressed.

When I can't do my hair the way I want it, and it isn't cute, and then it makes me depressed.

I look in the mirror and don't like something about me, my hair, my body, and I get depressed.

My nose and my feet are too big, and then I look at other people's and its depressing.

Competence

I watch the people in sports do what seems to be an easy sport and then when I try it, it doesn't even *look like* the sport so I get depressed.

Once I was trying to draw something and I couldn't do it so I hated myself and then I got depressed.

I mess up at my school work and then I hate myself and get depressed about it. I'm capable, but I just don't work hard enough.

I was pitching, and the first two batters I walked, and then I hit the third one with the ball, and then the coach took me out. I was really down on myself and felt depressed the rest of the game.

I played really bad at soccer and felt like the loss was my fault, so it made me depressed.

Social Behavior

First I think I'm not a good friend, and then that makes me feel depressed.

I disobeyed my mom and didn't do my chores, and felt bad about it, and depressed.

I blew up at my best friend. I get mad at myself for losing my temper and then I felt depressed.

I first feel like I don't like myself because I yelled at my mom and then I felt depressed.

GROUP B. DEPRESSED AFFECT PRECEDES LOW SELF-ESTEEM

Rejection

I was feeling depressed because all of my friends went to the amusement park, and they acted like they didn't want me to go with them. Then I felt like I was a boring person and I didn't like myself.

I got depressed because I felt left out of something and then I feel like I don't have any friends and that nobody likes me and then I didn't like myself.

I got depressed because people called me a nerd, half of the people *I know* say I'm a nerd, so I don't like myself and how I act.

My mom got on my case because of my grades, and said she was really disappointed in me, which made me depressed, and then I got disappointed in myself.

TABLE 2 (continued)

Conflict

Every time I get into it with my mom, she always yells at me and then I get depressed and think of things that make me hate myself.

I got depressed because I got into a fight with my friend, and thought I wasn't a good person.

My mom got really mad at me for not doing my chores; at first I got mad, and then I became depressed about it, and wondered if I was a good person or not.

Loss

I usually get depressed because I can't accept my father's dying and then I usually feel that its my fault that he died and I don't like myself.

My grandfather died, and I thought it was my fault cause I didn't visit him often enough.

My boyfriend broke up with me, and I got really depressed; I wasn't sure what happened, what I had done, and I felt terrible about myself.

My parents got divorced, and my dad moved out, and it made me really depressed, and I didn't like myself as much as before.

of responses could be captured by three categories (that do not overlap with the categories described by the first group). (1) The most common was *rejection* by others, e.g., "I was feeling depressed because all of my friends went to the amusement park, and they acted like they didn't want me to go with them. Then I felt like I was a boring person and I didn't like myself." (2) *Conflict* with others, typically parents, represented another major category, e.g., "Every time I get into it with my mom, she always yells at me and then I get depressed and think of things that make me hate myself." (3) Experiences of *loss* of a person or pet, either through death or the termination of a relationship, represents the third most common category, e.g., "I usually get depressed because I can't accept my father's dying and then I usually feel that its my fault that he died and I don't like myself."

A more complete list, representing the range of examples, is provided in Table 2. In our most recent study, we employed a checklist procedure allowing us to examine the pattern of causes more systematically (Harter, Harter & Jackson, in press). *Peer* rejection and conflict were by far the most common causes of depressed affect (58%), followed by *parent* conflict or rejection (13%) and *loss* (13%). There were no gender differences in this pattern.

Correlates of directionality group membership. The findings presented above document the fact that adolescents in each directionality group systematically cite a different cluster of causes. These differences further suggested that the two groups may predictably be distinguished on a number of *correlates*, specifically, physical appearance and support or approval from significant others. We were particularly interested in those students who were below the midpoint on both depression and self-esteem, since these individuals were more likely to have experienced depressed affect, low self-esteem, and their co-occurrence. Thus, we identified a subgroup of adolescents from our normative sample whose scores on our affect and self-esteem subscales were 2.5 or below (on these four-point

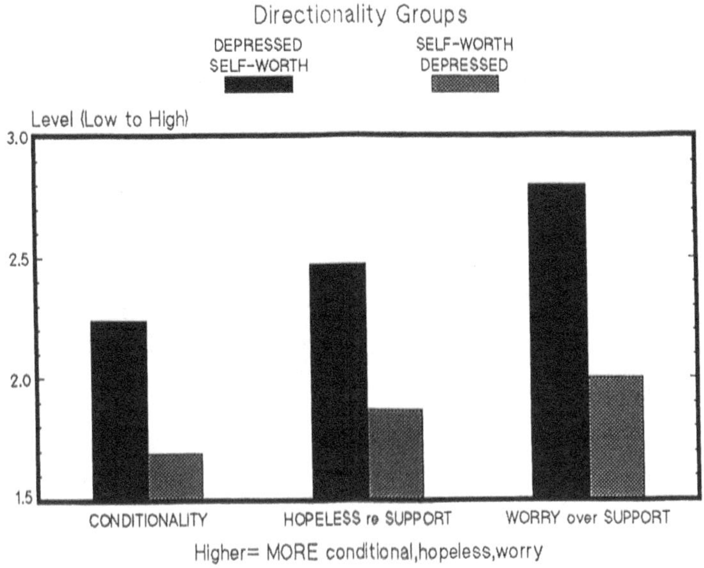

FIGURE 6. Directionality group differences for appearance variables.

scales). The two directionality groups had equally low scores on both self-esteem and depressed affect.

Given that the vast majority of individuals in the low self-esteem to depressed affect directionality group cite concerns over their physical appearance as the primary cause of their low self-esteem, we predicted that on our standardized questionnaires tapping appearance-related issues, this group would report higher levels of concern compared to those in the depressed affect to self-esteem directionality group. The results supported our prediction in that the low self-esteem to depressed affect group reported greater hopelessness about appearance, more concern over their appearance, and a greater link between appearance and popularity, namely that how one looks is a major determinant of one's popularity (see Figure 6).

Given that the depressed affect to low self-esteem directionality group cited examples of actions of the others against the self, we predicted that this group would have lower scores on variables tapping support or approval from significant others than would those in the low self-esteem to depressed affect group. Measures of five such variables, for four sources of support, peers, mother, father, were included in our battery: (a) level of support, (b) conditionality of support, (c) hopelessness about support, (d) worry over support, and (e) worry over being likable (by peers, only).

Figures 7 and 8 present the findings for peer and mother support (there were no significant differences for father support). As can be seen in Figure 7, the depressed to low self-esteem group reported more *conditional* peer support, more

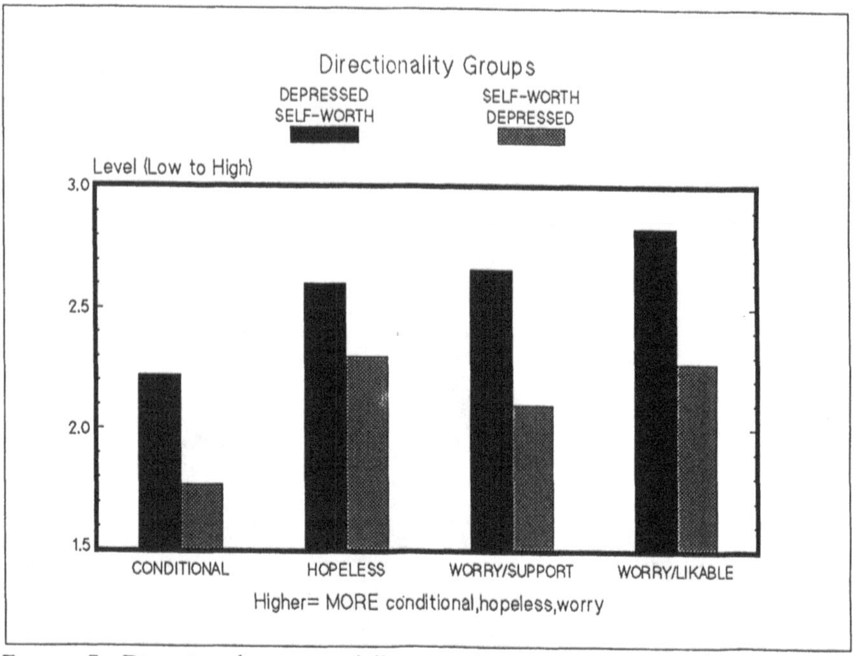

FIGURE 7. Directionality group differences for peer support variables.

hopelessness about peer support, greater *worry* over peer support, as well as greater worry about whether they were likable by peers. Level of support, per se, did not differentiate the two groups. Figure 8 documents a similar pattern for *maternal* support. Those in the depressed to low self-esteem group reported more *conditional* support, more *hopelessness* about support, and greater *worry* over support from mother. As with peer support, the actual level of maternal support did not differentiate the groups.

Thus, not only do the two groups clearly differ on the concerns that provoke their experience of directionality, but they can be predictably distinguished with regard to appearance-related concerns as well as peer and maternal social support variables. The converging evidence provided by the differences obtained further argue for the meaningfulness of directionality group membership.

Finally, we anticipated group differences in the *affects* experienced as part of the depressive experience. Both groups were expected to report high levels of *sadness*, i.e., sadness should *not* differentiate the two groups. However, the two directionality groups should differ on anger toward the self and anger toward others. We predicted that the low self-esteem to depressed affect group, given their focus on dissatisfaction with attributes of the self, would report greater anger at the *self*, as well as greater shame, than would the depressed to low self-esteem group. Given that the depressed to low self-esteem group reports actions of others against the self as the cause of their depression, in addition to concerns about support, we predicted that the depressed to low self-esteem group should report greater anger toward *others* than the low self-esteem to depressed affect

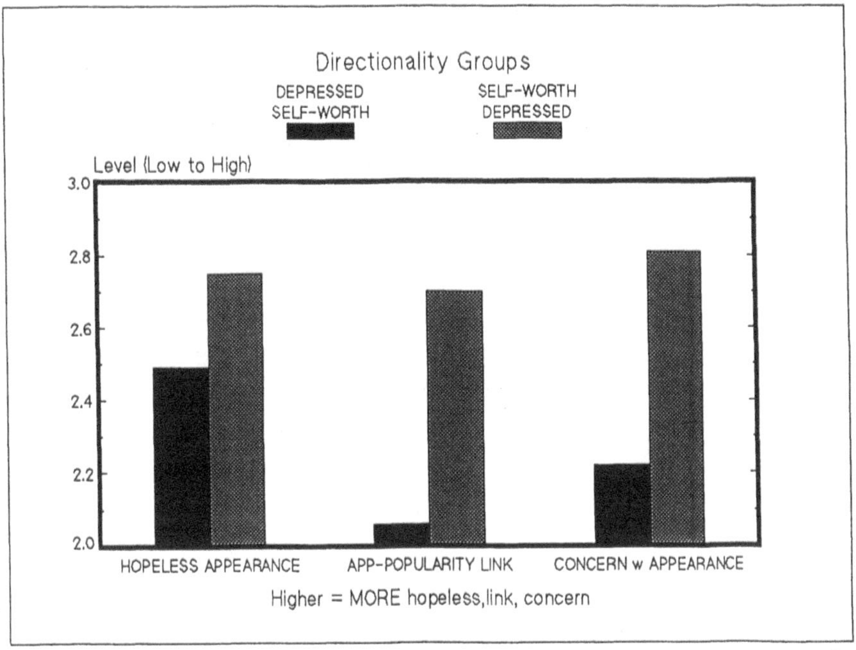

FIGURE 8. Directionality group differences for mother support variables.

group. The findings clearly supported these predictions. Thus, across three types of variables, (a) perceived causes, (b) correlates, and (c) affects associated with depression, we find a predictable pattern of differences, further suggesting that there may be different models or pathways of influence for each directionality group.

Different models for each directionality group.

Our excursions into the phenomenology of depression, including the directionality of the link between self-esteem and depressed affect, as well as associated emotions, point to potentially different pathways to depressive symptomatology. Two different prototypical models are proposed, models that represent refinements of the basic model presented in Figure 3. Model A describes the primary pathways for the directionality group that experiences the self-esteem component prior to affect. Model B depicts the primary pathways for the directionality group that experiences the affective reaction prior to self-esteem. The thicker arrow in each represents the strongest path for that particular model. Figure 9 presents each of these models diagrammatically.

Model A: Self-esteem precedes affect. For the group that experiences the self-esteem component prior to affect (Model A), concerns about the inadequacy of the self should predominate, based upon our data on the causes and correlates of

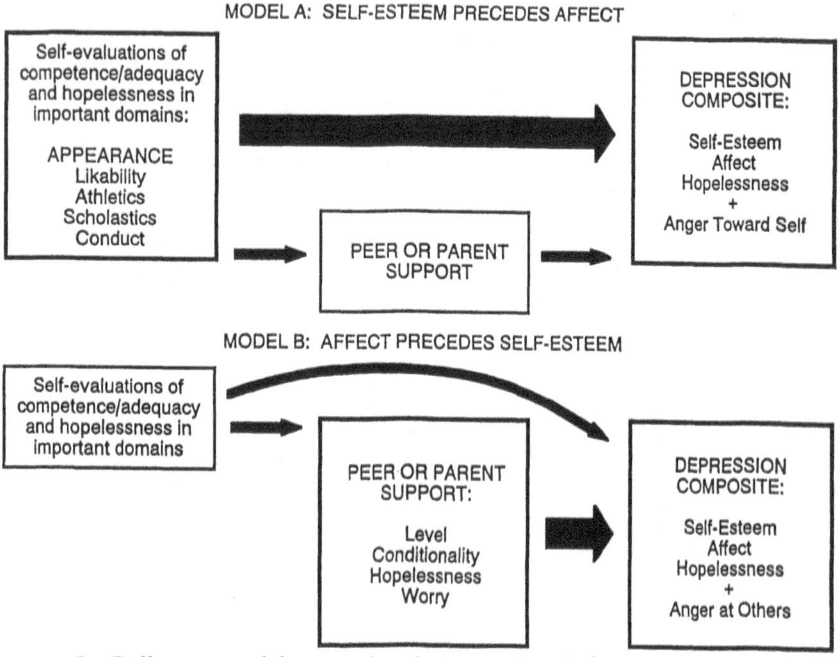

FIGURE 9. Different models postulated for each of the two directionality orientations.

this pattern. Thus, the strongest pathway should be the link between self-evaluations of competence or adequacy and the depression composite. More specifically, the self-evaluative construct is defined as competence or adequacy, as well as hopelessness, in domains where success is deemed important to the self. Thus, failure and hopelessness in a domain judged important will lead to the constellation of low self-esteem, depressed affect, and hopelessness, where the first two components are reported to be *experienced* in the order of self-esteem prior to affect.

In keeping with numerous findings to date (Harter, 1990, in press), the domain predicted to have the greatest impact, (Harter, 1990, in press), is *physical appearance*. Consistent with the general model in Figure 3, there will undoubtedly be a path from self-evaluations of competence/adequacy to peer and or parent support, and from support to the depression composite. However, these paths will be much smaller in magnitude. Moreover, based on our earlier model, it is anticipated that self-evaluations of appearance, peer likability, and athletic competence will bear stronger links to *peer* (than parent) support. In contrast, self-evaluations of scholastic competence and conduct should bear a stronger relationship to *parent* (than peer) support. Thus, in our statistical modeling procedures, the two clusters of competence/adequacy domains will be kept separate, as will peer and parent support. However, the main feature of this model is that pathways to and from support will be much weaker than the direct path from self-evaluations to the depression composite. Finally, consistent with our most recent results on the affective correlates of depression, the self-esteem to affect group should report greater anger toward the *self, if* they are below the midpoint on the depression composite.

In our normative efforts to model such a pattern, we will include all subjects, such that the range of scores will be quite broad. Thus, contributing to this pattern will be individuals who feel adequate in domains of importance, and who, therefore, will report relatively high self-esteem, as well as cheerful affect and hopefulness. From the standpoint of identifying, as well as understanding, adolescents at risk, however, those displaying lower scores are obviously of greater concern.

To portray a prototype of this pattern, we describe one student in our normative sample, a 15-year old, female adolescent. Her lowest self-evaluation scores are to be found among the first cluster of domains (see Figure 3) namely *appearance* (2.5), *peer likability* (1.3), and *athletic* competence (2.0), where 1 is the lowest and 4 the highest. In contrast to her perceptions of adequacy, she judges all three of these domains to be *important*, thus creating a potentially debilitating discrepancy between her real and ideal self-concept. Moreover, this student reports low *peer* support (2.4), consistent with our general model. (In contrast, she reports high levels of competence/adequacy in the domains of scholastic competence and conduct, along with considerable parent support, also consistent with our general model.) Although she is a straight A student, and a talented musician, it was reported to us by her counselor that she does not fit in with her peers at school and has great difficulty forming relationships with others her age. In fact, she is teased by her classmates.

Of critical relevance to Model A are her scores on the depression composite. This young woman reports low self-esteem (2.3), depressed affect (2.0), as well as general hopelessness (1.8), scores that are all below the midpoint of the scale. Interview data further corroborate the hypothesis that her disappointment with appearance and likability, in particular, contribute to her feelings of low self-esteem, depressed affect, and hopelessness. She blames herself for her inadequacies, and related lack of peer support, suggesting that the pathway from self-evaluation to the depression composite is the most salient.

Model B: Affect precedes self-esteem. For the group experiencing the affective component prior to self-esteem, concerns about support from either peers or parents should predominate, based on the causes and correlates of this pattern that have been documented. Therefore, the strongest path should be the link between the support variables (e.g., level, conditionality, hopelessness, and worry over approval) and the depression composite, where the components are *experienced* in the order of depressed affect prior to self-esteem. It is anticipated that for most adolescents in this pattern, lack of either parent support *or* peer support can lead to the experience of depression, followed by low self-esteem, though it is conceivable that for some individuals they may experience the absence of support from both sources.

The direct paths from competence/adequacy to the depression composite, and from competence/adequacy to support, are predicted to be less strong. That is, this orientation focuses primarily on lack of support, in the form of rejection, conflict, and loss, as a cause of depressive affect. Needless to say, however, there must be factors that legitimately *contribute* to the nonsupport of significant others, some of which represent characteristics of those others, and some of which undoubtedly reside in behaviors of the individual adolescent that provoke reactions in others. For example, parents may respond negatively to the adolescent's poor school performance, or peers may shun the adolescent whose appearance does not measure up to the prevailing stereotypes. However, the adolescent's focus is primarily on rejection or lack of support, not his/her role in producing such outcomes. Nevertheless, there should still be somewhat weaker paths from cluster # 1 (appearance, likability, athletic ability) to peer support, and from cluster # 2 (scholastic competence and behavioral conduct) to parent support. Finally, individuals displaying this directionality orientation should be more likely to report *anger toward others* as an affective correlate of depression.

A 15-year old male in our normative sample exemplifies this pattern. From the counselor, we learned that this adolescent has been under constant pressure from his family to achieve academically. He has done poorly in school, and several months before our testing he had been placed in a special education class. Perpetually, he has gotten into trouble. Not surprisingly, he reports on our measures that he receives little parental approval (2.5), and whatever support is forthcoming he views as conditional. He indicates that his *parents* consider scholastic competence and behavioral conduct to be extremely important (3.8 and 3.5, respectively). However, he is not performing in these areas, giving himself ratings of 1.8 for his scholastic competence and 2.0 for his behavioral conduct. Thus, consistent with our general model, parental support is low given his failure to meet parental expectations in the areas of scholastic competence and conduct.

In contrast to the lack of perceived parental support, this young man is reported to do reasonably well with his male peers, and is described as fun to be with. He works hard to one of the group, socially, and his peer acceptance score reveals that he is reasonably popular (3.2). He has also been relatively successful at sports, and was actively involved in wrestling at the time of testing. His athletic competence score was 3.0, considerably higher than his scores for scholastic competence and behavioral conduct.

This young man was initially identified as an "at risk" student given his scores on the components of the depression composite. He report depressed affect (2.0), low self-esteem (2.0), and general hopelessness (1.8). His causal focus would appear to be the lack of support he is receiving from parents, rather than his own inadequacies, per se. He reports that he takes little personal responsibility or blame for things that go wrong for him. Thus, it would appear that his seemingly realistic perceptions of lack of support from his parents are primarily responsible for his depression, related low self-esteem and hopelessness.

There is a second variant of pattern that defines Model B, namely one in which the adolescent is concerned about lack of *peer* support, and appears to be primarily angered over rejection by others his/her age. For this subgroup, lack of peer approval, conditional peer support, and worry over such support constitute the primary causes of depressed affect, low self-esteem, and general hopelessness. These are the adolescents who provided descriptions of peer rejection, conflict, or loss of a peer relationship, major factors that also provoke depressed affect that in turn leads to low self-esteem. Adolescents exhibiting this pattern typically report relatively low scores for appearance, peer likability, and/or athletic competence, perceived deficiencies that may lead to lack of peer support. However, for adolescents displaying this pattern, the beacon of attention, as well as anger, is directed at the absence of peer support, rather than one's inadequacies, per se.

While it is certainly plausible that rejection by significant others, loss of a relationship, lack of approval and conditional support from peers or parents should provoke *depression*, why, in turn, should depression necessarily trigger low self-esteem? In our original model, where the direction of effects underlying the robust correlation between self-esteem and depression was assumed to flow from lack of self-esteem to depression, it was plausible that harsh indictments of oneself as a person, tantamount to loss of self, should cause individuals to become depressed. With regard to the contrasting directionality orientation (depressed affect precedes low self-worth), it is also plausible that loss of another, through rejection, death, conflict, should provoke *depression*. It is less obvious, however, why depression caused by actions of others against the self should so predictably produce low self-esteem.

Pyszczynski and Greenberg's (1987) self-awareness theory of reactive depression, against a backdrop of Cooley's looking glass self formulation, provides some compelling clues. Self-awareness theory posits that the loss of a significant other may typically signify the loss of central source of self-esteem, a contention that finds empirical support (see also Oatley & Bolton, 1985). Thus, in addition to a depressive reaction to loss or rejection, one should also experience a loss of self-esteem, to the extent that the significant other represented an important source of self-esteem.

There is certainly clear evidence from our own work (Harter, 1986, 1987, 1990) documenting Cooley's looking-self formulation that peer support and parental approval are both critical sources of self-esteem for many adolescents, though not all (see Harter, Stocker, and Robinson, 1992). Adolescents who are highly invested in approval from others as a source of esteem, therefore, are particularly vulnerable to losses of self-esteem, if this external approval is in any way threatened. For such individuals, rejection from significant others should usher in not only affective reactions of depression but serious doubts about one's worth a person, if such worth is no longer confirmed by those others.

Clinical implications

Recently we have turned our attention to these directionality orientations among a group of adolescents with psychiatric diagnoses of depression who were hospitalized on an in-patient unit. Half of this sample also had diagnoses involving conduct disordered features. Of particular interest was our discovery that the percentage of males and females in each directionality group approximated that of our normative sample. Thus, girls are over-represented in the low self-esteem to depressed affect directionality group, whereas boys are over-represented in the depressed affect to low self-esteem orientation. The concerns provoking each reaction were also similar to those evidenced in our normative sample. Noteworthy among the low self-esteem to depressed affect individuals was the relentless focus on *appearance* as a cause of low self-esteem, particularly among the girls. The next most common themes were school failure and conduct problems, not surprising given that these represent common presenting problems among this psychiatrically hospitalized sample.

Among those reporting that depressed affect precedes low self-worth, the most common concerns for both males and females were peer rejection or loss, conflict with parents, and lack of parent support. Descriptions of themes involving parents were more prevalent among this clinical sample, compared to our normative sample. Such a pattern is understandable, given that the presenting problems of many of these psychiatrically hospitalized youth involved conflict between adolescent and parent.

It is tempting to speculate that there may be some relationship between patients' diagnosis and their choice of directionality orientation. In our clinical sample, where half of the adolescents were comorbid for both depression and conduct disordered features, there was a tendency for more of the latter group to be represented in the depressed affect to low self-esteem group. In contrast, more of the depressed only individuals adopted the self-esteem to depressed affect orientation. However, the relationship was neither striking nor significant.

One can entertain hypotheses pertinent to other diagnostic groups. For example, adolescents with eating disorders (e.g., anorexics, bulemics) may be more likely to be observed in the self-esteem to depressed affect group, given the salience of appearance concerns for those adopting this orientation. One might also speculate that adolescents with learning disabilities would be more likely to adopt this same orientation, if their focus is the denigration of their academic competence. Conversely, perhaps adolescents with a history of physical or sexual abuse may endorse the depressed affect to low self-esteem orientation, given that such individuals tend to view the negative actions of significant others against the self as responsible for their mood states.

However, such parallels are likely to be too simplistic, in the absence of knowledge about one's accompanying *attributions*. Our two directionality orientations are undoubtedly mediated by perceptions of responsibility, blame, and locus of control. For example, consider the abused adolescent who takes personal responsibility for the abuse, concluding that she, herself, provoked the attacks. Such an individual will invariably experience shame, feelings of unworthiness (not an uncommon pattern among abuse victims), which may result in the pattern whereby low self-esteem ushers in feelings of depression. However, other abuse victims may display indignance and anger at the abuser, leading to the opposite pattern in which there is a greater focus on the negative actions of the other against the self. One can imagine similar analyses for any given diagnostic category, namely different scenarios with regard to attributions concerning the role of self versus other, that would lead to different directionality orientations. Thus, it is unlikely that these orientations will bear a direct relationship to diagnostic category. Rather, it will be necessary to examine mediators such as perceived locus of control, the ratio of internalizing to externalizing defenses, etc. in order to both predict and interpret directionality orientation.

Suicidal ideation. It is also tempting to make predictions about the likelihood of suicidal ideation or gestures, based on directionality orientation. There is evidence in the data from our normative adolescent sample (Harter, Marold, & Jackson, 1992) that among individuals below the midpoint for both self-esteem and depressed affect, the low self-esteem to depressed affect group reports significantly more suicidal ideation than those in the depressed affect to low self-worth group. The former group also reports significantly greater hopelessness. The impetus for suicidal behavior, therefore, may well reside in feelings of unworthiness that provoke what Baumeister (1990) has identified as a solution to the need to escape from oneself. Thus, the suicidal behavior is directed against the self, both physically and psychologically.

However, among both our normative and clinical samples, we also observe suicidal ideation, and a history of attempts, among certain individuals within the depressed to low self-esteem directionality group. Interviews and/or material in their charts reveal that for these adolescents, suicidal behavior is often an act against *others.* A number of these subjects explained their motives and thought processes quite clearly, with phrases such as "I'll show them", "they'll be sorry when I'm dead", "I'll get back at them for what they did to me". Among those in our clinical sample who are comorbid for depression and conduct disordered behavior, the pattern is even more complicated. Such individuals may display alternations between behaviors involving aggression against others and gestures involving aggression against the self. Often it is difficult for the clinician to predict which set of behaviors will occur. Our observations are consistent with the caution that we not categorically dichotomize individuals into internalizers and externalizers, given findings throughout the literature that these two types of symptom patterns and defensive styles are often quite highly correlated.

Treatment implications. It is highly likely that a knowledge of an individual's directionality orientation may, in conjunction with information concerning a client's presenting problem and diagnosis, have implications for intervention. For those in the low self-esteem to depressed affect group, a focus on the basis for negative self-evaluations may well be the most fruitful avenue to pursue. Questions such as (a) what are the individual's most salient attributions, (b) how *realistic* are their self-perceptions, etc. may profitably be posed. In certain cases, the individual may require therapeutic interventions that support the alteration of unrealistic self-representations. In other cases the goal may entail the lowering of unrealistically high expectations of the self. In still other cases, the profile of self-evaluations may highlight areas where skill training may be profitable. Finally, the client may need to shift one's investment from a domain in which one is, in reality, not that competent, and may have little potential to improve, to a domain where one can achieve greater success. Each of these strategies should produce, as outcomes, a heightening of self-esteem, a reduction in anger toward the self, and the alleviation of depressed affect.

For those endorsing the depressed affect to low self-esteem directionality orientation, the initial focus of treatment will undoubtedly be conflictual or non-gratifying relationships with significant others. Thus, one would want to explore the basis for feelings of rejection, conflict, or loss. Critical questions will include (a) how realistic are these perceptions, (b) whom does the client see as responsible, (c) what role does the client's own behavior play in this pattern (d) can the client realistically expect to obtain support from these others, (e) how critical is the support of these others as a source of the client's self-esteem, (f) are there alternative people to whom one might turn for support that can be more validating or enhancing and less conditional. In working through these issues, preferably with inclusion of the family in treatment, it is anticipated that there will be an alleviation of the client's depression, his/her anger at others, and an enhancement of self-esteem.

Although there are a number of avenues for obtaining information relevant to both the diagnostic and treatment enterprise, we have found adolescents self-perceptions to be extremely valuable. Moreover, it should be noted that within the field of developmental psychopathology, in general, as well as depressive symptomatology and its correlates, in particular, there has been a call for self-report measures that can be used as screening instruments, diagnostic aids, and indices of potential change (Harter, 1990b; Kazdin, 1990; LaGreca, 1990; Pfeffer, 1988; Plutchik & Conte, 1989; Rutter, 1989; USPHS report on the Secretary's Task Force on Youth Suicide, 1989). There has been a particular need for screening instruments that can be used with *normative* populations within the school system (see Garrison, 1989; Pfeffer, 1988). The Dimensions of Depression Profile for Children and Adolescents (Harter et al., 1987) employed in the present study represents a self-report instrument that meets many of these needs. It is particularly useful in identifying dimensions of depression e.g., low self-worth, hopelessness, suicidal ideation, that may not be as readily observable as depressed affect or low energy level. Our Self-Perception Profiles for Children and Adolescents (Harter, 1985a, 1988), as well as our Social Support Scale for Children and Adolescents (Harter, 1985b) have also be very useful indicators of the particular determinants leading to depressive reactions. Through the use of such self-report instruments, children and adolescents about whom there is some concern, as well as those not previously identified, can be better understood, in our efforts to improve the processes of identification, intervention and treatment.

REFERENCES

Abramson, L. Y., Metalsky, G. I., & Alloy, L. B. (1989). Hopelessness depression: A theory-based subtype of depression. *Psychological Review,* 96, 358–372.

Abramson, L. Y., Seligman, M. E. P., & Teasedale, J. D. (1986). Learned helplessness in humans: Critique and reformulation. In J. C. Coyne (Ed.), *Essential papers on depression.* New York: New York University Press.

Alcohol, Drug Abuse, and Mental Health Administration (1989). *Report of the Secretary's Task Force on Youth Suicide.* (DHHS Publication No. ADM 89-1621). Washington, DC: U.S. Government Printing Office.

Asch, S. S. (1966). Depression: Three clinical variations. *Psychological Study of the Child, 21,* 150–171.

Battle, J. (1987). Relationship between self-esteem and depression among children. *Psychological Reports, 60,* 1187–1190.

Baumeister, R. F. (1990). Suicide as escape from self. *Psychological Review, 97,* 90–113.

Beck, A. T. (1967). *Depression: Causes and Treatments.* Philadelphia: University of Pennsylvania Press.

Beck, A. T. (1975). *Depression: Causes and Treatments.* Philadelphia: University of Pennsylvania Press.

Beck. A. T. (1987, May). *Hopelessness as a prediction of ultimate suicide.* Paper presented at the joint meeting of the American Association of Suicidology and the International Association for Suicide Prevention, San Francisco.

Bibring, E. (1953). The mechanism of depression. In P. Greenacre (Ed.), *Affective disorders; Psychoanalytic contribution to their study.* NY: International Universities Press.

Blatt, S. J. (1974). Levels of object representation in anaclitic and introjective depression. *Psychoanalytic Study of the Child, 29,* 107–157.

Bonner, R. L., & Rich, A. R. (1987). Toward a predictive model of suicidal ideation and behavior: Some preliminary data in college students. *Suicide and Life-Threatening Behavior, 17*(1), 50–63.

Brown, B. (1990). Peer groups and peer cultures. In S. S. Feldman & G. R. Elliot (Eds.), *At the threshold: The developing adolescent* (pp. 171–196). Cambridge, MA: Harvard University Press.

Cantor, P. (1987). *Young people in crisis: How you can help.* A film presentation of the National Committee on Youth Suicide Prevention and American Association of Suicidology, in consultation with Harvard Medical School, Department of Psychiatry, Cambridge Hospital.

Carlson, G. A., & Cantwell, D. P. (1982). Suicidal behavior and depression in children and adolescents. *Journal of the American Academy of Child Psychiatry, 21,* 361–368.

Carlson, G. A., & Gerber, J. (1986). Developmental issues in the classification of depression in children. In M. Rutter, C. E. Izard & P. B. Read (Eds.), *Depression in young people: Developmental and clinical perspectives* (pp. 399–434). New York: Guilford Press.

Carver, C. S., & Scheier, M. (1981). *Attention and self-regulation.* New York: Springer-Verlag.

Cicchetti, D., & Schneider-Rosen, K. (1986). An organizational approach to childhood depression. In M. Rutter, C. E. Izard, & P. Read (Eds.), *Depression in young people: Clinical and developmental perspectives* (pp. 71–134). New York: Guilford Press.

Cooley, C. H. (1902). *Human nature and the social order.* NY: Charles Scribner's Sons.

Cooper, C. R., Grotevant, H. D., & Condon, S. M. (1983). Individuality and connectedness: Both father and adolescent identity formation and role taking skills, In H. D. Grotevant & C. R. Cooper (Eds.), *Adolescent development in the family: New directions for child development.* San Francisco: Josey-Bass.

Coopersmith, S. (1967). The antecedents of self-esteem. San Francisco, CA: W. H. Freeman.

Curran, D. K. (1987). *Adolescent suicidal behavior.* Washington, DC: Hemisphere.

Donaldson, S. K., & Westerman, M. A. (1986). Development of children's understanding of ambivalence and causal theories of emotions. *Developmental Psychology, 22,* 655–662.

Emery, P. E. (1983). Adolescent depression and suicide. *Adolescence, 18,* 245–258.

Epstein, S. (1973). The self-concept revisited or a theory of a theory. *American Psychologist, 28*, 405–416.

Epstein, S. (1991). Cognitive-experiential self theory: Implications for developmental psychology. In M. R. Gunnar & L. A. Stroufe (Eds). *Self Processes and Development: The Minnesota Symposium on Child Development, 23*. Hillsdale, NJ: Lawrence Erlbaum.

Fenichel, O. (1945). *The psychoanalytic theory of neurosis*. New York: Norton and Company.

Fischer, K. W. (1980). A theory of cognitive development: The control and construction of hierarchies of skills. *Psychological Review, 87*, 477–531.

Frank, E., Carpenter, L. L., & Kupfer, D. J. (1988). Sex differences in recurrent depression: Are there any that are significant? *American Journal of Psychiatry, 145*, 41–45.

Freud, S. (1968). Mourning and melancholia. In J. Strachey (Ed.), *The standard edition of the complete works of Sigmund Freud* (Vol. 14). London: Hogarth Press (Original work published 1917).

Frijda, N. (1986). *The emotions* (Part III: Synthesis). New York: Cambridge University Press.

Garrison, C. Z. (1989). The study of suicidal behavior in the schools. *Suicide and Life-Threatening Behavior, 19*, 120–130.

Gispert, M., Davis, M. C., Marsh, L., & Wheeler, K. (1987). Predictive factors in repeated suicide attempts by adolescents. *Hospital & Community Psychology, 38*, 390–393.

Glick, M., & Zigler, E. (1985). Self-image: A cognitive-developmental approach. In R. Leahy (Ed.), *The development of the self*. NY: Academic Press.

Grotevant, H. D., & Cooper, C. R. (1985). Patterns of interaction in family relationships and the development of identity exploration in adolescence. *Child Development, 56*, 415–428.

Hammen, C., & Goodman-Brown, T. (1990). Self-schemas and vulnerability to specific life stress in children at risk for depression. *Cognitive Therapy and Research, 14*, 215–227.

Harris, P. L. (1983). Children's understanding of the link between situation and emotion. *Journal for Experimental Child Psychology, 36*, 490–509.

Harter, S. (1982). The perceived competence scale for children. *Child Development, 53*, 87–97.

Harter, S. (1985). *The Self-Perception Profile for Children*. Manual, University of Denver, CO.

Harter, S. (1985). *The Social Support Scale for Children and Adolescents*. Manual, University of Denver, CO.

Harter, S. (1986). Processes underlying the construction, maintenance, and enhancement of the self-concept in children. In J. Suls & A. G. Greenwald (Eds.), *Psychological perspectives on the self* (Vol. 3, pp. 137–181). Hillsdale, NJ: Lawrence Erlbaum Associates.

Harter, S. (1986). Cognitive-developmental processes in the integration of concepts about emotions and the self. *Social Cognition, 4*(2), 119–151.

Harter, S. (1987). Developmental and dynamic changes in the nature of the self-concept: Implications for child psychotherapy. In S. R. Shirk (Ed.), *Cognitive development and child psychotherapy* (pp. 119–160). NY: Plenum Press.

Harter, S. (1988). *The Self-Perception Profile for Adolescents*. Manuscript, University of Denver.

Harter, S. (1990). Issues in the assessment of the self-concept of children and adolescents. In A. La Greca (Ed.), *Childhood assessment; Through the eyes of a child* (pp. 292–325). Boston, MA: Allyn and Bacon.

Harter, S., & Buddin, B. J. (1987). Children's understanding of the simultaneity of two emotions: A five-stage developmental acquisition sequence. *Developmental Psychology, 23 (3) 388–399.*

Harter, S. & Jackson, B. K. (1993). Young adolescents' perceptions of the link between low self-worth and depressed affect. *Journal of Early Adolescence*, 13, 383–407.

Harter, S., & Marold, D. (1989). A model of risk factors in adolescent suicide. Paper presented at the Society for Research in Child Development, Kansas City, Kansas.

Harter, S., & Marold, D. B. (1991). A model of the determinants and mediational role of self-worth: Implications for adolescent depression and suicidal ideation. In G. Goethals & J. Strauss (Eds.), *The self: An interdisciplinary approach.* Springer Verlag.

Harter, S., Marold, D., & Jackson, B. (1991 April). *The directionality of the link between self-esteem and depressed affect as experienced by adolescents.* Paper presented at the Society for Research in Child Development, Seattle, WA.

Harter, S., Marold, D., & Whitesell, N. R. (1992) A model of psycho-social risk factors leading to suicidal ideation in young adolescents. *Development and Psychopathology, 4,* 167–188.

Harter, S., Stocker, C., & Robinson, N. (under review). The perceived directionality of the link between approval and self-worth: The liabilities of a looking glass self orientation among young adolescents.

Harter, S., & Whitesell, N. R. (1989). Developmental changes in children's understanding of single, multiple and blended emotion concepts. In C. Saarni & P. L. Harris (Eds.), *Children's understanding of emotion.* Cambridge University Press.

Hawton, K. (1986). *Suicide and attempted suicide among children and adolescents.* Beverly Hills, CA; Sage.

Higgins, E. T. (1987). Self-discrepancy: Theory relating self and affect. *Psychological Review, 94,* 319–340.

Higgins, E. T. (1989). Self-discrepancy theory: What patterns of self-beliefs cause people to suffer? In L. Berkowitz (Ed.), *Advances in experimental social psychology, 22.* NY: Academic Press.

Higgins, E. T. (1991). Development of self-regulatory and self-evaluative processes: Costs, benefits, and trade-offs. In M. R. Gunnar & L. A. Stroufe (Eds.), *Self processes in development.* Twenty-third Minnesota Symposium of Child Psychology. Hillsdale, NJ: Erlbaum.

Hoffman, M. (1986). Affect, cognition and motivation. In R. M. Sorrentino & E. T. Higgins (Eds.), *Handbook of motivation and cognition* (pp. 244–280). Guilford Press.

Izard, C. E. (1983). Emotion-cognition relationships and human development. In Izard, Kagan, & Zajonc (Eds.), *Emotions, cognition and behavior.* New York: Cambridge University Press.

James, W. (1892). *Psychology: The briefer course.* NY: Henry Holt & Co.

Khan, A. U. (1987). Heterogeneity of suicidal adolescents. *Journal of the American Academy of Child and Adolescent Psychiatry, 26,* 92–96.

Kaslow, N. J., Rehm, L. P., & Siegel, A. W. (1984). Social-cognitive and cognitive correlates of depression in children. *Journal of Abnormal Child Psychology, 12,* 605–620.

Kazdin, A. E. (1990). Applications of self-report measures with children and adolescents. In A. M. La Greca (Ed.), *Through the eyes of the child* (189–233). Boston, MA: Allyn and Bacon.

Kendall, P. C., Cantwell, D. P., & Kazdin, A. E. (1989). Depression in children and adolescents: Assessment issues and recommendations. *Cognitive Therapy and Research, 13,* 109–146.

Kovacs, M., & Beck, A. T. (1977). An empirical-clinical approach towards a definition of childhood depression. In J. G. Schulterbrandt & A. Raskin (Eds.), *Depression in childhood: Diagnosis, treatment, and conceptual models. NY: Raven Press.*

Kovacs, M., & Beck, A. T. (1978). Maladaptive cognitive structures in depression. *American Journal of Psychiatry, 135*, 525–533.

Kovacs, M., & Beck, A. T. (1986). Maladaptive cognitive structures in depression. In J. C. Coyne (Ed.), *Essential papers on depression.* New York: New York University Press.

LaGreca, A. M. (Ed.). (1990). *Through the eyes of the child.* Boston: Allyn and Bacon.

Lazarus, R. S. (1982). Thoughts on the relations between emotion and cognition. *American Psychologist, 37*, 1019–1024.

Lazarus, R. S. (1984). On the primacy of cognition. *American Psychologist, 39*, 124–129.

Leventhal, H., L., & Scherer, K. (1987). The relationship of emotion to cognition: A functional approach to a semantic controversy. *Cognition and Emotion, 1*, 3–28.

Maris, R. (1985). The adolescent suicide problem. *Suicide and Life Threatening Behavior, 15*, 91–100.

Markus, H., & Nurius, P. (1986). Possible selves. *American Psychologist, 41*, 954–969.

Marold, D. B. (1987). Correlates of suicidal ideation among young adolescents. Unpublished Doctoral Dissertation, University of Denver.

McCauley, E., Mitchell, J. R., Burke, P., & Moss, S. (1988). Cognitive attributes of depression in children and adolescents. *Journal of Consulting and Clinical Psychology, 56*, 903–908.

Mead, G. H. (1934). *Mind, self, and society.* Chicago: University of Chicago Press.

Nolen-Hoeksema, S., Girgus, J. S., & Seligman, M. E. P. (1986). Learned helplessness in children: A longitudinal study of depression, achievement, and explanatory style. *Journal of Personality and social Psychology, 51*, 435–442.

Pfeffer, C. R. (1986). *The suicidal child.* NY: Guilford Press.

Pfeffer, C. R. (1988). Risk factors associated with youth suicide: A clinical perspective. *Psychiatric Annals, 18*, 652–656.

Pfeffer, C., Lipkins. M. A., Plutchik, R., & Mizruchi, M. (1988). Normal children at risk for suicidal behavior: A two-year follow-up study. *Journal of American Academy of Child and Adolescent Psychiatry, 27*(1), 34–41.

Pfeffer, C., Zuckerman, S., Plutchik, R., & Mizruchi, M. (1984). Suicidal behavior in normal school children: A comparison with child psychiatric inpatients. *Journal of the American Academy of Child Psychiatry, 23*(4), 416–423.

Plutchick, R., & Conte, H. (1989). Self-report scales for the measurement of depression. *Psychiatric Annals, 19*(7), 367–371.

Puig-Antich, J. (1982). Major depression and conduct disorder in prepuberty. *Journal of the American Academy of Child Psychiatry, 21*, 118–128.

Pyszczynski, T., & Greenberg, J. (1987). Self-regulatory preservation and the depressive self-focusing style: A self-awareness theory of reactive depression. *Psychological Bulletin, 102*(1), 122–138.

Renouf, A. G., & Harter, S. (1990). Low self-worth and anger as components of the depressive experience in young adolescents. *Development and Psychopathology, 2*, 293–310.

Riley, W. T., Treiber, F. A., & Woods, M. G. (1989). Anger and hostility in depression. *Journal of Nervous and Mental Disorders, 177*, 668–674.

Rogers, C., & Dymond, R. (1954). *Psychotherapy and personality change.* Chicago, IL: University of Chicago Press.

Rosenberg, M. (1979). *Conceiving the self.* NY: Basic Books.

Rosenberg, M. (1986). Self-concept from middle childhood through adolescence. In J. Suls & A. G. Greenwald (Eds.), *Psychological perspectives on the self* (Vol. 3, pp. 107–136). Hillsdale, NJ: Lawrence Erlbaum Associates.

Rudd, M. D. (1989). The prevalence of suicidal ideation among college students. *Suicide and Life-Threatening Behavior, 19*(2), 173–183.

Rutter, M. (1988). Epidemiological approaches to developmental psychopathology. *Archives of General Psychiatry, 45*, 486–495.

Rutter, M. (1989). Isle of Wight revisited: Twenty-five years of child psychiatric epidemiology. *Journal of the American Academy of Child Adolescent Psychiatry, 28*(5), 633–653.

Rutter, M., Izard, C., & Read, P. (Eds.). (1985). *Depression in childhood: Developmental perspectives.* New York: Guilford Press.

Sandler, J., & Joffe, W. G. (1965). Notes on childhood depression. *International Journal of Psychoanalysis, 46*, 88–95.

Savin-Williams, R. C., & Berndt, T. (1990). Friendship during adolescence. In S. S. Feldman & G. R. Elliot (Eds.), *At the threshold: The developing adolescent.* Cambridge, MA: Harvard University Press.

Seligman, M. E. P. (1975) *Helplessness: On depression, development, and death.* San Francisco: Freeman.

Seligman, M. E. P., & Peterson, C. (1986). A learned helplessness perspective on childhood depression: Theory and research. In M. Rutter, C. E. Izard, & P. B. Read (Eds.), *Depression in young people: Developmental and clinical perspectives* (pp. 223–249). New York: Guilford Press.

Shaffer, D. (1974). Suicide in childhood and early adolescence. *Journal of Child Psychology and Psychiatry*, 275–291.

Shaffer, D. (1985). Depression and suicide in children and adolescents. In M. Rutter & L. Hersov (Eds.), *Child and adolescent psychiatry: Modern approaches* (2nd ed.). Oxford: Blackwell Scientific Publications.

Shaffer, D., & Fisher, P. (1981). The epidemiology of suicide in children and young adolescents. *Journal of the American Academy of Child Psychiatry, 21*, 545–565.

Smith, K., & Crawford, S. (1986). Suicidal behavior among normal high school students. *Suicide and Life-Threatening Behavior, 16*, 313–325.

Spirato, A., Brown, L., Overholser, J., & Fritz, G. (1989). Attempted suicide in adolescence: A review and critique of the literature. *Clinical Psychology Review, 9*, 335–363.

Sroufe, L. A., & Rutter, M. (1985). The Domain of developmental psychopathology. *Child Development, 55*, 17–29.

Steinberg, L. (1990). Autonomy, conflict, and harmony in the family. In S. S. Feldman & G. R. Elliot (Eds.), *At the threshold: The developing adolescent* (pp. 255–276). Cambridge, MA: Harvard University Press.

Tesser, A. (1988). Toward a self-evaluation maintenance model of social behavior. In L. Berkowitz (Ed.), *Advances in experimental social psychology* (Vol. 21). NY: Academic Press.

Tesser, A., & Campbell, J. (1983). Self-definition and self-evaluation maintenance. In J. Suls & A. G. Greenwald (Eds.), *Psychological perspectives on the self* (Vol. 2, pp. 1–32), Hillsdale, NJ: Lawrence Erlbaum Associates.

Weiner, B. (1985). An attributional theory of achievement motivation and emotion. *Psychological Review, 92*, 271–282.

Wicklund, R. (1975). Objective self-awareness. In L. Berkowitz (Ed.), *Advances in experimental social psychology* (Vol. 8, pp. 233–275). New York: Academic Press.

Withers, L. E., & Kaplan, D. W. (1987),. Adolescents who attempt suicide: A retrospective clinical chart review of hospitalized patients. *Professional Psychology: Research & Practice, 18*, 341–393.

Wylie, R. C. (1979). *The self concept, Vol. 2. Theory and research on selected topics.* Lincoln, NE: University of Nebraska Press.

Zajonc, R. B. (1980). Feeling and thinking: Preferences need no inferences. *American Psychologist.*

Zajonc. R. B. (1984). On the primacy of affect. *American psychologist, 39*, 117–123.

XI Adolescent Suicide and the Loss of Personal Continuity

Michael Chandler

In the main, this chapter reports upon an ongoing program of research specifically aimed at working out some plausible developmental explanation for the dramatic increase in suicidal behaviors known to occur during the adolescent years (Hendin, 1982). More broadly, the studies on which I will report were further fueled by a wider ambition to add to the short list of known ways in which theories of normal and theories of abnormal development can both be made to leverage our understanding of health as well as disorder. In particular, in what follows I will argue that the class of normative developmental theories that are fundamentally dialectical in character (theories, for example, such as those of Piaget and Kohlberg) hold out a largely untapped potential for making comprehensible certain otherwise poorly understood psychological disorders by re-reading them as evidence of that brand of momentary systems failures that periodically reoccur when self-organizing systems upgrade by restructuring themselves to some higher, more differentiated level of order or organization (Roth, 1981). The new evidence that I will bring out is meant to offer a specific illustration of the morbid potential inherent in such deconstructive processes by showing that, in contrast to their more typical age-mates, suicidal adolescents are typically bereft of any and all of their previously constructed conceptual means for judging themselves to be persistent or continuous through time. Instead, as this chapter undertakes to show, such self-destructive young persons generally register as having somehow lost their way while attempting to navigate those routinely difficult transitions leading from developmentally less, to developmentally more mature ways of reasoning about their own so-called "numerical identity," or continuous existence through time. No longer able to splice together the various strands of their own self-narrative, such young persons, I will

The author wishes to extend his appreciation to Lorraine Ball who collaborated in all phases of the program of research reported here, and to Dr. Michael Boyes and Terry Estrin who provided valuable assistance in parts of the data collection. Special thanks are also owed to Drs. D. Bilsker, M. Gilbert, S. Bayrakal, and T. Barnett, and to Ms. L. Cox and the nursing and child care staff of the Adolescent Unit of the Vancouver General Hospital, for their support and assistance. Thanks are also due to the Vancouver School Board and to all of the adolescents and their parents for their cooperation and participation in the studies reported here.

argue, lose any sense of ownership of their own past and, more to the present point, their commitment to their own future. As a consequence, otherwise commonplace, if unactionable, self-destructive impulses become emptied of their ordinary personal significance, and so move decisively forward in the ranks of conceivable solutions to life's frustrating moments. While continuity, then, doth make cowards of us all, young persons who, at moments of developmental transition, end up dropping the thread of their own personal persistence are cost this important protective factor.

Each of the three subsequent sections that make up this chapter are meant to help in unpacking the foregoing train of heavily loaded claims about developmental psychopathology in general, and about suicidal behaviors in particular. Part One proceeds by filling in more of what was intended by suggesting that the new discipline of developmental psychopathology has so far seriously underutilized those explanatory resources already available within constructive theories of normal development. Part Two begins the more specialized job of concretely illustrating these claims by first focusing attention on what is presently understood about the place of self-continuity in the normal identity formation process, and by detailing how the thoughts of young persons concerning their own continuous identity ordinarily progress through a common sequence of increasingly adequate self-continuity warranting practices. Finally, the third and last section offers an empirical demonstration of how the ordinary process of constructing more mature solutions to the recurrent problem of numerical identity can and does sometimes totally collapse, leaving those who have failed to make it over these developmental hurdles entirely without that ordinary sense of commitment to a personal future that would otherwise insulate them from routine self-destructive impulses. Here, comparative data will be presented that lend strong support to the theoretical expectation that suicidal adolescents are particularly characterized by such general systems failures. Before coming to these empirical matters, however, more first needs to be said about the contrastive ways in which various normative developmental theories inform, and fail to inform, our understanding of psychopathology.

PART ONE: Theories of normal and pathological development

In keeping with the common ambition of all of the chapters in this volume to further extend the list of ways in which theories of both normal and pathological development can be shown to leverage one another, this introductory section begins with an assay of such currently available interpretive practices. As a way of getting started with this agenda, it is perhaps worth drawing attention to our common, if often tacit, commitment to the idea that theories of both normal and deviant development ought to be somehow "complementary" (Cicchetti, 1984, 1990; Keating, 1990), or, as Nannis and Cowan (1988) have put it, available in "matched sets." That is, even if not always honored in practice, it is generally agreed upon in principle that every theory of normal growth necessarily contains within it some perhaps latent theory of developmental deviancy, just as every adequate theory of psychopathology needs to have been worked out against the back-cloth of some more or less explicit account of the normal developmental course.

A natural corollary of all such claims about "complementarity," or what Keating (1990) describes as "the unity of developmental theory," is that if every account of deviant development is necessarily constrained by the normative theory upon which it is predicated, then the same problems of radical incommensurability that have haunted the study of canonical development necessarily await the newer study of developmental psychopathology. That is, without the arrival of some unforeseen consensus concerning the nature of the ordinary developmental course, the immediate prospects of also moving toward some single, unified theory of developmental psychopathology will have to be regarded as faint at best. In the place of any such unlikely ecumenical view, we are obliged, I suggest, to work out instead just how it is that this or that particular theory of normal development both creates interpretive opportunities and sets explanatory limits upon the different kinds of psychopathologic processes we might hope to understand. The paragraphs that follow are meant to form the beginnings of such a general accounting scheme.

Step one in any first attempt to work out the possible ways in which various theories of normal development differently constrain one's understanding of psychopathology should probably be to take stock of just how many importantly different kinds of normative theories one need take into account. After setting aside as uninteresting those various directionless models that try to do without any real distinction between development and simple change (Blasi, 1983), an at least provisional answer would seem to be that the residual set of such importantly different contenders amounts to only a handful of competing theory types, all of which can be located within the cross-hairs of two orthogonal dimensions. One of these subtends the differences between theories that emphasize *quantitative* as opposed to *qualitative* change. The other divides those accounts that portray development as *unified* or monolithic from those that characterize the same growth process as simultaneously unfolding along a manifold of *multiple* independent developmental routes. Situated within this axial framework Piaget's theory, for instance, provides an example of what van den Daele (1969) has referred to as "simple unitary progression models," in which discontinuous, qualitative changes are characterized as proceeding along a more or less unified or monolithic developmental front. By contrast, much of contemporary "life-span developmental theory" takes just the opposite stance by portraying development, especially mature development, as proceeding along a manifold of more or less independent growth trajectories, while generally viewing progress on these several fronts as the cumulative result of a series of more or less gradual or continuous quantitative changes (Van Den Daele, 1969). The other cells of this contingency table, while generally less well populated, are, nevertheless, "manned," in one case by theorists who view ordinary developmental change as both fitful and multidimensional, and, in the other, by those who read the normal growth process as being somehow simultaneously holistic and continuous.

While subject to easy abuse, this rough organizational framework will have served its purpose if it can be made to draw attention, not only to what is unique, but also what is common to the various models of canonical development under consideration. Such a framework already supposes, for example, that all so-called "strong" or self-consciously developmental theories not only regard ontogenetic change as inherently directional, but also hold out some sort of temporal standards or durational expectancies regarding the usual *rate* and *cadence* of such progressive moves. Consequently, all such fully-fledged developmental theories necessarily leave room for the possibilities that persons can go wrong either: a) by somehow lagging behind normal developmental schedule; or b) by persistently doing what is more rightfully expected only of much younger persons. By contrast, where such progressive growth models are left free to vary is with reference to the still open question of whether such notions of simple *fixation* and *delay* do or do not make up the full complement of all theoretically permissible moves for explaining psychological disorder. As I mean to go on to show, it is on precisely this matter that the differences between alternative developmental psychopathologies most decisively turn.

What has not been subject to serious doubt is the evident clinical fact that there is no end to the number of troubled persons who, having previously arrived at certain age appropriate solutions to various problems in living, later prove unequal to these same tasks, and so end up once again relying upon simpler or formally less complex problem solving strategies. "Mental" hospitals and clinics are literally filled to overflowing with once better adapted persons, whose current symptoms are, in certain respects, reminiscent of immaturities common to still younger persons. In such cases easy talk of fixation or delay clearly won't do. Exactly how it is that various theories go about making interpretive room for these often dramatic instances of apparent backsliding or dilapidation can be shown to depend upon how they suppose that the normal developmental process ends up disposing of its own outmoded adaptational strategies.

One classical way of understanding such evidently regressive ways of behaving—a way remote from what would ordinarily count as a proper developmental theory—has been to simply suppose that everyone is some kind of unremediable hedonist who merely adopts or discards different ways of behaving according to schedules that merely maximize available rewards and/or minimize local punishments. By such largely ahistoric lights persons who come to behave in what might be thought of as "regressive" ways are simply taken to be those unfortunate enough to find themselves in a set of contingent circumstances that no longer support what polite society happens to define as mature. While getting good marks for simplicity, the nagging problem with such early 20th century associationistic accounts is that they offer only a "conventionalist" interpretation of regressive behaviors which, to paraphrase Kohlberg (1969), are thought to be picked up in much the same way as are social dance steps.

By contrast, more avowedly developmental theories, that is, theories which actually allow for the possibility of real progress (Chandler, 1993), have typically pursued one or the other of two very different sorts of interpretive strategies in dealing with apparent instances of behavioral regression. According to the first of these, those various childish ways of behaving that one has long since outgrown are not thought of as having been literally expunged from one's behavioral repertoire, but are said to persist instead as back-up routines, that can again be brought into play should access to one's more recently acquired, and arguably more mature ways of proceeding somehow become blocked or lose their competitive edge. By such lights, the route to maturity, whether seen to be paved with holistic stages or simple associative connections, is explicitly regarded as a two-way street. That is, development is thought of as a change process with both a forward and a backward gear, and regression is simply progress run off in reverse. The work of Looft (1972) as well as that of Hooper and his colleagues (e.g., Hooper, Fitzgerald, & Papalia, 1971), which portrayed senile dementia as a process of neural decay that literally stripped off one layer of Piagetian cognitive development at a time, constitute clear examples of this particular take upon the process of regression.

The second of these general interpretive possibilities is that later occurring levels or stages of development, while naturally understood to be the outgrowth of what has come before, are thought to incorporate or literally subsume, rather than merely mask, those earlier forms upon which they are predicated. The problem with all such up-dating models, of which, according to Bearison (1974), Piaget's particular form of genetic structuralism is perhaps our best example, is that they effectively disallow the easy kind of reversibility supposed by associationistic models that equate development with simple change. As Berlyne (1965) put it, with Piaget's theory one does not get, and can not get, an earlier patterning when the child has moved on to a more advanced pattern. Bearison (1974) and Berlyne (1965), and still others who make the same point do not intend, of course, to deny that people's performance, including their performance on various Piagetian tasks, sometimes actually does deteriorate over time. What such commentators have generally concluded instead is that "the behaviors that some theorists have cited as being regressive in form are better understood as failures in 'performance' rather than 'competence' " (Bearison, 1974). That is, because it is generally supposed that there can be "no takebacks" when it comes to progressive structural development, it is also widely imagined that disordered persons, who do sometimes behave in ways that lend themselves to being described as child-like, still retain their best developmental accomplishments, that are only somehow masked or suppressed by internal or external performance factors.

If that were all there were to it, that is if Piagetian and other structural theories of progressive development actually had no real contribution to make to our understanding of regression, then there would be little reason for continued interest among developmental psychopathologists in any or all such accounts. As it is, any such conclusion would be ill advised. This follows, I want to suggest, because there are in fact more ways in which contructivistic models, including that of Piaget, can speak to the clinical reality of behavioral regressions, broadly conceived, than by imagining that they are all simply the products of superficial performance difficulties. In particular, the very real prospect exists, I mean to urge, that more mature patterns of behavior can and do give way to less mature forms of behavior, not because the usual mechanisms of ontogenesis somehow have been blocked or otherwise put in reverse, but rather because, in the process of transforming themselves from lower to higher organizational states, self-organizing systems regularly put themselves at risk to "fibulating" of "crashing" or otherwise somehow "going nova" (von Uexkull, 1981). Seen in this light, functionally pyramidal organizations of the sort commonly thought to operate during the course of cognitive development are understood to intermittently arrive at "bifurcation points" that not only allow for transformative change in the direction of some new, more differentiated, higher level of "order" or organization, but that also sometimes operate in such a way as to put the entire system in danger of disintegrating into "chaos" (Roth, 1981). That is, during such unstable "singular" or "revolutionary" moments what would otherwise constitute only small perturbations to, or fluctuations within, such systems are thought to become greatly amplified, causing the entire organizational structure either to evolve toward some qualitatively higher regime, or to suffer some structure-breaking devolution toward total randomness.

This is hardly the place to try and further rehearse those various novel concepts recently brought to our attention by contemporary uncertainty and chaos theorists (e.g., Prigogine, 1980; Prigogine & Stengers, 1984). Rather, it is hopefully enough for present purposes to simply take note of the fact that recent contributions from these fields have served to introduce a set of new terms into the more traditional equations of structural developmental theories—terms that make provision, not only for radical qualitative transformations of the progressive sort required to understand canonical growth, but also for those other regressive forms of special interest to theorists charged with working out a coherent developmental psychopathology. What, for the moment, would appear to best advance our understanding of such theoretical prospects is not, I suggest, more in the way of heady abstractions about chaos theory, or the beating of butterfly wings on distant continents. Rather, what seems called for instead are concrete examples of how otherwise promising "revolutionary moments" in the course of ordinary child development can sometimes fall into structure-breaking tail spins that we would all recognize as familiar forms of serious developmental psychopathology.

In a way that is meant to follow this bit of homey advice, I mean to offer up the problem of adolescent suicidal behavior as such an illustrative case in point. I will, in the process, begin by first drawing your attention to several aspects of the problem of adolescent suicide that recommend it as a possible example of developmental deconstruction. I then go on to back this candidate notion by presenting a set of empirical findings that I think clearly portray suicidal adolescents as having suffered what amounts to a total collapse in that aspect of their identity system that is meant to insure a sense of self-continuity or sameness in the face of personal change. The pages that immediately follow pick up this agenda by briefly reviewing what little is known about the development of self-continuity and by undertaking to make clear why disruptions in the ability to maintain a sense of so-called numerical identity might be the occasion for taking steps to end one's own life.

PART TWO: On the deconstruction of diachronic identity

Although still largely in the form of a promissory note, the line of argument laid out in the preceding pages is meant to help rehabilitate the otherwise suspect idea that constructivistic theories of development both allow for, and can serve to make more comprehensible, certain species of structural regression. In particular, it was argued that such dialectical accounts do in fact make a theoretical place for the possibility that, at critical transformational moments, elaborately constructed developmental hierarchies can sometimes topple and crash, leaving no stone standing on any other stone.

The aim of the present section is to move beyond such wholesale theoretical remarks and on to the more retail business of pointedly re-reading the problem of adolescent suicide as a concrete instance of just such a deconstructive process—in this case a deconstruction of diachronic identity. More plainly put, it will be argued that a primary reason that adolescents so often attempt to take their own lives is that the identity formation demands endemic to this developmental period can sometimes trigger the destructuring of that entire system of self-continuity warranting practices responsible for insuring an abiding stake in one's own future. Stripped of their persistent sense of identity, such suicidal young persons, it will be argued, have no more investment in their own future well-being than in that of some complete stranger. Getting clearer about why this should be so will require taking the time, not only to spell out more of what is meant by the generally unfamiliar notions of diachronic identity and self-continuity, but also to better detail why it is that adolescent suicidal behaviors should especially require a developmental explanation. Making that case is the immediate task of the section that follows.

The Demographics of Adolescent Suicidal Behaviors

The reason that adolescent suicidal behaviors especially call out for some developmental explanation is that, even though adults, particularly elderly adults, succeed in killing themselves in equal or greater numbers (Carlson, 1983; Diekstra & Moritz, 1987; Shneidman, 1985), young persons in their teen-age years actually take steps to end their own lives at rates that are variously reported to be anywhere between 20 to 200 times higher than those observed in any other age group (Hendin, 1982; Petzel & Cline, 1978). That is, while pre-adolescents almost never attempt suicide (National Task Force on Suicide in Canada, 1987; Statistics Canada, 1970), and while the ranks of adult suicide "attempters" do not greatly exceed the number of those who actually finish up killing themselves (Baumeister, 1990), adolescents, as a group, temporarily court death in such large numbers that any suicidology that fails to provide an explanation for these remarkable age-graded differences simply won't do.

Once clearly brought out, the existence of evidence indicating that adolescents are dramatically over represented among suicide attempters serves to help restrict the range of any further search for possible explanations for this appalling fact. Particularly in view of the fact that developmentalists have lavished most of their attention on still younger age groups, the roster of classical developmental theories aimed primarily at this adolescent group quickly narrows, and ends up including the writings of Erikson, and precious little else. The one small virtue to be found in this otherwise serious shortfall is that at least Erikson's views on adolescents (e.g., 1968), and especially his idea that developing a coherent sense of identity is the principal psycho-social task of that age period, are already widely known. What is perhaps less well remembered is that, according to Erikson (1968), the achievement of such a stable sense of selfhood is a process that must be pursued simultaneously on two quite different fronts. The first and more familiar of these centers upon the essentially synchronic or cross-sectional task of figuring out some way of understanding how it could be that all of the simultaneously present features or aspects that go into making up one's current identity could possibly be counted as parts of one and the same "unified" self. Persons who suffer various role conflicts, or who, in the extreme, are labeled as having multiple personality disorders, give concrete expression to the difficulties associated with working out just this problem of the synchronic unity of the self.

Less well remembered is the fact that Erikson attached equal importance to a second and more historical, or diachronic dimension of the self. That is, along with numerous other past and present philosophers and theorists of mind (e.g., Gergen & Gergen, 1983; Harré, 1979; James, 1910; MacIntyre, 1977; Rorty, 1976) Erikson saw and drew attention to the fact that it is unavoidably constitutive of what it ordinarily means to have or be a self that all of one's constantly changing ways of being must be understood to be paraphrases or alternative expressions of one and the same continuous or numerically identical person. As Shotter (1984) has put it, continuity represents a necessary condition over which the term "self" is reasonably allowed to operate. This follows for the reason that a self that was not conserved in this fashion, and which stood apart from its own past and as yet unrealized future, would be fundamentally nonsensical (Rorty, 1976).

What is not made clear by all such tough talk about the abstract necessity of conserving one's sense of self across those personal changes to which we are all inevitably subject is just how such arguments in favor of self-continuity could possibly be won. That is, it is one thing to insist that the concept of selfhood formally requires that some way be found to effectively bridge the exceptionless changes we all experience, and quite another to figure out concretely just how this might be, and ordinarily is, accomplished.

Whether or not available theories have any way of explaining these issues, it nevertheless is a matter of practical certainty that ordinary people must have already worked out what is of necessity a range of more or less complex ways of argumentatively redeeming such a sense of personal continuity within change. At least it has been on the strength of this conviction that some of my research colleagues and I (Ball & Chandler, 1989; Boyes, 1987; Chandler, in press; Chandler & Ball, 1989), as well as a few others (e.g., Damon & Hart, 1982, 1988), have recently undertaken to ferret out exactly how it is that persons at various life-stations actually do go about the business of securing or warranting their own self-continuity.

One consequence of these empirical efforts has been a gradually clarifying picture of the several ways that young persons variously situated along the usual course of their social-cognitive development differently reason about the conditions that might secure their own sense of continuous identity. The several such continuity warranting practices that so far have been identified sort themselves into something of a "soft" developmental sequence (Kohlberg & Armon, 1984) of more or less formally adequate problem solving strategies. That is, while not thought to form a hierarchy in which earlier practices are necessarily subsumed by later occurring alternatives, these different self-continuity warranting strategies appear to be orderable in terms of the adequacy with which they successfully argue for sameness without also finding it necessary to ignore change. The sections that follow lay out this proposed developmental sequence, beginning with what are characterized as first *structural* and then *functional* continuity warrants.

A Typology of Sequentially Ordered Self-Continuity Warrants

Following an assessment strategy to be detailed in a later section, more than 200 adolescents have so far been examined with regard to the argumentative grounds upon which they rest whatever convictions of personal continuity they might harbor. A first rough cut through these data has yielded a working distinction between those subjects who subscribe to what Barclay and Smith (1990) have termed an "entity," as opposed to a more "narrative" conception of the self. Young persons in the first of these two categories are forced to adopt one or another of what my research colleagues and I have called *structural* continuity warrants. By these lights, all hopes for justifying a sense of personal persistence in the face of evident change are thought to be pinned upon successfully finding some enduring aspect of the self that has managed to somehow stand apart from the ravages of time. As is spelled out in greater detail below (see also Table 1), what varies across the distinctive *Simple Inclusion, Topological,* and *Essentialistic* warranting strategies that together make up this generic class of structural solutions to the self-continuity problem are the particular trade-offs between persistence and change that they promote.

By contrast, those young persons whose ontological view of the self is generally more narrative or process oriented all end up subscribing to what seems to be a more *functional* approach to the problem of warranting self-continuity. Such persons treat as suspect all vain claims about parts of the self that are somehow imagined to be altogether immune to change, and proceed instead to the more winnable argument that the self is altogether less a thing than a process. So far, two such *functional* arguments have been identified. As is further detailed below, one of these, labeled here as *Foundational continuity warrants,* reads history back to front by viewing the present self as an *effect* of which past selves are the *cause.* Finally, attention will be turned to what are labeled *Narrative continuity warrants,* which attempt to provide a more presentist historiography of the self (Polkinghorne, 1988), by continually undertaking to re-read the past in light of one's self of the present moment. In what follows, these five different continuity warranting strategies are lined out from least to most complex, with special attention devoted to how each differently deals with the problem of change.

Simple Inclusion Warrants. Young, typically pre-adolescent persons who hold to this simplest of continuity warranting strategies tend to view the self as a kind of loose mosaic of isolated autobiographical facts. Changes to this arbitrary conglomerate of attributes are thought to occur in a piecemeal fashion, with various bits and pieces being simply added on or sloughed off without any

TABLE 1 A Typology of Possible Continuity Warrants.

Level	Warranting Strategy	Grounds for Continuity	Characterization of the Self	Interpretation of Change
1	Simple Inclusion Warrants	Structural	a figural collection or mosaic of parts	change is discounted
2	Topological Warrants	Structural	a multifaceted typologic structure	change is denied
3	Essentialistic Warrants	Structural	an unchanging genotypic core	change is trivialized
4	Foundational Warrants	Relational or Functional	an effect or logical implication of a determining past	determinate change is rationalized
5	Narrative Warrants	Relational or Functional	an autobiography or narrative center of gravity	change triggers a hermeneutic re-reading of the past

real consequences for the assemblage as a whole. Personal continuity, in this interpretive context, is seen to be guaranteed so long as some minimal subset of one's atomistic features present at time "T minus One" continue to survive as part of the colony of one's personal attributes at time "T One." Continuity warrants of this small caliber succeed, in so far as they are successful, by effectively turning a blind eye to real change, and by staking all of one's reputation for personal sameness on whatever stubbornly persistent attributes of the self come most readily to hand. In this fashion those who practice such *Simple Inclusion Warrants* tend to rest their case for personal continuity on various durable, but otherwise superficial matters of fact such as their name or street address. In the course of our own identity development each of us presumably went on to other more mature solutions to our own personal continuity problems whenever similarly resting our identities on such simple demographic matters began to trivialize who we take ourselves to be.

Topological Continuity Warrants. The most common self-continuity warranting strategy found among the 12- to 16-year-olds that we have tested is one which rejects the arbitrary feature lists that make up the self-concepts of still younger children and substitutes in their place a better organized and altogether more architectural view, according to which the various attributes that contribute to one's identity are seen as forming the distinct facets of an otherwise empty polyhedronic self-structure. By these new lights young people see themselves, for example, as having a good and a bad side, or a shy and a more forward side, each of which is thought to periodically shoulder its way forward as its opposite number is temporarily eclipsed or somehow put in the shade. On this view what would otherwise have to count as evidence of real personal change tends to be written off as merely presentational, amounting to no more than a temporary spatial rearrangement of one's parts (Shotter, 1984). Those who think of themselves as having an "ugly side" that comes out only when they drink, or who proceed as though they have a devil on one shoulder and an angel on the other, are examples of practitioners of such level 2 *Topological* warranting practices. While an advance over simpler shared parts arguments, such approaches to the continuity problem nevertheless come up short because they attempt to "manage" the problem of real change while ultimately denying it.

Essentialist Continuity Warrants. What are termed here *Essentialist* strategies ffor warranting beliefs about personal sameness go beyond the earlier occurring *Simple Inclusion* and *Topological* arguments outlined above by postulating the existence of a self structure with a certain kind of depth or internality, the deeper lying aspects of which are seen to come closer to one's hidden "essence" or "true" nature. Given this proposed hierarchical arrangement of parts it becomes possible to see beneath the phenotypic surface structure of one's changing attributes to the possibility of some more subterranean and genotypic core that is not only more enduring, but also is capable of preserving and productively paraphrasing itself in endless superficial variations. Armed with this new genotype-phenotype distinction the adolescents who acquire this strategy are now able, for the first time, to successfully justify convictions of persistent personal sameness without at the same time having to turn a blind eye to the real changes occurring in the self. Rather, such changes are "finessed" or trivialized by re-reading them as alternative surface variations upon the same rock bottom essentialist core.

Although an important step toward maturity beyond those simpler and less robust approaches to the problem of self-continuity that tend to precede it, *Essentialist* warrants of the sort currently under discussion nevertheless suffer a range of important limitations latent in all such "entity" approaches to selfhood. The most fundamental of these shortcomings is that, while free to discount certain personal changes as only superficial, some other even deeper lying aspects of the self still need to be seen as somehow fixed and insulated from the workings of time. Something like this search for a part of the self totally immune to change is perhaps what has driven theologians to suppose that immortal souls are themselves featureless and attributeless. Clearly, as soon as a self, or a soul for that matter, is outfitted with some one or more concrete characteristics then, no matter how abstract or deeply buried such attributes might be, the threat arises that these "essential" attributes too may prove amenable to change.

The difficulty, then, facing those who attempt to perfect such *Essentialist* warrants arises from the fact that what may well work theologically may not have a prayer in the more secular world of identity development. Only God needs to be able to distinguish one soul from another. By contrast, it falls to each one of us not only to warrant our own self-continuity, but also to achieve some understanding of our own nature as well. A self that attempts to overcome the self-continuity problem by arranging to be essentially unknowable is at best self-defeating. Nor do the problems with such essentialist notions of self-continuity end here. As Barclay and Smith (1990) have pointed out, such views also automatically sponsor a kind of perilous dualism that effectively decouples the self from the mundane activities of the whole person. The effect is that the self comes to be treated as a kind of indwelling spirit or "ghost in the machine" that serves as the hidden and unknowable cause of one's concrete actions. Continuity arguments that belong to the general class of *Functional* warranting practices taken up in the next section work to overcome these and other shortcomings characteristic of all still simpler "entity" notions of the self.

Foundational and Narrative continuity Warranting Strategies.

Both the *Foundational* and the *Narrative* problem solving strategies that form the highest levels in this proposed typology of increasingly adequate self-continuity warranting practices are distinct from the three *structural* approaches already discussed in that they abandon as unrealistic all hopes of finding material or structural attributes of the self that are imagined to have somehow escaped the ravages of time. In the place of any such common parts arguments, practitioners of these two more *functional* approaches to the self-continuity problem substitute the more thematic alternative of searching out those various relational forms that work to stitch together the multiple episodes of one's life.

What divides these otherwise similar functional approaches is the point of departure they assume when attempting to move between the past and present. As is the case with most traditional forms of historiography, so-called *Foundational* approaches to the self-continuity problem begin in the past and move forward, with the aim of demonstrating that one is continuous in time for the reason that events from one's ancestral past (i.e., that fall from the high-chair; that reoccurring "primal scene; that football scholarship) can be demonstrated to be the antecedent cause of one's unfolding present. The primary drawback to such otherwise effective approaches to the continuity problem would seem to be that they tend to be rather fatalistic, in that they make one's future a totally fated effect or byproduct of one's deterministic causal past.

Narrative arguments for self-continuity, by contrast, practice a more "Wiggish" or "presentist" form of historiography (Ricoeur, 1983) by interpretively re-reading and re-editing the past in light of the present (Polkinghorne, 1988). By these more constructivist lights one's diachronic identity is not so much a sequence of causally related time-slices as it is what Dennett (1978) has called the "narrative center of gravity" of one's constantly unfolding autobiography. Self-continuity, framed in this more *narrative* fashion, amounts to the ability to tell and re-tell a coherent story about the constantly shifting course of one's life.

While only a longitudinal study could convincingly demonstrate that the five increasingly elaborate continuity warranting strategies outlined above actually form a fixed developmental sequence in the mental lives of individual persons, there is some cross-sectional data consistent with that possibility. For example, the results of these studies do demonstrate that individual subjects typically employ only one of these warranting strategies, and that movement along this proposed sequence is both age and ability related. Findings from one such pair of normative studies (i.e., Boyes, 1987; Chandler et al., 1986) show, for example, reliable correlations, on the order of +.45, between movement through this five level sequence and chronological age. In general, level 1 *Sim-*

ple Inclusion warrants are most often observed in pre-adolescents, while Level 2 *Topological* arguments are preferred by young teenagers. Finally, Level 3 *Essentialist* and the two "functional" arguments appear to be the solution strategies of choice for those in later adolescence, although still only approximately a third of high-school juniors and seniors seem to have already adopted what I have referred to as Level 4 and 5 *Foundational* and *Narrative* continuity arguments. Other work (e.g., Ball & Chandler, 1989; Boyes, 1987) has further demonstrated that only subjects who succeed on measures of Piagetian formal operations are capable of Levels 3, 4, or 5, and that subjects can typically paraphrase self-continuity claims that are less, but not more complicated than their own usual level of argumentation. Taken together these findings are seen to make a sufficiently good case in favor of their being a predictable age- and ability-graded sequence in the ways normal adolescents attempt to come to terms with the problem of self-continuity to justify a decision to explore the possible adaptational consequences of this developmental sequence somehow going wrong.

Before going on in Part Three to report upon how two different clinical populations responded to measures meant to draw out their thoughts concerning self-continuity it is worth pausing for a moment to first reflect upon how progress toward some mature solution to this problem could, in theory, conceivably go wrong. The least extravagant of such prospects would have to be that the progress of certain troubled adolescents might be *delayed*, or, worse yet, altogether *fixated*, so that their ability to reason about their own personal persistence would seem immature relative to that of their better adjusted peers. Exactly what the upshot of such slow or stalled progress would be is not, however, self-evident. While it is undoubtedly somehow better to go about things in as mature way as possible, there is some sense in which any personally acceptable grounds for counting one's self as persistent in time may do as well as any other. We might, for example, look askance at an adult who, like some middle-school child, judged him or her self to have a continuous identity simply because they had suffered no change of name or address, but it is not obvious that such an evident bit of immaturity would necessarily count as a problem for the individual in question.

Alternatively, disturbed individuals could, if theory and practice allows, show signs of having regressed from more mature to less mature ways of thinking about their own persistence in time. Even if such things are seen to be possible given the inner-workings of available theories, it is not immediately apparent how, in the absence of longitudinal data, such cases could be distinguished from still simpler instances of delays or fixations. Nor, even if there were clues that would allow us to reliably differentiate backsliding from simply having made too little progress in the first place, is it apparent how being regressed is importantly different in practice from being delayed, if they both end you up in precisely the same place.

The third and potentially much more interesting possibility is that there might be clinical groups characterized by the fact that, while working their way up from some developmentally less to some developmentally more mature ways of thinking about matters of personal continuity, may have been thrown into a complete structural tail spin, or otherwise suffered a kind of total systems "crash" that left them without any kind of workable means for preserving a sense of identity in the face of change. Such individuals, if they exist, would lose what ever basis they might once have had for feeling responsible for their own past and for feeling a sense of proper care and concern for their own future well being. Imagine, for example a Methuselah who, while perhaps living 900 years, could only keep his experiences in mind for 100-year stretches. Would such a 99-year-old Methuselah choose, for example, to quit smoking or practice safe sex on behalf of a person he would never remember becoming? Perhaps more to the present point, would he shy away from killing himself to escape some seemingly intolerable situation when the person he was slated to become, should he live, would mean no more to him than a perfect stranger. Methuselah, of course, is a special biblical case. What is not so hypothetical, and what the studies to be summarized in the following pages were meant to help determine, is whether suicidal adolescents could be just such a group of young persons who, having lost all sense of self-continuity, no longer have any investment in choosing long life over a short escape from some seemingly impossible situation of the moment.

PART THREE: Adolescent suicide & the loss of self-continuity

Two hard questions motivated the ongoing program of research to which attention is now turned. The first of these is how anyone, of any developmental station, could come to override the all but universal impulse to preserve their own life (Linehan, Goodstein, Nielsen & Chiles, 1983). The second is why, with all of life's potential sweetness full upon their lips, adolescents would engage in such self-destructive behaviors at rates some 20 to 200 times greater than any other age group. Based upon all that has just been said, the hypothesized answers to these questions that the research under discussion was meant to test, are: a) that suicide becomes a live option primarily to those who have wholly lost a sense of connectedness to their own futures; and b) that adolescents, more than any other age group, are put at special risk to such a loss each time the normal course of their identity development carries them toward yet another transition to some still another more complex way of warranting their own personal continuity. That is, recurrently poised on the cusp of yet another transition from one set of continuity warranting practices to the next, such young persons often abandon older, less mature ways of preserving their sense of personal sameness before some more adequate solution strategy is yet in place. Caught in this fashion "between stays" they go adrift, losing all proper care and concern about their own future well-being. It is during these periods of selflessness, it is proposed, that, when confronted with those inevitable hardships that make one's life seem momentarily intolerable, that suicide becomes for such young persons an actionable possibility.

In order to test out the explanatory framework just outlined, two resources were required. The first was an available sample of suicidal adolescents, along with appropriate control groups. The second was some workable procedural means of reliably locating each of these young persons with respect to the five level typology of alternative self-continuity warranting practices introduced earlier.

Assessing Alternative Self-Continuity Warranting Practices. At the time this research was initiated, there was little or nothing to choose between in the way of already available instruments for measuring self-continuity. It consequently was necessary to begin constructing such assessment procedures from the ground up. In view of the fact that persons are unaccustomed, at best, to open discussions of the argumentative grounds for their beliefs in their own diachronic continuity, what was seen to be especially required was some comfortable means of broaching this subject with them. What was eventually hit upon was an assessment technique that relied in some measure on tests of subjects' understanding of the persistent identities of various characters drawn from children's literature (Ball & Chandler, 1989; Chandler & Ball, 1989). The kernel idea here was that, because the authors of such biographies typically undertake to craft their stories with an eye toward showing continuities in the lives of their characters, the ability of young subjects to understand and paraphrase these stories could be used as a way of marking their developmental progress in coming to a mature understanding of the problem of self-continuity. With this prospect in mind, better than 200 adolescents of various ages and mental health statuses have so far been pressed for explanations, first about why various familiar fictional characters went on being themselves despite often dramatic changes, and then about the existence of possible continuities in their own lives. More concretely, in the specific studies to be summarized, both suicidal and nonsuicidal adolescents were first shown "Classic Comic Book" versions of Victor Hugo's *Les Miserables* and Charles Dickens' *A Christmas Carol*, and then questioned concerning whether, and if so how, Jean Valjean and Ebenezer Scrooge qualify as being one and the same continuous person from the beginning to the end of their stories. Subjects were then asked to provide current and retrospective descriptions of themselves, and were again pressed for explanations as to how, given the changes reported, they themselves might qualify as one and the same continuous person.

Blind scoring of verbatim transcripts of these structured interviews have shown that the responses of almost all ordinary and psychiatrically hospitalized adolescents can be reliably located within one of the five continuity warranting strategies detailed earlier, and that most subjects responded in only one of these ways, whether commenting upon their own life or the lives of the fictional story characters.

The especially interesting exception to this general pattern, to be described in greater detail below, is that, in stark contrast to their normal and psychiatrically hospitalized but nonsuicidal peers, the suicidal adolescents so far tested have almost all thrown up their hands in response to probes about their own self-continuity, showing themselves wholly unable to find any personally acceptable grounds whatsoever for judging themselves or the story characters to be continuous across time.

The Subject Sample. The original design for the research under discussion included a planned three-way comparison between psychiatrically hospitalized

TABLE 2 Type of Continuity Warrant by Suicidal Status.

	Type of Warrant		
Suicidal Status	None	1. Simple Inclusion 2. Typological	3. Essentialist 4. Functional
High Risk (N = 17)	14 (82%)	1 (6%)	2 (12%)
Low Risk (N = 23)	3 (13%)	18 (78%)	2 (9%)
Control (N = 41)	0	16 (40%)	25 (60%)

Note: N = 81

groups of suicidal and nonsuicidal adolescents, along with a nonpatient group, matched for age, sex and socio-economic status. On careful study, however, it proved a practical impossibility to identify hospitalized adolescents about whom no concern over the prospect of suicidal behaviors had ever been expressed. Consequently, an alternative coding system was devised for rating each subject's medical record in terms of perceived risk to suicide. These data were then collapsed in such a way as to yield a "low" and "high" suicide risk group. No subject in the low risk group was known to have made a frank suicidal gesture, and all of those classified as high risk had been independently placed on an "active suicide precautions" regimen during some part of their current hospital stay. To date 81 subjects (40 hospitalized and 41 nonpatient controls) have been tested in this design. The hospitalized sample consists of those consecutive admissions to the adolescent psychiatric inpatient unit of an urban general service hospital who, over an 18 month period, met a list of selection criteria that included having provided personal and parental consents, as well as psychometric evidence of at least normal intelligence. Sixty five percent of the adolescents screened met these criteria, of which 23 were rated as being at low, and 17 at high risk to suicide.

Results. The results of these analyses reduce down to one clear and decisive point (see Table 2). As can be seen from an inspection of this table, roughly 5 out of every 6, or more than 80% of the high risk subjects so far tested wholly failed to find any means whatsoever of warranting their own or other's self-continuity in the face of change. This is all the more remarkable in view of the fact that only 3 out of 23 (i.e., approximately 8%) of the "low" risk adolescents, and no nonpatient control subject showed this same across-the-board failure to find any means of warranting self-continuity. All this was true despite the fact that these suicidal subjects were generally no less cooperative, or verbally productive than their nonsuicidal counterparts, and in almost every instance offered up various continuity arguments which they then went on to reject as unacceptably immature.

The general picture offered by these data is not without its exceptions. There are, for example, as evidenced by the 2 high risk cases in the upper right hand corner of Table 2, subjects who apparently went on trying to take their own lives, despite the availability of high level self-continuity warranting strategies. Note should also be taken of the 3 low risk subjects who entirely lacked any means of justifying personal sameness, but whose medical histories were nevertheless free of any known evidence of serious attempts against their own life. Still, in view of the long history of failed attempts to identify factors that powerfully discriminate between suicidal and nonsuicidal persons, and in light of the fact that nothing else in the literature seems to offer any theoretically coherent way of understanding the anomalously high rate of suicide attempts among adolescents, the strong results emerging from this program of research seem especially promising. Over and above any contribution that these efforts might make to our eventual understanding of adolescent suicide, these data are also viewed as providing a hopefully persuasive illustration of how constructivistic theories of normal growth can be employed as a way of coming to a better understanding of certain profound forms of developmental psychopathology.

CONCLUSION

On the verge, perhaps, of having lost you in the machinery of what was intended only as a working example, it may prove useful, as a way of concluding, to step-back from the particulars of the foregoing work on adolescent suicide and to attempt a last lingering look at what is being held out here as a novel form of explanation for certain types of developmental psychopathology. If there is a single take-away point here, beyond the specific demonstration that the numerical identity of suicidal adolescents appears to have gone missing, it is that past interpretive practices have so far failed to fully exhaust the explanatory resources of structural models of progressive development. What is meant to have been added here, by way of the illustrations provided, is a demonstration that certain forms of psychopathology are best understood, not as the result of some form of developmental delay or arrest, but rather as the expression of a kind of structural collapse brought on by those dangers lurking near the cusp of normal transitions from one stage of development to the next.

By way of a further example, it has also been claimed, in certain quarters, that infants who are lost to so-called crib death may be those whose emerging abilities to intentionally clear their own airways have not yet come fully on line before other still earlier involuntary mechanisms for accomplishing the same task have already dropped away. Whether or not such claims will eventually prove to have merit is not a matter about which I have an informed opinion. The *form* of argument upon which such accounts rest is of interest, however, and illustrates the sort of explanatory mechanism being advanced here. As in the case of my own more detailed example of evident failures in the self-continuity warranting practices, the interesting prospect that such accounts help to highlight is that perhaps every important developmental transition is marked by moments of heightened vulnerability when growing persons can easily end up with both of their feet off the floor. That is, while having set aside still earlier and more childish ways, and while still reaching out for some developmentally more advanced way of being, one can often end up being all stretched out and exposed, and altogether unprepared to ward off the next sharp jab that life may hold in store. If, on further study, all this should prove to routinely be the case (that is, should moments of developmental transitions regularly prove to be times of heightened risk to psychopathology), then the number of explanatory arrows in the quiver of developmental theorists will have shot up by some appreciable number. More than simply adding to some general arsenal of explanations, interpretive accounts of this new sort also appear to have the virtue of working best upon what, to date, have proven to be the hardest cases. It takes no blinding insight to recognize, for example, that the brakes can sometimes be put upon various developing abilities, or that circumstances might prevail that could bring the course of progressive development to a full stop. What, by contrast, have always proven to be most mysterious are those harder instances in which otherwise progressive development appears to utterly fall upon its face. Simple regression, in which the workings of progressive development are imagined to merely run themselves off in reverse, often will not do. This follows because too much evidence exists in support of the view that developmentally earlier structures are not always simply sidelined, but are, rather, radically transformed as they become incorporated into still later occurring ways of being. If this is what actually happens, then easy explanations about developmental regression are blocked (Bearison, 1974). What must be brought in to take their place, I have attempted to argue, are new ways of understanding the hazards of developmental transitions. Adolescent suicide attempts, of the sort documented here, are offered as instances of that broader class of developmental psychopathologies potentially open to such structural explanations.

REFERENCES

Ball, L., & Chandler, M. (1989). Identity Formation in Suicidal and Nonsuicidal Youth: The Role of Self-continuity. *Development and Psychopathology, 1*, 257–275.

Barclay, C. & Smith, T. (1990). Autobiographical remembering and self-composing. *International Journal of Personal Construct Psychology, 35*, 59– 65.

Baumeister, R. (1990). Suicide as Escape From Self. *Psychological Review, 97*, 90–113.

Bearison, D. (1974). The construct of regression: A Piagetian Approach, *Merrill-Palmer Quarterly, 20*(1), 21–30.

Berlyne, D. (1965). *Structure and direction in thinking*. New York: Wiley.

Blasi, A. (1983). "The self and cognition." In B. Lee and G. Noam (Eds.), *Developmental Approaches to the Self* (pp. 178–210). New York: Plenum Press.

Boyes, M. (1987). *Epistemic Development and Identity Formation in Adolescence*. Unpublished doctoral dissertation, University of British Columbia, Vancouver, B.C.

Carlson, G. A. (1983). "Depression and Suicidal Behaviour in Children and Adolescents." In D. P. Cantwell and G. A. Carlson (Eds.), *Affective Disorders in Childhood and Adolescents - An Up- date* (pp. 335–352). New York: Spectrum.

Chandler, M. (1993). "Contextualism and the postmodern condition: Learning from Las Vegas." In S. Hayes, L. Hayes, H. Reese, & T. Sarbin (Eds.), *Varieties of Scientific Contextualism*. Reno: Context Press.

Chandler, M. (in press). "Self-continuity in suicidal and nonsuicidal adolescents." In G. Noam (Ed.), *Developmental approaches to child and adolescent suicide.* San Francisco: Josse-Bass.

Chandler, M., & Ball, L. (1989). "Continuity and Commitment: A Developmental Analysis of Identity Formation Process in Suicidal and Non-suicidal Youth." In H. Bosma and S. Jackson (Eds.), *Coping and Self-concept in Adolescence* (pp. 17–26). Heidelberg: Springer Verlag.

Chandler, M., Boyes, M., Ball, S., and Hala, S. (1986). "The Conservation of Self-hood: Children's Changing Conceptions of Self-continuity." In T. Honess and K. Yardley (Eds.), *Self and Identity: Individual Change and Development* (pp. 108–120). London: Routledge & Kegan Paul.

Cicchetti, D. (1984). The emergence of developmental psychopathology. *Child Development, 55,* 1–7.

Cicchetti, D. (1990). "A historical perspective on the discipline of developmental psychopathology. In J. Rolf, A. Masten, D. Cicchetti, K. Nuechterlein, & S. Wientraub (Eds.), *Risk and protective factors in the development of psychopathology* (pp. 2–28). New York: Cambridge University Press.

Damon, W., & Hart, D. (1988). *Self-Understanding in Childhood and Adolescence.* New York: Cambridge University Press.

Damon, W., Hart, D. (1982). The development of self– understanding from infancy through adolescence. *Child Development, 53,* 841-864.

Dennett, D. (1978). *Brainstorms.* Hassocks: Harvester Press.

Diekstra, R., and Moriz, B. (1987). "Suicidal behaviour among adolescents: An overview." In R. Diekstra and K. Hawton (Eds.), *Suicide in Adolescents* (pp. 7–24). Dordrecht: Martinus Nijhoff.

Erikson, E. J. (1968). *Identity: Youth and Crisis.* New York: W. W. Norton & Co.

Gergen, K., and Gergen, M. (1983). "Narratives of the Self." In T. R. Sarbin and K. E. Schebe (Eds.), *Studies in Social Identity,* (pp. 254–273). New York: Praeger.

Harré, R. (1979). *Social Being: A Theory for Social Psychology.* Oxford: Blackwell.

Hendin, H. (1982). *Suicide in America.* New York: Norton, 1982.

Hooper, F., Fitzgerald, J., & Papalia, D. (1971). Piagetian theory and the aging process: Extensions and speculations. *Aging and Human Development, 2,* 3–20.

James, W. (1910). *Psychology: The Briefer Course.* New York: Holt and Co.

Keating, D. (1990). "Constructivism and Diversity." In. D. P. Keating and H. Rosen (Eds.), *Constructivist perspectives on developmental psychopathology and atypical development* (pp. 1–23). Hillsdale, NJ: Lawrence Erlbaum Associates.

Kohlberg, L. (1969). "Stage and sequence: The cognitive developmental approach to socialization." In D. A. Goslin (Ed.), *Handbook of socialization theory and research* (pp. 347–480). Chicago: Rand McNally.

Kohlberg, L., and Armon, C. (1984). "Three types of stage models used in the study of adult development." In M. L. Commons, F. A. Richards, and C. Armon (Eds.), *Beyond Formal Operations: Late Adolescent and Adult Cognitive Development* (pp.383–394). New York: Praeger.

Linehan, M., Goodstein, J., Nielsen, S., & Chiles, J. (1983). Reasons for staying live when you are thinking of killing yourself: The reasons for living inventory. *Journal of Consulting and Clinical Psychology, 51,* 276–286.

Looft, W. (1972). Egocentrism and social interaction across the life span. *Psychological Bulletin, 78,* 73–92.

MacIntyre, A. (1977). "Epistemological Crisis, Dramatic Narrative, and the Philosophy of Science." *The Monist, 60,* 453–472.

Nannis, E. D. & Cowan, P. A. (Eds.), (1988). *Developmental psychopathology and its treatment.* San Francisco: Jossey-Bass.

National Task Force on Suicide in Canada (1987). *Suicide in Canada.* Ottawa: Health and Welfare Canada.

Petzel, S., & Cline, D. (1978). "Adolescent suicide: epidemiological and biological aspects." In S. Feinstein and P. Giovacchini (Eds.), *Adolescent Psychiatry* (pp. 239–266). Chicago: University of Chicago Press.

Polkinghorne, C. (1988). *Narrative Knowing and the Human Sciences.* Albany, NY: SUNY Press.

Prigogine, I. & Stengers, I. (1984). *Order out of chaos: Man's new dialogue with nature.* New York: Bantum Books.

Prigogine, I. (1980). *From being to becoming: Time and complexity in the physical sciences.* New York: W. H. Freeman.

Ricoeur, P. (1983). "Can Fiction Narratives be True?" *Analecta Husserliana, 14*, 3–19.

Rorty, A. O. (1976). *The Identities of Persons.* Berkeley: University of California Press.

Roth, G. (1981). "Biological Systems Theory and the Problem of Reductionism." In G. Roth and H. Schwegler (eds.), *Self-Organizing Systems: An Interdisciplinary Approach* (pp. 106–120). Frankfurt: Campus Verlag.

Schneidman, E. S. (1985). *Definition of Suicide.* New York: Wiley.

Shotter, J. (1984). *Social Accountability and Selfhood.* Oxford: Basil Blàckwell.

Statistics Canada (1970). *Causes of Death.* Ottawa: Health and Welfare Canada.

van den Daele, L. (1969) Qualitative models of developmental analysis. *Developmental Psychology, 1*, 303–310.

von Uexkull, T. (1981). "Systems and Crisis in Human Physical and Mental Development." In G. Roth and H. Schwegler (Eds.), *Self-Organizing Systems: An Interdisciplinary Approach* (pp. 132–144). Frankfurt: Campus Verlag.

Author Index

C

D

E

F

H

I

J

K

L

M

Q

R

T

U

V

W

Y

Z

Subject Index

T

W

Y

www.ingramcontent.com/pod-product-compliance
Lightning Source LLC
La Vergne TN
LVHW090002031026
849161LV00027B/3075/J
* 9 7 8 1 8 7 8 8 2 2 3 1 4 *